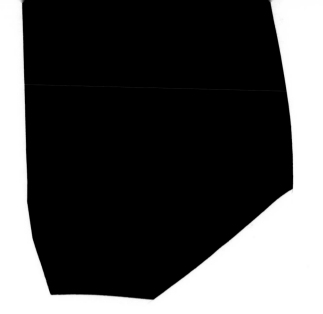

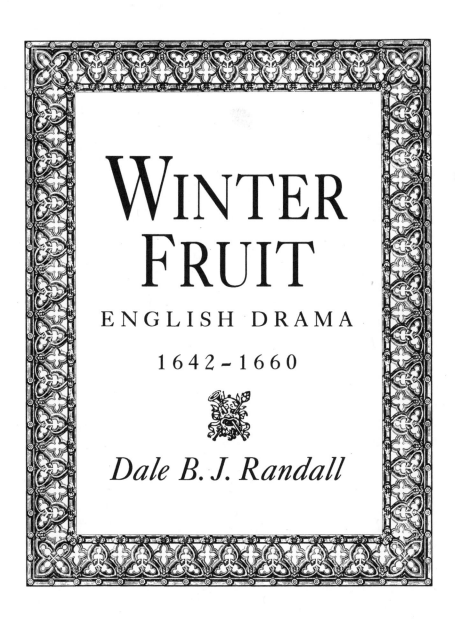

WINTER FRUIT

ENGLISH DRAMA

1642–1660

Dale B. J. Randall

THE UNIVERSITY PRESS OF KENTUCKY

This book has been supported by a grant from the
National Endowment for the Humanities,
an independent federal agency.

Copyright © 1995 by The University Press of Kentucky
Scholarly publisher for the Commonwealth, serving Bellarmine College,
Berea College, Centre College of Kentucky, Eastern Kentucky University,
The Filson Club, Georgetown College, Kentucky Historical Society,
Kentucky State University, Morehead State University, Murray State University,
Northern Kentucky University, Transylvania University, University of Kentucky,
University of Louisville, and Western Kentucky University.

Editorial and Sales Offices: The University Press of Kentucky
663 South Limestone Street, Lexington, Kentucky 40508-4008

Library of Congress Cataloging-in-Publication Data
Randall, Dale B. J.
  Winter fruit : English drama, 1642–1660 / Dale B.J. Randall.
    p.   cm.
  Includes bibliographical references (p.   ) and index.
  ISBN 0-8131-1925-1
    1. English drama—17th century—History and criticism.   2 Great
Britain—History—Civil War, 1642–1649—Literature and the war.
3. Great Britain—History—Commonwealth and Protectorate,
1649–1660.   4. Literature and history—Great Britain—History—17th
century.   5. Theater and state—Great Britain—History—17th century.
6. Cromwell, Oliver, 1599–1658—Views on drama.   7. Puritans—
England—History—17th century. I. Title.
PR680.R36 1995
822′.409—dc20   95-7634

To Phyllis

It was in the dead of a long Winter night.
  —James Howell, *A Winter Dreame* (1649)

CONTENTS

ILLUSTRATIONS

PREFACE

... this Mad, Sad, Cold Winter of discontent.
—John Taylor, *Crop-Eare Curried* (1644)

'Twould grieve one's heart, to see men drop like ripe fruit in a strong
wind, and never see their enemy. ....
—Richard Atkyns, *The Vindication* (1643)

What I have now to say is but to the ingenious Reader, that
Hee will value these, noe other then as the writer gives them
Leaves, and perhaps Budds of a tree, which (if this long winter
of generall Calamitie had not nipt, and nere perished) might
have brought forth a more noble, and better relishing Fruit.
—George Daniel, "To the Reader" (1647)

IN THIS BOOK I OFFER the reader a reasonably inclusive analysis of dramatic writings in English during the 1640s and 1650s, and in the process I explore particularly some of the many ways in which these works are interrelated with various aspects of the period that produced them—a period of civil strife often referred to at the time as a "winter."[1]

For me, the title *Winter Fruit* has personal as well as historical and literary applications. I set to work on this project in the late 1960s, in fact in the year when a number of disaffected students at Duke University barricaded and threatened to burn Duke's main administration building, where as a dean I had an office. I remember clearly the smell of tear gas drifting up to my windows from the University's well-kept gardens, which were suddenly teeming with angry students and worried lawmen. Everything I saw that day seemed alien and unsettling—most strikingly, even things that had not really changed. The perceived threat of chaos was universally affecting and, I now see, a fitting prologue to a book concerned with the transformative power, good and bad, of civil strife.

Since this book has now had an unusually prolonged gestation—many classes, duties, and projects have intervened—its position with regard to the work of other scholars is unusually difficult to define. Some readers might like to know, however, that with regard to both chronological subject

---

[1]Earl Miner, who makes much of the matter, observes that "Those who have encountered such images as 'the North,' winter, storms, and battle again and again in unquestioned political contexts will likely think the political reading inevitable" (186).

and contextual approach, I have come to see it as situated somewhere between Martin Butler's study of slightly earlier English drama (that is, Caroline drama before 1642) and Robert Hume's study of Restoration drama (that is, drama after 1660). To attempt placing it in a different way, one might relate the book to some of the work that has been published by Stephen Orgel, Lois Potter, Annabel Patterson, and Kevin Sharpe. Though I did, indeed, choose a similar approach in the earlier 1970s in my own book on Jonson, such scholars have helped to reassure me of the interest and validity of pursuing an historico-literary course.

Since one early reader of the present book has told me that it manifests an inclination toward royalism, and another that it reveals my whiggism, perhaps I should take this opportunity to state that I hold no brief for either (or any) side engaged in England's mid-seventeenth-century strife. In fact, my attempt to be evenhanded is based on the conviction that both the varied kinds of royalists and their miscellaneous opponents were variously right and wrong at different times and on different issues. On the other hand, if indeed there is some apparent inclination toward royalism here, I would trace it less to any personal predilection than to the fact that the royalists tended to be more tolerant of, interested in, and productive of drama. Their opponents were capable of producing the potent *Tyranicall-Government Anatomized* and *Marcus Tullius Cicero*, but the fact is that the royalists were generally more likely to read, write, and translate plays. Then again, if despite my goal of impartiality the book occasionally seems tilted, so be it. There is plenty of factual ballast in the hold. Besides, viewing this book in conjunction with or in opposition to certain other studies that have appeared in the last decade or two may incidentally revive for us (or aid the survival of) a useful dialogue. When all else is said and done, we are likely to fare best if we recognize the provisional aspect of historical truth.

Like many books that target a large number of texts for discussion, this one is indebted to the work of virtually (and perhaps literally) innumerable scholars, only some of whom finally made it into the list of "Works Cited." Let it be said here, however, that my most constant companions have been the seven volumes of Gerald Eades Bentley's *Jacobean and Caroline Stage* (1941-68) and the Harbage-Schoenbaum-Wagonheim *Annals of English Drama* (1940, 1964, 1989).

Along with facing a staggering amount of raw data and deciding how best to select from it and deploy it as clearly, helpfully, and interestingly as possible, I have been concerned from the beginning with apportionment. Considering that none of the dramatic works treated here is frequently studied or even read, and that it would be undesirable (even if possible) to give equal space to each play, I have had to select certain plays for emphasis. Generally speaking, I give fuller attention to some because the specificity of their historical or political pertinence can be ascertained and the context of their writing documented. For my purposes here, part of the value of such works is that they help to illuminate and confirm what is more conjecturally going on in other, less fully or less carefully historicized plays. Then again, certain plays have received more attention here than others because they seem particularly helpful for making a different sort of point. Finally, however, I freely confess that some choices regarding apportionment have been arbitrary.

Among other subjects involving choices, perhaps the method of dating and the quoting of sources deserve comment. Granted the fact that a fair number of the dates to be dealt with here are conjectural, the citing of days and months follows as closely as possible the Julian mode of reckoning current in the seventeenth century. As in most studies nowadays, however, calendar years are considered to have begun on 1 January rather than 25 March. With regard to the quotation of sources, I have tried to reproduce texts faithfully, warts and all, on the grounds that modernizing and partial modernizing both seem to be more misleading. In keeping with this decision, furthermore, I generally refer to works by the titles of the editions I have used—which means that titles cited in the text of this book should, the Fates permitting, match those recorded in the list of "Works Cited."

At this late date I am only too well aware of the impossibility of acknowledging all the assistance I have received while working on this project. Nevertheless, I want to give public thanks for generous support from the John Simon Guggenheim Memorial Foundation, the Folger Shakespeare Library, the National Endowment for the Humanities, the American Philosophical Society, the Duke Endowment, and the Duke University Research Council. Among individuals, Professor John L. Lievsay and Lilly Stone Lievsay take the crown for years of extraordinary kindness, hospitality, and moral support. Especially important in the final stages of the project were Professors Cynthia Herrup, Annabel Patterson, and George Walton Williams, all of whom offered helpful comments on a late printout of the manuscript, and J. Samuel Hammond, who, beyond serving as Rare Book Librarian and University Carillonneur at Duke, has produced the index for the volume.

I am grateful also to a trio of (now former) Duke students who at various stages helped to nudge my work forward: Jane M. Kinney, Jonathan Nauman, and Ryan Holifield. Graduate students whose dissertation work has heartened me in mining the literary-historical ore of the 1640s and 1650s include Vivienne Stevens Johnson, Marilynn Strasser Olson, and Patricia Haim (formerly Yates).

Librarians everywhere have been endlessly helpful and resourceful in answering offbeat questions and running down such out-of-the-way material as the project has required. Pride of place here must go to the librarians—indeed, friends—at the William R. Perkins Library, Duke University, followed closely by their compeers at the Folger Shakespeare Library. Their "pains / Are regist'red where every day I turn / The leaf to read them" (*Macbeth* I.iii.150-52).

My gratitude is great also for the help I have received at the British Library, the British Museum, the Bodleian Library, the Library of Worcester College (Oxford), the Louis Round Wilson Library and the Walter Royal Davis Library at the University of North Carolina at Chapel Hill, the Library of Congress, the Library of Cambridge University, the Library at Lambeth Palace, the Huntington Library, and the Beinecke Rare Book and Manuscript Library at Yale University.

Among individuals who have helped signally with various matters from classics to computers, I am glad to name Peter Beal, Hilton Kelliher, Lynn Hulse, Walter Melion, Joanna Parker, Joseph A. Porter, Kent Rigsby, Susan Ryman, Louise Smith, and Georgianna Ziegler. My thanks to each and every one.

Then, to finish all, a few shards. Having had to correct myself so frequently during the course of writing and revising this work, I must assume that there still remain errors here of both commission and omission. For all of these, my apologies: *Gradatim vincimus*. Moreover, having spent a long while trying to emulate the Mediterranean chameleon who can aim its eyes in two directions and simultaneously see both sights as part of one reality, I am well aware that my own historico-literary reality here cannot be the same as (though it may resemble) that of any other scholar or reader. In the words of Antonio Hurtado de Mendoza—a seventeenth-century Spanish dramatist noted herein—everyone's writing tends to reveal *Cada loco con su tema*. "What is truth?" said jesting Pilate. It is chastening to remember that for all his learning, Faustus misreads the message written in blood on his own warm arm. Nevertheless, one continues to read and write, *Scripta litera manet*, and, at last, *Senex saltat*.

[I]

A Case of Cultural Poetics

Look to your Hats and Clokes, the Red-coats come.
D'amboys *is routed*, Hotspur *quits the field*,
Falstaff's *out-filch'd, all in Confusion yield,*
Even Auditor and Actor, what before
Did make the Red Bull *laugh, now makes him roar.*
—Thomas Jordan,
prologue to *Walks of Islington and Hogsdon* (1657)

Is it unlawfull since the stage is down
To make the press act: where no ladies swoune
At the red coates intrusion: none are strip't;
No Hystriomastix has the copy whip't
No man d'on Womens cloth's: the guiltles presse
Weares its own innocent garments: its owne dresse,
Such as free nature made it. . . .
—R.C., "To Mr. Alexander Goughe," *The Queene* (1653)

Then 'tis no matter what *the Captious say,*
Wee'l read, and *like,* and *think* we see *thy Play.*
—J. Cole in George Gerbier D'Ouvilley,
The False Favourite Disgrac'd (1657)

THE DATE 1642 has for too long afforded students of English drama a
comfortable point of closure. When the theatrical companies were silenced
that year by Parliament, the many-splendored arc of Tudor and Stuart
drama came at last to an end—or so we have been told—with a dying fall.
Having looked on splendid and undoubted greatness, we are asked to
believe that little or nothing happened in English drama for the next
eighteen years, at the end of which time, with the restoration of the Stuarts
to the throne and the banishment of Puritan gloom, the theaters reopened,
the players resumed playing, and the whole enterprise of English drama
got under way again.

This book presents a different view.[1] The fact is that the 1642 procla-
mation against stage-playing, whatever else it did, also acknowledged

---

[1] That it appears useful, even necessary, to do so is all the more remarkable when one realizes
that as long ago as 1934 Louis B. Wright thought that "all the world knows since the
publication of studies by Professors Graves, Rollins, and Hotson that . . . [the drama's] light
never went out completely" (73).

implicitly the danger and hence the effectiveness of dramatic performances of the day. Furthermore, throughout the ensuing official hiatus in playing, dramas continued to be composed, translated, revived, transmuted, published, bought, read, and even acted. Naturally all of these activities underwent different phases as the years slipped by, but the larger fact to be explored here is that drama, which had so much interested the English in earlier years (William Prynne complained in 1633 of "This play-adoring age" [**1v]), continued to interest many and to provide English writers, readers, and sometimes audiences with many forms of expression, whether for persuasion or pleasure or both. The very recurrence of prohibitions against playing attests to the persisting life of drama.

Historically, one of the signs that drama (or any kind of literature) is functioning significantly, that it is approaching life in some vital way, has been the attempt of authority to contain it. It is valuable to recall, therefore, that for many years before the 1642 proclamation, Renaissance drama in England had been monitored and sometimes suppressed by the Bishop of London, the Privy Council, the Lord Treasurer, the Court of High Commission, the Lord Chamberlain, the Master of the Revels, and even the monarch.[2]

As such a state of affairs implies, the topical infringement of drama on life reaches back to the beginnings of early modern English playmaking, to Medwall's *Fulgens and Lucres* (1497) and Heywood's *The Play of the Weather* (1528), to Bale's *King John I & II* (1538 and ca. 1558), Udall's *Respublica* (1553), and Norton and Sackville's *Gorboduc* (1562). Like writers of other times and places, in other words, early modern English dramatists were from the beginning alert to the problems and possibilities of topicality.

Since many scholars—including Thornton S. Graves, David M. Bevington, John N. King, and Annabel Patterson—have helped to explore this complex issue, a small handful of specific instances should suffice here. In April 1559, very early in Elizabeth's reign, Paulo Tiepolo wrote to the Venetian Doge and senate that players in London "brought upon the stage all personages whom they wished to revile, . . . and amongst the rest, in one

---

[2]For example, on 29 September 1639 there was an "Order of the King in Council" about *The Whore New Vampt:* "[T]he stage-players of the Red Bull [have for] many days together acted a scandalous and libellous [play in which] they have audaciously reproached and in a libel [represented] and personated not only some of the aldermen of the [city of London] and some other persons of quality, but also scandalized and libelled the whole profession of proctors belonging to the Court of [Probate], and reflected upon the present Government" (Hamilton 529). Two helpful studies on the earlier period are Clare's *"Art made tongue-tied by authority": Elizabethan and Jacobean Dramatic Censorship* (1990) and Richard Dutton's *Mastering the Revels: The Regulation and Censorship of English Renaissance Drama* (1991). One might note, furthermore, that censorship of the English stage was not abolished altogether until the Theatres Act of 1968.

play, they represented King Philip, the late Queen of England, and Cardinal Pole, . . . saying whatever they fancied about them" (Graves, "Some Allusions" 546). In the prologue to *Damon and Pithias* (1571) Richard Edwards took attention-rousing pains to specify that when "Wee talke of Dionisias Courte, wee meane no Court but that" (Aii,r). It was clear to Thomas Bowes, the translator of a 1594 edition of La Primaudaye's *Academie françoise*, that the players *"dare to gird at the greatest personages of all estates"* (b4v). In 1605 George Calvert wrote to Ralph Winwood, "The players do not forbear to present upon the stage the whole course of this present time, not sparing the king, state, or religion, in so great absurdity and with such liberty that any would be afraid to hear them" (Richard Simpson 375).

Whether comic or otherwise, the topical allusions so acknowledged were largely a form of political critique. Furthermore, some of the boldest may be forever beyond our retrieval because they were the product of the actors' extemporizing and because, as Shakespeare writes in another context, "There was . . . language in their very gesture" (*Winter's Tale* V.ii.13-14). Certainly the critical rhubarb could be served with flattering sugar. In *The Gypsies Metamorphos'd* (1621) Ben Jonson not only cheerily displayed the taking ways of George Villiers and his gypsy entourage but also had Villiers assure King James that he was James the Just. Jonson had earlier put the rhetorical case quite directly: "Phant'sie, I tell you, has dreams that have wings, / And dreams that have honey, and dreams that have stings" (*Vision of Delight* [1617], ll. 61-62). Sometimes, obviously, the stings might be foregone. Not merely courtly masques but also plays of the public theater—such as *Macbeth* and *Perkin Warbeck*—could be shaped in part by an intention to gratify the powers that be.

So obvious are some of these observations that most students of the period will have no difficulty recalling a few examples of their own. Best known of all is the ill-fated revival of *Richard II* by Shakespeare's company at the time of the 1601 Essex Rebellion. (On the other hand, we are likely to forget that *Richard II* was also put on—and silenced—in the later 1670s, when once again the problem of succession became critical.) Well known also is the staging of Middleton's *Game at Chess* (1624) following the collapse of negotiations for the marriage of Prince Charles to the Spanish *infanta*. Still closer to the years that most concern us, the chronological proximity of William Prynne's *Histrio-mastix* (1633) and Walter Montagu's *Shepheard's Paradise* (1633), in which Queen Henrietta Maria performed, was a factor in the now-famous clipping of Prynne's ears. No harm will be done if we leave ourselves room to ponder the possibility of universal implications in all these varied plays, but we are nevertheless likely to understand them a little more fully if we stay alert to their specific Renaissance resonances.[3]

The power of topicality, of course, is discernible in many periods other than sixteenth- and seventeenth-century England. Our plays here may even be perceived as constituting a microcosm helpful for providing perspectives on a vast number of dramatic works between then and now. To cite but a scattered sampling, David Mallet's *Mustapha* (1739) took up a subject that previously had attracted two of our seventeenth-century playwrights, the story of Solyman the Magnificent, a ruler misled by an unscrupulous adviser into believing that his son Mustapha was disloyal. In 1739 this general situation could be paralleled more or less readily to that of George II, Walpole, and Frederick, Prince of Wales—to whom Mallet dedicated the work. In 1754 an audience wrecked Thomas Sheridan's theater because he forbade an actor to repeat a politically topical speech in James Miller's tragedy *Mahomet the Impostor*. And Verdi's *Masked Ball* (1859) as we know it was the result of a major revamping intended to blur the political parallels in its original form.

In the earlier twentieth century John Millington Synge's *Playboy of the Western World* (1907) occasioned riots on both sides of the Atlantic. In 1941 Hitler's Reich Chancellery banned performances and school study of Schiller's *William Tell* (1804). Arthur Miller's *The Crucible* (1952) used a seventeenth-century façade to facilitate the exposition of twentieth-century, McCarthy-style witch-hunting. Tom Stoppard chose to reflect in *Cahoot's Macbeth* (1979) the Czechoslovakian dramatist Pavel Kohout's efforts to create a "Living-Room Theatre": "[W]hat we don't like is a lot of people being cheeky and saying they are only Julius Caesar or Coriolanus or Macbeth" (63). When Leonid Brezhnev died on 10 November 1982 and the Czech National Committee decreed that the only suitable dramatic genre for the day was tragedy, the Ypsilon Theater canceled its scheduled comedy and performed *Macbeth* "with inordinate pauses at the relevant points, and a full minute of silence after 'Yet who would have thought the old man to have had so much blood in him?' It was a black mass" (Adler 1413). Andrzej Wajda's *Danton* (1983), a motion picture about the French Revolution, caused shock waves that reached the highest levels of the French government. Caryl Churchill's *Serious Money* (1987) made serious jabs at the venality of not only the business world but also the British government. In the latter part of 1992 the Vice President of the United

---

[3]As Dutton writes, "The topical meaning of a play is not its only meaning, and arguably not its most important one (whether or not it was intended by the dramatist), but it remains part of the living response to a text in the real world, and wilfully to ignore it diminishes the vitality of that text" (14).

States, Dan Quayle, touting goals of the Republican election campaign, voiced disapproval of an unwed mother in a television series, whereupon that character, a television anchorwoman played by the actress Candice Bergen, was given an episode in which to respond to "her" viewers across the nation. In the summer of 1993 Susan Sontag was reported to be in war-ravaged Sarajevo rehearsing actors in a Serbo-Croat translation of Samuel Beckett's *Waiting for Godot*. In the summer of 1994, while the present book was in press, the Cameri Theater in Tel Aviv caused a furor by presenting a Shylock who first came onstage in a homburg and gray suit and finally appeared as a bearded and prayer-shawl-and-white-skullcap-wearing, ultra-orthodox religious fanatic. And so it apparently will continue to the last syllable of recorded time.

One needs to bear in mind, furthermore, that modes of analogous thinking in dramatic works are paralleled in other kinds of writing. Readers of this book are likely to remember that Milton's typical thoughtful man fancies old romances "Where more is meant then meets the ear" ("Il Penseroso," l. 120), and various scholars have shown that this insight may be applied not only to famous fictions such as Sidney's *Arcadia* and Barclay's *Argenis* but also to more obscure ones like Brathwaite's *Royal Romance*—which is a transparent version of events in England during the period of our concern. Analogous thinking is and was ubiquitous. In the seventeenth century it undergirded coats of arms, sermons, songs, tapestries, and even penny pamphlets. Though we should bear in mind that some playwrights were less interested than others in this sort of thing, a good many might have said with the pamphleteer Richard Overton, "The figure is but the shell; will you not crack the shell to take out the kernell?" (*Baiting* A1v). In fact, one of our mid-seventeenth-century playwrights, Samuel Sheppard, turns to this very image in writing of masques, comparing the unlearned, to whom they seem "Riddles, and Nulls," to "the knowing, who are able to explain the sense and meaning, and to crack the shell . . . [to] finde a sweet and pleasant kernell" (*Famers Fam'd* 15).

Edmund Ludlow in his *Memoirs* records a moment in the life of Charles I at Carisbrooke when those about the King were unsure—and as intrigued as one might be about interpreting a scene in a play—whether or not there was a kernel in the shell. "At the same time that the Scots were coming to the King," Ludlow writes, "Commissioners were also sent to him by the Parliament with offers of a personal treaty, on condition that the King in testimony of his future sincerity, would grant the four preliminary bills formerly mentioned. Whilst these two sorts of Commissioners were one day attending the King as he walked about the castle, they observed him to throw a bone before two spaniels that followed him, and to take great delight in seeing them contesting for it; which some of them thought to be intended by him to represent that bone of contention he had cast between the two parties" (1:179). Ludlow's words about intention are crucial. Where analogy is concerned, the creator of the work is sometimes creating also some comfortable personal leeway.

The mid-seventeenth century, then, had a particular concern for what is obviously a universal phenomenon: the impulse to compare. As the playwright William Cavendish put it, "Whensoever we see, we are always similizing" (*English "Prince"* 177). The resultant metaphors can be interesting, provocative, useful, memorable, beautiful, dangerous, and many things else. In the form of allusions to earlier times, they may serve as aids to either praise (Charles I as Christ) or blame (Charles I as Richard II). Narrative "similizing" or "exampling" even had reassuringly firm authorization from the ancients. According to Quintilian, examples from history are valuable because "as a rule history seems to repeat itself and the experience of the past is a valuable support to reason" (3.8.66-67). Hence, at a comic level, Don Armado's wish that he might "example" the description of his love with "some mighty president" (*Love's Labor's Lost* I.ii.116-17). Exampling is especially useful in a period of strife because it allows some writers to proclaim outrageous, even libelous, parallels, others to choose the shadowy safety of parallels, and still others to seek an intermediate position between such extremes.

In the writing of George Wither—sometime Anglican and later militant Puritan—we have one of the most extended of all midcentury commentaries on literary indirection. Though the playwright-poet John Denham held him to be the worst poet in England, Wither provides in *The Dark Lantern* (1653) some direct and useful information of the sort we must usually infer:

> The *times* are dangerous; and, I am told,
> By that which is my *Guide*, I should not bold
> Beyond *discretion* be; which makes me talk
> In *riddles*, and with this *Dark Lantern* walk:
> That, I may see my way, and not be seen
> By ev'ry one, whom I may meet, between
> My goings *out*, and *in;* and that it may
> Give *light* to some, who are beside their way. . . .
>
> [A3r]

In other words, Wither feels impelled to be discreet, indirect, and didactic. A dark lantern, after all, has an aperture that enables one to control both the direction and the amount of light to be cast. After going on to remind readers of Jesus' example of indirection in his parables, and after many other lines on the nature and use of indirection, Wither offers the following advice to would-be interpreters of his lines:

Observe them well, with enquiring, what
Their *Authors* meaning was, in *this,* or *that,*
Till, you *your selves,* have search'd, how they *in reason,*
Suit our *affairs,* our *persons,* and the *season,*
According to your *judgements;* for, that, shall
Be somewhat to the *purpose,* though not *all.*
But, where no sense that's likely, you can rear,
Leave it, as that, which lies without your *sphear.*

[9]

As the author of the most ambitious English emblem book of the day—*A Collection of Emblemes* (1635)—Wither certainly had had plenty of experience with this sort of communication.

The Dark Lantern provides both a comment on tensions in the period and a fair prognostic regarding much of the material to be discussed here. Because Wither has been frustrated by the publisher's commercially motivated three-month delay in bringing out *The Dark Lantern,* he even makes clear that timing has been important to him: "*Providence* hath permitted these [verses] to be delayed, until their publication came too late, for effecting that which was intended" (A1r).[4] Thus Wither acknowledges directly that his writing is meant to interact in some intricate and even timely way with his readers' intellectual systems or capabilities.

There can be no doubt that English dramatic writings during the time of the Civil Wars, Commonwealth, and Protectorate played a significant part in the life of their time. It is not too much to say, therefore, that they are one way of reading their time. Conversely, it is necessary to read their time in other kinds of documents in order to understand these plays. Hence the citation here of such writers as Prynne, Ludlow, and Wither, and hence, in fact, the title of the present chapter. To a greater degree than usual with creative works, many of these dramatic writings would remain inert and puzzling if we did not know something—and the more the better—about their cultural context. The more we learn about that time—about midcentury matters of a literary, social, political, religious, moral, and economic nature—the better we will understand its drama. Although no truly great writers may be found among the many who contributed to the body of plays we will be considering, their works constitute a subject of considerable complexity and interest, both in themselves and for the light they cast on other aspects of English culture at midcentury. Moreover, without exam-

---

[4]As part of his extended title, Wither includes the dating of his work; it is the result of "his *Solitary Musings,* the third of *November* 1652. about *Midnight.*" The entire business of the Commons that day was the "Debate upon the List returned by the Commissioners for compounding, of Persons sequestered for Omissions or Underevaluations" (*Journals of the House of Commons* 7:208).

Mr: William Prynne, for writing a booke
againſt Stage-players called Hiſtrio—maſtix
was firſt cenſured in the Starr-Chamber to looſ
ſe both his Eares in the pillorie, fined 5000ᵗ & per
petuall impriſonment in the Towre of London
After this, on a meer ſuſpition of writing other
bookes, but nothing at all proved againſt him,
hee was again cenſured in the Starr-chamber t
looſe the ſmall remainder of both his eares i
the pillorie, to be Stigmatized on both his Cheek
with a firey-iron, was fined again 5000ᵗ and ba
niſhed into yᵉ Iſle of Ierſey, there to ſuffer perpe
tuall-Cloſs- impriſonmᵗ: no freinds being per
mitted to ſee him, on pain of impriſonment·

Figure 1. William Prynne
(1600-1669), after
Wenceslaus Hollar. (By per-
mission of the British Mu-
seum.)

ining the continuous life of the drama in the 1640s and 1650s we cannot
fully understand either the similarities or the differences between pre-1642
and post-1660 drama.

Though a contextual approach here provides a multifaceted means of
perceiving both the plays and the historical reality of which they are a part,
it must be admitted that seeing either literary or historical facts accurately
is always a relative business. As Robert Burton put the matter in his *Anatomy
of Melancholy,* "Some understand too little, some too much" (10). When
William Prynne lost his ears and was branded in reprisal for his antitheatrical
Histrio-mastix, Thomas Fuller later recalled, "So various were mens fancies
in reading the . . . letters, imprinted in his face, that some made them to
spell the *guiltiness* of the *Sufferer,* but others the *cruelty* of the *Imposer*"
(*Church-History* Bk. 11, p. 155; see figure 1).

Differences among readers are inevitable. Integral to any question
about signs, moreover, is the problem of whether or to what degree

meaning is inherent or construed—the problem of Charles and the spaniels, as it were. With regard to Prynne's branding, even if one knew neither the words *Seditious Libeller* nor *Stigmata Laudis*, interpretative phrases pointing in opposite directions, the letters *S* and *L* had multiple possible meanings. Like nearly any of the plays we shall be considering, therefore, perhaps these mere two juxtaposed letters will serve to show how writing, be it simple or complex, may be more complex than first seems likely. In short, Laud's *S* and *L* should help to prepare us for the possibility of literary alternatives.

Given our different orientations, it is obvious that we are all bound to create different alternatives, different patterns of intelligibility for ourselves and, if we try to share them, for others as well. If it is not totally true that we half create what we perceive, it certainly is true that we more than half create what we can convey to others. Such thoughts can explain in part why the present book differs so markedly from its predecessor, Alfred Harbage's ambitious and erudite *Cavalier Drama* (1936).[5] Confronted with a mountain of complex and conflicting data, Professor Harbage accomplished a great deal. Unfortunately both for him and for us, however, he apparently lost or never had much sympathy for the material he was studying. At the beginning of his book he assumes that a scholar in the field will be "[d]epressed by the knowledge that he is dealing constantly with the trivial" (3), and at the end he offers the conclusion that the plays he has studied are "the petty creations of a petty circle" (258).

What concerns us most here is that in the process of dealing with many plays Harbage understandably felt the need to generalize, and some of his generalizations are now due for reexamination. For instance, whereas Harbage took the view that these plays are in the main soberly serious—and some surely are—many are brightened or sharpened by comic scenes and satire. (Jonson, after all, was still an admired model.) Of even greater consequence—and this will be a major theme here—the plays are far richer than Harbage acknowledges in both kind and quantity of allusions to their times. Most pervasively of all, however, the image that Harbage gives of "cavalier drama" is unnecessarily constricted. Perhaps we may say that he

[5]Harbage's book is the only previous one to survey the plays of the 1640s and 1650s, but we now have also Martin Butler's provocative book on the period 1632–42—an invaluable lead-in to the present study. Other scholars who have written major volumes in the field (but without attempting to survey the dramatic writing) are Leslie Hotson, Annabel Patterson, and Lois Potter. Others who have made significant contributions include Isaac Disraeli (a true pioneer), Hyder Rollins, Thornton S. Graves, and Louis B. Wright, among earlier scholars, and, more or less recently, Geoffrey Aggeler, Margot Heinemann, David Underdown, Michael Wilding, Kevin Sharpe, Albert Tricomi, Derek Hirst, Ira Clark, and Nancy Klein Maguire. Numerous others are noted here in the text.

has half perceived and half created a scholarly order that centralizes the nervelessly effete—at the cost, it seems, of his own patience and, certainly, of the marginalizing of some very interesting works.

Arguing, as the present book does, for an approach that is culturally contextual has a number of implications. Among them, and so important and obvious that one might overlook it, is a factor that both limited and freed the playwrights themselves: namely, the plays to be studied are *writings*. Furthermore, numerous as they are, they are survivors from a still larger body of writings. Even in the heyday of the playhouses, not all plays reached print, not even all successful ones. Some that were printed were destroyed. (One wonders what dramas disappeared forever when the play-books stored in the vaults of St. Paul's were burned in the Great Fire of 1666.) And manuscripts, of course, survive but spottily.

That most of the extant plays of the period are likely to remain available to us only in writing is, in any case, a reality that puts us on a footing roughly similar to that of those seventeenth-century men and women who found it difficult or impossible to attend theatrical performances. Had Ben Jonson lived five years longer, he might have raised a brimming cup to the triumph of textuality over theatricality. Of course, a totally opposite and non-Jonsonian view is also possible. Richard Baker wrote that "a Play *read*, hath not half the pleasure of a Play *Acted;* for though it have the pleasure of *ingenious Speeches;* yet it wants the pleasure of *Gracefull action;* and we may well acknowledg, that *Gracefulness* of *action*, is the greatest pleasure of a Play" (34).[6]

Many of our playwrights have something to say on the subject. Robert Baron wrote that "Playes written are not finished, made they are / I' th' study first, next on the Theater" (*Pocula Castalia* 114). Thomas Jordan held that performances in "all their glory" were "much advantaged with the illustrative faculties of Musick, Painting, and Dancing" (*Fancy's Festivals* A2r-v). Richard Flecknoe warned of his *Erminia* (1661), "It will want much of the grace and ornament of the Stage, but though there it be better seen, yet here 'tis better understood; mean while, a lively fancy may imagine he sees it Acted: and to help the imagination, I have set down the Scenes, the Habits, and Names of the Actors" (A3r). Whatever reasons they may have had, the fact is that some midcentury playwrights did begin to include more stage directions than had been customary in earlier years. It is a fact also that when we are confronted with a text on a table rather than players on a stage, we are likely to catch more of the author's words. A reader can always reread. The

---

[6]Thomas Rymer, writing late in the century, expressed what may be the most extreme view of this matter: "*Action* is speaking to the Eyes; and all *Europe* over, Plays have been represented with great applause, in a Tongue unknown, and sometimes without any Language at all" (4).

reading audience of *The Famous Tragedie of King Charles I* (1649) was reminded that

> Though *Johnson, Shakespeare, Goffe,* and *Devenant,*
> Brave *Sucklin,* Beaumont, Fletcher, Shurley *want*
> The life of action, and their learned lines
> Are loathed, by the Monsters of the times;
> Yet your refined Soules can penetrate
> Their depth of merit. . . .

[A3r]

James Shirley himself, in an address to readers of the Francis Beaumont and John Fletcher folio (1647), offers a wry variation on the venerable comparison of stage and life, then tries to put on a happy face: "*And now Reader in this* Tragicall Age *where the* Theater *hath been so much out-acted, congratulate thy owne happinesse, that in this silence of the Stage, thou hast a liberty to reade these inimitable Playes, to dwell and converse in these immortall Groves, which were only shewd our Fathers in a conjuring glasse, as suddenly removed as represented, the Landscrap is now brought home by this optick, and the Presse thought too pregnant before, shall be now look'd upon as greatest Benefactor to Englishmen*" (A3r-v). A play in a book is, indeed, a far cry from a rhetorical, visual, and social event, and thanks to such thinking as Shirley's, plays continued to be printed and read.

Although some of the play-texts that concern us here were never meant to be performed (Robert Knightley, translator of *Alfrede* [1659], says as much [1v][7]), others would take on a good deal more life if we could see them presented by actors possessed of wit, skill, and charm. Since we are focusing here mainly on texts, it will be well to bear in mind, therefore, that often what strikes us as textual weakness might well be concealed in a skillfully managed rush of action on a stage. The anonymous creator of *The Cyprian Conqueror* understood this. Surely he was not unique in realizing his own shortcomings as a playwright ("I wish in this play I had donne better" [5v]), but he is unusual and helpful for recording his hope that performers will compensate for them. He writes that "what is wanting in it I hope those eloquent tongs of ye actors will not bee defectiue in; action beeing ye greatest of winning force, & a greater conquerour, y^n ye Cytherean" (4v).[8] With or without knowledge of Shakespeare, he asserts that "action . . . is ye eloquence of ye body" (5v; cf. *Coriolanus* III.ii.76). Nevertheless, he says, what is most desirable of all is "a well composed & eloquent play, well represented" (4v).

---

[7]Interestingly, however, as we shall see in chapter 6, the author of Knightley's Latin source did intend for his work to be performed.   [8]The writer hopes we will recall that the island of Cythera was associated with Venus.

At this point, to help readjust a commonly skewed view, one might observe also that when Parliament took over the control of printing in 1640, it revealed no animus against plays. Despite Milton's scorn for "what despicable creatures our common rimers and play-writes be" (*Of Education* 405), he knew well enough, when occasion suited, how to make use of the fact that "*Gregory Nazianzen,* a Father of the Church, thought it not unbecoming the sanctity of his person to write a Tragedy" (preface to *Samson* 332). An example closer to home might have been the Protestant John Foxe, famed mainly for his *Book of Martyrs* (1563), who also tried his hand at writing plays. So did the Protestant polemicist John Bale, now best known for his *King John* (1538 and ca. 1558), with its dramatis personae including the widow England, Usurped Power (the Pope), and Private Wealth (a cardinal). Later on, Steven Gosson, whose high-decibel, late Elizabethan scorn for stage-players gave place to no man's, was grievously offended when he found that some of his own plays had been unearthed by enemies and (strange punishment for a playwright) actually produced. Most telling of all, perhaps, the acerbic Prynne chose the extraordinary course of structuring his antitheatrical *magnum opus* with acts and scenes, prologue and chorus.[9] An essential fact for clarifying all of these data is that throughout the long years of wrangling about drama, it was not the play but the player that drew the heavy fire. Hence in his *Histrio-mastix* we find Prynne actually recommending the reading of plays (831-36, 928-31).[10]

Whatever reasons they had, readers continued to buy plays even during the grimmest years of the century. Then or now, we all know, a book bought is not necessarily a book read, and from the disputes of scholars on the makeup of early modern English theater audiences we surely may extrapolate the need for caution when it comes to generalizing about readers. On the other hand, we need not be hesitant about collecting such clues as come our way. Humphrey Moseley, for example, explains in an address to readers of the Beaumont and Fletcher folio that he is bringing forth only new plays, not a complete collection, because "*Gentlewomen* would have found it scarce manageable, who in Workes of this nature must first be remembred" (A4r). Taking a less approving stand on the matter, Samuel Torshell in *The Womans Glorie* (1645) fretted that too many women read only "*Love-stories* and *playes*" (127). "Away," he urged, "with your *Tragedies,* and *Comedies,* and *Masques,* and *Pastorals,* & whatsoever other names they have, that soften

---

[9]Jonas Barish observes that "Prynne evidently wishes both to exploit the possibilities for order inherent in such an arrangement, and also to perpetrate a running irony, to turn the terminology of dramatic structure against its usual practitioners and make it serve a godly rather than a satanic purpose" (85).   [10]Then again, the very title page of *Histrio-mastix* announces that "*the penning, acting, and frequenting of Stage-playes, are unlawfull, infamous and misbeseeming Christians.*"

the spirit, and take away your savour of heavenly matters" (124). One might call to mind also that young miss in Aston Cokayne's *Obstinate Lady* (1657) who squanders so much of her time reading plays (B4r). And of course some writers were worried about the weakness of the stronger sex. Henry Edmundson believed that "*the feeding of mens mindes with . . . Play-books . . . (if there be no other iniquity in them) is apt to make men unapt for the duties of life*" (a2r). Conversely, while he was in London between January and November 1653, Sir Daniel Fleming of Skirwith bought no fewer than seven playbooks (Rollins, "Commonwealth Drama" 58). At different stages of his life the pious Nicholas Ferrar apparently shared the views of both Edmundson and Fleming: as death drew near, he burned his collection of playbooks (Maycock 298). And elsewhere—who can say if it magnified the danger or merely the fun?—we find that William and Margaret Cavendish, two of the dramatists we shall be considering, sometimes read plays together.

Indubitably some Englishmen were building libraries. The printed catalogue of Dr. Francis Bernard's collection eventually came to an amazing 450 octavo pages (Lawler 191). Another big buyer, Richard Smyth, secondary of the Poultry Compter, owned the first folios of Shakespeare, Jonson, and Davenant. The library of Walter Rea is said to have contained "a good sprinkling of poems, plays and Roman Catholic Literature" (Lawler 20). And whether he bought the books or borrowed them, John Cotgrave somehow managed to mine about sixteen hundred passages of verse, all from plays, for his *English Treasury of Wit and Language* (Bentley, "Cotgrave's Treasury" 190).

As for readers higher in rank, the library at Castle Ashby, home of the Earl of Northampton, another of our playwrights, had at least seventeen volumes of plays, including the works of Shakespeare and Jonson.[11] It is often noted that Sidney's *Arcadia* figured in King Charles's final days because he thought Pamela's prayer there provided rhetoric suitable for addressing his own God, but a lesser-known and slightly earlier bit of historico-literary flotsam is even more relevant here: in December 1648, while imprisoned at Windsor, the King was reported to be "*most delighted with* Ben Johnson's *playes, of any bookes that are here*" (*Perfect Occurrences*, no. 102). It is not surprising that Abraham Cowley had one of his characters in *Cutter of Coleman-Street* (1663) predict that the Puritans' "first pious work will be to banish *Fletcher* and *Ben Johnson* out o' the Parlour, and bring in their rooms *Martin Mar-Prelate*, and Posies of Holy Honey-suckles" (27-28).

---

[11]This information is taken from a typescript by William P. Williams (cited in Kelliher, "Cavalier Dramatist" 167).

The future Charles II, of course, would have none of that. A number of the plays we shall be discussing turned up in his personal library.[12]

At certain booksellers, fortunately, a reader's choice of plays was comfortably large. In the first and only edition of Thomas Goffe's *The Careles Shepherdess*, a pastoral tragicomedy acted before Charles and Henrietta Maria at Salisbury Court and later published in Cromwell's time (1656), one comes across a list purporting to be an "Alphebeticall Catalogue of all such Plays that were ever printed." Compiled and printed for Richard Rogers and William Ley, this extraordinary document includes more than five hundred plays. In the same year, and apparently in competitive response, the bookseller Edward Archer came out with a longer list. At the back of the first and only edition we have of the Jacobean comedy called *The Old Law* (by Middleton, Rowley, and Massinger), Archer offered "An Exact and perfect Catalogue" of 622 plays. Furthermore, these works were not simply known to him; he claimed that they could be purchased either "at the Signe of the *Adam and Eve*, in Little Britain; or, at the *Ben Johnson's* Head in Thredneedle-street, over against the Exchange."[13]

That there was competition among booksellers with a special interest in drama is demonstrated further by Francis Kirkman. In 1661 Kirkman compiled *A True . . . Catalogue*, listing some 685 plays, all of which might be bought or sold at the four several shops of Nathaniel Brook in Cornhill, Thomas Johnson in St. Paul's Churchyard, Henry Marsh in Chancery Lane, and Kirkman himself "at the John Fletchers Head." Any suspicion we might have that this trade in plays was fueled in part by personal zest, moreover, is supported by Kirkman's words that same year in what proves to be our only edition of a 1620s comedy called *A Cure for a Cuckold* (probably by Webster, Rowley, and Heywood). Kirkman explains that

> It hath been my fancy and delight . . . to converse with Books; and the pleasure I have taken in those of this nature, (viz. Plays) hath bin so extraordinary, that it hath bin much to my cost; for I have been (as we term it) a Gatherer of Plays for some years, and I am confident I have more of several sorts than any man in England, Book-seller, or other: I can at any time shew 700 in number, which is within a small matter all that were ever printed. Many of these I have several times over, and intend as I sell, to purchase more. [A2r]

In fact, though details of the business are bound to remain obscure, some booksellers even collected—and therefore may well have sold—plays in manuscript form.[14] Theatrical history must concern itself with the anguished

---

[12]The library of Worcester College, Oxford, has Charles's copies of, for instance, *Marcus Tullius Cicero* (1651), Manuche's *The Just General* (1652), and *The Hectors* (1656).   [13]Quoted from a leaf following page 76 of *The Old Law*.   [14]Harbage records various kinds of evidence on the subject in his "Elizabethan-Restoration Palimpsest."

closings, furtive openings, and reactive demolishings of the playhouses, but the availability of plays for readers can scarcely remain in doubt.[15]

Since the number of plays to be dealt with in the present study is large, some kind of taxonomy is necessary to confront them. The major approach here will be in chapters that are shaped so as to emphasize either the actualization of various dramatic genres or the impingement of historical events on dramatic texts. Insofar as any literary taxonomy is a pragmatic construction, such an approach runs the risk of seeming arbitrary. The facts are that genres borrow constantly from one another, that within a given genre one work may differ greatly from another, and that some works may fit conveniently in more than one genre. Leonard Willan's *Astraea* (1651), for example, yields different insights if viewed as a romance, a tragicomedy, or a pastoral. Beyond mere classification, in other words, genre provides an avenue to meaning—and perhaps especially where it seems most inadequate as a category. In any case, the chapters here may be viewed as supplementing and clarifying one another, and themes and modes that have once been introduced are likely to recur in different shapes and places. Tragic themes and modes, for example, appear not merely in the chapter devoted to tragedy (chapter 13), where a hurried reaper might expect to harvest them, but also in "Arms and the Men" (chapter 5), "The Famous Tragedy of Charles I" (chapter 6), "*Anglo-Tyrannus*" (chapter 7), "The Craft of Translation" (chapter 11), and "Fruits of Seasons Gone" (chapter 12).[16] Overall, of course, the goal is to provide a fuller sense of the plays, the genres to which they belong, and the world that made them possible.

Fortunately, one need be of no particular persuasion to respond with interest, feeling, and even fascination either to the plays themselves or to the endlessly ramifying pressures of their world. No special eyeglasses are required to see the problems and possibilities posed by England's mixed goals and moral paradoxes at midcentury, or by the erosion of old ideals and the gradual growth of new. Clearly there was a continuing human need for making pretty façades and speaking from behind masks, for teaching, persuading, railing, and amusing by means of a variety of dramatic forms. Whatever impulses sustained it, the dark lantern of drama continued to cast its gleam throughout the 1640s and 1650s.

---

[15]Some years after the close of our period, Langbaine reported his purchase of "*all the Plays I could meet with, in the* English *Tongue,*" totaling "*above* Nine Hundred *and* Fourscore *English* Plays *and* Masques, *besides* Drolls *and* Interludes." What is more, he claimed "*having read most of them*" (*Momus Triumphans* A2r).   [16]Besides its chronological listing of plays, the *Annals* of Harbage, Schoenbaum, and Wagonheim indicates the genre of each work. For these and other reasons, it provides a helpful complement to the present study.

[2]

THE SUN DECLINING

He's in his Court;
And now me thinks his presence guilds the walls.
      —William Strode, *The Floating Island* (1636)

. . . the mortall Sunne from whom we Brittanes receive our safest
warmth.
      —*Five Most Noble Speeches Spoken to His Majestie* (1641)

Ye'have showne it, *Brittaines*, and have often donne,
Things that have chear'd the weary setting *Sunne*.
      —Abraham Cowley, *The Civil War* (1642)

. . . let no Nobles hope their worth will shine,
Who make the Sun of Majesty decline. . . .
      —Thomas Fuller, *Andronicus; or, The Unfortunate Politician* (1646)

. . . the Suns withdrawing leaves one world,
Into a Winters Tyrannie t'be hurld. . . .
      —Mildmay Fane, *Otia Sacra* (1648)[1]

IN ORDER TO GLIMPSE some of the continuities and discontinuities in English drama before and after the official closing of the theaters, obviously it is necessary to consider the period just prior to 1642.[2] As soon as one does so, the importance of the court—and often its idealization—become apparent. In 1633 Thomas Carew had had Religion assure Britain's King and Queen in *Coelum Britannicum* that "*Mortality cannot with more / Religious zeale, the gods adore*" (183). Even in 1640, when unease was spreading throughout the kingdom, Edmund Waller virtually prayed to the Queen: "Great Goddess give this thy sacred Island rest" (134). George Ridpath, author of *The Stage Condemn'd* (1698), recorded that King Charles, for the first Sunday in Epiphany, 1638, requested a masque (Davenant's *Britannia Triumphans*) "for his own praise, upon that day, which by Divine Institution was set apart for the praise of our Redeemer" (13–14, 25). And after Charles was beheaded, at least one writer was moved to write of the event as a "*Deicide*" (Glover 9).

---

[1]Solar imagery of the sort illustrated in this cluster of passages is paralleled in the other arts (see figure 2).   [2]The single most potent fore-and-aft studies of the drama are those by Martin Butler (on the years 1632–42) and Robert Hume (on Restoration drama).

Figure 2. A medal struck in 1633 depicting Charles I (obverse) and the sun over London (reverse). The motto on the latter may be translated "The sun returning illuminates the world; so the King does the city." (From Pinkerton, *The Medallic History of England to the Revolution* [1790].)

One did not need to be of any particular political or religious persuasion to have reservations about such adulation. On the other hand, English monarchs had long enjoyed being elevated to the status of breathing icons. To go back no earlier, one might cite Jonson's famed praise of the sixty-eight-year-old Queen Elizabeth as the goddess Diana, "Queen and huntress, chaste and fair." When James VI of Scotland came to the English throne in 1603, reinforcing his position with reminders that kings are like gods on earth, there was little reluctance on the part of writers to entwine divine and imperial themes. John Taylor, the self-styled "Water Poet," who went to visit Charles after his 1647 flight to Carisbrooke Castle on the Isle of Wight, reported that the King was still "touching" and curing faithful citizens.[3] Even as late as 1662 the playwright Margaret Cavendish had one of her characters, Lady Sanspareile, endorse the old creed: "Kings and Royal Princes should do as Gods, which is to keep their Subjects in aw, with the Superstitious fear of Ceremonies" (*Youths Glory*, pt. 2, p. 155).

Speaking for the opposition and writing in exile some time after 1660, the republican regicide Edmund Ludlow provides a statement that is equally clear and rather more subtle: "The question in dispute between the King's party and us being, as I apprehended, whether the King should

---

[3]Taylor provides a number of interesting details in *Tailors Travels, from London, to the Isle of Wight* (1648), collected in his *Works*.

Figure 3. Charles I (1600-1649). (By permission of the British Museum.)

govern as a god by his will, and the nation be governed by force like beasts: or whether the people should be governed by law made by themselves, and live under a government derived from their own consent" (1:18). Finding Ludlow writing on the matter as a "question in dispute" may help us see the value of Christopher Hill's statement that "Divine right had to be proclaimed because it was being challenged" (22).

In the days of Elizabeth and James, extravagant praise had sometimes served political ends, first helping to shore up the Tudor monarchy when it was weak within and threatened from without, and later establishing and reinforcing the authority of the new monarch from Scotland. Ironically, therefore, the rhetorical mode that once appears to have strengthened both England's throne and the pride of its people almost certainly served later to broaden the gap between Charles and his people. In particular and with the benefit of hindsight, the lavish Caroline masques of the 1630s may be viewed as emblems of the distancing of the King from his people. At the center of these shows, as Stephen Orgel has argued, there lies "a belief in the hierarchy and a faith in the power of idealization" (*Illusion* 40). Both immediately and ultimately, the masques depict "the triumph of an aristocratic community." Kevin Sharpe adds, "That a monarch as hard-working as Charles devoted much time to the entertainments . . . alerts us to their political significance" (*Personal Rule*

227). Despite some interesting criticism integrated in their mix of ingredients, in other words, the masques as a whole present a basically true and potentially unsettling image of Charles's cultural and political views.[4]

Students of the period have been assiduous in trying to gauge the distance between the monarchs and their people (the questions of *what* people and *when* make the subject extremely complex), but they have tended sometimes to overlook the cracks within Whitehall itself. Terms such as *court* and *cavalier* are of limited use unless we keep in mind that, as Edward Hyde, Earl of Clarendon, observed later, "the court was full of faction and animosity" (1:187).[5] John Suckling included in his play *Brennoralt* (1639–41; printed 1646) a speech to a king that in retrospect seems especially pointed:

> Nor are you, Sir, assur'd of all behinde you:
> For though your Person in your Subjects hearts
> Stands highly honour'd, and belov'd, yet are
> There certaine Acts of State, which men call grievances
> Abroad; and though they bare them in the times
> Of peace, yet will they now perchance, seeke to
> Be free, and throw them off.
>
> [III.ii.93–99]

Brennoralt concerns Somewhere Else, of course, but Suckling wrote it soon after returning from the First Bishops' War in Scotland, and Brennoralt himself, as Suckling's editor L.A. Beaurline suggests, "probably was

---

[4]Conrad Russell makes the supplementary point that the actual presentation of the masques brought together people who would take different sides in 1640 and 1642 (*Fall* 4), and Malcolm Smuts concludes that "the early seventeenth century witnessed a weakening of cultural bonds uniting the monarch with the political nation and the largely illiterate populace" (187). P.W. Thomas writes of the "breakdown of the national culture" (184).

[5]Keeping the matter of factions more or less realistically complicated and at the same time clear enough to be understood is a problem that must be confronted either directly or indirectly by nearly anyone writing about the court in particular or the country at large. Knights, for example, observes that "in the middle years of the century . . . one finds, not a sharp division into opposing 'sides,' but a series of fluctuating alliances of groups of persons that only at crucial moments—such as the outbreak of war or the trial and execution of the King—have even the appearance of massive cohesion. Not only were there sharp divisions within each camp, even after the war had started men changed sides, and there were those too—often the best—who were closer to some men of the opposing party than they were to many within their own. Looking back, we can see certain economic, political and intellectual movements that were to shape the future government of the country and—broadly speaking—its political philosophy; but the closer one gets to the events of the time, the broad stream of history is less apparent than the swirls and eddies and the occasional whirlpool" (61–62).

intended to represent one or more of the disaffected young noblemen who openly criticized the pacification of Berwick" on 18 June 1639 (Suckling 2:289).[6]

Having arrived at conjugal happiness with Henrietta Maria only after weathering several stormy years in the 1620s, and having dismissed a troublesome Parliament in 1629, Charles, at least for a while in the 1630s, was able to enjoy what was to be the best period of his life. These were the so-called "*Halcyon* dayes" that one encounters in writings of the time (e.g., Carew, "In Answer of an Elegiacall Letter," l. 96). Richard Fanshawe wrote at the beginning of the decade: "White Peace (the beautiful'st of things) / Seemes here her everlasting rest / To fix" ("An Ode," ll. 37–39, in *Shorter Poems*). So far as Parliament was concerned, Charles really may have thought he had tidied up and essentially done away with a messy problem. Such thinking surely would have been encouraged by those at court who, in Sir Dudley North's words, "Theyr Princes errors . . . applaud in Halcyon dayes" (Randall, *Gentle Flame* 144). As early as 1636 North wrote also that his countrymen lacked "nor Art nor Courage for a civill warr" (146). Nevertheless, and despite a variety of destabilizing elements that gathered force during the remaining years when he ruled without a Parliament, Charles was able to perceive himself as the happiest king in Christendom.[7]

During this period he enlisted William Laud, Archbishop of Canterbury, in the cause of strengthening religion by means of making everyone embrace the same form of it. Albert Tricomi puts the matter thus: "Perceiving the instability that Puritanism was bringing to England, Charles and Archbishop Laud undertook to revivify Anglicanism by shifting the emphasis from divisive pulpit sermons to ritual and ceremony" (168). Laud, a hard-working, methodical, self-disciplined man, later said of himself, "I laboured nothing more, than that the External Publick Worship of God . . . might be preserved" (224).

During these same years Charles also launched a series of proposals for replenishing the strained royal treasury. Edward Hyde, who for a while served as leader of the King's party in the Commons, looked back with a

---

[6]After the so-called First Bishops' War with the rebelling Scots ended in June 1639, and a Second Bishops' War followed when the Scots invaded England in August the next year. The King's army was defeated in about a week.   [7]Cited in Sharpe's *Personal Rule* from a letter that Charles wrote to his nephew, the Elector Palatine, in 1637 (770–71). Assessing the antebellum climate has proved difficult for scholars because of the complexity of the relevant evidence. Sharpe provides a good deal of valuable information and commentary on the question, and Anselment observes that, later on, "[h]owever much the civil war led to an exaggerated impression of England's lost happiness, the sense of her unique peace had been well established before the outbreak of armed conflict. Charles and his contemporary historians, in fact, recount an inseparable blend of myth and history fashioned in the context of international and not civil war" (23).

cold eye on Charles's moneymaking projects of the 1630s, saying that "many ridiculous, many scandalous, all very grievous were set on foot" (1:85). The King who was being exalted in his masques at court could be—and sometimes was—perceived as a threat to his own realm. He was, indeed, a "Hieroglyphic King" (Vaughan 370).

When conflict over Charles's Laudian policies began to build toward the Second Bishops' War in Scotland, and when Charles realized that the gentry would not provide so-called Ship Money to aid him and that he could not secure credit elsewhere to raise military support, he was finally compelled to call another Parliament—the first since that of 1628–29.[8] When it met on 13 April 1640, Charles naturally wished to talk of funds and supplies, but Parliament wished to talk of reform and redress. Again the King closed Parliament, but before the year was out, he had to call another. This one began to meet on 3 November 1640, and what remained of it in January 1649 would put Charles on trial.

With hindsight one can see signs of approaching danger throughout the 1630s, and some that are reflected in the drama have been analyzed with great skill by Martin Butler. Although Butler occasionally claims too much, he is nonetheless pervasively convincing in his readings. An invaluable lead-in to the present study, Butler's book explains how those dramatists who wrote for Whitehall "were limited in the material they could use, the diversity of opinion they could express, the range of conflicting or conventional attitudes which they could incorporate in their plays" (*Theatre and Crisis* 4). And yet Butler's main point is that this courtly narrowing is by no means the whole story. In fact, some of the works he calls "courtier plays" prove to be more critical than complimentary. He demonstrates at length that the best courtier plays of 1632–42 "show the stage acting not as an extravagant and narrowly 'Cavalier' plaything but as an important focus and voice for anxieties and dissent existing in tension within the court. The writers . . . perceive the injustice, instability and unpopularity of Charles's regime with considerable clarity and concern" (82).

The dramatic bill of fare was further varied on the other main stages operating in London during the 1630s.[9] At the opposite end of the social scale from Whitehall was the huge and raucous Red Bull. In 1640 John Tatham described the Bull as a place of "din, and *incivility*." There one

---

[8]In 1634 Charles succeeded in collecting tax from coastal towns and counties with the argument that it would be used for protection against enemy shipping and pirates. In the following year the taxable territory was expanded to inland towns and counties. Finally, however, in 1641, the collection of Ship Money aroused so much opposition that it was declared illegal.   [9]Attention here will be focused on London, but we should bear in mind that there were also many provincial performances.

might expect to find "a noyse / Of *Rables, Applewives*, and Chimney-boyes" as well as overreaching players with "mouth enough to teare / *Language* by th'eares" (*Fancies* H2v-H3r).

Besides recognizing the different limitations and capabilities of drama at Whitehall and the Red Bull, we have also to consider an important middling tradition that spoke mainly to a somewhat elite and gentlemanly audience. We catch sight of it in the words of James Jones in a poem to Tatham: "Thou didst not meane thy *Theater* sho'd be / Common (though publique) to th'Obliquity / Of ev'ry duller eye" (*Fancies Theater* A1r). We find it in *The Actors Remonstrance* (1643), which speaks of the actors as "friends, young Gentlemen, that used to feast and frolick ... at Tavernes" (6). We find it in the words of Edmund Gayton, who recorded in 1654 how interested auditors might invite actors to repeat their scenes in taverns (*Pleasant Notes* 140–41). And we glimpse it, too, in the words of Simonds D'Ewes, who in May 1641 complained that parliamentary business was being impeded in the afternoons because "the greater parte" of the members were being drawn to "Hide Park & playes & bowling grounds" (Butler, *Theatre and Crisis* 134). In short, whether one delves into the history of the theater or turns to the surviving play-texts, one finds a range of offerings that together invite a broader and more complex sense of the times than may be suggested by the term *cavalier drama*.

In thinking about this body of plays just preceding the order to close the theaters, moreover, we should bear in mind that while we know what lay immediately ahead, the dramatists, players, and booksellers themselves were able to do no more than catch glimpses of the handwriting on the wall. It appears that in 1640 (or maybe 1641) they could have read in a pamphlet called *Vox Borealis*—probably by Richard Overton—about "a lamentable Tragedie, acted by the Prelacie, against the poore Players of the *Fortune* Play-house" (B2r).[10] Though there is good reason to have doubts about the accuracy of this document, the fact is that it must have been close enough to reality to pass for truth at the time. In the course of a few lines it concerns itself not only with what the Fortune players presumably had attempted by way of comment on religious matters, but also with how they excused

---

[10]Somewhat oddly, the pamphlet claims to have been printed in "the yeare coming on, 1641," which conceivably indicates its appearance during January-March 1640-41. Laud, a key figure in the anecdote, had been imprisoned since 18 December 1640. Combing through records of cases heard by the Court of High Commission in 1640 through 7 December yields a handful of references to the Fortune, but none to any raid such as the pamphlet describes. Complicating matters further, Bentley assumes that the anecdote is a later telling of an incident elsewhere reported—also with suspect detail—in May 1639 (*Jacobean and Caroline Stage* 1:278 and 5:1235).

themselves to an ecclesiastical court worried about being depicted onstage, and how the actors then proceeded to use their playing skills yet again to comment on a related matter. The players, we are told, had chosen to revive

> a new old Play, called *The Cardinalls conspira[c]ie*, whom they brought upon the *stage* in as great *state* as they could, with *Altars, Images, Crosses, Crucifexes,* and the like, to set forth his pomp and pride. But wofull was the sight to see how in the middest of all their *mirth,* the Pursevants came and seazed upon the poore Cardinall, and all his Consorts, and carryed them away. And when they were questioned for it, in the High Commission Court, they pleaded *Ignorance,* and told the Archbishop [Laud] *that they tooke those examples of their Altars, Images,* and the like, *from Heathen Authors.* This did somewhat asswage his anger, that they did not bring him on the Stage: But yet they were fined for it, and after a *little Imprisonment* gat their *liberty.* And having nothing left them but a few old Swords and Bucklers, they fell to Act the *Valiant Scot,* which they Played five dayes with great applause, which vext the Bishops worse then the other, insomuch, as they were forbidden Playing it any more; and some of them prohibited ever Playing againe. [B2r-v][11]

Apocryphal or not, the silencing reported here of certain players is probably no more than would have been approved at about the same time by that former masque-writer John Milton in his *Reason of Church-Government* (1642). In Milton's view, "it were happy for the Commonwealth if our magistrates would take into their care . . . the managing of our public sports." He continues, "Whether this may be not only in Pulpits, but . . . in Theaters . . . or what other place, or may win most upon the people to receiv at once both recreation, & instruction, let them in autority consult" (820).

Just who was to be in authority was, of course, the big question. When we begin to consider various kinds of dramatic and quasi-dramatic writings, we encounter it repeatedly. In 1640, and most ostentatiously of all, Davenant's great masque called *Salmacida Spolia* conveyed the official royal image. Whatever "*malicious Fury*" (B1r) might threaten, Davenant writes, the land will be guided by "*a secret power,*" namely, the wisdom of Philogenes ("*Lover of his People*"), who was presently dancing at Whitehall in silver and blue. In 1640 nearly anyone could see clearly enough and even say in a masque that "*tis his fate, to rule in adverse times*" (C1r). Within this same masque, on the other hand, coming to Charles as a helpmeet, descending from a huge cloud and accompanied by martial ladies, was "the

---

[11]*The Valiant Scot* by J.W. had been published in 1637 but dates back to approximately 1626. Allusion in the present context—whether onstage, in the pamphlet, or both—is to Charles's unsuccessful encounters with the Scots in the Bishops' Wars.

chiefe Heroin" of the piece (D2r), a woman of whom it might be said this early, "*The valiant take from her their Fire!*" (D2v). (That Henrietta Maria was pregnant again was for some reason thought to enhance the occasion [Bentley, *Jacobean and Caroline Stage* 3:214].)

Some serious questions are implicit in the narratives that undergird all this laudation. As Davenant points out in his introduction, *Salmacida Spolia* takes its theme mainly from two ancient sources. The first concerns the fountain of Salmacis, which reduced fierce and cruel barbarians to the sweetness of Grecian ways, and the second concerns some Thebans who counterattacked and decimated some Argives, an invading foe. In effect, we have here two responses to the troubles seething in Scotland: the magical waters of conciliation and bloody, self-righteous force. Then again, lavishly mounted with stupendous settings and packed with antimasques of mad lovers, "antick" cavaliers, and much else, the masque concludes with a climactic view of heaven itself, thanks to the still-operative skills of Inigo Jones. Above all, *Salmacida Spolia* says that the King seeks civil concord by any means, and he plans to "out last / Those storms the peoples giddy fury rayse, / Till like, fantastic windes themselves they waste" (D1v).

Both the Scottish problem and the exaltation of England's royalty are manifest also in John Sadler's lesser-known *Masquarade du Ciel* (also of 1640), a strange sort of closet show that presents Charles and Henrietta Maria as Phoebus and Phebe, the sun and moon, light and life of the world.[12] Ignoring any signs that the sun's rays might be weakening, Sadler nevertheless acknowledges "The late Commotions . . . about the Northern THULE," which is "*a cold North Iland, belonging to the Crown of SCOT-LAND*" (title page and A1v). Sadler also includes dramatic hints of threatening "Horror" and "Chaos," suggested in part by "harsh unpleasing kroaking, and hideous Scritchings of *Nights Forlorne Creatures*" (B1r). Since the fault seems to lie in the stars, Phoebus sends Mercury to Thule, but Saturn, like a dour Scot, drives him back. Thus Phoebus himself, who is endowed with "much Goodnesse, condescendeth to take a *Northern* Progresse toward Thule" (A2v). Eventually, observing that such matters have "a while detained the *Thoughts*, rather then the *Eyes*, of the *Trembling* Spectators" (B1r), Sadler calls for the sun-king to enter "in his glorious Chariot" (B2v). Thanks to Charles's solar power, and thanks, too, to Henrietta Maria—to whom the work is dedicated—"a Perpetuall and Inviolable *Peace*" is settled "through all the *Little World*" of Britain (C3v).

---

[12]In later years John Evelyn recorded finding in a field a medal that showed Charles, armed and crowned, sitting hand in hand with Henrietta Maria, a sun over his head, a moon over hers, with both treading down a serpent representing "a Viperous brood" (*Numismata* 111). The medal was dated 1642.

Elsewhere in the "*Little World*" were other masques and masquelike entertainments, sometimes so different in nature as to suggest a different genre, sometimes so much simpler as to remind one of the origins of masquing in costumed dance. Down in Derbyshire at the seat of Philip Stanhope, first Earl of Chesterfield, Sir Aston Cokayne's 1640 Twelfth Night *Masque Presented at Bretbie* (printed in 1658) had a pleasant air of structured informality (its prologue was "to be spoken by whom the Masquers shall appoint" [118]). The text calls for a *Lar familiaris* and some nimble satyrs, the "excellent" little sons of Chesterfield, and ladies dressed as goddesses. Rather pointedly it claims not to be prompted by "Necessity, or pride, / Or empty prodigality" (119). To the west, at Knowsley, for the pleasure of James Stanley, Lord Strange (later Earl of Derby), Sir Thomas Salusbury in 1641 wrote another Twelfth Night masque that took as its theme the merry death of Father Christmas, followed by the dance of the New Year and its twelve months. And for the last day of that same year Salusbury wrote A *Show or Antimasque of Gipseys*, a modest home entertainment modeled on Jonson's famed *Gypsies Metamorphos'd* (1621) and designed as part of the festivities following a wedding at Chirk Castle. Likewise reflective of the widespread need to provide one's own entertainment were a couple of allegorically inclined and scenically ambitious works by Mildmay Fane, Earl of Westmorland: *Raguaillo D'Oceano*, the most masquelike of all Fane's several efforts, and *Candia Restaurata* ("Candy" was an old name for the island of Crete), in which the patients of Dr. Synodarke (Parliament) include the three ailing but curable daughters of Signior Cosmus: Albinia, Ibernia, and Callidonia.

Also touching the times—and especially the Caledonian problem— was another sort of show that, not unlike a masque, simultaneously celebrated and *became* part of an event. One may find it worthwhile to know about the series of speeches composed for the return of Charles out of Scotland in November 1641, though they were dramatic only in a limited sense. When "performed," these works depended on written scripts, were presented to thousands of people, and partook in the direct shaping of ongoing current events. More particularly, the various components of *Five Most Noble Speeches Spoken to His Majestie Returning Out of Scotland into England* (1641) were assigned to the recorder of York, the mayors of Stamford and Huntington, and the Lord Mayor and recorder of London— the latter two of whom were knighted in the process. Charles was welcomed home as "the mortall Sunne," but less predictably there was clearly a concern about "how dangerous times are, brother is timerous and fearefull to trust the other, Sects and Schismes doe daily increase" (A3v). Just as in masques of the period, the Londoners who were supposed to be joyful at this "Entertainment" of 25 November 1641 are said to have been dejected during the King's absence, "since the *Rayes* of his Majesty (our great *Luminary*) were over-clouded by his absence from us" (*Ovatio Carolina* A2r). Only three days earlier, it turns out, the Commons had narrowly passed John Pym's Grand Remonstrance, which was essentially a vote of no confidence in the King's governance. Now, embedded in the celebratory written record of men's crimson velvet robes, golden chains, truncheons, and torches, there were signs of major stress. We find that "because some *seditious* Libels were at that time dispersed, which bred a *Panique* feare in some, order was likewise taken, that there should be two *Companies* of the *Cities* trained Bands, placed in severall parts of the Citie upon that day; as also that at every dore a man should be placed, sufficiently appointed, to be ready upon all occasions, to appease any Disorders" (A3v).

Cushioned by security measures—an armed man "at every dore"—and buoyed by cheering crowds and trumpets with banners and the ringing of bells in over a hundred parish churches, Charles was moved to make a statement that, whatever its impact at Moorfields at the time, may be offered here as a general indication of his character, with its tender pride, ill-founded hopefulness, and fundamental political naïveté: "I Must desire you (because my voice cannot reach to all those that I desire should heare me) to give most hearty *thanks* to all the good Citizens of *London*, for their hearty expressions of their *love* this day to me. And indeed I cannot expresse the *contentment* I have received therein: for now I see, that all these former *Tumults* and disorders, have only risen from the meaner sort of people: and that the affections of the better and mayne part of the *Citie*, have ever beene *loyall* and affectionate to my *person*, and *government*" (*Ovatio Carolina* B2r). Here one may sense something of the inclination to reshape reality that led Charles a little over seven years later to what was to become the most famous stage of the day, a scaffold erected outside the Banqueting House at Whitehall.

Turning now to some performance texts of 1640–41 that are shaped variously as comedies, tragicomedies, and tragedies, we might observe first that comedies are plentiful and, in the main, good-natured works full of characters concerned with amorous pursuits. Then again, many have darkening topical touches. Of comedies by writers who were well recognized at the time, two of the best remembered now are Richard Brome's *The Court Beggar* and *A Joviall Crew*. The former was banned in 1640 for its sharp reflection on the King's 1639 "journey into the Northe" at the time of the First Bishops' War (Freehafer 367). It has particular barbs for the courtier-poet-playwright-soldier John Suckling in the cowardly character of Sir Ferdinando. (Though he was not a coward, Suckling had made himself vulnerable to jeerers by raising a troop of horse arrayed in more-pretty-than-practical scarlet and white.) There were probably also some barbs for

William Davenant as Court-Wit. Martin Butler's analysis goes much further than such suggestions, however: "the court's furious reaction shows that it recognized how dangerous the play was; *The Court Beggar* is a full-blooded and uncompromising demonstration of the bankruptcy of the personal rule and an attack on all that the court, by 1640, had come to represent" (*Theatre and Crisis* 220).

A Joviall Crew was presented the following year at the Cockpit in Drury Lane, but it did not reach print until 1652, at which time it was accompanied by references to "*these* anti-ingenious *Times*" (A2r) and "*these sad and tragick daies*" (a2r). Deemed by Butler "a profoundly historical play, giving vigorous expression to the most central preoccupations of its time" (*Theatre and Crisis* 279), it shows Oldrent kindly opening his heart and barn to a troop of beggars who are joined by some attractive young folk in disguise. The whole thing moves with brisk, cheerful confidence and simultaneously manages to pose thought-provoking questions about governance, civil strife, escapism, human kindness, treatment of the poor, and the nature of liberty. Ira Clark summarizes well: "Brome presented pressing issues in a pressing time" (157).[13]

Shirley's *The Brothers* appeared first in 1653.[14] At this late date, instead of writing witty prologues that in earlier days used to be "*keen | Upon the tyme*," "*wee... | In corse dull fleam, must preface to our playes*" (A4r). Performed at the Blackfriars in 1641, this play is a rather mechanical working out of the marital fortunes of the *madrileño* brothers Fernando and Francisco (there is a light seasoning of hispanisms), but a somewhat warmer center of interest is provided by the madcap Luys. The writing as a whole is a little disengaged and underpowered, and yet, as the noble Don Pedro says of Luys, "I like his wit, his spirit, and his humor" (71).

There is scarcely room here to do more than name a cluster of less professional comedies, some rather livelier and more appealing than Shirley's *Brothers:* Robert Chamberlain's *The Swaggering Damsel* (1640), con-

---

[13]Unusual among plays in this study, *A Joviall Crew* has been revived on the London stage in our own time. The Royal Shakespeare Company played it to full houses at The Swan in Strafford in 1992 and The Pit (Barbican Centre) in 1993. Valuable for conveying the serious undertones in the text, this production also may be said to have provided support for Clark's contention that Brome's plays generally offer the "combination of an exhortation to face sociopolitical problems with an absence of principles on which change might be based or goals to which it could conform" (161). Unfortunately from a scholarly viewpoint, the RSC version, an adaptation by Stephen Jeffreys, differed greatly from the seventeenth-century text. [14]Shirley's *Six New Playes*, which includes *The Brothers*, gives the date 1653 on its title page, together with the information "*Never printed before.*" Within the volume, each play is provided with its own separate title page, each of which again proclaims first-time printing. In five out of six instances, however (the exception being *The Court Secret*, dated 1653), the individual plays are dated 1652.

cerned with "A woman Cavellier" ("Virgins . . . shall applaud thee as . . . / The
sole restorer of their liberty" [A3v]); Thomas Jordan's *Walks of Islington and
Hogsdon* (1641), a bustling, colloquial depiction of "Woodstreet-Compter,"
said to have had an extraordinary run of nineteen consecutive days at the
Red Bull; Shackerley Marmion's *The Antiquary* (1641), acted at the Cockpit,
set in Pisa, and poking fun at a rich old man with "a humour easie to be
wrought on" (E2v)—and probably expressing misgivings about Charles's
autocratic handling of the bibliophile Charles Cotton (see Gair, "Poli-
tics");[15] Robert Wild's *The Benefice* (1641), concerned with the scrambling
of various people for a church living and designed to be played in a barn by
children; and William Cavendish's *The Variety* (1641), a Jonsonian work to
which we shall return later.

A rather striking presence among these comedies, because the play-
wright is better known in another context (his emblem book has been called
the most popular book of verse in the seventeenth century), is Francis
Quarles's *The Virgin Widow*. This was acted privately by some young gen-
tlemen in Chelsea in 1641 and then eight years later was finally published,
according to the stationer, "*to sweeten the brackish distempers of a* deluded *age.*"
Time and again the plays printed during the theatrical blackout display
straightforward signs of frustration such as this. Quarles's *Virgin Widow*
proves to be a thoughtful, careful, alert, and complicated work, possessed
of more bite of wit than one might have expected from a man known best
for moralizing verse. Reasonably enough for a work from an emblem writer,
however, it also has a more abstract quality than most plays of the day, its
life somehow emanating less from its characters than from the authorial
mind that produces words for them to speak. For example, we have more
than an in-character comic malapropism when an unwell Lady Albion is
said to be "troubled with a Liturgie." In fact, the physician on duty is
allowed simultaneously to clarify and to backtrack on the author's behalf
by saying, "A Lethargie you meane" (I3v).

Aside from Brome's *Court Beggar* and *Joviall Crew*, the most potent
comedies of the day were Abraham Cowley's *The Guardian* (which would
metamorphose later into *Cutter of Coleman-Street*) and Thomas Killigrew's *The
Parsons Wedding*, both the work of men now thought of mainly as Restora-
tion figures, though these particular plays were first performed in 1641–42.
When *The Guardian* was printed in 1650, its prologue acknowledged the
difference in the times: "*How can a Play pass safely, when we know, / Cheapside-*

---

[15]In his *Personal Rule* Kevin Sharpe has a brief but interesting section called "The Control
of Private Papers and Archives" (655–58). He writes: "In 1630, suspecting that Cotton's
library had provided ammunition to those who framed the Petition of Right, the king ordered
the closure of the finest repository of medieval and contemporary records in England" (655).

Cross falls for making but a show . . . ?" (A2r). (The elaborate old market cross was demolished in 1643, presumably, in Laud's wry words, "to cleanse that great Street of Superstition" [203].) On the other hand, *The Guardian* still conveys a sense of the city going about its social business. When Aurelia has caught her man and "got'um knighted," she says, she "shall be drest up to play at Gleek, or dance, or see a Comedy, or go to the Exchange i'the afternoon" (C2r).

Killigrew's *Parsons Wedding* is cut from a similar bolt but in its earliest surviving form (1663) claims a wider range of moral acceptability.[16] The names tell much: Lady Wild is courted by Constant and Sadd, Lady Love-all is a stallion-hunting widow, and the captain's punk, who is married off to the parson, is Wanton. All in all, *The Parsons Wedding* is a loose, lively, bawdy city play, nonetheless interesting because its pre-Interregnum elements are now impossible to factor out with certainty. Among the likeliest older bits, one might think, is Jolly's reference to a playwright knighted "In the North, the last great knighting, when 'twas Gods great Mercy we were not all Knights" (111).

From about 1640–41 (and subsequently, of course) we also have a certain number of manuscript plays. The comedy called *Grobiana's Nuptialls*, though difficult to date, is sometimes assigned to 1640 and associated with the names of Roger Shipman and William Taylor, both of St. John's College, Oxford. Based on a tradition going back to Grobian, patron saint of boors, as depicted in Sebastian Brandt's *Narrenschiff* (1494), and fueled anew by current feats of undergraduate crudity (members of the audience are addressed as "fellow Grobians" [13r]), the play brushes lightly on events of its time but now serves chiefly to remind one that grubbiness springs eternal in the human breast.

Over in Denbighshire, meanwhile, Sir Thomas Salusbury tried his hand at a comedy he called *Love or Money*. For readers now, the most valuable insight from this manuscript may be one that comes indirectly when Salusbury stands back briefly from what he has written and acknowledges the unconventionality of the disjunction between his plots. He rationalizes, "Its soe much the more like the worlds great play" (69).

Of all the on-the-eve dramatic manuscripts that come down to us, however, the most interesting may be *The Cyprian Conqueror.* Here an anonymous writer (we know only that "Our author is a country man" [49v]) retells Petronius's story of the widow of Ephesus who is wooed and won by

---

[16]*The Parsons Wedding* is accorded a separate title page with the date 1663 in Killigrew's *Comedies, and Tragedies* (1664). One might note that of the ten plays in that volume, all have separate title pages dated 1663 except the final two, *Claracilla* and *The Prisoners*, both dated 1664.

a Roman soldier at her husband's tomb. The interest of the document lies less in the play itself, however, than in the author's prefatory remarks. Though undeniably pedestrian, these are the product of a concerned and educated intelligence. After noting the genesis of his play ("having met with a story yᵗ did somthing please me, coming nigh what I find daily by experience verified, I could not chuse but digest it into action" [2r]), he comments on the nature of his characters, the usefulness of depicting evil on the stage, and the different kinds of speaking voices to be heard there. Unfortunately he also lards his thoughts almost beyond decipherability with citations from Horace, Ovid, Virgil, Martial, Cicero, the elder Seneca, Plato, and—especially—Julius Pollux.[17]

Tragicomedies of the pre-closure period make up an equally diverse group. An offering by the prolific professional James Shirley, *The Imposture* (acted at Blackfriars in 1640, but not published until 1653),[18] opens in a Mantua that is under siege. A stand-in princess (the impostor) provides the focus of interest, and for variety the play is equipped with a cowardly courtier ("Here comes our mirth" [10]). In a rather modest way *The Imposture* displays a willingness to comment on state affairs ("when Princes break faith / Religion must dissolve" [2]) and goes so far as to include a provocative soliloquy from the hero Honorio, which begins, "This Court is like a twilight" (34).

A more interesting work, however, produced both at court and at Blackfriars, is *The Queene of Arragon* (1640) by the courtier-amateur William Habington—best known now for his lyrics in *Castara* (1634). At the outset one of the Aragonese ladies opines that love is not "in season, when an Armie lyes / Before our Citie gates" (B1r), and war thereafter permeates the play ("these Generalls by a Noble warre, / Resolve to try their fate" [B3r]). Predictably, love proves to be the avenue that makes possible the writer's exploration of matters both military and political. Deserving of more attention than may be given it here, *The Queene of Arragon* is worthy of study not only as a superior literary achievement but also, Martin Butler argues, as a subtle exploration of the idea of "government as an agreement involving the *consent* of both ruler and ruled" (*Theatre and Crisis* 70).

John Gough's *The Strange Discovery* (1640) is a far less sophisticated attempt, yet deserving of mention for reminding us specifically of the mine

---

[17]Julius Pollux of Naucratis (Egypt) was a Greek grammarian and sophist in the time of Commodus. His *Onomasticon* in ten books includes information on the Greek theater, among much else. The English playwright seems to have turned particularly to 2.116–17 of the edition of Pollux published by Rodolphus Gualtherus in Frankfurt in 1608—a work that afforded the convenience of parallel columns in Greek and Latin.   [18]*The Imposture*, from *Six New Playes* (1653), is one of the works in that collection with a separate title page dated 1652.

of still-useful motifs and plot elements in Heliodorus's *Aethiopica* (third century B.C.), a romance that had fascinated Renaissance English writers for most of a century. Gough chooses the main plot of the romance for dramatization—his "strange discovery" therefore being the famed revelation of how two black parents came to have a white daughter.

On the grounds of its much greater timeliness, Henry Burnell's *Landgartha* (1640) warrants a somewhat closer look here. Acted at the St. Werburgh Street Theatre in Dublin and printed in that city in 1641, *Landgartha* brings to the fore Charles's current and very real troubles in Ireland. In 1632 Charles had sent his friend Thomas Wentworth to Ireland as Lord Deputy. Whatever Wentworth's virtues by way of honesty, hard work, and self-discipline, he is said to have ruled there almost like a king, eventually becoming unpopular not only with the native Irish but also with the English colonists. An approach that Wentworth called "Thorough" was by some called tyranny. Nevertheless, recalled to England in 1639 to help resolve the complex Scottish situation, Wentworth was created first Earl of Strafford in 1640. Matters shortly afterward came to such a pass that he was accused of raising Irish troops to invade England on Charles's behalf, convicted by a bill of attainder (a parliamentary bill that decreed guilt rather than proved it), and then abandoned by Charles out of fear of a popular uprising. Strafford was beheaded on Tower Hill on 12 May 1641, and on 1 November news came of rebellion in Ireland.[19]

Burnell's *Landgartha*, however, is not set in Ireland. Instead, Burnell turns back to Scandinavian lore for his subject (*Saxo Grammaticus*, bk. 9) and claims to offer Landgartha, a Norwegian, as a pattern for ladies to imitate. Wicked King Frollo of Sweden is a tyrant come to conquer Norway, where he is resisted by Landgartha and other ladies, *"all attyr'd like Amazons"* (B2v). Before act I concludes, Frollo is defeated by Landgartha, whereupon King Reyner of Denmark enters and says to the ladies, presumably punning on his own name, that "those, by whom we raigne, shall be our guides" (C2v). At the end, even though she has married Reyner and it is ascertained that her descendants will gain the throne, Landgartha staunchly abstains from her husband's bed. Apparently it was actual audience complaints about this provocative conclusion that drew a miffed response from the dramatist: *"I answer . . . that a Tragie-Comedy sho'd neither end Comically or Tragically, but betwixt both: which* Decorum *I did my best to observe, not to goe against Art, to please the over-amorous"* (K1v).

Perhaps more to the point than genre decorum, however, is the figura-

---

[19]Some of the complexities of Strafford's fall are intimated nicely in an anonymous "epitaph" reprinted by Saintsbury: "Here lies wise and valiant dust / Huddled up 'twixt fit and just; / Strafford, who was hurried hence / 'Twixt treason and convenience" (3:67).

Figure 4. A personification of Ireland lamenting ("Myne eyes do fayle with teares . . . "), from *A Prospect of Bleeding Irelands Miseries* (1647). (By permission of the British Library.)

tiveness that lurks in the play. Female personification of a country is, of course, an age-old device, and from a few years after Burnell's *Landgartha* we have a helpfully parallel pictorial representation of Ireland as a sorrowing woman (figure 4). A number of problems raised in the play begin to be resolved, furthermore, when we heed Catherine Shaw's explanation that Landgartha may be—probably should be—viewed as Ireland herself, wooed and won by Reyner (England), then betrayed when he takes up with another woman (Scotland). When Reyner comes under attack in his own land, he turns to the abused Landgartha for aid—as Charles turned to Ireland at just about the time the play was composed. It may be that the play's ending is rather odd and inconclusive because Burnell wrote at a time of uncertainty, when it was still possible to hope for political union and religious coexistence between England and Ireland.

One further tragicomedy, so-labeled in its published form and said to have been *"Acted with great Applause"* in Paris, skittered past almost all normal boundaries of the kind. The very title of *Mercurius Britanicus* (1641), a work by the versatile miscellanist Richard Brathwaite, suggests a kinship with the news pamphlets (or "mercuries") of the day. Though presumably the scene is Smyrna, both title and play clearly allude to a "languishing Island" (A2v) many hundreds of miles to the west. Apparently the work was so pointedly timely and telling as to call for five or perhaps even six editions.[20]

By means of speeches so extended sometimes as to take us into the realm of the dialogue pamphlet, the work all but explicitly turns our minds to the career of Strafford.[21] Concerning the "Strafford" figure in the play, for example, we read that

> This man is honored in the sight of his Prince, enioyeth his delights, stretcheth upon beds of yvory, and is crusht with honours . . . : in the meane while one small cloud obscureth all these false beames in a day, ye[a] in a minute of an houre, his Prince leaveth him, his glory departeth like a dreame; and [t]his *Atlas* who carried such heapes, such mountaines of honour upon his shoulders, hath his *exit* with reproach. . . . Yet no sooner hath this *Hero* suffered an inrevocable fate, but he is wisht alive againe by them, who in his life and glory prosecuted him with extremest violence: They hate him alive, lament him dead, and with pious teares desire his restitution: but great mens heads are sooner taken off, then set on againe. [A3r]

On 1 December of that same year—1641—Parliament would present its Grand Remonstrance of 22 November to Charles, urging that he "have

---

[20]Two were in the play's original Latin, the remainder in English.   [21]James Compton, third Earl of Northampton, likewise seems to have designed a play giving dramatic form to Strafford's story. For a brief discussion of this manuscript fragment, see chapter 13.

cause to be in love with good counsel and good men" (Gardiner, *Constitutional Documents* 232).

Not only was Strafford gone by that time, but Laud, impeached by Parliament in December 1640, was imprisoned. In March 1644 Laud would be tried, and in January 1645 his head, too, would be "taken off." In the view of the poet John Cleveland, "The state in *Strafford* fell, the Church in *Laud*" ("On the Archbishop of Canterbury," l. 39).

The main order of Brathwaite's play, however, is to judge certain judges. One by one they are accused of "perturbing the Halcyon days of a peacefull king and an obedient state" (D2v), and much is said about their handling of Ship Money.[22] Arriving at the end of act IV, however, we suddenly find ourselves at the end of the play, served with notice that "*the fift Act shall be acted upon* Tyber, I *should say* Tyburn. . . . Vive le Roi" (E2r). Somewhere here we have stepped out of the realm of allusive political drama, even beyond that of propagandistic drama, into that of the propagandistic pamphlet in dramatic form. Between the latter two forms lies a sort of twilight zone in which, as we shall see in chapter 4, a number of writers chose to work.

Tragedy also was touched by topicality. One of the strongest plays James Shirley ever wrote, one that he himself regarded as "*the best of my flock*" (A3r), was *The Cardinal*, performed at Blackfriars in 1641 but unpublished until 1653.[23] As Charles Forker demonstrated some years ago, this play alludes indirectly but unmistakably to men's attitudes toward Archbishop Laud. To understand Shirley's decision to swathe boldness with indirection here, one need only recall the anecdote of those unfortunate players at the Fortune who are said to have revived *The Cardinalls Conspiracie* a year or so previously. Safely set in far-off Navarre, where it could pretend to be uninvolved in English matters, Shirley's *Cardinal*, for all its borrowing from earlier drama, is a potent play. As would continue to be true of most of the tragedies written in the years just after it, in fact, *The Cardinal* appears to achieve a broader significance and deeper seriousness precisely because it touches upon issues of the day.[24]

---

[22]As Martin Butler points out, however, Brathwaite distinguishes between good and bad Ship Money judges, in fact completely exonerates three of them. Butler concludes that this "dramatization of the downfall of the scapegoats for Charles's misrule . . . could have spoken powerfully to a wide and plebeian audience offended with the crimes of the judges and enthusiastic for a reformation" ("Case Study" 953).   [23]*The Cardinal* is another of the works in *Six New Playes* (1653) that comes with its individual title page dated 1652.   [24]This is hardly true, one might observe, of Samuel Harding's *Sicily and Naples* (1640), which perhaps influenced Shirley's *Cardinal* (see Roberts). *Sicily and Naples* concerns the aborted match of the King of Naples with the Princess of Sicily. The latter is plunged into melancholy because her father has been killed by the man supposed to become her husband, and along the way we meet a page who proves to be not merely female but also pregnant, a wicked black rapist who is only pretending to be black and mistakenly rapes his sister.

Another strong and late tragedy is *The Sophy*, written by the poet John Denham (of "Cooper's Hill" fame), performed at Blackfriars in 1641, and published in 1642. Relating the same violent story of tyrannical government in Persia that we will encounter again in Robert Baron's *Mirza* (1655), the play opens with the monetary and military problems of the sophy (or, as we would now say, the shah). Also presented to us early is the knowledge that because of flattery "stretch't even to Divinitie," rulers cannot rely unconditionally on their advisers: " 'Tis the fate of Princes, that no knowledge / Comes pure to them" (2). For a number of reasons, bad councillors were to become one of the most common of all motifs in the midcentury drama. Denham's boldest thrusts in *The Sophy* call up the now-tarnished image of Archbishop Laud and at the same time manage to excuse Charles himself. The courtier Abdal observes,

> Poore Princes, how are they mis-led,
> While they, whose sacred office 'tis to bring
> Kings to obey their God, and men their King,
> By these mysterious linkes to fixe and tye
> Them to the foot-stoole of the Deity:
> Even by these men, Religion, that should be
> The curbe, is made the spurre to tyrannie;
> They with their double key of conscience binde
> The Subjects soules, and leave Kings unconfin'd. . . . [26]

This outspoken and rather moving work clearly engaged the political consciousness as well as the pen of a skillful writer.[25]

Far less can be said for Thomas Rawlins's *Rebellion* (1640). Despite its arresting title, this work proves to be a free-ranging and inept gallimaufry by a young goldsmith who went on to the more practical job of being chief engraver to the Mint under both Charleses. (It is Rawlins who designed the famous "Oxford Crown" of 1644, showing the King mounted and wielding a sword, and displaying a view of Oxford beneath the horse [Nathanson 11].) Performed at the Red Bull for an impressive nine consecutive days, *The Rebellion* offers a malcontented villain named Machvile, a nurse on loan from the Capulet family, an enacted dream with Cupid, a heroine tied to a tree for purposes of raping ("doe you weep, you / Puritanicall Punke!" [G1v]), and the execution of a dog in a chair, to say nothing of

---

[25]It is with good reason that John M. Wallace takes *The Sophy* as a starting point in an essay exploring the nature of "application" and "exampling." He writes: "*The Sophy* works well as a deliberately chosen historical example, quite different from the present, but related to it by application. . . . To readers in later years who had forgotten all about the Attempt on the Five Members, Mirza's projected crime would continue to exemplify a general truth, but in 1642 the topical inferences would have made the whole play appear allegorical" ("Examples" 288).

the titular war. A sense of humor will help a modern reader here, much as it probably helped at least some in the play's original audience.

Even so rapid and partial a survey as this of dramatic writings from our brink years, 1640 and 1641, should suffice to suggest their range.[26] We should also bear in mind, however, that the dramatic mix is further complicated and enriched by the simultaneous printing of earlier plays. Among these in 1640 were several by John Fletcher, John Webster's *Duchess of Malfi*, and a new edition of *Terence in English*, as well as a number of plays by James Shirley. Perhaps most notably of all, the years 1640–41 brought to light more works by Ben Jonson—who had lived until 1637 and would remain an important point of reference throughout the next two decades. Hence we find Nicholas Downey assuring his friend Samuel Harding, concerning *Sicily and Naples*, that

> BEN is deceas'd, and yet I dare avow,
> (*Without that booke*) BEN's *redivivus* now,
> I could beleeve a *Metempsycosis*,
> *And that thy soule were not thine owne*, but *his*. . . .
>
> [Harding *2v]

When all is said and done, it should be clear that dramatic writings of the period immediately preceding the closing of the theaters were numerous, lively, and varied, indebted in many ways to earlier dramatic traditions, and traditional not least in their tendency to touch social, political, and religious issues of their day. As far-reaching crises continued to occur, the urge to expression would flourish both in the theaters and in the streets, churches, and bookshops. Whenever he composed the lines, Robert Herrick could still exclaim in print in 1648, "Give way, give way, now, now my *Charles* shines here" ("To the King," l. 236). As forces against Charles gathered strength during the 1640s, however, the English Phoebus actually was embarked on a long and painful decline. From Milton's perspective, "the whole course of his raign . . . resembl'd *Phaeton* more than *Phoebus*" (*Eikonoklastes* 463). The goldsmith-playwright Thomas Rawlins was moved to offer the silly and yet somehow terrible warning that "Kings are in all things Gods / Saving mortality" (E4v).

---

[26]Because of its arresting title, John Day's *Parliament of Bees* (1641) probably should be mentioned here also. Judging from the death year of Day's dedicatee (1634), however, the work dates back to the earlier 1630s. Moreover, as Lehmann writes, the *Parliament* "is not actually a drama, a pastoral eclogue, or a masque, though it could easily be dramatized because of the set speeches which formulate its contents" (206).   Despite the difficulties involved in dating, brink plays from the first eight months of 1642 (i.e., just before the order for closure) will be cited in subsequent chapters as further on-the-eve examples.

KINDS OF CLOSURE

Buy a new Ordinance of the Commons,
  against S[t]age-players: New-lye printed,
  and new-lye come forth.
Saints now alone must *Act* for Riches,
The Plott out-smells old *Atkins* breches.[1]
  Thus goe the cryes of Westminster. . . .
                    —*The Cryes of Westminster* (1648)

Affrighted with the shadow of their Rage,
They broke the Mirror of the times, the Stage. . . .
    —*Prologue to His Majesty at the First Play . . . Novemb. 19* (1660)

. . . the Stage . . . lies now undar a heuier censure, then any wise
nation euer loaded her with, being to my knowlig the beast tutor our
ignorant gentary & nobility had. . . .
        —Francis Osborne, *The True Tragi-Comedie* (ca. 1654)

ONE SUBSUMING FACT of this study—that English plays between 1642
and 1660 were radically affected by social, religious, and political forces—is
perhaps no different than we should have supposed. In the years 1640-41
we have now seen numerous signs—from *Salmacida Spolia* and the
Masquarade du Ciel through *Landgartha, Mercurius Britanicus,* and *The Car-*
dinal—of a tendency that would grow stronger still. It came to be mani-
fested in so many ways, in fact, and so many illustrations of it lead into so
many neighboring fields, that a relatively broad study such as this one
requires that we proceed suggestively, concentrating on some areas, briefly
noting others, and letting still others go.

  In sorting matters out, however, the importance of official governmen-
tal boundaries quickly becomes clear. Whatever the subject of a play, it was
either within these boundaries or outside and against them that writers,
players, and booksellers had to work. Hence part of the life and interest of
these writings derives from the constraining tension imparted to them by
the law. Furthermore, the stakes of the game were raised for all its partici-

---

[1]Having served previously as Sheriff of London (1637–38) and Lord Mayor (1644–45),
Thomas Atkins was an alderman at the time of the publication of this broadside (22 February
1648). His alleged bowel problem is memorialized in Nedham's satiric *The Reverend Alderman*
Atkins (The Shit-Breech) (1648), Crouch's *New-Market-Fayre* (1649), and elsewhere.

pants because the perimeters within which it was played were unstable. Sometimes they altered according to changes of wording in the rules, sometimes according to the severity or laxness of enforcement at the moment, and sometimes according to an individual's current impulse toward self-censorship or bravado.

Immediately preceding the period of our main interest here, Sir Henry Herbert was serving as Master of the Revels. He had purchased the post in July 1623, back in the time of James, and from the beginning of Charles's reign in March 1625 there was wrangling about drama. *A Shorte Treatise against Stage-Playes*, published in May by Alexander Leighton, urged Parliament "*to restreyne them for ever hereafter*" (A2r).[2] Clearly the serious but rather modest kind of courtly surveillance provided by Herbert fell far short of satisfying such men as the author of *A Shorte Treatise*, the title page of which carried the motto "*He that loues pastime shall be a poore man.*" Once inside the *Treatise*, one finds that the Christian Church first admitted plays "when that great scarlet coloured whore of Babylon with her golden cup of abhominations in her hand . . . was set in Peters chaire at Rome as the Papists say; then did the king of the Locusts, called *Abaddon* and *Apollyon*, hauing the key of the bottomeles pitt, . . . sette the church doore wide open for sundrie sportes and playes to enter freely in the house of God" (8-9). It is obvious to the writer of the *Treatise* that the "matter acted in tragedies is murther, treason, rebellion, and such like; and in comedies is bauderie, cosenage, and meere knaverie" (11).

The most conspicuous proponent of such views was William Prynne, whose thousand-page *Histrio-mastix*, made available to the public in 1633, was begun in the mid-1620s. For Prynne, stage-plays and playhouses came from the devil via "Idolatrous Infidels, and voluptuous Pagans" (18), and stage-players were "the very greatest mischiefes which can befall" a nation (734).[3] One should add that most of the complaints against plays, if not playbooks, are substantiated by the playwrights themselves, some wearing long faces, some grins. Beyond the fundamental fact that men and boys wore female clothes to perform female roles, there was the workaday

---

[2]Parliament on 18 June 1625 actually produced "An Acte for punishing divers Abuses," including the Sunday performance of "Interludes, Common Plays or other unlawful Exercises and Pastimes" (*Statutes*, 1 Car. I, cap. 1). Later the same month (24 June), nevertheless, Charles renewed his father's patent licensing his "welbeloved servants" Heminges, Condell, and their colleagues—the King's Men—to exercise their "Art and facultye" (Hazlitt 57).

[3]To bring Prynne's mind-set and overall career into focus, it is worth knowing that he subsequently became "popular," in William Lamont's words, "at two levels: he was Parliament's official apologist for its cause (and later for the trial of Laud); his pamphlets enjoyed a wide readership" (74). As Lamont observes, "the readiness of Parliament to commission Prynne is . . . solid recognition that his words did indeed 'take with the people' " (75).

presence in the theater of whores and pimps. In the prologue to *The Obstinate Lady* Aston Cokayne acknowledges, "*Troth Gentlemen, we know that now adayes / Some come to take up Wenches at our Playes*" (a2r). There was also the problem of personating or impersonation. Thomas Jordan in his *Walks of Islington and Hogsdon* has a character allude to the actors' knack for portraying real people onstage; his Tripes recalls that "The Players brought me oth' Stage once" in a version of *Moll Cutpurse* (E3r). William Strode has one character inform another in his *Floating Island*, "Sir you and we were acted at the Court. / We loosers are made laughing-stocks" (D3v). For a more fully grounded example, a performance at the Red Bull of *The Whore New Vampt* on 29 September 1639 libeled some aldermen (Hotson 4). Jordan, moreover, in *Fancy's Festivals* provides a further hint concerning an actor's skill that may have been equally incendiary. When the playwright has a figure named Poetry protest about actors improvising "without premeditation" (thus acknowledging a source of trouble noted in *Hamlet* half a century earlier [III.ii.38-45]), Verity replies, "Yes, yes, you know Extempore's in fashion" (B1v). Some of the wittiest, boldest, unkindest cuts of all, it would appear, were ostensibly spontaneous thrusts—verbal and gestural—that are now beyond hope of recovery.

For a ready-made, self-accusatory catalogue of actors' wrongdoing, we need look no further than *The Actors Remonstrance* (1643). Here, in the process of vowing reform, the author admits to the actors' former "obscene and scurrilous jests," their crowd-pleasing "bawling and railing," their inveigling of "young Gentlemen, Merchants Factors, and Prentizes" to treat them and their harlots in taverns, and their borrowing of money at first sight from gullible gallants (A2r-v). On the last page—in fact, in his closing sentence—the remonstrator admits also that some players have even spoken their parts "in a tone . . . in derision of some of the pious" (A4v). Such an admission might strike one now as an anticlimactic afterthought, but at the time it probably looked very different.[4]

For every champion of suppression of the players, one can find a defender. Francis Osborne, a shrewd and sharp-eyed observer, believed that England's stage had served as the best "tutor our ignorant gentary & nobility had" (*True Tragi-Comedie* 18r). Richard Whitlock wrote a little more expansively: "*Wisedome* is *Debtor* . . . to the *Sock,* and *Buskin;* Nor is it such a *Paradox* as it may seem to sound to some *halfe-witted Eares;* for I dare aver

---

[4]G.E. Bentley, concerned with an earlier period, summarizes five bases for censorship: critical comments on the government, negative presentation of friendly foreign powers, commentary on religious questions, obscene or blasphemous language, and personal satire of influential people. During the period with which we are concerned, the most important of these probably would have been the first and last, with the second, perhaps, being least important (*Profession of Dramatist* 167).

what hath been *writ* for the *Stage* (*ancient,* or *modern*) is not inferiour to any *writings* on the same *Theme* (excepting the *Advantages* of *Christianity,* and our better *Schoolmasters* for *Heaven*) of never so *severe* an *Authority*" (473). Sir Richard Baker remarked more tartly in his *Theatrum Redivivum* (1662) that Prynne's "*Reason* proves it no more *unlawfull* to *see a Play,* then to *eat a Pudding*" (17). "If all things must be *cast away,* that may be . . . *abused,*" he asks, "why doth not this man pull out his *Eyes* with *Democritus?* or *geld* himself with *Origen?*" (27). And in the anonymous and self-justifying *Stage-Players Complaint* of 1641—ostensibly a conversation between Andrew Cane of the Fortune and Timothy Reed of the Blackfriars—the playhouses are credited with providing recreation for strangers in town, for citizens to feast their wits, for gallants who might spend their money in worse ways, for the learned to increase their wit, and for gentlewomen to avoid idleness and increase their knowledge (4).

Though the weakening effect that the plague had on the theaters is a factor that must be considered in the period preceding the 1642 order for closure, an equally telling antecedent may have been the Root and Branch Petition of 1640. Signed in December by some fifteen thousand citizens of London (although it would be naive for us to assume that all who signed the document had read it), the petition proposed abolishing episcopal government, including "all its dependencies, roots and branches." In due course the petition became a bill that was introduced into the Commons the following May and eventually dropped, but it serves to inform us nonetheless of a significantly widespread public aversion to licentious publishing, including that of "lascivious, idle, and unprofitable books and pamphlets, play-books and ballads" (Gardiner, *Constitutional Documents* 139).

Riots in Westminster during the Christmas season of 1641 were followed by the King's charge of treason against five parliamentary leaders, then by his extraordinary personal appearance with three hundred armed men at the House of Commons to arrest those leaders on 4 January 1642, and not least by the hasty and momentous departure of the King and his family from Whitehall to Hampton Court on 10 January, and afterward to the still more distant safety of Windsor. Parliament's quick assumption of military control of the capital, Conrad Russell observes, "was perhaps the greatest victory of the whole civil war" (*Origins* 30).[5]

---

[5]Russell also remarks that "The King's action [against the five members of Parliament], which had been designed to reassert his authority, had simply alienated the Lords, and tipped the Commons' majority over the edge into what was very near a state of legal rebellion" (*Fall* 450). Equally interesting is Russell's observation that "It is so well established in English folk memory that the charge against the Five Members was a political disaster, and the belief contains so much truth, that it is hard to remember that Charles's legal case against them might have been very strong" (447).

As a matter of fact, Parliament's "Order for Stage-plays to cease" did not come until after war had actually erupted. Charles raised his standard at Nottingham on 22 August 1642 (after Dover Castle had already fallen to parliamentary forces), and nearly two more weeks passed before the order of 2 September. The order, then, was not precipitous. Moreover, as Butler has argued, it by no means constituted a simple moral or doctrinal conquest by emotional, Prynne-like M.P.'s. Instead, it was a reasoned and rhetorically careful statement issued at a moment of political and social crisis. Its importance justifies presenting it here in full:

> Whereas the distressed Estate of Ireland, steeped in her own Blood, and the distracted Estate of England, threatened with a Cloud of Blood by a Civil War, call for all possible Means to appease and avert the Wrath of God, appearing in these Judgements; among which, Fasting and Prayer, having been often tried to be very effectual, having been lately and are still enjoined; and whereas Public Sports do not well agree with Public Calamities, nor Public Stage-plays with the Seasons of Humiliation, this being an Exercise of sad and pious Solemnity, and the other being Spectacles of Pleasure, too commonly expressing lascivious Mirth and Levity: It is therefore thought fit, and Ordained, by the Lords and Commons in this Parliament assembled, That, while these sad causes and set Times of Humiliation do continue, Public Stage Plays shall cease, and be forborn, instead of which are recommended to the People of this Land the profitable and seasonable considerations of Repentance, Reconciliation, and Peace with God, which probably may produce outward Peace and Prosperity, and bring again Times of Joy and Gladness to these Nations. [Firth and Rait 1:26-27]

Collectively and vividly fearful that "a Cloud of Blood" was about to burst over their heads, the members of Parliament could not countenance "Spectacles of Pleasure." A mere glance at the journal of the House of Lords for 2 September confirms the dangerous context of the moment. The "Order for Stage-plays to Cease" is immediately preceded by an "Order for 2000 l. for Lord Kerry to raise Men for Ireland," and it is immediately followed by an order for the "E. of Warwick to send Two Ships for the Relief of Ireland, and suppressing Pirates" (*Journal of Lords* 5:336). Under the circumstances, the 1642 order concerning stage-plays, which was passed by both Lords and Commons, could have been much more extreme. And its major successor would be. Over time, it must be judged in a context of other moves to achieve reform—the institution of public fasts, the regulation of alehouses and gaming, and even legislation regarding sexual relations. Judged by its wording, however, this document of September 1642 is not fueled primarily by moral outrage. Instead—and despite the fact that it must have gratified play-haters—it appears to be informed by a deep concern that nothing further be allowed to rock the ship of state. Surely nothing, one might suggest, like the preceding years' *Landgartha, The Sophy,* or *The Cardinal.* Perhaps nothing, to tell the truth, that might draw a crowd.[6]

From October 1642, the following month, we catch a glimpse of the now-crowdless Cockpit and "Revelling Rooms" at Whitehall. With the King away at war—the drawn battle at Edgehill was fought that month—and his Queen in the Netherlands, working to procure arms for England, one might "goe in without a Ticket or the danger of a broken-pate, . . . enter at the Kings side, walke round about the Theaters, view the Pullies, the Engines, conveyances, or contrivances of every several Scaene And not an Usher o'th Revells, or Engineere to envy or finde fault with your discovery" (*Deep Sigh* A3v). One might, if so disposed, "pisse in the Porters Lodge" (A2v).

As for playbooks as opposed to performances, Parliament seems to have taken a milder stand. At any rate, it manifested far more concern about other kinds of publication. When Parliament took control of the licensing of published works in 1640, a stringent 1637 Star Chamber decree on licensing was still in effect. That decree had placed all printing under the control of the Stationers' Company, giving the Stationers greater powers than they had ever before known. Dissolution of the Star Chamber itself in July 1641, however, in effect opened the printing floodgates. Understandably, the licensing of newsbooks appeared to be necessary, and in March 1642 it became compulsory. Then in August—several weeks before the theaters were closed—came a "Special order . . . concerning Irregular Printing, and . . . the suppressing of all false and Scandalous Pamphlets" (Siebert 182). Problems continued to abound, however, and in June 1643 it proved necessary to bolster both of the 1642 orders with an ordinance requiring that *all* books and pamphlets be licensed. It is this document that provided Milton with the impetus to write *Areopagitica* (1644). There Milton not only defends publication of scandalous pamphlets but also, regarding the *vetus comoedia*, argues that no records exist to suggest that "the writings of those old Comedians were supprest, though the acting of them were forbid." And he adds: "that *Plato* commended the reading of *Aristophanes* the loosest of them all, to his royall scholler *Dionysius* is commonly known, and may be excus'd, if holy *Chrysostome,* as is reported, nightly studied so much the same Author . . . " (495-96).

---

[6]Similar English thinking is reflected explicitly in the Venetian ambassador's report to the Doge and senate in November 1655: "They have absolutely forbidden plays suspecting that these gatherings of the people might occasion some disadvantage to the present state of affairs" (cited in Louis B. Wright 75). Wright suggests that the authorities were particularly nervous in 1655 because of the royalist uprising headed by Colonel John Penruddock in March of that year.

Whether or not Milton's learned and impassioned essay had an effect on anyone's thoughts about licensing, the printing of unlicensed words continued to be a threat, commercial as well as political. Authors and printers alike simply proved to be ingenious and determined. Thus there were still further official attempts to control the presses, most notable among them the military measures that began in January 1649 (the month of Charles's execution), the Printing Act of September of that year, another one in January 1653, and Cromwell's order of August 1655—which, according to Fredrick Siebert, "reached a high point in the stringency of regulation and almost equaled Elizabeth in the degree of compliance enforced on printers and publishers" (3). The timing of this "high point" is worth noticing here, because the 1650s saw an upsurge in the number of published playbooks.

As for the actors, part of the strain throughout the period came from not knowing how long or, indeed, how completely the playhouses might be closed. Many went off to war, and most joined the royalists. According to James Wright's recollection in his *Historia Histrionica* (1699), "Most of 'em, except *Lowin, Tayler,* and *Pollard,* (who were superannuated) went into the King's Army, and like good Men and true, Serv'd their Old Master, tho' in a different, yet more honourable, Capacity. . . . I have not heard of one of these Players of any Note that sided with the other Party, but only *Swanston,* and he profest himself a Presbyterian, took up the Trade of a Jeweller, and liv'd in *Aldermanbury*" (7-8). Presbyterian or not, Ellaerdt Swanston was sufficiently reconciled with his fellow players in 1647 to join them in signing the dedication of the Beaumont and Fletcher folio.

Before 1642 was out, some of the King's Men left for Oxford, where the King had set up his new headquarters. In effect, Oxford would be his capital for the next three and a half years. (Extraordinary though the royal removal surely was, Laud's chancellorship of the University there, since 1630, may have helped to make the move seem more reasonable. Moreover, Christ Church, a royal foundation, provided a natural base of operations.) Once the players joined the Oxford court, they were asked to put on plays. It is therefore the more interesting to find a parliamentary "proposition" addressed to the King at Oxford on 24 November 1644 asking that he lend his authority to "the suppressing of interludes and stage plays: this Act to be perpetual" (Gardiner, *Constitutional Documents* 275-77). After all that had happened in the intervening years—most recently Charles had made a nighttime escape following the Second Battle of Newbury (27 October)—one hopes he was mildly amused. Eventually, however, few could smile. In September 1645—after the royalists had suffered major defeats at Marston Moor (July 1644) and Naseby (June 1645)—the King's players returned to

London and tried to make their own separate peace with Parliament. Even then, of course, not all smiles ceased in Oxford. It has been suggested, in fact, that the final dramatic entertainment for the Oxford cavaliers did not take place until 5 May 1646, shortly before the city fell to Parliament's forces on 24 June (Cutts, "Dramatic Writing" 16). Martin Llewellyn's *The King Found at Southwell* (1646), the entertainment in question, is quasi-dramatic at best, but merry, musical evidence of cavalier spirit at the time.

As for the years of actual fighting, Hotson observes that "even during the height of the war, plays were given with remarkable frequency in the regular playhouses in London" (16). *Remarkable* may be too capacious an adjective. Still lacking much quantifiable data after all these years, we nonetheless find that Sir Humphrey Mildmay attended plays even during the summer and fall of 1643 (Bentley, *Jacobean and Caroline Stage* 2:680). On 1 October 1643, however,

> The Players at the Fortune in Golding Lane, who had oftentimes been complained of, and prohibited the acting of wanton and licentious Playes, yet persevering in their forbidden Art, this day there was set a strong guard of Pikes and muskets on both gates of the Play-house, and in the middle of their play they unexpectedly did presse into the Stage upon them, who (amazed at these new Actors) it turned their Comedy into a Tragedy, and being plundered of all the richest of their cloathes, they left them nothing but their necessities now to act, and to learne a better life. [*Weekely Accompt* 6]

Moreover, surveying all such evidence as we now have, Judith Milhous and Robert Hume have concluded that professional playing "virtually ceased" between 1643 and 1647 (491). In 1644 the Second Globe, built in 1614, was pulled down and replaced by tenements. Conversely, in October 1644 players at the Salisbury Court off Fleet Street made bold to perform Beaumont and Fletcher's *A King and No King* (the title itself might draw a crowd), a fact that comes down to us because city officials broke up the performance and seized at least one of the major actors, Timothy Reed.

In 1647, finding that they could get away with it, the players were once again acting more or less openly, not only at Salisbury Court but also at the Fortune and the Cockpit in Drury Lane. They were also setting plans in motion to make Blackfriars playworthy once again. The surest evidence of all regarding their activity, however, is provided by the next major official effort at closure. In July 1647, almost five years after its first effort in the matter, the Commons drafted another order to suppress plays and play-houses—though the impact of the measure was subsequently softened by the Lords, who wished to extend it only to 1 January 1648.

Meanwhile, the army entered London on 6 August 1647, and on 22 October there came a more potent "Ordinance for the Lord Mayor and City of London, and the Justices of Peace to suppress Stage-playes and Inter-ludes." This time the Lords and Commons required officials to enter wherever plays were acted and to commit any players, upon oaths by two witnesses, "to any common Gaol or Prison, there to remain untill the next general Sessions of the Peace ... or sufficient security entred for his or their appearance at the said Sessions there to be punished as Rogues, according to Law" (Firth and Rait 1:1027). This ordinance had a harder edge. It had been many years since every acting actor was really considered a rogue.

Whatever their reasoning, the actors, apparently heartened by the time limit specified in the document of July 1647, laid plans to resume perform-ances in January 1648. Certainly there was an audience for them, and when the time came, many plays are said to have been produced. On 27 January no fewer than 120 coaches are reported to have delivered spectators to the Fortune, while still others made their way to the Red Bull to see Beaumont and Fletcher's *Wit without Money* (Gildersleeve 225)—the title itself looking like a comment on the players' circumstances.

This flurry of theatrical activity provides the backdrop against which to view the important ordinance of 11 February 1648. By this time the King had fled to Carisbrooke Castle on the Isle of Wight (he arrived there in November 1647) and signed an agreement—the so-called Engagement—to obtain aid from the Scots. Parliament, incensed, declared that as of 17 January 1648 it would receive no further messages from him. Though the purging of moderate members from Parliament was yet to come (6 Decem-ber 1648), this February 1648 document—not the more famous one of 1642—is the first to reveal the extreme Puritan position on drama. The sternness of the piece is conveyed by its title, "An Ordinance for the utter suppression and abolishing of all Stage-Plays and Interludes," and the tenor of the whole is conveyed in its opening phrases: "Whereas the Acts of Stage-Playes, Interludes, and common Playes, condemned by ancient Heathens, and much less to be tolerated amongst Professors of the Chris-tian Religion is the occasion of many and sundry great vices and disorders, tending to the high provocation of Gods wrath and displeasure, which lies heavy upon this Kingdom, and to the disturbance of the peace thereof ..." (Firth and Rait 1:1070). Henceforth any actor caught acting was subject to punishment as a rogue, "notwithstanding any License whatsoever from the King or any person or persons." Royal protection was irrelevant. Further-more, enforcers of the ordinance were "required, to pull down and demol-ish, or cause or procure to be pulled down and demolished all Stage-Galleries, Seats, and Boxes, erected or used, or which shall be erected and used for the acting, or playing, or seeing acted or plaid, such Stage-Playes, Interludes, and Playes aforesaid, within the said City of London and Liberties thereof." Thanks to the "company of Saints" now in ascendancy, wrote an anonymous pen in *A Key to the Cabinet of the Parliament* (June 1648), "we need not any more *Stage-playes*, we thanke them for suppressing them, they save us money; for Ile undertake we can laugh as heartily at *Foxley, Peters*, and others of their godly Ministers, as ever we did at *Cane* at the *Red Bull, Tom: Pollard* in the humorous Lieutenant, *Robins* the Changeling, or any humorist of them all" (8).

Despite everything, some players continued to play. G.E. Bentley is perfectly correct to point out that "As a viable profession the theatre was dead" ("Theatres" 122). Nevertheless, Milhous and Hume have been able to identify no fewer than twenty-five actors in London in 1648 (491, 495). James Wright, writing about fifty years after the event, recalled that their activity was sufficient to occasion a major raid:

> [I]n the Winter before the King's murder, 1648 [Charles was beheaded on 30 January 1649], They ventured to Act some Plays with as much caution and privacy as cou'd be, at the *Cockpit*. They continu'd undisturbed for three or four Days; but at last as they were presenting the Tragedy of the *Bloudy Brother* [or *Rollo, Duke of Normandy*, by Fletcher and others], (in which *Lowin* Acted Aubrey, *Tayler* Rollo, *Pollard* the Cook, *Burt* Latorch, and I think *Hart* Otto) a Party of Foot Souldiers beset the House, surprized 'em about the midle of the Play, and carried 'em away in their habits, not admitting them to Shift, to *Hatton-house* then a Prison, where having detain'd them sometime, they Plunder'd them of their Cloths and let 'em lose again. [8-9][7]

The punishment, of course, might have been worse. On that same day (1 January 1649), Parliament charged the King with treason against the state. Rick Bowers, noting the juxtaposition of events, suggests that "plays were plundered on this day in order to remove any further threat of public disorder in advance of trial and sentencing" (470).

From 1649 we also have *The Terrible, Horrible, Monster of the West*—the monster being Parliament—which relates how the benches, galleries, and stages at Blackfriars and the Fortune had been gobbled up—"nay, their very Hell and Heaven to boot" (5). The interior of the Cockpit, scene of *The Bloudy Brother*, was likewise demolished, as was the interior of Salisbury Court.

With matters gone from bad to worse, the actors of the Blackfriars and the Cockpit made bold the following year to petition Parliament. They described themselves as "having long suffered in extream want, by being prohibited the use of their qualitie of *Acting*, in which they were trained up

---

[7]Milhous and Hume point out that this account is partially garbled, perhaps a conflation of events (494).

from their Childhood, whereby they are uncapable of any other way to get a subsistance, and are now fallen into such lamentable povertie, that they know not how to provide food for themselves, their wives and children: great Debts withall being demanded of them." Hence they asked for permission "to *Act* but some small time (for their trial of *inoffensiveness*) onely such Moral and harmless Representations, as shall no way be distast-full to the Common-wealth or good manners" (*To the Supream Authoritie*). They were even willing to donate part of their proceeds to Cromwell's campaign against the Irish rebels.

Dire as all this sounds, the Red Bull in Clerkenwell—perhaps because it was somewhat out of the way—survived throughout the Interregnum and occasionally even mounted shows of various kinds. Other venues operated as well. The passage previously cited from James Wright proceeds thus: "Afterwards in *Oliver's* time, they used to Act privately, three or four Miles, or more, out of Town, now here, now there, sometimes in Noblemens Houses, in particular *Holland-house* at *Kensington*, where the Nobility and Gentry who met (but in no great Numbers) used to make a Sum for them, each giving a broad Peice, or the like. And *Alexander Goffe*, the Woman Actor at *Black-friers*, (who had made himself known to Persons of Quality) used to be the Jackal and give notice of Time and Place" (9).[8]

We shall never be able to count the surreptitious performances of the period or even estimate their frequency with any assurance, but there are scattered signs that theatrical life persisted throughout the remainder of the Interregnum: a performance of Killigrew's "*Claracilla* at one Mr *Gibbions* his *Tennis Court*" (*Mercurius Democritus*, 1654); a barn converted to "a very fine play house" in Hyde Park (noted in a letter by H. Smith); and, most famous of all (as we shall see more fully in chapter 9), William Davenant's crafting of a musical form of dramatic entertainment that was officially acceptable in 1656 and nowadays is generally held to constitute the found-ing of English opera. By April 1656, in fact, it appears that besides Davenant's own quarters at Rutland House, he had other "houses" for performance in Lincoln's Inn Fields, Drury Lane, and elsewhere (Hotson 144). Perhaps each of these glints of dramatic performance shines a lumen

---

[8] Holland House was a splendid Jacobean mansion, the home of Henry Rich, first Earl of Holland. In the 1620s Holland had been engaged to negotiate the marriage of Charles and Henrietta Maria, but in 1642 he joined Parliament's side. In 1643 he returned to Charles's side, and on 9 March 1649, despite the efforts of Fairfax on his behalf, he was beheaded. Holland House then passed into the hands of his son Richard, second Earl of Holland.   Though the term itself did not come into vogue until after the Restoration, a "broadpiece" was a twenty-shilling coin. In calling Gough a jackal, Wright is remembering the old belief that a jackal was good at seeking prey for a lion.

or so brighter when set against the fact that the threat of the 1648 ordinance officially remained until the Restoration.

Things appear to have gone a little better in the earlier 1650s. In 1653 Alexander Brome, bringing out a collection of plays by Richard Brome (apparently not a relative), was glad to think that

> *now new* Stars *shine forth, and do pretend,*
> *Wit shall be cherisht,* and Poets *finde a* Friend.
> *This makes these sleeping* Poems *now creep forth,*
> *As innocent of wrong, as full of worth.*
> [Richard Brome, *Five New Playes* A4r][9]

Though the verb *pretend* here may give us pause, the versifier adds boldly,

> *May this* Work *prove successefull, and we finde*
> *Those men, that now are* Pow'rfull, *to be kinde!*
> *And give encouragement to* Wit, *and* Worth,
> *That things of* Weight *may come with boldnesse forth!*

Predictably, however, the starlight dimmed again, as evidenced by Cromwell's "Orders . . . for putting in speedy and due Execution the Laws, Statutes and Ordinances made and provided against Printing Unlicensed and Scandalous Books and Pamphlets, and for the further Regulating of Printing" (28 August 1655).

However effective the various efforts were to forbid unlicensed printing or to close the public stage, we may suppose that some families or groups of friends occasionally gathered privately to put on plays for one another, much as play-reading groups nowadays perform for their own mutual pleasure, or, a closer parallel, much as some of the tsarist aristocrats are said to have read plays—especially Shakespeare—during their exile. On 27 December 1655 Elizabeth, Queen of Bohemia, also an exile, wrote to her exiled nephew Charles that "wee now haue gotten a new diuertissment of little plays after supper, it was heere the last week and now this week at your Sisters."[10] Mark Girouard finds evidence that plays were sometimes

---

[9] Sometimes overlooked is the fact that Alexander Brome himself had apparently tried his hand at playwriting. The title page of *The Cunning Lovers*, a comedy printed for William Sheares in 1654, claims that that play, "Written by Alexander Brome, Gent.," had been "Acted, with great Applause, by their Majesties Servants at the private House in *Drury Lane*." Rollins held that Alexander Brome "was such an outspoken critic of the government that he deserves a prominent place in a history of the drama" ("Commonwealth Drama" 61).

[10] Elizabeth refers here to Mary, Princess of Orange. She then goes on to say, "I hope the Godlie will meach [grumble] against it"—a statement that is interesting on several counts. She neglects to give the year of her letter, but it may be deduced from her news that the Queen of Sweden had recently been brought to bed of a boy. Charles XI, the only son of Charles X and his Queen, was born on 24 November 1655.

given even in very modest English country houses (80), and the manu-
scripts of Mildmay Fane and Thomas Salusbury provide interesting spe-
cific information on dramatic performances at great houses. For instance,
in Salusbury's epilogue to a private performance of Beaumont and
Fletcher's *The Scornful Lady*, he indicates that

> It was not our intent to gett by hart
> Each one of us soe perfectlie his part,
> As those that doe at London show yow sport
> All days i'th weeke and take your money for't.[11]

A modest stage or none at all would suffice for such a reading.

On the other hand, whatever communal or individual readings we may
conjure in our mind's eye should not altogether block out the fact that most of
the English people at the time could not read. David Cressy has concluded
that "more than two-thirds of the men and nine-tenths of the women were so
illiterate at the time of the civil war that they could not even write their own
names"(2). For any and all play-lovers who depended on the spoken word,
sporadic and more or less clandestine performances had to suffice.

The wonder may be that so many play-texts were available. Quite aside
from their efforts to censor or block new publications, the Lords and
Commons in an ordinance of 20 November 1643 directed that "whole
Libraries, and choice Collections of Printed Books of several Arts and
Faculties" might be sequestered—and hence made unavailable to their
owners (Firth and Rait 1:343). In the spring of 1649, for example, all of the
books and papers of the playwright-pamphleteer Samuel Sheppard were
seized (*Calendar . . . 1649-1650* 1:529). And some libraries were periodically
searched. John Donne, son of the poet, wrote in the dedication of his
father's *Biathanatos* (1648) that after the beginning of the fighting his study
and all his books were frequently examined. And yet old playbooks con-
tinued to be sold, as we have seen, and new ones to be printed. Though
individual specimens sometimes must have looked dangerous or marginal,
they were clearly not a generic target of the authorities.

Playbooks were sold, then, licensed and unlicensed, and plays were
read. The rub was that the playhouses were either closed or subject to
closure. One of the introductory poems to *The Queene* launches a rhetorical
query on the subject:

---

[11]This particular performance was given at Thornton House, Buckinghamshire, on 12
January 1638 (Gair, "Salusbury Circle" 74). Thornton was the seat of Sir Edward Tyrrell,
whose daughter had become Salusbury's wife in 1633. When war broke out and Salusbury
was commissioned, Newman reports, his "industry . . . was prodigious. He raised an infantry
regiment to full strength, 1,200 men, in time for Edgehill." However, "Salusbury's mysterious
death in 1643 deprived the King of a profoundly committed North Welsh supporter" (271).

Is it unlawfull since the stage is down
To make the press act: where no ladies swoune
At the red coates intrusion: none are strip't;
No Hystriomastix has the copy whip't
No man d'on Womens cloth's: the guiltles presse
Weares its own innocent garments: its owne dresse,
Such as free nature made it. . . .

[R.C. A3r]

Before it comes to a close, the question has turned into a statement—and raised an image of the press that, unfortunately, then or now, will not bear scrutiny. In any case, during this period when the theaters were closed and not closed, and books were licensed and not licensed, plays continued not only to provide pleasure but also to explore issues of the day. More than in most other times, as we shall see, their direction was often masked by indirection, and neither stage nor press could lay legitimate claim to any garments of innocence.

[4]

THE PAPER WAR

... the *Presse*, like an unruly horse, hath cast off his bridle of being *Licensed*, and some serious books, which dare flie abroad, are hooted at by a flock of pamphlets. . . .
—Thomas Fuller, *The Holy State and the Profane State* (1642)

What Pamphlets the World in these latter times hath swarmed with, the studious *Shop-keeper* knoweth, who spendeth no small time at the *Bulk* in *reading*, and *censuring modern controversies*, or *News;* & will be readier to tell you *what the times lack*, than *to ask what you lack.*
—Richard Whitlock, *Zootomia* (1654)

. . . *the slightest Pamphlet is now adayes more vendible then the Works of learnedest men. . . .*
—Humphrey Moseley, *Poems of Mr. John Milton* (1645)

But some Historians will gather them together, and make a great swell'd Hydropical History of them.
—Margaret Cavendish, *Plays* (1668)

IT IS TEMPTING but too simple to say that the closing of the English theaters triggered the appearance of many midcentury pamphlets that bore the formal trappings of plays. It is too simple for a number of reasons, but most of all because the inclination toward short, playlike pieces of eight or so pages had already become manifest before September 1642. In 1641 Robert Wild had a character suggest in *The Benefice* that pamphlet dialogues were killing off comedies (13). Even before that, in 1637, Peter Heyleyn was lamenting *"No times more full of odious Pamphlets, no Pamphlets more applauded, nor more deerely bought; then such as doe most deeply wound those powers, and dignities, to which the Lord hath made us subject"* (a3r). In the latter part of 1640 the scattered hopes that were raised by the convening of the Long Parliament led some to anticipate a new era of cooperation and reform.[1] The ensuing disappointment, however, plus the waning of Charles's powers, the gradual shift of allegiance within the Stationers' Company

---

[1]William Cartwright, the playwright and poet, recorded both his hopes and eventual disillusion regarding this Parliament in a poem called "November; or, Signal Dayes." Those members he perceived at first as "Cull'd and Trusted Men" finally proved to constitute what he called "the unhappy Parliament" (*Plays and Poems* 561).

(Charles's main hope to control the press), and the printing of the first newspaper to report events happening in England (November 1641) were all elements that converged to invite or encourage the production of yet more pamphlets.[2] At least one further reason for their proliferation may be suggested: at the same time the pamphlet newsbooks of the day were disseminating news (largely slanted, of course), other kinds of pamphlets provided outlets for reactive, complementary, no-holds-barred editorializing. The flood of paper was phenomenal. As Richard Whitlock put it, "We live in an Age wherein never was lesse *Quarter* given to *Paper*" (229). Fredrick Siebert has counted some twenty Thomason pamphlets of various sorts for the year 1640, a figure that rocketed to over a thousand in each of the next four years, reaching a record of nearly two thousand titles in 1642 (191).[3] Not unlike those occasional earlier pamphlets that had cropped up in times of stress ever since Thomas Cromwell found them useful back in Henrician days, these mid-seventeenth-century pamphlets, especially those cast in dialogue and treating contemporary people and current events, continued to be visible incarnations of dissonance throughout most of our period and on into the Restoration.[4]

That the pamphlets were effective may be suggested in a number of ways. Reinforcing the Heyleyn statement just cited, John Bond wrote in *The Poets Recantation* (1642) that "The inumerable multitude of Pamphlets, which have been surreptitiously inserted above this twelve months and halfe to the ignominious scandall of the State, did not only exasperate his Majesties just indignation against them, but also highly incensed his Parliament" (1). Parliament protested in an ordinance of 14 June 1643, claiming that religion and government were both being defamed by the printing of "books, pamp[h]lets and papers, in such multitudes, that no industry could be sufficient to discover or bring to punishment all the several abounding Delinquents" (Firth and Rait 1:184). Clearly the outburst of pamphlet writing was unnerving to those in authority. No one knew how susceptible the public might be to a press that behaved as though it were free. Moreover, the continuing effectiveness of the pamphlets was great enough to warrant more ordinances. One that is dated 30 September

---

[2]Nelson and Seccombe (25) record that the printing of this newspaper was the achievement of John Thomas, who in November put forth *The Heads of Severall Proceedings in This Present Parliament*. Beginning with the third issue, Thomas called it *Diurnall Occurrences; or, the Heads of Several Proceedings*.   [3]George Thomason, a bookseller at the Rose and Crown in St. Paul's Churchyard, collected many thousands of English publications from 1640 to 1662. In 1762 this invaluable historical resource was presented by George III to the British Museum.   [4]Concerning Henrician times, John King observes that the "Rediscovery of Plato and Lucian permitted the humanistic revival of the dialogue as a vehicle for philosophical discussion and satire" (285).

1647 gives a hint of the pamphlets' range of distribution: "[M]any Seditious, False and Scandalous Papers and Pamphlets [are] daily printed and published in and about the Cities of London and Westminster, and thence dispersed into all parts of this Realm, and other parts beyond the Seas" (Firth and Rait 1:1021).

In attempting to deal with the short, drama-like pieces that played so lively a part among the pamphlets, one may be inclined occasionally to assign them to some segment or other of the dramatic spectrum. Probably it is best, however, to deny them any but a peripheral place, illuminating but ancillary. Since it seems unfair to the facts of the day to pass over them in silence, perhaps the most valid way to handle them in a book on the drama is to consider them as dramatic—but not dramas. If such a course is acceptable, what label should we use? The terminology of the period provides as much confusion as aid. For instance, *The Levellers Levell'd; or, The Independents Conspiracie to Root out Monarchie* (1647), by Mercurius Pragmaticus (that is, Marchamont Nedham), proclaims itself to be an "INTERLUDE."[5] *The Second Part of Crafty Crumwell; or, Oliver in His Glory* (1648), also by one of the Mercurius Pragmaticus team (either Nedham, John Cleveland, or Samuel Sheppard), is presented as a "Trage Commedie," as is a racy, late satire on the Reverend Zachary Crofton called *The Presbyterian Lash; or, Noctroff's Maid Whipt* (1661)—a work, incidentally, said to have been "acted" at the Pye Tavern at Algate. *Lamberts Last Game Plaid* (1660), which depicts John Lambert in the Tower after his unsuccessful attempt to prevent General Monck's march from Scotland to London, is called a "Mock-COMEDY." And a 1643 satire on the cavaliers that bears a title referring more to its time than to itself (for the work ends positively) is called *The Tragedy of the Cruell Warre*. Whatever may be inferred from any of these labels, their main pertinence relates less to genre—the works they designate are not comedies or tragedies—than to mode. That is, they are capable of simulating or borrowing certain comic or tragic devices and of appealing, broadly speaking, to one's comic or tragic sense. Granted some latitude for occasional parodic, reversed intentions, then, the labels on the various title pages of the pamphlets do afford their own limited kinds of mainly adjectival helpfulness.

The appeal of these pretend-plays must have been considerable. We might recall that a tolerance for dramatic or quasi-dramatic writing extended even into some unlikely quarters. What motivation, one wonders,

---

[5]Nedham, the most prominent journalist of the day, found it expedient to take different stands at different times. Joseph Frank points out that while working under various pen names, Mercurius "Britanicus-Pragmaticus-Politicus Nedham wrote well enough for some of his prose to be attributed to Milton" (*Beginnings* 272).

must William Prynne have had to cast the great mass of materials that went into his *Histrio-mastix* into the "acts" and "scenes" of two "tragedies"? What rationalization might he have had for working thus closely with the formal elements of drama? Could it have been to fight fire with ironic fire or to acknowledge in another key that there is nothing wrong with reading certain kinds of drama? By way of explanation, George Ridpath recalled at the end of the century that Prynne had holy precedents, for he "had heard some preachers call their Text . . . a Play or Spectacle, dividing their Texts into Actors, Spectators, Scenes, &c as if they had been Acting a Play" (11). The larger fact is that metaphors from the theater had been powerful analytical tools for many years, and not even mid-seventeenth-century Puritans were immune to the fact. At Oxford in 1653, yet another divine, the Reverend John Rowe, published a book that he called *Tragi-Comoedia*, which is actually an account of how the floor of the White Hart Inn at Witney collapsed during a recent, well-attended performance of the old Elizabethan chestnut *Mucedorus:* "So," writes Rowe on his final page, "by the just hand of God came it to passe."

As for the quasi-dramatic pamphlets at hand, one should note not merely that they are equipped with some accoutrements of regular drama but also that they are a timely development of a much older form, namely the dialogue. Here, perhaps, is the word that most frequently suits our need. Educated writers and readers were familar with the (very different) dialogues of Plato, Cicero, and Lucian as well as with a good many more recent examples, such as those of Machiavelli and Tasso, of More (*The Dialogue of Comfort* was composed in 1534), of Ascham (*Toxophilus*, 1545), and even of James VI and I (*Daemonologie*, 1597) and Izaak Walton (*Compleat Angler,* 1653).[6] In fact, the very catechism of the English church represented voices in dialogue—and became an instigatory factor in the creation of more than thirty other "catechisms" during our targeted years (Yates 170).[7] As Pedanto observes in Wild's *Benefice,* "a Dialogue is . . . the Muses Hodg-Podg" (8).

Whereas most of the foregoing examples imply at least some Renaissance amplitude of possibility, some space for dialogic exchange, the short, mid-seventeenth-century dialogues under consideration here are generally designed to drive home their authors' beliefs—or, in some cases, the beliefs that the author has been hired to present. The old didactic technique of breaking a topic into manageable bits is still pursued here, but seldom is it

---

[6]More's place in the history of English dialogues is especially important. The polemical dialogues of the German Reformation, once they had been imported to England, were "answered" by More—who in the process introduced the leavening of irony, puns, and characterization (Yates 170). [7]The latter include, for instance, *The Cavaliers Catechisme* (1643) and *The Souldiers Catechisme* (1644).

utilized for any intellectual airing or even for friendly persuasion. Instead, the quasi-dramatic form serves to sharpen the position-based satiric darts. The demand for (or assumption of) agreement rather than the invitation to thought is so pervasive in the pamphlets, in fact, that one is scarcely prepared to come across an occasional thoughtful work such as R.P.'s appropriately named *Discreet and Judicious Discourse betweene Wisdome and Pietie* (1642), especially since R.P. writes on the ticklish problem of how to deal with church government. By and large, the atmosphere created in the dialogues is one of hasty and harsh political and religious polemic, a realm characterized by the satiric, coarse, and comic, and often drenched with the bile of hate and frustration. Indirection is frequently the name of the game, but given the anonymity of the authors, the transience of their presses, and the mercuriality of some of their hawkers, it can afford to be the sort of indirection by which one may readily find direction out.[8]

A foray into the midst of the pamphlets will suggest something of their temper and the milieu from which emerged the plays to be discussed here in later chapters. A reasonable beginning point might be the highly conspicuous close of the careers of the King's chief pillars in matters civil and religious, Strafford and Laud. In *A Description of the Passage of Thomas Late Earle of Strafford, over the River of Styx* (1641), Strafford is presented confessing his own overreaching to the expectantly waiting William Noye, the former Attorney General, who had died in 1634. This pamphlet-Strafford admits that during his lifetime he sought "T'untye three Realmes" (A3r). He is also moved to report on the current flood of "*Mercury's,*" or news pamphlets: "Why, there are men *Mercury's,* and women *Mercury's,* and boy *Mercury's; Mercury's* of all sexes, sorts and sizes; and these are they that carry up and downe their Pasquils, and vent them unto shops" (A4r-v).

In 1644 a dramatic monologue entitled *The Earle of Straffords Ghost Complaining of the Cruelties of His Countrey-Men* presented a woodcut of Strafford in a shroud along with a directive rhyme beginning "Let not my shape affright you, but my crimes" (title page). Still a potent political symbol well after his death, Strafford confesses here, "Was it not I that arm'd the *Irish* Catholikes, and disarm'd the Protestants . . . ?" (A2v). And he explains his own continuing relevance with a metaphor from the drama. Whether in York, London, or Ireland, "many times, as in a Theater, the bloody Tragedies I made way for in my life time, are presented to my view"

---

[8]Concerning the hawkers, and despite the fact that his characteristic device is hyperbole, John Taylor may be understood to have some factual grounds for writing that distribution of the pamphlets was effected in part by "Vagrants and Vagabonds from all the Shires round about *London,* and they were all suddainely Metamorphis'd and Transform'd into wandring Booke sellers; every one of them . . . had quickly learn'd the Art to Cry, *Will you buy a new Booke, new lye come forth*" (*Henry Walker* 3).

(A3v). Such a publication is clearly intended less to woo royalist sympathiz-
ers into considering an alternative stand than to reinforce the already-sym-
pathetic views of the opposition.

In 1641, the year of Strafford's beheading, when Laud was already a
prisoner in the Tower, a dialogue called *Read and Wonder* has the Pope
proclaim, "my tripple Crowne / I give to Englands Canterbury, if / He can
but step to Rome and fetch it thence" (A2v). As the Pope knows, however,
"Brave Canterburies cag'd" (A1v). The pamphlet dialogue of the period
that is probably best known nowadays has a woodcut of England's Arch-
bishop of Canterbury actually in a birdcage. Presented along with other
pictures, and with more carefully worked out dramatic trappings than can
be found in most pamphlets, it is specifically labeled *A New Play Called
Canterburie His Change of Diot* (1641). In act I, Laud personally cuts off the
ears of a doctor, a divine, and a lawyer. The first two represent John
Bastwick and Henry Burton, and the last, William Prynne, all of whom had
received savage sentences—but not from Laud, though he approved of
them.[9] Hence we find Laud here ordering a medical, divine, and legal
harvest of ears to be dressed for his supper.

Act II depicts Laud preparing to sharpen his knife on a grindstone, but
instead a carpenter holds Laud's nose to the latter (figure 5). Since no
real-life carpenter appears likely for this role, one might suppose that it is
meant to be generally suggestive of popular resistance to Laudianism.
Perhaps preferably, however, one might suggest that the author alludes
specifically to Richard Carpenter, a "Theological Mountebank" (Wood
1:440) of the day who puns in his book *Experience, Historie, and Divinitie*
(1641): "This is not the rich Jesuits Rule, but the poor *Carpenters* rule"
(2.246). Newly reformed from Romishness, the frequently renovated Car-
penter describes himself as "a convert to the Church of *England*, in a time
which needs a man of a bold heart, and a good courage like my selfe; to
resist the craft, encroaching, and intrusion of Popery" (5.214). Fair or not,
such words as these—especially since they are dedicated to the House of
Commons—may be read as attacks on Laud.[10]

---

[9]Bastwick (M.D., Padua) was the author of the scurrilous *Litany of Dr. John Bastwick* (1637),
which proclaimed bishops enemies of God; and Burton was a Puritan cleric who for more
than a decade had accused Laud of popery. Brought before the Star Chamber, all three men
were sentenced to stand in the pillory and have their ears cut off, pay fines of five thousand
pounds, and face imprisonment for life. Regarding their treatment, Russell makes an
important observation: "The Laudians . . . failed to communicate their sense of the danger-
ousness of Burton, Bastwick, and Prynne to the public at large, and so only alienated the
public by measures taken against them" (*Fall* 23).   [10]Linking Carpenter with the carpenter
in the anti-Laud pamphlet at hand is all the more tempting when we discover in Laud's
private papers a deposition made by one Dr. Lowe, a pastor from Surrey. Lowe was for some
reason moved to record how Richard Carpenter had been given permission to recant his

Figure 5. Archbishop William Laud and carpenter as depicted in *Canterburie His Change of Diot* (1641). (By permission of the Bodleian Library.)

At this point in *Canterburie His Change of Diot* a Jesuit confessor enters to comfort the bleeding bishop, and in act III Laud and the same Jesuit are placed in a big birdcage. William P. Williams has argued that Laud's comforter here is a shadowing of an English Jesuit named John Percy—a man with whom Laud actually disagreed vigorously (*"Canterbury"* 39-40).[11] In fact, it is most unlikely that Laud ever leaned toward Rome at all. Considering the case made by F.G. Stephens, however, one may more readily believe that the confessor in the playlet is meant to call to mind the Queen's own confessor, Robert Philips (134-35). Certainly Philips was a

Romishness in St. Paul's itself, how he petitioned Laud for a benefice, how Laud tried to provide one, and how no benefice was forthcoming. Though we do not know how the maverick Carpenter may have expressed his disappointment and frustration, something moved Lowe to set down his own knowledge about events in the Laud-Carpenter relationship. He stated that "I neu[r] heard one Syllable that Eu[r] [ever] his Grace dishartened the said M[r]Carpente[r]." Instead, Lowe reports, Laud merely "advised him to carrie himself discreetly, & prudently & [spake] words to that purpose." However he came by the post, Carpenter in 1657 was vicar of Poling, a small seaside village in Sussex. Previously, in 1656, he had preached and published a sermon called *The Jesuit, and the Monk* in which he wrote, "*A Malignant is he that is full of evil Fire*.... They break, burn, *blow up all* Barrs, Yokes, Ligaments, *Civil, Ecclesiastical, Divine*, of *Nature*, of *Man*, of *God*" (123). And later he wrote *The Pragmatical Jesuit New-Leven'd* (ca. 1660–65), a spirited and original work in which, as the title page asserts, "The Dev'l himself is turn'd Jesuit." [11]William P. Williams's *"Canterbury His Change of Diet"* is one of a series of helpful editions of pamphlets published in *Analytical and Enumerative Bibliography*.

notable public figure. Commissioned by Henrietta Maria to solicit aid against the Long Parliament from Pope Urban VIII, he was questioned by the Commons several times in 1641. For a while, like Laud, he was even "caged" in the Tower. Eventually the matter was dropped, however, and in 1642 Philips accompanied the Queen to The Hague.

In act IV of the pamphlet the King learns that his bishop has been caught, his informant being a jester—a sure reference to Archibald Armstrong. Archie, as he was known, had served the Stuarts as court jester from the very beginning of James's reign—in fact, until he made the mistake of irritating Laud, who got him fired and thus opened himself to some comic revenge. Sample evidence in the case would be the pamphlet called *Archy's Dream, Sometimes Iester to His Maiestie, but Exiled the Court by Canterburies Malice* (1641). Clinching the identification is the jester's single line in act III: "Ha, ha, ha, ha, who is the foole now" (A3r). Earlier the story had got about that Archie, sufficiently in his cups at the White Lion in Westminster, had been heard to declare that "My Lord of Canterbury is a monk, a rogue and a traitor"—then added, as if speaking to Laud, "Who's the fool now? Did you not hear the news from Stirling about the liturgy?" (Carlton 155). Archie referred to the disastrous attempt in July 1637 to impose in Scotland a prayer book based on the English Book of Common Prayer. A riot had ensued.

Finally, the gleefully vicious *Canterburie His Change of Diot* comes to a close with a "Gig"—a clear reminiscence of such song-and-dance jigs as traditionally followed the performance of real plays.[12] Here it is performed by the jester from act IV and a paritor (that is, a summoning officer of an ecclesiastical court).

In reading this pamphlet demi-drama on Laud—which appears to be the work of Richard Overton—one might recall not only that *cage* was the proper term for a certain sort of jail, but also that similar belittling imagery had come to the fore earlier when James Shirley ironically dedicated his *Bird in a Cage* (1633) to the theater-hating Prynne on the occasion of Prynne's enforced "*happy* Retirement" (A2r). The relevance of cage imagery has still further ramifications in Laud's case. None other than Prynne himself in his *Breviate of the Life of William Laud* (1644) records that Laud was born in Reading "of poore and obscure Parents, in a Cottage, just over against the Cage: which Cage since his comming to the Arch-bishoprick of *Canterbury* . . . was removed to some other place; and the Cottage pulled downe, and new built by the Bishop" (A1r).

---

[12]Martin Butler observes that jigs occur in a number of the pamphlet plays (*Theatre and Crisis* 239). Whether or not one believes they were actually performed, they certainly constitute part of the pamphlets' dramatic disguise.

The falls of Strafford and Laud were both shattering national events and also—we can now see—preludes to the fall of the man they served. Later we shall take a look at some dramatic writings that are related to Charles's own story, but here we may note *A Tragi-Comedy, Called New-Market-Fayre*, written by the Man in the Moon (now recognized as John Crouch [Werstine 74]) and said to be "Printed at *you may goe look*. 1649"—probably in late May or early June. On 21 March an order had been issued to inventory and appraise the goods and personal estate of the late King, his Queen, and the Prince, and on 16 and 21 July two acts were passed regarding their sale.[13] Meanwhile, arising out of the whole volatile situation, Crouch's lively piece—utilizing hyberbole to heighten one's sense of how far matters had gone—opened with a crier selling off the King's effects ("O Yes, O yes, O yes, Here is a Golden Crowne" [3]) and the welcoming of Oliver Cromwell and his crew to Newmarket by Sir Thomas Fairfax ("Victory was proud to honour us at *Nasby's* happy Field" [4]). Each man—Cromwell and Fairfax—thinks the crown would look good on himself, and hence each bids against the other for it. Then Mrs. Cromwell and Lady Fairfax enter, quarreling like fishwives. Energized throughout by a keen bitterness, *New-Market-Fayre* ends when a messenger comes in to say that the "Prince" has landed in the West with thirty thousand men, news that causes the now-devastated would-be rulers of the realm to fall upon their swords, crying, "All People here behold our *miseries*, / Who lives by *Treason;* thus by Treason dies" (8).[14]

Apparently popular enough to warrant three subsequent editions, this work led Crouch to write a sequel—*The Second Part of the Tragi-Comedy Called New-Market-Fayre* (1649)—which is longer, more ambitious, and more stage-oriented in its wording. The sequel itself enjoyed two editions. The prologue of *The Second Part* even predicts how the now-resurrected rebels will rage "To see themselves thus acted on the Stage." A few lines earlier, however, the metaphorical quality of the theatrical references is probably clarified sufficiently when we are told that the author "prayes you *reade*." Equipped with more characters (enough for a full-fledged history play) than with pages of text, the work offers two loyalists (Constantius and Fidelius), Fairfax and Cromwell (both now possessed with devils), the wives of each, together with their attendants (Ruth Incontinence and Abigail Concupiscence) and their paramours (Lady Fairfax's Gorge and Mrs. Cromwell's Morley[15]), to say nothing of three "traitors" (the promi-

---

[13]Werstine cites these and gives various related details.   [14]Contrary to one's first impression, the "Prince" here is probably Rupert, who from 1649 to 1652 functioned partly as a pirate and partly as commander of the royalist fleet. In July 1649 young Charles was on the opposite coast, sailing for Scotland.   [15]These names may refer to Sir Ferdinand Gorge and Colonel Herbert Morley, but probably the names of various men whom either lady had met would have served much the same defamatory purpose.

nent regicides Henry Ireton, John Hewson, and Thomas Pride), as well as various others. Once again the conclusion (which includes Lady Fairfax's murder of Mrs. Cromwell) anticipates restoration of the Stuarts, this time specifically invoking the Prince of Wales: "Come Royal CHARLES, and with a cloud of thunder / Disperse this bed of Snakes, and keep them under" (20).

Here and elsewhere the authors' caricaturing of actual people conveys some of the bite of political cartoons of a later day. And as with such cartoons, the more we know about their human targets, the more completely we can react. In reading both parts of *New-Market-Fayre* it helps to know, for instance, that Thomas Fairfax had served as commander of Cromwell's New Model Army, defeated Charles at Naseby, and agreed to the King's trial—though he then declined to serve as a judge on the court that condemned him. In fact, in the year following Charles's execution and the publication of these two pamphlets, Fairfax resigned his military commission because he was unwilling to invade Scotland. For the next few years he retreated to Nun Appleton, his estate in Yorkshire, inspiring the admiration of his daughter's tutor, Andrew Marvell—and, of course, Marvell's "Upon Appleton House." One would not expect the writer of *New-Market-Fayre* to know, care, or acknowledge that Fairfax was for the most part a brave, honorable, thoughtful, moral man.[16] His one great error probably was his legitimate but perhaps vengeful execution at Colchester of Sir Charles Lucas and Sir George Lisle in 1648. Somehow Fairfax seems not to have seen that killing Lucas and Lisle was an act that pointed down the road toward killing their royal master. When Charles died, Fairfax wrote privately, "Oh lett that Day from time be blotted" (281).

One of the largest and most interesting groups of pamphlet dialogues concerns Parliament, which was frequently personified (Sir Pitifull Parliament, Mister Parliament, Mistress Parliament) and usually vilified, especially after the term "Rump Parliament" was invented to describe those members of the Long Parliament who survived the "purge" given it by Colonel Pride's soldiers in December 1648. *Ding Dong; or, Sr Pitifull Parliament, on His Death-Bed* (1648) was produced by the royalist writer Mercurius Melancholicus. *Ding Dong* depicts Sir Pitifull in bed, wasted "with a *Scotch* Feaver" and shaken by a "*Welch* Ague" (2), with Sir Ralph Rebellion holding his head. Parliament confesses his wrongs, explains that "*Machiavill* was my master" (4), and presents his last will and testament "In *the name of* Lucifer, *Amen*" (5). Hell and the devil, in fact, lend color and force to a good many of these dialogues. The background for Milton's mighty debate in

---

[16]To readers of this book it may seem important that thanks to Fairfax the Bodleian Library at Oxford was not pillaged when the parliamentarians took control there in June 1646.

the nether world certainly includes such works as *The Devill and the Parliament* (1648), in which the devil says, "I meane to call a Parliament in Hell" (2).

One cannot be sure whether or not the several Mistress Parliament dialogues are indebted in any specific way to the "Mistress Missa" dialogues that flourished in England a hundred years earlier during the debates on the mass (John King 287, 290). Be this as it may, the central metaphor here is that of a woman giving birth to a monster. The full title of another Melancholicus pamphlet from 1648 suggests some of the matters involved: *Mistris Parliament Brought to Bed of a Monstrous Childe of Reformation. With Her 7 Yeers Teeming, bitter Pangs, and hard Travaile, that she hath undergone in bringing forth her first-borne, (Being a Precious Babe of Grace.) With the cruelty of Mistris London Her Midwife; and great Affection of Mrs. Synod Her Nurse, Mrs. Schisme, Mrs. Priviledge, Mrs. Ordinance, Mrs. Universall Toleration, and Mrs. Leveller Her Gossips.* Presumably one might choose to see this (and, indeed, many of the Rump-related writings) as illustrative of the politicized carnivalesque. Peter Stallybrass and Allon White observe of such low, body-oriented humor that "[t]he openings and orifices of the carnival body are emphasized, not its closure and finish. It is an image of impure corporeal bulk with its orifices ... yawning wide and its lower regions ... given priority over its upper regions" (9). Written at a time when many women died in childbirth, the pamphlet raises doubts about Mrs. Parliament's survival. At the very end, however, discarding dialogue and turning to straight prose, the pamphlet describes how the room where she lies grows dark, the candles go out, the wauling of cats and the howling of dogs and the barking of wolves are heard, and the goggle-eyed monster is born. The episcopal church having been deconstructed, this newborn "Childe" is the national church that the Westminster Assembly brought forth in its stead.[17]

Somewhat different but recognizably of the same breed of pamphlet is *The Disease of the House* (August 1649), which presents a French quack who is to administer physic to "Madame le Parlament" (4) but who at the close admits, "begar, me have no *Cure* . . . ; this be dying Nation, lost, lost, begar utterly lost" (7).

Among the most interesting of the dialogues focused on Parliament is *The Terrible, Horrible, Monster of the West* (1649)—and "*doe not thinke Sir, / 'Tis* [Balthazar] *Gerbiers Puppet-play*" (title page).[18] Lest there be any doubt

---

[17]Potter explores the issues raised by this work and tentatively ascribes it to John Hackluyt ("*Mistress Parliament* Dialogues"). [18]Gerbier, a courtier, painter, architect, minor diplomat, and Master of the Ceremonies (1641), was a man of some cultivation, uncertain ethics, and many projects. In September 1648, when *Mercurius Pragmaticus* presented a prospectus for Gerbier's new academy to introduce arts and sciences to the young, its pretensions amused the pamphleteers (see Hotson 134–36).

about the identity of this horrible creature, the monster is directly called "the *Embleme* of this *Parliament*" (3). It has swallowed bishops, bishoprics, and recusants' estates, devoured St. Paul's ("Organ-Pipes, and all"), chopped off the head of the owner of Whitehall and consumed all his goods, and then gone on to the House of Peers, where it ate up most of the nobility (4-5). It has even devoured the Man in the Moon's press, letters, and books—and, as we have seen previously, strategic parts of the Blackfriars and Fortune playhouses. All this is colorful but standard fare. More striking is the dialogue's turn to an elegiac, pastoral mode in a long speech by an old shepherd named Carolina:

> This monstrous *Wolf* has seiz'd on all my *Flock*
> Kill'd the *chiefe Shepheard* of *Arcadia;*
> . . . .
> I cannot speake for griefe, his tender *Lambs*
> Are forc'd from the soft Teats of their owne *Dams*.
> Their *snowy fleeces*, (white as Innocence)
> Tore from their Flesh by *pricking Bryers*,
> All *means* of Life is from them tane away,
> And *Albion* white, become a *Golgotha*.
>
>   [2]

Here in a moment of enfigured, royalist adoration we find some respite from the vengeance and spleen that permeate most of the pamphlet dialogues.

Variation amid the paper flood is provided also by a scattering of dialogues dealing with other kinds of subjects. For instance, *Newes Out of the West; or, The Character of a Mountebank* (1647) is a thirty-page work—a mini-comedy, one might say—that relates the misfortunes of Hodge Lether-Pelch and Tym Hob-Nayle, who have come up from Taunton to London to see a physician. Though the serious target of this work is the mountebanks who have set up fleecing operations in the city, its chief attraction, probably in its own time as well as ours, is the lively detail afforded by the Somerset bumpkins. Hodge, for instance, tells the wherry-man who rows them over the Thames that he is a lazy harlot for charging a groat—a day's toil with plow and cart—for a little paddling in the water with two oven-shovels (5).

For verbal play of a rougher sort one can hardly do better than an eight-page "mock comedy" called *The Gossips Braule; or, The Women Weare the Breeches* (1655). Smacking more than a little of old-fashioned, hard-core misogyny, this is a tongue combat between Jone, Doll, Meg, and Bess (a dunghill raker, a fishwife, a washerwoman, and a hostess). At least, says Bess, "I was never *down-diddl'd* by a Barbers Boy, on a *Coblers stall*" (6). Since it is hard to say how guffawing about lecherous, lower-class working women has any useful social or political purpose, one is left to ponder other reasons why the author wrote this piece. A pursuit of possible answers would take us off course here, but meanwhile one might suggest that the pamphlet's subtitle points in a likely direction.

Whatever their subject or temper, one of the questions to be posed about the pamphlet dialogues is whether or not some were performed. Historians of the theater have been unable to give a sure answer. Perhaps this is not such bad news, however, for keeping the question of performability in mind is a good way to keep us alert to details in the individual texts themselves. In most instances one can say with reasonable assurance that the work at hand was never meant to be performed. As we have seen in a complimentary poem in the 1653 publication of *The Queene*, it was generally safer "*To make the press act.*" And yet sometimes the texts invite doubt. *The Levellers Levell'd* has a prologue said to have been "spoken" by the author, Mercurius Pragmaticus—a persona, as we have seen, assumed by Marchamont Nedham during one of his royalist phases. *Levellers* also includes the statement that "this Play was acted once indeed" (A1v). The valuable ambiguity here of the verb *acted* resides in the fact that it serves as a perfectly good term for either the theater or life. And act I, scene i, of *Levellers* opens with the provocative stage directions, "Confused Musick: Enter *Englands Genius*" (A2v). Since experienced theatergoers had long been exposed to the implications of "confused" music in such plays as Marston's *Malcontent* and Webster's *Duchess of Malfi*—both realms of disharmony and disorder—we may conjecture that the mere mention of it here would suffice for some communication to take place. On the other hand, all such dramatic signals in *The Levellers Levell'd* are restricted and qualified when we who take the pamphlet in hand come across the words "you must onely read" (A1v).

Ironically, the strongest indication of some sort of performance of the pamphlet dialogues may be found embedded in the language of an ordinance of 30 September 1647. In the process of delineating who is to be punished for violating it, the ordinance specifies "what person soever shall Make, Write, Print, Publish, Sell or Utter, or cause to be Made, Written, Printed, Published, Sold or Uttered any Book, Pamphlet, Treatise, Ballad, Libel, Sheet or Sheets of News whatsoever (except the same be Licensed by both or either House of Parliament . . .)" (Firth and Rait 1:1022). Perhaps the verb *utter* should give us pause. Does it mean simply "publish" or "display for sale"? Is it used here as a synonym for "express in writing"? One can only suggest that if its range of reference includes audible expression, it probably does not allude solely to the performance of ballads. If it did, why not use the word *sing*? The term *Ballad-singer* occurs elsewhere in the document. Perhaps, then, *utter* is meant to cover both speaking *and* singing. Which of the designated kinds of publication might be spoken? Perhaps the ordinance is intended merely to prohibit, for example, the reading of a newsbook to one's illiterate friends. Whatever the case, the oral reading of unlicensed pamphlet dialogues is also prohibited after this time, perhaps suggesting that previously they had been read aloud.[19]

Though a handful of midcentury dialogues may have been performed or at least given oral readings, many include indications (inadvertent or intended) of their own circumscribed nature. The prologue to the *"Tragi-Comedie"* called *Craftie Cromwell* (February 1648), for instance, begins thus:

> An Ordinance from our pretended State,
> Sowes up the Players mouths, they must not prate
> Like Parrats what they're taught upon the Stage,
> Yet we may Print the Errors of the Age. . . .
>
> [A1v]

And Mercurius Pragmaticus, the author of *The Second Part of Crafty Crumwell* (1648), addresses himself pointedly "To the Readers of my former peece," concluding that he *"Writes for your sollace, somewhat for his owne"* (3). Here, then, as we shall see also in subsequent chapters, the evidence suggests strongly that old habits formed by the writing and reading of plays proved too useful to abandon even if actual performance was not the goal.

In fact, the form of some of these writings serves sometimes to reinforce their belligerence. The author of *Rombus the Moderator* (1648), which proclaims its political stance in a wishful subtitle, *The King Restored*, tries to imagine punishments suitably harsh for the likes of Fairfax and Cromwell, as well as William Lenthall, Henry Martin, and Thomas Rainsborow. Tarring all of this crew with the same brush denies any individual virtues that any one of them might have had, and also, less obviously, it blurs their individual failings. Henry Martin was probably the man here most richly endowed with failings. Early in the war he is said to have seized certain belongings of the King, urged that the royal family be destroyed, and generally aroused attention with his violence and womanizing.[20] In any case, the author of *Rombus* achieves a sort of closet-theater coup when he has his titular "moderator" ordain of them all that

---

[19]One possible candidate for oral presentation would be Sheppard's *Joviall Crew* (1651)—to which we shall return in chapter 14. Whether it is a "pamphlet" or a "comedy" is hard to say. In either case, postponing examination of it to a later chapter should help to make the point of its generic ambivalence. [20]C.M. Williams summarizes helpfully: "Everything about Henry Marten, from his irreverent humour to his immorality, his religious heterodoxy, his indiscriminate concern for justice, and his association with Levellers and Quakers, might have been calculated to alienate a sizeable part of his noble and gentle contemporaries" (136).

you shall be assembled together, to take upon you the faculty of fooling, as you terme it, and be made players in spight of your teethes.

You shall be called; the society of *Goblins;* you shall practice tumbling: picking of pockets, and plackets, with all the Science of *Legerdemaine;* the play you shall be alwayes presenting shall be famous, and entitled, *The English Gipsee, and her damned Crue:* which shall be capable of enlargement, for variety, but never loose the Tittle.

Of this Company, you *Fairfax* shall be King . . . , King of the vagabonds; *Oliver* shall be your *malus genius,* or evill Counsellour. *Lentall,* the Prologist, and Treasurer, *Martin,* the Humorist, or Mad-Lover. *Marshall, Annanias,* or the White Devill. *Rainsborough,* the Intelligencer, or Scout. *Hamon,* the Door-Keeper. *Madamoiseille Fairefax,* the Gipsee, or Stigan Proserpine. And *Chaloner,* though exempt from publick Trial, shall likewise passe upon his part, and play the Fool egregiously. [12-13]

In pamphlet dialogues such as this one, the subversive nature of the playlike form emphasizes the subversiveness of the message. In this instance the effect is enhanced because the villains are condemned to be cast in a play on a stage in hell. What greater damnation could there be for such rogues?

Though writers from various parts of the political and religious spectrum made use of playwriting techniques in their pamphlets, generally those with royalist sympathies produced the most potent specimens. Then again, probably so many dialogues were produced partly because the pamphlets of various factions were themselves engaged in dialogue with one another. Indeed, it seems likely that some writers used the engagement in unbuttoned verbal violence as a substitute for physical violence. As Dudley North, fourth Lord North, observed ruefully in looking back on this period from the relative calm of his Restoration retirement, the mid-century English found themselves hotly engaged in a paper war (29).[21] The pity was that it came to have such deadly parallels in the war played out at Edgehill, Cropredy Bridge, Hopton Heath, Marston Moor, Naseby, and Preston, as well as at Drogheda and Wexford and Dunbar.

---

[21]Though the concern in this chapter has been with printed works, of course there was a concomitant surge of unprinted diplomatic papers. Writing in particular of the period when Sir John Hotham, following an order from the Commons, denied Charles entry into Hull (23 April 1642), Russell observes: "For the next month after the King's attempt . . . , the paper war was at its peak" (*Fall* 504).

[5]

ARMS AND THE MEN[1]

Here first the *Rebell windes* began to roare,
Broke loose from those just fetters which they bore.
Here mutinous waves above their shores did swell,
And the first storme of this dire *Winter* fell. . . .
                    —Abraham Cowley, *The Civil War* (1642)

Noe pestilence so bad as civil wars.
All evill to a Kingdome y^t doth bring.
It doth destroy ye Subject & ye King.
                    —*The Disloyall Favorite* (1650s)

. . . we Vow
Not to Act any thing you disallow. . . .
Aspiring *Cataline*, shall be forgot,
Bloody *Sejanus*, or who e're would Plot
Confusion to a State; the Warrs betwixt
The Parliament, and just *Henry* the sixt,
Shall have no thought or mention, cause their power,
Not only plac'd, but left him in the *Tower*. . . .
                    —*Rump* (pub. 1662)

To a playe of warre, 9d. . . .
                    —Humphrey Mildmay, 16 November 1643

THOUGH OTHER MATTERS sometimes deflect us from the fact, soldiers
and their wars had long been staples in English dramatic fare. From
Roister Doister and Tamburlaine through all the history plays and down to
their numerous progeny in the cavalier plays of the 1630s, soldiers had
marched across the English stage, ongoing reflections of a perennial con-
cern of English life. There is reason enough, of course, to hold that the
country became somewhat less oriented toward the military in the mid-
1630s. G.M. Trevelyan writes of England at the time as the "most civilian
of societies" (188).[2] Then again, it is of considerable importance here that

---

[1]Seeing the title of this chapter, one might think first of Virgil, but "*Armes, and the Men*" are
the opening words of Richard Fanshawe's translation from Camoëns's *The Lusiad* (1655).
[2]Regarding the period after Charles fled with his family from London on 10 January 1642,
Conrad Russell has suggested that "the historian's major task is not to explain why there
was a civil war: it is to explain why there was not a civil war for another eight months" (*Fall*
454). The subject should not be oversimplified, but Russell believes that the delay at this

between 1639 and 1642 Charles found himself facing armed resistance from all three of his kingdoms—first Scotland, then Ireland, and then, most killing of all, England itself. In an age when at least some young men of position might be expected to seek part of their training in the finishing school of Mars, even when England was at peace, and when some common soldiers found themselves sloshing through foreign mud (the earlier lot of Ben Jonson), the dramatists (including Jonson and, later, his literary descendants) naturally included soldiers and wars in their theatrical refractions of the world.

Clearly some care about what a soldier said and did, onstage or off, was always in order for the circumspect. Just as it had not been a safe idea to reenact the overthrow of Richard II in 1601, so it would have been risky at midcentury to stage the wars between Henry VI and his Parliament. But the dramatic writings of our later period are nevertheless often invaded by military concerns. It could hardly be otherwise during times

> When armed men each day we meet
> In every lane and every street:
> When as our streets are chained streight,
> And Ordnance plac'd at every gate.
> [Rollins, *Cavalier and Puritan Ballads* 148]

In the same season that these lines were written, the "Ordnance" at Edgehill had already begun to kill Englishmen. As a sort of counterbalancing reminder, we are fortunate to have Bulstrode Whitelocke's observation that the years with which we are concerned were not "*altogether of a piece, every day brings not forth a* Petition of Right, *nor an* Edge-hill *Battel; there are Intervals, there are Flats where Fortune drives swimmingly without Rattle or Disturbance, as well as Ups, and Downs, and Precipices, where She jolts, and tumbles, and overturns every thing in the way*" (1r). Still, for many of the English and much of the time, these years brought war and rumors of war.

When civil war first broke out, it was possible for many to believe that they faced only a limited rebellion, a brief resort to arms as a means of readjusting the social machine. Probably few dreamed that the conflict would develop into a full-scale revolution, with all that that meant for soldiers and citizens alike. And probably some, especially when great property holdings were at stake, took care to have relatives represented on both sides, so the family might have powerful friends no matter which side prevailed (William Compton 99). In any event, from the beginning and

---

point was at least in part "a measure of how extraordinarily demilitarized a country England had become. That England had reached January 1642 with no unquestionably legal method of raising troops is a symptom of this demilitarized condition" (455).

throughout, many people wanted to be as neutral as possible as long as possible. As Paul Hardacre notes, "Nonintervention . . . commended itself to men who were never satisfied in their conscience as to the justice of either faction, and who were torn between allegiance to the king and resistance to personal government" (1). J.S. Morrill has found "attempted neutrality pacts in twenty-two English counties and in many boroughs" (36-37). Nevertheless, militarism was thrust into many British lives in ways that could not be resisted.

Not surprisingly, then, militarism is a major element in plays of the period. Sometimes it is a cause and means of questioning, sometimes a device for externalizing and carrying fictional conflicts to an extreme, sometimes a magazine of evocative details, sometimes a means to make thematic or polemic points, and, naturally, sometimes a mix of these. In his *Fancy's Festivals* (1657) Thomas Jordan mounted a debate between Power, habited as a soldier, and Policy, habited as a scholar, in which he has Policy observe that each of them should serve the other. However, writing at the end of that interval when the country was divided into ten, then eleven, military districts, each governed by a major general, Jordan eventually has the soldiers draw their swords on the scholars, after which "*all ascend, the Souldiers into the supream places*" (B4r).

What one now sees and understands about military elements in plays of the period will be determined to a large extent by both one's point of departure and one's means of entry into the subject. For example, one might come fresh from a study of prose romance bearing insights from relevant fictions both ancient and modern, foreign and domestic (romances such as the *Aethiopica, Arcadia,* and *Argenis,* and perhaps others not so well known). Or one might consider to what degree militarism functions as a source of conflict in a play, or as a means of echoing, paralleling, or reinforcing the major conflict, or as a background that provides useful coloration. Then again, one might follow Marilynn Olson's lead and consider the different kinds of soldiers that these writings deploy.[3]

We shall begin with this last approach, since the question of dramatic character converges usefully with sociopolitical and economic issues, and so keeps the facts of military history in view. With taxonomic possibilities in mind, we see very quickly that this drama affords a good many mirrors of military nobility. Of course there were numerous literary models for such characters, figures like Baltazar in Dekker's explicitly titled *The Noble Soldier* (1626), Massinger's Lord Lovel in *A New Way to Pay Old Debts* (1622),

---

[3]Building on this last possibility, one might test the hypothesis that the quite different lives of noble and common soldiers, of officers and men, tended to be paralleled structurally in the drama by a playing out of plot and subplot.

and Jonson's Lovel in *The New Inn* (1629). Furthermore, contemporary events were now producing real-life models, the king himself among them. Though civil war had not yet broken out in England when Van Dyck painted Charles as an armored warrior king (the great Fleming died in 1641), Charles did, indeed, prove eventually to be a brave and noble soldier. Robert Herrick exclaimed fervently, "War, which before was horrid, now appears / Lovely in you, brave Prince of Cavaliers!" ("To the King . . . ," ll. 7-8). Among many other names of soldiers that come down to us, perhaps none shines brighter than that of General James Graham, fifth Earl and first Marquess of Montrose. A brave, gracious, capable, Scottish cavalier, Montrose proved to be a superb leader, a man acknowledged by many to be a bona fide hero.[4]

Among midcentury dramatic works that attempt to depict nobility in military characters, one might cite Cosmo Manuche's *The Just General* (1652), which provides a noble titular character who is seasoned, loyal, and—as advertised—just. In fact, he is exactly the kind of soldier that Manuche, himself a former soldier, seems to have valued most. One might point also to the noble Alphonso in Davenant's *Siege of Rhodes* (1656) or to the king in Knightley's version of *Alfrede* (1659). Various kinds of pressure—including love, honor, friendship, faith, and pride—serve to elicit manifestations of nobility in various good soldiers. Throughout the plays, moreover, one of the most striking pressures of all is that of loyalty to a king who is supposed to be more noble than oneself but who, too frequently, is not.[5]

Breathing an altogether different sort of air from these noble beings are the common soldiers. Largely lacking in fine feelings and, of course, in fine rhetoric to express such feelings as they have, these are the "stragling Souldiers with Wenches" who make an appearance in William Chamberlaine's *Love's Victory* (1658). In Jasper Mayne's *Amorous Warre* (1648) three of them parcel out "Three daies to one / Dryed *Bisket*, and horne *Stock fish*, both which might / Be shot for *Battery*" (42). In Burnell's *Landgartha* (1641) they need to pillage because their allowance is only three pence a day (35). The tailor's wife in *The King and the Cause* (1642?) tells her creditor-ridden

---

4Unfortunately, however, Montrose may be remembered best for his abandonment by the younger Charles—who was himself harried and desperate at the time. One should note also that the subsequent cruel execution of Montrose by the Scots (1650) was perceived north of the border as just retribution for a man who had been responsible for the deaths of many of his countrymen.   5Though there is generally and obviously some leeway between technical and figurative nobility, it is helpful to have Newman's conclusion on the historical record. He writes, "The *nobiles minores* and *nobiles majores* accounted for 90 per cent of the regimental commanders: the *minores* for 67 per cent, the *majores* for 23 per cent, showing that a clear majority of them were untitled gentlemen or knights at the time they were commissioned into the King's armies" (126).

husband of a pillaging soldier who has been able to snatch up for his wife such treasures as two pillowcases, a flaxen towel, and a pair of yellow shoes (18v). To be sure, the poor estate of the common soldier is of no concern at all to some romance-oriented playwrights, but enough of the others touch on the subject to catch our eyes and minds, and occasionally to conjure up moments of apparent realism. In J.S.'s *Andromana* (1642; published 1660) we come across such a moment in a speech by a stouthearted captain. Complete with its touch of anatomical comedy, it may stand as a reminder that in pondering the word *common* we are engaged in matters of social class as well as military rank:

> Sir, We wear as sound hearts in these torn breeches
> As ere a Courtier of them all.
> We are not afraid of spoyling our hands for want
> Of gloves, nor need we Almond butter when we go to bed.
> . . . .
> You shall see us dye as handsomely in these old cloaths
> As those wear better, and become our wounds as well,
> And perhaps smell as sweet when we are rotten.
>
> [C3v]

In fact there were degrees of impoverishment among the common soldiers at different times and in different places, and we need not picture all as pathetically barefoot, undernourished, and forlorn as the poor soul depicted in figure 6. Nevertheless, the fact is that if he appears at all in a play, the common soldier is likely to be not only of low social and military rank but also poor.

Crude, comic, and poor, as a rule, and sometimes portrayed with the aid of concrete details (an old biscuit, a dried stockfish, a moldy scrap of cheese[6]), the common soldier of these works is as much a distillation and distortion of life as the noble one. The author of *The Female Rebellion*, probably Henry Birkhead, sums up the two types succinctly, writing that "wealth, autority, & armour are / The portion of Comanders; want, submission, / And nakedness the share of private Soldiers" (175v). When the types are juxtaposed or made to interact in a play, each a foil to the other, such characters sometimes acquire sufficient life to remind us of the broad, real spectrum from which they both are drawn.

That real spectrum included also some braggart soldiers. Sir John Byron, for instance, was known among parliamentarians as a "Bloody Bragadochio" (Burne and Young 134). Onstage, braggarts certainly had had

---

[6]Helping to put this bleak picture in perspective is Rogers's observation that "The armies of both sides lived and fought mainly on biscuits and Cheshire cheese, and this, in fact, was almost the only food ever issued" (35).

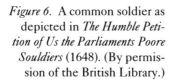

Figure 6. A common soldier as depicted in *The Humble Petition of Us the Parliaments Poore Souldiers* (1648). (By permission of the British Library.)

a long and successful career. From the time of Aristophanes and Terence down to Udall's Ralph Roister Doister and Lyly's Sir Tophas, we proceed— naming but a few—to Shakespeare's Armado, Falstaff, and Parolles, Jonson's Bobadill and Glorious Tipto (the name a takeoff on the classical *miles gloriosus*), and Beaumont and Fletcher's Pharamond and Bessus. Considering such a well-established dramatic heritage, perhaps we should wonder that more braggart soldiers do not appear in our midcentury plays. Then again, perhaps the braggart as an ingredient for leavening may be said to have developed into (perhaps merged with) more contemporary kinds of comic military fraud. Since real hacksters and cutters sometimes roistered their way through the taverns and streets of London, it is only natural that the midcentury playwrights paid heed to them. At any rate, whereas one can find the likes of Cowley's Cutter and Blade—talkers, swaggerers, and sharpsters claiming a military past—one rarely encounters such an old-fashioned specimen as Quermero in Meriton's *Love and War* (1658), who at one point examines a hole in his stocking to see if he has been wounded and at another "*Falls as if he were dead, & while he lies, eats up his pottage*" (M2r). Another such is Bragadocia in *Alfrede*.[7] (For a crude representation of the type, see figure 7.) Says Knightley's Bragadocia, "let me blow doune Kingdoms with my breath, and blow vp townes" (6r). In fact, it turns out

---

[7]Despite the feminine ending of the name, *braggadocia* is indeed one of the variants of *braggadocio*.

The Braggadocia Souldier

Figure 7. A braggart soldier as seen in *The Braggadocia Souldier; and, The Civil Citizen* (1647). (By permission of the British Library.)

that this character's real name is itself a sort of heavy weapon: Polemobombardifragosogigantomiomachopomponides (29v). There are better laughs and more convincingly sinister implications in the likes of Cutter and Blade.

In contrast, the blunt soldier is a straight-talking man who knows his job in the field and is instinctively suspicious of braggarts, courtiers, and carpet knights. Once again, a search would turn up numerous precedents from the earlier drama. Among the more famous are Chapman's Bussy d'Ambois and Shakespeare's Coriolanus. As a matter of fact, claims of bluntness are made by several of Shakespeare's better military speakers, including Richard III, Hotspur, Iago, and Mark Antony. In his attempt to win over the Roman crowd, Antony presents himself as "a plain blunt man" (*Julius Caesar* III.ii.218). James Shirley's *Maid's Revenge* (1626; published 1639) has a character named Sforza who is defined in the list of dramatis personae as "*a blunt Souldier.*" Some fifteen years later, in his more famous *Cardinal* (1641; published 1653), Shirley gives us in Columbo a soldier whose honest bluntness seems all the more worthy because it is juxtaposed with artifice, hypocrisy, and subterfuge. In other years we find a "blunt soldier" in Salusbury's *Love or Money* (ca. 1638-42), a downright Danish soldier in the Fletcher-Field-Massinger *Knight of Malta* (ca. 1616-18; published 1647), another downright soldier in Glapthorne's *Revenge for Honour* (ca. 1637-41; published 1654), and yet another in D'Ouvilley's *The False Favourite Disgrac'd* (1657). In Compton's *Bassianus* we find Bassianus claiming that "Some rudiments I haue of arts & arms / but nere could frame my tongue to compliments" (23v). In *Love in Travell* (1655) Manuche presents Bolster as an impoverished former soldier who is especially tough-minded, outspoken, and admirable for his honesty. Many years later we continue to encounter the type. In Shadwell's *The Volunteers* (1692; published 1693), for instance, we have an old cavalier officer, "somewhat rough in Speech," who is called, frankly, Major General Blunt (A4v). Variations of this durable character must have played well (and read well) not merely because they sometimes provided an efficient means of expressing the playwright's brand of right-thinking, but also because they appealed to an enduring esteem for the sort of plain speaking that many of the English found difficult in real life.

However traditional the literary figure of the blunt soldier was, his validity was reinforced by living models. Sir Arthur Haselrig, a parliamentarian commander, was known for his downrightness. William Cavendish, sometime commander of the royalist forces and also one of our playwrights, assured his wife "That Rhetorick was fitter for Falshoods then Truths" (Margaret Cavendish, *Life* b2v). And Prince Rupert, the most dashing of them all, thought fit to claim in a speech of 1642 that "I may by my education in the military art (having been nursed in the Low Countries, that Seminary of warlike discipline) claime the priviledge in my blunt souldiers phrase, briefly to deliver my opinion" (A2r). Thus does life appear to mirror an art that appears to mirror life.

Setting aside for a few moments one further kind of military character type, let us note briefly a different and major means of presenting the military in drama, then proceed to a sampling of plays.

Thanks to the traditional intrication of love and war in narrative fiction and drama, midcentury playwrights instinctively fell into the habits of their predecessors and managed sometimes to produce newly powered variations on the old combination. For some striking earlier evidence of the dual tradition one might turn to Shakespeare's *Troilus and Cressida*, where Agamemnon exclaims, "may that soldier a mere recreant prove, / That means not, hath not, or is not in love" (I.iii.287-88)—a declaration that has its counterpoint in Thersites's later "Lechery, lechery, still wars and lechery, nothing else holds fashion" (V.ii.194-95). It is not simply that sensual indulgence may prove to be a foe of heroic virtue, or that matters sexual and military often share patterns of strategy, combat, and conquest. It is, rather, that they compete and yet seem inseparable. "*I am compelled by duty,*" says a character in Meriton's *Wandring Lover* (1658), "*to praise your fidelity in the war-like attempt of* Venus" (5). Priests of both Mars and Hymen pass over the stage together in Compton's Leontius (ca. 1649), where we are presented with the rhetorical question, "When Mars and Hymen both agree / Who then can doubt of Victory" (4r-v). Though the linkage of love and war had had countless incarnations through the centuries, this particular period of strife appears to have triggered more thought on the topic than ever.

Presumably a soldier would prefer to enjoy both of the loves of his life, but the soldiers in our plays are sometimes committed more to a woman, sometimes more to a war. "He is a Lover," says Flecknoe in his prose character of a Gallant Warrior, "and the Warre is his Mistresse" (*Enigmaticall Characters* 68). In *Cola's Furie* (1645; published 1646) Henry Burkhead provides a like-minded song, acknowledging (as did Lovelace) not only that military life separates young lovers but also that it may command greater love than the ladies themselves:

> *Come away, O come away,*
> *Couragious youths, O doe not stay,*
> *Now's the time, brave Mars Will prove*
> *More powerfull then the god of love.*
>
> [12]

Killigrew's Cicilia in part 1 of *Cicilia and Clorinda* confesses that "of all the services the Prince did to win esteem from me, I loved him more for running from me when his honour call'd him, then if he had staid, and pin'd at my feet" (218). On the other hand, Cartwright's *The Siedge; or, Love's Convert* (1628-38; 1651) closes with a tableau of "five Commanders," Hercules, Theseus, Pyrrhus, Atrides, and Achilles, placing their weapons at the feet of five ladies on pedestals (178).

In Jasper Mayne's suggestively titled *The Amorous Warre* we have a specifically amatory-military play that was written we know not when but certainly published in 1648 and then again in 1659. Mayne held a doctorate of divinity from Oxford (1646), and we find him preaching earnestly against divisiveness: one of his sermons was titled *Against Schisme; or, The Seperations of These Times*. In fact, Mayne progressed far beyond most of his fellow Englishmen—indeed, beyond some of our own contemporaries—by arguing against the use of such pigeonholing terms as "Puritan," "papist," and "cavalier." In his dramatic *Warre*, however, he has lighter aims. He equips this play with an Ovidian epigraph ("*Militat omnis Amans; Et habet sua Castra Cupido*"), and he opens it with "*a Warlike sound of Drummes and Trumpets within*" (1). There is some first-scene questioning among courtiers who ask, "How, without losse of fame, can we avoid / To accompany the King?" (3), since the conflict may prove to be a mere "*Smocke-Warre*" between two kings, each smitten by the other's sister. The relative seriousness of all this may be gauged even better when we find some of the court ladies with "*faces discolour'd to a comely Browne*" (32) presenting themselves as Amazon visitors at their own court. Furthermore, the now-somewhat-outworn Neoplatonic cast of the amorousness may be sampled in the following declaration by Eurymedon, King of Thrace, to Barsene, sister of Archidamus, King of Bithynia:

> I did frame such *Ideas* of you, so pure,
> So free from these grosse figures, which do stirre
> The vulgar admiration, that, if I said,
> A *Minde* was worshipt by a *Minde,* And that
> My thoughts supply'd the place of Sacrifices,
> Which flew betweene us; And, like winged prayers,
> Maintain'd a sacred Entercourse, & traffique,
> With the Originall of what I fancy'd,
> I doe but rudely, but halfe expresse my selfe.
>
> [22-23]

Whether or not such a passage dates back to earlier, more lighthearted days, it is far removed from the world of Mayne's own common soldiers, whom we have earlier seen sharing a biscuit. It is perhaps closer to his six "Warlike *Moores*" who later come in to dance wearing nothing much but pearls above the waist and blue satin with silver fringe below it (34). In any case, the play as we have it is a rather loose medley of theatrical elements.

The whole is not so loose, however, as to absorb unnoticed certain passages, sharper in tone, that must have accrued to it in the 1640s. In act V the young Lord Theagines, addressing the parcel-gilt gentleman Artops, alludes to some non-amatory wars that are at once English and foreign:

> . . . you were imploy'd
> In our late *Civill Warres,* by the factious Members
> Of our *Synedrium,* when they arm'd their *slaves,*
> And made their *Bondmen Curiasseirs*[8] against
> Th' *Equestrall Order;* And did enact it lawfull
> Ith' *Kings* Name to take Armes against Him; And
> Out of Obedience to Him to rebell.
> And 'mongst their other Wilde and furious *Votes,*
> Decreed it lawfull, for the *Good* oth' Subject,
> To rifle their *Estates;* slaughter their *persons;*
> Ravish their *Wives,* and to defloure their *Daughters.*
>
> [63-64]

It is interesting to find Mayne, a man elsewhere concerned with defining *cavalier,* writing here of the "*Equestrall Order*" and their pro-Synedrium foes. Equally striking is an outcry from Lord Theagines against those who

---

[8]The term *cuirassier,* introduced in the seventeenth century, was applied during the Civil Wars to the heavy cavalry—usually troops in three-quarter-length armor (*OED*). In this play, then, enslaved horse soldiers are pitted against "cavaliers."

tried to "reforme" the "*Temples*," "Deface" the "*Altars*," and "erect strange *Preists*, / Taken from *Awles* and *Anvills*, to deliver / False *Oracles* unto the *people*" (64). Thus the Oxonian divine-poet-scholar expresses himself on the attempted takeover of religion by an untrained citizen clergy. Perhaps most striking of all is a still later passage referring to "the *Red nos'd Burgesse*, / Who enacts *Ordinances* in *Sacke;* Or with / The Life and Death of *preaching Nol*, and *Rowland*" (68). Overt references to the nose of "Noll" Cromwell began to appear about 1647 (Johnson 21) and afterward became common in royalist writings.[9] Notwithstanding such relatively late touches, however, The Amorous Warre ends as it probably did when first conceived— with a reconciliation of lovers and a symbolic sheathing of all their swords. In Jasper Mayne's playbook world, if not in life, *amor vincit omnia*.

The Amazonian element in *The Amorous Warre* may serve as an introduction to one last military character type. An interest in Amazons is traceable from Homer and Aeschylus to Chaucer, Sidney, and Shakespeare, and on to Jonson's *Masque of Queens* (1609), in which Queen Anne danced as Queen of the Amazons, and to Davenant's *Salmacida Spolia* (1640), in which Queen Henrietta Maria gave what was to prove the most famous Amazonian performance of the prewar period. Instead of a warrior woman, however, Henrietta Maria played in this masque a discreetly armed figure of peace, a woman in harmony with her people-loving mate, King Philogenes as played by King Charles. All the more striking it is to know, therefore, that a few years later the poet-playwright Cartwright, writing "On the Queens Return from the Low Countries" (March 1643), would exclaim that even when there was no script to follow, "Courage was cast about Her like a Dresse / Of solemne Comelinesse" (11. 13-14 in *Plays and Poems*). Soon thereafter she would be seen riding with the royalist army of William Cavendish, proud of her stamina, calling herself "Generalissima" and leading thirty companies of horse and dragoons.

Civil war called forth other deeply engaged women. Setting aside the suggestion that some may have been descended from real Amazons (Sir Thomas Urquhart claimed descent from Ourqhartos, the husband of an Amazon queen [Seccombe 48]), probably the most famous of English "Amazons" besides Henrietta Maria herself were Charlotte Stanley, Countess of Derby, defender of Lathom House in Lancashire; Lady Mary Bankes of Corfe Castle in Dorset; and Blanche, Lady Arundell, defender of Wardour Castle in Wiltshire. In striking contrast are such women as Mrs. Webster and Mrs. Maine, both noted in *The Kentish Fayre* (1648) and said to

---

[9]The title page of *The Kentish Fayre*, a pamphlet published in 1648, the same year as Mayne's play, contains a poem that begins: "Good *Oliver*, lend me thy nose; / 'Tis darke, all lights are out: / For now I meane to write in prose, / But guided, by thy snout."

be "now in Armes in *Kent*," bragging that "*Wee two* [are] *like* Amazons *of old*" (A2v). The popular song "When Cannons Are Roaring" provides a more sympathetic reference to women's war efforts; here we read of "Women with stone in laps, / To the walls bringing" and "Women great timber logs, / To the walls bearing" (Winstock 42-43).

In contrast to all of these women, the courtly maidens who don the disguise of Amazons in Mayne's *Amorous Warre* do so merely to attain matrimonial goals. Despite such myths and masques as touch on martial women, the obvious truth is that soldiering was fundamentally a masculine pursuit. On the other hand, continued outcroppings of female warriors in the plays suggest that they answered certain needs. If such figures are largely decorative in Mayne's play, a more or less mechanical acquiescence to fashion, one still may be inclined to wonder what drove that fashion. Besides giving some extra visibility to feminine sentiments that for a number of years circulated at Whitehall, Amazons, one may suppose, provided an appealing sexual frisson because of the cross-dressing required of warrior women. Their enactment of unwonted empowerment probably provided a special current of excitement. Possibly the externalization of dread or desire or both could provide pleasure so long as it came in the form of play. There may even have been some tentative, court-approved gesturing in the direction of a protofeminism. Conversely, to the extent that any such gesturing was basically sympathetic, untroubled, and untroubling, it may be supposed to indicate the lack of any notable feminist strength.

Henry Burnell, whose *Landgartha* deals primarily with a strong and probably allegorical woman, specifies that his prologue is to be spoken by an Amazon wielding a battle-ax. Such a choice of speaker is validated not only by the play's martial theme but also by Landgartha's centrality throughout and by Burnell's own wish to respond aggressively to the fact that a former play of his had "met with too much spite" from its public (A4v). In William Cartwright's significantly titled *The Lady-Errant* (ca. 1628-38; published 1651), which opens with the assumption that women will "turn the / Politique dore / Upon new hindges very shortly" (1), we are specifically invited to think of Amazons as "Types" of the Lady Errant (17).[10] And Robert Howard's *The Blind Lady* (1660)—which is particularly interesting for its rather hard-boiled depiction of the fighting for a country dwelling besieged by one set of soldiers and defended by another—

---

[10]Anyone wishing to push this door further will be interested to know that the prologue of the play notes that "*each Sex keeps to it's Part*" and, even more pointedly, that "*the Female's Habit is / Her owne, and the Male's his*" (a2r). Apparently the play was performed some time in the earlier 1630s by a cast of both male and female actors—the latter being, doubtless, not professional performers but women of position. Evans discusses the matter in his edition (Cartwright, *Plays and Poems* 84–85).

presents an admirable young woman who takes up arms to rescue her suitor.[11] Outreaching all three of the foregoing dramatists, Margaret Cavendish creates for *Bell in Campo* (1653-62; published 1662) a lady named Victoria who proves to be not only a critic of male military management but also one who leads a whole female army and thereby wins power and prestige for women. In this play as elsewhere, however, Cavendish finally backs off from the feminist issues she raises.

The Female Rebellion (ca. 1657-59), possibly the work of Dr. Henry Birkhead, is an altogether different matter. Sometime Fellow of All Souls and founder of the Oxford Chair of Poetry, Birkhead gives us women who are not merely powerful but also evil. In Orithya, Queen of the Amazons, as Birkhead says in his dedication to the King, "I aimd at yᵉ character of a good Sovereign" (174v).[12] The problem is that the Queen's subjects, being more typical Amazons, are rebelling against her because she is insufficiently tough in handling her captive Scythians. Her diehard associates hold that "Rapin & slaughter are our Rights & Vertues" (177r), whereas she asserts that " 'tis rational to vanquish, / To destroy too is brutish" (175r). Orithya is also perceived as too soft in managing the collection of Trojan consorts whom the women keep as inseminators. (That the latter are as much Englishmen as Trojans is suggested by the remark of one that "my back's as unfit for fine garniture, as a Schismatic's head is for a Mitre" [178v].) At one point Orithya's erstwhile supporters appear to have succeeded in casting off both their mates and their monarch, but eventually the Queen is both restored to power and matched with her former prisoner, the Scythian King.

If the rampant misogyny in *The Female Rebellion* is to be read as anything beyond the expression of personal feeling, perhaps it may be viewed as an upside-down effort to valorize conventional marriage as a means of curbing female sexuality and violence. Then again, Amazonianism is not the only subject that the writer means to explore. In fact, it may not even be the main one. Throughout the drama he has characters convey criticism for rebellion and praise for monarchy. Thus we come to see that the rebellious women are bad not merely because they are madwomen on the loose but

---

[11]Margaret Lucas Cavendish, wife of the royalist General, wrote: "I have heard that in our late Civil Wars there were many petty skirmishes and fortifications of weak and inconsiderable houses, where some small parties would be shooting and pottering at each other; an action more proper for bandits or thieves than stout and valiant soldiers" (*Life* 144).

[12]Orithya's story had been retold recently in a chapter on her successor, Penthisilaea, in Heywood's *The Examplary Lives and Memorable Acts of Nine the Most Worthy Women of the World* (1640). Heywood writes that "Orythia . . . for her martiall discipline, and many glorious victories, and for the constant vow of Virginity, as she was much famed, so shee was much honoured" (101).

also because they represent those who have proved so mad as to become rebels in England. Subtlety is not the order of the day. Bad Antiopa says, "Since we are for the Good Cause, we should cort the people with some selfdenying Ordinance" (188v). The phrase "Good Cause," of course, is a barefaced reminder of the "Good Old Cause," which referred loosely to the complex of goals held by those who opposed King Charles; and the Self-Denying Ordinance of 3 April 1645, passed because of Parliament's frustration with inadequate army officers, had required all members of Parliament to resign from every civil office or military command to which they had been appointed since 20 November 1640—with the understanding that they could later be reappointed. Echoing all the old occupational slanders against Cromwell, we read here of "That State Hocus-pocus who dissembled Himself from a Brew=house to a Throne" (189v). Using a term that had been used to stigmatize all kinds of royalists, one of the women complains, "These sanguin Malignants are . . . intoxicated with Allegiance" (192r). We may suspect that the femaleness of the martial villains here (perhaps like the femaleness of the pamphlets' Mistress Parliament) is in part a means to convey the author's sense of outrage while dealing with something that he perceives to be repellant and contrary to nature. In other words, unlike the Amazons of Jasper Mayne, the Amazons of Birkhead (if he is, indeed, the author) are anything but decorative. The aim of the play, we read in the epilogue, is "to silence, if not reconcile," the opposition (176r).

Fashionable though they proved to be, Amazons of course offer but one way of exploring the love-war nexus. Three further plays with a significant martial and amatory component are William Chamberlaine's *Love's Victory,* Thomas Meriton's *Love and War,* and Gilbert Swinhoe's *The Unhappy Fair Irene,* all published in 1658. While Chamberlaine's *Love's Victory* places considerable emphasis on mingling love and war, it also contrasts war to wisdom. In a dedication to the teenaged Sir William Portman, Baronet, Chamberlaine notes that his work has long lain dormant, *"being then in the embryo, when with us, War first made the present Age unhappy"* (A2v). Though details of the matter are scarce, Chamberlaine in his monumental poem called *Pharonnida* (1659) tells of setting aside his pen for a sword—that is, leaving for the Second Battle of Newbury in October 1644 (II.v.513-36).[13] Having waited so long, he now writes for his audience not a prologue but an apology, *"That so in private each Spectator may / Singly receive his welcome to a Play"* (A3v). Years later the work was adapted and performed (Langbaine records its presentation after the Restoration under

---

[13]A prose abridgment of *Pharonnida,* called *Eromena; or, The Noble Stranger,* was published in 1683, four years after Chamberlaine's death. It, too, was dedicated to Portman.

the trendier title *Wits Led by the Nose* [*Account* 57]), but the version that
concerns us here was meant to be read.

Not surprisingly, *Love's Victory* begins with soldierly material: first the
tragic, then the comic. Immediately after a military funeral procession
moves over the stage, it is contrasted to the attempt of two buff-coated
cheats (buff being the tough-but-light hide coat worn in battle) to gull the
lumpish clown of the play ("cham no Zodier," he weeps, "Cha been better
bred than zo" [2]). In fact, we never leave totally behind either the military
material or the constant contrasting of tragic and comic modes.

Chamberlaine depicts here a young lord named Zannazarro who has
been dispossessed in a rebellion. Determined to claim his dead father's
rights, Zannazarro must prolong the old struggle and go against the
kindly reassurance of General Oroandes, leader of the current King's
army. When Zannazarro's sister, Eurione, meets Oroandes, it begins to
appear likely that we have at hand the "victory" credited to love in the
title. Despite the healing power of love evinced here, however, the
current King is provided with some lines that must have been both
written and read with a special alertness. His first words are the excla-
mations "How full of fatall changes are our lives! / What is't to be a
Monarch, and yet live / Trembling at every blast of passion thus!" (17).
And when Zannazarro and Eurione are brought before him as prisoners,
he speaks as he must on the subject of rebellion:

> . . . that's a sin whose black infection strikes
> Damps to the heart of Monarchie, and cannot
> Be nurst within a States ejecting womb
> Without distempering every vitall part.
>
> [19]

In fact, the young rebel and his sister are prepared for sacrifice by the
priests of Mars and Minerva. (At this point one might recall not only the
figures of Theagenes and Chariclea from Heliodoran romance but also the
playwright's own claim in his dedication: "*I sacrificed to* Minerva *in the Temple
of* Mars" [A2v].) Allegorical elements begin to grow clearer when the priest
of Minerva makes advances to Eurione, claiming to prefer her to "Our
Common-wealths Protectresse" (26), namely, Minerva herself. Then
shortly afterward, as the brother and sister, clad in crimson and white, are
led to an altar for sacrifice, a five-stanza song begins, "*See, each winde leaves
Civill Wars, / The gods approve your Sacrifice*" (32). Fortunately, some unex-
pected miracles at the ceremony induce the King to forgive his captives.
After Chamberlaine has woven in a few comic subplot elements, he lets us
see that the King, like the General, has been smitten by the rebel maiden.
When the King therefore orders the General to draw a sword against him,
that noble soldier answers thus:

> . . . your sacred person
> Is circl'd with divinity, which without reverence
> To touch is sacriledge, to look on sin
> Unlesse each glance is usher'd with a prayer,
> Kings are but living temples, wherein is
> As in the Nations center, the chief seat
> Of their protecting God, and shall I then
> Pollute my hands in bloud, whose every drop
> Would swell my Countreys tears into a floud?
>
> [64]

Later, believing that he has indeed killed the King, General Oroandes is stricken with remorse: "I cut the heartstrings of the Land" (82). The King still lives, however, suitably paired now with the Princess Heroina, and at the close of the work he proclaims (recalling and explaining the title), "Our cares are conquer'd by Victorious Love" (87).

The mix of love and war takes on a tragic guise in Meriton's *Love and War* and Swinhoe's *The Unhappy Fair Irene*. The former is an instance of well-intended amateurism, now interesting largely as a means of suggesting how a lay writer responded to the achievements of his professional predecessors. So toplofty in language as to be confusing, especially toward the beginning, the play offers a King Aberden, who despite his name is ostensibly not a Scot but a Bruzantian now invading the neighboring Numenia. Meriton is not shy about directing our thoughts. He has the Numenian General Burgargo assure us in so many words that the Numenians "stand for right" (E1v). Moreover, the invader Aberden is equipped with a suggestively but grotesquely rabid partner, Queen Adrenimia, who cries that

> . . . it's blood that I
> Crave of my King, untill the day I dye.
> If none can have from forraign Countries then,
> Constrain'd I must take then our innocent men. . . .
>
> [E3r]

Thus it is good news when "*Ensign, Drums, Flagge*" (F1v) are brought onstage and we learn that certain trenches have served the Numenians well and that their use of heavy armor (certainly on the decline in Britain in the 1650s) has worked against the Bruzantians.[14] Burnomoy, a valiant Numenian soldier, reports, "My stomack n'er did faint with killing till / This

---

[14]Spencer Compton, the second Earl of Northampton and father of one of our playwrights (James Compton, the third Earl), is credited with winning the battle at Hopton Heath on 19 March 1643. Unfortunately, though his armor protected him well during most of the battle, he lost his helmet and thus enabled one of his foes to kill him with a blow to the back of his head.

day" (F2v). Immediately, however, his admirable, serious soldierliness is contrasted to the humours of Quermero, the old-style braggart we glimpsed earlier. Aberden, unfortunately, proves triumphant. "The best politick way that must come here," he says, "Is to destroy both branch and root of them" (G1v). Such a choice of words is eye-catching. Presumably the real-life Scots would have liked nothing better. When the Numenians regroup, however, *their* king cries, "Fall on brave souls, let's ruine root and branch" (M1v). Thus what flickers as a momentary sign of concern with the London petition of December 1640 to abolish episcopal government (followed by the resultant bill proposed in 1641) proves to be merely a current, multipurpose phrase expressing totality of destruction. Not until the final act does the Numenians' King Celerinus tip the playwright's topical hand so far as to use the phrase "we *Albions*" (M4v).

Meanwhile the love interest designated by the title has been provided by young Hollarro, Prince of Bruzantia, and his lady Lerenica. The name "Hollarro" may anagrammatically suggest "royal," possibly with connotations of seeking (from Spanish *hallar*), and "Lerenica" certainly is an anagram of *eirenical*, peaceful. If indeed the play may be considered in some sense figural, we should note also that the lovers' relationship ends with the suicide of Lerenica—that is, the death of peace—and the continued wandering of Prince Hollarro. Scattered and inconclusive though the topical gestures in the play have proved to be, it closes with some words from one of the Graces, Euphrosyne ("heart-easing," Milton had called her), who clearly invites us to think of the heart-troubling wandering of England's own Prince Charles:

> The hoysting sayls of all his hope must be,
> After foul cross to have community,
> Until the spangled skies doth give such rays,
> I wish bright *Sol* may turn all nights to dayes;
> But if my wish be too severe in sight,
> I wish all native Princes had their right.
>
> [N4r]

That final line is about as direct as a line in drama can be.

The Unhappy Fair Irene, written by a young Northumbrian ("On then, auspicious Youth!" [***r]), has much the same energy and intensity as Meriton's *Love and War*, a similar naïveté, and perhaps a tad less skill in composition. Set in far-off Hadrianople and heavily populated with military personnel, Swinhoe's play depicts the capture by the Turks of a beautiful Greek maiden named Irene, whose "espoused love" is Paeologus (6). If we are prepared to consider Irene (Greek *eirene*) as another lady figuring peace, we may listen the more carefully as her captor, great Mahomet, a sort of

Turkish Mark Antony, claims his willingness to throw over all his other conquests for her.[15] That we are invited to read "Irene" thus is suggested by a Bashaw who worries that "the sweet Lullabies of an alluring Peace / Hath epileps't [Mahomet's] ... active Spirits" (17). In fact, Mahomet himself says to her, "Come, come, thou Center of my Peace" (20). By simply being herself, Irene conquers a conqueror as entirely as Cleopatra or Zenocrate ever did—and yet she keeps her "untainted fruits" at arm's length from him (21).

Not so her historical prototype, if we are to believe the story told of Mahomet II, first Emperor of the Turks, and the Grecian maid, who is indeed described by Richard Knolles as "the fair *Irene*" in his *Generall Historie of the Turkes* (350). The wicked Mahomet, Knolles relates, after conquering Constantinople in 1453, was presented with a Greek woman of surpassing beauty who became both "mistres and commander" of the great conqueror (350). Whatever source or sources the playwright may have used, the rest of his story is much as Knolles tells it.[16]

So thoroughly is Mahomet distracted from his military duties that some of his henchmen begin to reflect on killing him. Even desperate Turks, however, unlike some Englishmen, are given pause by the thought of acquiring the "unmatched stain of Kill-Kings" (Swinhoe 22). When Irene herself is, instead, attacked by Mahomet's subjects, he—true Turk that he is—cuts off her head to forestall things yet more terrible. The play then ends with the arrival of Irene's distraught fiancé, Paeologus, and with his suicide by stabbing. The best thing about this work may be that it poses some questions and then leaves the mind free to ponder them. In both this play and Meriton's, peace dies. Even more interesting here, however, one is left to ask how "Mahomet" is to be read. Something parabolic is clearly under way. On the other hand, Swinhoe was well aware that he was working within a theatrical tradition. At the end of the play he recalls Shakespeare: "This is a Spectacle of like Woe / To that of *Juliet*, and her *Romeo*" (30).

Probably we have now seen sufficient evidence to suggest that military elements are often presented so as to provoke thoughts of civil strife. Nor is it surprising that somehow or other they frequently seem to allude to strife within England. The work that may be the most extraordinary of all the war plays, however, totally eschews indirection and presents actual current events in England in dramatic form. Unfortunately this work—now at the Beinecke Library, Yale—survives only as an untitled, anonymous,

---

[15]For good measure, one might note also the figure of Eyrene in *Time's Distractions* (1643), who is supposed to wear a loose white robe and a palm and olive chaplet (46v).   [16]That other sources were available we may deduce from such a work as *The Turkish Mahomet and Hiren [Irene] the Fair Greek* (ca. 1594), a now-lost play sometimes attributed to George Peele.

fragile, and fragmentary manuscript. Though it lacks both beginning and ending, its twenty-four leaves (forty-seven pages) include twelve complete scenes and two partial ones, enough to touch on a good many subjects that claimed public attention in 1642. To suggest something of the play's contents and provide some means of referring to it, one might call it *The King and the Cause*.

The fragment opens with its two most talkative characters, a cowardly tailor named Littlewit and his ambitious wife. Mrs. Littlewit is nagging her husband to respond to the Militia Ordinance (5 March) by enlisting in Parliament's service. Such a move, she argues, will enable him to elude their creditors, enhance her status, and respond to "The necesitie of the cause" (3r). Besides,

> . . . oʳ: Preacher . . .
> Tells us that all
> That die in the Cause
> Must needs goe to heaven.
>
> [5r]

Short, prosaic lines such as these, laid out as verse, are a constant throughout the work.

The second act opens with John Pym, presented here as leader of a group that includes John Hampden, Denzil Holles, William Strode, and Thomas Harrison.[17] "Well Gent[lemen]," says Pym,

> . . . wee have prevailed[.]
> Our p[ar]tie in the house
> Have careyed itt
> And the tame Lords
> Dare not butt Assent[.]
>
> [6r]

Harrison is delighted to see how many citizens have tumbled forth to contribute to Parliament's war coffers, bringing "their plate / Their wedding rings / And their bodkins" (6v). (On 9 June Parliament had issued an ordinance designed to bring in money and plate, ostensibly for preserving

---

[17]When King Charles went to the House of Commons on 4 January 1642, it was to arrest Pym, Hampden, Holles, Strode, and Sir Arthur Haselrig. Harrison, who would later gain prominence as one of Cromwell's generals, associated himself with the King's foes from an early date, joining Essex's bodyguard in 1642. In October 1645, as the First Civil War ground to a close, he became known for an action that may be recorded here: at the taking of the great castle of Basing House, Harrison shot Captain William Robbins, a sometime comic actor who was best known for his role of Antonio in Middleton and Rowley's *The Changeling*.

the peace by defending both the King and the Parliament.[18]) Hampden reflects: "Such is the vigo[r] of y[e] cause / Itt bears doune the Lawes" (6v).

A third group of characters, the King and his supporters, is introduced next. As he will in each scene where he appears, Charles speaks thoughtfully and well:

> My Lords: and Gent[lemen]
> Yo[r]: true Loyalltie is noe smale comfort
> To o[r] afflicted Soule
> Aflicted wee saie
> To see o[r]: selfe: devided
> Against o[r]: selfe
> The head against the bodie[.]
>
> [7r]

Despite the striking metaphor, the King hopes for "a happie end," and Prince Rupert, now Lieutenant General of Horse, expresses an eagerness for the King's army and Parliament's to meet.

The following scene (II.iii) returns us to the tailor and his wife. Littlewit now appears with a great sword (which he wears on the wrong side) and in the company of some freed apprentices-turned-soldiers who welcome him as a brother. Tomorrow, we learn, all are to march.

Act II, scene iv, then takes us to their commanders, most notably Robert Devereux, third Earl of Essex—appointed to the post of Captain General of Parliament's forces on 15 August 1642. Rather than satirizing Essex in the manner of the pamphleteers, the writer allows him to speak plainly and simply: "Gent: to yo[r]: seuerall Regiments / And putt them in order" (10v).

Thus are we prepared for the battle of Edgehill (23 October). At this point in the play we have only a very succinct scene, the main event of which proves to be the leap of Philip, Lord Wharton, into a saw-pit for safety. (Colonel Wharton did, historically, give up soldiering when his regiment was routed at Edgehill.) Essex's army, confronted by the King's somewhat superior forces, was by no means overthrown during the encounter, and yet the royal camp concludes correctly here that it has been hurt. (Some accounts nowadays conclude that the battle was a draw, but the royalists probably came out better in that Essex had not blocked the King's advance toward London. At the time, both sides claimed victory.) The King—still thoughtful, still aggrieved—observes that "who soe now gaines / The loss is o[rs]" (11r). It is noteworthy that while the Earl of Lindsey

---

[18]John Taylor later wrote scornfully, "Many of your Faction (like decoy Ducks) brought in their Plate and Monies at the beginning of this Rebellion, in large proportions to the *Gull-Hall* of *London*, whereby thousands of people were gull'd" (*Generall Complaint* 6).

has appeared earlier in the play in a group scene, he is given no lines, and no mention is made of the fact that he was to have served as Charles's commander in chief at Edgehill but resigned shortly before the battle when Charles exempted Prince Rupert from his command. In fact, Lindsey was wounded and captured at Edgehill, and as his son looked on, he died there.

Meanwhile, as Pym and his companions are wondering what has transpired, a soldier runs in seeking the Committee of Safety.[19] When Harrison responds, "wee are they," the terrified soldier bids them save themselves, for "All is lost, alls lost" (11v). He goes on:

> . . . I saw a madd man
> they call Prince Rupert
> And his dogg to
> They charged cleane through us
> And I saw him sett uppon
> The waggons; and Carriages. . . .
>
> [11v-12r]

Soon, however, a messenger from Essex comes in with a corrective report that all is not lost, though the bold and daring Rupert has, indeed, "Putt all in daunger" (13v).[20] Moreover, the King is now marching toward London "On the Westerne Road" (14r). Pym sees at once the need to "fortefey the Cittie" and have the Trained Bands readied for action (14r). It is needful also to turn to the preachers to sell Parliament's cause to the people. Thus is Hugh Peters (recently returned from New England) introduced into the play. Pym assures Peters that Providence now puts into his hands the opportunity "To bee fullie revenged / Uppon these yor: tiranicall enemies" (14v), and members of the Committee of Safety charge him "To goe preach in the Cittie / To stirr them upp to show / Their zeale to the Cause" (15r).

We then return to the Littlewits, in particular to Captain Littlewit. From a gentleman's house in Northampton he has taken a pair of brass andirons and a pair of small iron dogs to hold up wood in the fireplace (18v).[21] (His wife wonders if there were no irons for sea-coal, which she

---

[19]Probably the play is more effective for retaining this group as behind-the-scenes machinators, but the historical truth is that both Holles and Hampden fought at Edgehill.   [20]After an impressive charge, Rupert apparently could not keep his men from pursuit of their foes. As Hibbert describes it, "They thundered through the village [Kineton] and way beyond it, coming upon the enemy's baggage train and thoroughly plundering it, burning wagons, killing wagoners" (80).   Rupert's famous white dog called "Boy," who seems to have accompanied his master everywhere, was described by John Cleveland as "that four-legg'd *Cavalier*" who "holds up his Malignant leg at *Pym* (*Poems*, "To P. Rupert," ll. 122-26). He met his end at Marston Moor.   [21]Hibbert writes that before Essex's soldiers "reached Northampton, they had pillaged villages and ransacked houses all along the way, several companies threatening to turn back unless they received their overdue pay" (66).

would prefer.) He also picked up some pewter spoons, a basting ladle, and four round trenchers—but retained none of them because Prince Rupert and a devil in the shape of a dog took all away. (One of the nuggets of truth here is that at various times both sides were guilty of plundering.) Littlewit therefore brings home nothing but his honor, together with the information that he has preserved it by leaping into the very saw-pit where Lord Wharton himself had leaped.

Act IV opens with London's Lord Mayor, Isaac Pennington (a wealthy fishmonger), the well-known alderman Thomas Atkins, and Hugh Peters.[22] Peters is urging that the city do more "To oppose this tiranicall king / And his prophane Court / And popishly affected gentrie" (20r). Sufficiently persuaded, the Lord Mayor agrees to send out the Trained Bands. In short, the Londoners prove to be so successful in warding off the royalist approach (13 November) that the King realizes "wee must draw back / ffrom this rebellious Cittie" (22r). Rupert now suggests that the King think of choosing winter quarters, and when the King agrees, it is George, Lord Digby, who reports that most of the officers believe Oxford would be the best choice, since it is "a place well scittuated for defense / And full of loyall hands" (22v). Historically, the royalist forces reached Oxford on 29 November.

Scene generally follows scene here in intelligent, connected ways, especially considering how many groups of characters are involved and how complex the events of the day really were. At this point we have yet to hear from Denzil Holles regarding how "They putt vs shrewdly to itt / At Brainford [i.e., Brentford, on 12 November]" (23r), where Rupert was clearing the way for Charles's advance on London. We have yet to have a final laugh at Littlewit, who fell sick and shook like a custard when the King's army came near to London, and, finally, we have yet to learn how the Lady Mayoress (Abigail Pennington) and some other citizens' wives show themselves to be zealous for the "Cawse," holding it to be a "sweete death" to be killed by Prince Rupert—provided he also ravish them. And then the play as we have it ends.

That the play originally continued beyond this point we may be sure from the catchword on the final page, but how much is lost, whether the play was ever finished, and how it might have ended are all now matters for conjecture. The upbeat tone of the work could be maintained fairly easily as far as the writer wrote. Still, just as Cowley felt compelled to give over his hopeful poem on the war when the historical reality turned bleak

---

[22]As an alderman, Pennington earlier had been the man to present the petition to abolish bishops, root and branch, and eventually he would serve as one of the King's judges—though not sign his death warrant.

for royalists, so the royalist writer of this work would have found it increasingly difficult to maintain his confident outlook and tone. Conceivably the King's safe arrival in Oxford, surrounded by loyal followers, provided an ending for the play. Perhaps, indeed, the play was written at Oxford by one who had come there with the King and thereafter had the leisure to ruminate on all that had happened thus far. Perhaps—the largest perhaps of all—such a play could have been performed for the court at Oxford. Though *The King and the Cause* poses a good many questions that cannot now be answered, we may safely observe its wide range of soldierly types, its pleasant combination of serious and comic elements, and its quite unusual and strikingly efficient encapsulation of events of the day.

Though the civil strife within England will continue to command most of our attention, we should keep in mind that both Charles and Cromwell also had their bouts with Scotland and Ireland. We have considered previously Thomas Meriton's rather lightweight depiction in *Love and War* of a King Aberden who invades the land of the Albions, and in chapter 2 we saw how Henry Burnell's more potent *Landgartha* shadows forth the strained relations between England and Ireland in about 1640. To bring the present chapter to a close, we shall take a closer look at a play that goes to the heart of the Anglo-Irish conflict.

In October 1641 some of the native Irish rose against the English and Scottish settlers who through the years had claimed their lands, and soon afterward their cause spread and strengthened itself into a national rebellion. The English Parliament, outraged, recorded that "the barbarous and bloody Rebels" slaughtered over a hundred thousand "Protestants" (Firth and Rait 1:340). Reports on the range of atrocities and numbers of slain on either side have varied greatly over the years, but there is no reason to doubt the great cost of life or the extremes of passion and suffering involved. Nor is there any doubt about the complexity of the political and religious dynamics then or later. Disastrously at odds even among themselves, the Irish were splintered into longtime Irish Roman Catholics (the so-called Old Irish), long-settled "Old English" Catholics seeking greater religious liberty, Ulster Puritans who supported the Parliament, and faithful Protestant royalists—all of whom put together armies of their own. *Cola's Furie; or, Lirenda's Miserie* is an impassioned reflection in drama of this explosive concatenation. It was written by a merchant named Henry Burkhead in 1645 (according to the title page), and in 1646 it was printed at Kilkenny, center of the Catholic Confederacy.

Burkhead's fervent topicalism begins with the obvious anagrammatic metamorphosis displayed in the name "Lirenda." (A parallel personification can be found in the picture of "Irelandes Lamentation" on a broadside from April 1647, which might just as readily have been labeled with the subtitle of the play [figure 4]). Major clues appear also in the dedication, which is addressed to Edward Somerset, Lord Herbert, heir apparent to the Marquess of Worcester. That the dedication was completed late in 1646 is suggested by the fact that Herbert succeeded as second Marquess in December 1646. In 1645 he was promised (or maybe even granted informally) the earldom of Glamorgan. It was as an earl, in any case, that he became known to both his contemporaries and historians. "The subject of this small worke," Burkhead claims, is "drawn from the historicall records of Forren countryes" (2r-v), but he nonetheless admits that the play is "fitly applyable to the distempers of this kingdome" (2v). That is, he specifically invites the reader to engage in what was known at the time as application. Still, in his dedication to Glamorgan, Burkhead continues quite directly:

> . . . forasmuch as your Honour out of the generosity of your nature, have been pleased with a glance of reall compassion to view and survey the modell of its sad afflictions, having with unspeakable toyle, charges, and dangers adventured hither (not unlike to NOAH'S Dove, with an Olive branche of Peace) to appease the raging fury of our intestine harmes; This enriching the Diademe of your renown with a particular Iewell of rare merit, are not these issues and ofsprings of a boyling & bleeding heart, boyling with impregnable love and loyaltie unto his Majestie, and bleeding for the continuall distempers of his kingdomes. [2v]

The site of the "modell" mentioned here was in fact of vital interest to the dedicatee because about the end of June 1645 he had arrived in Dublin on a mission on behalf of the King. A royalist, Catholic, and friend of the Crown, Glamorgan was supposed to assist James Butler, Earl of Ormonde, the Lord Lieutenant of Ireland, in rounding up troops to be sent as soon as possible to aid the royal cause in England. Charles had just been defeated at Naseby and needed from the Irish not only troops but as much quietude as they could muster. More privately, therefore, Glamorgan was supposed to carry on negotiations for peace in Ireland. In August when he went to Kilkenny—the place where Burkhead's play would be published— he was welcomed both as an envoy from the King and as a peace negotiator, and on 25 August 1645 he signed a treaty with the confederated Catholics. The satisfaction of certain religious demands made by the Irish, however, was conditional on reaching agreement with Ormonde on some other business, and presumably all was to remain secret until an army from Ireland could be landed in England. Unfortunately a copy of the agreement made its way to London, where it was printed by Parliament's order. On 26 December Glamorgan, returning to Dublin, was arrested and charged with treason. Back in Kilkenny, the incensed General Assembly declared that negotiations for peace would cease unless and until Glamorgan was freed— as indeed he was on 22 January 1646. Small successes in Glamorgan's story were followed by great disasters, however, and eventually—leaving historians to wonder about the actual facts of the case—the King disclaimed everything that Glamorgan had done in Ireland in the name of the Crown.[23] To carry the story no further, we may say that the dedicatee of *Cola's Furie* was a significant figure in part of the struggle that it depicts, and that at the time the play was written, the ending of the historical story had yet to be enacted.

Following some conventional verses that praise Burkhead's work in excess of its merit (*"Iohnson* for all his wit / Could never paint out times as you have hit, / The manners of our age" [3v]), the prologue designates the Irish subject matter in unequivocal terms: *"Kind Natives of this poore afflicted Ile, / To your oppressions we addresse the style / Of this our tragicke pen"* (¶4v). We then enter into a play that begins with a constable, a citizen, and a couple of soldiers bearing halberts.

At once we hear of the "Romish Recusants" who "thinke to subvert the true reformed Gospell" and threaten "This City Castle" (2), much as the royal castle in Dublin was threatened in October 1641. That the castle is secure, however, we soon learn from one of the Angolean (obviously "English") governors appointed to Lirenda, an old veteran named Berosus, based on Sir John Borlase, Master General of the Ordnance in Ireland. King Charles had made the mistake of appointing Borlase as one of two Lords Justice of Ireland—a mistake because both Borlase and his fellow justice were Puritans who proved to be Parliament men. Together they managed to drive even the most loyal Roman Catholics to rebellion. The other leading Angolean in the play (Osirus/Ormonde plays a lesser role) is Pitho, based on Charles's other justice, Sir William Parsons, a man who managed to gain considerable power, if not affection, by becoming the first master of an Irish Court of Wards. Pitho hopes that the Angoleans will be able to earn the sympathy and support of "the Palans"—a plain reference to the "Old English" who lived within the Pale, where English jurisdiction had been established—while awaiting "new supplyes from the grand Parliament" (4).

Meanwhile, Berosus suggests that the Angoleans employ "that warlike / Leader brave *Carola, Cola*" (4). This wild-eyed "Machavillian" (14) or "demi-divell" (16) is a dramatic transmutation of Sir Charles (hence Carola) Coote, a New English colonist who had been chosen to break the Wicklowmen and rapidly became known for his military atrocities. Word went out that Coote engineered the slaying in their beds of many of the King's loyal subjects, saw to it that others were hanged by martial law

[23]Coonan is especially helpful in interpreting these murky events in a chapter called "The Glamorgan Episode" (194–201; see also 206–13).

without cause, and had still others killed by means that seem almost to have been calculated to enhance reports of his madness (Gilbert 1:35, 248). His burning of Santry and Clontarf may stand as representative of the sort of "furious" violence that Burkhead wishes to decry, with "many townes and villages . . . destroyed in / dreadfull flames" (15).[24]

Following a victory by the admirable Lirendans, which draws forth a violent outburst from Cola, there is by way of contrast some singing and dancing by the Lirendans, despite their worries about "*Angolias* furie" (13). (Thus does the word *furie* link the Angoleans to their major on-the-scene agent.) As one woman is permitted to say (and the women say very little), "this cruell rage is in their owne defence, least we who have been still as slaves to them should now endeavour to regaine our owne religion, lawes, and liberty" (13). In fact, Cola himself, true to his billing in the title, is soon quoted as crying out, "kill, kill, spare neither man, woman, child / regard not age or sex" (16). Ironically and doubtless with some fidelity to human nature, the invading Angolean soldiers subsequently march in to claim that "through the power and helpe of heaven we are, / in safe possession of their strongest holts" (21). Thereafter two Lirendan gentlemen are put on a rack and stretched onstage, and a lady with burning matches between her fingers is drawn aloft.

Another change of pace is provided by one of our finest noble soldiers, admirable Abner, Lord General of Stelern (that is, Thomas Preston, General of the Leinster army). Like the Abner of scripture, Burkhead's Abner is a valiant man who calls for peace (see 1 Sam. 26.15 and 2 Sam. 2.26). Patricia Coughlan argues plausibly that the positive presentation of this figure helps to support the view that Burkhead was personally more committed to the Old English party than to the native Irish one (6, 7). In any case, Abner has a dream in which the Queen of Fates calls him a second Mars, and presently Mars himself (along with Bellona, Pallas, and Mercury) comes onstage. Thus even in the midst of a passionate and quite immediately political dramatization of the times, a masquelike interlude—with verse, song, and dance—seems to the playwright an appropriate means of communication.

Yet another change of pace is provided when next we see the furious Cola, plagued now with ghastly visions of hags and monsters. Revenge itself enters with a bloody sword and flaming torch ("true Emblems of thy furious strategemes" [47]) to lead Cola to "eternall punishment" (46)—a preview

---

[24]Harbage believes that "the name 'Cola' must derive from Collooney in Connaught where this cruel English colonist held lands" (*Cavalier Drama* 179). One might point out also that it approximates the last sounds of "Angola," with the initial *C* both substituting for a *G* and standing for the first letter of Coote's name. Then again, "Cola" is an anagram for the Spanish *loca*, which means "mad."

of his sudden death by pistol at the close of act IV, which in turn reflects Sir Charles Coote's somewhat mysterious death on 7 May 1642, about six and a half months after the rebellion began.[25] The contrasting dreams or visions that the playwright invents for Abner and Cola are reminiscent of those dream-ghosts whom Shakespeare parades before Richard III and Richmond just before the Battle of Bosworth. The allusion is reinforced when Cola is promptly shot and the Angolean General of Horse, Lysana (Philip Sidney, Lord Lisle), comes in to call for "a guide, a guide, a thousand pound for a guide." He offers even "my whole estate / to him who will be my guide" (53).

With Cola off the scene, his function is more or less taken over by one Tygranes.[26] As the play ends, however, Abner is able to credit heaven with the Lirendan success thus far. A courier comes in with news of an armistice that is to last a year and a day—a reference to the one-year peace, ending in September 1644, that Charles had wanted Ormonde to arrange with the rebels, and probably also a reference to the peace efforts of Burkhead's dedicatee. Old Abner says that "if our wrongs be not repaired thereby / we will againe, renew this Tragedie" (61). Thus the play ends equivocally, as it must, since it has been sailing so close to the shores of fact. No great length of time would pass, though, before it became clear that despite the hopes of both Abner and Burkhead, the Irish problem was to remain unsolved.

Altogether a highly charged work, *Cola's Furie* may serve here as an example of a drama that displays numerous soldiers of differing factions and classes, briefly makes the Mars-Venus connection, and concentrates on the righteous rights and damnable wrongs of opposing sides—rights and wrongs that reflect real oppositions in the political, religious, and military life of the day. If not a work for all time, *Cola's Furie* was emphatically a work for its own. Probably a large part of the interest in reading it either in its own time or ours lies in its inherent invitation to see the real behind the fictional or, better, the real *through* the fictional, as in a palimpsest. The possibility that such a play was meant to be played on a stage as well as read, despite the turbulence of the time, is hinted by the author's call for music and dancing (of limited use in a closet drama) and also by his request in the epilogue that his "Noble, worthy Audience / . . . clap hands" (62). Then again, all such touches may be metaphorical.

Looking back over the range of militarism serving as a focus or frame

---

[25]Coote's tomb in Dublin was inscribed with the words "England's honour, Scotland's wonder, Ireland's terror here lies under" (Coonan 132).   [26]Tygranes is described as "A Tyger, / truly by name and nature" (Burkhead 57). Coughlan suggests that he represents "Lord Moore of Mellifont, who was in fact spectacularly shot to pieces by Owen Roe O'Neill's gunner at the battle of Portlester (September 1643 . . .), just as Tygranes is killed by a cannon shot at long distance at the end of the play" (8).

in midcentury drama, we might say that whereas the anonymous *King and the Cause* conveys a sense of trying to catch history-making military events on the fly, Mayne's *Amorous Warre* and Chamberlaine's *Love's Victory* use the subject of war to raise questions; that Burnell's *Landgartha* and Swinhoe's *Unhappy Fair Irene* use it to carry conflicts to a bloody extreme; Howard's *Blind Lady*, to help bring a sense of vividness to a small-scale conflict; Burnell, Birkhead, and Swinhoe to make thematic points in *Landgartha*, *Female Rebellion*, and *Irene;* and Burkhead in *Cola's Furie* to do all of the above. Time and again, military strife continued to provide, as it always had, a natural source, pattern, and parallel for dramatic strife. The figure of the soldier could be readily dramatized as an entity divided against itself (Venus and Mars, love and honor, passion and precept) or as a force against which other forces might be deployed. Noble soldiers could be contrasted with common ones, and plain soldiers with fancy courtiers, and by exploiting the interest that had grown up in Amazons, male soldiers might be played off against female ones. Banking on a tradition that had long kept alive the repute of the martial arts in literature (despite Falstaff's shrewd catechizing back in the 1590s) and equipped with a spectrum of possibilities that tested literary fantasy against freshly experienced historical fact, writer after writer brought military concerns into the body of midcentury dramatic writings—and did so in ways that reflect both the untidiness of experience and the usefulness of traditional literary characters and genres.

Moreover, as men of the day shaped their art in accordance with their views of life, so with remarkable frequency they viewed their lives in artistic terms. Sir William Waller, for one, wanted Lord Hopton of Stratton to know that his affection remained unaltered despite their marching now to different military drums. "Wee are both upon the stage," wrote Waller, "and must act those parts that are assigned us in this Tragedy" (Haythornthwaite 64).

Strangely, perhaps, it is in a brief entertainment written by James Shirley for a small group of boys that we find—along with a touch of comedy and some music by Edward Coleman—what may be the most moving of all responses in our dramatic literature to the wars that had ensnared the English people:

> The Garlands wither on your brow,
>   Then boast no more your mighty deeds,
> Upon Deaths purple Altar now,
>   See where the Victor-victim bleeds,
>   Your heads must come,
>   To the cold Tomb,
> Onely the actions of the just
> Smell sweet, and blossom in their dust.

[Contention 118]

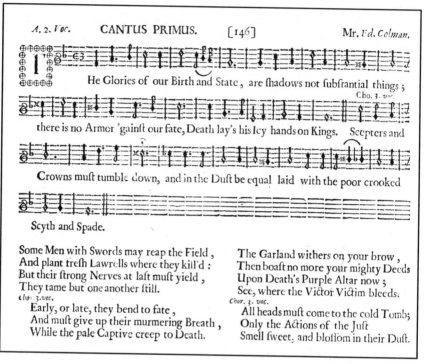

A. 2. Voc.   CANTUS PRIMUS.   [146]   Mr. *Ed. Colman.*

He Glories of our Birth and State, are shadows not subftantial things;

Cho. 3. *voc.*

there is no Armor 'gainft our fate, Death lay's his Icy hands on Kings.   Scepters and

Crowns muft tumble down, and in the Duft be equal laid with the poor crooked

Scyth and Spade.

Some Men with Swords may reap the Field ,
And plant frefh Lawrells where they kill'd :
But their ftrong Nerves at laft muft yield ,
They tame but one another ftill.
Cho. 3. voc.
　Early, or late, they bend to fate ,
　And muft give up their murmering Breath ,
　While the pale Captive creep to Death.

The Garland withers on your brow ,
Then boaft no more your mighty Deeds
Upon Death's Purple Altar now ;
See, where the Victor Victim bleeds.
Chor. 3. voc.
　All heads muft come to the cold Tomb;
　Only the Actions of the Juft
　Smell fweet, and bloffom in their Duft.

Figure 8. "The Glories of Our Birth and State," a song by Shirley and Coleman from *The Contention of Ajax and Ulysses* (1658), as it appeared in Hilton's *Catch That Catch Can* (1667). (By permission of the Folger Shakespeare Library.)

In its original context this well-known song functions as a comment on the body of fallen Ajax in ancient Troy (see figure 8). Equally to the point, it bespeaks an awareness of the bloody outcome of military strife in any New Troy.

6

THE FAMOUS TRAGEDY OF CHARLES I

> . . . Where e're you goe
> All else are but Spectators, not the Show.
> > —*Ovatio Carolina* (1641)

> . . . the Stage growes great with horror. . . .
> > —*The Famous Tragedie of King Charles I* (1649)

> The Sun shined that morning very clear without intermission, until
> the King came to the Fatal Block and lay down, and then at that
> moment a Dark thick Cloud covered the face of the Sun. . . .
> > —*The Bloody Court* (1649)

> Winter doth untwist, and doth unweave the Suns bright Golden
> Beams, and wind them on dark bottoms.
> > —Margaret Cavendish, *The Comicall Hash* (ca. 1653-62)

> Our SUN went down at *Noon.*
> > —*An Elegie upon the Death of Our Dread Soveraigne* (1649)

THE MOST DRAMATIC historical action in seventeenth-century England—
and probably the most significant and symbolic as well—was the public
decapitation of King Charles I. The grip of this event on the English
imagination is everywhere to be found, and frequently in images pertaining
to the stage. Hence we have a sort of impassioned, multiple mirroring of
history tinged with art's words and concepts, and of art—or dramatic
writing, at any rate—that displays some of the varying distances possible
between historical fact and itself.

We need make no heavy weather about the figural linkage of kings
and courts with plays and theaters. Sir Thomas More had long since writ-
ten that kings played "king's games, as it were stage plays, and for the more
part played upon scaffolds" (Greenblatt 13); Elizabeth that "we Princes . .
. are set on stages, in the sight and view of all the world" (Neale 2:119); and
James that "It is a true olde saying, That a King is as one set on a stage"
(*Basilikon* 3.103). In fact, a king in a play-text could acknowledge the
conceit: says Genzerick in Henry Shirley's *The Martyr'd Souldier,* "A Play, a
Comicall Stage our Palace was" (B2r). No wonder, then, that William
Cartwright could write of the royals who attended his *Royall Slave* that "*the
Spectators only made the Play*" (g2v). No wonder, either, that afte the trauma
of that final winter day on that newly erected platform outside Whitehall,

many were moved to record their feelings in images drawn from tragedy. Samuel Butler wrote bitterly: "We perceive at last, why Plays went down; to wit, that Murthers might be acted in earnest. Stages must submit to Scaffolds, and personated Tragedies to real Ones" (21). Long having served as a means to reaffirm the power of sovereignty, the public show of execution had now been used in England to enact the death of it.

A number of years previously Parliament had discussed "the Disposall of the Person of the King" (see Ker), but not until 6 January 1649 did it pass an ordinance establishing the court that would try him. Charles is said to have laughed when the solicitor for the Commonwealth called him a tyrant, traitor, and murderer (the Queen had been declared a traitor in 1643), denying to the end the authority of the court to try him. He thought it a strange world, indeed, in which royalists were accused of being rebels and he himself was charged with inciting these "revolters" to further his own evil designs (Gardiner, *Constitutional Documents* 373). On 27 January, nonetheless, he was condemned to death, and on 30 January he was beheaded.

Though some Englishmen saw that bloody event as a necessary path to reform, the words that come down to us are mainly those of anguished outrage, among them innumerable references to tragedy.[1] The stage was set, so to speak, by the commissioners themselves, who ordered that "the Scaffold, upon which the King is to be executed, be covered with black" (*Catalogue of the Names* 7). Thus could an author write of "those pure-crimson streamlings which were shed / On th'*Sable Stage*, where He resign'd His Head" (*Princely Pellican* 39). Not only was the scaffold proper and its rails "hung round with black" (*Charles I . . . His Speech* 4), but the flooring itself was covered with black baize (*England's Black Tribunall* 65).

Students of the theater have not made much of the fact, but the stages of the public playhouses in the preceding period were similarly draped when a tragedy was performed.[2] As far back as Sir Philip Sidney's day, a casual but telling metaphor appeared in *The Countesse of Pembrokes Arcadia*: "darke cloudes . . . had blacked ouer all the face of heauen; preparing (as it were) a mournfull stage for a Tragedie to be played on" (2.125). At about the same time, Shakespeare referred in *The Rape of Lucrece* to a "Black stage for tragedies and murthers fell" (l. 766). The induction to *A Warning for Fair Women* (1599) draws attention to a similar scene: "The stage is hung with

---

[1]Maguire observes that "Royalists and non-Royalists enlisted the terminology, structures, and expectations of the theatrical tradition to politicize (and work through) the act of regicide—theatrical in itself—by transposing the events of 1649 into the more familiar concepts of drama" ("Theatrical Mask/Masque" 6).   [2]As Neill writes, "The effect of this proleptic announcement of catastrophe was to supply a continuous visual commentary on the action, often creating (particularly in scenes of romantic intrigue and so-called 'comic relief') a sharply ironic effect" (163).

Figure 9. Charles and his masked executioners on the scaffold outside the Banqueting House, Whitehall. One executioner asked Charles to put his hair under his nightcap and then—along with Dr. Juxon (right)—helped him do it. (By permission of the Folger Shakespeare Library.)

blacke: and I perceiue / The Auditors preparde for Tragedie" (A3r). Nor was the tradition forgotten at midcentury. In Manuche's *Just General* (1652) the stage direction "Enter upon a black Stage" leads into an execution scene (63). Still more explicitly, one of John Fountain's directions in *The Rewards of Vertue* (1661) reads, *"There appears a Scaffold covered with black, with many Spectators about it"* (76). Unfortunately one cannot say just where the hangings and curtains were hung or draped in the playhouses, but hung or draped they certainly were. More problematic—though common sense might suggest the answer is "no"—is the question of whether or not the floor itself of the stage was ever covered or partly covered in black like the floor of the scaffold at Whitehall. What we may be sure of, in any case, is that black cloth had long been displayed in English playhouses to convey a solemn sense of tragedy, and that, long-lasting as the custom was, bringing forth funeral "blacks" must have proved an effective way of preparing an audience for a tragic end.

However alert the commissioners ordering Charles's execution may have been to relevant parallels, their efforts certainly were designed to make an impact on an audience. Foucault has argued that in ceremonies of public execution "the main character was the people" (57). Probably it suffices to say merely that the audience is potent mainly as witness and validator, similar to its function at a wedding. The important point here, however, is that the commissioners who gave orders and the people who attended the final scene played by Charles I—complete with headsmen whom Whitelocke describes as "Two men in disguises and vizors" (370)— clearly were aware of a spectacle-spectator dynamic (see figure 9). James Howell would soon report how "That black tragedy which was lately acted heer . . . hath fill'd most hearts among *us* with consternation and horror" (*Epistolae Ho-Elianae* 3.40). Of course, the whole affair was a matter of tragedy and history combined. In fact, history plays, too, generally ended with major scenes involving impressive ceremonies and eye-fixing tableaux.

Given what we know now, one well might wonder whether the commissioners would have staged the scene quite as they did had they been able to foresee what use the royalists would make of it. Reasons relating to crowd control may help explain why they chose as a site the space just outside the Banqueting House at Whitehall. Also, making Charles step out onto a platform immediately in front of a building associated with his masquing days, with all that that implied, must surely have played a part in their motivation. This is a point that comes into slightly better focus if we turn to a book of fiction well known to Charles—and to his father before him (see Randall, "Some New Perspectives" 189). One of the "tragical histories" in John Reynolds's *Triumphs of Gods Revenge* (1621 et seq.) tells how Idiaques, a bona fide evildoer, is "brought to the place of execution, which for the greater example and terrour to others, and of ignominy to himselfe, was before his owne house, wherein hee had acted and perpetrated all his enormous crimes. Where the scaffold is no sooner erected, but there flock an infinite number of people from all parts of the City, to be spectators of this last scene of his Tragedy" (259).

What the commissioners did not foresee clearly enough is that Charles, whatever he had been in life, would play his final scene with a dignity sufficient to guarantee the idealization of his memory. Nor did they fully fathom the idea that one of the scriptural passages appointed for the day of Charles's execution was that of Christ's Passion, wherein it is written that "*they* . . . *crucified their King*" (Warwick 345). "This *Scene* was like the *Passion-Tragedie*," one writer exclaims. "His *Saviour's Person* none could Act but He" (*England's Black Tribunall* 77). Another claims that "never was there any who expressed so great conformity with our Saviour in his sufferings, as he did" (*Life and Death of King Charles* 3). Another simply states, "*Our KING is* Crucifi'd" (*Mercurius Pragmaticus, Communicating Intelligence*, title page). And the chopping block on which the King placed his neck was cut into pieces that were then sold as relics (Bates 1:157). The underlying gist of all this should have been foreseeable. Charles himself, who for some time had understood what he was about in the matter, had informed the Prince of Wales quite specifically, "I may (without vanity) turn the reproach of my sufferings . . . into the honour of a kind of martyr-dom" (*Letters* 265-66). Though it is impossible to say how long such an idea had been in the King's mind, Archbishop Laud had stated as early as May 1640 that "no man in England [was] more ready to be a martyr for our religion than his Majesty" (*Calendar . . . 1640* 234). In fact, when one of our playwrights, James Compton, third Earl of Northampton, set down his own personal record of the events, he called it *The Martird Monarch.*[3]

One need be no Mr. Dick, obsessed with the subject of King Charles's head, to be struck by the amount of writing on the monarch's death. Then again, Charles's "true tragedy" began long before January 1649. Edward Hyde believed that both King and kingdom were lost in 1645 at Naseby (4:46). For our present purposes we shall move back a couple of years earlier still in order to consider first a play from January 1643, a play that, quite amazingly, warned Charles of what the future might hold. Three years after he had danced in *Salmacida Spolia*, and about four months after the theaters were closed, the Commons committee on printing took the ex-traordinary measure of presenting the King with a playbook. It bore the no-holds-barred title *Tyrannicall-Government Anatomized; or, A Discourse Concerning Evil-Councellors*. From the title alone one could hardly guess that the play concerned John the Baptist and Herod. Originally it had been written in Latin by George Buchanan, a brilliant Calvinistic Scot who once had served as tutor to Charles's father. In its earliest days in the 1540s, when Buchanan was teaching at the Collège de Guyenne in Bordeaux, it was called *Baptistes sive Calumnia*, and under this title it was first printed in London in 1577. Buchanan had spent many years in France, where he became a significant figure in French drama. Indeed, nowadays he is considered as a forerunner of Corneille and Racine.

Buchanan's *Baptistes* is a strong, spare play that from the time it first appeared invited glossing. With a prefatory hint from Buchanan himself that his version of the story was intended to suggest new applications, scholars have associated his Herod Antipas with Francis I, James V of Scotland, and Henry VIII (in his dealings with Thomas More or perhaps John Fisher). According to the later assertion of Buchanan himself, the play was written to comment on the confrontation of Henry VIII and More. In

---

[3]Despite the frequency of the Christ/Charles comparison, one should not infer that such comparing was unique to the period. As Zwicker points out, the "king as *typus christi* is prominent in medieval political theology" (116).

a trial before the Lisbon Inquisition, Buchanan testified under oath that "so far as the likeness of the material would permit, I represented the death and accusation of Thomas More and set forth before the eyes an image of the tyranny of that time."[4] In other words, we have here a rare and valuable statement by a playwright on the specific subject of paralleling in one of his plays. Furthermore, whatever references he had in mind either when he wrote it or when he testified about it, Buchanan sent down to posterity a play about kingship, religion gone bad, and martyrdom for true religion. Hence its reappearance a century after he wrote it is unsurprising.

The anonymous English version of 1643, written as blank verse but printed as prose, is probably not the work of Milton—though Milton's authorship has been argued and Milton certainly did commend the use of drama for some kinds of state purposes. Be this as it may, the play is a good deal better and more subtle than its tendentious title suggests. Surely no mice-eyed decipherers (as Nashe once wrote) are required to recognize that in 1643 the subject of *Tyrannicall-Government Anatomized* was not merely scriptural. The irony is that this play about an ill-advised king who orders the beheading of an outspoken good man would be followed six Januaries later by the beheading of the same (presumably ill-advised) king who was its current addressee. In a curious additional irony, then, Samuel Butler could write of the Commons that "these *Herods* can behead without the allurements of a Dance" (22).

Tyrannicall-Government Anatomized opens with a chorus and two Pharisees, Malchus and Gamaliel. "O This old wretched Age," laments Malchus, "That we should behold our Temples lewdly, cursedly defil'd, our holy things prophan'd, our Country slav'd" (B2r). There has arisen in the desert a religious leader who "deceives, with shew of sanctity severe, the simple people . . . ; And now unto himselfe he hath reduced an Army of the vulgar following him" (B2v). Gamaliel's is a voice of moderation, but Malchus proceeds with a zeal that in 1643 could have called Laud to mind. According to Malchus, the Baptist is one who "our Laws contemnes, new Sects doth teach, besides new Ritts [i.e., rites], reviles our Magistrates, and our high Priests with calumny pursues" (B3r). When Malchus goes off to seek action from King Herod, Gamaliel gives a contrasting, insider's view of the priesthood. He knows that priests "deceive with shew of sanctitie, the common sort" (B4r), that they know well how to cut down their enemies, and that if the King fails to satisfy Malchus, "another dart more cruell hee'l invent, hee'l cry the sworne Bands that attend the King do secretly con-

---

[4]This translation is provided in Berkowitz's fine edition of the play (Buchanan, *Critical Edition* 114).

spire, some wicked plot preparing." Then the chorus laments, "O what a night of darkenesse doth possesse the minds of mortalls!" (B4v).

The lines of Queen Herodias to Herod may be read as a reasonable gloss on what some thought about Henrietta Maria. A couple of years later one writer went so far as to say "that the Kings Counsels are wholly managed by the Queen; though she be of the weaker sexe, borne an Alien, bred up in a contrary Religion, yet nothing great or small is transacted without her privity & consent" (*Kings Cabinet Opened* 43). In the play, Queen Herodias warns her husband of "that vulgar Preacher," asks, "If private Conventicles you permit, how can you sleep secure?" and argues that if a choice must be made it is better to destroy one's enemy. She goes so far as to say, "but if you had the spirit of a King—" (2d B1r-v). What has not been apparent from the play's subtitle, *A Discourse Concerning Evil-Councellors*, therefore, becomes evident now: the Queen herself is an evil counselor. In Charles's case, of course, the Queen was but one of several major counselors. The plural of the term is therefore insisted on in, for example, *King Charles His Defence* (1642), which holds that "our gracious Soveraigne Lord King *Charles* hath been, and still is seduced by evill Counsellours" (2). Considering the sponsors of the play in 1643, we should note particularly a parliamentary order of 9 June 1642 that speaks of the King as "seduced by wicked Counsel" and asserts that "wicked and malignant Counsellors . . . seek to engage the King in . . . a Civil War, and destroy the Privileges and Being of Parliaments" (Firth and Rait 1:6-7).[5]

When at last John appears in the play, Herod upbraids him for reviling the old ways, deceiving the vulgar, spreading "the deadly venime of a new sect," and promising new kingdoms (2d B2r). With almost startling relevance to 1643, Herod then muses to himself about his own course of action: "All things to me are lawfull without Law" (2d B3r). And John, shortly thereafter, having talked of kingship with the King, talks of priestcraft with Malchus. Using imagery that was traditional long before "Lycidas," the translator has John say, "You are the Wolves your selves that flee [i.e., flay] your flocke, cloth'd with their Wooll"; "your selves you feed, but not your flock" (2d B4r).[6]

Only as we draw near the end of the play can we see that except for

---

[5]Peter Donald points out that bad counseling was "in general terms a line of criticism quite common in the Europe of the day" (1). More specifically, in a chapter entitled "An Uncounselled King," he writes that "it cannot be doubted that Charles I was intentionally a counselled king, and that his subjects likewise expected this" (320). He continues, saying that "criticism levelled at counsellors was ambiguous. It could be attacking the individuals in question, for personal or political reasons . . . but it could also be a message that the king was to desist from 'ill-advised' paths" (321).   [6]Traditionally, of course, this imagery had political as well as religious uses. Ezekiel warned that tyrant princes are as wolves (22.27).

John the only speakers to the King—and hence the evil counselors of the subtitle—are the powerful priest, the willful Queen, and, finally, her daughter. Rebecca Bushnell believes that Buchanan's play portrays the Queen's tyranny as much as the King's (108). One may say also that the Queen's daughter, Salome, seems to function as a sort of extension of her mother. Both in a sense rule the ruler.[7] Once the girl has requested John's head, in fact, it is she who argues that a king can make just what is unjust. Now Herod quite reasonably begins to see how he might be called a tyrant. He protests that fear is not the best preserver of kingdoms, and his final words to her, far from those of a wild-eyed tyrant, are those of a man warning a girl of her guilt and begging that an execution be averted.

A simply designed play (Milton's *Samson Agonistes* is comparable in its classical handling of a biblical story), *Tyrannicall-Government* moves plainly and intelligently to its inevitable end. In quality of both language and thought it far exceeds most polemical publications of the day. John the Baptist contemplates death and eternal life thus:[8]

> If *Caucasus* rough-growne with hoary frost,
> The Ayre with Tempests and the Sea with stormes,
> And the whole Region with excessive heate,
> Should all resist me, thither I would goe;
> To see so many Leaders, Prophets, Kings,
> And pious Iudges, shall I not make way,
> Though with a thousand deaths I be oppos'd?
> My spirit therefore from this body freed,
> (This carnall prison) thither longs to flye,
> Even whither all the world betimes or late
> Shall be dispatch'd; For long life I conceive,
> Is nothing but a gentle Servitude
> In a hard painfull prison; O sweet death,
> That art of heavy Toyles the sole Release,
> The Haven where all grief and trouble cease,
> Yet unto few men profitable known:
> Receive this shipwrackt body in thy bosome,
> And bring it where eternall peace abides,
> Whither no impious violence, deceit,
> Or calumny shall follow it.
>
> [C3v]

---

[7]Though one cannot say what specific examples he had in mind at the time he wrote, Osborne offers the assertion that *"the greatest are not Free, but led in triumph by the Affections of others, through the mediation of their own, by which means Women come to Govern, and Children to dispose of Common-wealths"* (*Miscellany* 257).   [8]The lineation here shows how the translator's words appear when set as verse. The original, like the rest of the play, is printed as prose.

A tissue of commonplaces, to be sure, such a passage nonetheless has a simplicity, clarity, and strength that may for the moment seem even more important than the boldly political purpose to which we know it has been put.

Who might "John" have been in 1643? John Pym is a possibility. Pym was a potent leader who had supported the Petition of Right (1628), moved Laud's impeachment (1640), figured importantly in creating the Grand Remonstrance (1641), been targeted by Charles as one of the five members of Parliament to be arrested (1642), and functioned as a leader of the so-called war party. In such a capacity we have seen him portrayed in *The King and the Cause*. Still, all in all, it seems best to relate the Baptist in Buchanan's *Tyrannicall-Government* not to any specific Englishman, martyr or otherwise, but to a bold and virtuous reformist spirit in whatever breasts it might have been stirring. Whatever specific targets the sponsors of the book had in mind, however, we have here the exploration of many pressing issues of the day. Almost equal in interest to the subject matter of *Tyrannicall-Government*, moreover, is that the Commons itself deemed the resuscitation, translation, and publication of a potent old play to be an appropriate and effective way of aerating serious contemporary issues for English readers, including the King.

In the spring of 1649 Charles himself would appear as a martyr in the misleadingly but calculatingly titled play *The Famous Tragedie of King Charles I*. In curious accord with the old custom of not bringing a living king to the stage, *The Famous Tragedie* provides no entrance for its tragic hero until the end—when the chorus draws aside a "travers" and reveals not only the dead body of the King but also those of Hamilton, Holland, and Capel, all three of whom were beheaded on 9 March 1649. Nor is this closing mortuary tableau strictly a collection of saintly remains. The closing chorus assures us that James, first Duke of Hamilton, "was the sole Causer of the strife / . . . Betwixt the King and Parliament" (42) and that Henry, Lord Rich, first Earl of Holland (who knew well "how to Drab" [43]), was brought to the block by his folly, not his faith. Then in contrast, and strangest of all if we have taken up the piece expecting Charles to command stage center, some of the last moments of the play are devoted to praise of Arthur, Lord Capel, Baron of Hadham, as "The glory of his Nation" (43). Capel had, indeed, been a committed royalist. He had attended Prince Charles to Bristol (1645) and escorted the Queen to Paris (1646). He had aided the King in his escape from Hampton Court (1647), and most recently he had helped to defend Colchester (1648). By this time he in effect commanded the royal army. Considering that the most "famous" tragedy of the day was that of the King, however, Capel's prominence here, apparently meant to be broadly supportive of the royal cause, is rather strangely deflective. *The Famous Tragedie* does, indeed, have things to say about the King (he is in prison offstage during most of the play), but to a large extent it is a passionate patchwork that gathers up a variety of events and names in the news in order to pass vindictive or vindicating judgment in one of the few ways that remained open to a royalist. To give the title page its due, it goes on to advert not only to the scattered range of characters to follow but also to the author's scorekeeping approach. Here is a work "IN WHICH IS INCLUDED, The several Combinations and machinations that brought that incomparable PRINCE to the Block, the overtures hapning at the famous Seige of *Colchester*, the Tragicall fals of Sir *Charls Lucas* and Sir *George Lisle*, the just reward of the Leveller *Rainsborough, Hamilton* and *Bailies* Trecheries, In delivering the late *Scottish* Army into the hands of *Cromwell*, and the designe the Rebels have, to destroy the ROYAL POSTERITY."

In its dedication to Charles's eldest son, then nineteen, *The Famous Tragedie* is given a definitively aristocratic frame: the "Loyall Gentry" are dying of grief or imprisonment, while the "*Plebeians,* who procure our ills / Feed high, sleep soft, have Kingdomes at their cals" (A2v). The prologue is addressed to the gentry and suggests that only such "refined Soules" as themselves can appreciate the great playwrights of England's recent past, whereas the plebeians would "raze, our Theaters to the ground" (A3r).

The first act of *The Famous Tragedie* opens with Oliver Cromwell asking his righthand preacher, Hugh Peters ("My fine *facetious Devill*" [1]), to prepare a formal speech against the power of kings. Peters—a highly visible Independent who in 1642 became army chaplain and eventually ascended so high that he moved into Laud's quarters at Whitehall—is rather unconvincingly allowed some jesting at his patron's expense. Cromwell's nose, he says, is "like a bright Beacon, sparkling still (the *Aetna,* that doth fame our English world)" (2). And as usual in political satire of the day, Cromwell's reassurance for Peters is cast in terms that throw more light on the writer's views than on Cromwell's: "Thou art that Load-stone, which shall draw my sense to any part of policy i'the Machiavilian world" (4). Even now he plans a trip northward to subdue the Scots.

The second act opens with Thomas Fairfax (that "bloudy *Marius*" [10][9]), Henry Ireton, and Thomas Rainsborow in arms at the siege of Colchester (June-August 1648), with the ill-fated Sir Charles Lucas, Sir George Lisle, Lord Capel, and Lord Goring upon the walls. For a while "the *Roundheads* are beaten off" (12) and there appear to be grounds for the defenders to hope, partly because the Prince of Wales is now in the Downs with most of the royal navy. In fact, "swarthy *Tom*" Fairfax is said to have

---

[9]Marius (157–86 B.C.), seven times Consul of Rome, ended his career in a bloodbath: as he passed through the streets, his guards had orders to kill everyone he did not salute.

flown off "with his timerous Troops" (15). Thus the act draws to an equivocal if not upbeat close, complete with a Herrick-like *carpe diem* song: "*Drinke then (Boyes) and down all sorrow, / Who knows if we shall drink to morrow?*" (17).

In the third act, after a scene with Cromwell gloating and planning, we return to Colchester, which has finally surrendered after all (28 August 1648). Now Lucas and Lisle are ordered to be shot—with the weight and execution of that decision falling on Rainsborow, not Fairfax.[10] Lucas, a noble blunt soldier and a brother of one of our playwrights, Margaret Lucas Cavendish, is depicted dying with classical allusions upon his lips. His friend Lisle, presumably with other and earlier English drama in mind, exclaims, "There crack'd the cords of life, Oh noble *Lucas!*" (29). Then in his own death speech Lisle acknowledges that "the Gods created Man but for their sport" (30).[11]

In act IV Cromwell, having returned from chasing the Scots (at Preston, in August 1648), turns next to wooing the wife of John Lambert—who is himself down in Lancashire disbanding troops of horse (see figure 11). The little that is known about the real Frances Lambert refutes all those who attempted to satirize her (Dawson 278). Wives of prominent men, however, were frequently brought into the more venomous writings of the day. Probably the main goal was to smear the reputations of their husbands, with the implicit understanding that unbridled will—expressed both sexually and otherwise—was traditionally associated with bad governors (Bushnell 51). In other words, the denigration of the women associated with such men was probably little more than a fringe benefit.

In order to divert *The Famous Tragedie*'s somewhat skittish Mrs.

---

[10]Henry King, in his impassioned "Elegy on Sir Charles Lucas and Sir George Lisle," writes of the scorn that Lucas had expressed for Rainsborow when royalist forces capitulated to him at the siege of Berkeley Castle (September 1645). He then remarks somewhat cautiously: "Some from this hot contest the world persuade / His [Rainsborow's] sleeping vengeance on that ground was laid: / If so, for ever blurr'd with Envy's brand, / His honour gain'd by sea, was lost at land" (ll. 243–46). On 29 October, assuming Rainsborow to be guilty, a group of cavaliers surprised and murdered him. Hyde's view of the deaths of Lucas and Lisle is very different. Hyde writes that "the manner of taking the lives of these worthy men was generally imputed to Ireton, who swayed the general, and was upon all occasions of an unmerciful and bloody nature" (4:389). Sir James Turner would concur: "Sir Charles Lucas and Sir George Lile were cruellie dealt with, having bot tuo houres given them to prepare for death; and after that short time, by the instigation of wicked Ireton, Cromwells sonne in law, mercileslie shot dead" (*Memoirs* 70). Two valuable tracts on the subject are *The Loyal Sacrifice* (1648)—which claims Ireton importuned Fairfax for the dispatch of both captives—and *An Elegy on the Murder Committed at Colchester upon Sir C. Lucas and Sir G. Lisle* (1648). [11]A drawing showing the terrain and accompanied by a description of events of the time was published in 1648 as *The Siege of Colchester* (see figure 10). The Lucas family had been seated near St. John's Abbey since the reign of Edward VI.

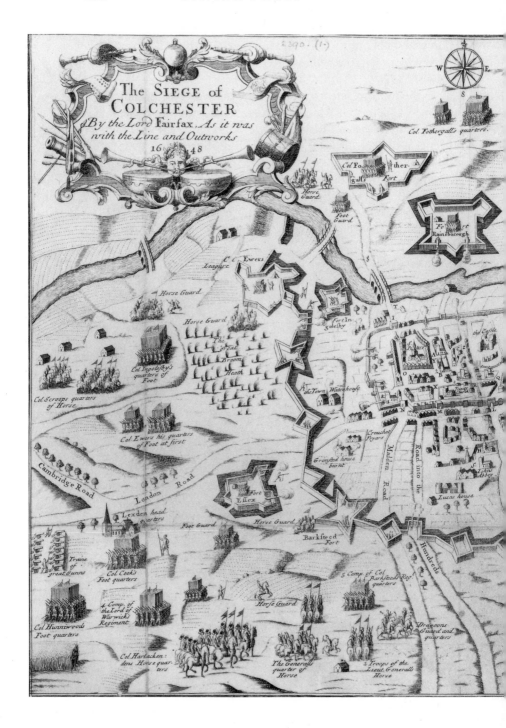

The SIEGE of COLCHESTER By the Lord Fairfax, As it was with the Line and Outworks 1648

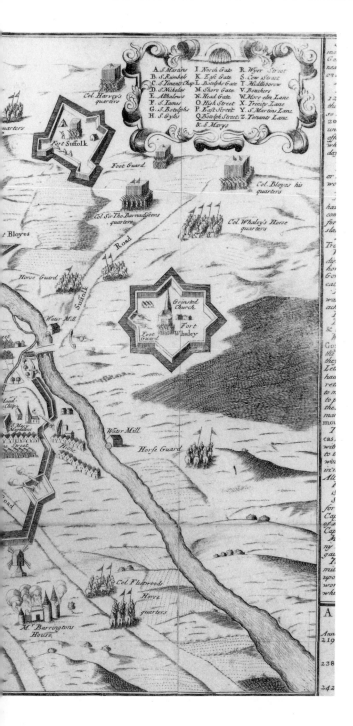

Figure 10. The Siege of Colchester (1648). The Lucas home and St. John's Abbey were directly south of the town wall, and "Fort Rainsborough" directly north across the river. (By permission of the British Library.)

Figure 11. Oliver Cromwell and
Frances Lambert as depicted
on a satiric Restoration play-
ing card. (By permission of
the Special Collections Li-
brary, Duke University.)

Lambert, its crafty Cromwell calls for a masque. Again and again one
realizes that when students of the masque put together their histories of
the form, they would do well to scrutinize the assumptions underlying such
out-of-the-mainstream works as this one, in which Cromwell summons
"six prime Westminsterian Senators" (35)—habited as Ambition, Treason,
Lust, Revenge, Perjury, and Sacriledge—with whom Cromwell and Mrs.
Lambert proceed to dance. Inverted like so many other things in this
topsy-turvy time, what once would have been an antimasque is now the
masque proper. Following its performance and before act IV ends, we are
taken elsewhere to witness the death of a now-conscience-stricken Rains-
borow at the hands of Blackburne, an avenging royalist soldier. Presumably
being justly punished, Rainsborow cries out, "Thou King of flames, let me
in Sulphure swim / Neare to that Caudron, holds my Patron, *Pim*" (39).

Act V calls again for Cromwell and Mrs. Lambert, this time following
some skirmishes in bed. Then quite suddenly we find that the King is dead
and his offspring outlawed (historically, 13 February 1649), and the whole
work comes to a close with the chorus speaking about that tableau of four
corpses.

Whatever life *The Famous Tragedie* can claim derives from its author's
impassioned response to real men and events in the years 1648 and 1649.
The King whom it honors is but recently dead, his heir presumptive figures
in both the text and the dedication, and an assortment of other characters,

good and bad, have lines with speech-tags that are the names of real people. Like life, moreover, the work is diffuse. Short on selectivity and restraint, as well as on many kinds of artfulness (despite using a number of theatrical conventions, such as the inset masque and tableau), *The Famous Tragedie of King Charles I* finally proves neither dull nor weak. To say also that it is similar in many ways to the dialogue pamphlets of the day only underscores the plasticity of genre at a time when content exerted stronger obligations than form.

Whereas *The Famous Tragedie* ends with Charles's death, *Cromwell's Conspiracy* (1660), according to its title page, begins there. The claim is inaccurate, however, for the play, strangely enough, opens with the same Cromwell-Peters scene that opens *The Famous Tragedie*. Eleven years later the first words are again Cromwell's "My fine facetious Devil," and in Peters's first speech Cromwell's nose is still "the *Aetna* that doth fame our *English* World" (B1r). Apparently the original author has returned to his material, rearranged some of it, and supplemented it extensively—there are many more characters now—so as to bring the work up to date as of the summer of 1660.

Announcing himself only as "a Person of Quality," the writer provides a prologue in which Cromwell, "A man of *mean extraction*," has outsoared Catiline and Caesar himself. After devoting act I to the seriocomic machinations of Cromwell and Peters, he re-presents in act II the Cromwell–Mrs. Lambert affair, complete with the Westminster masquers. Not until act II, scene iv, do we come upon the stage direction "*Enter* K. Charles *as on the Scaffold, Dr. Juxon, &c. with men in Vizards*" (B4r). "Is this," Charles asks, "The effect of all their Fastings and long prayers / Their Solemn League and Covenant . . . ?" (B4v). He gives his "George" to Bishop William Juxon for Prince Charles, forgives his executioner and his enemies, and bids "Adieu dear friends, adieu to all the World."[12] Then comes the fateful stage direction "*Executioner cuts off his Head*" (B4v).

Immediately, and not without effect, Cromwell is again shown disporting with Mrs. Lambert. When Ireton, Cromwell's well-trusted son-in-law, sends word that the King is dead and "we are now modellizing the Commonwealth," Cromwell exults, "Then now I am above the reach of Fate" (C2v). After bidding Mrs. Lambert adieu, he falls asleep, and in a

---

[12]Many would have known the gesture of passing along the George to be heavily weighted with significance. Sharpe discusses the "enormous importance" that the King placed on the Order of the Garter and cites Herbert's information that every morning without fail Charles put on his George, a jewel that depicted St. George on horseback encountering the dragon. Enhancing its meaning further, the King's George bore on its reverse side a picture of Henrietta Maria (*Personal Rule* 219).

song we hear the voice that he hears in his dream: *"This is the state of Kingly glory / Kings they are but transitory"* (C3r).

In succeeding scenes it becomes clear that the rising Cromwell has resolved upon the death of Sir Henry Slingsby (a Yorkshire gentleman who is said to have conspired on behalf of young Charles Stuart) and Cromwell's supposedly chiefest foe, the eminent royalist divine John Hewet (who reportedly tells people that Cromwell is tyrannous). A scene in which Cromwell's daughter Elizabeth (or "Bettie") Claypole pleads for Hewet (he had officiated at her wedding) ends with Cromwell proclaiming both Slingsby and Hewet as his sacrifices and Elizabeth herself exclaiming, "No longer Father, Monster now farewell, / Blood-thirsty Tyrants have their place in Hell" (D2v).

We then move into Hewet's trial (1 June 1658), at which one of the regicides, John Lisle, presides. During his trial, Hewet, like Charles before him, questions the authority of the court.[13] After a brief moment in court for Slingsby, too (historically it came first, on 25 May 1658), both men are sentenced to die. The fact that both are supporting players in the larger royal tragedy—like George Lisle and Charles Lucas in *The Famous Tragedie*—is made clearer still as Slingsby prepares himself for the block. In terms that echo the historical words and action of the King, Slingsby pardons his executioner, then bids him "use me kindly, / And when I stretch my hands out—Then—" (E2r). Hewet was beheaded on 2 June 1658, and Slingsby six days later. History tells us further that the mourning rings given to Hewet's friends were inscribed "Herodes necuit Johannem" (*DNB* 9:758).

The final act of the play is retributive. Cromwell, sick upon his bed and raving, sees the King's body and severed head and then the ghosts of Hewet and Slingsby. "Now Daughter *Claypool*," he says, "I begin to feel / Thy Curses light too heavy upon me" (E3v). With his last breath he announces his departure for hell. As a matter of fact, the death of Elizabeth, Cromwell's second and favorite daughter, on 6 August 1658 not only came a few weeks before Cromwell's own death on 3 September but also probably hastened it. In any case, the people in the play appear to be dubious when Richard Cromwell is proclaimed Lord Protector ("Hum, hum, hum," they say [E4r]). When General Monk (that is, General George Monck) appears, however, they shout, *"a King, a Monk, a Free Parliament; a King"* (F2r), thus clearing the way for Monk to speak the final lines: "Go home, Ring Bells, and make good lusty fires; / A King you crave, you shall have your desires" (F2r).

Written mainly in verse, more and less fluent by fits and starts, this "TRAGY-COMEDY, Relating to our latter Times," gains much of its force

---

[13]A version of this scene is presented in *Beheaded Dr. John Hewytt's Ghost Pleading* (1659).

from its focus—which is clearer than that of its predecessor, *The Famous Tragedie*. Uniting the varied segments of action and the characters who phase in and out of view is the author's powerful animus against Cromwell. Symbols of virtue (the King's virtue being replicated here by Hewet and Slingsby) are of course essential to the author's purpose, but the sure aim of his scorn provides the play's chief strength. Whether or not it was the original author himself who went back to borrow from his own *Famous Tragedie*, in this cannibalizing sequel we have not only an updated and still-fervent editorial on the news, and a blood-cousin to the pamphlets, but also a more unified work.

Any grouping of these dramatic writings is bound to be arbitrary (*Cromwell's Conspiracy*, for instance, would fit comfortably in a chapter on tyrants), but placing Robert Knightley's translation called *Alfrede; or, Right Reinthron'd* in the present chapter should help to show how much it probably gained in its own day by being read with Charles's story in mind.

A manuscript play bearing the date 1659 and now held by the Bodleian Library, *Alfrede* is the product of a scholarly gentleman's spare time. More precisely, as Lois Potter has shown recently (*Secret Rites* 106), it is a translation of William Drury's Latin play entitled *Aluredus sive Alfredus* (1619). Drury began his studies in London, pursued them in France at St. Omers (one of the best-known of Continental schools for English Catholic youths), and then proceeded to the English College at Rome. After receiving minor orders (1606) and being ordained (1610), he returned as a missionary to the English (1612), whereupon he was arrested and put in prison. In June 1618, when King James freed a number of recusant prisoners as a goodwill gesture toward the then-departing Spanish ambassador, the famed Conde de Gondomar, Drury was among the lucky ones to depart from England under Gondomar's wing. Subsequently placed, with Gondomar's aid, at the English Seminary at Douai, Drury there began to teach rhetoric and poetry and to write plays. In fact, he made something of a name for himself as a writer. Drury probably expressed genuine gratitude, therefore, when in 1620 he dedicated his *Aluredus sive Alfredus* to Gondomar.[14]

Drury's midcentury translator signed himself only as R.K. Recently identified by Albert Tricomi as Robert Knightley,[15] he was bred of a prominent Worcestershire family, studied at Douai, and presumably produced his *Alfrede* for the private reading of his half-sister Mary, Lady Blount (wife of Sir George Blount). We are very much concerned here with families

---

[14]Later editions of Drury's play appeared in 1620, 1628, and 1641. The information here on Drury comes largely from Freeman's essay in *Recusant History*. [15]Tricomi has both deciphered the initials and provided a valuable introduction in his 1993 edition of Knightley's *Alfrede*.

evincing strong Catholic allegiance—and sometimes suffering for the fact. The Blount family estates had been confiscated by Cromwell in November 1652. Despite its royalist orientation, however, and despite its extensive concern with things military, the play that Knightley translated deals with faraway times (ninth-century Britain) in a manner that somehow both conveys and yet diffuses its political implications. The temper of the piece may be suggested best by the detail that the first speaker is St. Cuthbert (d. 687), who has returned to earth to serve as Alfrede's "Patrone." In the prologue he explains the situation:

> Piety's no Captiue to the Orbs aboue
> But oft vnto afflicted lands doth moue.
> This makes me to forsake the glorious skyes
> To visit my poore Cuntry wch exhausted lyes
> A prey to Mars, where the inhuman Dane
> with sacrilegîous Crueltys doth staine
> Our holy Alters; but Im come to bring
> Help to th' afflicted, mindfull of that King
> Of my deare England, who zealously intent
> so oft his prayres vnto my eares hath sent.
>
>   [3v]

St. Cuthbert's rather startling involvement here may be explained to some degree when we read elsewhere about his "Miracle of bodily Immortality after Death," and especially that he was supposed to be so dear to "King *Alfred,* that he made him share with him in his Soveraigntie, and honoured his name upon his own Coyne"—traditions that were reported by Robert Hegg in *The Legend of Saint Cuthbert* (10, 16).

   Alfred the Great was quite possibly England's noblest king and probably came close to deserving even such extravagant praise as he has sometimes received. According to Knightley's play, which in the main is faithful to Drury's original, Alfrede is a flawed but nevertheless essentially good and pious English monarch who is so beset by bloodthirsty foes that he can "scarse refuge find at home" (4r). Why, one might ask, would Knightley turn his mind to such a king in 1659? Or better, perhaps, how could Knightley have done so without thinking of the comparable woes of England's latest— possibly England's last—king? Or of the protracted homelessness of Charles's successor? Alfrede's mother bemoans the lot of her son:

> Alas! death would be lesse painfull to me
> then a life, wch hath seene my son disthron'd,
> and fertile Britain groaning vnder
> th' oppression of a cruel tyrant.
>
>   [7r]

If topical shadowing seems almost inescapable here, moreover, we probably should pay particular attention to St. Cuthbert's words in the prologue: "Thus heau'n to th' Britans punishment doth send, / Till taught by evells they their liues amend" (4r). The tragic elements in this "Tragi=comedie" have been brought on not only by bad men, we find, but also and specifically by a ruler who has not been good enough.

As the play begins, it is nighttime in a woods—symbolic enough, one might think—and Athelrede, Alfrede's General in charge of foot, wonders, "Whither tends th' expiring fate of England?" (4r). He is joined by Humfrey, General of the Horse, and then by the King himself and the two princes. Alfrede sends one boy to fetch the Queen and the other the Queen Mother, his goal being to reunite his family on the Isle of Athelnea and there to rebuild his forces. (Though we should not expect too many parallels when an old story is concerned, Athelney is a real place in Somersetshire, long famous as Alfred's retreat in 878-79, and a reader may be struck by the fact that in desperate times King Charles, too, sought refuge on an island.) The noble soldier Humfrey volunteers, "Lets be associates in y^r flight, as well as griefe" (5r). The King, however, asks Humfrey to levy forces to "embody / Our dissipated troopes" (5v). And he himself, putting his royal robes in a pit and donning the habit of a common soldier, gives us a *Lear*-like glimpse of the failings Cuthbert has referred to: the "poysenous glory" of royal robes can lead to tyranny (6r).

We then meet the villains. Gothurnus, King of the Danes (otherwise known as Guthrum, and a very tough warrior), gloats, "England I rise from thy ashes / As a Phoenix from his reviving fflame" (6v). In Gothurnus, as we learn from Alfrede's mother in the next scene, we have "th' oppression of a cruel tyrant" (7r) such as may follow upon the disenthronement of a legitimate if overly willful king.

A variety of episodes follow: Humfrey finds it expedient to put on the clothes of a Danish soldier—and then, in a noble gesture, gives them to his friend Athelrede. Of course Humfrey himself is then caught by the Danes. He faces death, however, in a specifically Christian way that is less reminiscent of tragicomedies of the day than of such real deaths as we have seen sketched for Lucas and Lisle, Hewet and Slingsby. In fact, when it looks as if he will not survive, Humfrey hopes to "receive a double triumph / flowing from Martyrdome and inocence" (14r).

Alfrede himself is no less aware of martyrdom, and he turns to such mingled thoughts on crowns as had been shared by most English readers at the time of Charles's death:

> Who makes a Crowne, beset with thornes of Cares,
> His Idoll and fancies the splendor of his scepter
> the lookinglasse of all glory; nor feares
> the proteous vicissitude of ffortune:

Let Alfrede, once King of England, be his
Obiect. . . .

[17v]

Having reached the island of Athelnea, Alfrede is visited by St. Cuthbert disguised as a beggar ("he / that trusts in it, needs not despeare of help" [20r]) and falls in with some comical, good-hearted country folk—a swine-herd, his wife, and his son—who welcome Alfrede to "liue here in safety / till better times apeare" (24v). As Robert Powell reports in his 1634 biography of Alfred, "some would have that [Alfred entered] in the service of *Denwulphus* a *Hogheard*" (14).

A good many events ensue: Prince Edward loses his sister for a while and has a scene with a helpful echo; a braggart Danish soldier puts on Alfrede's robes ("Now I am a King ev'ry inch of me" [36v]); and the holy hermit Neothus (St. Neot was sometimes reputed to be a brother of Alfred) counsels Alfrede well: "God Created you a king, and you make / y'selfe a Tyrant; wretched, Nobody" (38v). Alfrede sees and acknowledges his wrong, asks that his people be spared punishment, and resigns the title of king. By such deeds he begins to mitigate God's anger, and it is clear to Cuthbert that "I may exhibite him / a Patern to the world, and a pious / example to future generations" (39v).

But hold—we are still only at act IV, scene iii, with sixteen more scenes left in this act, plus all of act V! Both Drury and Knightley were clearly committed to this major project and probably would have agreed with Humfrey that "Idlenesse is oft bought at a deare rate" (51r). Moreover, the villainous Danes remain to be conquered—in this case by Alfrede's newly assembled troops, as well as by his wit, faith, and piety. At the end Alfrede not only converts the Danish leader and many of his followers (as did the real Alfred) but also makes the now-reformed Gothurnus ruler over the eastern part of Britain. Then Cuthbert reappears to deliver an epilogue (truncated from Drury's original) that is helpful if we wish to ponder the work's unusual emphasis on Christian faith:

> O wretched England! would thou still did'st know
> that ancient happy state; thou wouldst not now
> As from ye world thou seperated art,
> So from ye world's true faith be kept apart:
> Thou wouldst not then be cald an Isle ingrate
> ffrom Heau'n rebelliously degenerate;
> Nor wouldst thou consecrated Temples spoile,
> Nor them with sacrilegious Hands defyle;
> Nor let vnparent-like thy Children bee
> Shipwrackt vpon ye Rockes of Herisy.

[61v]

It had been some time since the banishing of the Book of Common Prayer (4 January 1645) and the abolishing of bishops (9 October 1646), to say nothing of the smashing of stained glass in the churches and the stabling of horses in St. Paul's, but the wording here points to a yearning for a dispensation older than the Anglican one.[16]

Whatever purposes Drury may have had in mind when crafting the original form of this play, Knightley's *Alfrede* appears to be a history-and-legend-based wish-fulfillment that enabled him to write not only about what might have been in King Alfred's time but also about the nightmares of his own time, about what sort of new era might have ensued if only Charles had acknowledged his own overreaching, and—last but not least—about what hopes one might dare hold regarding a second Charles. The subtitle, after all, is *Right Reinthron'd*.

To simplify, unfortunately, is generally to falsify. In the present case, it is best to acknowledge that in contrast to what one might anticipate, a fair fuss is made over Alfrede's tendency to "tyranny." Why should this be? Answers enough are embedded in some of the older sources (which include William of Malmesbury and Holinshed), but if we turn back to the title page of Powell's panegyric of Alfred—written between the times of Drury and Knightley—we may find the probable answer stated most clearly. The full title of Powell's book is *The Life of Alfred; or, Alured: The First Institutor of Subordinate Government in This Kingdom*. Alfred was not only a great king, in other words, but one who became great in part because he had developed the grace and humility to share his power. Furthermore, writing well before the downward curve of Charles's real-life story had been completed, Powell in 1634 was for some reason moved to publish along with his biography a separate essay that parallels Alfred and Charles. Both were younger sons of a king, travelers abroad, men noted for piety, and models of meekness, temperance, abstinence, "conjugall castimony, and all other vertues." Powell's parallels are many, but the sum of them all is that this "paire of Peerlesse Princes" is capable of standing as "presidents of imitation to all Princes and people" (151-52). This itself makes a fair precedent for St. Cuthbert's and Knightley's claim to exhibit Alfrede as "a Paterne to the world, and a pious example to future generations" (39v). Drury could not have put it better. Knightley knew how Charles would end, as Powell did not, but the depiction by each man of the earlier king suggests what might be thought about the later one.

In the chapters that follow, many of the plays brought forward will spark further thoughts of King Charles. He and Cromwell were, after all, the most

---

[16]Samuel Sheppard, one of our playwrights, wrote an epigram titled "On the Pollution of a Well Known Temple," in which he alludes to the horses in St. Paul's (*Epigrams* 148).

conspicuous men of their time. Even the small cluster of works gathered here, however, should suffice to show that Charles's story could be approached in vastly different ways. We have seen how some writers seem to set down their own reactions as spontaneously and passionately as a man might curse, and how some choose to express themselves indirectly through the dramatic forms of other men in other times. Whether it was set in ancient Galilee or early Britain, or on the black-draped scaffold outside the windows of the Banqueting House at Whitehall, the tragedy of Charles I was the most compelling story of the age.

7

ANGLO-TYRANNUS

So, so, the deed is done,
    the Royall head is severd
As I meant, when I first begunne
    and strongly have indeavord.
Now Charles the I. is tumbled down,
    the second, I not feare:
I grasp the Septer, weare the Crown,
    nor for Jehovah care.
—*A Coffin for King Charles* (1649)

Tarquin taught his son Lucius to secure his tyranny by striking off
the heads of those poppies in his garden which grew higher than
their fellows. . . .
—Marchamont Nedham,
The Case of the Commonwealth of England (1650)

. . . a tyrant, like a king upon the stage, is but the ghost or mask of
a king, and not a true king.
—John Milton, *First Defence* (1651)

We have had the private Stage for some years clouded and under a
tyrannical command. . . .
—Francis Kirkman, "The Stationer to the Judicious Reader" (1661)

THE CHANGEOVER FROM Charles Stuart to Oliver Cromwell was for some
in England a change from enskied saint to bloody, bawdy villain. Among
the fifty-nine men who signed the order for the King's execution, the most
substantial group comprised New Model Army officers, chief among them
Cromwell. Hence the image of Cromwell as a crown-seeking Machiavel
was easy for many royalists to see. In earlier years, ironically, if J.S. Morrill
is correct, what may have been Cromwell's underlying irresolution could
be perceived by some as "serpentine self-advancement" (27). In 1649,
however, Cromwell was resolute enough. The 1648 labels of "*King* Crom-
well" (see Mercurius Urbanicus) and "King *Noll*" (*Rombus* 4) would retain
their relevance up until the time of Cromwell's death, when his funeral
effigy was dressed in a purple robe and outfitted with an orb, scepter, and
many-colored crown.[1] Like but also vastly unlike Charles in his later years,

---

[1]Johnson's fifth chapter ("I Saw Him Dead") provides many relevant details.

Cromwell was a king and no king. And like Charles, he was perceived by his enemies as a tyrant.

The subject of tyranny was of compelling interest at midcentury, but in approaching the fact as it is manifested in drama we should bear in mind that it had seldom been out of view since Tudor times. From even earlier days when Herod raged in the streets of medieval cycle drama, through the times of *Cambyses, Tamburlaine, Richard III*, and *Sejanus,* English audiences had witnessed repeated reincarnations of tyrants onstage. In John Fletcher they had a veritable specialist in tyrannical rulers. *Cupid's Revenge, The Maid's Tragedy, Valentinian, Rollo, Wife for a Month*, and *Custom of the Country* (to cite only a few) enabled Fletcher and his collaborators to display so many tyrants that, as Robert Y. Turner puts it, "he must have found that it touched a responsive chord in his audience" (123). In fact, Turner goes on to observe, "It is hardly stretching plausibility to see in the number of tyrants that begin to appear on stage about the time of *Cupid's Revenge* (ca. 1607-12) a reflection of discouragement consequent upon a growing acquaintance with James's behavior and an exploitation of anxieties about being trapped under a bad monarch" (134). The point is important here because of the continuing significance of Fletcher at midcentury. In fact, the prominence of stage tyrants throughout Charles's reign is notable. One thinks of such Caroline plays as *The Roman Actor* (1626), *Albovine* (1628), *Believe as You List* (1631), and *Aglaura* (1637).

In considering the concern with tyrants in midcentury drama, we should mark also a parallel concern in other kinds of writing. In 1639, for example, someone thought it pertinent to resurrect Bishop John Ponet's *Short Treatise of Politike Power* (1556), which back in the days of Mary Tudor had questioned whether monarchs have absolute power, how far subjects are bound to obey them, and whether it is lawful to kill a tyrant. The year that civil war broke out in England brought forth the anonymous *Briefe Discourse upon Tyrants and Tyranny* ("I . . . comprehend under this title such as encroach upon the just liberties of their subjects" [7]). Another revival was *Vindiciae contra Tyrannos: A Defence of Liberty against Tyrants*, perhaps originally by the French Huguenot Hubert Languet. In 1648 its translator assumed that this 1569 book might help to mold current thinking. "*The whole body of the people,*" we read here, "*is above the King*" (51). Notable for its historical paralleling and its dedication to John Bradshaw (who presided over and pronounced sentence at Charles's trial) is George Walker's *Anglo-Tyrannus; or, The Idea of a Norman Monarch Represented in the Paralell Reignes of Henrie the Third and Charles Kings of England* (1650). It is among such works that we encounter also the now-much-better-known *Tenure of Kings and Magistrates* (1649), a prose polemic by the greatest poet of the age, followed by *Joannis Miltoni pro Populo Anglicano Defensio contra Claudii Anonymi, alias Salmasii Defensionem Regiam* (1651).

Naturally such publications were balanced by royalist ones. An old manuscript by Sir George Buc (d. 1623) was brought forth as *The History of the Life and Reigne of Richard the Third* (1646 and 1647), and naturally it had something to say about "that Vocable, or term *Tyrannus*": we find, basically, that it means "evil King" (1647:133). Well-apprised of the technique of smearing with "Paralogisms" (135)—Buc had served for a while as Master of the Revels—he himself chose to use them in a clean contrary way. He concluded that "where tyrannical acts be objected against [Richard] . . . , they must be conceived done by other men, or by their practice, or else before he was King; and what he did then, was not, nor could be properly called Tyranny" (134). Usually, of course, Richard III served as a negative model. One of the dialogue pamphlets of 1660 had a tyrannical "Cromwell" speak of "my Parrallel *Richard* the third" (*Conference Held* 2), and one of our playwrights, Abraham Cowley, wrote that "we have had . . . such a Protector as was his Predecessor *Richard* the Third to the King his Nephew; for he presently slew the Common-wealth . . . and set up himself in the place of it" (*Discourse* 346). The subtitle of *The English Tyrants* (1649) clarifies its stance at the outset: *A Brief Historie of the Lives and Actions of the High and Mighty States, the Lords of Westminster.* Yet another royalist voice is to be heard in Robert Filmer's *Necessity of the Absolute Power of All Kings* (1648), which asserts, "The subject is never to be suffered to attempt any thing against the Prince, how naughty and cruel soever he be" (11). For many in England, even those not fond of Charles, the instinctive default position was support of the monarchy, but Filmer articulates support of an ominous kind.

Whatever regime was in power—Tudor, Stuart, Commonwealth, or Protectorate—tyranny was a specter that could always be conjured up by someone. What distinguishes the midcentury years, in addition to the urgency with which the subject was pursued, is that *tyranny* became a floating term no longer reserved for monarchs. Once the republic was established and the throne and the traditional estates dismantled, the much-contested boundaries between the rights of the ruler and the rights of the ruled became still more uncertain. The terms *tyrant* and *tyranny* became weapons available to anyone who chose to brandish them. From the time that Charles began to rule without Parliament (1629) until the time that his dealings with the Scots brought on the Second Civil War (1648), he was perceived by some of his subjects to have "over-king'd it" (Hunton 4). In Milton's phrase, he was guilty of "Monarchical Tyranny" (*Eikonoklastes* 388). It is all the more ironic, therefore, that when he tried to arrest and impeach those five members of the Commons in January 1642, he accused them as traitors attempting "to place in subjects an arbitrary and tyrannical power" (Gardiner, *Constitutional Documents* 236). Insofar as arbitrary power is concerned, the sentence that Charles received from the High Court of Justice, Westminster, on 27 January 1649 makes clear that some of his subjects thought he himself was the culprit: "For . . . treasons and crimes this Court doth adjudge, that . . . the said Charles Stuart, as a tyrant, traitor, murderer, and public enemy to the good people of this nation, shall be put to death by the severing of his head from his body" (Gardiner 380). In the view of three Cambridge students moved to write on the subject, Charles had "degenerated from a king unto a Tyrant" (Fidoe, Jeanes, and Shaw 15). On the other hand, Charles had not been gone long when it became treasonous for anyone to write or say that the Commonwealth was either usurped or tyrannical (act of 17 July 1649: Gardiner 389). The obvious impetus for such an act was that some men were saying exactly that.

For many who were hurt or threatened by Cromwell and his associates, or simply appalled by what they represented, they appeared vulnerable on grounds of class.[2] John Hewson, whom Cromwell made Governor of Dublin, was said to have cobbled old shoes in a stall; John Barkstead, to have sold needles, bodkins, and thimbles; and Edward Whalley, to have been a broken clothier (Bates 2:222). Hence a typical diatribe such as *Cromwell's Bloody Slaughter-House* (1660) by John Gauden may be found claiming that "most" of the opposition were of "base extraction, of meane education, [and] strangers to all good Literature, Honour, or Civility" (9). However we are meant to flesh out that striking word *Literature*, Gauden points to significant and felt differences of background, training, inclination, and habit. Henry Leslie wrote on the matter with more indirection but equal scorn: "As it is in the parable of *Jotham* [Judges 9.7-15], they have advanced the Bramble above the Cedar of *Lebanus*, while they set the People, even the basest of the People on the Bench" (10). Though we are not dealing here with a simple or clearly defined class struggle in either the politics or the plays of the period, we may rest assured that a class element is involved in both.

No matter how far back the heralds might trace his ancestry, Cromwell himself could be perceived as an upstart. "Sing old *Noll* the Brewer," goes a song of 1649 (Rollins, *Cavalier and Puritan Ballads* 289). Though Marvell might write of "Angelique *Cromwell*" ("The First Anniversary," l. 126) and Milton might hold him to be "instructed by all-but-divine inspiration"

---

[2]This would include Cromwell's wife, Elizabeth, who played a background role but was nevertheless "*commonly called Protectresse Joan and vulgarly known of later years by no other Christian name, even in the greatest Heighth of her Husbands power, and that chiefly out of Derision and contemptuous indignation*" (*Court & Kitchin* B3r).

(*Second Defence* 674), this East Anglian country squire who shortly after Charles's death rose to be Lord Lieutenant of Ireland (1649), then commander of Parliament's forces (1650), and then Lord Protector of the Commonwealth (1653) was bound to be accused by many as a base and ruthless usurper. Even before he came fully to power he was attacked as a "Turkish" tyrant in *The Tyranny of Tyrannies* (1648). Later we find both him and the Commonwealth attacked by the indefatigable William Prynne (who certainly had suffered under Charles) in *A New Discovery of Free-State Tyranny* (1655). Later still, Edward Sexby (using the *nom de plume* William Allen) put forth in *Killing Noe Murder* (1657) a good many reasons why someone should actually kill Cromwell: "let every man to whom God hath given the Spirit of Wisdome and Courage, be perswaded . . . to endeavour by all Rational means to free the World of this Pest" (B4r). And to some, after his death, he became *Oliver Cromwell, the Late Great Tirant* (1660.)

We have already seen some low-comedy jibes at Cromwell's appearance (that ruby nose) and sexual life (those bouts with Mrs. Lambert), jabs that trivialize him like a comic devil. (Figure 12 provides us with as straightforward a visual image as we are likely to find.) More deadly are the allusions to his heavy-handed dealing with some of the royalists (Henry Slingsby, John Hewet) and perhaps especially his massacre of the Irish at Drogheda in 1649. In any case, when Richard Perrinchief wrote of Cromwell in 1661, he had no hesitation about paralleling the English Protector's methods with those of the Syracusan tyrant Agathocles: "that which was obtruded upon ['the Multitude'] . . . as the Oracles of Heaven, or as the generous dictates of Free Souls, were but the acustomed cheats of former Tyrants, newly proposed to an Ignorant and Credulous Generation" (*Syracusan Tyrant* A6r).

Considering the allegations of tyranny that filled the air during this period, it is little wonder that the dramatists remained interested in tyrants. We have already seen evidence of this in such works as Burnell's *Landgartha*, Denham's *The Sophy*, and Buchanan's *Tyrannicall-Government Anatomized*. In the present chapter we will examine four more plays—all tragedies and all concerned with the artistic and dialectic technique of paralogism. Despite far-flung settings in Constantinople, Naples, Persia, and Gaul, each has been fashioned to take a stance or make a statement concerning its own time and place.

The first of these is Thomas Fuller's *Andronicus*, published in 1661 but evidently written in the early 1640s. Because most students of the period know Fuller as the prolific Anglican divine who produced *The Historie of the Holy Warre* (1639), *The Holy State and the Profane State* (1642), *The Church-History of Britain* (1655), and *The History of the Worthies of England* (1662),

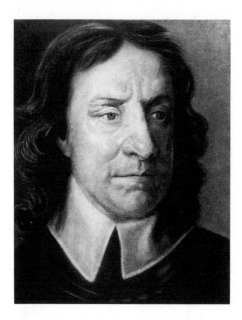

Figure 12. Oliver Cromwell
(1599-1658), after a painting
by Samuel Cooper. (By permis-
sion of the British Museum.)

his dramatic writing may come as a surprise. Despite the fact that several
other Oxford clergymen of the period set their pens to writing drama—
among them William Cartwright, William Strode, and Jasper Mayne—one's
surprise concerning Fuller may be the greater because of his expressed
doubts about drama: "*Some sports being granted to be lawfull, more propend to
be ill then well used.* Such I count Stage-playes" (*Holy State* 184). Fuller writes,
in fact, that "wanton speeches on stages are the devils ordinance to beget
badnesse; but I question whether the pious speeches spoken there be Gods
ordinance to increase goodnesse, as wanting both his institution and bene-
diction" (186). Providing us with evidence of some non-Puritan doubts
about the stage, these passages were published only about a year before
Fuller put his hand to the play *Andronicus.*

In previous writings Fuller had considered both tyranny and Androni-
cus. Chapter 17 of *The Profane State* is a prose characterization of a tyrant:
"A Tyrant is one whose list is his law, making his subjects his slaves. Yet it
is but a tottering Kingdome which is founded on trembling people, which
fear and hate their Sovereigne" (425). Chapter 18 is called "The Life of
Andronicus." In fact, the latter is Fuller's follow-up of a one-paragraph
handling of the Byzantine emperor Andronicus (A.D.1118-85; r. 1183-85) in
The Holy Warre (bk. 3, chap. 3), and a springboard for his separately pub-
lished prose tract called *Andronicus; or, The Unfortunate Politician* (1646)—for
which he borrowed chiefly from Nicetas Choniates.

There is, therefore, less self-contradiction than one might otherwise assume in his creation of *Andronicus: A Tragedy, Impieties Long Successe, or Heavens Late Revenge* (1661). Various other writers during the century (Samuel Bernard, John Wilson, and William Banister) took it upon themselves to write plays about the same twelfth-century tyrant (see Klause), but Fuller's interest in the subject seems exceptional. Although his dramatic treatment was published anonymously, the play's preface clearly points back to 1643 and Fuller's authorship (see James Wood). *"Let me Acquaint thee,"* it begins, *"with a Pedigree and Progresse . . . of this Tragedy. It was born some eighteen years since in* Oxford."[3] At that time and place, Fuller had retired for a while to Lincoln College, having previously served as curate of St. Mary Savoy in London, preached for peace between King and Parliament, and lost both his post and his worldly goods. Soon after the Battle of Edgehill (October 1642) the King established winter quarters at Oxford, and subsequently Fuller preached before him there. As it happens, Fuller's conscience inclined him to preach against the ungodly ways of the cavaliers—a fact that is interesting to juxtapose with Charles's final sovereign proclamation, issued from Oxford on 3 February 1646 and intended to prevent "Disorders in the Night-time, in the Garrison of Oxford" (Hughes and Larkin 1071-72). Fuller himself, one might suggest, was not unlike the hermit Monodius in his play, a thoughtful man who leaves his cell to go to court. Says Monodius, "there my Councel I'le dispence" (9). Consequently, when someone in the play presumes to make use of a lute, Monodius smashes it, maintaining that even "Musick's now but discord, and doth Jarre / With these sad times" (11). Whatever Fuller's reason—probably because he was not himself wholly in tune with either royalists or roundheads—it appears that during his stay in Oxford he lived a rather isolated life which proved conducive to writing. ("Monodius," one might note, is a suggestive name for a somewhat solitary man to choose for his major mouthpiece in a work.) Later on, the only manuscript of the play was lost, possibly when someone took it to York, but then at long last it turned up in London. Looking backward in 1661 (figure 13 depicts him at this later time), Fuller observed that in the early 1640s the work had been a *"Diversion . . . from the troubles of the Times,"* and yet he also admits to the play's seriousness of purpose. Pointing us with an inaccurately recollected quotation from George Herbert, Fuller says, "A verse may finde him out, who shuns a Sermon."[4]

Andronicus proves to be a fascinating document—and also, not surprisingly, an unplayable play. The latter results partly from the author's deployment of a rather large cast of characters. We may conclude that Fuller, who

---

[3]Quoted from the verso of a leaf following the title page of Fuller's *Andronicus: A Tragedy.*
[4]Ibid.

Figure 13. Thomas Fuller, D.D., author of *Andronicus: A Tragedy* (1643). This picture and the publication of the play both date from 1661, the year of Fuller's death. (By permission of the British Museum.)

was writing when the theaters were closed and who did not much approve of the public stage anyway, intended his drama, like his prose, for the closet. But why would he assay any play at all? For those willing to accept Fuller's own words, it was because once "*the Historian, . . . gave the* Groundwork," the poet was freer to provide the "Varnish."[5] The bottom line must be that, having told the story in other ways, he was especially interested here in the art of varnishing.

Part of the interest of Fuller's *Andronicus* lies in the fact that its story of a bloody Byzantine tyrant has no very close English parallel, despite, say, Charles's tragic abandonment of the Earl of Strafford to the headsman in 1641. One might perceive larger parallels by granting that the play could have undergone some reshaping in the years between its original composition and its Restoration publication. Nevertheless, the play's most interesting glossing of the mid-seventeenth century relates less to the main line of the tyrant story than to its atmosphere, its incidental relationships, and its commentary.

The play relates how Andronicus, a kinsman of the debauched young Emperor Alexius (r. A.D. 1180-83), murders and succeeds him, then proceeds to do still more of the terrible things that ancient tyrants did. When Andronicus and his forces arrive at the port of Constantinople, however,

[5]Ibid.

the words of the chorus sound as reminiscent of 1642 or 1643 as 1182. One part of the chorus speaks thus:

> There is danger in delay,
> In a tottering State to stay,
> In those Ruins we'd be loath.
> To be Slaine, and buried both. [18]

Though many royalists were gathered in Oxford with the King, some had begun migrating to the Continent. The other part of the chorus continues:

> But pray tell us is it faire,
> Now to seek a forreign Aire?
> In our Sins you bare a part,
> From our sufferings now you start.
> And on us throw all the Load,
> By deserting your Aboad.
> We're resolved not to fly,
> Here we liv'd, and here we'le die. [19]

While this is hardly great verse, the straightforward, jingling, colloquial quality of such lines somehow helps to bring their English relevance to the surface.

In a later interchange between Paleologus (a young courtier) and Crato (a statesman), the subject of "Juntoes" arises. Though Andronicus has claimed to be going to Santa Sophia to pray, Crato tells his friend, "The Devil hee's at's devotions, he is gone / Unto his Junto, there they do debate, / How to confer the Imperial Crown on him" (28). And Paleologus replies,

> I never had a Fancy to these Juntoes. . . .
> Let me have things discuss'd at Councel Board
> In free and full appearance, where 'tis no Treason
> With solid reason to displease a Prince. . . .
> Now things in private ways are smothered. [28-29]

In 1643 the word *junto* is likely to have referred to John Pym's war party. A satirical broadside called *Pyms Juncto* from May of that year goes thus: "Then weel [members of Pym's Juncto will] resume the House, and so adjourne / Till five at night, the moderate (wearied thus) / Will quit their seats, and leave here none but us" (Frank, *Hobbled Pegasus* 88).[6]

Fuller's handling of the Patriarch of Constantinople, Basilius, is per-

---

[6] *Junto* was a flexible term, however, and was also used to refer negatively to such presumably cabalistic groups as the Oxford Parliament (loyal members of both Houses who were to meet at Christ Church), the remnants of Parliament after it was "purged" in 1648, and the group conspiring to execute Charles.

haps still more striking, insofar as it shadows forth the views of the author on the primate of all England. Monodius, the hermit, addresses Basilius thus: "Sir, I come to chide your Holiness / That earth you practise, and yet profess a heaven." The hermit also says, "Y'ave bin of late, / An over-active stickler in the Nation" (31). Writing while Archbishop Laud was a prisoner in the Tower, the ejected clergyman Fuller has Monodius continue, "*Mark Clergy-Sticklers on the Civil Stage, / A quiet death doth seldome crown their Age*" (32). One is never altogether safe, of course, in maintaining that a play-wright holds the ideas of certain of his characters, but with Monodius we can feel as safe as ever. In his *Church-History* the characteristically equable, good-natured Fuller reports that Laud is most accused for meddling in state matters, "more then was fitting, say many, then needfull, say most, for one of his profession. . . . At home, many grumbled at him for oft making the *shallowest* pretence of the *Crown* deep enough . . . to drown the undoubted right of any private Patron to a Church-living" (bk. 11, p. 217). Thus writes the moderate Anglican churchman who in 1644 was himself appointed chaplain to Princess Henrietta.

In short, the original story's cruelty and double-dealing, including Andronicus's wooing of Alexius's widow, Anna (after the manner of Richard III's wooing of the royal widow, Anne), are all present, but Fuller's seven-teenth-century "varnish" provides the work with an intriguing new dimen-sion. At one point Princess Maria in the play is furious with the courtier Paleologus, reminding him that it was her father who made him "honour-able, rich and great" (48). "What would you have us do?" asks Paleologus, "destroy our selves?" "No," she replies, "I would have you to preserve your Prince" (49). In other words, we both are and are not at the court of Constantinople. Paleologus continues:

> If any whisper but the lowest word
> Of Loyalty, there's one to cut his throat.
> Hence houses rifled, goods pillag'd, lands forfeited,
> Our selves disabled from all further service. . . .
>
> [49]

The Princess retorts, "let no Nobles hope their worth will shine, / Who make the Sun of Majesty decline" (50). It is hard to maintain many doubts about Fuller's paralogism, and perhaps hardest of all when we find the tyrant Andronicus actually pointing out in the final act that "my hair is short" (80).[7] He is, in brief, a Byzantine roundhead. A performable play

---

[7]The term *roundhead* is said to have been introduced in 1641 and "applied to the Puritans in general or to the Independents and sectaries in particular" (Boyce 72). Cromwell's own hair, however, fell down over his collar (see figure 12).

Andronicus is not, but as an historico-literary work by one of the best-known clergymen of the day, it is a significant document.[8]

A tyrant play of a very different character is T.B.'s *The Rebellion of Naples* (1649), which also deals creatively with real events, but with a crew of plebeians and a clash of systems. In the summer of 1647 a young fisherman from Amalfi named Tommaso Aniello—better known as Masaniello—became the leader of a popular revolt against Spanish rule in Naples. Fueled by various kinds of fiscal oppression, the revolt ignited suddenly on 7 July 1647 because of a new tax on fruit. The troubles began at the city gate with a riot between the fruit vendors and the customs officers, and it moved on to the palace of the Spanish Viceroy, who was forced to flee to nearby Castelnuovo. Instead of proceeding totally at random, the rioters at an early stage chose Masaniello as their leader. Somehow they acquired arms and then more arms, drove off all attempts at opposition, and proceeded to terrorize the city, a place of nearly six hundred thousand souls, if we are to believe James Howell and his sources (*Exact Historie* A2v). Many of the nobility are said to have been murdered, and Masaniello, acting as judge, condemned even some of the rioters themselves to death. Finally the Viceroy, Count D'Arcos, was forced to grant all of the revolutionaries' demands, and on 13 July, with the help of the Archbishop of Naples, an agreement was signed by D'Arcos and by Masaniello as leader of the people of Naples. For a while Masaniello claimed to want to return to a life of fishing and fishmongering, but after being presented with a gold chain and a silver suit, and perhaps with some poison as well, he began acting so wildly that his friends deserted him. Finally, on 16 July—the tenth day after it all began—he was murdered while haranguing a crowd.

The playwright has here a violent and compelling story that the bookseller can describe on the title page as "really Acted upon that bloudy Stage, the streets of NAPLES." Further, the playwright himself, who puts the book forward as both *"true, and reall"* (A3v), claims to do so as an eyewitness authority. Though we do not know who he was, he signs himself "T.B." and dedicates the play to his kinsman, comrade, and fellow traveler John Caesar of Hyde Hall in Hertfordshire. Given the incentive of knowing that the Hertfordshire Caesars were of Italian extraction, one may hope that someday an appropriate T.B. will be found among their relations.[9]

Whoever he was, T.B. was aware that some readers would say, "*I*

---

[8]The usefulness of Andronicus as a referent is suggested further in a pamphlet called *A Conference Held between the Old Lord Protector and the New Lord General* (1660). Here Cromwell exults over the fact that in the eyes of the devil he himself ranks higher than Cain, Nimrod, Nero, Mahomet, and Andronicus (2).   [9]In 1647, upon the death of his father, Sir John Caesar, T.B.'s friend John inherited the fine mansion of Hyde Hall, which he sold in 1656. Lodge credits him with a "disposition to utter carelessness in private affairs" (54).

warrant you this man drives at notable and remarkable passages of State, if we could understand him. And though Naples *be the Scene, yet he plasters his bills upon the walls and gates of* London" (A3v). To this, T.B. responded in anticipation, understandably though disingenuously, "*if there be any thing in my booke which points at the present condition of our affairs, I assure you the times are busie with me, and not I with the times.*" Though genuinely concerned with telling about the strife in Naples, he is clearly aware that his book points as well to current English conditions, and he knows that English readers accustomed to "paralogism" will know it, too. As the prologue has it, "if you'r pleas'd with seasonable things, / Here's fightings 'twixt the people and their Kings" (A4v). That should be clear enough. The clearest evidence of all, however, that T.B. is consciously riding a dual track may be found in his epilogue:

> *Let Kings beware how they provoke*
> *Their Subjects with too hard a Yoke,*
> *For when all's done, it will not doe,*
> *You see they breake the Yoke in two:*
> *Let Subjects no rebellion move*
> *On such pretences least it prove,*
> *As sad a thing, (which God forbid)*
> *And fatall as to us* [Neapolitans] *it did.*

[F6v]

The overthrow of the Neapolitan Viceroy is possible mainly because he pays heed to evil counselors regarding taxation—a "Yoke" that may be paralleled readily enough in Caroline England.[10]

T.B.'s *Rebellion of Naples*—which is subtitled *The Tragedy of Massenello*—has a firmness of texture and fullness of detail such as rarely characterize plays of the period. Thanks to its large supply of convincing details and to the playwright's familiarity with those details, and despite the application of some authorial varnish (the play opens, for example, with a prophetic hermit carrying a death's head), it has surprising power. Though sufficiently varied in incident—embracing even a love theme—it nonetheless has some of the concentration and efficiency of good drama, focusing mainly on the fisherman-tyrant who would pull down two hundred houses to build himself a palace in the *mercato*, who orders offending bakers to be baked and butchers butchered, who commands that the heads of all Frenchmen be cut off, and who breaks his wife's neck ("O, how God-like it is, to rule and sway!" [D2v]). All in all, this study of oppressive monarchy and

---

[10]Aggeler suggests that "The Neapolitan Lord Treasurer seems clearly to be modelled on Weston, the Lord Treasurer who encouraged the King to raise his revenues by fines, the enforcement of forest laws, the issue of ship-money writs and other measures that effectively alienated many subjects of every class" (58–59).

Figure 14. In this frontispiece from *The Rebellion of Naples* (1649), the verses to the left pun on Massenello's ability to catch both fish and men. (By permission of the British Library.)

plebeian revolt gives a frightening picture, one whose range of reference reaches far beyond Naples. The mind has difficulty staying fixed on Naples, in fact, when an English playwright publishing in 1649 has one of his characters tell the Viceroy (sometimes called "King"), "Sir, they will not be satisfied with all you grant, except you will grant your self to be nothing" (B5v).

Probably we should note in particular the social level of the major troublemaker in *The Rebellion of Naples*, a wild-eyed plebeian who cries out for liberty and, once possessed of power, becomes an egomaniacal tyrant. The frontispiece provided for the play depicts a fine-clad Massenello with a sword at his side, yet at the same time it manages to make much of the fisherman theme (see figure 14). Massenello is supposed to be saying "Acchiappato il pesce via la rete": "Caught is the fish in the net" (perhaps an ironic allusion to Matthew 4.18-19). Probably it also would be well to recollect the dismay and outrage registered by such English people of the period as saw hopeless confusion in their own social structures. In a 1645

Figure 15. A seventeenth-century Dutch satiric medal comparing Cromwell with Masaniello. (By permission of the Folger Shakespeare Library.)

poem by Alexander Brome called "The Commoners," we read that "the scum of the land / Are the men that command, / And our slaves are become our masters" (MacKay 9).[11] And an anonymous broadside of the following year fumes: "The meaner sort of men have all the power; / The upper end is now beneath the lower" (Frank, *Hobbled Pegasus* 136). Such complaints are easy to find. Probably worth considering, too, is the insight later provided by Cowley that "when God only intends the temporary chastisement of a people, he does not raise up his servant *Cyrus* ... or an *Alexander* ... but he makes the *Massanelloes*, and the *Johns* of *Leyden* the instruments of his vengeance, that the power of the Almighty might be more evident by the weakness of the means which he chooses to demonstrate it" (*Discourse* 362). Indeed, looked at from this angle, T.B.'s *Rebellion of Naples* is closer than any other play discussed in this chapter to what many in the English population thought they had experienced. The best hard evidence now to be found, moreover, that English parallels to the Masaniello story continued to retain their relevance for a while is a Dutch medal that depicts Cromwell on one side, Masaniello on the other (figure 15).[12] Here is parallelism with a vengeance.

Robert Baron's *Mirza: A Tragedie, Really Acted in Persia, in the Last Age* (1655) is yet another historically grounded tyrant play.[13] Back in 1627,

---

[11]Edward Phillips refers to Alexander Brome as "an Atturny of the Mayors Court, yet Poetically addicted" (*Theatrum Poetarum, Moderns* 6).   [12]A suggestion by Henfrey that this medal is rather late may be said to strengthen and further validate the parallel (161–62). One might note also D'Urfey's Restoration *Massaniello*, parts 1 and 2 (1699).   [13]Though 1647 has been suggested as the date of *Mirza*, the Norwich author was then only seventeen. In that year he published his *Cyprian Academy*, which Maule correctly describes as "a juvenile and

Figure 16. Robert Baron as depicted on the frontispiece of his *Pocula Castalia* (1650). (By permission of the Folger Shakespeare Library.)

during Charles's third year on the throne and toward the end of the forty-one-year reign of Abbas the Great (1588-1629), Shah of Persia, the English King had sent Sir Dodmore Cotton to Persia as his ambassador. In fact, Baron reports having received the original hint for writing this play from a letter by Cotton himself in the hands of a friend at Cambridge— where Baron had been admitted to Caius College on 22 July 1645 (figure 16 depicts Baron as a youth). Baron regrets that he was unaware of John Denham's *Sophy* (1641; published 1642) when he himself first began to write and that he had finished "*three compleat* Acts" of his own play before learning of it; "*nor was I then discouraged from proceeding, seeing the most ingenious* Author *of that has made his seem quite another story from this*" (A5v).

---

highly derivative political romance" (393). Despite its interest as early royalist fiction, *The Cyprian Academy* is a less mature, more amateurish work than *Mirza*. Furthermore, though one might find the dedication "TO HIS MAIESTIE" (A2r) rather ambiguous, *Mirza* refers to "our late King *Charles*" (108; i.e., 180) and has a complimentary poem from John Quarles, "*Fell. of Pet. House* Camb." (A3v). Quarles became a Fellow in 1651.

Figure 17. The historical model for the character in Denham's *The Sophy* (1642) and Baron's *Mirza* (1655): Abbas, King of Persia, from Thomas Herbert, *A Relation of Some Yeares Travaile* (1634). (From the copy in the Rare Book Collection, University of North Carolina at Chapel Hill.)

Titles of the King of Persia may be these.

Bbas *is King of* Perfia, Parthia, Media, Bactria, Cho-razon, Candahor, *and* Heri , *of the* Ouz-beg Tar-tar, *of the Kingdomes of* Hircania, Draconia, Euer-geta, Parmenia, Hydafpia, *and* Sogdiana, *of* Aria, Paropa-niza

Baron explains also that he has learned certain of his Persian facts from Sir Thomas Herbert's *A Relation of Some Yeares Travaile, Begunne Anno 1626* (1634). Herbert, who traveled in Cotton's retinue, not only recorded events concerning the ambassadorial visit but also related the story that Baron dramatizes. He even included a picture of Abbas (figure 17). Maintaining that his work is designed chiefly for scholars, Baron gives page references to the main passages in Herbert's *Relation* to which he is indebted, and at play's end he reinforces his claim to scholarly interest with over a hundred pages of annotation.

Among Baron's contemporary readers, in all likelihood, were those who contributed poems to help launch the volume. And among these was John Quarles, whose lines serve less as customary bombast than as indicators that Baron's play concerns the present as well as the past. "Advance Great *Mirza,*" he begins, "let the base world see / *Vertue* is *Vertue* though *in misery* (A3r). Such a sentiment suits the plight of royalists generally, but since Mirza is the noble and persecuted Prince of Persia, the application seems variously fit for either the English King or the Prince of Wales. "Vertue is highly priz'd," Quarles continues, "though overthrown." Writing from the perspective of one who has seen Mirza's tragedy played out until his death, Quarles seems to know, too, the fate of at least one English counterpart to Mirza:

> We mourn thy loss, admire thy worth, and grieve
> Our *Isle* a *Mirz'* and *Allybeg* can give.
> Thus Text and Time doe sute, and whilst you tell
> Your Tale, wee'l easily find a Parallell.
>
> [A3v]

Wee'l easily find a Parallell—the final line of the poem indicates as straightforwardly as possible that this is something good readers are supposed to do.

The Ally-Beg mentioned by Quarles is the Machiavellian favorite of King Abbas, whose tyrannical tendencies need little encouragement from anyone. Unfortunately Ally-Beg succeeds in arousing the King's doubts about his son, Prince Mirza. The latter is an all-virtuous and long-suffering soldier and family man, much beloved by his followers and yet inevitably brought down—in other words, a reasonable Charles figure. Why, then, does Quarles single out the monarch-and-favorite relationship for emphasis? That it is important we may be sure, for in Baron's dedication "TO HIS MAIESTIE" he claims to present *Mirza* to his royal reader "Not onely to *delight*, but *profit YOU*, / In warning to *eschew* what spoild his Right, / The *Flatterer*, and too powerful *Favourite*" (A2r). Moreover, he repeats this message within the play. The chorus of act II exclaims, "What dire effects evill Counsell workes / Even to unhinging greatest states!" (40), and it ends,

> O Kings, be sparing to make those
> Whom well you love, your Favourites;
> For them you give to vulgar spights,
> Or else, for them, your selves, depose.
>
> [42]

Charles I, of course, was for years cushioned from reality by miscellaneous flatterers, and in 1643, as we have noted in exploring the Parliament-sponsored *Tyrannicall-Government* of Buchanan, his "Evil-Councellors" seemed to many a cause for alarm. In 1655, however, Baron's play would impinge on the world of Charles II. According to royalist lights, the younger Charles certainly was of proper rank to be addressed as "Highness." Though the gesture was mainly symbolic, he had assumed the title King of England in January 1649; the Scots had crowned him at Scone in January 1651; and in 1655 he was old enough to look back on the phenomenon of favorites at his father's court. Indeed, he had favorites of his own among those who remained faithful to the royal cause. In any case, the most interesting thing about the admonitions from both Baron and Quarles is that they can expand our thoughts beyond a Mirza-Charles parallel to an Abbas-Charles one. More subtle than first we might think it, *Mirza* offers exotic Persian images of both tyrant and martyr.

Abbas is addressed in the play's opening speech by the ghost of his brother, whom he has murdered. The ghost reminds the tyrant of the colorful spectrum of his frightful deeds, including the murder of their father—and also including, one should note, many sexual crimes. The turning point comes when Mirza, finally driven mad, takes revenge on his father by breaking the neck of his own blameless daughter, Fatima, on whom the tyrant dotes. One may find it surprising, then, to read in other sources about some of the historical Abbas's considerable virtues, and even to discover at the end of Baron's play that the King repents his ill treatment of Mirza (including blinding him) and prepares to be succeeded by Mirza's son, Soffie.

Beyond the basic display of a tyrant untrammeled, this very long play (159 pages) offers many incidental insights: the royal children are shown a picture of a story that is to be enacted (the apposite story of Procne, who kills her son [16]); a home performance of *Medea* is arranged at the residence of Madam Omay, a court lady of the secret opposition party (21); the "new sect of Platoniques"—such as thrived at the Caroline court—are scorned as "the best Pimp that ever enter'd Court" (28); and in far-off Persia we encounter a character's brag that

> . . . these mercenary Priests
> Are the best fire-brands, such I've ready kindled,
> They are at work in every Conventicle,
> Their empty heads are Drums, and their hoarse voyces
> Are Trumpets to the war. . . .
> [54]

We also come upon a clear echo of Richard Lovelace's lyric conundrum: "yet could I not / Love thee so much, lov'd I not honour more" (94). *Mirza* is a fully developed, complex work, obviously a labor of love. Baron did not blot enough lines, and perhaps he borrowed too much, but he seems really to have been caught up by his theme. The story of the tyrant and his son has plenty of interest, and probably Baron was genuinely fired by its relevance to his own time, not to say buoyed by the hope that on occasion he might come close to Ben Jonson's "miraculous *Poem*" *Catiline*, which he claimed for a pattern (161).[14] His generous friend Robert Hills was ready to assure him that he had, indeed, matched Ben.

---

[14]Under the circumstances and despite the number of parallels that Bradley musters, it seems a little unfair of him to write of Baron's "plagiarism" of Jonson in *Mirza* (407).

Leonard Willan's *Orgula* (1658)—our fourth and final tyrant play—is a very different sort of work. Unlike *Andronicus, The Rebellion of Naples,* and *Mirza,* it eschews the frame of a specific story from history and nudges the tyrant figure somewhat off stage center in order to put there the woman he marries. Sufficiently important to give the play its title, Orgula bears a name that suggests her essential pride.[15] Plays that represent historical episodes certainly may include abstractions: the aged councillor in Fuller's play is called Cleobulus (after Clio and the ancient sage), and the tutor to the young emperor, Philobiblus. But Willan's move toward abstraction extends further. When he places his play in the neverwhere of Segusia, a city of ancient Transpadane Gaul, it is just part of a broadly generalizing gesture. That Willan has his own time and place firmly in mind is suggested by the tyrant's name and attention-grabbing title—Sinevero, Lord Protector—and by the thoughtful analysis of drama that Willan makes in his prefatory essay to *"the most accomplisht . . . Lady* FRANCES WILDEGOSS" (A2r).[16]

Like the play that follows, Willan's preface is marred by an unwillingness or inability to write clearly. Nevertheless, his remarks on the nature and virtues of drama make clear his earnestness about *Orgula* and provide us with an extended midcentury statement that largely compensates for the patience required to read it. A complete text of the document is provided here in Appendix A, but for the moment we might note Willan's contention that playwriting is an intellectual pursuit, despite the fact that of late it has been "vilified with vulgar Obloquie" (A2r). Willan holds that when an historical subject is attempted in *"Poesie"* (A2r), as in all three of the preceding plays here, one may expect to find "interwoven certain enlargements and digressions" (A3v). This is fair enough: every historian is a rhetorician. Furthermore, poesie is enhanced, not vitiated, when it works extensively with imaginary material. Willan believes that "we find our most authentique precepts couched in such forms of texture, as Allegories or Parables; a winning method to attract the grossest tempers, and infix in All most durable impressions" (A3v).

Willan defends not only writing and reading dramas but also seeing them and playing in them. He argues that "the well composed illustrations of a *Theater*" may "conduce to form the Judgement, compose the mind, . . . [and] rectify the manners" (A4v). Useful as a means of conveying regal messages to the people, useful for furthering "mutuall Amities" (a1v), and

---

[15]The name is related to *orgoglio* (Italian) and *orgullo* (Spanish) and akin to Shakespeare's *orgillous* (*Troilus and Cressida,* prol. 2).   [16]The Wildigos (Wilgos, Wildgoose) family had been seated at Iridge Court in Saleshurst, Sussex, since the fourteenth century. In 1645 the Ladies Wildigos, senior and junior, were each assessed four hundred pounds by the Committee for Advance of Money. Both were eventually discharged, the younger—Willan's probable addressee—on account of "her affidavit that she has no considerable estate" (Green 2:588).

useful for "requisite relaxation" (a2r), dramatic presentation is also "usefull in the Education of our Youth" (a2r). Willan is well aware that beyond the silver sea that rings his own island such usefulness is widely recognized. The production of plays, he writes, is "a frequent exercise in Forreign Seminaries, Societies and Schools" (a2r).

Though Willan claims in his essay that *Orgula* is an old work, his presentation of a lecherous, treacherous, tyrannical Lord Protector is un- likely to antedate December 1653 by very much, for it was then that Cromwell accepted that title. As the play opens, Sinevero is planning to ascend to the "Summet . . . / By secret paths" (2), and we overhear his musing on the recent death of General Castrophilus,

> Whose Glories, still surviving, in his Sonn,
> The People rule more powerfully than Law:
> And by *Ambigamor* his friend pretends
> To wed fair *Orgula*. So fooles conclude
> E're they consult those powers do them preside.
> I am their Fate. . . .
>
> [2]

Judged by his name (a *castra* was a Roman camp), Castrophilus is more likely to represent armed royalism generally than King Charles specifically. In any case, the lost leader's son is Ludaster. *Lud* will do as a pronunciation of "lord," and in *aster* we have a suitably bright and steadfast name to suggest great Sidney himself. Beyond both of these prospects lies the possibility of King Lud (or Ludd), who founded and gave his name to London, the New Troy (as Geoffrey of Monmouth would have it). The function of Ambigamor is defined still more surely by his name: he is both Ludaster's friend and Orgula's brother. Other major characters include the Lord Protector's daughter, Zizania (whose name means cockle or tare, as in Matthew 13.25), and his son, Filathes (suggestive of atheism), both of whom he finally liquidates, thereby keeping pace with Andronicus, Mas- senello, and Abbas, each of whom murders within his own family. The present powers of the Protector are presumably justified because the gracious Princess Eumena is slightly underage. She is old enough, however, to be interested in young Ludaster and he in her, and we are allowed some hopes that he might win her hand. But it is not to be, for both grace and light are snuffed out at play's end.

The ever-sinful tactics of Protector Sinevero are manifested early: to the funeral of Castrophilus he sends a sergeant at arms to accuse the dead General of treason, and he also issues a "severe injunction" to silence the people (3). (At this point one might recall, for example, the parliamentary act of 17 July 1649, which declared it treason to call the current government tyrannical.) Ludaster uses such fancy language to protest on his father's behalf, first here and then later when the case comes to court, that he approaches incomprehensibility; but part of what he says on this second occasion is clear enough:

> The Function of General, solely being
> To Soveraignty inherent; whose presence
> Heretofore authoris'd all proceeding,
> Till a corrupter Age, through ease and lux,[17]
> Induc't a substitute, who still retains
> Th'essentiall marks of his Original;
> Exacts the Rites of National Laws abroad;
> Supports the course of civill laws at home;
> And with his moving Commonwealth transports
> A Law peculiar to his Ministrie. . . .
>
> [11]

The Protector's desire to degrade the dead hero is carried through, of course, and young Ludaster is sentenced to banishment.

Orgula herself then enters with her waiting women, Vergona (French *vergogne*, shame) and Amasia (Latin *amasio*, lover), one of whom carries a cabinet of jewels, the other a mirror. Wooed by the Lord Protector (though we have heard him say, "my care rests onely on my own / Security" [46]), Orgula herself fancies the good-looking Fidelius, page to Ludaster. Her servant Mundolo's advice on the subject is suitably worldly:

> Wealth moves the world, yet is Loves Minister:
> First we contract with this, then joyn with that.
> Husbands are us'd, as Properties in Scenes,
> To keep the inward motions undiscover'd.
>
> [49]

To have her cake and eat it too, Orgula agrees to marry Sinevero, but on their wedding night she has him drugged so that she can sleep with Fidelius—who presumably will be delivered to her by Mundolo. Unwittingly she is bedded instead by Mundolo himself, who has not been able to enlist the services of Fidelius. Having been served by her own servant, then, Orgula appears, amorous in her night robe, and encounters Fidelius— who, to make a point that must be made, *"Opens his bosome"* and reveals (ah!) the breasts of Fidelia (71). Orgula is enraged, and in trying to kill Mundolo kills instead her new husband, the Lord Protector. Then she goes mad.

A very involved work, the language of which tends to mist over whenever the writer reaches after a poetic strain, *Orgula* is a violent,

---

[17]As one might guess, *lux* (from French *luxe*, Latin *luxus*) means luxury (*OED*).

latter-day descendant of *Philaster* and *The Maid's Tragedy*. Harder and coarser, though, with more convolutions and less grace, and with an allegorical dimension such as Willan's preface commends, it is at least clear about some of its basic aims. Not really a good play, it nonetheless offers a provocative image of a tyrant Protector wedded to dangerous pride.[18] This linkage provides a variety of insights into the mind of a thoughtful, politically disaffected, theater-loving Englishman. That Willan regarded his subject matter seriously may be inferred from his later publication of *The Exact Politician; or, Compleat Statesman: Briefly and Methodically Resolved into Such Principles, Whereby Gentlemen May Be Qualified for the Management of Any Publick Trust* (1670). It is not likely to be more than historical coincidence, however, that the deaths of both Sinevero and Cromwell—one in ancient Gaul and one in Whitehall—both reached the English press in 1658. Recollecting also that the play begins by depicting the revisionary, postmortem degradation of Castrophilus and the banishment of his successor, one might note the further coincidence that in 1661 the body of England's Lord Protector was dug up, taken to Tyburn, hanged, and beheaded, and his head placed aloft upon Westminster Hall.

Among the tyrant plays sampled here, one is set in Asia, where according to Aristotle despotism was a normal way of life because everyone there agreed that only the leader was free. In the handling of all four of the tyrant leaders in these tragedies, however, we find a fascination with the abnormal, the terrible, the bestial, the monstrous—and not least in *The Rebellion of Naples*, where the proletarian revolution casts up a fisherman tyrant.

It therefore behooves us to recognize that each of these plays reflects seventeenth-century England. Whether working with older historical material (*Andronicus*) or newer (*Mirza* and *The Rebellion of Naples*) or creating a reasonably original construct (*Orgula*), the dramatic writers in this grouping all refract ideas, problems, and events that to them were pressingly current. How did they—and others like them—dare to say as much as they did? We can hardly be sure, but Quintilian's answer comes as close as we are likely to get: "You can speak as openly as you like against . . . tyrants, as long as you can be understood differently, because you are not trying to avoid giving offense, only its dangerous repercussions. If danger can be avoided by some ambiguity of expression, everyone will admit its cunning" (Patterson, *Censorship* 15). Working with paralogism, parable, and allegory so as to "shadow" more than first meets the eye, our writers here have produced plays offering not merely some "requisite relaxation" but also a window to

---

[18]Robert Herrick's appraisal of Willan's writing ability is appropriately guarded: "I might extoll thee, but speake lesse, / Because thy selfe art comming to the Presse" ("To M. Leonard Willan His Peculiar Friend," ll. 9–10).

thought, specifically to timely political thought. No matter how artificial their "varnish" may be, these writers share an impulse to view drama through the lens of life.

We have also seen the reverse. The image passed down to us of King Charles as an actor on a stage in the final scene of his life is but one particularly dramatic product of a widespread habit of paralleling that in 1661 enabled the bookseller Francis Kirkman to observe, "*We have had the private Stage for some years clouded and under a tyrannical command, though the publick Stage of* England *has produc'd many monstrous villains, some of which have deservedly made their* exit" ("Stationer to the Reader" A1r). In October 1660, twenty-nine of the fifty-nine signatories of Charles's death warrant were convicted of treason. Thirteen were executed, and in a resolutely symbolic display, three who were already dead were exhumed and hanged. Though tyrants had trod the English stage off and on for many years, one may conclude that the treatment of tyranny in drama flourished in the middle years of the seventeenth century partly because so many people were sure that they had seen tyranny stride across the stage of life.

8

SHOWS, MOTIONS, AND DROLLS

The severest and in other matters most rigid . . . Common-wealths
(to wit the *Spartan*, and *Lacedamonian*, and *Athenian*) smooth'd the
rugged Front of their power in this *Punctilio* and reason of State, and
Plato and *Aristarchus*, and *Aristides* (though never so just, never so
strickt) indulg'd alwaies these Ingratiations to the People.
> — Edmund Gayton, *Charity Triumphant* (1655)

Yes, the next day after *Simon* and *Jude*[1]
. . . all your liveries go a feasting
By water with your gally foist and pot-guns,[2]
And Canvas Whales to *Westminster;* I am not
Affear'd of your green Robin-hoods, that fright
With fiery club your pitifull Spectators
That take pains to be stifled, and adore
The Wolves and Camels of your company.
Next whom the children ride, who innocent things,
What with the Gyants, and the Squibs and eating
Too many sugar-plumms, take occasion to
Perfume their Pageants, which your Senators
Ride after in full scent.
> —James Shirley, *Honoria and Mammon* (1659)

. . . you may talk of your Playes, but give me . . . Pretty harmless
Drolls for my money.
> —Thomas Shadwell, *The Miser* (1672)

THREE YEARS AFTER the death of Cromwell, in a show designed for
Charles II as he passed through the city of London, John Ogilby called for
the placement of a female figure named Rebellion on the north side of
Leadenhall Street (*Entertainment* [1662], 13). She was to wear a crimson
robe and be mounted on a Hydra, "*her Hair snaky, a Crown of Fire on her
Head, a bloody Sword in one Hand, a charming Rod in the other.*" "*Stand! Stand!*"
she was to cry, "*who 'ere You are! this Stage is Ours*" (47; i.e., 41). On the

---

[1]One of the fixed holy days, the day of St. Simon and St. Jude falls on 28 October. This
passage as a whole offers a medley of details meant to conjure up a typical Lord Mayor's show.
[2]A galley-foist is a state barge, especially that of the Lord Mayor, and a potgun is a short piece
of ordnance with a large bore (*OED*).

opposite side of the street stood Brittain's Monarchy, wearing a mantle on which was drawn the map of Great Britain (17). Brittain's Monarchy was to tell Rebellion to go to hell and say to Charles, "*Enter our* Sun, *our* Comfort, *and our* Life" (42). Beyond doubt, the "glorious Restauration" (1) thus celebrated had unleashed a burst of pride and patriotism such as England had not seen for many years.

In antebellum days Londoners had become accustomed to annual autumn shows when the newly elected Lord Mayor and other dignitaries processed to and from Westminster in order that the Mayor's election might be confirmed by the sovereign, or at least by someone representing the sovereign. Over the years these shows had called for various combinations of pageants, barges, costumes, songs, and speeches, the whole generally tending to be lavish, colorful, and allegorical. The shows ceased in 1640, however: in August of that year a Scottish army invaded England, and December brought the Root and Branch Petition. People may well have thought that Thomas Heywood's 1639 *Londini Status Pacatus* would be the last of the series. Fifteen years later, however, in Cromwell's time, the story resumes.

Though such civic entertainments are only marginally dramatic, we will fare better in the long run if we know something about them, as well as about such other minor forms as the motion and the droll, both of which continued to be performed at least sporadically. Many of the dramatic writings discussed in this book have come to life (both then and now) only in the minds and closets of their readers, but the three types of entertainment now before us all served as midcentury sources of communal dramatic pleasure and helped keep the thespian spark visibly alive.

Common to both medieval drama and the Renaissance civic show was a dependence on the interest, pride, and cash of the trade guilds. Also common to both was the concept of visual allegory—and its fellow traveler, didactic purpose. Moreover, both medieval drama and seventeenth-century show partook of the mingled nature of tableau and processional. Just as the old pageant wagons moved through the city, so too did the pageants in the Lord Mayor's procession. And sometimes the Mayor's procession paused by fixed scaffolds where Rebellion, say, might hurl her wrath, or where (in that same show) eleven hundred children clad in blue might break into song.

The possibilities for fragmentation and discontinuity were obviously great in any processional show, but there was always the chance that some meaningful coherence could result from an author's handling of theme. Constructing allegorical scenes from a wealth of traditional, mythological, and historical materials, and reinforcing verbal and visual art with one another, authors usually created complex, message-laden shows that probably intrigued even those who were puzzled by their meaning. Rather optimistically, the dramatist Leonard Willan assures us that "the illiterate and orebusied multitude," in fact "their very children," are likely to understand such entertainments (*Orgula* alv). Willan also claims that "Peoples intercourse with one another" and "mutuall Amities" are no slight benefits from them. So long as they are not going to conspire, there is something to be said for people's commingling (alv). Most important from a political viewpoint, however, is what the shows say. It is a "happy piece of policy," writes Willan, "to inform with delight the meanest member of the civill frame in what he is concerned" (alv).

The unconcern of Charles I about such a policy was one of the factors that enabled him to cancel the splendid entertainment planned in 1626 for his grand entry into London to celebrate his coronation. Almost worse than the last-minute cancellation, he ordered the pageants torn down immediately, despite the fact that his subjects had gone to great expense to build them (Bergeron 106-8). Never a man of the people, Charles found his natural and most comfortable habitat to be the court.

One might suppose that the monarch's faint interest in civic shows would either dampen the city's interest or be counterbalanced by the city's greater attention to them. To a large extent, David Bergeron maintains, it is the latter phenomenon that occurred. Equally noteworthy is the fact that, after the cessation of pageant entertainments, followed by the trauma of war and the death of the King, regular civic shows were reinstituted by the city in 1655. In January Cromwell had dissolved the Protectorate Parliament, and in May he had appointed ten major generals to control the country. Order there may have been, but it was hardly a time for widespread celebration. Probably starting the shows again, even on a modest scale, marked a calculated effort to pull things together, to construct an image of normalcy and get on with life. It may even have been a contra-royalist move. Such, in any event, we may infer with the help of Gail Paster, who writes that generally a "pageant's . . . insistence on the city's independent ability to produce, nurture, and finally celebrate its own worthiest citizens reveals the extent to which the pageants ministered to the city's self-esteem by challenging the aristocratic assumptions of the masques that birth, courtly graces, and royal favor matter more than anything else" (62).

Whatever the motivation may have been, Edmund Gayton writes somewhat edgily in the dedication of the pamphlet discussing his 1655 Lord Mayor's show, *Charity Triumphant*. "I cannot here set forth the reason," he says, "of the late extinguishing these *Civick Lights* and suppressing the Genius of our Metropolis" (4). Thus are we left to surmise not only the reason but also why he cannot express it. Ancient Rome, he observes, whether "under many happy KINGS, or in its change from Monarchy to

Democracy, or in its little resurrection to Aristocracy," always offered "Shewes and Pomps to the People, who are naturally pleas'd with such Gleames and Irradiations of their Superiors" (3). Indeed, the people "rejoyce alwaies to see some of their money spent upon themselves" (4). As a source of intimations about Gayton's own attitude and the current state of affairs, such passages are not much more helpful than his sketchy comments on the show's "Scenicall Contrivement & Pageant Bravery" (5). All that survives is what he calls "a written Pageant" (5), a brief description *sans* text. On the whole, however, judging from such evidence as remains, we may suppose that the "real" *Charity Triumphant* was comparatively underpowered. The Mercers may have managed but a single pageant featuring a crowned virgin wearing satin ("See how she rides! See how she comes! / Alarum'd in with Fifes and Drumms" [6]). No matter how appealing the music, satin, and virgin may have been, moreover, the show was surely muted and dampened by the October winds and showers that day (7).[3]

The Lord Mayor's show of the following year was not only more ambitious but also determinedly upbeat. Its author, John Bulteel, like Gayton, clearly knew that some people were not yet ready for such celebrations, but he had little patience for these folk. "What Infamy could there have been greater," he wrote, "then now to be morose, sullen, and niggardly, when all eares are listening for no news but those of Feasts and Triumphs?" (9). Professing to desire *"nothing more then the prosperity and glory of this renowned City"* (4), where "the rich live splendidly, and the poorest are free from want" (8), Bulteel goes so far as to claim that there is "no City that hath more flourish'd, nor any City that hath been lesse afflicted with calamities" than great *"Lud's* Town" (5). At least Bulteel might say so— while simultaneously boasting of the city's military force, presumably consisting of more than two thousand horsemen "and threescore 1000 footmen fit for war" (8). There were salutes to the Lord Protector, a mock battle on the Thames, aldermen riding in scarlet gowns, and a twelve-foot giant, as well as symbolic pageants to please and puzzle the eye and mind, and particularly to dazzle the common folk so as "to make them know, there is something more excellent in Magistracy then they understand, whereby they may be drawn to a stricter and greater obedience" (9). Who among them, one might wonder, ever read Bulteel's pamphlet? Toward the close of the show, in Soper Lane, Orpheus appeared in a wilderness, playing his

---

[3]Kenneth Richards makes a good observation: "Of course, . . . the dramatic, visual, and intellectual substance of pageant shows is notoriously difficult to determine, and there is constant danger of doing gross injustice to a pageant-maker's work when so little is available on which to base even tentative comment" ("Restoration Pageants" 49).

harp for an assortment of dancing monkeys, bears, tigers, and lions (the new Lord Mayor, Robert Tichburn, belonged to the Company of Skinners). As a tamer of beasts, Orpheus presumably resembled a just magistrate who is able to tame "the wild affections of men" (14). If few of the Georges and Nells in the audience thought much about the imagery of dancing monkeys, it was probably just as well.

The next eight Lord Mayors' shows (1657-64), a series which takes us well into the Restoration, were all the work of John Tatham. In 1657, after Richard Chiverton, the new Lord Mayor, had taken his customary oath at Westminster Hall and returned down the Thames on his barge, the pageants were waiting for him "*at that place where Cheap-side Crosse stood*" *(Tatham, Londons Triumphs* B1v)—another reminder that that landmark icon had fallen prey to the reformers. Mounted on the first of these pageants there was again a wilderness with wild beasts (Chiverton, too, was a skinner), accompanied this time by an old man carrying a staff and wearing a long gray gown and a hat turned up on one side so as to display a scallop shell. With such signs of being a venerable pilgrim, he could command with authority, "Wander no farther!" One is scarcely surprised to learn that in all the course of his wanderings the old man has found London to be the true nursery of "Arts and Arms, Fames Garden Military. / The Merchants Treasure, and their safety too" (B2r).

In 1658 Tatham presented Honour ("a Man with a grave Aspect" [*Londons Tryumph* 11]) as the chief figure in a chariot drawn by griffins and guided by a golden-helmeted Prudence. Honour acknowledged Cromwell's death the previous month (*"Clouds do interpose our joy"*) but nevertheless insisted *"that this day may not obscured be"* (12).

In the following year, when England's future began to seem more uncertain than ever, Tatham prefaced his pamphlet on the show (produced by the Company of Grocers) with a story about certain ancient Romans whose games in honor of Apollo had been interrupted by war. In due course these athlete-soldiers became *"returning Conquerours, assisted by an unknown hand; Clouds of Arrows and Darts, having covered their Enemies, they found an old man dancing, and their sports in some manner continued, whereat with much joy they uttered forth,* Salva res est, saltat senex, *which afterwards became a Proverb, & is properly spoken when a sudden evill is seconded with a good event, beyond Hope or Expectation. Gentlemen, the inference needs little explanation; tis sufficient Providence affords us that happinesse to return to our Tryumphs, the glory of the City, [and] an encouragement to Arts"* (*London's Tryumph* A3v).

Not until 1660, however, when Tatham wrote *The Royal Oake*, did a Lord Mayor's show shake off its Long Parliament fetters. The oak, of course, was an old symbol that had been infused with new vigor by the story of how the younger Charles, after the royalist defeat at Worcester in 1651, escaped from his foes by seeking shelter in an oak tree at Boscobel. Tatham knew that from this show the people expected "more then hath been in ordinary Triumphs heretofore" (A3v). Significantly dated, on the title page, "in the 12th Year of his *Majesties* most happy, happy, Reign," *The Royal Oake* is said to have offered twice as many pageants and speeches as its predecessors. The King's own trumpeters and kettledrummers participated in the show, the new Lord Mayor, Sir Richard Browne, was praised for his "superlative loyalty" (A3v), indeed for his help in bringing Charles back, and the King was lauded as God's vicegerent, restored at long last and plainly said to have come "To rescue us from Wolves" (9). In short, the notes of true celebration had at last returned to the civic show.

Unlike his father, furthermore, Charles II did not cancel the dazzling coronation celebration mounted in his honor in April of the following year. Also the work of John Tatham, *Neptunes Address* displayed again the Royal Oak, now joyously adorned with glistering scepters and crowns (5).[4]

Among other shows of the time, one might note the flurry of entertainments associated with General George Monck's arrival in London in early 1660 to arrange for Charles's succession. Most notable among these, perhaps, Thomas Jordan's *"Musical Representation"* called *Bacchus Festival* was presented for Monck at Vintners Hall on 12 April 1660. Performers playing a Frenchman, a Spaniard, a German, and a Greek all paid honor to both Bacchus and the guest of honor by providing the latter with assorted varieties of vinous refreshment. Edmund Ludlow would later grump that it was Monck's "custom not to depart from those publick meetings till he was as drunk as a beast" (2:244), and the General himself after this particular event was pleased to request a cessation of invitations on the grounds that such occasions were not suited to the distemper of the times.

Civic entertainments like these, datable and assignable to specific occasions, leave a far better paper trail than the "motions" or puppet shows of the period.[5] Students of the drama are likely to have a fair notion of the latter, nonetheless, thanks to the attention lavished on them by Ben Jonson in several scenes of *Bartholomew Fair* (1614) and thanks to the additional fact that puppets are great conservators of tradition. In Jonson's play the

---

[4]Paula Backscheider's comments on "Charles II's London as National Theater" are helpful regarding such civic shows. In connection with this particular entertainment, she observes that Charles himself grew trees from acorns of the Boscobel Oak and that others of its progeny were cultivated in places such as the Physic Garden, Chelsea (17).   [5]George Speaight writes: "Motions have been accepted as synonyms for puppets by all the competent authorities, and in many cases this is quite certainly the sense of the word, but if we examine the references carefully we shall find that the term was used extremely loosely to describe *any kind* of moving mechanism" (55). Where puppets are clearly intended, Speaight adds, they frequently appear to have been glove puppets (66).

puppeteer Lanterne Leatherhead draws his wooden actors from a basket and puts them through their comical-mythical-topical-tragical paces until interrupted by a Puritan heckler. The latter, Zeal-of-the-Land Busy (" 'tis I, will no longer endure your prophanations" [V.v.1-2]), disputes vigorously with the Puppet Dionysius. His main argument, applied to the stage with equal vigor by Prynne some twenty years later, is that "the Male, among you, putteth on the apparell of the *Female*, and the *Female* of the *Male*" (V.v.99-100)—a notion that the puppet refutes by lifting up its garment. Whatever other goals the incident achieves, one should not overlook the fact that it effectively conveys a puppet show's invaluable potential for spontaneity.

The major place in London for the motions was Smithfield in August at the time of Bartholomew Fair. But other places and times also served— for instance, Fleet Street in Term, when litigants and lawyers were in residence.[6] In *The Actors Remonstrance* (1643), after war had broken out and the theaters were closed, the author complains that "Puppit-plays, which are not so much valuable as the very musique betweene each Act at ours, are still up with uncontrolled allowance, witnesse the famous motion of *Bell* and the *Dragon* so frequently visited at *Holbourne-bridge;* these passed Christmas Holidayes, whither Citizens of all sorts repair with far more detriment to themselves then ever did . . . Playes, Comedies and Tragedies" (5).[7] The author's sense of injury here, stated on grounds of relative value, is understandable. While it is true that the puppets sometimes borrowed from such plays as *Tamburlaine* and *Julius Caesar,* we may suppose that their literary merit was generally slight. They were dramatic and they were entertaining, but probably they never aspired to be much more than brief and broadly popular entertainment. George Speaight cites a "Song of Bartholomew Fair" (1655) that conveys this point with the aid of a visiting Hobbinoll:

> For a penny you may zee a fine puppet play,
> And for twopence a rare piece of art. . . .
> Their zights are so rich, is able to bewitch
> The heart of a very fine man-a;
> Here's Patient Grisel here, and Fair Rosamond there,
> And the History of Susannah. . . .
>
> [71]

---

[6]Speaight provides a "Plan of London" that indicates a dozen different places where puppet shows were presented in the seventeenth century (61). He also makes the point, however, that most puppet showmen earned their living by traveling through the countryside (62).
[7]Bel and the Dragon are two separate stories that constitute one book of the Apocrypha. Bel was the main god of the Babylonians, and the dragon was a physical manifestation of evil.

One might observe that this song conveys also what was probably a typical potpourri of fictional, historical, and scriptural stories.[8]

We now know too little to make much of the matter, but topical allusions were clearly a stock-in-trade of the puppet master. Presumably at least part of the crowd in earlier days cheered delightedly to see the puppet show brothels of Sodom and Gomorrah wrecked by a crowd of Elizabethan apprentices (Speaight 64). And one recalls Leatherhead's remark that his rendition of *The Gunpowder Plot* was the most successful of his shows (Jonson, *Bartholomew Fair* V.i.11-14). As for the later period, of course, while the puppet masters are not likely to have changed their ways, they also would not have been allowed to continue performing had they been perceived as dangerous.

The borrowing of selected bits from earlier drama is one of several devices that the motions shared with the drolls. A comparison of these two forms might be instructive, though too little information survives for anyone to do it well. In any case, and despite the survival of more information on the drolls than on the motions, the drolls remain frustratingly elusive, partly because of their variegated character and career, partly because of the scarcity of surviving texts, and partly because the word *droll* itself was used so loosely. For example, the comic character Rifaloro in Fanshawe's *To Love Only for Love Sake* (1654) is referred to as a walking "Drole" (*Querer* b2v). Apparently *droll* might signify "jesting," as when Manuche has a fiddler in *Love in Travell* (1655) say to a chamberlain, "prethee, Bolster (without droll) Does S^r peirciual: Lye in his old Chamber" (7r). In Tatham's welcoming show for Charles (and the Dukes of York and Gloucester) in July 1660, the first pageant, featuring Time, was appropriately and predictably "very glorious" (*Londons Glory* 7), but it was followed by "another Pageant in the Nature of a Droll" (8) wherein appeared the figure of Industry, together with some carders and spinners. Offputting in a comparable way, Tatham's Lord Mayor's show of the next year calls for "*a Droll of* Indians *who are labouring*" (*London's Tryumphs* 21; i.e., 13). And later in this same show there is another "Droll" in which tumblers are expected to "play their Tricks" (8). Even within the latter two totally different segments from a single civic show, then, we have signs of the broad range of uses to which a mid–seventeenth-century writer or speaker might put the term *droll*.

---

[8]Though one cannot say how the puppeteers handled the material, it is certain that they drew heavily from scriptural stories. Even Milton could point out that when God gave Adam reason, "he gave him freedom to choose . . . ; he had bin else a meer artificiall *Adam*, such an *Adam* as he is in the motions" (*Areopagitica* 527). Robinson has charted the biblical subjects treated in puppet plays and tried to relate them to other more or less contemporary drama.

At least it is clear that the prevailing tone of drolls was comic. The oldest known uses of the term have a comic thrust, and indeed the title page of part 2 of Francis Kirkman's *The Wits; or, Sport upon Sport* (1673) describes that anthology as "A / Curious Collection of several / DROLS and FARCES."[9] According to Kirkman, furthermore, the performers of these works were strolling players, fools, fiddlers, and mountebanks' zanies. However much he writes tongue-in-cheek here, his choice of words helps to clarify the fundamental nature of the entertainment.

Bobbing to the surface at a time when conventional, full-length plays were officially banned, these brief dramatic shows were generally so simple to perform and so easy to mount that they could be—and were—presented nearly anywhere. Kirkman observes that even the costumes in the droll, unlike those in the plays of prewar days, were kept simple, for they "*were in great danger to be seiz'd by the then Souldiers*" (Elson 169). And Henry Marsh, in bringing out part 1 of *The Wits* in 1662, said he did so not only for the sake of individual readers but also to assist extemporaneous performance at private social gatherings. Both early and late, in other words, drolls could be readily performed by amateurs.

Just a few years before Marsh published this last information, of course, the more public a meeting was, the more daring. Gerard Langbaine observes, not too surprisingly, that drolls were applauded "in the University" (*Account* 89), and Anthony à Wood adds that they were particularly favored at degree time (quoted in Elson 23). Kirkman says that they also were put on at fairs down in the country. Somewhat more dangerously, one might suppose, they were performed at Bartholomew Fair, as well as at taverns and at Charing Cross and Lincoln's Inn Fields. In fact, Langbaine reports that "when the . . . Reformers of the Nation suppress the Stage," drolls, "under the Colour of Rope-dancing, were allow'd to be acted at the *Red-Bull* Play-house by stealth, and the connivance of those straight lac'd Governors" (*Account* 89). Determined performers of drolls, if they were somewhat discreet, could at certain periods hope for the helpful inattention of the authorities, even within the precincts of one of the old theaters.

We should also note in passing that the rope-dancing that could serve as a cover for the performance of drolls was in its own right a crowd-pleasing form of entertainment. Moreover, given the mix of "acts" at the Red Bull, one ought not be hasty about assuming the constituency of the crowd. The cautious but endlessly curious John Evelyn, for example, may provide us

---

[9]Part 1 of *The Wits*, containing twenty-seven drolls, had been gathered together and published over a decade earlier, in 1662, by the printer Henry Marsh. Marsh died in 1665, however, without producing part 2, and in 1672 Kirkman brought out a second edition of part 1. In 1673 he followed it with part 2, containing ten more drolls, in both octavo and quarto editions. Elson's 1932 edition of both works is invaluable for sorting things out.

with a mild surprise when he writes about going to see the Turk, a famous rope-dancer, on 15 September 1657: "I saw even to astonishment the agilities he perform'd, one was his walking bare foote, & taking hold by his toes onely, of a rope almost perpendicular & without so much as touching it with his hands" (*Diary* 197).

As for drolls themselves, beyond doubt they owed much not only to earlier plays but also to jigs. In the days of Richard Tarleton (d. 1588) and Will Kempe (fl. 1600), the jig was characteristically a short, farcical, song-and-dance entertainment that followed the performance of a play. Thus we read in *Jack Drum's Entertainment* (1600) that "the Iigge is cal'd for when the Play is done" (Baskervill 107). Although texts and bits of music survive for a mere handful of these essentially ephemeral pieces, a good many allusions to them enable us to surmise much. After coming in for a barrage of scorn in the early 1600s (when Shakespeare had Hamlet say that Polonius wants "a jig or a tale of bawdry, or he sleeps" [II.ii.500-501]), the jig eventually regained favor in the time of Charles I, even at some of the better theaters. Hence when we come to 1641 and the jocularly vicious pamphlet called *Canterburie His Change of Diot*, we find that it ends with a song called a jig. Nor should we be surprised that in Marsh's collection of "Select Pieces of Drollery" in the first volume of *The Wits* we find *The Humours of Singing Simpkin*, one of the most famous of Elizabethan jigs. Not only was there overlap between the genres of droll and jig; sometimes there was identity.

A brief excursus into latter-day jigging may help to reinforce the point. Fortunately, a very late example comes down to us from John Balshaw of Brindle, Lancashire. Written in verse intended to be sung (each of the jig's four parts is set to a different tune), the work has a simple comic plot that is given an unusually firm historical underpinning. At the outset we meet one Captain Causlesse, who is delighted that Fortune has chosen to raise him "from a plow man to Honnour." He says,

> . . . for when as our kingdome was lately devided
> I tooke up a commission a captaine to bee
> While some from their dignityes downeward haue slided
> now I am advanced to a higher degree[.]
>
> [1v]

Causlesse (whose name is an inverted reminder of the "Good Old Cause") then elaborates:

> ffrom toyle and from labour now I am a ffreeman
> who formerly worked both early and late
> for gould and for silver I haue att commandment
> and thinke my selfe fitt for each gentlemans mate
> This sword it hath purchas[d] both riches and Honnour

> & this my commission did make mee beare sway
> for whiles I did fight vnder Olivers banner
> I had what I pleased and none durst say nay[.]
>
>   [1v]

While the topsy-turvydom of revolution has made a captain of this plowman, his neighbor Justice Trueman, once a man of position, enters fretting that

> . . . the States haue determind to sequester mee
> And if for delinquency I bee detected
> both I and my son shall bee quite overthrowne
> Tis pitty true subiects should bee thus reiected
> and others enioy what is none of their owne.
>
>   [1v]

Captain Causlesse responds that Trueman's words show him to be still corrupt: "And if you before our committy bee taken / your life is in danger with out ffurther doubt." To this Trueman replies, "I hope for kinge Charles longe lookett for Arivall" (1v).

The plot, simple but well developed for a jig, involves the possible betrothal of the captain's daughter, Juviana, to Trueman's son, Samwell. Such a match is unlikely, however, for Samwell prefers the captain's niece and ward, Lucina. In any event, old Trueman has no intention of marrying off his son to one "of baser blood" (3r). Such action as there is takes place in 1660, and its resolution brings forth Lucina to sing "My Vncle hath receiued newes / our kinge hee is arrived" (5r). Trueman exults, "god blesse our kinge / And hange disloyall Subiects" (5r). The show as a whole was doubtless a light and lively affair when performed to such tunes as "Yorkshire Redcaps" and "Theres Noe One Shall Prove Loue Soe Faithfull as I"; and yet Balshaw's jig has a dark side that is understandable only in historical terms.

As for authorship of the drolls in *The Wits*, Kirkman can say only that they were "Written I know not when, by several Persons, I know not who" (title page). This perhaps suggests the folk humor of some of the pieces as well as the contemporary need for anonymity. Such a statement certainly does not reveal the fact that many midcentury drolls were made up of scenes from well-known plays. For example, one of the drolls is called *Bottom the Weaver*, and another *The Bouncing Knight; or, The Robers Rob'd* (most readers will be on familiar ground here from the very opening line: "How now *Jack*, where hast thou been?" [*The Wits*, pt. 1, in Elson 47]).

Though it is unlikely that we will ever be able to draw aside the veil of anonymity concealing the creators of midcentury drolls, the name of Robert Cox, "An Excellent Comedian that liv'd in the Reign of King *Charles* the First" (Langbaine, *Account* 89), is a major one that survives. Not traceable among the members of any London company, Cox probably was a strolling or country player who came to London late in the game. Langbaine reports, in any case, that when plays were suppressed, Cox "betook himself to making Drolls or Farces"—and note the repeated linkage of these terms—such as *Acteon and Diana* and *Oenone* (89). Apparently Cox not only put these skits together but usually took the leading parts, "and so naturally, that once after he had play'd Young *Simpleton* at a Country Fair, a noted Smith in those parts, who saw him act, came to him, and offer'd to take him as his Journey-man" (89).

Cox died in December 1655, and in 1656 his *Acteon and Diana, Oenone,* and *Simpleton*—"Acted at the *Red Bull* with great applause"—were printed for Edward Archer in Little Britain. The bibliographical facts are unusually confusing, but apparently we have here Cox's presentation of his work "To all the Worthy-minded GENTRY." Like Langbaine's and Wood's references to a university audience, this dedication is a reminder that the drolls' appeal was not confined to lower social levels or intellects. We also have Cox's statement of intention, which is probably for the most part true as well as indicative of the reason he was allowed to perform: he declares that his drolls were created "*rather to provoke a laughter, then occasion a contemplation*" (A1r). In June 1653, nevertheless, the Redcoats raided a performance of his comically swashbuckling *John Swabber* ("by the beard of my great Grandfather, I swear, I will so sashado, mashado, pashado, and carbinado thee, that thou shalt look like a Gallimafry all the days of thy Life" [Elson 192]). The attending gentry were compelled to pay five shillings apiece as an exit fee.

Since generalizations tend to falsify, it will be well to have a glance at a sampling of drolls. Cox's *Oenone* runs to about ten quarto pages (in *Acteon and Diana*) and has a dozen or so roles (depending on the number of "Satyres" available). Hence it is rather larger in scale than most of its kind. Starting with the famous mythological topos of Oenone deserted by Paris, it presents a mournful Oenone whose birthday is being celebrated by assorted shepherds and shepherdesses. The main energy of the piece, however, derives from the contrast of such pastoral figures as Amintas, Strephon, Cloris, and Phillis with Hobbinoll, a rustic swain who believes Oenone to be enamored of him. A Bottom-like figure, and surely the role that Cox designed for himself, Hobbinoll considers himself "one of the understandingst, sweetest, neatest, and compleatest Shepherds that ever took hook in hand," so handsome that when he sees his reflection in a pail he has much ado to keep from drowning himself (21). Oenone smiles at his rude actions in order to draw "a false vail of mirth" over her melancholy (24). There is a shepherds' dance, a morris dance, and a satyrs' dance, a rather lyrical speech from late-arriving Pan, and then an invitation from

Oenone for all to repair to her bower. The whole is light, musical, and pleasant, enlivened by farce rather than dominated by it.

Cox's Hobbinoll and Simpleton spring from similar soil. Running to thirteen quarto pages in *Acteon and Diana*, *The Humour of Simple; or, Simpleton the Smith* opens with Old Simpleton complaining of his son, Young Simpleton: "He will not work, and yet no sooner is his nose out of the Alehouse, but his head is in the Cupboard: His insatiate stomach may well defie a Giant, or the great Eater of *Kent*" (1).[10] Then Simpleton enters with a huge piece of buttered bread—a stage prop memorialized in the famous frontispiece of *The Wits* (the upper-right portion of which is reproduced here as figure 18). When the old man suggests that the young one marry Mistress Dorothy, who has youth, beauty, and money, Young Simpleton obligingly goes to Doll's window with a viol to play and sing, assuring her, "I love you better and dearer, then a Bear does honey, and I hope you will affect me as much as a Sow does a bunch of Carrots" (6). At this point Doll offers to throw a chamberpot down upon him. In the last half of the work Doll is indeed wedded to Young Simpleton, though she is also entertaining two gentlemen. All ends reasonably happily when Young Simpleton, aided by Old Simpleton, manages to send the two interlopers forth with a good beating. A straightforward, fast-moving work, *Simpleton* is reminiscent of jestbooks from both the sixteenth and seventeenth centuries and carries forward a strain of broad humor something like that in *John John, Gammer Gurton's Needle*, and probably many a now-lost jig.

To keep our understanding of *droll* properly complicated, however, we might also consider *Philetis and Constantia*. Perhaps by Cox, this work was based on a narrative poem called *Constantia and Philetus*, which had been written by Abraham Cowley at the age of twelve and published in 1633 in his *Poetical Blossoms* (Elson 395). Here is a mini-tragedy complete with love, conflict, revenge, murder, and suicide. No sooner does Constantia confess her love for Philetis than her father enters and orders that she never see Philetis again. The lovers secretly agree to meet while the old man is out hunting, but at the time of their rendezvous an angry rival of Philetis appears and runs him through. The girl's brother, Philocritus, then comes in and kills the rival (who has spoken a mere nine lines), leaving Constantia to take up her dead lover's hand and kill herself with his sword: "Oh, my *Philetis*, for thy sake will I / Make up a full and perfect Tragedy" (Elson 289). The basic plot is reasonable enough, surely no worse than some of its

---

[10]Missing from some copies of *Acteon and Diana*, the *Simple* addition can be found in, for example, BL 644.b.14. Nicholas Wood of Harrietsham, Kent, known generally for his amazing gastronomic achievements, was celebrated more particularly by John Taylor in *The Great Eater of Kent* (1630).

Figure 18. Simpleton the Smith with his chunk of bread, from the frontispiece of Kirkman, *The Wits* (1673). (By permission of the Bodleian Library.)

day that received full-length treatment. Whatever of the farcical pertains to it probably lies less in what one might call the work's sense of itself than in our sense of it, and especially in our reaction to its extreme compression and oversimplification. Whoever the author of this droll may have been, and whether he really wrote for puppet, not human, players (one meaning of *droll* is puppet play), it is improbable that he wrote "*to provoke a laughter.*"

The term *droll*, besides referring to mini-tragedies, durable old jigs, resurrected scenes from old plays, mythological scenes, and new comic skits, embraces also some brief forays into scripture. Keeping matters relating to drolls complicated is no problem: it has even been suggested that the droll that Kirkman printed as *King Ahasuerus* was performed by puppets (Elson 406-7).

Stretching the boundaries of the form to its opposite limits, Kirkman also includes one droll, *Wiltshire Tom*, that has the distinction of having been designed originally as "An Entertainment at Court." It was, in fact, borrowed from a court masque of 1636 called *The Entertainment at Richmond.*

Mainly an excuse for some dancing and singing, *Wiltshire Tom* is of particular interest for its stage directions. "*As soon as the Queen had taken her place*," we read, "*a Gentleman-Usher standing at the entrance of the Scene . . . sayes thus*" (Elson 297); and "*The next thing that offer'd it self to the sight was a pleasant Countrey, for the most part Champain, from whence issued the Countrey Fellows, and first, Tom*" (Elson 298). Unlike most drolls, this one calls for a painted backdrop.

Perhaps most interesting of all, the second in the list of characters (Tom being first) is one Mr. Edward, described as "*a Courtier, standing near the Queene*" (Elson 298). Probably Mr. Edward was the young (b. 1622) second son of Edward Sackville, fourth Earl of Dorset, Lord Chamberlain to the Queen. At the close of the droll, Wiltshire Tom says, "when you have a mind to more of this, tell but Mr. *Yedward,* and we'l come at a whistle" (Elson 304). Unlike others of its kind, then, and indeed not unlike an antimasque, *Wiltshire Tom* is an occasional piece. Furthermore, it enables us to add the masque and the court to our range of sources for drolls.

For one last example, let us consider Thomas Jordan's *Cheaters Cheated* (1659)—which should not be confused with another similarly named droll that makes use of scenes from Marston's *Dutch Courtesan.* Jordan (who, as we shall see, proved to be a rather prolific writer) called this "A Representation in four parts to be Sung," a description that immediately calls to mind the old-time jig. Nowadays denied the jigging music, we still can read of the antics of Nim and Filcher, two London cheats who pick the pockets of Wat, a West-countryman ("This vamous zitty of *Lungeon* / Is worth all *Zomerset-zhere*" [36]), and of Moll Medlar, a woman of no particular good fame who wishes to dispose of a basket that proves to have a baby in it ("Farewell *Bloomsberry,*" she says, "and *Sodom*" [41]). Jordan designed this lively business "*for the Sheriffs of* London" (title page) and closed it with Wat's singing of a merry song about the twelve companies of London: "The *Cloth-workers* trade is a very vine thing, / And of all the Trades may be counted the King" (55). Perfectly irrelevant to the skit that preceded it, the song was, of course, relevant to its original audience and occasion. In fact, the likelihood that some such entertainment might be expected on other similar occasions is suggested by Wat's promise "chil come here agen next Winter" (55). Here is yet a further expansion of our notion of the range of audiences for whom drolls might be appropriate. Moreover, by a circuitous route we have returned once again to the London companies and the subject of civic entertainments.

For the most part, the clandestine drolls and the civic shows are contrasting kinds, alike mainly in being continuing manifestations of the impulse to performance at a time when the theaters were all supposed to be closed. As for differences, the major excuse for a civic show was its implicitly topical nature, whereas the more portable and innocuously irrelevant a droll might be ("Pretty harmless Drolls," Thomas Shadwell has a character in *The Miser* call them [III.iv]), the less likely it was to offend.

This last point is worth pursuing. John Elson concludes that "No contemporary political allusions occur in the drolls; no interpolations are made to satirize contemporary happenings, and very few excisions can be detected of passages which might be thought to touch on dangerous current issues. The drolls were designed to entertain, not to propagandize" (22). One might demur that sometimes there is eloquence in laughter. To the extent that Elson is right, however, the drolls constitute an exception that highlights and tests the main thesis of this study. As examples of excision he notes that the Falstaffian *Bouncing Knight* either expurgates or modifies Shakespeare's "Lord," "Zounds," "Sblood," and "God," and also drops all references to civil war and rebellion (370). And Horatio, in a droll called *The Grave-Makers*, is made to address Hamlet not as "My Lord" but as "Sir" (376).

On the other hand, and recalling Ben Jonson's words on the importance of endings, perhaps one should note also that this same droll ends with the words

> Imperial *Caesar* dead, and turn'd to clay,
> Might stop a hole to keep the wind away;
> Oh that that Earth which kept the World in awe,
> Should patch a Wall t'expell the Water Flaw.
>
> [118]

One might note further that a droll called *The Loyal Citizens* (from Beaumont and Fletcher's *Cupid's Revenge* IV.i) concerns some loyal royalists who rise to rescue their prince. A droll that is interestingly titled *The Lame Common-Wealth* (from Fletcher and Massinger's *The Beggars' Bush* II.i) begins with the question of who is to be the king of the beggars: "*Higgen* your *Orator*, in this *inter-Regnum*, ... doth beseech you all to stand faire," and Prig announces himself as "A very Tyrant, I, an arrant Tyrant" (78, 79). The terms *inter-Regnum* and *Tyrant* are both arresting. Most thought-provoking of all, however, is the cast of mind that may have led to the choice of Beaumont and Fletcher's *Philaster*, act V, scene iv, for a droll called *The Club-Men*. In it, according to the "argument," "*An old Humourous Captain animates the rout to Rebellion on the behalf of Philaster*" (146), the dispossessed prince. "Come my brave mirmidons, lets fall on," he shouts. Soon the overreaching intruder Pharamond is reduced to begging, "O spare me Gentlemen" (147), and at the close all shout, "Long may'st thou live brave Prince, brave Prince, brave Prince" (149).

Brave prince, indeed! Granted that the surviving droll texts are few and that no printed words can give us a full sense of the improvisatory dimension of the form, and that players and writers alike had long demonstrated a recurring tendency—perhaps even a come-what-may need—to comment on the world in which they found themselves, one reasonably may suspect that at least some of the drolls, like all civic shows, were tinged with topicality and therefore capable of occasioning some timely contemplation.[11]

---

[11]For a corollary phenomenon beginning in 1655–56, one may consider the word *drollery* as it refers to "an anthology of miscellaneous verse . . . compiled by the Cavaliers for the sake of registering protest against the Puritans in a jocose, mocking, and often frankly sensual fashion" (Courtney Craig Smith 42). With some of their material garnered from earlier poets (as the drolls were sometimes borrowed from earlier dramatists), the drolleries were distinguished by "their quality of protest: they were compiled by and for Cavaliers as a weapon against their social and political foes" (45).

[9]

MUNGRELL MASQUES AND THEIR KIN

Inigo Iones cannot conveniently make such Heavens and Paradises
at *Oxford* as he did at *White-hall;* & . . . the Poets are dead, beggered,
or run away, who were wont in their Masks to make Gods and
Goddesses. . . .
          —George Wither, *Mercurius Rusticus* (1643)

All musique's turn'd to croaking froggs. . . .
          —Mildmay Fane, *De Pugna Animi* (1650)

. . . do not all wise men know, that a Morall Masque is profitable to
see?
          —Samuel Sheppard, *The Famers Fam'd* (1646)

If *Musick, Dancing, Poetry*, and *Painting*,
(Free from scurrility, or obscene Ranting)
May please your Apprehensions, we'l not feare. . . .
          —Thomas Jordan, *Fancy's Festivals* (1657)

PRODUCING A DEFINITION of *masque* that is both inclusive and accurate
constitutes a problem that has proved well-nigh unsolvable for students of
Renaissance English drama. A subject sufficiently complex for the years
before 1642, moreover, leads on to yet greater complexity during the time
of the Civil Wars, Commonwealth, and Protectorate—a period when some
think the form ceased to exist. One might therefore be tempted to retreat
to the broad suggestiveness of Shakespeare's collocation of "revels, dances,
masks, and merry hours" (*Love's Labor's Lost* IV.iii.376) or to Jonson's
seriocomic reductionism in *A Tale of a Tub*, where Pan asks, "A Masque,
what's that?" and Scriben replies, "A mumming, or a shew. / With vizards,
and fine clothes." Clench adds simply, "A disguise, neighbour" (V.ii.29-
30).

    At its fullest development a masque was made up of five parts: a poetic
induction, antimasque (or antimasques), main masque, revels, and epi-
logue. In other words, the main masque was preceded and followed by
framing elements. The main masque itself, which was both the jewel in
the crown and the core of the form, was the appearance of a group of
disguised persons who came to dance, and the purpose of the written text,
whatever else it achieved, was to explain their presence. At court, before
the appearance of the masked dancers, an antimasque (later, more than
one) served as a sort of appetizer and became increasingly popular because

of the contrasting (often comedic) qualities that it (or they) could contribute. It might be helpful to think of the antimasque as embodying what we may now call a "droll" element. When at last the main masquers appeared in their finery, they first performed their special, rehearsed dancing. Then they took out members of the audience to dance the so-called revels, at which point there was an explicit and notable merging of the idealized fictional world of the masque (a realm of heroes and heroines, gods and goddesses) with the actual world of the English court—which in turn certainly had its own provocatively fictional dimensions. The epilogue rounded out the whole.[1]

Jonson, the chief shaper of the masque, insisted that no matter how dazzling the silks, jewels, and torchlight, and no matter how elaborate the stage machines, the spoken "*voyce*" of a masque should refer to the immediate occasion for which it was made, and its "*sense* . . . should always lay hold on more remou'd *mysteries*" (*Hymenaei*, ll. 18-19). That is, Jonson held that a masque should be celebratory in a more or less immediate way, in keeping with its nature as an occasional piece, and it also should point beyond the particulars of the moment. The provocative nature of the pointing, one might add, owed far more to the parabolic aspect of the masque than to any Socratic invitation to thought. At bottom the education that a masque provided was mainly inculcatory.[2] In this regard it was not unlike the civic shows discussed in chapter 8. To be sure, the juxtaposing of antimasque with masque, and of main dance with revels, was capable of suggesting educational opportunities of a dialogic kind, but these generally remained merely suggestive—for the simple reason that the court and its writers (again like the writers of civic shows) typically had their authorized answers at hand. Though some interesting exceptions to the rule can be identified, the fact is that assertion, not dialogue, was most characteristic of the masque.

In the 1630s, as Charles maneuvered his course without a parliament, the cavalier Thomas Carew observed that "Tourneyes, Masques, Theaters . . . become / Our Halcyon dayes" ("In Answer of an Elegiacall Letter," ll. 95-96). This statement was the more true insofar as the court had itself become a sort of theater. In a masque significantly titled *Tempe Restored*, Aurelian Townshend seems intentionally to have blended the images of Charles as king and Charles as masquing ideal. "In Heiroicke vertue," he writes, "vertue is figured in the King['s] Majestie, who therein transcends

---

[1]Studies of the masque have proliferated in recent years, but Stephen Orgel's *Jonsonian Masque* (1967) still provides the best overview. One of the best shorter studies is the article by Dolora Cunningham (1955).   [2]As Lindley observes, a masque presented to the King might well have a "hortatory dimension" (3). Hence it makes sense to speak of "hortatory inculcation."

as farre common men as they are above Beasts, he truly being the prototipe to all the Kingdomes under his Monarchie, of Religion, Justice, and all the *Vertues* joyned together" (104). Stephen Orgel has pointed out that such writing presents "the triumph of an aristocratic community; at its center is a belief in the hierarchy and a faith in the power of idealization" (*Illusion* 40). It is not necessary to deny the strong infusion of flattery in the masque, one might add, in order to agree with Orgel's resounding conclusion: "The full force of Caroline idealism, the determination to purify, reorder, reform, reconceive a whole culture, is here fully realized in apparitions and marvelous machinery" (87). Nor need we deny all traces of a tendency in the masques toward cultivated escapism. Masque-viewing, after all, was limited to relatively few. On the other hand—and it is proof positive that we are dealing with no simple issue here—their potency as images of power was, on the eve of the midcentury wars, significantly qualified by disturbing internal elements such as north winds, parasitical courtiers, and even rebellious military leaders (these last two from William Davenant's *Britannia Triumphans*).

A broad view enables us to see also that masquing was not restricted to Whitehall. Part of the story of the masque includes the creation and performance of works like Thomas Salusbury's *Masque . . . at Knowsley* and *A Show or Antimasque of Gipseys*, Mildmay Fane's *Raguaillo D'Oceano*, and Aston Cokayne's *Masque Presented at Bretbie*. Such examples suggest that the term *masque* was broader and more flexible at midcentury than some students in our own time have acknowledged. People who were actually creating and writing about what they called masques used the term to embrace a fairly broad spectrum of shows calling for the combined use of costume, dancing, and verse. In fact, after the great court masques vanished, these other masques and masquelike shows came on all the stronger.[3]

One of the most notable practitioners of the form proved to be James Shirley. At the time the theaters closed, Shirley, chief dramatist for the King's Men, was one of the two most skillful dramatic writers in England. Nowadays perceived not only as a critic of Laud in *The Cardinal* but also as a writer who dared to offer advice to Charles himself in the stupendous Inns of Court masque called *The Triumph of Peace* (1634), Shirley was nonetheless a committed royalist who followed his patron, William Cavendish, into battle. Cavendish himself, however, suddenly went into exile in July 1644, and Shirley turned—or, rather, turned back—to teaching. As partial evi-

[3]The discussion that follows is devoted to some of the same works that Lindley has in mind when he writes that the term *masque* "in the later seventeenth century . . . is applied very randomly to entertainments whose connection with the earlier genre is at the level of theatrical ingenuity and splendor, of an operatic musical style . . . , and of the employment of classical myth (though usually in a far more decorative and enhumanised form)" (7).

dence, one might consider his *Rudiments of Grammar: The Rules Composed in English Verse for the Greater Benefit and Delight of Young Beginners* (1656). Probably Shirley was ahead of his time for bothering to factor delight into the educational equation. At any rate, it must have been partly for the pleasure of his schoolboys that he wrote *The Triumph of Beautie* in 1646.

Though the title of this piece parallels that of Shirley's spectacular Inns of Court masque in the previous decade, and though this later work also calls for fancy costumes, songs, and dancing, *The Triumph of Beautie* is far smaller in scale. Moreover, it celebrates no discernible occasion, honors no particular person, does not integrate audience and players, and at the level of plot clearly relates its single antimasque to the main show that follows.

The work opens with a drollworthy clutch of shepherds (Crab, Clout, Toad-Stoole, and so on), the name of whose leader, Bottle, invites us to think of Shakespeare's Bottom, especially when the men decide to put on a play for Prince Paris and Bottle argues that in their *Tragedie of the Golden Fleece* he will portray the fleece, "as I am the best Actor, and Master of the Company" (8). Paris then enters, briefly interacts with the bumpkins, and falls asleep. When Mercury descends with a golden ball, the country folk flee, and the rest of the masque is devoted to the awakened Paris's famous problem of deciding whether to present the ball to Juno, Pallas, or Venus—each of whom appears to plead her case. Slighter by far than Peele's staging of the old myth in *The Arraignment of Paris* (which relied on the presence of Queen Elizabeth for its resolution), Shirley's *Triumph of Beautie* has the virtues of grace, simplicity, and clarity, together with an appealing juxtaposition of antimasque and masque.

Equally neat but more ambitious is his *Cupid and Death* (1653 and 1659). Based on one of Aesop's fables and originally intended as a private entertainment, this work was later chosen for presentation on 26 March 1653 before the Ambassador from Portugal, Don João Rodrigues de Sá e Menezes, Conde de Penaguião.[4] In 1659 the work was presented yet again "att the Millitary Ground," a house near the present Leicester Square that was used by the Military Company (Bentley, *Jacobean and Caroline Stage* 5:1104). Both the 1653 and the 1659 productions called for three different settings that (at least in the performance for the Ambassador) "wanted no elegance, or curiosity" (A2r). They also required machinery enabling Cupid to fly and Mercury to descend on a cloud; they offered various kinds of music that "had in them a great soul of Harmony" (A2v); and, instead of

---

[4]The story of the successful peace treaty negotiated during this period between Cromwell and John IV of Portugal took a tragic turn with the execution at Tyburn of the Ambassador's brother (see Prestage).

Figure 19. The traditional back-
ground of Shirley's *Cupid and
Death* (1653) as illustrated in
Ogilby's *Fables of Aesop* (2d
ed., 1668). (By permission of
the Folger Shakespeare
Library.)

an antimasque, they wove antimasque elements into a plot that led eventually
to a scene in Elizium "*where the grand Masquers*" appeared "*in glorious Seats,
and Habits*" (D3r). Because both Shirley's text and the complete 1659 score
composed by Matthew Locke and Christopher Gibbons still exist in
Locke's own hand, Dennis Arundell has been moved to write of *Cupid and
Death* as "the one surviving example of a late Commonwealth near-opera"
and to observe that "to the musical historians of opera it is of immense
value" (71-72).[5]

The basic conceit of the work concerns a visit of Cupid and Death to
an inn. Upon their departure, each mistakenly takes the other's arrows.
(An illustration in Ogilby's *Fables of Aesop* suggests some of the incongrui-
ties that ensue; see figure 19.[6]) Somewhat bolder than *The Triumph of
Beautie* in its incidental allusions, the masque has jibes for those tippling
gentry who scatter coins and "rore, and fancie / The Drawers, and the
Fiddles, till their pockets / Are empty" (B1v). Ill models, indeed, for youth!
"Pickel'd" at last, these roaring boys shed their clothes in the morning
streets. Shirley's partial glimpse here of the cavalier world ends with an

---

5 Another indication that the historical importance of *Cupid and Death* has been recognized in
our own time is its selection in 1984 for presentation at London's Queen Elizabeth Hall under
the direction of Anthony Rooley. Shirley's text and the 1659 score are available at the British
Library (Add. MS 17799).   6The Shirley-Ogilby connection suggested here is grounded not
only on appropriateness of subject but also on Shirley's prior work with Ogilby in Ireland. In
fact, Bentley points out that two years before Shirley wrote *Cupid and Death*, he had written
commendatory verses for Ogilby's translation of Aesop (*Jacobean and Caroline Stage* 5:1103).

ambiguous statement: "But all their dancing dayes are done, I fear" (B1v). There is notice also that the devil is not engaged these days in "low employments" such as overseeing suicides because "Hee's busie 'bout Leviathans" (B3v). This comment serves well enough for a general reference to monstrous problems, but it can hardly have been written or spoken in 1653 or 1659 without remembrance of Thomas Hobbes's politically volatile *Leviathan* of 1651.

Mainly, however, the masque is concerned with the switched weapons of Love and Death. Death shoots arrows that cause old folks with crutches to dance and a leader of apes to fall in love with his charges, and at length the lovers whom Cupid has slain prove to be none other than the happy main masquers, now residents of Elizium. All in all, Shirley's own shafts fly to no great height here, but he has turned out another interesting variety of masque, one that must have been pleasant, lively, and genuinely entertaining. Beyond that, and despite Shirley's basically royalist sympathies, the masque's bits of criticism of the unbuttoned gentry were doubtless acceptable to those for whom the show was performed.

Much the same can be said for *The Contention of Ajax and Ulysses*, another work that Shirley evidently wrote for performance by his pupils ("young Gentlemen of quality," according to the title page). Working again with universally known classical materials (Ovid, *Metamorphoses*, bk. 13), he depicts an Ajax whose "big heart seems to boil with rage" (101) and a Ulysses who is calm and well-spoken. Each is attended by a diminutive page who contributes to the show's comic strain by chirping up for his master. As the two heroes contend for the armor of dead Achilles according to ground rules laid down by Agamemnon, Ajax brags, "The honour of my birth and blood must lift me" (104). Eventually, though, Agamemnon proclaims that "Wisdom, not down-right Valour wins the day" (118). Calchas the prophet, nevertheless, reassures Ajax that "what you lost alive by humane Judges, / Their divine Justice shall restore with honour / To your calm dust" (125). Then Shirley's most famous song (the same one noted in chapter 5) brings the little entertainment to a close in a way that masterfully reprises the themes of both *The Contention* itself and the times: "*The glories of our blood and state, / are shadows, not substantial things*"; powerful men "*tame but one another still*"; "*Then boast no more your mighty deeds*"; and, last of all, "*Onely the actions of the just / Smell sweet, and blossom in their dust.*" Sung first by Calchas, then in parts to music "*excellently composed*" by Edward Coleman, this closing song of *The Contention*—with its text by one who himself had served Mars—must have provided one of the finer moments in the dramatic presentations of the day (see figure 8).

Although literary historians of the seventeenth century tend to hasten onward as quickly as possible to the work of William Davenant—who, indeed, played a major role—the fact is that some masquelike shows by two other interesting writers preceded Davenant's famed achievements of 1656. In 1654, the year after Shirley's *Cupid and Death*, the prolific Richard Flecknoe also turned to the ancients for the subject of his *Ariadne Deserted by Theseus, and Found and Courted by Bacchus*, whose title conveys the action. The next words on the title page are also significant, for they not only suggest Flecknoe's attempt to sidestep the forbidden realm of plays but also anticipate the kinds of evasion that soon would appear on Davenant's title pages. Flecknoe calls his work "A Dramatick Piece Apted for Recitative Musick." He explains in the preface, "Tis many years since I proposed unto a Soveraign Prince" certain ideas about an elevated music in which sound and subject are "all of one piece" (A3r). Some time later, while traveling in Italy, he continues, "I found that Musick I intended to introduce, exceedingly in vogue, and far advanced towards its perfection. . . . I mean Recitative Musick, being a compound of Musick and Poetry together, affecting the mind and sense with redoubled delight, since if a thing but barely pronounced has such force to move the Soul, how much more forcible must it be, when the Harmony of Musick is added to the pronuntiation?" (A3v-A4r). In his dedication to Mary, Duchess of Richmond and Lennox (Flecknoe was ever a cultivator of titled ladies), he comments on the suitability of various languages to the music he attempts to describe, notes the general difficulty of singing in English, and concludes that in English recitative "the words . . . are to be made as facile as may be, the better to be understood" (A6v). This is the same man who argues elsewhere that one of the prime virtues of the now-silenced English stage was its "perfectioning of our Language," and specifically its function as a "*Mint* that daily coyns new *words*" (*Miscellania* 103-4). Flecknoe's interest in the kind of words best suited to "Recitative Musick" was not without precedent in England. So far as can now be determined, the first English use of the Italian phrase and art of *stilo recitativo* dates back to Jonson's and Nicholas Lanier's masque called *The Vision of Delight* (1617). Perhaps after being introduced, the style faded from sight for a while.

Less notable than Flecknoe's attempts to theorize, in any case, are the actual results of his pursuit of the "facile," with its rhetoric of "short periods and frequent rithmes" (A7r). Ariadne begins,

> Ay me! and is he gon!
> And I left here alone!
> Ah *Theseus* stay—
> But see he sails away,
> And never minds my moan—

Yet sure he do's not fly me,
But only dos't to try me. . . .

[B1r]

It is probably such lines that underlie Langbaine's jibe that Flecknoe "was as Famous as any in his Age, for indifferent Metre" (*Account* 199). Some might argue, in fact, that Flecknoe came near to deserving those celebrated poetic put-downs wherein Marvell presented him as "Fleckno, an English Priest at Rome," and Dryden transformed him to "Mac Flecknoe." On the other hand, to give him his due, Flecknoe presumably kept his lyrics simple because he recognized the difficulty that listeners have in understanding words that are sung. Furthermore, Flecknoe even set himself the task of composing the music for his text. Some legitimate doubt has been expressed as to whether he ever actually wrote the music (Edmond 129), but one can build no iron-clad case for such doubt on the fact that no such music has survived.

More interesting for its text, if not its theory, is Flecknoe's *Mariage of Oceanus and Brittania* (1659), which he terms on the title page an "Allegorical Fiction" designed "*To be Represented in Musick, Dance, and proper Scenes.*" This work, too, is said to have been "Invented, Written, and Composed" by Flecknoe, but its most notable feature may be Flecknoe's choice of subject—England's sea power. After the opening "*Symphony,*" the setting is shown to be "*the Maritime coast of Albion or England, by its white cliffs encompassed with Seas*" (B1r). Oceanus himself is described in masquelike terms: he wears a mantle of sea green and silver, carries a trident, and rides in a scallop-shell chariot drawn by sea horses. Brittania holds a cornucopia, is seated upon a throne, and also wears a green mantle, but hers is supposed to be richly embroidered with cities and towns (as on the famous title page of Drayton's *Poly-Olbion* [1612]). Though indeed she is allowed to remark on "the unhappinesse of civil wars" (14), it is now other nations, not Britain, that are thus afflicted, and she exclaims, "How happy am I of all other Lands" (15). England had not long since defeated two Spanish treasure fleets, providing a motive for praising Brittania as "The richest Ile of all the world" (29). In foreign affairs the British fleet had indeed become England's chief tool, enabling it not only to safeguard commerce but also to enforce recognition from otherwise recalcitrant foreign powers. Besides keeping the Dutch in check, the navy was making significant progress in the Mediterranean, the Baltic, and the New World. Roy Strong points out that all the British monarchs from the time of Elizabeth had been "celebrated as sovereigns of the seas" (161), yet clearly such sovereignty had never been greater than under Cromwell. In a panegyric on the Lord Protector, Flecknoe elsewhere exulted that the English were "absolute and sole masters of the Sea, and every where soveraign Arbiters of peace and war" (*Idea of His Highness Oliver* 40-41).[7]

Flecknoe's earlier goal of creating a unity of parts is set aside in this show so as to include some tumbling and rope-dancing (the latter executed by Castor and Pollux in Grecian military garb [*Mariage* 21]), skills that English audiences had helped to keep alive throughout the time of their troubles. Providing yet another sort of contrast in the last of the work's five contrasting parts, a ragtag rabble comes in *"hoarsly and ridiculously singing . . . to the tune of* Packingtons pound" (39).[8] After this antimasquelike faction "vanishes," some gallantly clad dancers "representing the Nobility and Gentry, . . . dance to a Courtly measure" before Brittania and her suitor, who are referred to—in 1659—as a *"Royall pair"* (43). Then, be it noted, *"Two in civil black Representing the Burgesse & Citizen"* dance a galliard. And then two *"Country swains"* dance a jig. The successive dances here by representatives of four different social levels are certainly noteworthy. Even more so is the implied message of unity and harmony when all—all but the ridiculous rabble—join together in the main and final dance. Group dancing, in which every participant is a part of the pattern, is an unmistakable image here of civilized social cooperation. Though exclusion of the rabble would doubtless exercise some of our own contemporaries, we may safely suppose that the overall effect was supposed to be inclusive and ameliorative. The fact is, however, that while many of the English in 1659 might indeed join in being proud of their country's successes at sea, whether or not the rabble was left out, by no means all were dancing in universal harmony. Everything considered, then, Flecknoe's *Mariage of Oceanus and Brittania* comes across as a chauvinistic, panegyrical, allegorical, idealistic, musical, varied, and—according to the lights of its time—politically correct show.

In the 1650s we also reencounter Thomas Jordan, a sometime actor, a busy dramatic writer (we have previously glimpsed his *Cheaters Cheated*), and generally "a man of no small impudence" (Bentley, *Jacobean and Caroline Stage* 2:487). When it comes to masquing, Jordan mined veins similar to those of Shirley and Flecknoe. The title page of *Cupid His Coronation in a Mask* reports that this entertainment was performed with "good Approbation at the Spittle diverse tymes by Masters and yong Ladyes y[t] were theyre scholers in the yeare 1654."[9] The masque opens with

---

[7]Waller sang much the same tune in his 1655 "Panegyric to My Lord Protector": "The sea's our own; and now all nations greet, / With bending sails, each vessel of our fleet; / Your power extends as far as winds can blow, / Or swelling sails upon the globe may go" (2:10). [8]Originating about 1560, "Packington's Pound" was, according to Claude M. Simpson, "the most popular single tune associated with ballads before 1700" (564). [9]The Spittle in question was probably Christ's Hospital near St. Paul's. Lindgren points out that "It was a foundling hospital and school with separate facilities for both boys and girls" (122).

assurances from a young priest of Apollo that no wronging of religion, government, or modesty will ensue. The year 1654 did, after all, bring fresh governmental efforts to discover "Enemies of the Peace" (Cromwell, *By the Lord Protector*), but this was a harmless, private show. Surely it would do no harm to crown Cupid? Performed with a curtain that rose and scenery that could be opened and closed to display new scenes, as well as with singing, dancing, and "symphonies," Jordan's *Cupid His Coronation in a Mask* includes an antimasque of seven neighboring "nations" whose squabbling is ended by Cupid. It then closes with a "Grand Maske" of twelve young virgins who first dance, then kneel, at Cupid's throne—the only speaker in the masque having been that "yong Priest of Apollo" (108r).

More ambitious is Jordan's *Fancy's Festivals* (1657), a masque performed privately "by many civil persons of quality" (title page). The original length of this work may only be guessed, however, for when it was published Jordan took the liberty of adding "many . . . delightful new Songs, for the further illustration of every Scene." He also was moved to embark on some theorizing, apparently to justify what he had created. "I have strayed from the regular road of Masks," he explained to his dedicatee, Francis Lenthall, Jr., "as they were formerly presented on publike Theaters, not aiming so much at concatination, as variation" (A2v). He continues: "I have in these concise Discourses, rather chosen to make my persons speak properly then highly, since (according to the rules of *Horace*) aptitude is more commendable then altitude" (A2v). Jordan's goal in this show, with its five acts, prologue, and epilogue, is to be "compendious, pertinent and clear" (A3r). Just as in *Cupid His Coronation*, he again assures any Politic Picklocks that nothing that follows will wrong religion, government, or modesty, and he says that anyone who "Shall Comment ill on what this hour discloses, / May extract venome from the veyns of Roses" (A3r).

This little apologia, however, proves somewhat disingenuous. For his first speaker, Jordan brings on Poetry (a gowned young man with a wreath of bays), who expresses surprise that Verity (a white-robed virgin with a chaplet of lilies) is to be found on earth—"and in this City too" (A4v). Soon Poetry is fingering the swelling belly of a pregnant woman named Fancy (who wears a parti-colored robe and a garland of flowers). The rather Hobbesian role that Jordan assigns Fancy is especially clear when, rising from a chair, she drops ribbons, balls, baubles, masks, and dancing shoes—as well as some papers with the "plot" of the masque that is to follow. The rest of act I is then devoted to a scene called forth by Verity: Cupid on his throne and seven dancing "nations." In short, Jordan has recycled a section of *Cupid His Coronation* into this later and bigger show.

The second "act"—which term here designates separate successive actions, not, as in drama, parts of a unified whole—brings on a debate between Power (a soldier) and Policy (a scholar). Dancing on Policy's side are a statesman, lawyer, divine, and physician, and, on Power's, four military commanders dressed in buff. As we have seen in chapter 5, Jordan eventually situates the soldiers in "the *supream places*," the "*Gown-men below*" (B4r). This unmistakably parabolic action is followed in act III by a lively divertimento between Mrs. Friendly, a woman of pleasure, and Mr. Frolick, a man willing to please her, along with various tavern folk. Then in great contrast act IV presents the King of Darkness and the Queen of Night dancing to the music of the spheres. Before they begin, however, a figure called Watch observes, "Where I am wanting all things must miscarry, / That are Divine, Moral, or Military" (D1r). Watch then turns to his companion, Sleep, and asks pointedly, "where wert thou, / When fruitful *Albians* Alabaster brow, / In the warm blood of Civil War was dyed?" (D1r-v). Sleep replies with singular clarity: "I was amongst them too on the Kings side"; he even says, "Sleep is . . . / The Freemans fetters" (D1v).

In act V, Poetry is brought back again and lays plans for the show's concluding grand masque of nine heroes who have died for their country. At least in the published version of 1657, Jordan goes so far as to suggest that these heroes, "lately stellified for merits" (how specifically, one wonders, were these men represented onstage?), are to be brought back for a while from Elysium

> Where pious Priests and Princes reassume
> The heads and Crowns they lost in Martyrdom,
> Where Poetry is mounted above chance,
> And the poor power of Pride and Ignorance. . . .
>
> [D3v]

The political case could hardly be stated more plainly. If we have had previous doubts, we now see the royalist stance of both Jordan and his audience. We also see how far one might venture in print in Cromwell's final years.

Equally explicit but less extended are some lines that were first spoken in French by English royalty, then translated to English in James Howell's *Nuptialls of Peleus and Thetis* (1654).[10] Princess Henrietta Anne, who had

---

[10]Howell's title continues: *Consisting of a Mask and a Comedy; or, The Great Royal Ball, Acted Lately in Paris Six Times.* Inside, following the mask, another title page reads: *The Nuptialls of Peleus and Thetis. A New Italian Comedy, Whence the Preceding Mask Was Extracted; Made English by a Nearer Adherence to the Original, Then to the French.* Though the "original" appears to be unknown, it has been conjectured to be *Le nozze di Peleo e di Theti* by Francesco Buti, or perhaps the *Tetide* of Diamante Gabrielli. The 1654 English incarnation of the "comedy" proves to be a short, masquelike play in verse. It shows how the courtship of the titular lovers is retarded when Thetis transforms herself into a lion, then a monster, then a rock—before yielding at last to Peleus. The finale displays, besides Peleus and Thetis, a choir consisting of various deities, Hercules, and Hymen, plus "*the Liberal and Servile Arts*" (D2v).

been born at Exeter in June 1644, only a couple of weeks before Henrietta Maria fled from England, was apparently considered old enough now to take the role of the muse Erato.[11] Certainly it was an Erato who came trailing clouds of the Princess who played her. After observing that her "stemm is more then of a mortall race," which is a sufficiently muselike claim, Henrietta presumably proceeded to explain that "to *great* Henries *Grandchild* all give place" (2), thus attributing her supramortal heritage to Henri IV. In a genuinely masquelike way, Henrietta was both Erato and herself. As for the English side of the family, she was to say:

> . . . he who loudly would complain
> of *Princes* falls and *Peoples* raign,
> Of angry starrs, and destiny,
> Let him but cast his eyes on me.

Quite explicitly, little Erato was meant to elicit "both pitty and respect" from her audience (2).

The English version of the entertainment that is cited here was available for purchase at the New Exchange in 1654. Working from a text that must have been in French, despite its Italian origins, the versatile Welsh translator—nowadays known best as a letter-writer—apparently took on his high-society task with relish. He informs his dedicatee, Katherine, Marchioness of Dorchester, that in Paris the show was performed with a cast of over a hundred "Representators" (A1v), including the King of France (as the sun god, Apollo), and that it cost an astounding half million "French liures." Basically, however, this extravaganza tells the simple story of how Peleus, King of Thessaly, aided by Prometheus, wins the Nereid Thetis.

Thetis was to appear, Venus-like, on a great shell, encompassed by a troop of twelve coral fishermen—and one of the latter was played by none other than young James, Duke of York, who expressed the following sentiments:

> T'is not for me to fish for Corrall here,
> I to another Coast my course must steer,
> A fatall ground
> Which Seas surround.
> There I must fish upon an angry Main,
> More then two Crowns and Scepters to regain.
>
> [8]

---

[11]One might add that Erato was traditionally the muse of mimic imitation and sometimes equipped with a lyre, but it would be pointless to muse long on the fact that Erato was also associated particularly with erotic poetry.

Figure 20. Sir William Davenant (1606-68). The famous disfigurement of Davenant's nose was caused by syphilis. (By permission of the British Museum.)

Though the thought is artfully constrained and Howell's language is controlled, we can hardly expect to find a more thorough merging of art and life. And this in a masque published in London just a few months after Cromwell was appointed Lord Protector.

Clearly Sir William Davenant's shows in the later 1650s were not without interesting predecessors and successors. It is also true, however, that Davenant was moving away from both courtly masques *and* masques such as we have been considering. Himself the author of England's last great court masque, *Salmacida Spolia* (1640), which had indeed dared to speak of strife, this sometime servant of the Queen and long-time poet laureate had served in the Bishops' Wars (1639, 1640) and subsequentl involved himself in the Army Plot (1641), joined the staff of William Cavendish as Lieutenant General of the Ordnance (1642-43), been knighted at the siege of Gloucester (1643), engaged in royalist gun-running (1644-45), been sentenced to death (1650), and suffered imprisonment in the Tower (1651)—from which he was not released until August 1654, only about two years before the playing of his *First Day's Entertainment at Rutland-House*. To give Davenant his due, this enterprising prewar court dramatist (pictured in figure 20) had long before—in 1639—obtained a patent to construct a theater in Fleet Street (though it was never built) where not only plays but also "musicall entertaynments" could be produced.[12] Therefore, while the works that he presented in 1656, 1658, and 1659 were all shaped by their particular moments in time and designed to differ from pre-closure entertainments, they were also in some sense a realization of ideas that he had generated back in the 1630s.

For ten days beginning on 23 May 1656 Davenant put on the "Declamations and Musick" that he called *The First Day's Entertainment at Rutland-House*. Rutland House in Charterhouse Square had previously been the home of the Roman Catholic Countess Dowager of Rutland, Cicely Manners. After the Countess's death in 1654, however, the mansion was sequestered, and now it was Davenant's own private residence. Nevertheless, by charging admission to the public to attend his entertainment, Davenant was straining the law against public playing.

Not masquelike at all, the text of *The First Day's Entertainment* begins with a prologue apologizing for the cramped quarters that had to be endured by audience members and performers alike. Then come two dialogues that are both introduced and followed by music. The first pair of speakers, Diogenes the Cynic and Aristophanes the Poet, declaim on the subject of "Publique Entertainment." Diogenes voices a string of Prynnian objections, and Aristophanes, clearly dealt the upper hand, is provided with arguments in favor of public assemblies, music, dramatic poetry (of which none is in evidence here), and painted scenes for public "*Opera*"—all such things, in fact, as Davenant would utilize in a show later that very year. When Diogenes and Aristophanes have had their say, the second dialogue of the *Entertainment* presents a Parisian and a Londoner as chauvinistic disputants. Naturally Davenant, who in exile had lived in Paris, weights the argument in favor of London. The work then closes with an epilogue and more music.

Dry as it may look now, the *Entertainment* probably achieved a reasonable sense of liftoff thanks partly to the music provided for it by Henry Lawes, Charles Coleman (father of Edward), Henry Cook, and George Hudson (Dent xiv). In any case, *The First Day's Entertainment* proved to be a sort of ice-breaking, temperature-testing, dialectical precursor.

Davenant's next show, *The Siege of Rhodes* (1656), would prove to be one of the most important dramatic creations of the century. Though its kinship with the masque, broadly defined, is our main concern here, it is nowadays generally held to be both the first English opera and a forerunner of the Restoration heroic play.[13] It employed elaborate movable scenery and a proscenium arch for the first time on a public English stage, and it called

---

[12]One might note also that Hotson turned up a ballad from March 1656 suggesting that Davenant previously had hired Apothecaries' Hall, Blackfriars, for "*Masques / Made a la mode de* France" (142). [13]As Maguire observes, Dryden himself considered *The Siege of Rhodes* to be "the first light" of heroic plays in England (*Regicide* 95). Indeed, the overlapping of

for what is generally regarded as the first appearance of an actress on a public stage in England. Catherine Coleman, the wife of Edward Coleman, had advanced from being a singer in the chorus of Davenant's *First Day's Entertainment* to being the singer of an actual role. Aware as we are that Mrs. Coleman and another woman, now unknown, had sung at Rutland House previously, and that even this later, rather rarefied performance was "public" only in a somewhat limited sense, we should be careful not to exaggerate the contemporaneous visibility of what was happening. Furthermore, although the all-musical *Siege of Rhodes* belongs as much to the history of opera as to that of drama, we should observe also that the show was registered with the Stationers' Company on 27 August 1656 as a "maske"— albeit a masque with a difference.[14] The entry in the *Register* is for "a mask called *The siege of Rhodes made a representac[i]on by the art of prospective in scenes, and the story sung in recitative musicke*" (Briscoe 2:81).

Whatever one decides to call the show, its printed title page from later that year uses the label "Representation" (one recalls Howell's 1654 term *Representators*), adding that the show is to be conveyed "by the Art of Prospective in Scenes, And the Story sung in *Recitative* Musick"—rather as Flecknoe had assayed in his *Ariadne* (1654). The difference this time, and another reason that the work is held to be a landmark, is that the show was put on for a paying audience. Though still complaining about the size of his stage (eleven feet high and fifteen deep), Davenant was proud of the varied backdrops produced for him by John Webb, a protégé, nephew, and son-in-law of Inigo Jones (see figure 21). Nowadays recognized as England's first professional architect, Webb had already proved himself sufficiently skilled to win King Charles's commission in 1647-48 to design a new palace for Whitehall (Bold 3, 5). That, of course, was to remain a palace built only in the air.

The five composers of the music for *The Siege of Rhodes* included England's leading songwriter, Henry Lawes (who had previously written the music for Milton's *Comus*), Henry Cook and Matthew Locke (both of whom sang roles), Charles Coleman, and George Hudson. Besides Mrs. Coleman, the seven singers included her husband, Edward, who played the role of her husband, and, as the Turk Mustapha, Henry Purcell (apparently the father of the famed composer).

Davenant's proclaimed goal in *The Siege of Rhodes* was to present an

certain generic traits enables Maguire to hypothesize that "the rhymed heroic play, ideologically close to the pure form of the court masque, functioned socially and politically for the sixties as the court masque functioned for the thirties" (83).   [14]Viewed in a Continental context, Davenant's *Siege* may be seen to have had numerous kinds of Italian precursors. Nevertheless, writes Carter, "The history of opera may really begin as recently as 1637, when the Teatro San Cassiano in Venice first opened its doors to a paying public" (19).

Figure 21. Backdrop designed by John Webb for the open-
ing scene of Davenant's *Siege of Rhodes* (1656). (Devon-
shire Collection, Chatsworth. Reproduced by permission
of the Chatsworth Settlement Trustees.)

"Heroical" story that would "intelligibly" (that is, not too obscurely)
"advance the Characters of Vertue" (which presumably the plays before
1642 often failed to do) and would accomplish this by using "the shapes of
Valor and conjugal Love" (A3r-v). It was a midcentury treatment, then, of
the old love-and-war theme or, one also might say, the love-and-honor
theme that Davenant, among others, had explored in prewar days (most
notably in *Love and Honour* [1634]) and that would subsequently dominate
the heroic drama of the Restoration. Presented in five "entries" (presum-
ably *entries* was a safer term than *acts*), each staged behind a fixed prosce-
nium arch and marked by the raising and dropping of a curtain, *The Siege of
Rhodes* was set in 1522 in the far-off island of Rhodes. The Sicilian Duke
Alphonsus and his bride, Ianthe—played by the Colemans—are visiting in
Rhodes when it is attacked and besieged by the great Solyman (historically
Suleiman I) and his termagant Turks.[15] After she has sold her dower and
jewels to assist the Rhodians and her husband, Ianthe is captured by the

---

[15]Curtis Price, who is concerned with operatic as distinguished from dramatic history,
observes that Davenant's *Siege* "is a remarkably good drama" and "unlike nearly all contem-
porary Italian librettos in being based on a historical event" (39).

Turks. Thus Mustapha may bring her before Solyman—and it is of interest that the script required Mrs. Coleman to make her historic first entrance wearing a veil. In fact, Ianthe refuses to remove her veil throughout her entire first scene, creating an interesting effect of appearing and yet not appearing. Instead, she remains "the Morning pictur'd in a Cloud" (10) and in the process draws forth the stunned admiration of Solyman: "Thou great example of a Christian Wife" (12).

The chaste nature of this first role professionally acted by a woman—indeed, by a wife—is noteworthy. No Doll Tearsheet nor Lady Wild she. In fact, the terms *Christian* and *Wife* in Solyman's address are worth pondering. Davenant's basic pitting of crescent against cross enables him to direct the spectators' eyes somewhere above the dangerous problem of mid-seventeenth-century internecine Christian strife. At the same time, he takes the opportunity to tuck in more references to the (obviously Christian) English than one might have expected to hear in Rhodes: those Britons who come to aid the Rhodians are "cheerful *English*" who fight "merrily and fast" (8), the Turks themselves have praise for "Those desp'rate English" (31), and it is among the English that Ianthe, when wounded, finds succor. Although Davenant is fairly heavily indebted for his factual background to Richard Knolles's *Generall Historie of the Turkes*, clearly he claims a playwright's usual liberties throughout. Like readers and viewers of his own day, we are therefore left to consider the possibility of parallels between Ianthe and Henrietta Maria, both of whom were not only virtuous Christians but also virtuous wives who felt obliged to assume a martial role (Ianthe appears on the ramparts of Rhodes clad as a soldier) and both of whom sold their jewels to aid their husbands in war. Ann-Mari Hedbäck goes so far as to say that Henrietta Maria's "activities during the first years of the Civil War parallel strikingly those of Davenant's Ianthe" (li)—which observation might trigger our recollection that during the same period Davenant served for a time as the Queen's agent on the Continent. We also are left to weigh for ourselves an insistence in *The Siege* on the conjugal virtues of Ianthe and Alphonsus, virtues that to some observers had appeared extraordinary in Charles and Henrietta Maria. Edward Hyde in his autobiography wrote that the King and Queen "were the true Idea of conjugal Affection, in the Age in which they lived" (cited in Hedbäck lv).

To what extent can we use such perceptions in reading *The Siege of Rhodes*? Like beauty, paralogism is likely to be found anywhere, but it ultimately lies in the eye of the beholder. One should not underestimate the boldness of a man like Davenant (after all, he countenanced reports that he was a bastard son of Shakespeare), and yet in 1656, recently out of prison and seeking ways to make theatrics work in an antitheatrical environment, he is likely to have held himself and his allusions somewhat in check.

In 1659 he would bring forth a sequel to *The Siege of Rhodes*, and eventually he would revise the original to include Roxolana (Solyman's wife and empress) and various female attendants. Not until 1663 were parts 1 and 2 published together and dedicated to Edward Hyde. (Back in the 1620s Davenant and Hyde had lived together in the Middle Temple, but Davenant in Restoration times is likely to have weighed more heavily the fact that Hyde was now Earl of Clarendon and Lord High Chancellor of England.) Five years later still—more than a decade after part 1 had premiered—John Dryden had one of the discussants in his essay *Of Dramatick Poesie* go so far as to observe "that no serious Playes written since the Kings return have been more kindly receiv'd by them ['the mix'd audience of the populace and the Noblesse'] then the *Siege of Rhodes*" (73-74).

Meanwhile, in 1658 and 1659, Davenant had turned out two other shows. Like *The Siege of Rhodes*, both were "Exprest by Instrumentall and Vocall Musick, and by Art of Perspective in Scenes" (*Cruelty of the Spaniards*, title page). Perhaps reminding one of the old technique of busying English minds with foreign broils, Davenant in both works aims his fire at Spaniards. Not only were Spaniards traditional targets, but they were also in the news. As early as 1655 Cromwell had formulated a design to conquer Spanish possessions and trade in the Caribbean. Summer that year brought him Jamaica. Not until February 1656 did Spain declare war on England, but then in short order Philip IV proceeded to make the situation worse for himself by concluding a treaty with the exiled Prince Charles. In the Treaty of Brussels, signed on 2 April, Charles promised that England would return Jamaica to Spain and suspend English penal laws against Catholics; in return, a Spanish army and Spanish-subsidized forces under Charles were to invade Cromwell's England. For multiple reasons, then, one of the great events of the year was the English interception of the Spanish treasure fleet on its route to Cadiz on 9 September. At the opening of Parliament about a week later (17 September), Cromwell was more emphatic than eloquent: "Why, truly, your great enemy is the Spaniard. He is. He is a natural enemy, he is naturally so. . . . And truly when I say that he is naturally throughout an enemy, an enmity is put into him by God. . . . And he that considers not the providential and accidental enmity, I think he is not well acquainted with Scripture and things of God" (*Writings* 4:261-62). In April 1657, under the command of the great parliamentarian naval commander Robert Blake, the English demolished the Spanish fleet at Santa Cruz, occasioning Edward Hyde to write, "The whole action was . . . miraculous" (6:36). The Spaniards thought that devils must have destroyed them. And in June 1658 the English, together with the French, defeated a Spanish army at the Battle of the Dunes.

Without the impetus of such events Davenant hardly would have chosen to create either *The Cruelty of the Spaniards in Peru* or *The History of Sᵣ Francis Drake*. As for a literary source, *The Cruelty* is likely to have been sparked by John Phillips's similarly motivated 1656 translation, dedicated to Cromwell and called *The Tears of the Indians*, from Bartolomé de las Casas. Phillips's agenda of readjustment certainly was clear: "*O men of* England, . . . *you are not now to fight against your Country-men, but against your Old and Constant Enemies*" (b3r, b3v-b4r).[16]

Davenant wanted to demonstrate not only the cruelty of England's old and more or less constant enemy but also, conversely, the glories of being English, however divided the English actually may have been. Probably even more he wanted to be allowed to put on another show, this time not within the walls of his own house but at a bona fide theater, the Cockpit in Drury Lane. In any case, as a setting for his anti-Spanish propaganda, *The Cruelty of the Spaniards in Peru* offers eye-catchingly exotic backdrops, the first entry calling for "*Coco-trees, Pines* and *Palmitos*" and a priest of the sun in a robe of feathers (2). The fifth entry calls for various "Engines of torment," with one Spaniard "turning a Spit" while another is "basting an *Indian* Prince, which is rosted at an artificiall fire" (19; see figure 22). Perhaps most extraordinarily of all, however, to those who, then or now, expect some "concatination" in a show, Davenant calls for various intervals wherein acrobats perform "the Trick of Activity, call'd the *Sea-Horse*" (8), the "*Porpoise*" (21), and the "*double Somerset*" (25), and wherein two apes are brought on to display their rope-dancing skills (6).[17]

When it comes to historical accuracy, Davenant is moved to confess, "These imaginary *English* Forces may seem improper, because the *English* had made no discovery of *Peru*, in the time of the *Spaniards* first invasion there; but yet in Poeticall Representations of this nature, it may pass as a Vision discern'd by the Priest of the Sun, before the matter was extant, in order to his Prophecy" (23-24). The theatrical man's need to modify history

---

[16]Edmond (132) suggests that Phillips's "main source" was a 1633 French translation of Garcilaso de la Vega's *Comentarios reales*, which had been published in Lisbon in 1609.

[17]Feinberg, who has reviewed the tradition of the ape in English drama, writes that generally "[t]he ape, though fascinating and amusing in his resemblance to man, pointed . . . to the degeneration of the human soul," but that "[t]he long-lived popular conception of the monkey pillaging a sleeping pedlar or a lover engrossed in lust is exploited by Davenant in a good-humoured, parodical way" in *The Cruelty of the Spaniards in Peru* (5). "Special costumes," Feinberg continues, "were designed for the ape-players" (6). One might add that the apes in this show probably should be related particularly to the English fondness for rope-dancing (see chapter 8).

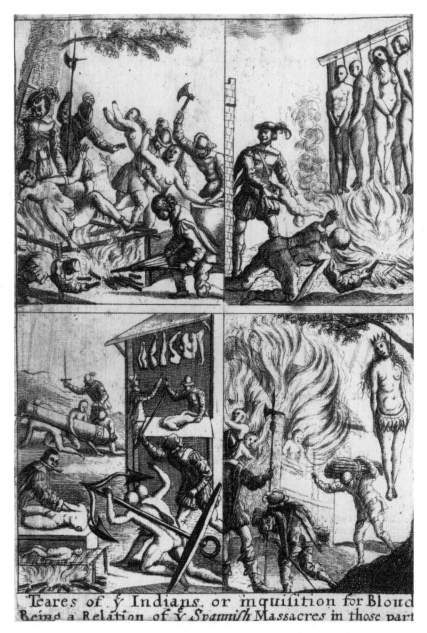

Figure 22. Torture of Indians as illustrated in John Phillips's translation *The Tears of the Indians* (1656) and relating to Davenant's *Cruelty of the Spaniards in Peru* (1658). (By permission of the British Library.)

for artistic or political reasons, and probably for both, will come as no shock
to such readers as have learned to live with the revelation that the historical
Hotspur was really over twice the age of Prince Hal. Any questions here
are more likely to concern the nature and ends of Davenant's wrenching.
What Susan Wiseman has called Davenant's "mythologisations of the
English as Conquerors" (194) first draws on an idealized past and then for
its resolution skips forward to the future, thus allowing the writer to
imply England's continuing greatness without actually looking into the
troubling realities of the moment. Aiding the entire maneuver, of course,
is the fact that the scene of *The Cruelty* is a more or less pristine New World.
Far removed from European messiness, such a place might even arouse
thoughts about colonizing. As usual, Davenant remains here the canny
and politically alert showman. It may even be that his percipient canni-
ness explains the absence of a woman this time among his performers.

During the winter of 1658-59 Davenant next mounted at the Cockpit
a still more playlike new work called *The History of Sr Francis Drake*. For all
Davenant's care to maneuver in terms of "opera," however, Richard Crom-
well, the new Lord Protector (Oliver died in September 1658), and the
Council of State named a committee to investigate not only the persistent
poet-impresario himself but also his actors. Fortunately for Davenant, the
business apparently came to little or nothing, for references to the "opera"
continue.

Davenant's Drake show returned its audience to colonial Peru and
economically used the same proscenium that had been designed for *The
Cruelty*. It offered a larger cast of solo performers, a male chorus and dancers,
and more action—though once again no woman. The new show was based
on Drake's voyage of 1572-73, when he captured the rich prize of Nombre
de Dios in the Isthmus of Panama. Assuming that Davenant's goals were
as usual not merely aesthetic, we may surmise that, in addition to such
motivation as we have seen regarding *The Cruelty of the Spaniards in Peru*, he
revived the great Elizabethan sailor in order to provide his new work with
a specific English naval hero.[18] All in all, he was operating from a base very
similar to that of an anonymous chauvinistic volume published five years
earlier as *Sir Francis Drake Revived*. The title page of this publication says
that Drake "is or may be a Pattern to stirre up all Heroicke and active

---

[18]Ironically, Drake in his own time came to be viewed negatively. Quinn writes: "In June
1589 Drake returned from his voyage to Portugal in disgrace. An investigation established to
the satisfaction of the Queen and her ministers that his inaction at crucial stages had
prejudiced the success of the expedition—the greatest single force sent against Spain during
the whole course of the war. Whether or not Drake was a principal cause of the failure, from
the summer of 1589 until 1593 he lived as a private gentleman in the West Country and was
excluded from state affairs" (182).

SPIRITS of these Times, to benefit their Countrey and eternize their Names by like Noble ATTEMPTS."[19]

Of particular interest in *The Cruelty of the Spaniards* is Davenant's presentation of his subject via the old Golden Age theme—"Whilst yet our world was new, / When not discover'd by the old" (4)—which is both understandable in a politically correct El Dorado story and interestingly at odds with the bleak theorizing of the author's friend Hobbes. Still more striking is Davenant's depiction in *The History of S* *Francis Drake* of Drake's alliance not only with the native Peruvians but also with "the Symerons, who were a Moorish People, brought formerly to *Peru* by the Spaniards, as their Slaves, to dig in Mines" (8). Historically speaking, these *cimmarones*, who by the mid-1500s were "identified exclusively with blacks" (Nuñez 126), had escaped from their Spanish masters and formed scattered settlements in remote and secluded areas. Some such villages in Panama, Ecuador, and Columbia survive today "as incomparable laboratories for the study of Afro-American culture" (Meiklejohn 140). Presumably portrayed at the Cockpit in blackface, these New World allies of the English must have provided one of the most striking and sympathetic appearances of a group of blacks in the whole range of early modern English drama. "Welcom!" says the Symeron king somewhat improbably to Drake, "and in my Land be free, / And pow'rfull as thou art at Sea" (12).

The inevitable climax of the entertainment is the English defeat of the Spaniards, specifically the capture of a mule train laden with silver and gold. Drake sings,

> Your glory, valiant English, must be known,
>   When men shall read how you did dare
>   To sail so long, and march so far
> To tempt a strength much greater than your own.
>
>   [37]

And all closes with a "Grand Dance" of land soldiers, seamen, Symerons, and a Peruvian. The exaltation of English sea power (Flecknoe's *Mariage of Oceanus and Brittania* was published about the same time) and the attractiveness of colonizing were timely topics to fuel this new show, but the disappearance of female roles both here and in *The Cruelty* calls to mind the restrictions that Davenant continued to face.

In August 1659 the well-seasoned cavalier showman was arrested, not

---

[19]Behind this 1653 publication lay an anonymous Dutch tract, *Franciscus Dracus redivivus* (Amsterdam, 1596), which put Drake forth as a champion of Protestantism in the struggle against Spain. In England it appeared as *Sir Francis Drake Revived* in 1626 and again in 1628 (Quinn 182).

Figure 23. "Ieroboam" Cromwell and the Devil, from the frontispiece of Sadler's *Subjects Joy* (1660). (By permission of the Bodleian Library.)

for theatrical reasons—he had been careful enough there—but because he had become involved in a royalist uprising. In only a matter of months, however, Charles II would return.

The spring of 1660 brought not only Charles himself but also a torrent of panegyrical writings, including Anthony Sadler's work called *The Subjects Joy for the Kings Restoration, Cheerfully Made Known in a Sacred Masque.* Inspired because he had envisioned "the Royal Sun, begin to rise" (2), Sadler included in this work not only the basic masquing ingredients of costume, song, and dance but also a coherently scriptural cast of characters and a unifying scriptural theme (the eighteen-year rebellion of Jeroboam against his king). The paralleling in the work was even depicted on its frontispiece, where a wheel of fortune appeared with a devil on one side and, on the other, an armored man labeled both "Ieroboam" and "O. Cromwell" (figure 23).[20] Finally, as the show concludes, England's current King Charles is specifically incorporated into the scene: "Psyche . . . *goes, to present the* King, *with the* Masque, *in writing*" (39).

If we are willing to grant such latitude of definition as the age itself

---

[20]Thus we have here a conspicuous example of Zwicker's observation that "the language of types, a rhetoric of high spiritual authority in the early part of the century, was insistently used in Civil War, Commonwealth, and Restoration England to argue questions that seem to us exclusively political in nature" (115). For multiple examples of scriptural typology of an opposite sort regarding Cromwell, one need look no further than Marvell's "First Anniversary of the Government under His Highness the Lord Protector" (1655). Here, as Zwicker elucidates in his essay, Cromwell is another David, Elijah, Noah, and Gideon.

claimed, masques and masquelike writings and entertainments clearly may be said to have retained a certain vitality in the English mind well after the last masques of the Caroline court had been dismantled and the perform- ances of plays forbidden. Not only were a variety of these shows performed and/or published, but a good many continued to be incorporated within plays. One should not overlook this latter phenomenon. At midcentury the inserted show, a device that had been available in English drama ever since *Fulgens and Lucrece* (1497), proves to be much more varied than Julia Briggs would have it when she writes that inset masques were aimed against the "general hypocrisy of the decadent state whose false surface was being presented in terms of ceremonial" (200).

Inga-Stina Ewbank, though not concerned with plays of the 1640s and 1650s, is more on target with her observation that "playwrights were attracted to the [inserted] masque . . . as a functional dramatic device—a way of starting, furthering and resolving plots and of adding meanings to plots" (410). Some of the best clues to attitudes toward masques, however (including attitudes toward attitudes), are to be found in comments scat- tered within the plays themselves.[21] In William Cavendish's *The Varietie* (1641), for instance, when a character asks who in their midst will write a masque, the Frenchman Galliard responds—perhaps remembering Van- goose in Jonson's *Masque of Augurs*— "Aw, de write? dat is noting alamode, your speesh two, tre, yard long, pshaw? give a me de quick a spirit, de fancie, de brave scene, de varietie of de Antimasque, de nimble a foot, no matre de sence, begar it vole be de brave ting in de christian varle" (18-19).[22] From the patron of Jonson and Shirley, this commentary on spectators with no patience for a masque's text has a special piquancy.

Another and better-known product of the year 1641 was Shirley's own *Cardinal*, which includes not only preparations for a wedding masque— with a scene of prattle about costuming and plotlessness—but also the arrival of six disguised cavaliers in vizards and rich habits. The latter have come to dance a while and then murder the bridegroom, thus merging masquers and audience, though hardly in the way characteristic of most masques. In later years we find that Cavendish's daughters Jane and

---

[21]Of course one may find further references elsewhere. For example, within *The Cyprian Academy* (1647) by Robert Baron (the young Norfolk author of *Mirza*) one comes upon *Deorum Dona a Masque*, which is presumably performed before the King and Queen of Cyprus, "Translucent twins of Love, and majestie" (90), the Queen herself being "From *Albions* Isle" (91). And inset within Samuel Holland's *Don Zara del Fogo* (1656) is a twelve-page masque (*Venus and Adonis*) that is all the more interesting for being a parody.   [22]Galliard had sufficient appeal to entice someone to make a droll (called *The Humours of Monsieur Galliard*) from two scenes in Cavendish's play. Its "argument" explains that Galliard "*undertakes with the Foot, to correct State-matters, and teach the Subjects Reverence and Obedience to their King*" (Elson 204).

Elizabeth wrote *A Pastorall* (ca.1645) that begins with two antimasques, one of hags ("hath not our mischeife made wars . . . ?" [52]) and one of clownish country folk. Also obviously referential is the *"Dumbe Shew"* with *"Solemne Musicke"* included in the fourteen-page "Tragi-Comedie" called *The Scottish Politike Presbyter* (1647). Ostensibly this features a player *"representing"* Directory, the Scotch Presbyter (that is, another player-actor who is witnessing the inset show), and it calls for a rabble of elders fleeing from soldiers with drawn swords. (This show is immediately succeeded and reinforced by an explicit interpretation: "an *English* Army hath extirpated *Presbyterie* root and branch" [13].) Dating from the same year, the second part of Samuel Sheppard's *Committee-Man Curried*, presents a figure named Loyalty who arranges for an entertainment in which Sleep and Death dance around a prone and naked young man, each claiming him until Mammon brings him gold and he revives. Equally overt but more bitter is the show we have considered within *The Famous Tragedie of King Charles I* (1649), where Cromwell, thinking to divert his paramour, Mrs. Lambert, calls for a masque of "six prime Westminsterian Senators" (35). Costumed to disclose what essentially they are—Ambition, Treason, Lust, and so on—these masquers give us an inverted form of what the high court masques presumably had long aimed at, as when, for example, Lucy, Countess of Bedford, danced as Aglaia in Jonson's *Masque of Blackness*.

In 1651, Leonard Willan's intricately ornamental *Astraea* called for a masque of shepherds, then closed with a stage direction that clearly invoked traditional masquing technique: *"Whereat the Theater is opened, and both Companies uniting themselves, spend the rest of the Night in their accustomed Dances"* (128). Also working in a pastoral vein, Richard Flecknoe in 1654 included in *Love's Dominion* a "Pastoral shew, or Rural masque" (71) to analyze the phases of a lover's state. Cosmo Manuche's *Love in Travell* (1655) has yet another masquing show that calls for players costumed as shepherds and shepherdesses. Three years or so later Henry Birkhead (or whoever wrote the *Female Rebellion*) called for both an inset masque of seven female warriors (79) and—probably recollecting Richard Brome's title—an antimasque of men clad in animal skins: "Are you the Jovial crew?" (30). In about 1658, Margaret Cavendish called for antimasques even in *The Publique Wooing* and *The Presence*, two of her numerous plays designed for reading. Surely such masques or antimasques as were merely mentioned in another work or at most designed to be read (a device that might have been radical enough to please Jonson himself) is worth a moment's pondering: the costumes and dancing were never to be seen but in the mind's eye, the voices and instruments never heard but in the mind's ear.

For a final example from the close of the period, one might cite *Cromwell's Conspiracy* (1660). Here, eleven years after their first appearance, those same "six prime *Westministerian* Senators" (B3v) who once danced in the anonymous *Famous Tragedie* were lifted out and brought forth to dance again, joined not only by Cromwell and Mrs. Lambert but also by Cromwell's clergyman friend Hugh Peters.

In sum, inset masques continued to interest those concerned with dramatic writing. Whether they were destined to be performed or merely read, masques were a source of foils within plays, a justification for some music and dancing, and a handy excuse for stretches of allegory, comedy, and satire. Most important of all for our purposes, masques continued to be vehicles for conveying ideas.

As we look back over the various midcentury mutations of the masque—writings that in their own time were usually *called* masques—some of the hard-won generalizations that scholars have wrought in recent decades begin to slip through our fingers like water. It is not altogether safe even to say with Orgel, for example, that their central quality concerns the relationship between masquers and audience. We might revalidate some such observations if we could agree that the last *real* masque expired in a blaze of glory in 1640, but then what are we to make of a text such as Anthony Sadler's *Subjects Joy for the Kings Restoration*?

With regard to masques of all sorts, early and late, many of us nowadays probably would be willing to confess that a concern for printed texts has sometimes inclined us to minimize what William Habington calls "the fine Rhetoricke of cloathes" ("To Castara," l. 6, in *Poems*), what Flecknoe calls "conjoyning the scattered limbs of *Orpheus*" (*Ariadne* A5r), and what Thomas Campion terms "*the mirth of feete*" (D1v): in other words, costume, music, and dance. We have always known but sometimes forgotten the measure of truth in Galliard's airy dismissal and in Samuel Daniel's early observation that the texts of masques are "the least part and of least note in the time of the performance thereof" (307).

On the other hand, at the same time that we acknowledge the continuing reliance of masques and masquelike shows on disguise, song, and dance, we should recognize not only that individual texts are quite different from one another but also that they are shaped to serve a variety of disparate and more or less discernible ends. They do different kinds of cultural work. Contrary to what one might suppose from conventional discussions of the masque, the exemplars garnered here have sometimes attempted something far removed from the aristocratic celebration of power, far removed from royal flattery or, indeed, from royal criticism. Even back in 1634, of course, Milton's *Comus* had offered not praise or disraise of royalty, but a lyric brief for private, personal virtue, presumably in the hope that society at large might be modified so as to parallel personal good. And in 1646, several terrible years later, we find Samuel Sheppard asking, "Do not all wise men know that a Morall Masque is profitable to see"? (*Famers Fam'd* 15). In 1658 Shirley in his *Contention* submitted a sober admonition on the limited value of military prowess—while in 1656, 1658, and 1659 Davenant in a series of shows glorified the military. Not least interestingly, in 1657—nearly two decades after King Charles's last masque, by Davenant—the wedding of Cromwell's daughter Mary was celebrated with a masquelike entertainment.[23] Its pastoral lyrics by Andrew Marvell were to be sung by figures called Endymion and Cynthia, and by Hobbinol, Phyllis, and Thomaslin, and it is now conjectured that the figure of Menalcus or Jove (perhaps both) was represented by the great Lord Protector himself. If this was not a court masque in the old antebellum sense, it was at least a deity-adorned, masquelike show at His Highness's court, and it stunningly confirms the survival of the spirit of masquing in a place and at a time when one might have assumed that it had been quenched.

---

[23]Three years or so earlier Richard Flecknoe had made bold to dedicate his *Love's Dominion* (1654) to Mary's sister, Lady Elizabeth Claypole.

THE PERSISTENCE OF PASTORAL

Fair golden Age! when milk was th' onely food,
And cradle of the infant-world the wood
(Rock'd by the windes); and th' untoucht flocks did bear
Their deer young for themselves! None yet did fear
The sword or poyson: no black thoughts begun
T'eclipse the light of the eternall Sun. . . .[1]
　　　　　　　　—Richard Fanshawe, *The Faithful Shepherd* (1647)

. . . she
Hath put the Sheephook into the hands of
A hundred Hero's, who wearied with Lawrels,
And the noise of the war, are here retir'd. . . .
　　　　　　　　—William Lower, *The Enchanted Lovers* (1658)

Happy & Blest Arcadia how glad
and merry growes old time here in thy Conffines
To se the plenty in a florishing peace
that fflowes and spreads it selffe through all this nation
onely my thought I saw a glimpse of danger. . . .
　　　　　　　　—*Time's Distractions* (1643)

WITH NO MORE than a glimpse of Andrew Marvell's pastoral songs at the court of Cromwell and, before that, of works such as Robert Cox's *Oenone* and James Shirley's *Triumph of Beautie*, one might begin to suppose that pastoral is not a genre but a mode.[2] As such, its cluster of themes, motifs, characters, and scenes can be mixed and matched in virtually any combination or proportion and put to use nearly anywhere—in Herrick's *Hesperides*, for instance, or Milton's "Lycidas" or *Arcades*, or in the translation of a play like Guarini's *Pastor fido*. Furthermore, because it is one of the most retentive and conservative of literary modes, heavily indebted to

---

[1] These lines are Fanshawe's version of the opening of the choral song that concludes act IV of Guarini's *Pastor fido*. Guarini's original was itself a virtuoso imitation and transformation of a song in Tasso's *Aminta*.　[2] Marinelli offers the still broader suggestion that pastoral is "a view of life, an *ethos* or informing principle which can subsist either in itself . . . or which can animate . . . forms of literature like the drama. . . . Hence the word pastoral refers both to form and to content" (9). Though Kegel-Brinkgreve does not concern herself with mid-seventeenth-century English drama, her book is one of the most helpful and compendious treatments of pastoralism to appear since Greg's famous study.

previous works, any approach to a given incarnation of pastoral is bound to benefit from our awareness of its predecessors.

When considering the presence of pastoral in drama, it is well to recall that from the time of the earliest eclogues of Theocritus (ca. 275 B.C.), pastoralism had an affinity with dialogue. Joseph Loewenstein observes, furthermore, that "for a variety of reasons, continental pastoral underwent a steady process of 'dramatization' from about the eighth century" (40). In Renaissance England the process eventuated in Peele's *Arraignment of Paris*, Lyly's *Gallathea*, Shakespeare's *As You Like It*, Fletcher's *The Faithful Shepherdess*, Milton's *Comus*, and countless other works, and it would go on to gain still more attention in verse and drama in the time of Charles and Henrietta Maria.

Because pastoral plays carry so many classical and Renaissance accretions, they sometimes have the aura of secondhand goods—a difficulty that is not mitigated by the fact that many of their timeworn lendings are so artificial. What frequently and fortunately saves the day, however, enabling pastoral to quicken into life, is that the image of Arcadian shepherds is so obviously artful that it may arouse thoughts of contrasting realities. In fact, the situation is often even more interestingly complicated. Because of its own pains, doubts, and wrongs, the pastoral world generally comes across as a sort of middle world situated somewhere between a longed-for-but-impossible Golden Age realm and the real one where kings and shepherds abide but seldom meet. Part of the appeal of such a middling realm lies in the implied dialogic relation between the work itself and the society that produced it (as witness Virgil's first eclogue, Tasso's *Aminta*, and Walton's *Compleat Angler*). Even the earliest annotators of Virgil were aware of the affinity between pastoral and allegory. Characters in *Aminta* are idealized pastoralizations of actual persons. Guarini claimed, among other things, that in the figure of Amarillis in *Pastor fido* he had tried to embody pure soul and divine happiness. Petrarch, Boccaccio, Spenser, and a good many lesser writers turned to pastoral to treat political and ecclesiastical topics. And Puttenham and Drayton are among those who made direct statements on the subject. Puttenham writes that pastoral eclogues, "vnder the vaile of homely persons, and in rude speeches [may be used] to insinuate and glaunce at greater matters, and such as perchance had not bene safe to haue beene disclosed in any other sort" (31). And Drayton, that *"the most High, and most Noble Matters of the World may bee shaddowed in them, and for certaine sometimes are"* (517). To bring the matter up to and beyond midcentury, furthermore, we have Edward Phillips, who may be relied on for an unoriginal view. Publishing in 1675, Phillips affirms that *"the* Bucolic *or* Eclogue, *pretends only the familiar discourse of Sheapheards about their Loves or such like concernments, yet under that umbrage treats oft times of higher matters thought convenient to be spoken of rather mysteriously and obscurely, then in plain terms*" (**5r). If, therefore, one can resist being put off by the convention-ally pretty or quaintly rustic façade of pastoral, one may begin to perceive various ways in which its old metaphors have been made to seem new. Then again, some pastoralists were indeed content to do little more than rear-range the old country counters. That, too, is part of the story.

No matter how inventive or lackluster a pastoral work may be, it almost inevitably involves irony and paradox. "These Shepherds . . . ," writes the playwright Leonard Willan in *Astraea* (1651), "Are of th' Extraction of Nobility" (63). In his translation called *The Noble Ingratitude* (1659) William Lower has a character exclaim that "this fair desert's like a Court" (26). And a character from Thomas Forde's *Love's Labyrinth* (1660) declares:

> . . . I will retire from
> The front of honour, to the rear of a
> Shepherds life: where whilst I do daily tend
> The harmless sheep, will I sing forth sad notes. . . .
>
> [16; i.e., 19]

Annabel Patterson argues that the frequent occurrence of aristocratic Arcadianism during Charles's reign was "due in large part to Henrietta Maria's famous preference for pastoral as the expression of *her* personal style, and the encouragement she gave to writers to articulate that style" (*Pastoral* 147). Sidney's *Arcadia* itself became "the center of a little renais-sance," Patterson writes, by virtue of new editions and dramatizations (*Censorship* 179). Two of the latter are now thought to have been by Shirley (*The Arcadia*, published in 1640) and by Glapthorne (*Argalus and Parthenia*, published in 1639). But there was also Thomas Randolph's *Amyntas* (pub-lished in 1640), in which a prologuing shepherd asks that the gentlemen in the audience "look not from us Rurall Swaines / For polish'd speech, high lines, or Courtly straines"—which is precisely what they had been condi-tioned to expect.[3] There was *Love in It's Extasie* (probably written by William Peaps when a student at Eton), published in 1649 as "A kind of Royall Pastorall" that "*appeares now . . . before you like a winter blossome in the middle of a boysterous and ill-boding season*" (A2r).

Most of all, one might say, there was Walter Montagu's pastoral called *The Shepheard's Paradise*, performed in 1633 and published in 1659. In this vast desert of a play Montagu produced such overinflated and frequently impenetrable writing that Patrick Carey dared wonder about it in rhyme: "But tell mee pray, if euer you / Read th' English of Watt Montague, / Is't not more hard then French?" (14). Montagu, a courtier who had converted

---

[3] Quoted from an unmarked leaf preceding page 1.

to Catholicism, designed his pastoral for an all-female cast—namely, the Queen and her ladies. Whatever the failings of his work, the fact that all its male roles were written for cross-dressing female players was indeed not old hat in England.[4] Furthermore, on a stage designed by Inigo Jones and with no fewer than nine changes of setting, they performed for nearly eight hours. Henrietta Maria's personal level of commitment to this project may be gauged by the extraordinary number of lines she had to speak and sing, especially since they were written in a language that always remained somewhat foreign to her.

While intrinsically commonplace, Montagu's *Shepheard's Paradise* nevertheless stands as a literary and historical landmark, interesting in retrospect partly because its production coincided so closely with the publication of William Prynne's near-hysterical *Histrio-mastix*—in the index of which Prynne went so far as to write of actresses as "notorious whores" (Rrrrr4r). Moreover, some critics have discovered a topical subtext in Montagu's play that might have given it a special purchase on the attention of its original audience. Both Lois Potter and Erica Veevers have suggested that the play first adumbrates Charles's failed wooing expedition to Spain in 1623 and then turns to and develops his successful courtship of Henrietta Maria, the star of the show (Potter, *Secret Rites* 79; Veevers 39-43).

Clearly no political, religious, or social group had a patent on pastoral, or we would be hard put to explain such writings as those songs that Marvell wrote for the Cromwell wedding. Nevertheless, pastoral was characteristically an instrument of the royalists, especially in dramatic and quasi-dramatic writings. We have already seen how this works in *The Terrible, Horrible, Monster of the West*. This vehemently anti-Parliament pamphlet opens with a cacaphony of creaking cart wheels and "hagger-wawling" cats (1), followed by a word combat between two drunken scolds. All of this discord constitutes an antimasquelike foil for the entry of a shepherd named Carolina and a country hind named Rusticus. When Carolina speaks, he conveys a veritable compendium of traditional pastoral elements, beneath which lies a subtext that energizes all of them:

> Here on these flowry Plaines, (now made a barren desert)
> With care I kept my thriving Flock,
> No *Wolf* nor *Fox* durst prey upon my *Lambs;*
> My teeming *Ewes* in safety here did feed:
> My tender *Lambs* forsooke their Teats
> To listen to my Pipe,

[4]Presumably one might argue that the pastoral die had been cast during Henrietta Maria's first Christmas season in England (1625–26), when the Queen not only appeared in a French pastoral but also played the main role—and some of her ladies were appareled as men.

Tracing Meanders o're the dew-swoln grasse,
Whilst every *Primrose*, and humble *Violet*
Did bend his unctious head,
Bedeckt with Morning pearls.
Rich as *Dame Natures* self did we[a]re,
To grace our innocent sports; but now alas!
This monstrous *Wolf* has seiz'd on all my *Flock*
Kill'd the *chiefe Shepheard* of *Arcadia;*
But his blest *Pipe*, that Angels stoo'd to heare,
His *Crook* is broke, his *Strip* [i.e., scrip] is tane away,
And all his *Shepe* scatter'd and gone astray.
I cannot speake for griefe, his tender *Lambs*
Are forc'd from the soft Teats of their owne *Dams.*
Their *snowy fleeces*, (white as Innocence)
Tore from their Flesh by *pricking Bryers,*
All *means* of Life is from them tane away,
And *Albion* white, become a *Golgotha.*

[2]

From the now-vanished flowery plains to the lament for a lost shepherd, pastoral tradition provides a context here for the story of the English King—and, through the Golgotha reference, of his martyrdom.

In a move back to prose, Rusticus next gives the views of a poor country fellow. Since socially minded critics of our own time have sometimes blamed pastoral writers for excising all traces of serious response to the laboring class, one may find it interesting to discover just such a response here, and to find it a complaint directed not at the King and his court but at those who have displaced both of them:

I'me zure they've undone me, and all the Country besides; they say 'tis *Cromwell,* but I think 'tis the Deel rules them, they've all my Horses before (a blague on 'um,) and now because I had not Money to give them for Zur *Thomas,*[5] they have taken my white Bullock too, and they've blundred me over, and over againe; now they come for Zur *Thomas* again, and because che had it not to give 'um, they drove away my red Cow too, and zold her before my vace; a pox take 'um vor a company of cheating Knaves: now

---

[5]One might compare Alexander Brome's poem "Upon His Mare Stolen by a Trooper" (*Songs* 118–19). The need for horses is reflected frequently in documents of the period—for instance, "An Ordinance for adding Commissioners for seising of Horses and Goods, and Chattels of Malignants" and an "Order to redress the Abuses in taking Horses for Supply of the Army" (2 May and 10 May 1643; Firth and Rait 1:138, 155). In March 1645 we find "An Ordinance for providing of Draught-horses for carriage of the traine of Artillerie to the Army, under the Command of Sir Thomas Fairfax" (1:653). Fairfax was commander in chief of the army until late June 1650, at which time he expressed a readiness to relinquish his commission rather than lead the expedition then planned to invade Scotland.

they have zited me before a Committee as they call it, & they may be as very Knaves as themselves for ought I know; my neighbour *Trudge* saies they will goe neere to hang me; chad better be hang'd then starv'd. . . . [2-3]

The pamphlet then sets aside both laments and turns to the hell-beast Parliament.

As for full-fledged pastoral plays, we will consider first such evidence as confirms England's continuing interest in the achievements of Italy. (The subject of translations will be addressed more fully in the next chapter, but noting a few of them at this point will help to light the pastoral scene.) The *Aminta* by Torquato Tasso, whom Langbaine calls "the Father of Pastorals" (*Account* 99), was translated into English by Abraham Fraunce (1591), Henry Reynolds (1628), and perhaps Kenelm Digby, and—the reason for mentioning it here—it was translated yet again by John Dancer in 1660. Langbaine is wrong to grant Tasso pastoral paternity, but his epithet "Father" nevertheless conveys the great popularity of the work and its influence in shaping a full-scale drama concerned with the loves and trials (including threatened deaths) of refined shepherds and shepherdesses. Unfortunately, though Dancer's version of *Aminta* is both an indication of late interest in Tasso and an honorable effort to bring the work into English, W.W. Greg is able to dismiss Dancer as a "certified poetaster" (*Pastoral Poetry* 241).

Without much doubt the best translation of Italian pastoral in our period is Richard Fanshawe's 1647 version of Giambattista Guarini's *Pastor fido* (1590).[6] Guarini's work, leaning heavily on Tasso and apparently performed in the 1580s, is an intricately plotted *tragicommedia* that continued to find extraordinary acceptance throughout the next century.[7] What has most intrigued some readers of Fanshawe's midcentury version, however, is its evident political pertinence. Fanshawe was a committed royalist who eventually served both Charleses as secretary, soldier, and envoy; and when it came to dedicating his *Faithful Shepherd*, he turned not to the Queen or to the King but to the Prince of Wales. Having composed his translation "midst noise of CAMPS, and COURTS Dis-ease" (*Querer* A2v), he purported to present in "masking clothes," for greater accessibility to a teenage prince, knowledge of a "*Morall, Politicall, and Theologicall*" kind (A3v). When Fanshawe tells the young Charles that he will find here "the image of *a gasping State* (once the most flourishing in the world)" and "*A wild Boar* (*the sword*) depopulating the *Country*" (A4r), his lessons are not constrictedly

---

[6]It was preceded by a translation of 1602 that apparently was made by a kinsman of Sir Edward Dymocke (Greg, *Pastoral Poetry* 242).   [7]Nicholas Perella has observed that "the *Pastor Fido* was the most widely read book of secular literature in all of Europe" (6). No wonder Ben Jonson has Lady Would-be exclaim, "All our *English* writers . . . / Will deigne to steale out of this author, mainely" (*Volpone* III.iv.87–89).

political, but political they are. Most obviously, he writes that because his translation is like

> a *Lantskip* of these Kingdoms, (your *Royall Patrimony*) as well in the former flourishing, as the present distractions thereof, I thought it not improper for your Princely notice at this time, thereby to occasion your Highness, even in your recreations, to reflect upon the sad *Originall*, not without hope to see it yet speedily made a perfect *parallell* throughout; and also your self a great Instrument of it. Whether by some happy Royall Marriage (as in this *Pastorall*, and the case of *Savoy*, to which it alludes[8]) thereby uniting a miserably divided people in a publick joy; or by such other wayes and means as it may have pleased *the Divine Providence* to ordain for an *end of our woe;* I leave to that Providence to determine. [A4v]

"A *Lantskip* of these Kingdoms"—a writer could hardly be more explicit. In the midst of his pastoral "recreations" Prince Charles is invited to ponder Britain's woe and consider how he might become an instrument to relieve it. Thus Fanshawe himself, through the medium of a skillful verse translation, could hope to affect events of his time. Furthermore, when he reissued the play in 1648, he added a motto from Horace: "*Patiarque vel inconsultus haberi*" (*Epistles* 1.5.15: "I shall . . . suffer you, if you will, to think me reckless").

Such hints as Fanshawe gives of the possible uses of his dark lantern point well beyond the work at hand. Guarini's play, however, is basically about a love-stricken shepherd and shepherdess whose chief problems vanish when their true parentage is revealed. Latter-day readers, if possessed only of the translation, not Fanshawe's dedication, might well be accused of full-fledged Fluellenism if they posited parallels between the plights of the shepherd and Prince Charles. Perhaps two morals are germane here: first, that seventeenth-century minds were programmed far better than ours to discern parallels; and, second and consequently, that we are much more likely to perceive fewer of them than did the writers and readers of the period.[9]

A third major Italian pastoral that made its way into English at this time was the *Filli di Sciro* (1607) by Guidobaldo della Rovere Bonarelli. Like Tasso and Guarini, Bonarelli tells a story of amatory shepherds and shepherdesses. Two children, Fillis and Thirsis, who are captured in infancy and betrothed to each other, are then informed of each other's death, but actually placed in the homes of different shepherds and eventually reunited. Jonathan Sidnam published a translation of this work in London in 1655, apparently long after he had turned both it and Guarini's *Pastor fido*

---

[8]"Molto imprecisa" is Ferdinando Neri's demurral at this point (quoted by Perella 219).
[9]Though Fanshawe's translation was designed for reading, a freely revised version of it was performed at Dorset Garden in 1676.

into English. Another version from about 1655 by John Pullen, a clergyman from Lincoln, is now preserved in a somewhat later manuscript at the Folger Shakespeare Library. Perhaps the most interesting version, because of its associations, is a third one in manuscript at the British Library. This is the work of Sir Gilbert Talbot, sometime usher of the Privy Chamber, who had served as Charles I's agent in Venice in the late 1630s and as a colonel in the royalist forces during the Civil Wars. Talbot's relationship to the younger Charles may be partially inferred from a couple of letters in Italian that he sent in March 1656, models of what Charles might care to write to the King of Spain and Don Luis de Haro, because "Italian will be the most proper language you can vse." Writing in Paris the following year, Talbot dedicated his translation of the *Filli* to Charles. He was responding to a request from the young man, but by the time he finished the job Charles himself presumably had attained sufficient "proficiency" to read the play in Italian (*Fillis* 5r). Like Fanshawe about a decade earlier, Talbot uses his dedication to Charles to give a political twist to the whole manuscript:

> I must confess I was desirous to represent to y^r Ma^{ty} the providence which herein appears soe highly miraculous, although but in the fictitious redemption of two captiue Lovers, and the consequentiall restitution of theyre Country to its ancient freedome: that I might take occasion from hence to giue the world this sad (yet cheerfull) account of my fayth: That as Heauen hath bin pleased to punish the sinners of y^r kingdomes, upon the most innocent of Kings, in the martyrdome of y^r royall father, and exile of your self: soe it's iustice will never suffer such horrid, and unparalell'd villany to prosper into generations, either through the open defection, or (wch little differs) the tame temporising of y^r Subiects vnder a tyrannicall Impostor. But that all your persecutions, and sufferings hitherto haue bin onely to render you more glorious, and magnify the day of y^r redemption. . . . [5r-v]

The punishment due the sinners of England has been shouldered by the martyred King Charles and his exiled son, but just as both the lovers and their country are finally rewarded with "redemption" in *Fillis*, so also will the Charleses and their England be redeemed. The instincts to make relevant and to hope spring eternal in the human breast.

Italy's contributions to England's swelling pastoral stream are supplemented, of course, by those of France. The author of the play called *Astraea* (1651), based on the famous romance *L'Astrée* (1607-9) by Honoré d'Urfé, was Leonard Willan, Gentleman—first discussed here as the author of the 1658 tyrant tragedy *Orgula* (see figure 24). Willan's dramatization dates from some years before its publication, before (as he puts it) the "*Eclipses*" of certain great "Lights, from whom essentially it should have had both Influence and Lustre" (*Astraea* A3r). Such a statement certainly meshes well with the report that *L'Astrée* was the favorite book of Henrietta Maria.

Figure 24. Leonard Willan, playwright, as depicted in *The Phrygian Fabulist* (1650). (From the Rare Book Room and Special Collections Division, Library of Congress.)

Inscriptions are but Epitaphs on the Dead :
Such may bee His ; to Action buried :
Nor but the Rites of Freinds: in wante of whome,
His Owne Hand wrought This Monumente for His Tombe :
How lasting the Materialls shall bee ,
This Age may Gess, the Next perhaps Decree

Now deprived of such "Lights," Willan has sought out a new star in Mary, Duchess of Richmond and Lennox, the same lady to whom Flecknoe would soon address his *Ariadne Deserted by Theseus.* And again, though this time taking a different approach from Fanshawe and Talbot, the writer insists on the relevance of his writing to life. This play belongs to the Duchess, he says, not just as property, "but by the advantage of Similitude" (A3v). The Duchess is the real-life version of Astraea. Astraea is the Duchess's "Counterfeit" (A4v). Like the views expressed by Fanshawe and Talbot, Willan's should help us toward an understanding not merely of the dialogic force of much pastoral but also of a mind-set common among midcentury English men of letters. He writes: "*Astraea* is figured to descend from noble *Progeny,* who to avoid the Military Fury of debording Multitudes ... were constrained to betake them to the humble Sanctuary of a *Pastorical* condition: This Circumstance will meet no trivial *Analogie* in the Eminence of your Extraction, and Consequence of your present Rural Retreat: So that (with permission) may evidently be concluded, that in reference to your Natural perfections, Civil Transactions, or Accidental Occurrence, *Astraea* may (in equity) presume to be either your *Type, Parallel* or *Character*" (A4r). Recognizing the emphasis that Willan places here on parallelism should help us to notice also that, like many another panegyrical passage of the day, this one may be read as a sort of cryptic royalist credo.

The play it introduces is a potpourri of episodes from *L'Astrée*. To mount the whole thing appropriately, Willan calls for a proscenium that displays garland-bearing "*Cupidons*," a shepherdess, and a shepherd—the latter to be imagined "in a pretty posture, merrily playing on a Flute" (A5v). Equally pretty, we may suppose, is the first entry, which brings onstage a shepherdess "with a little Dog parried in Ribbons of several colours" (A6r). We are operating here, as Ben Jonson might say, at cream-bowl depth. Then again, one of the more interesting features of this English *Astraea* is precisely such stage directions. Phillis enters "Hastily and in some distraction" (4); Astraea speaks "to her self, somewhat mov'd" (10); Leonida enters "With a little stop, strook with a kind of wonder" (16); Tyrsis, Leonice, and Hylas sing a song "at far end of the Scene" (23); Sylvander makes "obeysance to the temple and goes in" (57); and, toward the close, "*A still kind of musick is heard with great Reverence*" (123). It may be that certain of these hints as to how one should imagine the action will provide thoughtful students with some clues to traditions of playing.

Also French in origin and related to d'Urfé's *L'Astrée* is T.R.'s translation called *The Extravagant Sheepherd* (1654) from Thomas Corneille's *Le Berger extravagant* (1653), which in turn had been adapted from Charles Sorel's *Le Berger extravagant* (1627; pt. 3, 1628). Rather than simply bouncing the realities of life off the varied artifices of literary pastoral, *The Extravagant Sheepherd* comically distances itself from both life and pastoral writings. That is to say, the work is a mock pastoral. Lysis, the shepherd of the title, who is actually the son of a rich Parisian merchant, has gone out of his mind reading romances:

> The Romance of *Astraea* was then publish't,
> Where reading *Hylas*, and *Sylvander*'s jarres,
> His braine being very soft in such a case,
> He needs would be their judge, and heare them plead,
> And so resolv'd to goe into the Forrests. . . .
>
> [7]

Attending François Tristan l'Hermite's 1652 stage-play *Amarillis* (from Jean de Rotrou's *Célimene*) appears to have nudged Lysis over the brink. Advised to engage in cross-dressing on a visit to his ladylove ("This Metamorphosis is very Past'rall" [26]), Lysis expresses minimal misgivings that his beard may spoil his disguise. Lest one suspect that such spoofing of a royalist taste is itself intrinsically anti-royalist, T.R. states in his dedication that his play is so innocent that it might *"without Gaule to the Spectators, have enter'd the Theater (had not the Guilty Ones of this Age, broken that Mirrour lest they should there behold their own horrible Shapes represented)."* [10] T.R. doubtless knew to whom he spoke: his specific addressee was Joanna Thornhill, wife of the Honorable Richard Thornhill of Ollantigh, Kent. A Colonel of Horse just a few years earlier (after his commander, Sir William Butler, was killed in 1644 at Cropredy Bridge), Richard Thornhill during the Interregnum became a voluntary exile and an active royalist conspirator (Newman 239).

Though such foreign-based works as the foregoing generally have an English flavor, pastorals concocted wholly at home provide different kinds of evidence. We will glance briefly at two such pastorals—one by Sir William Denny and one by Sir William Lower—and then give a bit more emphasis to four more—one anonymous, one by Thomas Forde, one by John Fountain, and one by Cosmo Manuche.

Reminding us of such pastoral strands as appeared in chapter 9, Sir William Denny observes that his *Sheepheard's Holiday* (which he dated 1 June 1651) "might heretofore haue passt for a Masque, had it not bene for Vizards" (3r). [11] He calls it instead a "Pöeme," an "Eclogue," and a "Pastorall" (3r). Whatever one calls it, his manuscript conjures up a world of innocent shepherds: "Harmelesse Sheepheards do not ken / The darke-borne Vice of Other men" (6r). In contrast to the intricate plotting of some pastoral drama, the action here is limited mainly to a few simple events: the reappearances of a commenting palmer who has come to help celebrate the marriage of Dalon and sweet Beta; a nuptial song-debate on the virtues of virginity versus those of marriage (argued by Vota and Lipsona); some festal singing and dancing ("This is The Sheepheards Holiday" [20v]); and finally an invocation to and response from Pega, who is called in to judge the debate. In sum, Denny's collocation of simple pastoral motifs accords well with his title.

The peculiar names of his characters draw attention to themselves, however. In Denny's dedication to Lady Kemp and Mistress Thornton he flatteringly assumes the ability of these ladies to divest his work of its "outward Dresse" (3r), but he nevertheless appends a "Key, or Clavis," which includes such explanatory information as few modern readers would fathom otherwise. For instance: "Beta is the Second Letter of the Greeke Alphabet. The Alphabet deciphers a Familie. Alpha is Paterfamilias, the Lord, & Master. Beta is the Lady, Mistris, or Dame of the House. The other Vowells are the Children" (3v).

The bridegroom "Dalon" proves to be simultaneously both wisdom and a brand alight at one end, "denoting Conjugall Loue" (3v). Lipsona

---

[10]Quoted from an unmarked leaf following the title page.   [11]This work by Denny should not be confused with Joseph Rutter's *The Shepheards Holy-Day*, published in 1635.

"signifies Chast Desire" (4r; see figure 25). "Vida" is experience, "Vota" virginity, and "Pega shadowes out Trueth" (5r). It may be ungentle to doubt the ability of Denny's dedicatees to decipher his manuscript *sans* "Clavis," but for us today that key may serve best of all as a warning to remain vigilant concerning the figural potential of pastoral writings.

Sir William Lower's *Enchanted Lovers* (1658) wears its pastoralism with a difference. More like the old Italian models than Denny's work, it presents three main sets of "noble strangers clad in pastoral weeds" (A3v) who have sought "sanctuary and repose" on the Portuguese island of Erithréa.[12] The best and core idea of the work is the enchantment of Diana (really Celia) and Thersander (really Cleagenor), the main pair of lovers, by the governing princess, Melissa, who causes each alternately to die and to mourn for the death of the other. A reader finds shipwreck here, and disguise and an echo-garden and fine talk, but most interesting is the enchantress: "By the effect, and strange force of my charms, / They shall have, without dying, every day / A thousand deaths" (D8r). All is at length resolved when the goddess Diana descends, deposes the enchantress, and grants eternal life and love to Celia and Cleagenor.[13]

Whatever temptations there may be to search for an allegorical dimension in all this, Lower seems interested mainly in turning out an accessible recreative work. On the other hand, we have here a group of noble characters (the hero is identified as a "Cavalier disguised") who travel abroad to seek "sanctuary and repose." Lower himself was a former Lieutenant Colonel in Charles's army and sometime Lieutenant Governor of Wallingford who went to Holland to escape from England's turmoil. There, in Langbaine's phrase, he "enjoy'd the Society of the *Muses*" (*Account* 332). We shall see more of him later.

Our four final pastoral dramas all concern Arcadia, and the first poses problems of several kinds. Suffering under the handicaps of being anonymous,[14] untitled, and long available only in manuscript, it has further receded into the bibliographical mist because the few who refer to it have assigned it such a dizzying array of labels: *Sight and Search* (from its first two speakers), *Time's Triumph*, *The Bonds of Peace*, *Juno in Arcadia*, *Juno's Pastoral*, and *Time's Distractions*. Of these titles, Diane Strommer's *Time's Distractions* is most helpful. Though the character named Time does not enter until the third act, Strommer's title directs us to the subsuming problem of the play. It also suits well with the date on the manuscript: 5 August 1643. The

---

[12]William Bryan Gates finds the play similar to Greek romance, and especially to one by Eustathius translated into French as *Amours d'Ismène et d'Isménias* (75).   [13]A librarian's note at the back of an anonymous and untitled Folger Shakespeare Library manuscript (J.b.2) identifies it as a synthesis of this play and Robert Davenport's *City Nightcap* (1624).   [14]Cutts, however, has suggested that it is a lost work by Richard Brome ("Anonymous Entertainment").

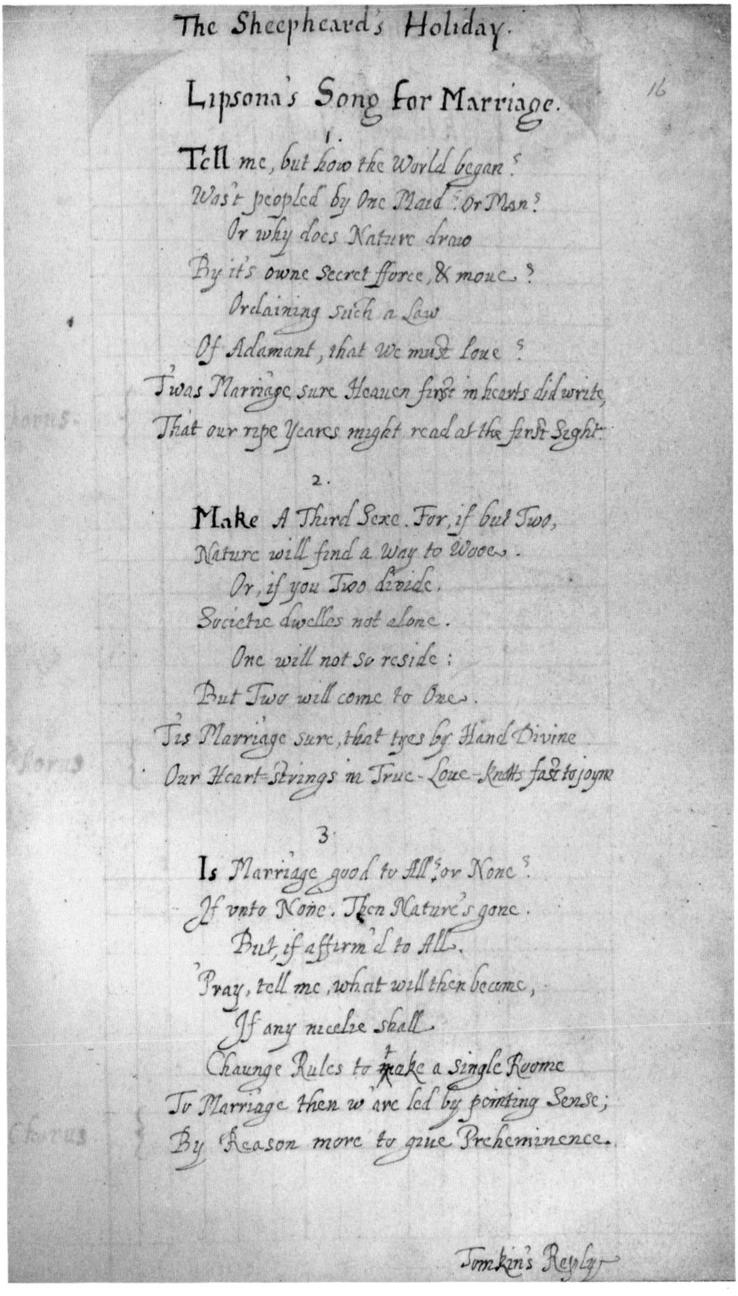

The Sheepheard's Holiday.

Lipsona's Song for Marriage.

1.

Tell me, but how the World began?
Was't peopled by One Maid? Or Man?
Or why does Nature draw
By it's owne secret fforce, & moue?
Ordaining such a Law
Of Adamant, that We must loue?
'Twas Marriage sure Heauen first in hearts did write,
That our ripe Yeares might read at the first Sight.

2.

Make A Third Sexe. For, if but Two,
Nature will find a Way to Wooe.
Or, if you Two divide:
Societie dwelles not alone.
One will not So reside:
But Two will come to One.
'Tis Marriage sure, that tyes by Hand Divine
Our Heart-Strings in True-Loue-Knotts fast to joyne

3.

Is Marriage good to All, or None?
If vnto None. Then Nature's gone.
But, if affirm'd to All.
'Pray, tell me, what will then became,
If any needie shall
Chaunge Rules to make a single Roome
To Marriage then w' are led by pointing Sense;
By Reason more to giue Preheminence.

Tomkin's Reply.

Figure 25. "Lipsona's Song," from Sir William Denny's manuscript of *The Sheepheard's Holiday* (BL Add. MS 34065, 16r). (By permission of the British Library.)

sequestering of royalist estates began that year, and the month of July had seen the Queen's journey from York to Oxford, bringing some four thousand men to Charles's aid. It also had seen the flight of the royalist cavalry to Oxford and Parliament's negotiations in Edinburgh for a Scottish army.

Overtly allegorical throughout, the play opens with Sight and Search—the servants, respectively, of Will and Judgement—conversing about "this earthly parradise / Arcadia" (213r). Will's mistress, Dessert, is being stalked by Danger, however; and Judgement's mistress, Virtue, by Envy. Nor is all sweet and sound in the outer world. When Juno, the goddess of the realm, enters with Fortune and Virtue, the latter reports that "The World / is out off fframe disorder gouerns it" (213v), and Fortune speaks of "unnaturall strife and bloody warrs" (214r). Clearly then, even before Time himself enters, the halcyon days of Arcadia are no more. Meanwhile, Will and Judgement, who are out fishing (not a bad conceit), catch Cupid in their net.

The time has come now to bring on Time.[15] Unfortunately, Time's mistress, Security, soon lulls him to sleep, thus unloosing a nightmare antimasque of hags—"Enuy Suspition Necessytey" and "5 or 6 hags more" (216r). When he awakes, Time is clearly beside himself—that is, "distracted"—and threatens that all Arcadia will feel his influence. The two old gentlemen, Judgement and Will, are "together by ye eares" (219r), and Fortune and Virtue exchange harsh words. The servant class is divided against itself, too, as Sight and Search squabble. In fact, something touching about the citizenry's helplessness is sounded in the line "all the shepheards in Arcadia are at it, & for they know not what" (219v). Though she has been slow to take action thus far, Juno knows she must do something to "purge" Time of his lunacy, and in a late turn toward the imagery of the 1640s pamphlets, she administers her medicine. One by one, Time vomits Envy, Suspition, Mallice, Revenge—in fact, a "damnable belly full" (221v). Associating Time still more explicitly with the times, the writer has Cupid report that the old man "ffarts diurnalls and weekely Intellegenses" (221v). Then at last all closes with various reconciliations and a dance—again "Thankes to greate Juno" (223r).

Something interesting has occurred here. Arcadia, an idyllic, microcosmic surrogate for England, with its fruitful valleys and pleasant plains, its tiers of alliances and friendships, harbors Danger and Envy from the start, and before it is restored to order by Juno it is first thrown so badly out of kilter as to become its own opposite, a little world turned inside out, the very sort of anti-Arcadia from which Arcadia has hitherto been a refuge. Creating an allegory of broad concepts, of parallels that offer no discernible

---

[15]Strommer observes that Time functions mainly as "a visual metaphor for the present—the times—but he also is temporality and, occasionally, the past" (*Time's Distractions* 22).

links between any one character in the play and a particular human being, the dramatist manages to suggest something about the complexity of various interacting forces and also his views on their role in England's current civil and social strife. He deplores the disorder and decline that are everywhere to be found, and yet he retains a hope that divine intervention may somehow, at some time beyond the violence of 1643, restore Time to his senses and harmony to the land. The finished play is no great work, surely, but its writer deserves credit for having crafted a thoughtful dramatic essay that is loosely applicable in many ways to its period. Most interesting of all, perhaps, its use of traditional pastoral elements is such that they appear not so much outworn as tragically at risk.

Thomas Forde's *Love's Labyrinth* (1660) is specifically labeled a tragi-comedy—and is therefore one of those works that might also be considered in a different chapter here. Forde himself is identified on the title page as "*Philothal.*" This has been taken to allude to the dramatist's love for the sea, but the tag might better be read as referring to a love for Thalia, the muse of comedy, who is mentioned in Forde's epigraph. None of these facts belies the reality that the play is a pastoral. More particularly, it is a dramatization of Robert Greene's *Menaphon* (1589), otherwise known as *Greenes Arcadia*.[16] The concern with complex plotting that is so frequently shared by writers of tragicomedy and romance (Greene himself was in-debted to both Heliodorus and Sidney) is acknowledged in Forde's title and very much in evidence within his play. His friend N.C. admired particularly how Forde's "*curious* inter-woven *Plots,* / Rich twine, *ty'd all in* Lovers-Knots" (*Love's Labyrinth* V2r).

While the play's subtitle, *The Royal Shepherdess*, doubtless called to mind in 1660 the long displacement of the pastoral-loving English Queen, Henrietta Maria, we are more specifically concerned here with a winter's-tale world in which an angry father, King Damocles, orders his daughter Sephestia, her "brat," and her "mate" to be thrust forth in a bark without oar, sail, or pilot (3). All three passengers are finally saved, it turns out, but tragedy is not averted. The Queen, Sephestia's mother, kills herself in protest against the King's monstrous behavior. On the other hand, the King's brother, Lamedon, survives shipwreck with Sephestia and provides her with some conventional—and at midcentury timely—counsel that is appropriate to pastoral writing: "Cares are companions of the Crown, the Court / Is full of busie thoughts, and envious strife, / Whilst peaceful sleeps attend a Countrey life" (25).

There is even a bit of perspective-adjustment regarding romance

---

[16]Notice has also been taken of the play's indebtedness to Robert Gomersall's *The Tragedie of Lodovick Sforza, Duke of Milan* (1628).

matter when the "silly" shepherd Doron observes that his brother has a whole tumbrel full of "Rogue-mances" (36). Menaphon, a song-prone character whose name Greene had utilized for the title of his narrative, is a man of substance in the pastoral world. In fact, he is "the Kings Shepherd" (V3v), one capable of providing hospitality for Sephestia as well as dazzled appreciation of her beauty. As befits pastoral romance, however, Sephestia's banished "mate," really Maximus, Prince of Cyprus, turns up with a new name and identity. Because Sephestia herself is disguised as the shepherd-ess Samela, the two do not recognize each other. Then again, Sephestia's noble beauties shine through her ignoble weeds, and because she resembles his long-lost wife, the supposedly bereaved Maximus is eventually moved to woo her: "*Why so nice and coy fair Lady / Prithee why so coy?*" (48). Meanwhile, their long-lost son, Plusidippus, now grown, impresses in different ways both his unperceiving grandfather and the Princess Euriphyla of Thessaly. Even at this late point Forde's labyrinthine plot grows more complex, enabling Sephestia to be wooed eventually not only by her disguised husband and Menaphon but also by her father and her son. At the end, with more or less equal measures of charm and conventional implausibility, the suddenly reformed King declares that "just men and lovers alwayes thrive" (72).

Rather akin in feeling to Forde's *Love's Labyrinth*, John Fountain's *Rewards of Vertue* also concerns a princess-shepherdess. At first we know only that Urania is a young maid who has been taken from her cottage by Prince Theander and presented as a gift to Princess Cleantha, whereupon she has become the observed of all male observers. Endymion, an attractive young poet and "*Vertiosi*" (2), who seems something of an authorial surrogate, decides that "No more, no more, we must scorne Cottages; / These are the Rocks from whence our Jewels come" (9). One Pyrrhus, a lord, comes to woo Urania on behalf of the King, bringing the problematic news that she will "be the Subject / Of his Revenge or Pleasure" (17). And Prince Theander himself decides he wants to marry her. The standard and steadily increasing intricacy of character and action that ensues leads at last to the near-execution of the heroine. Anyone familiar with the major events of the period might well be struck by the author's call for a "*Scaffold covered with black, with many Spectators about it*" (76).

As a writer of pastoral tragicomedy, however, Fountain is most notable for his insistent exploration of a central theme. Frequently focused on the mean status of his heroine, he seems intent on discussing the relationship between marriage and class. The Princess Cleantha argues well against those who uphold marriages of convenience "Like petty Countrey folks" (41), and Endymion decries marriages of "great folks" that are constrained "By Law and Policie" (49). The old King, however, reacts more traditionally: despite his lustful hankerings, he finally refuses to "mingle blood with those small folks / Who dwell in Cottages" (73). Especially striking, therefore, is Princess Cleantha's objection to those who condemn marrying beneath one, "as though the rich and poor / Were different species" (60). Thus, when Urania is apparently to be executed for her clandestine union with the Prince, the nurse of the frustrated Princess exclaims,

> Why Madam, here was now a marriage made
> According to your Highness principles,
> Purely for Love; without consideration
> Of Portion, or equality, of friends;
> And here you see the end on't.   [75]

Dealing extensively with a subject that was perhaps personally pertinent, certainly socially pertinent, and conceivably brought to the fore by some of the amorous liaisons of England's own current princes, Fountain finally chose the easy way out. At the end we have a shepherdess and no shepherdess. In a 1669 adaptation of the play, Thomas Shadwell would let the cat out of the bag from the outset with a new title: *The Royal Shepherdess.*

Our fourth and final specimen here of pastoral drama is Cosmo Manuche's *The Banish'd Shepheardesse* (1660), another play still in manuscript.[17] Within Arcadia itself, we discover here, there has been a terrible reversal in which proud rebels have dared to strike "at the Heads of kings" (prol. ii,r). Thus our main concern is with Arcadians who have fled to Thessaly for refuge. In presenting this pastoral play about exile to Henrietta Maria herself, the exiled Caroline queen of pastoral, Manuche addresses her as "Queene Dowager," thereby acknowledging Charles II as sovereign. Himself he describes as "a poore suffering subiect," one whose loyalty has occasioned "many Crewell imprisonments" (dedication iv; see figure 26).[18]

Having served the royal cause as a captain, then as a major of foot, Manuche in his play appears to project himself into the character of a

---

[17]The Huntington Library version is cited here. Complicating the textual situation, however, Manuche also presented a copy of *The Banish'd Shepheardesse* to James Compton, Earl of Northampton, which is now in the British Library. After analyzing both versions, William P. Williams has reported finding "a class of variants which certainly are explicable only in terms of audience, although they do not so clearly indicate performance" ("Evidence of Performance" 14).   [18]Manuche goes so far as to speak of his children as threatened by "a staruing death, for want of bread, which they haue Often, with teares (not tongues) begg'd for, Their father Haueing no other Dish for Them to feede on, but his Loyalty Seru'd vp in irons." Though we will probably never know the whole story, the glare of modern scholarship reveals that in 1656 Manuche was trying to obtain money also from Cromwell, on the grounds that he had passed on "discoveries of the disturbers of our present happy Government" (Phelps 209).

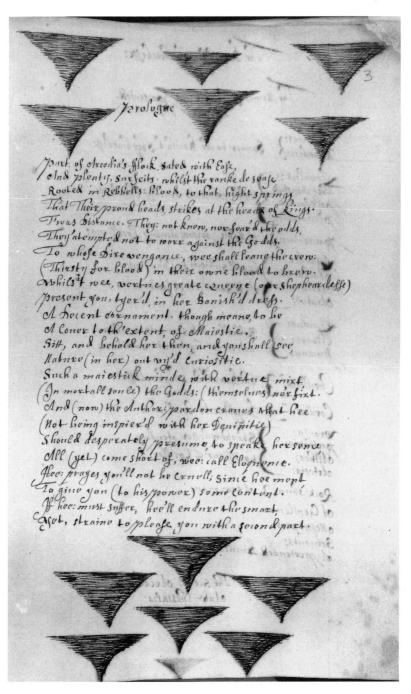

Figure 26. Prologue addressed to Queen Henrietta Maria in Cosmo Manuche's *Banish'd Shepheardesse* (BL Add. MS 60273). (By permission of the British Library.)

captain named Lysander, one of those loyal subjects—now in need of a loan—who has remained true to Charilaus, eldest of the two sons of the banished shepherdess. At the same time that the name "Charilaus" carries obvious overtones of "Charles," it also means "People's Joy" (as we read in Plutarch's *Lycurgus* 3.4). Unlike the allegorical abstractions that populate *Time's Distractions*, however, Manuche's characters are partly generic types of the day (for instance, the nobles attending Charilaus) and, more important, partly disguised representations of actual people. Seventeen years had passed since the relatively early dismay expressed in *Time's Distractions*, and now, in the opening scene between Lysander and a sailor, "Wee, heare, some muttering of a chainge" (1). In fact, "roundnesse" (presumably a term derived from "roundhead") is "out of fashion," and the sailor tells of three knavish servants of those in power who are hoping to make alternate plans, "In case, Their: politicke Masters: are put to flight" (1, 2). It is in Lysander's explanation to his landlady, Thais, however, that the plenitude of parallels makes clear the extent of Manuche's aim in summarizing the recent past and savoring the bittersweet promise of the present. The captain explains how the Arcadians some time earlier had come to enjoy too much ease and plenty "Vnder, a neuer to be forgotten, vertuous prince" (4). He tells how religion, a common cloak for rebellion, was used by those who wished to impose uniformity of belief. Then "The rable: arm'd, They: dare Article with Him" (4). They engrossed his treasure and seized his navy. Then

> The Rebells (by the permission of the Godds:)
> Stood Victors. And, to the amazement
> Of the Christian world, Murdered (most barberously)
> Their iust, And innocent prince. . . .
>
> [5]

This brings us to the present and to Corilliana, "that matchless Jem," "that suffering miracle of vertue, / The Banish'd: shepheardesse" (9)—and to her exiled daughter, Corilla. There is no room for doubt that Corilliana stands for Henrietta Maria, since in his prologue Manuche has assured the Queen that she is "Our shepheardesse" (ii,r). Corilla, then, personates Princess Henrietta Anne, now about sixteen years old. Fortunately, things have been looking better of late for these two, and the widowed Corilliana is somewhat less bowed by grief. But at no time has she ever doubted heaven's goodness. As she puts it, "Dispare: ne'r (yet) presume'd / To knock: which, if hee had, / H'had found Mee fortified, gain'st all his politick opposition" (12). As the mood lightens somewhat, there is psychological space for music and a dance, and then all the women go off to dine.

The most involved action in *The Banish'd Shepheardesse* occurs in the subplot and consists of an old-style Jonsonian gulling of some traitorous servants of the rebel leaders. Engineered by Captain Lysander, this business is drawn out by being interspersed with other matters, including a scene in which the noblest of all shepherdesses reports on hearing of that "Royall mine of vertue" (20), her son Charilaus. (Far less attention is accorded her other son, Nicandrus.) Her noble supporter Pausanius lauds Charilaus as that

> Braue young Man: with what magnanimitie, And pacience,
> Hath Hee: induered a burden, would haue made Atlas: stoope.
> His: story: being read,
> Heathens: Themselues (admiering) fell at odds,
> Whether, They: should adore, Him: or Their Godds.
>
> [20]

The name assigned here to the young man's praiser is perhaps most likely to call up thoughts of the second-century traveler, famous for his *Description of Greece* in ten books (bk. 8, *Arcadia*).[19] If, however, we wish to find a seventeenth-century counterpart of the Pausanius in Manuche's play, the peripatetic Henry Jermyn is the most obvious candidate. A handsome, agreeable, and useful man, Jermyn had held a variety of offices in Henrietta Maria's service, beginning as early as 1628. After the death of Charles, in fact, he had become the Queen's chief adviser, general factotum, and closest male associate (Bone 84).[20] Not too surprisingly, he was created Earl of St. Albans in 1660. Still, Manuche presents "Pausanius" in such a way as to preclude affirming more than that he is, indeed, a noble observer and supporter of the Queen.

In another passage Corilliana and her drowsy companions fall asleep, whereupon an angel "Desends from aboue: with a Goulden Croune: and septer" (24). Though modest in scale, this episode is like a scene in a masque. In this ultimate royalist wish-fulfillment sequence—which proves to be the ladies' communal dream vision—Charilaus enters and is crowned by the angel. Eventually Charilaus enters *qua* Charilaus, not merely as a dream man, and after a while, it being observed that he is inclined to mirth, one of his noble attendants proposes a toast to "our Noble Masters Lady," who "will bring forth Boyes" (33). Not surprisingly, one is left to conjecture who the real-life parallel of this "Lady" might be. From a vantage point some three hundred years after the fact, the most likely candidate would seem to be Barbara, born Villiers in 1641 and in 1659 married to a complaisant Catholic royalist named Roger Palmer. Fairly soon after the writing of

---

[19]The 1602 notes to *Il pastor fido* point out Guarini's own indebtedness to this Pausanias (Greg, *Pastoral Poetry* 196). Because of largely negative implications, the playwright probably would have preferred that we not call to mind certain other well-known ancients bearing the same name. [20]The *Kingdomes Weekly Intelligencer* for 16–23 February 1647 reported that "The Lord *Jermyn* continues still in great favour with the Queene," but added, "He beginneth to grow very corpulent, and to looke gray, either through care or age" (Hhh1r).

the pastoral at hand she would become Countess of Castlemaine (1661) and, later, Duchess of Cleveland (1670). Before wearing out her welcome, this lady would bear some five or so children for her King. Indeed, as Antonia Fraser puts the case, "she was already in the months before the Restoration contributing in her own way to the King's royal good humour" (175). Whether the lady be named, unnamed, or unnameable, the wonder is that Manuche did not sidestep the business entirely.

Unlike the gulling subplot, which slowly moves forward, the royal main plot is in some ways obviously constrained, even though we are informed that "the doune=fall of our Enemies, is certaine" and Charilaus "hourly, expects / A sommons, to inioye His owne" (53). If the phrasing in this last line is at all odd, probably it is because Manuche hopes to remind his audience of Matthew Parker's famous ballad called "When the King Enjoys His Own Again." Originally written to buttress the cause of King Charles in 1643, the tune was later put to use in the service of his son (Claude Simpson 766). Toward the close of Manuche's play we even hear about a general who is said to be advancing in Arcadia "More like a proffest states Man: / Then A souldier" (58). Whenever the play was begun, then, its conclusion seems to have been composed about the time that General George Monck made his celebrated march toward London in January and February 1660. The latest news in the play is that the General is proclaiming throughout the city that Charilaus is King, and as the work draws to an end, the expectation is that that long-suffering young man will be summoned back to Arcadia at any time. Meanwhile, the exiled ladies decide to celebrate by giving a little entertainment, after which Corilliana forgives the rascally rebels and all exit to the "Temple."

Throughout the period of the English infatuation with history plays, playwrights almost always drew their materials from periods significantly earlier than their own. Hence, like the Tudors and Stuarts themselves, later readers are implicitly invited to compare era with era. In *The Banish'd Shepheardesse*, however, Manuche reaches back only a couple of decades and then brings us up to the final days just before the Restoration of the Stuarts. Ironically, working in one of the most artificial and derivative of all literary modes, he gives the impression of putting current events into dramatic form with relatively little indirection.

Within the dedication of a later play to his patron Compton, Manuche gives the further but tantalizingly incomplete information that his *Shepheardesse* was made to order for a "Lady." Referring to *The Banish'd Shepheardesse* by name, he informs Compton that "in the writeing . . . I was vtterly deny'd the Current of my owne fancy: to please a Lady of Hon^r whose dictates I was tyed to follow" (*Feast* 1v). Who was this Lady of Honor? The Queen is one possibility. Henrietta Maria's fascination with pastoral had been demonstrated many times, in many ways, and long before civil strife and escape from war gave the old imagery of rural retreat a painful immediacy. Then again, perhaps the Lady of Honor might be "our Noble Masters Lady," that is, the lady designated in the play as capable of bearing royal boys—perhaps Barbara Villiers Palmer. In any case, whoever she may have been, why was Manuche "tyed to follow" her fancy rather than his own? Was this play simply requested, or was it commissioned? Do we have here in the comment to Compton a royalist playwright's private and disgruntled distancing from his own propagandistic drama? How many of our other plays were shaped in accordance with the wishes of someone other than the playwright?[21] When young Charles asked Talbot for a translation of Bonarelli's pastoral, did he expect it would be given any particular sort of spin? Firm answers to such questions will continue to elude us, but this brief passage from Manuche is valuable, nonetheless, for informing us of their existence.[22] Then again, even without it, one may see that *The Banish'd Shepheardesse* is both a tribute to endurance in adversity and a fervent expression of royalist hope that a well-remembered near-paradise might soon be regained.[23]

A thorough tilling of midcentury literary fields would turn up still more examples of dramatic pastoralism. Robert Cox's droll *Acteon and Diana* comes to mind, as does Robert Baron's *Gripsius and Hegio*, a three-act pastoral show that that busy young author inserted in his *Cyprian Academy* (1647). It will interest some to know that in Fane's *Raguaillo D'Oceano* the pastoral roles of a shepherd and a husbandman were played by two of the real-life gardeners on Fane's estate (3r).[24] In chapter 15 we shall consider a pastoral by the Cavendish sisters, Jane and Elizabeth. And doubtless some such works will remain obscured forever, as probably is the case with John Tatham's lost *Daphnes, A Pastorall*.[25] In any case, from the evidence here we may conclude that

---

[21]To cite another instance, we have Jasper Mayne's *The City Match* from 1637-38. In an address to the reader published in 1658, Mayne named King Charles as the instigator of the work and claimed that "*it was meerly out of Obedience that he first wrot[e] it*" (*Two Plaies* A1r).   [22]Elsky has explored an earlier instance involving Bacon's *Declaration of the Practices and Treasons . . .* (1601). Having betrayed his benefactor Essex in this work, Bacon later felt compelled to insist in *Sir Francis Bacon His Apologie* (1604) that at the time it was not he but Elizabeth and her councillors who controlled his pen.   [23]Maguire believes that this play demonstrates "Manuche's shrewd use of recent political history and his formal recovery of the masque and Fletcherian-Caroline tragicomedy" (*Regicide* 46).   [24]The question of casting becomes still more complex and interesting when we find that Fane sometimes also assigned roles to his guests. Morton observes that the latter included "prominent Royalist figures, some of whom were later involved with the covert activities of the Sealed Knot" (*Biography* 52). The Sealed Knot was a group endeavoring to bring Charles II to the throne.   [25]This example comes to mind because a 1651 title page for *Daphnes* has only recently been recorded in a Quaritch catalogue (*English Books*, no. 1091, 1988: p. 41).

despite the imitativeness that is a *sine qua non* of pastoral, the mid-seven-
teenth century displays a wide range of pastoral tones, methods, and aims.
This is a point worth emphasizing. Any would-be student who is predis-
posed to yawn at the mere thought of seventeenth-century pastoral drama
might well be surprised to discover that it affords such breadth.

Not enough breadth, of course, to please everyone. In these latter years
of the twentieth century, certain writers have rediscovered the fairly obvi-
ous fact that sixteenth- and seventeenth-century pastoral flourished de-
spite minimal attention to the working class. James Turner, for one, writes
that a major scholarly contribution of Raymond Williams is his perception
that in pastoral writing "landscapes are made by human labour and that
idealization involves spiriting away the labourer" (*Politics* xii). Louis Mon-
trose hopes a thoughtful reader may turn to good use the facts that "[n]ine
out of ten people in Elizabethan England were rural dwellers, and sheep
outnumbered people, perhaps by as many as three to one" (421). And
Turner rather scornfully compares pastoral literature to "a new colony,
[where] the land is cleared of its troublesome natives and planted with a
new and more loyal population—hilarious bumpkins, contented morons,
fauns, fairies and demigods" (185).

To offer a response that risks obviousness, one might say that such
complaining meshes badly with the goals of those who wrote most pastoral
literature, whether in England, France, Italy, or Spain. It ignores the fact
that the point of writing pastoral probably never was to hold the mirror up
to nature. Had it been so, all writers of Renaissance pastoral as we know it
would be failed realists. Instead, the artificiality and selectivity of Renais-
sance pastorals are devices or strategies designed to be attractively familiar
and interesting in themselves, and often also to make possible the meta-
phorical means of achieving nonpastoral ends. To put this last point another
way, one might suggest that *Time's Distractions* and even *The Banish'd
Shepheardesse* do not deal with England so much as they do—as both works
claim—with Arcadia, a traditional imaginary land (whatever its geographic
origin) that is configured to remind one of certain aspects of England. It is
perfectly understandable, of course, that some of our own contemporaries
might wish to remark on the marginalization of actual rural life in early
modern pastoral literature and to note that some of the native country
residents who appear among the dramatis personae of our plays are charm-
ing bumpkins. This is indeed no world of tar-boxes, raddle, manure on the
hobnails, unfinished sheepfolds, or cauld blasts on rocky crags. But to
perceive cultural obtuseness or conspiracy where there is more likely to be
cultural concentration on something else is to miss much of what traditional
pastoral writing has been about. It is to forget that a courtly element had
been inscribed in pastoral ever since Theocritus praised Ptolemy. From its

Figure 27. Death medal depicting Oliver Cromwell partly in pastoral terms (1658). The shepherd tends his flock beneath a suggestively relevant olive tree. (By permission of the Folger Shakespeare Library.)

earliest days, part of the purpose of pastoral was to praise or blame the nonpastoral. Even if common folk are rarely brought onto the scene, there is plenty to contemplate in the mid-seventeenth-century spectacle of gentle folk who have retreated to the country in order to find refuge from the strife and strain of their former lives.

All things considered, we have a better chance of understanding mid-century pastoral drama if we supplement the question "Where are all the callous-handed peasants?" with the question "Why did it seem appropriate to depict Charles II on his coronation medal as a shepherd?" During his wanderings in real life, Charles certainly had to resort to humble disguise, but on the medal he is perforce a shepherd of no common kind. If we turn back to 1630, the year of his birth, we find Herrick writing, "I a Sheep-hook will bestow, / To have his little King-ship know, / As he is Prince, he's Shepherd too" ("A Pastorall," ll. 42-44). To the extent that there is any puzzle here, surely it is solved by the motto on Charles's medal: DIXI CVSTODIAM, "I have said that I will keep them" (Pinkerton 80, 82).[26] Nor will it take anything away from the fundamental point to add that one side of Oliver Cromwell's funeral medal depicts a shepherd, his sheep, and an olive tree (figure 27). However many levels of reading this invites, it is in numerous ways appropriate that the mode is pastoral. As Drayton put the matter, in pastoral writings *the most High, and most Noble Matters of the World may bee shaddowed . . . , and for certaine sometimes are.*

---

[26]If we turn back further still to 1603, we find Charles's grandfather James writing, "I am the Husband, and all the whole Isle is my lawfull Wife; . . . I am the Shepherd, and it is my flocke" (*Political Works* 272).

[I I]

THE CRAFT OF TRANSLATION

You have Translations statutes best fulfil'd.
That handling neither sully nor would guild.
—Andrew Marvell, "To His Worthy Friend Doctor Witty" (1651)

'Tis good to have Translations, because they serve as a Comment,
so far as the Judgment of Man goes.
—John Selden, *Table-Talk* (ante 1654)

It speaks our *Land*, as well as *Tongue*, and cares
Not onely for our *Words*, but our *Affayrs*.
—commendatory poem in Christopher Wase, *Electra* (1649)

Translators are but like those that shew the Tombs at *Westminster*,
or the Lyons at the Tower, which is but to be an Informer, not the
Owner of them.
—Margaret Cavendish, *The Worlds Olio* (1655)

ALTHOUGH THIS STUDY has now skimmed off several translations for
a chapter on pastoral drama, and before that borrowed Buchanan's *Tyran-
nicall-Government Anatomized*, Knightley's translation of Drury's *Alfrede*, and
Howell's *Peleus and Thetis*, we still have before us a varied pool of ancient
and modern foreign plays that were rendered into English in the middle
years of the seventeenth century. Coming toward the close of England's
greatest period of translation—this was the century, one recalls, of the King
James Bible, Florio's Montaigne, Shelton's *Quixote*, Mabbe's *Rogue*, and
Chapman's Homer—these plays partake of a metamorphic tradition greater
than themselves. Like a good many foreign books imported in their original
languages, they also constitute a noteworthy infusion into England of
noninsular ideas and techniques.[1] Though Douglas Bush (who is usually
right) is not altogether correct in suggesting that these translations are the
work of "Renaissance humanists with a mission" (such a label is too heavy
for some), they certainly did provide a useful glass in which English readers
could glimpse other peoples and therefore, sometimes, themselves.[2]

---

[1]Robert Burton, one might observe, purchased volumes from Amsterdam, Antwerp, Hamburg, Cologne, Frankfurt, Paris, and Geneva within a year of their publication.   [2]Bush writes, "From the beginning of English history the translation of ancient and modern books had been a main agent in the development of religious and secular culture and of literary style" (57). This is true enough, but he also claims, too broadly, that "the translators were not dilettantes of leisure" (60).

That the glass would be dark was a given. It is and doubtless always was apparent that complete translation is impossible. Whether one thinks of Augustine's principle of a shared *significatio* or of a formal correspondence of linguistic units or of carryover at an affective level, equivalence is impossible. One of our spunkier play-translators, Christopher Wase, writes of the "insuperable defects in rendring Languages each by other, which are often inadaequate, and in signification, credit, phrase, variety, incommensurable one with the other" (*Cicero* A2v). Even within the same language, one cannot use different words and express the same thing. Hence style is important. In fact, as soon as we advance beyond some major correspondences between any translated play and its source, new and interesting questions arise: In what ways are these two works different? Granted the successful transmission of some kinds of data, in what ways is the translation a commentary on its source? In what ways is it an interpretative re-creation of its source? This is not the place to plumb individual translations deeply, but such questions may be borne in mind as helpful signposts to learning more about any particular work.

As for analytical tools of the day, Dryden's famed triad of metaphrase, paraphrase, and imitation—that is, literal translation, free translation, and original creation based on elements in the source—is a little late for us but still helpful (see Dryden, preface to *Ovid's Epistles* A8r-v). It elides, however, the element of creativity inherent in all translation. One might argue that a translator's creativity begins with the selection of a text. What the translator may be up to in this (knowingly or unknowingly) is always a fair question. Since we are concerned here with a politically sensitive period, this means among other things that we should be as alert as ever to contemporary relevancies. Behind the personal safeguard of a foreign source, the translator of a play may be inviting us to ponder Why this play? Why now? Why shaped thus? Why thus dedicated? On the other hand, and despite the fact that, willy nilly, a translator is an interpreter, we should be ready to recognize also that any translation may, after all, be little more than the end product of such goals as self-amusement, public display, and flattery.

In 1640, on the fore-edge of our period, we at once encounter a notable translation from Hugo Grotius, the polymath Dutch humanist. One of the major intellectuals of the day, Grotius wrote not only books on religion (*De veritate religionis Christianae*) and international law (*De jure belli ac pacis*) but also closet dramas in Latin, among them *Christus patiens*. In September 1639 the English poet and translator George Sandys (best known for his trim rendering of Ovid's *Metamorphoses*) dedicated his *Christs Passion* (published 1640) to the English King: "Thus in the Shadow of your Absence . . . have I, in what I was able, continued to serve you" (a5r).

Absent in the earlier part of 1639, Charles had been trying to negotiate with his northern realm. From Newcastle on 14 May he issued *A Proclamation Declaring the King's Intention toward the Scots*, and on 7 July came his last Scottish proclamation, "Given at Our court at Barwick" (Larkin 686). Then from Whitehall on 20 August came his "Proclamation declaring those of Scotland, who have entred, or shall enter this Kingdom in a Warlike manner, and their Adherents, to be Rebels and Traitours to His Majestie" (726-28).

Sandys was a gentleman of His Majesty's Privy Chamber, and as a writer he had long enjoyed Charles's favor. In *Christs Passion* he now offered his royal patron a dignified, formal, potent play that dared to turn scripture into drama. In fact, fortified with scholarly annotations and a reminder that the subject had been dramatized previously by Apollinarius of Laodicea and Gregory of Nazianzus, *Christs Passion* opens with a long speech by Jesus.

A second translation from Grotius, and again one that springs directly from scripture, was produced by Francis Goldsmith in 1652. It was to Henry, Lord Marquess of Dorchester, that Goldsmith dedicated this rendering from the work of a man he deemed "one of our best modern Latin Poets" (1st B2r). Giving its original author top billing, the volume is called *Hugo Grotius, His Sophompaneas*. Pharoah's new name for Joseph was "Sophompaneas" (Gen. 41.45), and it is with an alert awareness of dramatic precedents in Sophocles, Aeschylus, and Euripides that Grotius's play retells the story of Joseph and his brethren.[3] Though Goldsmith offers *Sophompaneas* to the English reader as the tale of a "Prophet, and Royall Favourite, famous in holy Writ . . . for wisdome and chastity" (1st B2r), there seems to be no particular reason for us to make much of the concept of "Favourite." The work as a whole suggests that Goldsmith's main aim was to make available a major work by a major modern writer. Then again, one should note that the translations by both Sandys and Goldsmith—one presented to the King and one, after the King's death, to a royalist—were derived from the publications of a man who himself had both written in support of the Arminians and worked for Christian reunion. One well might say that both books support Bush's point about an extended, latter-day Christian humanism.

Likewise religiously oriented and rendered from a modern Latin source is a translation from the *Tragoediae sacrae* (Paris, 1620) of Nicolas Caussin. Caussin was a Jesuit who at various times expressed his intense piety as a teacher, a preacher, a confessor to Louis XIII—and a dramatist. In the martyr play *Herminigildus*, which is based mainly on events related by Gregory of Tours, we read how a Visigothic King of Spain, Levigildus, a follower of the Arian faith, is induced to turn against his son Herminigildus. The latter, thanks to the machinations of his Arian stepmother

---

[3]The name is variously recorded as "Saphenath-paneah," "Saphaneth-phanee," and "Zaphenath-paneah."

(the Queen) and to his own conversion from Arianism to Catholicism (his wife inspires him to become "a Christian & a Roman one" [12v]), finds himself at war with his father. "If wee must fall by civill war," says his friend Erasistratus, "Lets . . . receiue o^r wounds with manly courage" (4r). After a period of attempted reconciliation, Herminigildus is finally sentenced by his aged father to beheading. No sooner is the sentence carried out, however, than the old King passionately regrets it, his only comfort now being that he can proclaim Herminigildus's innocence, become his supplicant, and adore him "as a Martir, a Miracle" (30v).[4] While reading this somber play about a sixth-century saint, one is given to understand that the two notable women in the story—the stepmother and the wife—are both important because of their impact on the hero. Quite strikingly, though, and with a certain strange effectiveness, neither woman ever appears.[5]

The English version of *Herminigildus* was discovered in 1977 by William P. Williams in a cache of manuscript plays at Castle Ashby, the seat of James Compton, third Earl of Northampton (see figure 28).[6] Since it comes down to us in the hand of Compton himself, and since it also has corrections in his hand, the work is now considered very likely to be Compton's own (Williams, "Castle Ashby Manuscripts" 402). However moved he may have been by the words he read or set down about the steadfast soldier-martyr Herminigildus, Compton knew from personal experience that great sacrifices are great sacrifices. Having served his King at Edgehill, Hopton Heath (where he was shot in the leg and his father was slain), Cropredy Bridge, and Naseby, Compton returned to Castle Ashby, which had been looted and despoiled.[7] On 7 September 1643 orders were issued for all of his goods in Crosby House to be sequestered, seized, and sold, and on 8 November 1644 Northampton House, by the Savoy, was designated as a center for receiving soldiers maimed in Parliament's service (*Journals of Commons* 3:231, 691). Irony of a different sort was created when an ordinance of 8 October 1645 decreed that revenues from Compton's properties in Islington and elsewhere in Middlesex were to go toward filling the coffers of Prince Charles Louis, Count Palatine of the Rhine—a surly nephew of Charles I who had sided with the parliamentarians (Firth and Rait 3:784).

---

[4]St. Hermenegild is said to have been killed on 13 April 585. Approximately one thousand years later his remains were acquired for the relic collection of Spain's Philip II, who is thought to have treasured them in part as a sort of surrogate for his own dead son, Carlos.   [5]McCabe observes that Jesuit regulations had earlier forbade female characters and costume on the stage, but in 1600 these restrictions were relaxed on condition that such usage be kept within bounds (178–84). Elsewhere Caussin did bring women onstage.   [6]On 8 March 1978 these plays were sold at Christie's to the British Library.   [7]Many details about the Battle at Hopton Heath, from a royalist perspective, are given in *Battaile on Hopton-Heath in Staffordshire, betweene His Majesties Forces under the Right Honourable the Earle of Northampton and Those of the Rebels*(1643).

Figure 28. James Compton, third Earl of Northampton (1622-81). (From the collection of the Marquess of Northampton.)

Young Compton confided in his private papers that he took it for granted "t^t those who inwardly repine must now outwardly submit," and he could not "thinke a fluent pen sufficient to blunt a sharpe sword" ("The former constitution" 39r). Though he applied as a "delinquent" to compound for his estates in 1646, and some might think that "General Cromwell hath been very kind to Lord Northampton about his composition,"[8] his fine was set at £20,820 10s.—enough to ruin him. Moreover, he was in and out of prison during the 1650s, apparently a watched man. All in all, and despite whatever self-protective rapprochement he ever established with Cromwell, one may reasonably surmise that Compton turned to the martyrdom of the royal Herminigildus with thoughts of his own King's execution. He devoted what he called a "volume" to Charles and named it *The Martird Monarch*. He also may have given more than passing thought to his own father, who had proved steadfast unto death in Charles's cause.

Among ancient writers who were translated during the middle years of the century, Seneca plays a significant role. By far the most influential of all classical dramatists in Elizabethan drama, Seneca—with versions of *Agamemnon*, *Hercules Furens*, *Medea*, *Hippolytus*, and *Troades*—was in fact the most frequently translated dramatist of the mid-seventeenth century. This is understandable at least in part because his declamatory plays were deemed to be well suited to private reading. As Robert Greene had observed back in 1589, "English *Seneca* read by candle light yeeldes manie good sentences" (*Menaphon* **3r).

James Compton's verse translations of both *Agamemnon* and *Hercules Furens* further expand our knowledge of the young Earl's linguistic and literary interests.[9] Generally speaking, and even though neither play reaches us in finished form, Compton's work is earnest and accurate. If it is true, moreover, that he wrote them in 1649 or 1650 (Williams, "Castle Ashby 404), he scarcely could have produced the following English words for Amphitryon without thinking of his own times and monarch:

> The world did find the author of it's peace
> was not on earth. prosperous & happy crime
> is vertue call'd. the good obey the bad.
> Right in ye Sword remaines. lawes yeeld to fear.
> ....
> . . . I Saw the crowne wth ye Kings head
> snatch'd off. Who can Sad Thebs Enough lament?
>
> [*Hercules Furens* 21v]

---

[8]These are the words of Compton's mother-in-law, recorded in her diary on 15 July 1650 (William Compton 101). [9]Mention should be made also of Compton's partial translation of Plautus's *Captivi* (BL Add. MS 60281).

Anyone may translate Seneca at any time, of course, but the suitability here of black Senecanism to defeated royalism is a phenomenon worth noting.

Edward Sherburne's translation of Seneca's *Medea* (1648) is a far more finished work, offering on its first page not only the opening eight lines of the play but also a marginal note and seven footnotes. At the back, further-more, there are more than fifty pages of further annotations. A man with decidedly scholarly leanings, Sherburne was a Roman Catholic who had succeeded his father as Clerk of the Ordnance in 1637-38, but the House of Lords relieved him of that responsibility when war erupted. As soon as possible, he reports, he went to the King, "who made me Commissary Generall of his Artillery. In wch Condition I serv'd him at the Battle of Edge Hill, and dureing the 4 years Civill Warre" (*Poems* xxiv). Afterward, Sher-burne's estate, personal property, and library having been seized, he moved to the Middle Temple. Here he established an important friendship with the translator and poet Thomas Stanley. Later still, from 1655 through 1659, he toured the Continent as a tutor to Sir John Coventry.

In *Medea*, his first publication, aiming to retain "the Majesty and spirit" of Seneca, "not the letter" (A2v), Sherburne claims to have produced a paraphrase. Whether or not this representation of bad acts in bad times was itself a comment on current bad times is perhaps beyond sure demonstra-tion. Anyone trying to decide the issue, however, should consider the words of Stanley. Himself both a classicist and a translator, Stanley writes that his friend Sherburne, in turning *Medea* into English, has seen to it that "our Times / Can speake, as well as act, their highest Crimes" (A3r).

In 1651 Edmund Prestwich published a young man's version of Seneca's *Hippolytus* (or *Phaedra*) along with some of his own "SELECT POEMS" (61). Prestwich's temptation-resistant Hippolitus is perhaps somewhat more a victim, more a martyr, than Seneca's uptight misogynist had been: "guiltlesse and chast / He fel" (46). Launched with a generous spray of gratulatory verse from, among others, James Shirley and Charles Cotton ("Thy work deserves an Ampitheatre," wrote the latter [Prestwich, *Hip-politus* B1v]), Prestwich's translation was in fact reasonably effective.

In the light of both Sherburne's and Prestwich's efforts, it is interesting that Samuel Pordage subsequently hoped he "might add the more lustre to, and set off with my distorts the beauties of *Medea*, and *Hippolitus*, so well translated by severall Hands" (*Troades*, "To the Reader"). Writing of his own "translation, or rather *Paraphrase*" of *Troades*, Pordage praises both "that noble *Philosopher*," Seneca himself, and also his own English prede-cessors, citing their "eligancy and skill." [10] Pordage composed these phrases in November 1660 and thereby provides interestingly late evidence of

---

[10] Quoted from the second leaf following the title page.

Seneca's prolonged and important presence in the English mind and imagination. In this particularly painful play, one should note, he has turned his attention to Seneca's depiction of the aftermath of the Trojan War, with its bloody retribution and, finally, for the victors, the wish-fulfilling reattainment of "Riches, and Glory" ("Argument"). Even as we read the play today, most can agree that always "It behoves us most / To know what Victors ought to do, and what / The Conquer'd suffer can" (12). As for its own time, Pordage's book appeared exactly when many in England were contemplating the fates of the regicides, twenty-nine of whom were convicted of treason (October 1660) and thirteen of whom were executed. Great Cromwell himself, dead in 1658, would in January 1661 be exhumed from Westminster Abbey and hanged at Tyburn.[11]

Though Thomas Stanley is best remembered for his polished lyrics and his imposing *History of Philosophy* (1655-62), we should note that he included in the latter a blank verse translation of Aristophanes' *The Clouds*—"*not as Comicall divertisement for the Reader,*" he explains, but "*as a necessary supplement to the life of* Socrates" (67). *The Clouds* takes Socrates as its chief target, satirizing him as a misguided and misguiding mentor, a "Priest of subtle trifles" (75). It is thus a landmark both in the story of Socrates' life and in the early history of personal satire in drama.

A second Aristophanic comedy, *Plutus*, was published in 1659 by "H.H.B.," perhaps Henry Burnell.[12] Long a favorite among Renaissance readers, surely because of the applicability of its satire to so many different times and places, *Plutus* caught H.H.B.'s eye at least partly for parabolic reasons. In a "Short Discourse" on *Plutus* he writes:

> Now amongst the ancient Fables, I find none that better unfolds the nature and state of Mankind then this, which *Aristophanus* takes for the subject of his Comedy; nor perhaps any that comes nearer to our own sacred Scriptures. *Plutus*, the Tipe of *Wealth* and *Plenty*, is said by *Jupiter* to be deprived of his Eyes, for aspiring to enthrone himself in his power and wisdome, that which at the first we read threw down the Angels, and next to them him, and in him that posterity that was created almost as happy as those Angels; so that *Plutus* with his *eyes open* may allude to us *Adam* in his *Innocency*, his *blindness* our *fall;* and his being brought to *Esculapius* his Temple to receive his sight again, may not unfitly emble[m] to us our seeking of a *Saviour* to bring us into that State again we fell from. . . . [33]

---

[11]If one is reluctant to find in Pordage's *Troades* an impulse to comment on current events, one surely need not be fainthearted regarding his *Poems upon Several Occasions*, published that same year. Here are poems praising both Charles II ("From whose arivall all our blessings Spring" [B4v]) and General Monck ("Great man by blood, by vertue greater made" [B2v]). The following year, 1661, brought Pordage's equally unequivocal *Heroick Stanzas on His Maiesties Coronation.*   [12]For discussion of the authorship problem, see Hines.

All of this serves to remind us that in staying alert to contemporary relevancies in these plays, we should bear in mind a ready tendency of some at the time to see also a scriptural dimension in drama's "Tipes and Figures" (33). Probably we should take seriously an assertion on H.H.B.'s title page: "Some dare affirm that Comedies may teach / More in one hour than some in ten can preach."

The fundamental vitality of *Plutus* had previously manifested itself in a thoroughly anglicized and unlaced comedy called *Hey for Honesty, Down with Knavery* (1651). Originally the work of a witty young Cantabrigian, Thomas Randolph, in about 1626-28, it was subsequently "augmented" and packed with midcentury allusions by one F.J. about 1648. "Prince Rupert knows what service I did at Marston Moor," says Mercurius, "when I run away" (478). Says Goggle, an Amsterdam-man, to Nevergood, a sequestrator,

> Now out upon thee for a roguish heretic!
> 'Tis not a Christmas, 'tis a Nativity pie.
> That superstitious name, I know, is banish'd
> Out of all England, holly and ivy too.
>
> [454]

The reference, of course, is to various parliamentary measures in the 1640s designed first to discourage the traditional celebration of Christmas and then to outlaw it. As of 19 December 1644 an ordinance made the Feast of the Nativity a fast day. Not only was feast changed to fast, but the very morpheme *mas* became politically and officially incorrect.[13] In a later passage of *Hey for Honesty* we read:

> I do remember thee in the archbishop's time,
> Thou madest me stand i' th' Popish pillory
> With Prynne and Burton, only for speaking
> A little sanctified treason.
>
> [456]

Also stitched onto the fabric of the older play is Clodpole's latter-day put-down of Poverty the trull: "What a silly woman's this to talk of nobility houses! Does not she know we are all Levellers, there's no nobility now" (423). Somewhere short of this reminder of John Lilburne and Levelling we have crossed over into Dryden's third realm of translation—imitation.

We must turn to Greek tragedy and specifically to Christopher Wase's version of Sophocles' *Electra* (1649) to find the most overt and passionate of midcentury editorializing translations. In an address to the recently bereaved Princess Elizabeth, Wase writes: "This dim Chrystall (sully'd

---

[13]The Puritan urge to suppress the *mas* in "Christmas" had long since provided Jonson with a mocking passage in *The Alchemist: "Christ-tide,* I pray you," urges Ananias (III.ii.43).

with Antiquitie, and a long voyage) will return upon your Highnesse some Lines and Shadows of that Pietie to your deceased Father, which seats you above the Age, and beyond your Years" (¶3r). Only thirteen in the year of both this book and her final farewell to her father, Elizabeth is offered here (by a verse writer who signs himself H.P.) "*A Christall for to dresse your Cypresse by*" (¶5r). She is assured (erroneously, as it turned out) that the "*next age may, / See the score of thy Royall Parents wrongs / Reveng'd by Kings which now sleep in thy Loynes*" (¶4v). In other words, both the Princess herself and the rest of Wase's original readers were well apprised of his drift. One who signs himself W.G. explicitly congratulates Wase on his "ingenious choice" of the play *Electra*, "Representing Allegorically these Times" (¶6v). Another notes "his apt *choice and seasonable translation*" (¶5v). Once again made explicit for us here is the concept of timely translation. This second writer continues:

> The *Calendar* that's stampt for *fourty nine*
> Suits not the *Year* more, then thy *Book* the *time:*
> Which comes forth in *such* day, that it *before*
> Had been *clean Verse*, and *English*, but *no more.*
> Now 'tis *Designe*, and *Plot*, and may be said
> Not to bring onely *forreign Wit*, but *Aid:*
> It speaks our *Land*, as well as *Tongue*, and *cares*
> Not onely for our *Words*, but our *Affayrs.*
>
> [¶5v]

In case the nature of "our *Affayrs*" is ever in doubt, pictures of both Princess Elizabeth, clad in black, and her eldest brother are included (reproduced here as figures 29 and 30); Electra is referred to in the play as the Princess Royal; and the volume concludes unequivocally with an "EPILOGUE Shewing the Parallell in two Poems, THE RETURN and THE RESTAURATION."[14] Wase had high hopes that "Here from a Popular bondage freed / The Countrey shall lift up her head," and specifically, for Elizabeth, that "Thy Prison too shall . . . fly ope" ("Restauration" F3v, F2r). The fact is that the English Electra would remain a prisoner and die at Carisbrooke Castle the following year.

The Greco-English correspondences that Wase wished to imply in his translation of the play are summarized by his friend W.G.: "Our *Agamemnon*'s dead, *Electra* grieves, / The onely hope is that *Orestes* lives" (¶6v). Though three members of the English royal family were thus accounted for, Wase obviously had to sidestep the implication that Henrietta Maria was a Clytemnestra. As it turns out, his words of rationalization may be applied to others' work as well as his own: "Here may not unproperly be

---

[14]Potter notes briefly some further parallels (*Secret Rites* 53).

Figure 29. Prince Charles, age nineteen, depicted in Wase's translation of Sophocles's *Electra* (1649). As the print suggests, Charles was in Jersey for a while in 1649. (By permission of the Folger Shakespeare Library.)

urg'd the old caution, that similitudes run not upon all foure: Yet may this be a fit pourtraiture of an accumulative or aggregative Lady, the queen politick, which hath trull'd it in the lewd embraces of the souldiery, and to consummate the scandall, shall have conspired with it, & together hainously upon agreement, destroys her just and undoubted Lord" (5).

Despite Wase's cautionary move of publishing his *Electra* at The Hague, one of the group of celebratory versifiers in it raises the possibility that now he "must / . . . be indited for . . . [his] per'lous Book" (¶7r). Another friend takes a more encouraging stance, in fact a remarkably frank one:

> And it is *Counsel* now to fight the times,
> Not in *pitcht Prose,* but *Verse,* and *flying rymes.*
> 'Tis safe too: For the Poet (as Men say)
> Can forfeit nothing but some *woods* of *Bay.*
> An old Lute, broken harp, torn wreath, or all
> Such *Goods* and *Chattels* mere *Poeticall.*
> . . . .
> . . . 'tis but *Sophocles* repeated, and
> *Eccho* cannot be *guilty* or *arraign'd*
> Thus by *flight* of *translation* you make
> Him *libell* 'em, who is *ten ages* back
> Out of their reach: and lay your ambush so,
> They see not who 'tis hurts 'em. *He* or *You.*
>
> [¶5v-6r]

From thy afflicted Vaile, that Cypresse Bower.
Still Watered fresh by thy Celestiall shower.
Come forth, come forth, Bright Captive, & Declare
With a Full Orb the Innocent, and Faire.

Figure 30. Princess Elizabeth in mourning as depicted in Wase's *Electra*. (By permission of the Folger Shakespeare Library.)

Although such a passage underestimates the obviousness of this particular translator's craftiness, it throws nonetheless valuable light on the self-protective indirection that a translator might claim.

The case of Christopher Wase, a young Fellow of King's College, Cambridge, who had received his bachelor's degree just a year earlier, is complicated by his having been caught sending "a feigned Letter from the King" (John Walker, pt. 2.152). Like many another of the time, Wase allowed his political passions to take him dangerously far, and for his combined offenses he was deprived of his Fellowship and turned out of the college. When he then tried to leave England, he was captured at sea and put in prison at Gravesend. Somehow managing to escape abroad, however, he proceeded to serve for a while in the Spanish army against the French. A further sign of his mettle is that when he eventually returned, Philip Herbert, first Earl of Montgomery, chose him as tutor for his eldest son—with whom, between Latin lessons, he followed the hounds (Anthony Powell 75). Subsequently he served successively as headmaster of Dedham and Tonbridge Schools, and finally, academic that he always was, he gravitated to Oxford, where he became Superior Bedel of Civil Law to the University (Deedes 39-40).

When we turn to plays in modern languages, we again find that most of our examples come from the 1650s. Supplementing the Italian pastoral plays discussed earlier—Tasso's *Aminta,* Guarini's *Pastor fido,* and Bonarelli's *Filli di Sciro*[15]—is a manuscript comedy (now at the Folger) called *Selfe Intrest; or, The Belly Wager* from the Italian *L'Interesse* by Nicolò Secchi (who lived ca. 1500-1560).[16] This was undertaken by William Reymes, a young Norfolk man, "per gusto suo" (title page), and it comes to us bearing hints of performance by players who hoped to provide some "gusto" for an actual audience. As one enters for a while into its hard-boiled world of greedy merchants, reckless youths, and bawds, a reader from our own spot in time is likely to be struck less by some resemblances to the plot of Shakespeare's *Twelfth Night* than by an unusually forthright depiction of gender subterfuge and cross-dressing. "I thought to force Dame Nature," confesses old Pandolfo of his daughter, "and would need's / make male of ffemale" (1).

A better Italian play from about the same period—indeed, sometimes considered the first and best of Italy's theatrical classics—is Niccolò Machiavelli's *Mandragola*. Probably written about 1519 and named for the mandrake root that, here, is supposed to help cure a young wife of sterility, this play is yet another work translated by James Compton, Earl of Northampton (Kelliher, "Hitherto Unrecognized" 173). More precisely, it was adapted by him. Though Compton's *Mandrake* raises the question of when a translation is not a translation, it is perhaps the best of his plays.

Transplanting the action from Renaissance Florence to Commonwealth London, Compton gives us a young man named Leaveland who returns from Paris to London in order to meet and obtain one Mrs. Soonewrought. That her husband, a barrister, is "the silliest fellow in London" (7v) facilitates Leaveland's pursuit. Nevertheless, a good deal of ingenuity is expended in achieving the actual conquest. For instance, our hero's first ploy is to pose as a physician from Paris, one who dazzles with volleys of Latin and complicates everything by claiming that the "man that hath first to do with her when shee hath taken the potion, will infallibly die within eight daies" (11v). The action throughout is expedited by a Mosca-like character named Lackwealth and enlivened by Lady Horner (Mrs. Soonewrought's mother) and Parson Renchetext (a self-interested accomplice in the entrapment). In the course of Renchetext's inveigling of Mrs. Soonewrought, he avers, "Truly M^{rs} as sure as ye holy couenant, to satisfie y^r husband in y^{is} is not halfe so bad as to see a play, whiche two sermons wipes of" (15v). So thoroughly Englished is the cleric in Compton's hands, indeed, that to help pass a sleepless night he is said to "read in Mr Prins

---

[15]Mention has previously been made here also (chapter 9) of James Howell's translation called *The Nuptialls of Peleus and Thetis* (1654), conjectured to be from an original work by Francesco Buti or possibly Diamante Gabrielli.   [16]In 1953 Helen Andrews Kaufman published an edition of the play.

workes" before walking out to see if he can "find any night congregations, to hearken after a new light" (19v). Like its Italian original, this English *Mandrake* raises a good many questions that are likely to make a reader think as well as smile. In fact, Compton's play is one of the best examples we have of a comedy so well adapted to its new cultural setting as to spark fresh meanings. Though unfortunately it appears to be undateable, the play certainly alludes to the 1650s and probably was written then.

Very different in appeal are the works from Spanish by the versatile diplomat and poet Sir Richard Fanshawe. One of the best and most industrious translators of the period—besides Guarini's *Faithful Shepherd*, noted earlier, he published Luis de Camoëns' *Lusiads* from the Portuguese (1655) and a Latin version of Fletcher's *Faithful Shepherdess* (1658)—Fanshawe had reinforced his Spanish connection by repeated state missions to Spain. Langbaine later would call him not only "a great Scholar; and a sincere, sweet natur'd, and pious Gentleman," but also "an able Statesman" (*Account* 191). More particularly, we learn in the introductory matter to his posthumously published *Querer por solo querer: To Love Only for Love Sake* (1670) that this work was the product of his confinement following the Battle of Worcester (September 1651). During that conflict, while serving as chief adviser to Charles II (crowned at Scone that year), he had been taken prisoner. Released on bail and in 1653 offered asylum at Tankersley Park, Yorkshire, by William, the second Earl of Strafford, Fanshawe planted some fruit trees and turned his mind back to Spain.

In Spain during the spring of 1622 a magnificent festival had been held at the spring palace at Aranjuez in honor of the new King, Philip IV, and his Queen, Isabel. The Countess of Olivares suggested to the poet-courtier Antonio Hurtado de Mendoza that he write an account that would preserve something of the event, whereupon he produced two such works, one in prose and one in verse. In fact, later that year he incorporated the version in verse within his own spectacular and sumptuous play called *Querer por solo querer*. Spain at the time was a place where dramatic entertainments could be delightfully and harmlessly performed by aristocratic young ladies—much as the French-born Henrietta Maria chose to do in Montagu's *Shepheard's Paradise*. As a matter of fact, not hesitating to cast the *meninas* themselves as kings, princes, and generals, *Querer por solo querer* naturally finds itself dealing directly and openly with the question of "*Manly Women*" and "Men effeminately bent" (9). But such matters are not much explored. One might even suggest that the title, which obviously advertises the value of love for its own sake, may be a gracious smile on the fact that only a limited sort of satisfaction could be promised by a cast made up entirely of women. None of the princes in the play, it turns out, wins either of the princesses.

Mendoza shaped his work, nevertheless, so as to suggest that the young Prince of Persia, Felisbravo, might represent King Philip (then seventeen), and Zelidaura, the Princess of Tartaria, Queen Isabel. Rendered into Fanshawe's native language, complete with fire-spitting serpents, shepherdesses wearing silver scarves, and Mars in a chariot drawn by lions, *To Love Only for Love Sake* fits into no standard English dramatic genre. On the other hand, granted the age's taste for high-flying, technicolor prose narratives, one sees at once why Fanshawe's title page calls it "A DRAMATICK ROMANCE." Nor must we set aside romance in order to consider looking more closely at such a passage as the following, spoken by Rifaloro, the droll:

> I quake: This *Prince* was born to rule the *World*.
> O the transcendent baseness of a pack
> Of Hounds, of us, who (with what we call Loyalty)
> Not follow, but ev'n *hunt* so sweet a King,
> And *worry* him!
>
> [16]

All this, significantly, has rather a different slant from Mendoza's Spanish original:

> Temblãdo estoy, que este espero,
>   q̃ ha de gouernar el mundo:
>   ò cuydado vagamundo
>   de tanto gran majadero;
> Pues, con lo que buena ley
>   los mentecatos llamamos,
>   todos, el dar, intentamos
>   sus consegitos al Rey. . . .
>
> [*Querer* 6v]

Though *To Love Only for Love Sake* was not published until 1670, several years after Fanshawe's death, some of the thoughts he expressed on dramatic genre were certainly timely in the 1650s, when he set them down. In his words, "These Representations . . . refused the vulgar name of Comedies, and aspire to that of *Opere*" (*Festivals* 3). In reading Fanshawe's translation of Mendoza's description of a Spanish occasion that took place in 1622, we find the view that an opera, instead of being "measur'd by the Common Rules of a Play (which is a Fable all of one piece) is made up of incoherent variety; of which the Sight got a better share than the Hearing, and where the Comedy (if it may be call'd so) was such to the Eye more than to the Ear" (17). The passage is all the more interesting when we realize that the thoughtful and basically fastidious translator has here updated a passage in which Mendoza does not refer to opera but instead writes of "Estas representaciones que no admiten el nombre vulgar de comedia, y se le dà de inuencion" (Hurtado de Mendoza, *Fiesta* A4r).

It is not Spain, however, but France that provides most of our midcentury plays from a modern foreign language. Since Caroline society was so strongly colored by French culture, one might be surprised that there were not even more. In narrative fiction, the middle years provide especially plentiful evidence of the French connection. In 1653, having been paroled from a Puritan jail, Sir Thomas Urquhart published part of his exuberant translation of Rabelais. More fashionable were the translations of romances: Gomberville's *History of Polexander* (1647), La Calprenède's *Cassandra* (1652) and *Cleopatra* (1652), Scudéry's *Ibrahim* (1652) and *Artamenes; or, The Grand Cyrus* (1653-55), and d'Urfé's *Astrea* (1657). Such books were bound to make themselves felt in subsequent English drama.

From the middle years of the century, in addition to such French dramatic writing as we have noted previously (Howell's *Peleus and Thetis* and T.R.'s *Extravagant Sheepherd*), we have a fragment from James Compton, Earl of Northampton—a few pages from the opening of Pierre Corneille's *Don Sanche d'Aragon*—and a series of products from the pen of Sir William Lower. Lower produced two works each from Paul Scarron, Philippe Quinault, and Pierre Corneille. Because we have previously seen his original wares deployed in *The Enchanted Lovers*, we should not now have exaggerated hopes. When it comes to translating, in fact, Lower's mediocrity is underscored by his tendency toward metaphrase. At worst, the result is opaqueness, a sort of verbal haze that simultaneously presents and obscures.

Lower's *Don Japhet of Armenia* (1657), translated from Scarron's *Don Japhet d'Arménie* and still in manuscript, takes us back to Spain in the time of Charles V and depicts some of the exploits of that Emperor's "vaine glorious" fool, Japhet (5v). Displaying the farcical humours of the egotistical, absurd Japhet is the main point of the work, but there is also a little to-do about Japhet's new servant, Alfonso, who is really a noble "Caualeer" (3v) in disguise. Thanks mainly to the verve of its original, this is the liveliest of Lower's surviving plays. One can only conjecture as to whether it might have held its own with Lower's *The Three Dorothies* from Scarron's *Les Trois Dorotées*.[17]

Two years later, Lower's version of Quinault's *La Généreuse Ingratitude* was published at The Hague as a twelvemo called *The Noble Ingratitude* (1659). During the latter 1650s Lower may have held a post at The Hague

---

[17] *The Three Dorothies; or, Jodelet Box'd* was created from Scarron's *Les Trois Dorotées; ou, Le Jodelet Souffleté*. The name "Jodelet," which had come to refer to someone so absurd as to incite laughter, was in fact assumed by France's leading comic actor, Julien Lespy Jodelet. It appears that no translation of *Les Trois Dorotées* ever reached print, however, and now the manuscript itself has disappeared. W.B. Gates's study of Lower's dramatic works and translations provides a helpful path through the bibliographical thicket.

in the household of Mary of Orange (eldest daughter of Charles I and wife of William II of Orange). By this means or some other he must have had some contact with Queen Elizabeth of Bohemia (sister of Charles I), then an exile in Holland. He not only dedicated *The Noble Ingratitude* to Elizabeth ("best of Queens, and ... most Juditious of Women" [A1v]) but also indicated that she had already approved it. Labeled a pastoral tragicomedy, the play is set in the *"Forrest of Argier"* (A3v), where the shepherds are descendants of

> Those Heros, who in time pass'd conquer'd Spain
> From those renowned Moors, whose great exploits
> Made the Kings of a hundred Christian people
> Tremble for fear, and who seeing *Tunis* conquer'd
> By *Charls the fifth*, conserve here in these places
> Their glory and their freedom. . . .
>
> [25-26]

Whatever this means, it provides further evidence that pastoralism played a lingering role in the drama of the day. When Almansor proclaims that "this fair desert's like a Court" (26), we are on familiar Renaissance ground. And as we should expect, the main business of these exiled courtiers is high-level matchmaking.

The Amourous Fantasme (1660) is another tiny book that Lower published at The Hague. Once more borrowing from Quinault (*Le Fantôme Amoureux*), Lower this time dedicated his labors to Mary of Orange herself, "the most accomplish'd Princesse of the Earth" (A3r). (A short time later, when Mary died of smallpox at twenty-nine, Lower published *A Funeral Elegy on Her Illustrious Highnesse the Princess Royal of Orange* [1661].) The amorous frustrations presented in this work are supposed to take place in Ferrara, and the "fantasme" of the title is actually a young man who is seen frequently after his presumed execution. Serious issues are raised ("if at any time / Those earthlie Gods ought to be punished, / It must be by a thunder bolt from Heaven" [36]), but attention is directed mainly to the stresses and strains of a conventionally fashionable tragicomic plot.

When we turn to Lower's two translations of French classical tragedy we may hope for more substance, since in both instances he follows in the footsteps of one of France's greatest playwrights. Lower published Pierre Corneille's *Polyeuctes; or, The Martyr* and *Horatius: A Roman Tragedy* in London, the first in 1655, the second in 1656. Some question regarding Lower's ethics has arisen from the fact that he gave no sign that these plays were not of his own invention. Whether or not a contemporary was supposed to be sufficiently *au courant* to know that both tragedies were from fairly recent French originals (published in 1643 and 1641, respectively), the fact is that the generally astute Langbaine mistook *Polyeuctes* for Lower's own. In any case, both plays are marked by Lower's general flat-footedness and occasionally humorous *faux pas*, and the main interest of the tragedies derives from what we can glimpse of their French originals.

Like the translations from Grotius and Caussin noted earlier, both of Lower's plays from Corneille dig deep into the past. Polyeuctes and his friend Nearchus are two "Cavaliers" in the year A.D. 250, living under the Emperor Decius in Melitene, capital of Armenia. The major tensions of the play derive from the fact that Polyeuctes converts to Christianity, finally going so far as to attempt the overthrow of Rome's "gods of stone and mettall" (24). *Polyeuctes*, then, is Corneille's *tragédie chrétienne*. Readers of the first French edition were treated to an engraving of the righteous hero, clad in seventeenth-century clothes, taking a hammer to some Roman idols. With or without pictorial aid, however, English readers might have recalled the Commons' resolution of 1 September 1641 requiring that "all crucifixes, scandalous pictures of any one or more persons of the Trinity, and all images of the Virgin Mary shall be taken away and abolished" (quoted in Kenyon 258). Not until 26 August 1643 did both Houses of Parliament finally pass a law ordaining the demise of altars, altar rails, crucifixes, and images, including pictures of the Trinity, the Virgin, and saints. Meanwhile, in exhorting repentance in a document of 15 February 1643, Parliament asserted that "Idolatry . . . is the Spreading sin of these latter times" (Firth and Rait 1:80-81). Then on 24 April the Commons appointed a committee charged with demolishing crosses and images both inside and outside churches.[18] The Cheapside Cross was destroyed on 2 May. While a troop of horse and two companies of foot did the deed, trumpets blew, drums beat, and caps were tossed in the air (figure 31 reproduces a somewhat later effort to record this event pictorially). A reader of *Polyeuctes* in our own time might well assume that the fear in Puritan London, as in Roman Armenia, was that signifiers would be displaced by merely physical signs, but even more threatening was the intended deconstruction of the meaning of both. Wherever one stood in relation to them, iconography and iconoclasm were matters of concern.[19] In Corneille's play, Polyeuctes (reminiscent of Herminigildus in Caussin's play) is sentenced to death by his own father-in-law, Felix, Governor of Armenia. Following the execution, Polyeuctes' tormented wife, Paulina, announces that she, too, has become a Christian. She begs: "Barbarous Father, finish thy black work, / This second sacrifice is

---

[18]Aston's study and, within it, chapter 3, "Iconoclasts at Work," are especially helpful.   [19]An interestingly complex passage on images turns up in *The Levellers Levell'd* (1647) by "Mercurius Pragmaticus." Here a figure called Conspiracie brings forth a picture of Catiline; on this "sacred Relique" various Levellers "swear not to lay down arms till the King is dead, all laws repealed, and *meum* and *tuum* never mentioned on pain of death" (4).

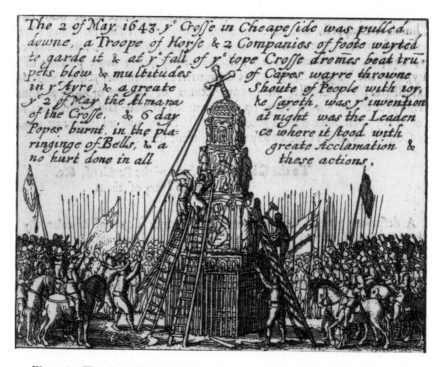

The 2 of May. 1643. y⁰ Croſſe in Cheapeſide was pulled
downe, a Troope of Horſe & 2 Companies of foote wayted
to garde it & at y⁰ fall of y⁰ tope Croſſe dromes beat tru-
pets blew & multitudes of Capes warre throwne
in y⁰ Ayre, & a greate Shoute of People with ioy,
y⁰ 2 of May the Almana- ke ſayeth, was y⁰ invention
of the Croſſe. & 6 day at night was the Leaden
Popes burnt, in the pla- ce where it ſtood with
ringinge of Bells, & a greate Acclamation &
no hurt done in all theſe actions.

Figure 31. The demolition of Cheapside Cross on 2 May 1643. From Vicars,
A Sight of y⁰ Trans-Actions of These Latter Yeares (1646). (By permission of the
British Library.)

worth thy rage, / Joyn thy sad Daughter to thy Son-in-Law" (57). Conse-
quently, providing an example of the miraculous power of grace, Felix
himself becomes a Christian. But a twist still more surprising is the closing
bid for all to be free to worship their own gods.

If *Polyeuctes* in 1655 might be thought to have afforded some usefully
relevant ideas on the contrasted torments of martyrdom and religious
accommodation, perhaps one might see in *Horatius* a picture of the entan-
gled agonies of war. Sabina, with her noble Roman husband, Horatius, and
his brothers on one side and her own three brothers on the opposing side
of Alba, laments at the outset, "I feare our Victory / as much as our destruc-
tion" (2). No matter what happens, she realizes, in Lower's words, "I will /
participate the ills without assuming / any thing of the glory" (4). When
Horatius's sister Camilla enters, we find that she also is pulled in two
directions, for she is betrothed to Curiatius, one of Sabina's brothers. True,
the oracle that foretells "Alba *and* Rome *shall be / to morrow in a faire
confaederacy*" (7) is bound to be right, but the prophecy overlooks the

painful means to that end. It turns out that the widespread civil strife is to be distilled and channeled into a mortal contest involving a mere six individuals, three on each side: Sabina's husband and his brothers versus Camilla's intended bridegroom and his brothers. Here is a stylized, formalized, rhetorical exploration of problems not altogether unlike those that had occasioned untold suffering in England.

In its fourth act the play becomes still bleaker and more tragic, for the passionate pacificism of Camilla and the intransigent patriotism of Horatius lead to a quarrel between them that results in the murder of sister by brother. The human cost of Horatius's commitment to Rome's political destiny inevitably raises far-reaching questions, though Lower's murky language throughout is the unhelpful vehicle of ideas and ideals that we glimpse almost in spite of him. Here is his Horatius on the forthcoming duel:

> Fortune, that opens us the lists of honour,
> offers a glorious matter to our constancy,
> she draines her force to strengthen a misfortune.
> To measure her self better with our Valour,
> as she esteemeth us not common souls,
> she doth exclude our fortunes from the common.
> To fight an enemy for the general safety,
> and to expose ones self alone to stroaks
> against a stranger, is but the effect of
> a simple vertue, thousands have already
> perform'd it, thousands can perform it still:
> to lay ones life down for his Country, is
> so faire a fate, so worthy an exposure,
> that all should strive to purchase such a death. . . .
>
> [16]

The complex appeal of Corneille's *Horatius* is more clearly manifested in the spirited translation by Katherine Philips ("the Matchless Orinda"), who at the time of her death in 1664 had completed all but the fifth act. Sir John Denham, therefore, finished the translation, and the whole was published in Philips's *Poems* of 1669 and 1678.[20]

Details about individual translations aside, the present chapter has achieved its main aim if it suggests the significant presence of foreign strains in midcentury drama. Though we are sometimes enjoined to perceive foreign influences in this or that Tudor or Stuart play (*Faustus*, say, or *Volpone* or *Bussy d'Ambois* or *The Duchess of Malfi*), we often overlook those foreign plays that were themselves actually turned into English. And

---

[20]Though Denham's continuation has its virtues, the 1710 edition of Philips's poems substitutes the fifth act as translated by Charles Cotton in a style better suited to Orinda's own.

perhaps one should remark (with the usual risk of being obvious) that many English men and women besides our translators were capable of reading Seneca or Corneille in the original—in their closets, cabinets, libraries, and arbors, and doubtless sometimes in their cells.

From the array of translations that crop up in our two decades, some conclusions may be drawn. For example, the large component here of manuscript material suggests that we cannot attain a clear picture of writing at the time if we restrict our reading to printed sources, and that questions about the relative authority of calligraphy as opposed to typography continue to be valid. Noteworthy also is the fact that most of the translations considered here are products of the 1650s, when the times, if not good, were nevertheless somewhat more settled. During these years Seneca maintained the general prominence he had earned in earlier decades and indeed proved to be the most fruitful source among the ancients. As for moderns, the French took the numerical if not the qualitative lead, mainly with the help of that industrious former army officer from Cornwall, Sir William Lower. Any prize for versatility, though, would have to go to the Earl of Northampton, who appears to have produced either complete or fragmentary translations of dramas originally in Latin, Italian, and French. Wherever the translators turned for subject matter, one might add, they tended to be strongly royalist and to make royalist points, implicitly, covertly, or overtly. Boldest of all in his craft was Christopher Wase, the young Fellow of King's College who published a translation of Sophocles' *Electra* that invites one to read England's current plight by the lightning flashes of ancient Greek tragedy.

As far as complete accuracy of translation is concerned, however, Sir Richard Fanshawe, probably the most gifted of the translating tribe, says most memorably what may be said in summary about all these books: "A *Translation* at the best is but the *mock-Rainbow* in the clouds, faintly imitating the true one" (*Faithful Shepherd* A4v). When all else is said, Fanshawe's observation resembles Stanislavsky's passionate but reasonable exclamation nearly three centuries later: "Plays cannot be translated, and there is an end of it!" (Granville-Barker 41).

FRUITS OF SEASONS GONE

... when our English Dramma was at hight,
And shin'd, and rul'd with Majesty and might,
A sudden whirlwind threw it from it[s] seat,
Deflowr'd the Groves, and quench'd the Muses heat.
Yet as in Saints, and Martyr'd bodies, when
They cannot call their blessed Souls agen
To earth; Reliques, and ashes men preserve....
            —[Jo.?] Hall, in James Shirley, *The Cardinal* (1653)

So though we've lost the life of plays the stage,
If we can be *Remembrancers* to the age.
And now and then let glow a *spark* in print
To tell the World ther's fire still lodg'd ith flint,
We may agen b'enlightned once and warm'd,
Men can't be civil till they be inform'd.
Walk wisely on: *Time's* changeable, and what
Was once thrown down, is now again reacht at.
            —Alexander Brome, "On a Comedie" (ca. 1656)

Then we shall still have *Playes!* and though we may
Not them in their full Glories yet display;
Yet we may please our selves by reading them
Till a more Noble Act this Act condemne.
            —Aston Cokayne, in Richard Brome, *Five New Playes* (1653)

IF WE HOPE TO THINK accurately about English drama as it was mani-
fested in the 1640s and 1650s, we must not forget the impact made by all the
earlier plays that first became available in print during this period. And we
must recall the supplementation of these works by a large influx of plays that
had been published earlier but were now for some reason brought forth again.

Few would deny the crudely served portion of truth in that passage of
Randolph's revived *Hey for Honesty, Down with Knavery* (1651) where the
Great God of Money is asked, "Did not *Will Summers* break his wind for
thee? / And *Shakespeare* therefore writ[e] his Comedy?" (6).[1] Plutus we have
always with us—and sometimes Grobianus, too. It is another motive,
however, that remains central here: though they manifested it in different

---

[1] Summers (d. ca. 1560) was Henry VIII's jester.

ways, many of the playwrights of early modern England were moved to treat issues of their day. Indeed, it could hardly be otherwise, then or now. Arthur Miller, three centuries after our focal period, observes that his own plays are a "response to what was 'in the air.' " Drama, says Miller, "is the art of the present tense par excellence" (11).

What was "in the air" in the seventeenth century obviously was in the mind of, for example, James Shirley—whose Laudian cardinal is a landmark of socially relevant dramatic indirection. As we see in his prologue to *The Cardinal,* moreover, where Shirley attempts simultaneously to arouse and derail suspicion, so we find in his prologue to *The Brothers* (published 1653[2]), a play *"Never Printed before,"* the claim that the "Author"

> . . . *saies the tymes are dangerous, who knowes*
> *What treason may be wrapt in giant prose,*
> *Or swelling verse, at least to sense? nay then*
> *Have at you Mr. Poet, Gentlemen,*
> *Though he pretend fair, I dissemble not,*
> *Y'are all betray'd here to a Spanish plot[.]*

[3r]

Licensed on 26 May 1641, *The Brothers* assuredly was launched in "dangerous" times. The Archbishop of Canterbury had been caged ever since December, and the Earl of Strafford had been executed only two weeks earlier (12 May), before a huge London crowd. Part of the jest, then, is that this playwright who "pretends fair" refers ambiguously to earlier known Spanish plots, to the current rumor-filled atmosphere of foreign plots, including Spanish ones, and—perhaps most deftly and directly—to the fact that the play at hand is set in Spain.[3]

All this is complicated enough, but the still more complex question

---

[2]As we have seen previously, *The Brothers* is one of the works in Shirley's *Six New Playes* (1653) which has a separate title page dated 1652.   [3]Though Shirley's reference is general and we should not suppose him privy to diplomatic secrets, Charles did, indeed, early in 1639 resort "to playing off France against Spain whilst staying out of any European engagements" (Sharpe, *Personal Rule* 829). Most interestingly, perhaps, the Conde de Olivares, well aware of Charles's problems with Scotland, thought in early 1640 that it was once again a good time to discuss an Anglo-Spanish match. Sharpe writes: "In March 1640 he [Olivares] resolved to send a special envoy to England to proffer proposals for a treaty of marriage between Prince Carlos and the Princess Mary, hoping thereby, as he argued in the council of State, 'to negotiate a breach between England and Holland, totally restore our fortunes in relation to France, and simultaneously restore the King of England's fortunes in Scotland, without his having to call parliament' " (896). From some time after the Scots defeated the King's army at Newburn (28 August) we have the popular ballad "Gramercy Good Scot," which glances at Charles's Spanish policy in the lines "Let Spain and the Strumpet of Babylon plot, / Yet we shall be safe, *gramercy good Scot*" (Wedgwood 63).

broached by the present chapter concerns whether or not such a play might have meant something in 1652 or 1653 that it had not meant in 1641. Clearly not every older play published between 1642 and 1660 was equally affected by the later environment into which it was introduced. Though Shirley's *Six New Playes* comes to a thought-stirring close with *The Cardinal,* the opening piece in the collection, *The Brothers,* turns out to be an innocuous drama about matchmaking of a sort that can be summarized in the lines of Ferdinand, one of the titular brothers: "Let Fathers look at wealth, tis all their Saint: / Hearts are freeborn, and love knows no constraint" (13). Such a declaration may incline a reader to agree with one of the watchful fathers, who decides, "So, so, I leave you to the amorous Dialogue" (17). *The Brothers* presents a stylized, constricted, and fundamentally non-English world that scarcely invites so much as a glance beyond itself.

In contrast, one may reasonably suppose that when Walter Montagu's *Shepheard's Paradise* was resurrected in 1659, it was in effect a statement on the potentially imminent return of the royal family with whom the work was so inalterably associated. In the preface, the bookseller Thomas Dring, though he says nothing precisely royalist, certainly takes the tack of aesthetic elitism. These pages, he says, now raised from sleep to put on the *"immortality"* of print, are addressed *"to the inspir'd and more refin'd part of men"* who *"have experienced those extasies and Raptures, which are the very Genius of Poetry"* (A3r). A cavalier like Prince Rupert would have guffawed. As for Montagu himself, he was long off the scene. After serving as a foreign agent for Henrietta Maria in the 1640s, then suffering imprisonment and exile by Parliament, he finally metamorphosed into the Abbot of St. Martin near Pontoise, northwest of Paris. His *Shepheard's Paradise* was left far behind, one of the "Reliques" of other days and also an example of the fact that the meanings of a play are likely to be less fixed over time than once was supposed.

Even without actors contributing their nuances of tone and gesture, to say nothing of adding or dropping lines, the 1655 published version of William Strode's *The Floating Island* necessarily had an effect very different from that when in the summer of 1636 it was performed at Oxford before the King and Queen. In 1636, sponsored by William Laud (then Chancellor of the University), it was given a splendid production by the students of Christ Church. In the mid-1650s, however, the implications of the play and the times had changed so drastically that readers were advised thus: "Before you read so farre as the *Prologue,* be pleased to consider this *Tragi-comedy* was both written and presented above eighteen years since; and if now it seem (in Language or Plot) to fit these times, it must be by *Prophesie,* the *Author* also himselfe having been long dead" (A2r).

The central action of *The Floating Island* concerns the disastrous results of deposing an island king named Prudentius, who himself asks ironically, "D'ee

long for action? have ye too much Peace? / Orecloy'd with blessings?"
(B2v-B3r). It is as though King Charles had asked whether his followers
surfeited with halcyon days. Later King Prudentius asks wonderingly,

> Have I these Vipers bred within my Brest
> With greater Care and Pangs then can a Mother
> The Childe within her womb? . . .
> . . . Ask Heaven and Earth, if I
> Have not with utmost care procur'd them Bread,
> Cloth, Health, Peace, Manners, and Religion!
>
> [B4r-v]

Were anyone so obtuse as to miss the Caroline application of such lines,
Strode took care to pin it down in his epilogue to Charles: "*No King so much
Prudentius as you*" (F4v). In fact, some details of the play as we have it are
sufficiently evocative of later events in Charles's story to make one wonder
if some hand has updated Strode's work. Such characters as Melancholico
("a Malecontent turn'd Puritan"), Audax (a soldier), and Malevolo ("a Mali-
cious contriver," quite clearly alluding to Prynne) conspire to depose and kill
Prudentius and replace him with Queen Fancie. After 1649, no matter what
one's personal place in the political spectrum might have been, this whole
business would have acquired a far deadlier hue. In the play, however, with
his trusty councillor Intellectus Agens at his side, the King wins through.

Under the circumstances it may seem obvious that the re-presentation
of a work may to some degree involve its reappropriation. Persistently
relevant, one might suppose, is the idea underlying some words written in
1633 by Henry Herbert, Master of the Revels from 1623 to 1642 (and then
again after the Restoration). Regarding his suppression of Fletcher's *Tamer
Tamed*—a play dating back to 1611—Herbert wrote plainly that "it concer-
nes the Master of the Revells to bee carefull of their ould revived playes,
as of their new, since they may conteyne offensive matter, which ought not
to be allowed in any time" (20).

Thus nearly any re-presentation of "ould" plays might implicitly vali-
date the queries Why *this* time? Wherein offensive? To what end? Even if
a dramatist originally managed little more than to introduce a subject (say,
kingship), or perhaps to explore his own ambivalence about it, the hindsight
enforced by events subsequent to his composition might, upon later pub-
lication or performance of a play, considerably modify its meaning. The goal
here, therefore, is to glance briefly into a variegated grab bag of revived
play-texts and to raise questions occasioned by the timing of some of them.[4]

---

[4]Though the path will not be pursued here, one should be aware that a full answer to the
question Why this time? would explore why and when *any* early modern English theatrical
company, playwright, or bookseller would be moved to publish a play. At this point one needs

In previous chapters we have seen that interest in drama did not expire with Parliament's 1642 order to close the playhouses, but one still may be surprised to find that at least some of the older drama was printed in every single year from 1640 through 1660. Clearly 1642 was a milestone, not a terminus. Furthermore, if we stand back and consider the whole sweep of "ould" plays first printed in the 1640s and 1650s, we find that the years of greatest productivity were 1640, 1641, and 1647. We see that beginning with 1642 and extending for about five years there was a notable drop in the annual number of resurrected plays. And we see that there was a wavering but significant increase of them in the 1650s.

Even as the storm clouds gathered, the vigorous publication of dramatic works in 1640 assures us of the continued viability of printed drama, including the intermingling of old with new. In that year, the third after Ben Jonson's death, his daring old *Gypsies Metamorphos'd* (1621) first appeared in print, as did Fletcher's *Night Walker* (ca. 1611) and *Rule a Wife* (1624).[5] Most of the earlier plays published in 1640, however, were rather recent. Among them were Richard Brome's *Sparagus Garden* (1635) and *The Antipodes* (1638), and Henry Glapthorne's *Hollander* (1636) and *Wit in a Constable* (1636-38). Most prominent of all were the works of James Shirley, who in retrospect may be viewed as marshalling his forces. The year 1640 first brought readers the texts of Shirley's *Humorous Courtier* (1631), *Love's Cruelty* (1631), *The Opportunity* (1634), *The Coronation* (1635), *The Constant Maid* (1630-40), *I St. Patrick* (1637-40), and *Arcadia* (if, indeed, the latter is his work; its date of origin is unknown). Even as Shirley began to erect a sort of bulwark of print against oblivion, however, he continued to be very much a man of the theater. In May 1636, when the London playhouses closed because of plague, he sailed to Dublin and for four years or so wrote for the Irish stage. All things considered, Shirley is a major candidate for the epithet given him by his friend Hall: "The last supporter of the dying Scene" (Shirley, *Cardinal* A4v).

Shirley's contemporary importance notwithstanding, the years 1640-41 may be most notable for three posthumous Jonson volumes—the 1640 and 1641 successors of the great 1616 folio. Of course these books were not the first or only evidence that Jonson would continue to be a commanding presence in the mental world of many in England. In 1638 he was honored with *Jonsonus Virbius*, the most impressive memorial book to be produced by a century known for its mortuary verse. Therein he was hailed by Robert

---

to recall that players in possession of good, viable scripts were generally reluctant to publish them, so we can assume that at least some plays were put forth in the 1640s and 1650s because the players then had few if any hopes of performing them.   [5]Jonson's masque appeared three times, in fact: in two different issues of *Q. Horatius Flaccus: His Art of Poetry* (the second issue incorporating the Windsor additions) and in the 1640 Jonson folio.

Waring as "*Poetarum Maxime!*" (66) and by Thomas May as "King of *English Poetry*" (21). Though Jonson lost much of his authorial steam well before his death, *Jonsonus Virbius* is merely the most extended sign of the high regard in which he was held. George Daniel of Beswick writes in his "Vindication of Poesie", that Jonson "was of English Dramatickes, the Prince" (l. 96). Thomas Fuller, author of *Andronicus* but no great friend to the stage, asserts that Jonson's works "will endure reading, and that with due commendation, so long as either *ingenuity* or *learning* are fashionable in our Nation" (*Worthies*, "Westminster" 243). Most surely putting the arrow on the mark for our purposes, however, is Richard West, who writes, "*Thou shalt be read as Classick Authors*" (*Jonsonus Virbius* 57).

Jonson would have been gratified. Supplementing a lifetime of performances, he had worked painstakingly to set down words that would be permanently accessible between the covers of books. His earliest published play, *Every Man Out of His Humour* (1600), was offered not as the script of a successfully staged work but as an author's text "*AS IT WAS FIRST COMPOSED*" and "*Containing more than hath been Publicly spoken or Acted*" (title page). Much later in his career he chose as a motto for the title page of *The New Inne* (1631) a revision of a passage from Horace's *Epistles* (2.1.214-15): "*me lectori credere mallem: / Quàm spectatoris fastidia ferre superbi*" ("I would rather trust myself to a reader than bear the scorn of a spectator"). In fact, Jonson stands out from all other writers of the century as the one most centrally concerned with the incarnation of drama in book form.

The 1640-41 volumes of his works added numerous if generally lesser titles to the Jonson canon: the later Jacobean masques (including *The Vision of Delight* [1617], *Pleasure Reconciled to Virtue* [1618], and *News from the New World* [1620]), some other entertainments (*Love's Welcome at Bolsover* from 1634, the year of Milton's *Comus*), *The Magnetic Lady* (1632), and the provocative but undateable fragments of *Mortimer* and *The Sad Shepherd*. Gathered together and brought forth by one of the devoted Sons of Ben, the quirky courtier Sir Kenelm Digby, these books, like the *Jonsonus Virbius* itself, were a notable form of homage. Their effect was to reinforce an already formidable reputation.

According to G.E. Bentley, more seventeenth-century allusions were made to Jonson's *Catiline* than to any of his other works (*Shakespeare and Jonson* 1:109). In the early years of the century King James himself had seen parallels between Catiline's plot and the Gunpowder Plot, and in later days other parallels seemed plausible. In February 1648 Mercurius Bellicus complained, "But now farewell Playes for ever, for the Rebels are resolued to bee the onely Tragedians, none shall act *Cataline* but themselves" (cited in Bentley 2:73). *Volpone*, *The Alchemist*, *Epicoene*, and *Sejanus* also came

frequently to writers' minds. Though this is not the place for any battle of
the allusions, perhaps one should add that the most frequently cited works
of Shakespeare appear to be, in order, *The Tempest, Othello,* and *Macbeth*
(Bentley 1:109)—each of which is cited less than any of the Jonson plays
just named. Moreover, Bentley finds Jonson "referred to more frequently
than Shakespeare in every decade of the century but the last." He con-
cludes: "Clearly, Jonson, and not Shakespeare, was the dramatist of the
seventeenth century" (1:132, 139). Whichever side of the scale most tempts
one's own thumb, the fact is that the middle years of the century saw no
new Shakespeare folio.

The other single most important publishing event in drama during the
1640s and 1650s was probably the folio *Comedies and Tragedies* (1647)
attributed to Francis Beaumont and John Fletcher. It is thus that the year
1647 suddenly made available a larger array of older drama than would
appear in any other year. Advertised as "Never printed before," the volume
was sent forth into the world with the accolades of many men of letters
whom we have previously encountered: John Denham, Aston Cokayne,
William Habington, William Cartwright, James Howell, Thomas Stanley,
Alexander Brome, Richard Brome, James Shirley, and more. That there was
safety in such numbers is a possibility that might have escaped us had
Humphrey Moseley, the bookseller, not assured readers that "I should
scarce have adventured in these slippery times on such a work as this, if
knowing persons had not generally assured mee that these *Authors* were the
most unquestionable *Wits* this Kingdome hath afforded" (A4v). Slippery
times, indeed: about two weeks before Moseley signed his address to the
reader, the Scots turned the King over to Parliament.

Moseley issued the Beaumont and Fletcher volume on behalf of a band
of now-unemployed, needy actors, and five years later, when yet another
Fletcher play, *The Wild-Goose Chase* (from 1621), was published, no bones
were made of the fact that it was for the "private Benefit" of old John Lowin
(who had played Fletcher's Belleur) and Joseph Taylor (Mirabell). " 'Tis
not unknown unto you All," the actors informed "Lovers of *Drammatick
Poesie,*" that "by a cruell Destinie we have a long time been *Mutes* and
Bound, although our Miseries have been sufficiently *Clamorous* and *Ex-
panded.*"[6] As Moseley phrased it in dedicating the 1647 collection to Philip,
Earl of Pembroke and Montgomery, the stage was now "*condemn'd . . . to a
long Winter*" (Beaumont and Fletcher A2v).

Obviously Moseley had been moved to consider the distinction be-
tween drama that was staged and that which was printed, for he raises
interesting questions about texts and playing when he writes of "All that

---

[6]Quoted from the recto of the leaf following the title page.

was *Acted*, and all that was not" (Beaumont and Fletcher A4r). The volume's most thoughtful comments on the subject, though, may be those of James Shirley, who was chosen to write an address "To the Reader." Availing himself of the endlessly useful *theatrum mundi* trope ("*this* Tragicall Age *where the* Theater *hath been so much out-acted*"), Shirley congratulates the reader on "*thy owne happinesse, that in this silence of the Stage, thou hast a liberty to reade these inimitable Playes, to dwell and converse in these immortall Groves, which were only shewd our Fathers in a coniuring glasse, as suddenly removed as represented, the Landscrap* [i.e., landscape] *is now brought home by this optick, and the Presse thought too pregnant before, shall be now look'd upon as greatest Benefactor to Englishmen*" (A3r-v). The theaters were closed, but this leading survivor of the King's Men was aware that readers might have some advantage over spectators.

Thanks to many hands, then, new life was given to such plays as *Bonduca* (1611-14), *Valentinian* (1610-14), *The Knight of Malta* (1616-19), *The Loyal Subject* (1618), *The Little French Lawyer* (1619), *The False One* (1620), *The Island Princess* (1619-21), *Beggar's Bush* (1615-22), and *The Maid in the Mill* (1623). Whatever complicated mix of playwrights had contributed to their creation, these essentially Fletcherian works were now granted the gift of textual survivability. Together they constituted a virtual summary of the ideals and attitudes of an earlier time, all set down in words by men who by and large cared a good deal about language. Here, surely, were rich and varied fruits for mulling in the long winter's night.

In 1653, six years after the Beaumont-Fletcher folio and the same year as Shirley's *Six New Playes*, Alexander Brome, sometime playwright and later songwriting attorney, brought forth *Five New Playes* by the seriously comedic Richard Brome. This was followed in 1659 by another *Five New Playes* by the same playwright: "We call them *new*, because 'till now they never were printed" (A3v). Having been the most prolific, successful, and outspoken of the playwriting Sons of Ben, Richard Brome seems to have wound down his career shortly before the theaters closed. On a number of occasions he may be found referring to his advancing age, and yet he produced *The Court Beggar* about 1639-40 and *A Joviall Crew*—his final known play—as late as 1641. By the time of the two collections of his plays in the 1650s, Brome may have died. We hear from him last in 1652, at which time he dedicated the first publication of *A Joviall Crew* to the scholar-poet-translator Thomas Stanley: "*You know, Sir, I am old, and cannot* cringe, *nor* Court" (A2r). Among other plays, the 1653 volume brought into print for the first time Brome's *Mad Couple Well Matched* (1638) and *The Novella* (1632); and the volume of 1659 presented *The Weeding of the Covent-Garden* (1632) and *The Love-Sick Court* (1639). Viewed from one perspective, then, Brome stands with Ben Jonson, Thomas Middleton, Philip Massinger, and

Thomas Heywood, and indeed with any other significant seventeenth-century dramatist whose career ended before our period began. Then again, because he comes so late in the line, he may be viewed also as sharing with Shirley the honor of producing the most significant body of plays on the fore-edge of our period.

Some of the many other works that came into print now for the first time (so far as one can tell) include Heywood's *Fortune by Land and Sea* (ca. 1607-9; published 1655); Middleton's *More Dissemblers Besides Women* (ca. 1615) and *Women Beware Women* (ca. 1620-27), both in *Two New Playes* (1657); Middleton and Rowley's *The Changeling* (1622; published 1653); and Massinger's *The Guardian* (1633), *A Very Woman* (1634), and *The Bashful Lover* (1636), all in *Three New Playes* (1655).

Some of the plays by smaller fry include William Heminges's *Fatal Contract: A French Tragedy* (1639; published 1653). Since he was the son of Shakespeare's fellow sharer and editor John Heminges, and hence the heir to shares in the Globe and Blackfriars, it is perhaps of more than passing interest that this younger Heminges dedicated *The Fatal Contract* to James Compton, Earl of Northampton, and his Countess, Isabella. At the very least, such a dedication constitutes some of the evidence for the significance of the Comptons as patrons of the drama. The printed version of *The Fatal Contract* also provides incidental evidence that in at least some quarters a reasonably lively circulation of manuscript drama took place. Though Heminges's play *"appears in a publike dress"* in 1653, we are told that previously it *"suffered very much by private Transcripts, where it past through many hands,"* acquiring along the way *"some dust and imperfections that too usually waits upon multipli'd Copies"* (dedication). Here Heminges unwittingly raises some questions for us regarding his dedicatee's own collection of manuscripts at Castle Ashby. For instance, how can we tell when or whether a transcriber is the author?

The year 1653 also brought forth an anonymous play called *The Ghost*. Apparently written in 1640 and conceivably put on surreptitiously after the theaters closed (Bentley, *Jacobean and Caroline Stage* 5:1432), this piece may serve as sample evidence of why some people justified that closing on moral grounds. Set in Paris and aiming for what the prologue calls *"City-chear,"* the play opens with young Octavian's apparent death-by-duel. This non-event serves to free his beloved Aurelia for pursuit by a range of lascivious suitors. Aurelia's father, Senio, favors old Philarchus, who is misperceived as a "drie weather-beaten Kix" (8) when actually he is as lewd and lusty as his juniors. Aurelia agrees to marry Philarchus but from the outset is determined to cuckold him. When she and her manservant Engin have occasion to undress the old man, Engin remarks, "These breeches would fit you Mistris passing well" (10). Aurelia agrees, puts in writing what she would have the old man sign, sits astride him, and has Engin mount the breeches on a pole that is to be carried before her. Hence the subtitle—*The Woman Wears the Breeches*—and the major symbol of the play.[7] Aurelia, however, instead of going on to march in triumph under any banner of liberated womanhood, finally proves to have been married from the outset to the still-alive Octavian. As for the main title of the play, when old Philarchus tries to sneak away for help during the de-breeching scene, Engin dons a sheet in order to become a ghost—specifically, the ghost of Octavian. Later in the play, for good measure, Octavian's brother Dauphine also plays ghost for a while. Even with its notable put-down of Philarchus, however, and even with a bawd named Erotia and her helper Cunicula tossed in, *The Ghost* is scarcely as risqué as an average hour of American television in our own day.

A couple of years later, and providing a rather different range of insights, the actor Andrew Pennycuicke brought forth Robert Davenport's *King John and Matilda* (1628-34; published 1655). In dedicating this work to Montague Bertie, Earl of Lindsey, Pennycuicke identified himself closely with actual performance of the play, "*my selfe being the last that . . . Acted* Matilda" (dedication). Matilda is "a chaste Dove" who is pursued by a "Lustfull King" (B3v). In fact, the volume is a rarity for its inclusion of a cast list. It includes also some brief remarks "To the knowing Reader" that are signed "R.D." (presumably Davenport himself), claiming that the dramatist "*had no mind to be a man in Print.*" Be this as it may, Davenport, if indeed it be he, now acknowledges that "*A Good Reader, helps to make a Book.*"[8]

What the reader finds is a book that opens with King John learning of the defiance of some rebels. Though a play need not be about politics in order to be political, here, obviously, is possible grist for our mill. We hear one of the rebels vowing that

> If but a hair of my betrayed wife,
> Or my poor boy do perish, a head royall
> Shall be sent back, slight scratches leave no scars
> But deep wounds are seeds of Civill wars.
>
>   [C3v]

Though the lustful, callous King John is no prototype of King Charles, some readers who had lived through the later 1640s might be forgiven for thinking of the latter when John observes, "he that would screw his ends / To his own aims, must mingle (when he wins) / Secret dissemblings

---

[7]After sifting a good deal of evidence and borrowing a term from Natalie Davis that is almost startlingly appropriate here, David Underdown writes: "The 'woman on top,' like the scold and the witch, seems to be primarily a phenomenon of the century between 1560 and 1660" ("Taming" 121).   [8]Quoted from a leaf following the title page.

'mongst his venial sinnes" (C4v). The play shows that during the reign of a bad king, when the crown sits but quaveringly and a "purple cloud" (F4v) shrouds England, men will talk of rebellion at home and intervention from abroad. That Pennycuicke meant no harm to the memory of Charles in bringing out the play, however, seems probable because of the fact that his dedicatee had been one of the King's most faithful adherents. Commander of a regiment at Edgehill and wounded at Naseby, Montague Bertie went with Charles to the Isle of Wight and after all else was one of the handful who accompanied the royal corpse to Windsor.

Very different in what it can suggest to us is Robert Daborne's *The Poor-Man's Comfort: A Tragi-comedy* (1610-17; published 1655), a play that catches the eye in part because it is one of those works that totally lack the directive, modulatory aid of introductory matter. It at once introduces the reader to Lucius, a Thessalian nobleman clad as a shepherd, who fled into Arcadia "when the King was overthrowne."[9] We have here another pastoral play, then. Under the circumstances, however, the lack of definition in its presentation may be akin to those eloquently plain brown wrappers in which a later day presents its pornography. Wherever *The Poor-Man's Comfort* takes us subsequently, some of its signs suggest non-royalist politics. The poor man of the title proves to be Gisbert, a kindly old shepherd who has provided Lucius, "a poor souldier in these wars" (G1r), with both a refuge and the opportunity to woo and wed his beautiful daughter. When the wicked rebel-usurper Oswell falls, however, the rightful King, Ferdinand, proclaims that all suffering and banished royalists such as Lucius shall be restored. Good reading, this, for English royalists of the 1650s, a decade that saw a series of plots and uprisings against the powers that be. Both the weight of the play and the significance of its title, however, derive from the fact that Gisbert, who comes on stronger as the play proceeds, voices eloquent underclass outrage (in the best speeches in the play) when the not-so-noble Lucius abandons his shepherdess wife. There are further dramatic convolutions, of course, but Lucius finally gets his comeuppance, and the restored and virtuous King makes the old shepherd his Chief Justice. One surely may see here an aristocracy that has strayed and a strikingly renewed and comforting coalition of a good king and the humblest of his subjects.

Such widely divergent and lesser-known plays as *The Fatal Contract, The Ghost, King John and Matilda,* and *The Poor-Man's Comfort* should help to convey some of the complexity of the dramatic landscape during the period. To try a different (but complementary) tack for a moment, one might take a closer look at a particular year. Among the plays brought into print in 1654,

---

[9]Quoted from the verso of the title page.

for example, we find the old *Appius and Virginia* attributed to John Webster. In this late-in-the-day, no-frills incarnation, the tyrannical Roman Consul Appius, only recently a plebeian ("the Heralds have not knowne you these eight months" [46]), confesses privately that "to catch this office; 'twas my sleeps disturber, / my dyets ill digestion, my melancholy / past physicks cure" (3). Appius is a calculating, ruthless arriviste, willing to sacrifice anything—the honor of an individual or the peace of Rome—for his own personal ends. An obvious question, therefore, is whether it is mere coincidence that his story was registered for publication in mid-May 1654, a relatively short time after Cromwell had become Lord Protector (December 1653) and dissolved the Parliament of the Saints (January 1654). (In January a pamphlet that "*Considered the Reasons of the Resignation of the Late Parliament and the Establishment of a Lord Protector*" was main-titled simply *Confusion Confounded.*) It behooves us to consider how a reader in 1654 might have responded to the character of Appius and especially to his ultimate consignment to the common hangman. For the sake of rounding off a play, Icilius proclaims, "*Rome* thou at length are free, / restored unto thine ancient liberty" (61). Before the year was out, the play was issued a second time, and, still more notably, it was put forth again in 1655 and yet again in 1659. Such a publication record suggests that *Appius and Virginia* had something of particular interest to offer at the time.

Approximately the same social and political background lay behind—and perhaps helped to motivate—an edition of the anonymous *Tragedy of Alphonsus*. Probably originating in Elizabeth's day, *Alphonsus* was in 1654 attributed to George Chapman. Its authorship, however, was not what interested the publisher, Humphrey Moseley, who states little directly except that "The Design is high, the Contrivement subtle, and will deserve thy grave Attention in the perusall." [10] Moseley's more significant statement probably lies in his action of selecting such a work for resuscitation (it was registered with the Stationers in September 1653), since from the opening speech of Alphonsus it is clear that the major subject of the play and the major subject of the time are one: "I will be King, and Tyrant if I please," says Alphonsus, "For what is Empire but a Tyrannie?" (B1r). Fortunately, there is much good to be spoken of Richard, Duke of Cornwall, who comes in to clean up the shambles created by Alphonsus. And Richard's nephew, Prince Edward of England, fallen into Alphonsus's hands, cries out stirringly to Richard,

> Uncle, you see these savage minded men
> Will have no other ransome but my blood,

---

[10] Quoted from the recto of the leaf following the title page.

> *England* hath Heirs, though I be never King,
> And hearts and hands to scourge this tyrannie.

[I2r]

To at least some readers in 1654, these would have been inspiriting words. The play is of interest for several reasons, including a fast-paced plot and a well-developed inset show (the Duke of Saxon's daughter, personating Fortune, rides in on a globe and has the various rulers who are present draw lots for the roles they are about to play). The driving force of the work, however, is strongly political and largely dependent on the canny machinations of the tyrant.

How such a play might strike a browser at an Interregnum bookstall obviously would depend on the zone of the political spectrum in which that person felt most comfortable. The book of *Alphonsus* would make a complementary purchase for one who sought mental reinforcement in J.P.'s new *Tyrants and Protectors Set Forth in Their Colours* (*"Tyranny makes Earth a hell, and a Tyrant is a Devil incarnate"* [A3r]). On the other hand, the political implications of *Alphonsus* clearly jar with those of Samuel Richardson's *Apology for the Present Government and Governor.* Therefore, even as we think we discern an aura of controlled royalist outrage behind *Alphonsus* (Moseley says only that it "will deserve thy grave Attention"), we need to recall that some Englishmen of the day, trying to make their way under the new dispensation, may well have been alarmed that year when coming across the *True Account of the Late Bloody and Inhuman Conspiracy Against H.H. the Lord Protector and This Commonwealth.* If it had not been aborted in time, the planned assassination of Cromwell would have plunged England into unbearable turmoil again. In any case, whatever other facts are now lost to us, polar-opposite publications—including plays—are part of the evidence in 1654 that England continued to be divided against itself.

Perhaps at this point one should in fairness acknowledge the riskiness of referring, both here and elsewhere, to the "first" publication of a seventeenth-century play. Some playbooks have simply disappeared. Many are said to have perished in the Great Fire that destroyed St. Paul's in 1666, and others had more everyday fates. Some may have acquired fresh titles, and hence a whole new lease on life. In short, one is left to wonder whatever became of such works as *The Tooth-Drawer, The King's Mistress, The Noble Ravishers, The Politic Bankrupt, The Supposed Inconstancy,* and *The Woman's Masterpiece.*[11] Though the matter cannot be pursued here, suffice it to say that enough older plays seem to have been first published in the 1640s and 1650s to warrant more extensive study of the phenomenon.

---

[11]These and many other such titles are recorded in "Supplementary List II" in the Harbage-Schoenbaum-Wagonheim *Annals.*

Moreover, an adjacent and equally interesting area of inquiry may be constituted by those older plays that, having been printed before, were now printed again. To suggest briefly something about the predictably great variety of this neighboring terrain, one might consider the dates of both the earliest known and sample later editions of the Fletcherian *Thierry and Theodoret* (1621; 1648); of *The Elder Brother* (1637; 1650) and *The Maid's Tragedy* (1619; 1650); of Carew's *Coelum Britannicum* (1634; 1651), which had a place in each new edition of the poet's collected works; of Shakespeare's *Merchant of Venice* (1600; 1652), which probably was encouraged by midcentury hopes and fears regarding religious toleration and readmission of the Jews to England;[12] Chapman's *Caesar and Pompey* (1631), the 1653 republication of which Derek Hirst calls "patently topical" (144); *King Lear* (1608; 1655) and *Othello* (1622; 1655); and a sprinkling of old-time crowd-pleasers such as Greene's *Friar Bacon and Friar Bungay* (1594; 1655), *The Merry Devil of Edmonton* (1608; 1655), *Mucedorus* (1598; 1656), and, eventually, Mr. S.'s *Gammer Gurton's Needle* (1575; 1661). The old-fashioned appeal of this last book is made visually explicit by its black-letter type.

There was also Henry Killigrew's newly titled *Pallantus and Eudora* (1635; 1653), revised from a play that had once been more boldly called *The Conspiracy*. Mildly interesting for its claim to some twilight praise from Jonson, *Pallantus and Eudora* is perhaps even more so because in its latter-day setting it seems to say so much about returning the Stuarts to the throne. The play is prompt in introducing men who plot to overthrow the reigning tyrant:

> When we have call'd our Party forth, the Work
> Will seem done, the thin Numbers that are left,
> Not deserving the Name of Enemies.
> The Tyrant then will see himself no more
> A King, but onely the Wretched Cause of Warre. . . .
>
> [B2v]

In April 1653, the year of this revival, Cromwell went so far as to expel the Rump Parliament. Furthermore, whatever parliamentarian foes he made, Cromwell continued to have fervent royalist ones, a fact perhaps best attested by the several assassination plots that targeted him. On the other hand, as David Underdown remarks, none of the latter schemes involved "more than a handful of Royalists in England, and the inspiration and

---

[12]Pleas for readmitting the Jews into England rose noticeably after about 1646. In 1648 the Council of War passed a resolution recommending toleration; in 1650 Rabbi Manasseh ben Israel published in Amsterdam the first edition of his *Hope of Israel;* and in 1651 he petitioned for readmission to England. Katz writes that "The campaign for the readmission of the Jews was . . . fairly well under way by 1652" (188).

control usually came from abroad" (*Royalist Conspiracy* 171). Killigrew himself, during the years after he wrote *The Conspiracy*, went on to become chaplain to the King's army and eventually chaplain and almoner to the Duke of York. His older brother, Thomas, of course, would come to the fore as the family's major playwright.

The Deserving Favorite (1629; 1659), by Lodowick Carlell, a young Scot, was written in the warm afterglow of George Villiers, the glorious Duke of Buckingham, and dared to picture a king who "passionately doth love the Duke" (3). Actually, problems relating to the historical Villiers had grown so serious in his last years that on 17 June 1628 the Commons produced a remonstrance condemning his influence over Charles. About two months later, on 18 August, all such problems were suddenly solved when the Duke was murdered. Thirty years later Carlell's *Deserving Favorite* was printed for Humphrey Moseley, and with it a cavalier demurral from the author: though performed at court, "This Play . . . was not design'd to travell so farre as the common Stage" (A2r). In 1659 there was no longer much need for a former groom of the Privy Chamber to muffle his royalist elitism.

Predictably, then, the configuration, aura, or even title of some older plays could cause their authors to be suspected of editorializing. Further candidates here might include Beaumont and Fletcher's frequently resurgent and title-potent *King and No King* (1619–"now the fifth time Printed" in 1655), Thomas Tomkis's *Lingua; or, The Combat of the Tongue, and the Five Senses* (1607; 1657), and Thomas May's *Tragedie of Julia Agrippina* (1639; 1654). Tomkis's *Lingua* is an academic allegory that was created back in King James's day to "*reprive*" a schoolboy's "*Sad hours, and serious studies*" (A2v). In later years it attracted fresh attention when the story got about that in a performance at the Free School at Huntington, the boy-actor who played Tactus was none other than Oliver Cromwell. Accurately or not, some would have it that sparks of ambition were struck in young Oliver's mind when he had to put on a crown and declaim:

> They lie that say Complexions cannot change:
> My Blood's ennobled, and I am transform'd,
> Unto the sacred temper of a King:
> Methink I hear my noble Parasites
> Styling me *Caesar,* or great *Alexander,*
> Licking my feet, and wondring where I got
> This pretous oyntment: how my pace is mended,
> How Princely do I speak, how sharp I threaten. . . .
>
> [A8v]

Tom May's *Tragedie of Julia Agrippina,* modeled (at a suitable distance) on Jonson's *Sejanus* and *Catiline,* offers as its central character the wife of

Claudius Caesar and the mother of Nero. The tigress Agrippina does not readily call to mind any major figure on the English scene either in the middle years of the century or in the late 1620s, when the play was written. England's foreign-born Queen, though she became something of a militarist in the 1640s and was coldly disliked by many Protestant Englishmen, fits the role of unscrupulous and power-mad empress only with considerable wrenching. And of course May's drama has its own self-concerned, tradition-bound story to tell, fleshed out with more or less predictable Roman characters and details. On the other hand, much is said in *Julia Agrippina* that would have had a powerful resonance at midcentury. In 1654, with the printed assurance that this play was "ACTED 1628"—that is, a safe long time ago—it opened with a speech that sounds one of the most pervasive themes in midcentury writing: "*Let Vertue lurke among the rurall Swaines; / Whilest Vice in* Romes *Imperiall Pallace reignes*" (A4r). These words are spoken by one of the Furies, Megaera, who would that "*no sacred ty / Of Nature, or Religious lawes restraine*" the "*Parricidall hands*" of those in power (A4v). The story that ensues concerns not only Agrippina but also other human monsters, not all of them royal. In the opening scene, for instance, one finds the humbly born Pallas musing thus:

> Let dull Patricians boast their aëry titles,
> And count me base, whilest I commend their lives,
> And for the furtherance of my high intents,
> Make noblest men my hated instruments.
>
> [A7v]

Meanwhile the steadfast Narcissus says of "the most hopefull Prince *Britannicus*" that "I rather wish / My selfe for ever lost, then that brave Prince / Should not succeed his father" (A8v). Narcissus is given other lines that would have lost no force after certain royalist defeats:

> . . . it beares the greater shew of justice,
> And honest service to my Roiall Master.
> Since wee must fall it is some happinesse
> To fall the honest way. . . .
>
> [A8r]

And the ill-fated Claudius Caesar later tells him that

> . . . tis 'th unhappy fate
> Of Princes ever (as *Augustus Caesar*
> Was wont to say) the people ne're beleeve
> That treasons were complotted 'gainst theire persons
> Untill those treasons take effect, and then
> Too late perchance they pity and beleeve.
>
> [B11r]

The good Crispinus goes so far as to say,

> I'de rather see (which all the Gods avert)
> *Rome* rent again with civill broiles, then hee [Britannicus]
> Should loose unjustly the Imperiall throne.

[A8v]

Striking as such passages are, their cumulative effect is ironically intensified for anyone aware that the dramatist May, who once enjoyed the favor of King Charles himself, eventually veered into Parliament's camp, perhaps as early as 1640 (Chester 56). In an overt attempt to expose the King's perfidy in 1645, in fact, May co-edited the private letters taken from Charles at Naseby, published as *The Kings Cabinet Opened.* The following year, to be sure, he was willing to commend his "Honoured Friend M. *Ja. Shirley*" in the latter's *Poems &c.,* but he also observed on that occasion that applause in the theaters *"now is fitly silenc'd by the Lawes"* (A5r).

Today May is probably best known for three things: his translation of Lucan's *Pharsalia; or, The Civil-Wars of Rome;* his postmortem skewering in a satire by Andrew Marvell ("Tom May's Death"); and his writings on the Long Parliament, most notably *The History of the Parliament of England: Which Began November the Third M.DC.XL.* Despite its apparent straightforwardness, the latter proves to be a kind of parliamentary apologia. On the title page May introduces himself as "Secretary for the Parliament" and offers the mutually reinforcing and self-justifying mottoes *"Tempora mutantur"* and *"Mutantur Homines."* In other words, May's *Julia Agrippina*, which is shaped to decry ruthless tyranny, was resurrected for reissue long after May had defected from the royalist cause. In fact, the 1654 volume appeared about seven years after he had published in his *History of the Parliament* an extended passage comparing Agrippina with the Italian-born French Queen, Marie de Médicis (1.109).

May's negative paralleling of Agrippina with Henrietta Maria's mother raises questions about his play of the 1620s. Nor are such questions inappropriate with regard to 1638, when May's play was registered with the Stationers, or to 1639, when first it was published. Marie de Médicis arrived in England for a visit to her daughter and son-in-law in October 1638, bringing with her some six hundred attendants. Charles, who in the previous year had expressly asked that she not come, found now that his own situation was worsening. When in March 1639 he felt that the situation warranted his journey to York, he had to depart without having solved his mother-in-law problem. In fact, Parliament itself finally had to invite the great woman to go. Whatever shades of denigration May could have meant to achieve with the Agrippina-Marie comparison, though, a broader point may be that he saw how such paralleling to some extent frees the reader from the author's grasp. He addresses this matter in a passage of his *History* that speaks of the Battle of Edgehill in light of Dion Cassius's report on the war of Brutus and Cassius against Caesar and Antony: "Whether the parrallel will in some measure fit this occasion or not, I leave it to the Reader" (3.31).

In determining the range of implications that readers may derive from *The Tragedie of Julia Agrippina*, moreover, we need to consider one further turn of the screw. About four years before the 1654 reissue of the play, Tom May died—choked, it was said, by the strings of his nightcap. After this time, if not before, men and the times, ever subject to change, were free to appropriate his text as they would.

Ben Jonson makes the wise observation in *Timber* that "likenesse is alwayes on this side Truth" (590). He warns that one should not expect to find reality in a writer's words, just something remindful of it. No one ever expected to find the "real" Roman court in Tom May's 1628 *Julia Agrippina*, nor for some of the same and some different reasons should we expect to find in the play the earlier Caroline court, the later Caroline court, or the courts of Louis or Oliver. The goals and capabilities of art are all circumscribed. But given the political sensitivity of the times and the ubiquitous convention of utilizing parallels, and even some of the other play-texts put forth in this same year, 1654, we may hypothesize that the publication of *Julia Agrippina* was inspired by something more than aesthetic and commercial impulses.

Three years later, when William Prynne felt compelled to comment on the third offering of the crown to Cromwell, he produced a pamphlet called *King Richard the Third Revived. Containing a Memorable Petition Contrived by Himself and His Instruments, While Protector, to Importune Him to Accept the Kingship* (1657). And everyone understood that, no matter how obvious or obscure, and no matter how bold or tepid the writing might be—and whether it occurred in a play, a history, or a pamphlet—readers bore some of the responsibility for realizing the meanings of the parallel.

Of course, an old play between book covers was a play and no play. As Dryden later recalled, "I have often heard the Stationer sighing in his shop, and wishing for those hands to take off his melancholy bargain which clapp'd its Performance on the Stage" (*Spanish Fryar,* dedication A2v). But reading afforded significant and counterbalancing compensations. Dryden in the same passage writes of "*the Lights, the Scenes, the Habits, and, above all, the Grace of Action,*" all of which he deems to be "*false Beauties*" and "*no more lasting than a Rainbow*"; for, he continues, "when the Actor ceases to shine upon them, when he guilds them no longer with his reflection, they vanish in a twinkling. I have sometimes wonder'd, in the reading, what was become of those glaring Colours" (A2v). Published in 1681, these timeless observations on the magic of theatrical art lead on to a major confession from the Restoration's greatest successor to Jonson, Shakespeare, and Fletcher: "*as 'tis my Interest to please my Audience, so 'tis my Ambition to be read; that I am sure is the more lasting and the nobler Design: for the propriety of thoughts and words, which are the hidden beauties of a Play, are but confus'dly judg'd in the vehemence of Action: All things are there beheld, as in a hasty motion, where the objects onely glide before the Eye and disappear*" (A3v).

That one might find it possible to think and write so is to be credited first of all to Jonson, and then to those who followed in his traces and made possible the folios of Shakespeare and Beaumont and Fletcher. Still more to the point here, during the 1640s and 1650s the relative status of plays both old and new as rhetorical art, not mere texts for the stage, was inevitably enhanced—perhaps we should say ironically enhanced—by the closing of the theaters. The life of plays both old and new now depended mainly on publication. There were also sporadic performances and playgoers' memories, of course, and there were plenty of antebellum play quartos lying about like "Reliques," but the aim of this chapter has been to show that a rich store of revived works now came to hand—and in the process spoke to ideas of continuity and return. The actors might complain that a printed play is no play, but even in an age that denied the stage what it granted the press, earlier drama continued to provide pleasure, profit, comfort (especially to royalists), and food for thought. During even the coldest, loneliest nights, *litera scripta manet.*

TRAGEDIES

Tragedies are the *Gentry*, I may say, of *Plays.* . . .
—Richard Baker, *Theatrum Redivivum* (1662)

The Tragick *Buskin traverses our stage*
In bloody Fillets, fitter for this Age,
Where Treason, Murder, Lust, and ev'ry vice
Grows impudent, and rifles for the Dice.
—prologue to *The Bastard* (1652)

Meethinkes the Chamber should haue mourn'd in Black
And the Sadd Owle haue Sung; The fatall Batt
Should haue put out the Candles. . . .
—Francis Jaques, *The Queene of Corsica* (1642)

War is a Tragoedy, that most commonly destroyes
the Scene whereon 'tis acted.
—Thomas Forde, *Times Anatomiz'd* (1647)

THOUGH HUMPHREY MOSELEY had it right—the English stage was indeed *"condemn'd to a long Winter"*—it is true also that many readers of the day realized that written drama constituted a kind of lifeline. In exploring various aspects of this lifeline we have already touched on a number of tragedies. These stretch all the way from Harding's heavy-handed *Sicily and Naples* (1640) through *The Famous Tragedie of King Charles I* (1649) to Pordage's translation of Seneca's grim *Troades* (1660). Other volumes that clearly prove the potential of pouring ancient tragic wine into new English bottles include Sherburne's rendering of Seneca's *Medea* (1648) and Wase's passionately politicized version of Sophocles' *Electra* (1649). Taken together, all of these works, together with such others as Fuller's *Andronicus* (1643; published 1661), Swinhoe's *Unhappy Fair Irene* (1658), and Willan's *Orgula* (1658), provide a considerable range of tragic matter. Viewed synoptically, moreover, they often raise as many thoughts about their own time and place as about either the universal ways of man or the eternal ways of God. Their likeness is always on this side truth (as Jonson says), yet time and again they call local truths to mind.

As we move into the final chapters of this study, perhaps we should retain some residual surprise that so many dramatic writings have come down to us from a time when the Truth for many excluded the theater. Not that fear and loathing of the theater were fresh phenomena. Milton had time-honored authority to write in his treatise *Of Education* (1644) about "what despicable creatures our common rimers and play-writes be" (405). Then again, for Milton as for others, it was the common playwrights and players more than plays themselves that inspired the hottest wrath. In the preface to his own *Samson Agonistes* (1671) he rationalized that "*Gregory Nanzianzen* a Father of the Church, thought it not unbeseeming the sanctity of his person to write a Tragedy, which he entit'ld *Christ suffering*. This is mention'd to vindicate Tragedy from the small esteem, or rather infamy, which in the account of many it undergoes at this day" (332). Perhaps most pertinently of all at the moment, the creator of *Paradise Lost* also wrote in his preface to *Samson Agonistes* that tragedy is "the gravest, moralest, and most profitable of all other Poems" (331). Nearly three decades later, at the close of the seventeenth century, George Ridpath made the same fundamental point. After venting over two hundred pages of spleen against plays, he conceded that there is "no Body against Writing a Poem in Nature of a Tragedy or Poetical Dialogue, with several Acts and Parts to add Life and Lustre to it" (193).

Considering the respect traditionally accorded tragedy—"the *Gentry . . .* of *Plays*," Richard Baker called it (25)—one might suggest that the heightened suffering and strife that marked much of the mid-seventeenth century made tragedy a particularly fitting form of expression. Moreover, the examples now at hand appear to be fairly well scattered over our two decades. Though several cannot be dated with assurance, four probably originated in the 1640s and six in the 1650s. Of the four works from the forties, two appear to have been unpublished until the 1660s, and two remained in manuscript. Three from the fifties made their way into print, and three did not. Of the plays that are more difficult to date, all but one remain in manuscript to this day. One in the aggregated group belongs to that class of play that makes its points through a biblical narrative (like Buchanan's *Tyrannicall-Government Anatomized*), at least four are directly and obviously concerned with political problems, and about half might be characterized roughly as presenting their varied ideas via the action of love and intrigue. We shall begin with the latter group, which includes Francis Jaques's *The Queene of Corsica* (manuscript dated 1642), J.S.'s *Andromana* (1642; published 1660), Thomas Killigrew's *The Pilgrim* (1646? published 1664),[1] and two anonymous plays called *The Bastard* (1652) and *The Disloyall Favorite; or, The Tragedy of Mettellus* (1650s).

The Queene of Corsica, which comes down to us in the famous British Library manuscript that lists plays burned by John Warburton's cook, presents the central enigma of a virgin queen (England had long since sung

---

[1]Included in the 1664 *Comedies, and Tragedies*, but assigned its own separate title page dated 1663.

the praise of such a one) who proves to be with child.[2] Rather than use this situation to make an anti- or pro-feminist statement, or to take a quasi-religious stand, or, as one might expect, to explore the political implications of an endangered succession, *The Queene of Corsica* makes Queen Achaea's dilemma the core of a complex and riddling intrigue. Achaea's basic problem is exacerbated by the arrival at court of young Calidor, a "Noble Stranger." Having been wounded by some thieves in a wood, Calidor is first rescued and then introduced to the Queen by her own betrothed lover, Florimond ("The sunne wee all must Looke on now" [4v]). When she returns from stag hunting ("Not Diana rides a Horse / With greater Maiestie" [4v]), Queen Achaea informs Florimond that although she has just brought down a stag, she too has had a fall: "I thought't had killd mee" (4v). Whatever one's final estimate of this play—Harbage found it generally "miserable" in execution and "atrocious" in taste (*Cavalier Drama* 131)—the action and imagery here prepare us for the main mystery of the work. Already in the second scene we hear the mutterings of Florimond's father, old Natolion, steward to the Queen, concerning his son's long-arranged marriage to her. We also are introduced to a more or less parallel subplot in which the Queen's sister, Princess Antiope, is wooed by two friends, Alceus and Phocillus. And still within the first act, we also meet a "ffrantique" named Beotto (6v), a Fletcherian madman who claims to be the rightful king and observes helpfully (for the benefit of textbound readers) that Queen Achaea's "fflanck is sufficientlie fill'd with something; but I'm a foole" (6r).

In the second act Achaea falls ill, and in dismay and misery on the morning when she and Florimond are to be secretly wed, she confesses to him, "I am with Child and know not how." He responds supportively, "soe Deare / You are to mee that I will putt my life / Betwixt you and yor Infamie" (8v). He even offers to say that he has previously married her in secret. This generosity is eventually undercut when we learn that he himself is the father-to-be, but meanwhile the playwright's new twist is that Achaea wants Florimond to woo the noble stranger, Calidor, on her behalf. Florimond responds badly, flinging away his sword (one may choose to ask why) and hurling out an "I will not doo't" (10r) along with some imprecations against female constancy.

Now the Queen's depiction begins to seem more complex. Her time fast approaching, she assures her intimate attendants that she is yet a virgin and laments, "Perhaps I shall giue Greife a Body, Girles." Adding to her torment is her realization that, despite all, she lusts after Calidor: "I must Enjoy him er to morrow night" (12v).

---

[2]The ink having bled and blurred on both sides of its leaves, the British Library manuscript can be read only with great difficulty. A Malone Society transcript became available in 1989.

With the wooing assistance of her cast-off fiancé, Florimond, the Queen is soon introducing Calidor to her court as her husband. As she leads him off to the "Closset where wee will unite / Two Bodyes to One Soule," Calidor is allowed to say hardly more than "I must not be soe rude to Underualew / What yor Opinion onely has made noble" (15v). Clearly he is no patriarchalist of the stamp so frequently decried in late twentieth-century scholarship. In fact, one of the play's most effective scenes occurs shortly afterward in the taper-lit bridal chamber, where Calidor, caught in a bad marriage by his sense of honor, is thinking that the room should be hung with fatal black. Then comes a woman's shriek, and the crazed Beotto enters with the announcement that the Queen has "miscaried a Little" (16v).

Though he knows only part of the story, old Natolion thinks he can "undoe the Ridle" (18r). He calls to mind Corsica's past "Black Dissentions" (19r), perhaps reminding us of England's present ones, and reveals that the wanderer Calidor, unbeknownst even to himself, is really Prince Lycomedon. Years before, when Corsica was invaded by Sardinia and forced into a union, Lycomedon was for safety whisked away to Sardinia by a noble soldier. Now at last come into his own, he vows to wield a "Sword of justice." To Natolion, who is ordered to be secured for having become too powerful a nobleman, the new King offers the observation, "I doe Appeale to your Owne Politique Principles" (20r). When Phocillus, one of the suitors dueling for Princess Antiope's hand, slays his rival, Alceus, Lycomedon again responds by invoking the proper duties of a good ruler: "Wee that are Kings must giue the Law his Right / Euen to a Brother. And you know that Duells / By it are justly Punished with Death." He even offers a stern rationale: a "Prince's Early Mercy / Is an Abortiue, and Emboldens Crimes" (21r).

From this scene of regality and high justice we move to a wood where the sometime monarch, Achaea, now clad in country weeds, is burying her newborn infant—"Pritty Babe Shame" (21v)—and strewing flowers on its grave. When Florimond, distraught and suicidal, comes upon her, we are asked to believe that he does not recognize her, that he is, in fact, moved to divulge the secret that once when Queen Achaea called for wine, he laced it with a witch's potion that for an hour both aroused her lust and suppressed her knowledge of what she did, thus enabling him to have his will of her. At last the central mystery of the play is clarified.

Following some intervening subplot action there comes the strange news that, despite everything, Florimond and Achaea have agreed to be married. In the most striking and problematic moments of the play, therefore, we are brought to a temple where a priest asks the image of Hymen to bless their union. Despite some soft music and garlands, we must presume that the atmosphere is now darkened by Achaea's looming bigamy.

Mindful of the equivocal place of priests and images in contemporary English life, we may be the more struck that the statue of Hymen begins to exude blood. Then suddenly the supposed bride stabs both Florimond and herself, thereby converting the couple into sacrifices to Hymen.

At this point the playwright provides yet another twist. He has Natolion exclaim that the man Achaea has stabbed is her own half brother. Florimond, already expiring at the time he realizes his rape of Queen Achaea was incestuous, now snatches a sword from off the altar and attacks Natolion. Hitherto known as Florimond's father, the dying old man explains that he also begat Achaea in the "Adulterate Sheets" of her mother. Lycomedon then attacks him ("Out Dog; dog"), and Achaea herself, a queen and no queen, expires (25r).

But still the play does not let up. Phocillus, the surviving suitor of Princess Antiope, has escaped from prison and is even now attacking. In a final flurry he accidentally kills his beloved and soon thereafter commits suicide by leaning upon his sword. Corsica's new ruler, King Lycomedon, is the last to die, wounded by Phocillus and also stricken by the knowledge that his mother was a whore: "Why what a Litter of Bastards are wee All" (25r). Showing no inclination to end, as some English tragedies do, with a glimmer of hope for better days, *The Queene of Corsica* affords merely a choric lord to close with two grim questions: "The Sickly state's endangerd to be Ruin'd. / What shall wee doe?" and then "O you Gods, / When you are Angry, who Can beare yor Rodds?" (27r).

Empowered by the secret rape at its center, *The Queene of Corsica* has a certain potency despite its flaws. Although it is overpacked with incident, the play has a kind of rude strength and self-consistency. The ending display of Hymen bleeding, for instance, is given perspective by Calidor's first-act wish that Hymen "And all his Blessings" (7r) will attend the wedding of Achaea and Florimond, as well as by Florimond's own subsequent cry that "Hymen will Rage" (7v) at how the marriage has been delayed. Similarly, the many scattered comments on governing tend to convey a sense of the importance of such issues, if not of their centrality here. And the evolution of the virtuous, victimized Queen Achaea into a woman whose desires and actions are no longer beyond reproach helps to complicate her suffering and strengthen our interest. A coarser, less adroit, but still rather urgent form of Shirleyesque play—Clifford Leech (117) compares it particularly to Shirley's *The Coronation* (1635)—*The Queene of Corsica* conveys the feeling of alert amateur work. Obviously Jaques, whoever he was, had a lively interest in various aspects of later Stuart drama, though somehow he never managed to establish priorities among his goals, and his hands became too full.

Andromana is a somewhat more sophisticated tragedy from about the same time (an allusion it makes to Denham's *Sophy* [1642] helps us with the dating).

Notwithstanding an attribution to James Shirley in the Stationers' Register (19 May 1660), the play is usually credited simply to the "J.S." of its title page. Whoever composed it, *Andromana* provides a good illustration of that harking back to Sidney that we have noted earlier, its central characters coming from various passages in book 2 of the *Arcadia*. Or, more precisely, as Michael Andrews has shown, *Andromana* harks back indirectly to the *Arcadia* through the qualifying intermediary of Beaumont and Fletcher's *Cupid's Revenge*.

Though Plangus, Prince of Iberia, is a central figure in the play, the title *Andromana* accurately indicates that the primary focus is on a woman. We may assume that Andromana's multifaced heinousness is supposed to be magnified by the fact that she is—as advertised in the subtitle—a "Merchant's Wife." The subject of her husband and his class appears to be introduced mainly or perhaps even solely to darken her affair with poor, love-snared Plangus. Sidney had only said, "This Prince (while yet the errors in his nature were excused by the greenenesse of his youth, which tooke all the fault vpon itselfe) loued a private mans wife of the principall City of that kingdome" (*Arcadia* 2.157). In any case, Andromana's cuckolded husband conveniently meets death by drowning "at the *Ryalto*" (B4v) when the play is still getting under way. Even before we learn that the father of Plangus, the foolish old King, Ephorbus, is also to be vamped by Andromana, the story of the havoc that may be wrought by an insatiate, unscrupulous, merchant-class woman is laid out for us plainly in the drama's second and suspiciously timely subtitle (one wonders when was it composed), printed on the first page of the 1660 text: "*The Fatal and Deserved End of Disloyalty and Ambition*."

Though the main action of *Andromana* can be summarized briefly, J.S. varies and expands his play in a number of ways. Any reader will note, for instance, that Plangus suffers from melancholy. On the second page we find that he has fallen "far beneath . . . the assurances all good men had of future gallantry. Hee's mellancholly now, and hath thrown off the spirit which so well became him, and all that sweetness which bewitcht men's hearts" (A2v). We learn this from a conversation between a couple of his fellow soldiers—who come in for a fair amount of attention in this play. One exclaims, "O this wicked Peace" (A3r) and supposes that some good fighting might rouse Plangus from his moodiness. A similar idea recurs later: "This ugly sneaking peace is the Souldiers rock, / He splits his fortunes on. Bawdry's a vertue to't" (C1v). Wherever the dramatist stood on the issue, he seems to express here an untried, younger man's view of war. What is a soldier if he be not fighting? The usual linkage of love and war, however ("I have . . . / . . . thought no women half so beautiful / As bloody gaping wounds" [C3r]), gives way to an intense misogyny that, for better or worse, contributes significantly to energizing the play. Here is Plangus after learning that Andromana has betrayed him:

> A woman! O heaven! had I been gull'd
> By any thing had born the name of man!
> But this will look so sordidly in story,
> I shall be grown, discourse for Grooms and Foot-boys,
> Be ballated, and sung to filthy tunes.
>
> [H2v]

And yet the playwright also recognizes the responsibility of great men who fall short. Early on, King Ephorbus exclaims, "What will this world come to at last! / When Princes that should be the patterns of all virtue / Lead up the dance to vice" (B3v). Before that scene is over, however, the Basilius-like old man has fallen prey to the merchant's wife: "Upon my life," he says, "shee is very handsome" (B4r). However we align or realign these various thematic elements, we clearly have here no straightforward panegyric of royalism.

To remove Plangus from the scene, King Ephorbus sends him off to war, and by the time he returns the King himself has married the now-widowed Andromana. More melancholy than ever (he "*Unbuttons his doublet*" [E2r]), Plangus feels the need to seek revenge. Like Shakespeare's Hamlet, however, he is hesitant to pursue it: "O the tameness of a conscience loaded with sin! / Which reasons and talks when it should do" (E2v). Andromana, now his stepmother, assures him that she will continue to be his mistress, using her queenship as protection for them both. (In Sidney's romance, Andromana makes advances to both Pyrocles and Musidorus.) When Plangus spurns her, however, she too decides to seek revenge. In fact, "a Queen must be more / Daring in her revenge, nor must her wrath / Be pacify'd under a whole Kingdomes ruine" (F1r). From this point on, the major characters are all on collision courses, and with some occasional further reminiscences of Shakespeare (for instance, "jealous husbands / Confirm their Cuckold-ships by ocular testimony" [F3r]), the play lurches toward various precipitous, violent deaths, last of all for Andromana herself, and ends with what may be the flattest closing couplet of the era: "But *Andromana* none could have begun it, / And none but *Andromana* could have done it" (H4r).

Viewed from our own time, the greatest puzzle concerning *Andromana* may be why J.S., writing in the earlier 1640s, took pains to make Andromana a merchant's wife and then did so little to capitalize on the fact. With the play's derivation from Sidney via Beaumont and Fletcher and an occasional borrowing from Shakespeare, with the steadying effect of its negative concentration on a single character, with a greater command of language than is displayed in, for example, *The Queene of Corsica*, and with its supposed production on the stage as late as 1671 (that is, about thirty years after its composition)—at least it is certain that the tragedy of *Andromana* has some claim on our attention. Even without demonstrating any real knowledge of the court or much interest in the political dimensions of the action, it nonetheless conveys a basic story, a feeling, and a gender-generated fear that may never go wholly out of date.

The same cannot be said for Thomas Killigrew's *The Pilgrim*, despite the fact that its author has a secure place in literary history, a highly visible place largely because Charles II in 1660 authorized two theater companies, one headed by Davenant and the other by Killigrew. In 1664 Killigrew identified himself on the title page of his *Comedies, and Tragedies* as a former page to Charles I and as a groom of the bedchamber to Charles II. He had, in fact, been a devoted servant of the royal family for many years. Not only had he served as a royal messenger both at home and on the Continent, but also he had reaped the rewards of such service by being arrested, confined by the Long Parliament, and then banished. In 1660, when at last he returned to England with Charles on the *Naseby*, he was soon made the head of the King's Company (which was composed largely of personnel from the old Red Bull) and *ipso facto* became a major figure in the theatrical world.

In 1664, when he was over fifty and was moved to publish a hefty folio of ten long plays, Killigrew assured readers, "*If you have as much leasure to Read as I had to Write these Plays, you may, as I did, find a diversion; though I wish it you upon better terms than Twenty Years Banishment*" (*Comedies* *2r). His *Comedies, and Tragedies* includes three comedies, six tragicomedies, and only one tragedy, *The Pilgrim*. Most unusually, all are identified according to the places and times that Killigrew presumably wrote them. Together the various dates and place-names (Basel, Madrid, Florence, and so on) suggest not only a personal claim to cosmopolitanism but also an abiding interest in drama that helps us to understand why Charles decided to honor Killigrew in a way that connected him so unmistakably with the theater. Harbage points out, however, that Killigrew's claim to have written *The Pilgrim* in Paris in 1651 is erroneous, for the playwright was in Italy that year. On the other hand, Harbage theorizes that while the date is wrong, the location may be correct. Killigrew may have written *The Pilgrim* in Paris as early as 1647, at which place and time not only he but also a company of English players were attached to the court of the exiled Prince of Wales (Harbage, *Thomas Killigrew* 191-93).

Not that one is tempted to argue for the performability of the play as we have it. Whatever its virtues as a literary artifact, *The Pilgrim* proceeds by sequences of rather prolonged prose speeches that, taken together, give the work a novelistic quality. Or better, perhaps, one might compare the dialogue with that in Sidney's *Arcadia* or in the series of then-fashionable French and English romances. While *The Pilgrim* deserves to be placed among Killigrew's most playable dramas (outdistanced only by his brisk

Parsons Wedding [1640-41]), it is difficult nowadays to imagine an actual production that might include the overextended comic subplot or even the persistently word-heavy discourse of the major characters. Here, for example, is Julia, the wicked Duchess of Milan ("an evil the Nation ought to arm against" [*Pilgrim* 157]), speaking to her secret lover, Martino, about their son, Cosmo: "O *Martino*, we are lost, for ever lost, if suddenly we attempt not some brave rescue; and the plot we have so gloried in (our breaking the friendship betwixt my Son and *Sforza*) as 'twas then the way to compass our ends, if the Duke dies, it will be our utter ruine" (160).

Faced with speeches that are sometimes both dense and prolonged, one well might wonder how plays like *The Pilgrim* ever could have been performed. Fortunately, a partial key to their stageworthiness lies in Killigrew's own annotated copy of his *Comedies, and Tragedies*, now in the library of Worcester College, Oxford. There, in his own hand, we have suggestions for the specific and numerous excisions that made the public performance of various plays possible (Van Lennep, "Thomas Killigrew").[3]

Cosmo, the pilgrim referred to in the title of the tragedy, is another noble stranger, a prince in disguise. Though such a figure was generally familiar from a good many earlier writings, he was still likely to have had particular appeal for the exiled Charles and his entourage. Cosmo is depicted as a devoted brother of the fair Fidelia, a staunch friend of Prince Sforza, and a lover-to-the-end of Sforza's sister, Victoria. In fact, Cosmo's friend Antonio broaches directly the theme of love and honor that runs through this and many other Caroline and Restoration plays:

> Sir, I find many Lovers complain of Love, and the heavy burthens he lays upon them; yet few or none make haste to discharge themselves, but rather patiently lie down under their loads; your Highness now complains of two hard Masters, Love and Honour, and you make a difficulty of obeying either; Reason counsels you to prefer one, your Passion t'other; and to me nothing appears easier then your part in both; for your Idle thought of coward, *Cosmo* is know[n] above it; and if the Princess be all your aim, if her favour be your ambitious hope, as you say, What need you thus hunt your own dangers, and pursue her Brother, and your Prince, upon a most unreasonable jealousie; unless you will give satisfaction to others, by disobliging her that you profess to love and value above the world. [180][4]

If the old world of Fletcher is discernible here, it is nonetheless reconstituted in the language of prose romance.

---

[3]Visser goes so far as to argue that "all the plays in the Killigrew folio were originally designed for the stage of a private playhouse, very possibly Blackfriars" (122) and concludes that the value of the annotated Worcester folio "lies in the relationship it demonstrates between the private playhouses of the early Caroline period, and the public theatres of the Restoration and Eighteenth Century" (136).   [4]Two printing errors in this passage have been corrected.

That Cosmo is the illegitimate offspring of Julia and Martino guarantees, unfortunately, that he is doomed to tragedy as surely as was Achaea in *The Queene of Corsica*. In the final act, as Martino dies, badly wounded, he informs Cosmo (as Natolion had informed Lycomedon) that he is the young man's real father. Julia, having mortally stabbed her son Cosmo by mistake (as Phocillus stabs Antiope), at last (like both Achaea and Andromana) stabs herself, leaving the near-cipher Duke Alfonso to speak the palely echoing lines, "Take up their Bodies, and let all Funeral Rites be given to these unfortunate people" (214).

Imitative passages such as this, we may assume, are not mere substitutes or crutches for invention. Instead, they are simultaneously supposed to display the writer's wit (Killigrew was known for his wit), to arouse a reader's pleased recognition, and sometimes, perhaps, to put an emotional lien on their originals. Killigrew surely would have us remember *Macbeth* when he has Julia claim that "since we are stept in, we must now go through with the work" (212). A short time later she says, "Make room, *Cosmo,* for thy mother: I struck not thee with half so good a will," presumably expecting us to think of the death of Shakespeare's Brutus; and a moment later, recalling for us the death of Webster's Duchess of Malfi, she says staunchly, "Thus I shall be *Julia* still" (213). It is to the point also that we find Harbage arguing that Killigrew's chief source for *The Pilgrim* is James Shirley's *The Politician*—which itself is indebted to *Hamlet* (*Thomas Killigrew* 194-95). The goal here is not to inspire further volleys in the old game of source-hunting, however, but to suggest the extent to which *The Pilgrim* and other midcentury plays, different as they may be from one another, nevertheless draw on a common matrix of characters, motifs, and sometimes even phrases, a matrix that is made up of both recent and earlier writings. Presumably part of a reader's pleasure is to be based on a recollection of what he or she (*The Pilgrim* is dedicated to the Countess of Carnarvon) had read or seen elsewhere, especially before the theaters were closed.

Surely this is true of the anonymous tragedy called simply *The Bastard* (1652), a play better known than either *Andromana* or *The Pilgrim*, though perhaps known better by title than by text. In our current cluster of Mediterranean intrigue tragedies we have seen that the motif of bastard-therefore-base ensures the tragic fall of would-be noble characters such as Achaea and Cosmo. In *The Bastard* we see how illegitimacy may engender villainy. Although we are no longer working here in the thin air of an imaginary royal court but, instead, in the conniving world of Spanish merchants, the underlying separateness of the titular bastard from his surroundings, despite his efforts to deny or surmount that separateness, provides a potent motive for his malignity. "I care not," says he, "if *I* rise, who fall" (48).

Despite the prologue's assertion that "*a* BASTARD *may have Noble* blood; / *And challenge* Kindred *with the best*" (A2v), Gaspar, the bastard of the title, is merely a high-level servant and "cousin" of the Sevillian merchant Alonzo. Trouble erupts because Gaspar covets Alonzo's daughter, Mariana. Mariana is even promised to him for a while, but she is also contracted to Balthazar, married to Picarro, and involved in amorous league with Chaves. As such a summary hints, Mariana shares with Gaspar much of our attention in the play. Together the intelligent, resentful servant and the willful, unscrupulous daughter of the house make a pair that is more than a little remindful of DeFlores and Beatrice-Joanna in Middleton and Rowley's *Changeling*—also a play set in Spain. A small but telltale link between the two works is the gloves that both Beatrice-Joanna and Mariana contrive to give their servant-admirers—sexually suggestive gloves that go back at least to the time when Kyd's Bel-Imperia dropped hers in order that they might be retrieved by Horatio. A more substantial connection between *The Bastard* and *The Changeling* is suggested by Mariana's need of Gaspar's assistance to be rid of the man her father has chosen for her husband. Mariana even turns to her maid, as Beatrice-Joanna turned to hers, with the problem of what to do when her new husband discovers that she is not a virgin: "Wilt thou supply my room?" (55). Middleton and Rowley had borrowed that part of their story from a genuine Spanish source, the *Gerardo* of Céspedes y Meneses, a work to which the author of *The Bastard* refers. Interwoven with *The Bastard*'s major strand of action involving Mariana, furthermore, is another and contrasting strain, for Alonzo has not only a marriageable daughter but also a marriageable ward. Effectively enhancing what therefore proves to be a dual-focused depiction of lust, jealousy, and revenge are some strongly misogynistic passages that parallel those we have cited earlier. Cries the cuckolded Picarro, "A plague upon this curst effeminate sex!" (62) and "Merits she not a *Chiliad* of deaths?" (69).

The tragedy closes with a jolting series of killings that prompt Gaspar's bitter remark, "More objects still of ruine? this will be / A bloody Poppet-play" (76). Here, too, we have his hubristic brag, "They're all o're-reach'd by one poor Bastards wit" (77). Shortly before he himself dies, Gaspar kills both Mariana and her father, telling the latter, in a nicely thought-provoking reversal, "know, *Alonzo*, 'twas your baseness, that / Urg'd me to this revenge" (80). In brief, we have here a violent revenge play about a hard and fragmented world of isolated people who hatch quick, hot plots and black betrayals. If it sometimes veers toward something that a moralistic or politically correct reader might label as a pornography of violence, at least it does so with flashes of wit.

The Disloyall Favorite; or, The Tragedy of Mettellus, another passion-driven play, purports to transport us to Egypt (see figure 32). Mettellus, the titular favorite, has the misfortune to be loved by both the King and the Queen of Egypt. When first we meet them, the Queen, indeed, is *in* love with Mettellus, who is perceived as "too Loyall to his Majesty . . . to defile his marriage bed" (286v). The plot thickens, however, when Mettellus suddenly kills Marsus, another favorite of the King, for suggesting that Mettellus, in loving the Queen, might be a traitor to the King. While the King is now plunged into melancholy because both killer and killed "were ye pillars of my life" (293v), the Queen and Mettellus waste little time in pursuing their own pleasurable ends. The Queen's sister warns the King what is happening, and he at first responds that he is sure Mettellus "is chast as any of ye Gods, & soe is She" (296r). Eventually, however, the evidence against the lovers is overwhelming. The King's little page has seen them together in bed (he reports that Mettellus "put his finger in her bublyes[5] and tickled them, & he did more to" [299v]). Furthermore, a little dog dies from poison that the Queen meant for her tattling sister, and the King intercepts an incriminating letter from Mettellus to the Queen. With evidence aplenty at hand, the King finally rouses himself sufficiently to banish the Queen and sentence Mettellus to be burned.

Interested in his task but amateurish, the playwright is never much concerned about persuading us that we are in Egypt. Perfunctory references to crocodiles, the Nile, and "ridiculous" images that the priests "call Gods" (292v) do not do the trick. Toward the end, in fact, our minds can hardly help turning to England. An ignorant rabble comes in to shout that the King is guilty of "perfect arbitrary government"—"tis very tyrannically done, tyrannically done," cries one, "I think I have pickt a proper word"— and a shoemaker proclaims, "I am as good a comonwealth man as any of them" (304v).[6] Even the final lines direct our thoughts more to England's tragedy than to that of Mettellus. Civil war, we now find, has "destroyed . . . many famous citys" and "wasted . . . many people" (305v). As a player-king conventionally should do, this one closes the play:

> Love one another & be free from jars
> Noe pestilence so bad as civil wars.
> All evill to a Kingdome yt doth bring.
> It doth destroy ye Subject & ye King.
>
> [305v]

One further "Mediterranean" tragedy will serve to suggest just how

---

[5]Perhaps *bubbyes*. Partridge gives *bubby* and *bubbies* for breast(s) from the late seventeenth century, citing D'Urfey and Congreve (143); probably related to *bubbing*, i.e. drinking. But see also *bubbles* for breasts (Cassidy 402).   [6]After it abolished the monarchy (17 March 1649) and the House of Lords (19 March), the Rump Parliament declared England to be a "Commonwealth" (19 May). *The Disloyall Favorite* would seem to postdate this last event.

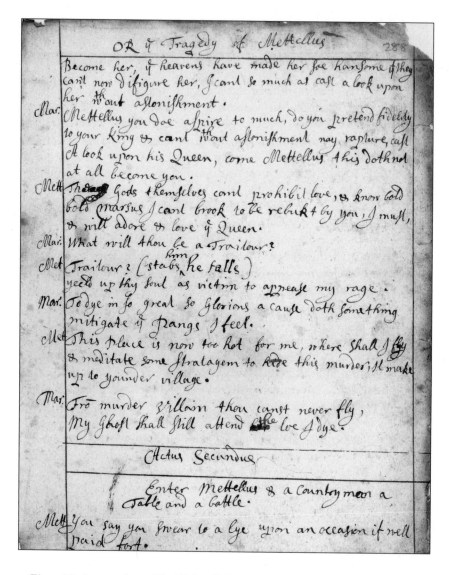

Figure 32. A page from *The Disloyall Favorite*, a tragedy (Bodl. MS Rawl. D.1361, 288r). (By permission of the Bodleian Library.)

English Sicily could be. John Tatham, whom we have thus far seen mainly as a writer of civic shows, published *The Distracted State* in 1650 or 1651—but did so with the unusual claim on the title page that he had written the work in 1641.[7] Understandably suspicious, John Wallace has argued that the claim is a ruse to divert us from seeing that *The Distracted State* alludes to the period of its publication ("Case").

When the play opens, King Evander has just been brought down by civil war, and his replacement, Mazares, is giving his subjects appropriate reassurances. A lord named Agathocles, speaking in asides, warns us that Mazares is a lying usurper—as indeed he soon proves to be. Hence Mazares, too, must be overthrown. A series of usurpers then strut their brief hour, in effect clearing the way for two competing military commanders to kill each other in the process of trying to grab power. Only then does the supposedly dead Evander return to the scene: "Ah poor *Cicily*," he exclaims, "How has thou been beaten and banded to / Promote the ends of turbulent Spirited Men?" (29). As Frank Occhiogrosso observes, *The Distracted State* shows that no matter what motivates rebellion, nothing can justify the havoc it brings (164).

Usurpation, of course, was no great problem in 1641. After Charles's death, however, it was decidedly on the table for discussion. In February 1649 Parliament ordered all members of the new Council of State to swear loyalty to a republic that now had neither king nor House of Lords. In January 1650 every man aged eighteen or over had to sign this "Engagement," the prevailing rationalization being that a usurping *de facto* power was not illegal if it was successful. Tatham, who depicts not merely one but a series of power-grabbing usurpers in his play, in effect presents a *reductio ad absurdum* of a political stance he abhors.

Wallace's strongest argument for dating the origin of the play closer to 1650 than to 1641 may be that an archbishop "Colder than th'Alpes in Charity" (Tatham, *Distracted State* 18) is more likely to represent a latter-day Presbyter than an Anglican prelate of the earlier period. Most striking of all on this score is a speech by Agathocles in which he tells the cleric that the realm would have been free of rebellion

> . . . had not your hot lungs
> Spet the Contagion. It was you gave Reines
> To the Licentious People, that, Like Negroes
> Shot their envenom'd Darts at th' Raies of Majesty,
> Whose carefull heat did warm e'm.   [10]

---

[7]Though the title page gives 1651, George Thomason's date of purchase was 29 November 1650. It is interesting that the 1642 order for stage-plays to cease (reproduced here in chapter 3) referred to "the *distracted Estate* of England" (italics added).

Obviously, interesting subjects other than dating and topicality arise with all of these plays, but since *The Distracted State* seems so clearly designed to do some political work, we are likely to get a plainer view of its nature if we regard the author's claim of 1641 composition skeptically.

Also of interest in *The Distracted State*, as Langbaine observed, is Tatham's "hatred to the *Scots*," manifested "when he introduces a *Scotch* Mountebank ... to poyson ... the Elected King" (*Account* 502). This carrying of coals to Newcastle is the more notable because the Scot has had to be imported all the way to "Cicily" for the job. He and his "Countramen," he brags, "ha peyson'd thra better Kingdoms as this" (*Distracted State* 23). Though animosity toward Scots is scarcely a dateable phenomenon in seventeenth-century England, one might observe that in many quarters there was fresh cause for it to flourish after the Scots in effect sold Charles to Parliament in 1647.

To round out this chapter, we will consider four tragedies that deal with "the times" and also move more decisively backward to ancient times—taking us finally within view of Jonson's classical world. All four of these plays come down to us as anonymous or quasi-anonymous works, but the first three, all from the cache of Castle Ashby manuscripts, appear to be yet further examples of the writing of James Compton, third Earl of Northampton.

Mariamne is a neoclassical play composed mainly in heroic couplets. It centers on the beloved first wife of Herod the Great, King of Judea, but it also depicts a guilt-ridden Herod who is misled by his brother and sister, Pheroras and Salome, first into doubting and finally into executing his Queen. "How loue & feare do in my bosome burne" (8), he exclaims at the close of the first act. We then come upon the first of the play's between-act choruses, this initial one being a dispute for precedence between Justice and Policie. Although Mariamne herself briefly considers revenge for Herod's misdeeds ("It is no sin to strike, usurped might, / revenge the injurd & restore ye right"), she soon decides that she "will not sin, but liue unfortunate," secure in the belief that "Vertue supprest on earth will mount the skie" (10). At the same time that such sentiments may call to mind the plight of aggrieved and suffering royalists, they also parallel to some extent the thoughts we have found expressed in Compton's own translation of Caussin's *Herminigildus*. In an extended and ambitious speech written in triplets, Mariamne even expresses a martyrlike commitment to suffer when confronted with death: "This world is guided by a higher power / The whiche swift time can't wast nor age devoure, / Which guides eache day eache minute & eache houre" (20).

Deriving ultimately from the Jewish historian Flavius Josephus, the story of Herod and Mariamne had a compelling and understandable appeal for medieval and Renaissance storytellers and dramatists of various nationalities. Maurice J. Valency—who did not know of Compton's work—located "at least a dozen new Mariamne plays" in the seventeenth century (7, 291), including Alexandre Hardy's *Mariamne* (ca. 1600; published 1625), Elizabeth Cary's *Mariam* (ca. 1602-5; published 1613), Gervase Markham and William Sampson's *Herod and Antipater* (ca. 1620; published 1622), Massinger's *The Duke of Milan* (ca. 1621-23; published 1623), Calderón's *El Tetrarca* (ca. 1635; published 1637), François Tristan l'Hermite's *La Mariane* (1636), and Tirso de Molina's *La vida de Herodes* (1636).[8] Whether or not Compton knew or used any of these—or, indeed, one of the many editions of Josephus—his own *Mariamne* is a major effort that deserves serious study. With formal debts to Greek and Roman drama and, perhaps, to Grotian and Jesuit drama as well, the play's greatest interest still lies in the story's two tormented protagonists. It is especially unfortunate, therefore, that the work comes down to us in a badly damaged rough draft: the upper portions of the opening pages have been lost.

The manuscript of Compton's *Bassianus* is likewise incomplete, breaking off in the middle of a conversation toward the end of the fifth act. This play presents the career of the Roman Emperor Bassianus (historically known as Caracalla) from the death of his father, Septimius Severus, in "frozen Brittaine" (4v) until, presumably, his own death at the hand of virtuous Romans who vie for the honor of killing him.[9] Inheriting the throne jointly with Geta, his virtuous younger brother, Bassianus personally murders him. In fact, he generally follows a path of ruthless self-interest—up to and including the wooing of his father's widow, Julia. In a play that is evidently the work of a royalist army officer, the thoughts attributed here to military men are noteworthy. Macrinus, a plain-spoken soldier (historically, prefect of the praetorian guard), meditates thus on how things stand in Rome:

> If all good men should still and quiet sit,
> The Bad alone, would onely beare the rule.
> And those so [i.e., who] thinke to shun harsh tirannie
> Are less secured from suspicions harmes
> And perhaps seeking selfe preservation,
> In vaine, ruine both themselues and country.   [15r]

Though our knowledge is incomplete, Compton himself clearly did not

---

[8]All told, Valency found more than forty plays dealing with the Herod-Mariamne story and recognized that even more must exist. As Beilin shows, the "brilliant, pious, energetic and talented" Cary appears to have used her version of the story to figure forth some of the difficulties encountered in her own life (49).   [9]Professor George Walton Williams has kindly pointed out that this same material provides the source for the Fletcher-Massinger *Bloody Brother* (1617; rev. 1627–30).

always sit "still and quiet." Kelliher records that at least a couple of his imprisonments in the 1650s were probably related to his involvement in royalist plots ("Hitherto Unrecognized" 164). In any case, this Roman tragedy in blank verse, amateur work though it be, is sensitive to the usefulness of borrowing from Shakespeare's *Richard III* and in fact displays a general alertness to the demands and possibilities of written drama.

Yet a third attempt on Compton's part to write original tragedy survives as a mere three-leaf (six-page) fragment (see figure 33). Despite its shardlike quality, its paralogistic technique may throw some indirect light on *Mariamne* and *Bassianus*. In any case, enough survives to suggest that Compton was exploring here the tragedy of Thomas Wentworth, Earl of Strafford (Kelliher, "Hitherto Unrecognized" 176). In the portion of act I that we have, the scheming "Pro." (whose abbreviated name survives only in speech-tags) explains to Pseudolon how the fall of Sophius will "dim ye princes power" (75v). The plan that "Pro." hopes to bring about will not be easy to effect. In fact, it will "sound so horrid in this peacefull land" (75v) that it will be necessary to pretend glorious goals. "Pro." explains that two types of men can be utilized: first, those "who like ye rule of gouernment, as now / It stands," but are envious "that they / Sit not at sterne"; and, second, those who

> . . . haue framed
> Themselues a false Idea both in churche
> And state, but that so senceless and seuere
> It cannot last, & of it selfe will sincke. . . .
>
> [75v]

Together, these two factions can "pull ye present power downe." Most notably, "They will their utmost skill employ" to show how indebted the royal Caliphilus is to Sophius. Then when the latter falls, the former's power will be weakened. Meanwhile, it will be good for the planners to feign humility and "pretend revelations" from God (75v).

In the next portion of text, from act II, we find a conversation between "Mega." and "Tim.," two friends with opposing views. "Tim." seems to express the author's thoughts: "I see great Sophius life is now the aime, / You all do levell at, but I see to / What hee hath don, merits not death by law" (76r). "Tim." believes that men such as "Mega." "are but ye stairs by whiche others clime" (76v). Not only is Sophius now marked for ruin, furthermore, but so is the church. "Tim." continues:

> . . . Phoebus is aimd at to,
> His shrines are thought to riche, his priests to learnd
> And truely less knowledge, may serue the turne
> Of those who will not heare but what they like.
>
> [76v]

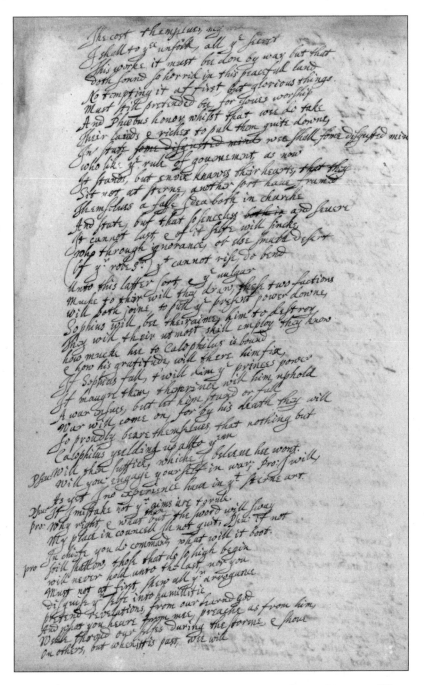

Figure 33. A passage from an untitled tragedy by James Compton (BL Add. MS 60281, 75v). (By permission of the British Library.)

In short, this dramatic fragment, even in its rough and unready state, provides fairly direct assurance that Compton, even when writing about ancient Greece, had one eye cocked skeptically on modern England.

Though none of the three tragedies by Compton noted here comes down to us whole, we can see in them a remarkable range, a lively spirit of experimentation, and a sheer knowledge of the drama that cannot but leave us wishing we had more information about both the plays and the situation in which (perhaps the situation *for* which) Compton wrote them. As matters stand, we must be grateful for the extraordinary glimpses they provide of amateur work at the time.

Finally, Rome in decline is once again the basic subject of *The Tragedy of That Famous Roman Oratour Marcus Tullius Cicero*. Harking back to Jonson's *Catiline* more than to any other play and reminding us that *Catiline* was the most frequently cited play of the period, *Marcus Tullius Cicero* is the most thoughtful and powerful tragedy to be discussed in this chapter. Unfortunately and perhaps significantly anonymous, it opens with Julius Caesar's ghost (as *Catiline* opens with Sylla's) and thence proceeds to depict with considerable historical fidelity the course of Cicero's final months.[10]

After the assassination of Caesar on 15 March 44 B.C., Cicero became head of the republican party that decried the rise to power of Antonius. Between 2 September 44 and 21 April 43 Cicero delivered a series of orations that he facetiously called *Philippics* because of their similarity to Demosthenes' speeches attacking Philip of Macedon. Twice mentioned in the present play, the *Philippics* mainly warned Rome about the dangers of Antonine ambition. Contemplating the killing of Caesar, in which he himself had played no part, Cicero says that he believed that "everybody who did not want to be a slave gained thereby, but particularly you [Antonius]; for not only are you no slave, you are a monarch" (*Philippics* 55). "Your abominable crimes," he assures Antonius, "make Catiline look tolerable in retrospect" (337). "What is there in Antonius," he asks, "save lust, cruelty, insolency, audacity? He is wholly compact of these vices" (125). Understandably, and as Shakespeare reminds us in *Julius Caesar*, Antonius and his fellow triumvirs, Octavian and Lepidus, soon called for the proscription of Cicero. He was murdered on 7 December 43, and by order of Antonius his head and hands were nailed to the Rostra in the Forum.

The mid-seventeenth-century play that dramatizes this story is highly literate in every sense. Its central character is both a statesman and a famous man of letters, and the words and thoughts of this "great *Patrician* of the speaking Art" (*Marcus Tullius Cicero* B1r) are both presented and discussed

---

[10]The tentative attribution of this play to Fulke Greville has been widely discredited (Randall, "Head and Hands" 52).

in the play.[11] Moreover, the playwright has created a spectrum of figures that includes a scholar named Philologus, a poet named Laureas, and a would-be historian named Tyro. Eventually we come also to a group of vatic soothsayers ("*Hetruscian* Vates" [D3r]), whom Cicero admonishes to "be not Aenigmaticall, nor shroud / Your Speeches in a dark mysterious cloud" (D3v). This varied array of word-men is deployed in the text in ways that draw the mind repeatedly to the functions and dysfunctions of each. Philologus sceptically holds that "scribling Fablers are sly," Laureas seems to see "the Soul / Of History" in a glass of wine (C1r), and Tyro summons up parallel tragic stories that juxtapose past with present. Antonius realizes that his stance and mien may "speak a mute Oration" (C3r). Cicero himself, however, best summarizes the playwright's own probable stance when he says of poetry and its mission,

> O 'tis the language of the Gods when Virtue
> Is made her theam; they prostitute the Muses,
> And turn *Parnassus* to a stews, that cloath
> Their unwasht fancies in these sacred weeds.
>
> [B2v]

The irony is all the greater, then, when Cicero is betrayed by his own manumitted man, a student of words, the scholar Philologus.

In the opening speech by Julius Caesar's ghost we are told directly that "*Caesar* must be reveng'd" (B1r). The central character, however, is not a revenger such as one finds in *The Spanish Tragedy, The Revenger's Tragedy, Hamlet,* or even *The Bastard,* but a victim somewhat reminiscent of the central characters in *The Duchess of Malfi, The Queene of Corsica, Herminigildus,* and *Mariamne,* all of whom are shown to endure a sort of martyrdom. More than this, however, it is clear in the present case that the victim is himself emblematic of free speech. Caesar's opening soliloquy includes the curse that

> . . . *Rome,* shalt bee plagued, and among
> Thy other evills lose thy sacred Tongue,
> The great *Patritian* of the speaking Art,
> Then shal thy griefs lie fettered in thy heart,
> And speak no other language but of tears;
> Words shall be strangled by thy stupid fears.
>
> [B1r]

At the end, finally, in keeping with revenge tragedy's tendency to display body parts for horrific dramatic effect—head, hand, heart, and leg—we have, in addition to Cicero's own head and hands, the heads of some of his

---

[11]In *Catiline* Jonson praises Cicero as "the *Consul,* / Whose vertue, counsell, watchfulnesse, and wisdome, / Hath free'd the common-wealth, and without tumult, / Slaughter, or bloud, or scarce raysing a force, / Rescu'd vs all" (V.304–8).

supporters. Furthermore, making the symbolic implications of the action more specific, Cicero's tongue, the famed "tongue" of the state, is savagely cut out of his head. Despite a moment at the end when a hint of revenge surfaces (Philologus is turned over to Cicero's enraged sister-in-law), ultimately no glimmer of light appears on the horizon. Instead, the final lines are given to Antonius, and the bleak irony of the whole is darkened for the last time as we hear that Caesar's initial call for revenge is eventually succeeded by the gloating words of his quondam friend. Triumphant amid the gore, Antonius says, *"my long wisht for aim, is wonne"* (E4v).

Contemplating this carefully wrought work, one might choose to say merely with Cicero's sister-in-law, Pomponia, that "I feel a kind of pleasure in the story / Of woes compleat and perfect" (E3v). Considering its publication in 1650-51,[12] however, one might prefer to stand with her son Quintus, of whom she asks, after he calls to mind the story of Croesus's mute son, "What Genius has inform'd my *Quintus* fancy, / That he still meditates on such examples?" (D2r). In either case, it is partly by means of Quintus's exampling that the playwright induces us to "meditate" on his own present "example." In 1650-51—about the time of Tatham's *Distracted State* and Hobbes's *Leviathan*—what possible reasons might there have been for a man of letters to present the public with a reminder of the republican Cicero's silencing?[13]

As frequently is the case with these plays, we are likely to draw a blank if we try to identify a real-life English model for Cicero. Furthermore, the play's action in many ways jars with what we know of the major historical events of the day. On the other hand, we are warned to be on guard in the matter of exampling here when, within the play itself, Pompiona protests rather dimly to her son that the narrative precedent he cites in his own commentary on current events "coheres not." For this intelligent Roman youth, coherence does not depend on congruence. The fact is that while the action of the play is in many ways at variance with what we know of the basic history of 1650-51, we could scarcely expect to find a drama that works more strongly with some of the ideas and passions, perhaps especially the fears, that then filled the air. In other words, we can hardly expect to find a better specimen of a play whose narrative incongruencies with its time are so complexly countered by its ideological and emotional relevance.

---

[12]George Thomason in his copy changed the printed "1651" to "1650." This is one of several places in the present volume where we may be grateful for Thomason's dates—at the same time acknowledging that they are not always accurate (see Greg, *Bibliography* 3:1328).   [13]As Hirst has written, "It goes without saying that appeals to the classical past could legitimate many present positions. Thus, while classical republicans, particularly in the frenzy of 1659, produced histories of republican Rome, plays about, histories of, Julius Caesar and other Mediterranean tyrants had a suggestive popularity throughout these years" (144).

An underlying "coherence" suggested by the play—parallel to that which young Quintus perceives between past and present—may be approached by various avenues, including the presentation of Julius Caesar, his "son" and heir, Octavian, and the ruthlessly ambitious militarist, Antonius. Though one should not press the matter too far, certain parallels are discernible between this trio and Charles I, Prince Charles, and Cromwell. In the key, opening speech of the play, the ghost of "butcher'd *Julius*" calls to mind not only Sylla or some other ancient, but also Charles I:

> My glory was, that Fortune did afford
> That royall power to doe thee [Rome] good I would,
> And Nature heart to will the good I could.
> But I was too too mild. . . .
>
> [B1r]

The play is by no means blind to the dangers Caesar posed, and yet it reveals also a lingering sympathy for him. As the first chorus sings—calling to mind the title of Cartwright's play of 1636—"*A King is but a Royall slave*," and "*A Scepter's but a glorious name*" (B4r).

Caesar's adopted son and successor, Octavian, is first viewed by Cicero, despite his own republican commitment, as "A youth / Ordain'd by Heaven to doe his Countrey good" (B4r). Octavian, however, who is twenty, we are told (the age of Prince Charles in 1650), has his own agenda, and soon we hear him musing, "The Senators, those Nestors of the State, / Disturb the fair *praeludium* of my Glories" (C3v). Despite Cicero's hope that the youth may be won "To have some pity on the State" (C4r), it turns out that his "Ambition cannot brook Plurality" (D1r). In fact, Octavian proves to be a threat even to some of his own would-be supporters.

As the historical story requires, Octavian proceeds to join forces with Antonius and Lepidus, the former being, of course, by far the more dangerous. Yet all "*State-usurpers think of nought but blood*," and inevitably "*when they consult tis to devour the good*" (D2v). As in the *Philippics* of both the historical and the dramatized Cicero, therefore, Antonius comes across as ambitious and self-serving. It is thus at his behest that the triumvirs mark Cicero for death. Though Cicero makes a reasonable attempt to avoid the inevitable, he nonetheless sees the handwriting on the wall and concludes that one ought "Not to survive ones countreys liberty" (D3v).

With the realization that these ancient Roman events conflict in multiple ways with current English ones, one still may find it noteworthy that Prince Charles, who shortly after his father's death was deprived of the succession by order of Parliament, was in some quarters considered to have succeeded automatically. Whatever signs of military power he was able to muster in support of his claims, however, all would come to nought with the death of Montrose and, finally, his own defeat at Worcester. James

Graham, Earl of Montrose, who was probably young Charles's best and noblest supporter, his Strafford, was hanged and quartered on 21 May 1650. A little more than a month later, on 27 June, Charles would come upon one of his friend's arms that the Scots had hung over the gate of Aberdeen. Not until September of the following year did Charles himself have to confront that crucial turning point of the period, defeat at Worcester by Oliver Cromwell.

A more commanding figure than Charles, Cromwell had become the first president of the Council of State soon after the execution of Charles I, and in March of the same year Parliament created him Lord Lieutenant of Ireland. He landed in Dublin that August and proceeded to exercise great severity in putting down the rebels, especially at Drogheda and Wexford. Large numbers of people were massacred by his troops, and, fairly or not, he was anathematized as a bloodthirsty man. He returned to London on 31 May 1650 and a short while later (26 June) was appointed commander in chief of all forces in the Commonwealth. In July he left to take up his command in the North, and in September, at Dunbar, he won one of the most decisive battles of his career. Then he marched on to Edinburgh and Leith, and eventually, in September 1651, he returned south to triumph over Charles at Worcester.

However one interprets the character, motives, and actions of the man, Cromwell was an imposing military figure who was frequently accused of monarchic ambition. In April 1649, in *A Coffin for King Charles: A Crowne for Cromwell,* a broadside polemicist had Cromwell saying to the people, "You *must be props* unto our *pride,* / and *Slaves* to our command," and in January 1650 we find him mocked coarsely in *The Right Picture of King Oliure.*

Even before the death of King Charles, the dangerous fault that threatened to separate Parliament and the army had become dramatically clear: in the winter of 1648 Cromwell and Ireton had given orders for soldiers to bar from the Commons about 140 members who were held to be antagonistic to the army. Thus the Rump came into being. Though presumably now purged of undesirables, Parliament in fact continued to contain a chorus of voices that were not always in tune with one another. The Engagement that followed—requiring a loyalty oath to the new Commonwealth—seemed to some to forbode tyranny. However one interprets Cromwell's motives, moreover, he was a threateningly powerful figure, and the breach between the army and Parliament would finally result in 1653 in his total silencing of the English "senate." "I say you are no Parliament!" he shouted. His armed troopers then entered, and when the chamber was emptied, Cromwell himself left last, taking with him the key. This was a grand climax, of course, and a turning point, but throughout the whole period silencings and reprisals of various sorts had occurred. Many men's hands and tongues were tied, if not cut off, and at about the time *Marcus Tullius Cicero* was published we find Milton himself, impassioned author of the *Areopagitica* (1644), serving as a licenser.

Whatever elements we call to mind from the English world of 1650-51, clearly some amalgam of them is seething in the interior of *Marcus Tullius Cicero*. This play about the tragic fall of a commonwealth whose "sacred Tongue" is silenced is in some ways safely off-target, and yet we may reasonably suppose that, in the playwright's words, its "dark mysterious cloud" (D3v) has been created in the hope that it will not remain totally impenetrable. There is something self-denying in the fact that the poet depicted in the play is so stricken by events—his own voice "strangled by a throng of strugling sighs"—that he feels he must desist and leave it to the historian to "Tell ... the Tragick story" (E3v). Probably the dramatist would have us reflect also on Cicero's earlier claim that poetry is "the language of the Gods when Virtue / Is made her theam." Probably he would have us recognize that the attempt to silence virtuous men in any time and place, Rome or England or elsewhere, is a tragedy sufficient to inspire real pity and terror in those left to watch.[14]

While considering a group of plays such as those examined in this chapter, we should recollect that, whatever its advantages, any selection inevitably directs our attention away from other cultivars of the species. For a fuller understanding of tragic writings in the period, we should ponder not merely the plays noted here but also as many others as we can garner. On the other hand, simply knowing that these tragedies exist is a step in the right direction. Such knowledge protects us from such errors as that which Wendy Griswold records when she writes that Shirley's *Cardinal* of 1641 is "often regarded as the last revenge tragedy" (67). Knowing these little-known plays enables us to see that revengers and tyrants continued to be major figures throughout the middle years of the century. They are no less interesting, furthermore, when we find that rather than confronting each other from opposing sides of a problem (roughly representing justice without law and law without justice, to use Thomas McAlindon's terms), revengers and tyrants show a disconcerting tendency to merge. Queen Andromana and Killigrew's Julia, like Antonius in *Marcus Tullius Cicero*, are double threats in the worlds of their plays. This complicates but by no means negates the convention that the villain somehow personifies rebellion—rebellion, that is, against the order of things as they ought to be. Order

---

[14]For a somewhat fuller discussion of this play, see Randall, "Head and Hands." Because of the present undeserved obscurity of *Marcus Tullius Cicero*, it is the more remarkable to find passages from it quoted by John Evans in his *Hesperides*. Though the latter was prepared for publication by Humphrey Moseley (Stationers' Register, 16 Aug. 1655, in Briscoe 2:8), it apparently remained in manuscript (Folger MS V.b.93).

and the bonds on which order depends are violated time and again in these plays. Inconstancy lies at the bottom of all the major tragic action, whether our attention is focused on lovers, spouses, friends, or heads of state. And the inconstancy is no less devastating for being that of a woman. Lisa Jardine writes about "the *frisson* of horror to be derived from ... representations of threatening womanhood" (97). In fact—and notwithstanding Elizabethan rationalizing on the subject—one might argue that depicting a threatening female at the top of the social pyramid is an effective way to suggest a world turned upside down.

It also falls out that the plays in this cluster that concern themselves centrally with amorous matters seem especially prone to treat adultery. Incest—broached long before in such works as *The Revenger's Tragedy*, *Women Beware Women*, *The Duchess of Malfi*, *Pericles*, and *'Tis Pity She's a Whore*—is brought forward less frequently, but represented here in *The Queene of Corsica* and *Bassianus*. One might therefore wish to note that, historically speaking, both adultery and incest were in the process of gaining even more tragic potential, for on 10 May 1650 Parliament approved an act that declared both to be felonies punishable by death (Gardiner, *History* 1:286).[15]

Like the violation of domestic order, the violation of civil order is a major factor throughout these plays. Here, as McAlindon has pointed out regarding tragedies from earlier times, the intertwining of "socio-political and sexual disorder is a constant feature," and "[w]hat happens in courtship and marriage is reflected in or directly affects what happens in the state" (39). For the most part these plays are very much based on man and his quest for power. Even when they in passing suggest some power beyond the merely human, their frame—despite their origin in a time of great religious turmoil—is generally far more cosmological than theological. Above the fog and filthy air, somewhere beyond human reach, the cosmos may be ordered, but our attention is seldom directed there. Even in those cases where transgression is at last contained, regeneration and redemption are notable largely for their absence.

---

[15]Keith Thomas writes, "If any single measure epitomizes the triumph of Puritanism in England, it must surely be the Commonwealth's act of 10 May 1650. ... This was an attempt, unique in English history, to put the full machinery of the state behind the enforcement of sexual morality" (257).   Another interesting approach to incest in drama can be found in Margaret Cavendish's play called *The Unnatural Tragedy*, probably an Interregnum work. Here a brother says to his sister concerning incest, "Sister, follow not those foolish binding Laws which frozen men have made, but follow Natures Laws, whose Freedome gives a Liberty to all" (349). Eventually he rapes and kills her, then commits suicide. In an epilogue written for the play by William Cavendish, we read, "To make it sadder, know this Story's true" (366).

The frequently cited requirements for tragedy as perceived by Jonson and laid down in his comments "To the Readers" preceding *Sejanus* are worth repeating here both because of the rarity of early keys to tragic theory and because the ghost of Jonson continued to be an important presence in the minds of midcentury Englishmen. The requirements are readily ticked off: truth of argument, dignity of persons, gravity and height of elocution, and fullness and frequency of sentence (350). Although each of us may walk inside each of these phrases and, looking out its windows, see a different view, it is at least reasonably clear that of the plays discussed in this chapter, *Marcus Tullius Cicero* comes closest to achieving Jonson's goals.

Probably not surprisingly, then, *Marcus Tullius Cicero* is also the play that comes closest to approximating old-fashioned Senecan tragedy.[16] Considering the long-term importance of Seneca, including the number of Senecan plays translated during the middle two decades of the seventeenth century, we might expect to find even more such traces than we do. The fact is, however, that besides Senecan and Jonsonian modes, more and newer ways were now available as models, including Grotian scriptural plays, Jesuit martyr plays, Corneillean neoclassical heroic plays, and, above all, the convention-filled plays that seem to have devolved primarily from Shakespeare and Fletcher.

If we press back a little further into the sixteenth century, moreover, we discover that Sir Philip Sidney seems to have singled out very early the definitive element that unites all of our tragedies: violence, sometimes even to be termed, as he terms it, "sweet violence" (*Apologie* F4r). Some of our own contemporaries have labored to show that with the Elizabethans the dramatic presentation of violence came to be a device for exploring and changing society. There is something to be said for this view, and yet one might choose to question those who go on to say that the drama declined when, though retaining its violence, it lost its drive to explore and change. Though the tragedies considered in this chapter all imitate earlier plays in innumerable ways, each also has its own idiosyncratic and exploratory range of qualities. As for the more problematic matter of a drive or will to change, it might be well to keep in mind the request that Picarro makes of Balthazar concerning the inset show in *The Bastard*: "Explain your Riddle, be our *Oedipus*," he asks, because "W'are yet in darkness" (56). This is a latter-day form of the question put many decades earlier when Faustus asked Mephostophilis, "What means this show?" In that earlier instance Marlowe crafted a devilishly subtle and endlessly appropriate response when he

---

[16]Senecanism in early modern England has long been a scholarly morass, but G.K. Hunter's salutary comments and Frederick Kiefer's listings should help nearly anyone arrive at a reasonable view of the subject.

wrote Mephostophilis's "Nothing, Faustus, but to delight thy mind" (v.83-84). Indeed, having once recognized the possible existence of "riddles" and "darkness" in drama, we should stay alert to the possibility that the violence that occurs in our tragedies is sometimes nothing but titillation for titillation's sake. It is a chastening fact that even when we feel most sure that a particular example of tragic violence reveals in some way the playwright's effort to make a point, we can rarely make our schools ring with *sic probo*. Nevertheless, it is our task (and, with luck, our pleasure) to keep inquiring of all these dramatists as Pompiona inquires of her son, "What Genius has inform'd my *Quintus* fancy, / That he still meditates on such examples?"

[14]

COMEDIES

Compositions of this nature, have heretofore been graced by the acceptance,
and protection of the greatest Nobility (I may say Princes) but in this age,
when the Scene of Drammatick Poetry is changed into a wilderness, it is hard
to find a patron to a legitimate muse.

—James Shirley, *The Sisters* (1653)

. . . We
Will dress our Scenes with various novelty,
And teach you wit enough for eighteen pence
Above the reach of the Common Councils sense.[1]

—*The Ghost* (1653)

I will winde up all, with a Use of Exhortation,
That since the Times conspire to make us all Beggars,
let us make our selves merry. . . .

—Richard Brome, *A Joviall Crew* (1652)

Come then! and while the slow Isicle hangs
At the stiffe thatch, and Winters frosty pangs
Benumme the year, blith (as of old) let us
'Midst noise and War, of Peace, and mirth discusse.

—Henry Vaughan, "To His Retired Friend" (1651)

PLATO'S SOCRATES ARGUED that the genius of tragedy is the same as
that of comedy. Puzzle over that as we may, we nevertheless sense that
Renaissance tragedies and comedies both rely on a basic desire for justice—
witty justice, violent justice, or both. Whether tragic disorder or comic disorder
is involved, audiences traditionally have hoped to see some eventual move-
ment toward order. Moreover, tragedy and comedy are both capable of
comment, including, as we shall continue to see, timely paralleling.

Contrasting genres, nevertheless, is probably more fruitful than com-
paring them. Concerning language, for instance, John Tatham warns a
reader of *The Rump,* "*Expect not here Language Three stories high,*" for "*Star-*
tearing Strains fit not a Comedy."[2] Juxtaposed to the language of tragedy, the
language of comedy is likely to seem earthbound. A buskin elevates higher
than a sock. A less obvious point is that while tragedies may be played

---

[1]The Common Council was the administrative body of the city of London. [2]Quoted from
the verso of a leaf following the title page.

(perhaps played best) in the theater of the mind, comedies thrive (some would say depend) on public viewing. The fact that clownage is best seen in a theater and wit best heard there naturally did not go unobserved in the seventeenth century. One reads in a note that John Marston appended to the 1606 preface of his *Parasitaster; or, The Fawne* that "*Comedies* are writ to be spoken, not read: Remember the life of these things consists in action" (A2v). It follows that during a period when many more plays were read than performed, genre-related losses and gains were part of the picture. Additionally we might recollect that from early times, perhaps beginning with Aristotle's *Poetics*, comedy was often held to be not only different from tragedy but also inferior to it.

All these facts and probably none more than this last one had an impact on midcentury plays. On the other hand, the lower critical status of comedy and the corresponding thinness of writing about it probably encouraged a healthy variety of comedic forms. George Greengoose himself could see the heterogeneity. The further good news is that he probably could see also a familial resemblance between jigs, drolls, entertainments (such as Martin Llewellyn's *King Found at Southwell*), and demi-dramas (such as Edward Fuscus's *Ovids Ghost*)—and between all of these and old and new comedies.

In the 1640s and 1650s, as we have seen, plenty of old comedies appeared alongside new ones. From Charles's reign, to cite a fresh example, we have Aston Cokayne's *Trappolin Suppos'd a Prince*, written in the early 1630s and published in 1658. A kim-kam, arsie-versie play based on a *commedia dell'arte* performance that Cokayne attended in Venice in 1632, *Trappolin* features a very common commoner (a pimp) who is for a while transformed into a duke. For an example from the more immediate fore-edge of our period there is Thomas Jordan's *The Walks of Islington and Hogsdon* (licensed 1641), published in 1657 with the commercially savvy claim that it had been "publikely Acted 19. days together, with extraordinary Applause." And for another example of lively prewar work, we might turn again to Richard Brome's *Joviall Crew*, accompanied in 1652 by the playwright's rueful recollection that "*it had the luck to tumble last of all in the* Epidemicall *ruine of the* Scene" (A2r).

Proceeding, then, with an awareness that both the generic and the temporal borders of comedy were protean, and with the hypothesis that adaptability of form helped the comic spirit to survive, much as a genus of plants adapts to harsher (or, indeed, merely different) terrain, we need to recognize also that comedy was often accompanied by satire. This will surprise no one mindful of the social, political, and religious upheavals of the day. The post-Star Chamber flood of pamphlets noted in chapter 4 has a high satiric content. Moreover, following the bleak period of the wars and Charles's death, as David Farley-Hills has observed, "There was . . . a sharp and quite sudden increase in the amount of comic poetry" (21). As luck and etymology would have it, our thoughts about what was happening in dramatic writing may be aided by the realization that a Greek synonym for *satirize* is *komoidein*, literally "to comedize" (Levin 195). Yet the larger wonder here—indeed, one of the wonders of this entire study—is that so many writers continued to find reasons to comedize after the playhouses were ordered closed.

As we watch comedy and satire moving toward the near-synonymity that they often achieve in the Restoration, we also encounter many signs of what may be called The Cavalier Phenomenon. Alfred Harbage, one recalls, thought the adjective *cavalier* a sufficiently broad umbrella to cover his pioneering work on midcentury plays. A major aim of the present study has been to convey instead a sense of the unruly multeity of the period, but let us here make sure that cavalierity receives its due as an element in the plays—including the comedies—of the period.

In 1650, according to Marchamont Nedham (at that time a hired pen for Parliament), "the several parties claiming an interest" in England were the parliamentarians, royalists, Scots, Presbyterians, and Levellers (51). In other words, a serious oppositional listing of "parties" of the day could afford to omit the term *cavaliers*. Nedham's nearest word here is obviously *royalists*. Almost as obviously, however, while *royalist* designates commitment to the royal cause, it cannot do much more, whereas *cavalier* has at least the potential of adding to *royalist* the residual implications of soldiery and, more specifically, connotations of being mounted on horseback, hence being superior, literally and figuratively. Edward Symmons wrote that a complete cavalier "is the onely Reserve of English Gentility and ancient valour" (Boyce 127). On the other hand, because royalist supporters might be found at every social level, a 1648 broadside could proclaim: "There's no true Subject, save the Cavaliere" (Frank, *Hobbled Pegasus* 211). Alexander Brome— a friend of Izaak Walton—tried his hand at rural dialect in order to suggest how even a good-hearted West Country clown might see himself as a cavalier: "Echave a be a Cavaliero, / Like most Weeze-men that escood hear-o."[3]

A multilevel social term used in such passages as a sign of honor, *cavalier* could be used by the enemy as an all-purpose term of opprobrium. According to Hyde, opponents of the royalists commonly referred to them as "*evil counsellors, malignants, delinquents,* and *cavaliers*" (2:314). And all the while friends and foes alike had in mind a similar range of referents. Complicating the situation still further, the image of the cavalier had not been unspotted even at the prewar Caroline court. Back in 1635 Davenant had introduced "An old over-growne debaush'd Cavalier" in his *Triumphs of the Prince*

---

[3]Brome's text (from *Songs* 137) reads "heaor," not "hear-o," but he clearly means to rhyme.

d'Amour (4), and Habington in 1640 had ironically offered a gambling, drinking, quarrelsome, profane, wanton man-about-court as "an absolute Cavalier" in his *Queene of Arragon* (E1v). Still, this kind of in-house satire was mild compared with the diatribes of the opposition after war broke out. John Goodwin makes his parliamentarian position tub-thumpingly clear in this 1643 title: *Anti-Cavalierisme; or, Truth Pleading as Well the Necessity, as the Lawfulnesse of This Present Warre, for the Suppressing of That Butcherly Brood of Cavaliering Incendiaries, Who Are Now Hammering England, to Make an Ireland of It.* "I mean," he explains, "that Colluvies, that heape, or gathering together of the scum, and drosse, and garbage of the Land, that most accursed confederacy, made up of *Gebal, and Ammon, and Amaleck, Philistims with the Inhabitants of Tyre,* of Jesuits, and Papists, and Atheists, of stigmaticall and infamous persons in all kindes, with that bloody and butcherly Generation, commonly knowne by the name of Cavaliers" (A2r). Here we have a wild-eyed caricature of cavaliers from a man who is also unwittingly caricaturing himself.

No one discusses the basic dichotomy of midcentury types better than David Underdown, who observes that the period's cavalier and roundhead "both reflected and heightened the division of the kingdom. Stereotypes—cultural constructions that express in a form of public shorthand the negative characteristics of opponents—are the inevitable product of deep-seated political divisions. When they acquire an aura of total moral exclusiveness, providing symbolic expression of fundamentally opposed ideologies and moral codes, they intensify pre-existing divisions and solidify group identities" (*Revel* 142). Such caricatures are not simply the two major images of their time. More interestingly, they are also consciousness-raising foils to each other. To keep the picture suitably complex, furthermore, we should bear in mind that the divergent negative images of cavalier and roundhead were counterbalanced by equally implausible idealized ones.

Naturally the negatives are more fun to read about, and in the case of the cavalier, libertinism is a much-harped-upon note. Although libertinism of a sort had been discernible in earlier years (in some of the Fletcher plays, for instance, and the verses of Carew), civil war brought it into clearer focus and made it a more obvious target. *An Exact Description of a Roundhead, and a Long-Head Shag-Poll* (1642) cites Revelation 9 to prove that shag-poll locusts "that wear hair like women" came up from "the smoaky pit" (A3v). It goes so far as to offer the titillating suggestion that the cavaliers' flowing locks are really wigs made from harlots' hair (A4v; see figure 34). The truth is that with an increased threat of physical danger after war broke out, libertinism may really have increased. A song in one of our plays, *The Famous Tragedie of King Charles I* (1649), yields the Herrickian admonition "*Drinke then (Boyes) and drown all sorrow, / Who knows if we shall drink to morrow?*" (17).

Meanwhile, the cavaliers tended to perceive their opponents as nasally

AN
EXACT DESCRIPTION
OF A
ROUNDHEAD,
AND
A LONG-HEAD SHAG-POLL :

Taken our of the purest Antiquities and Records.

Wherein are confuted the odious afperfions of Malignant Spirits:
Efpecially in anfwer to thofe moft rediculous, abfurd and beyond
comparifon, moft foolifh Baffle-headed Pamphlets fent into the
World by a Stinking Locuft, viz.

The Devill turn'd Round-- Head.	*The Vindication of the Round-Head.* and
The Refolution of the Round-Head.	*Jordan the Players exercifing.*

This Man of haire whom you fee marching heere,
Is that brave Ruffian Mounfieur Cavilier.
But let him not make fo much haft for hee,
Muft be drawn back; and ftayd by Gregore.

London, Printed for George Tomlinfon, and are to fold in the Ould-Baily. 1642.

Figure 34. Title page of a pamphlet on roundheads and royalists (1642). The "shag-poll" royalist is associated with York because Charles (and therefore his court) moved there in 1642. (By permission of the British Library.)

intoning hypocrites. In an untitled fragment of a comedy now in the Essex Record Office, a woman named Mincing recalls seeing "a poore simple cobler, get vp into a hollow tree, and hee would doe nothing but turne vp the white of his eyes, wagge his lipps halfe a quarter of an houre before hee spoake, and yn repeat, O lord, lord, throw his nostrills" ("Copt Hall Interlude" 24).[4] And William Cavendish has one of his characters say of another who is attempting to impersonate a Puritan that he fails "for want of twanging it deepe enough in the Nose" (*Witts Triumvirate* 12r). Much worse, of course, the roundheads often were seen as inflexible purveyors of repression and negation. It is therefore one of the ironies of history that the personal freedom claimed at the outset of our period by courtiers such as Carew and Suckling came to be subordinated to fighting and dying for traditional order, whereas freedom from tradition, indeed freedom from other men, was cried up in the polemic of the protesting factions.

Perhaps the single most important thing to observe about the cavaliers, in the drama and elsewhere, is the diversity of their images. The diversity is so great because so many variables of time, place, and circumstance appertain. In a 1642 pamphlet by "Agamemnon Shaglock van Dammee" we have comic-dyspeptic satire of raffish want-to-bes such as really walked the streets of London at the beginning of the civil wars (*The Speech of a Cavaleere to His Comrades*). In sobering contrast, we find the 1648 "Ordinance for Putting All Delinquents, Papists, Ministers, Officers, and Soldiers of Fortune, That Have Adhered to the Enemy . . . Out of the Cities of London and Westminster . . . and Twenty Miles Distant" (Firth and Rait 1:1166-68)—a document that reminds us that we can expect to read about real cavaliers acting in places other than taverns or battlefields. Some—like Compton, Killigrew, Fane, and Cowley—were imprisoned, at least for a while. Shortly after war broke out, according to Hyde, "all the prisons about London were quickly filled with persons of honour" (2:318). In fact, "Now not to suffer shews no loyall heart, / When Kings want ease Subjects must learne to smart" (*Liberty of the Imprisoned Royalist* A1v). Some cavaliers, of course, went to the Continent. Some, like the speaker of Lovelace's "Grasshopper," retreated to the haven of a country hearth. In other words, no one's view nowadays of the cavaliers should be restricted to a stereotypical image of bold and blaspheming young blades roistering off to battle. More than twenty years after "Agamemnon Shaglock van Dammee" wrote his *Speech of a Cavaleere*, Charles Hammond still thought it worthwhile to distinguish between virtuous, civil cavaliers and "*Roaring, Dam-me, Coun-*

---

[4]The first surviving words of text in the untitled manuscript—sometimes called the Copt (Copped) Hall Interlude—are spoken by the merchant Pennywise: "There's more tradesmen broke this year ith city than painted windows" (3).

terfeit Cavaliers" (22). Whatever they did during the 1640s, moreover, royalists in the 1650s had to work out a *modus vivendi* during the Commonwealth and Protectorate. In *The True Cavalier Examined by His Principles* (1656) John Hall finally went to the extreme of explaining to Cromwell that previously, when fighting for Charles, "our then present Protector, we did fight for You your self, our present Protector now" (A2r).

Although this chapter has much more to do than pursue the complexities of cavalierity, we shall next consider four different playwrights who can be considered cavaliers. First, for a clear instance of a real-life dammee cavalier, we shall return to Thomas Killigrew, that longtime courtier and eventual founder of the Theatre Royal (see figure 35). We have previously taken brief notice of Killigrew's bawdy comedy called *The Parsons Wedding*, in which a group of characters agrees that "any thing that breeds mirth is welcome" (98). One should always have demurrals at the ready, of course, when approaching a playwright's views via the remarks of his characters, but the libertine component in this writer's economy of mirth is not unfairly indicated when he has a character in *The Princesse* (1635-37)[5] observe, "They are the prettiest kind of commodities, these women, that a man can deal in, there is nothing like 'em, but ready money" (6).

Since the two Killigrew comedies now at hand are both called *Thomaso; or, the Wanderer* (parts 1 and 2), a reader should note that "Thomaso" is a continentalized version of Killigrew's own name and is, in fact, one that he applied to himself (Harbage, *Thomas Killigrew* 226). In a high-strung work called *The Life of Tomaso the Wanderer* (1676), Richard Flecknoe proclaimed to his readers that Killigrew was "born to discredit all the Professions he was of; the *Traveller, Courtier, Soldier, Writer*, and the *Buffoon*" (6). A conscienceless man, according to Flecknoe, Killigrew "car'd not in whose light he stood, so he might see" (6). Although the voice of a fellow showman is shrill with personal pain in this passage, the fact is that Killigrew traveled with little moral baggage. In 1652 he was expelled from Venice.

France, of course, was the usual cavalier destination. In Sheppard's *Committee-Man Curried*, part 1, Loyalty cries out, "*France*, I come into thy armes, thou spreadst them wide to entertaine those loyall Subjects [who] flie to thee for shelter" (A3v). And in 1647 Killigrew joined Charles in Paris. The two *Thomaso* plays, however, remind us that many cavaliers turned up in Spain. One of the byproducts of republican England's alliance with France was that young Charles became entangled with Spain. Hence in *Thomaso*, part 2, we find an Englishman in Spain lamenting, "would I were at *Paris*, or the *Hague*, again; did I leave those places of pleasure and quiet civil life to come to this where mischiefs only swarm; whose very air is

[5]Published in *Comedies, and Tragedies* (1664) with its own individual title page dated 1663.

CLARICILLA
THE PRISONERS
THE PRINCESSE
THE PILGRIM
THE WANDERER
THE REVENGE
Thomas Killegrew Page of Honour to King
Charles the first Groome of the Bedchamber to King
Charles the Second and his Ma:ties Resident with the
Republique of Venice in the yeare 1650.

Figure 35. Thomas Killigrew (1612-83) with a stack of his plays and, in the medallion above his head, a portrait of Charles I. From a copy of Killigrew's *Comedies, and Tragedies* (1664) in The John Work Garrett Library of The Johns Hopkins University.

lowsie, and that curse would destroy the Country but for another curse that wars with it, that of the dust which flies so hot it would fire powder as it passes; ev'ry sand is so many sparks in the air: yet here we walk in this furnace without a miracle" (455).[6]

Even such a brief passage may serve to suggest Killigrew's gift for detail. Unfortunately, the details are sometimes so profuse as to suffocate nearly everything else. Though we know little or nothing of the personal speech of Tudor and Stuart playwrights, much less how such habits might relate to their writing, one might consider here the hypothesis that Killigrew's written prose to some extent parallels the oral manner of the living man. At any rate, Flecknoe claims that his foe "talkt madly, *dash, dash*" (*Life of Tomaso* 8).

Killigrew's Thomaso, described as "An English Cavaleer, who had serv'd in the Spanish Army" (pt. 1, 312), is one of a handful of Englishmen ("Royal and Loyal Fugitives" [pt. 1, 320]) who are depicted as engaging in some mainly amorous escapades in Spain. The prevailing tone is set when we find that Angelica, a fashionable and expensive courtesan, has just become newly available. Indeed, half of the female characters here are bawds or whores and specifically not examples of "those tender-hearted Lovers you find in Comedies, that sigh at first sight; and run mad for strangers in the second act" (pt. 1, 325). What is more, Angelica and her bawd Anna are politically attuned. Says Anna: "There's no Rogue like your Round-head, a dissembling, insolent, bloody, blasphemous traytor" (pt. 1, 328). As for the unhappy English cavaliers, says Don Pedro, late commander of the Spanish army, they "have been kill'd or banish'd, sunk, hang'd and starv'd" (pt. 1, 343). His friend Carlo protests that the cavaliers are as proud of their persecution as the Jews, as proud of their impoverishment as a Castilian of his blood. Pedro believes nevertheless that "if poverty or vertue can plead, sure the English Court will find a reward" (pt. 1, 344).

Although there is much else that is historically interesting about this pair of plays, special mention should be made of the character named Harrigo. When Thomaso and Harrigo first encounter each other in part 1, the stage direction reads, "Thomaso *runs to him, and they embrace*," and Harrigo exclaims, "My Friend, the *Wanton Wanderer* still; what new ill luck drives thee hither again?" (320). Brought into the action as an instrument to further Thomaso's wooing and winning of Serulina, Don Pedro's sister, Harrigo is a representation of Henry Proger. A steward to Edward Hyde and Francis Cottington at the royal embassy in Madrid in 1649-50, and a personal friend of Killigrew, Proger also was ringleader of a group of cavaliers who thought they were achieving some worthwhile royalist re-

---

[6]Killigrew expects one to remember the story of Shadrach, Meschach, and Abednego, who emerged unharmed from the furnace where Nebuchadnezzar had cast them (Daniel 3.12–30).

venge by killing Antony Ascham, the newly arrived envoy to Spain from the Commonwealth (Harbage, *Thomas Killigrew* 227-28).[7] Killigrew's efforts to place his sordid high jinks in a particular social and political milieu could hardly be more direct. It turns out that in this pair of Spanish comedies the sometimes revealing and sometimes concealing veil of indirection is often lifted, apparently because Killigrew had little doubt that his readers would be royalists in politics and latitudinarians in just about everything else.

Cosmo Manuche was another playwriting royalist soldier. He served the King as a captain and major of foot from the beginning of the Civil Wars to their close, and for his pains he was imprisoned and impoverished. Though not of the court or even of gentle birth, Manuche was nevertheless a cavalier in word and deed. We encountered him in chapter 10 as the professedly reluctant writer of *The Banish'd Shepheardesse*, in which he presents idealized pastoral representations of Henrietta Maria and Prince Charles. Encouraged by the patronage of James Compton, Earl of Northampton—his former military commander—Manuche was not hesitant to express his gratitude. In the bits of extradramatic writing with which he equipped his comedy *Love in Travell*, he conveys his appreciation for Compton's support and, more intriguingly, his confidence that Compton "will find some thing in it, I lay'd not in Euery bodies Way" (3r).

Manuche's *Love in Travell*, though never published, is a lively, plot-packed comedy capable of holding its own with many plays that made their way into print. It differs from most, however, in that it depicts the period of readjustment that followed the wars and preceded the Restoration. Set in a Holborn inn, it offers not only denizens such as Smale-Peck the ostler and Bolster the chamberlain, but also a dramatically useful range of visitors. The latter consist mainly of the family of Sir Peircival Fondlin, a rich knight who happens to be the father of three eligible daughters, all supplied with suitors. When we meet him, old Fondlin is in the dumps because his favorite, young Arabella, has disappeared—actually gone off to join some gypsies while in search of her departed true love, a cavalier colonel named Allworth. Not too surprisingly, Colonel Allworth eventually turns up at the inn, though he has assumed a disguise in order to ascertain just how Shylockian his creditors are going to be. Perhaps because of his own painful debts or his patron's, Manuche warms to this hero as "A braue deseruing" man (4v), indeed

> . . . a Noble soule
> Lodg'd, in a Man of Men. where the true Hon[r]
> Of a deseruing souldier (seldome rewarded)
> Is seated, with a strong guard of vertue.
>
> [6r]

---

[7]This murder, which took place in Madrid in 1650, echoed that at The Hague of Isaac Dorislaus, envoy to the States-General, in 1649.

Eventually we learn that Bolster, who has worked at the inn for more than two years, once served in Allworth's own regiment: "I was not idle, S^r, when base Rebellion: / Storm'd a Noble cause" (27r). There is even some negative allusion to current "state policy" (6r), but the specific targets of the comedy are safer: a "Crooked Jewe" broker who may be out-tricked (4v), a country attorney's son named Fogg, and a rich farmer's son named Muck-Worme. As a matter of fact, Jews in the 1650s were much in men's minds because of Cromwell's personal inclination toward a policy of toleration. Thanks partly to the indefatigable Rabbi Manasseh ben Israel, Jews in the 1650s were permitted to live in England, in fact to have a synagogue and a cemetery in London.[8] In the major jest of the play, however, the two comic suitors, Fogg and Muck-Worme, are induced to cudgel each other—while dressed, respectively, as a Spaniard and a Turk. Toward the end of the action, as in so many plays of the period, there is also an inset masque. Whether or not the latter suggests actual staging capabilities at Compton's Castle Ashby or elsewhere, it calls for the goddess Phoebe to descend "in a Mashiene" (42v), and it occasions the long-postponed entry of Arabella in gypsy garb. Fortunately the delighted-to-distraction old Fondlin proves to be a sort of father-in-law *ex machina* who promises to pay off Colonel Allworth's creditors himself. In the playwright's imagination, if only there, an impoverished cavalier's reintegration into England's social fabric could be achieved with gratifying ease.

Though set against a backdrop of the times, the travail of the lovers in the play takes stage center. To call the work *Love in Travell*, in fact, is to opt for a pun. With sufficient emphasis in the text on travel (Allworth first appears at Sir Peircival's house "In's way of trauell" [14r], and Arabella has been out searching on the road for three months), Manuche very likely wants to call our attention also to the lovers' travail, caused for Allworth by the adverse times and for Arabella by love itself.[9]

Though Manuche's versified dedication to Compton expresses his realization that "ffew: there be / Is Crittick-prooffe, in Commick poetry," it also ventures to ask Compton "ffor aprobation" (3v). More, in his "Prologue: intended for the Stage," in fore-conceit "haueing stricktly veiw'd this Audience," Manuche is glad to suppose that "this Audience" will view his work with welcome "impartiallitie," in fact be so different from usual audiences as to forgive the "faults h'has writt" (4r). One is

---

[8]Another of our playwrights, Thomas Fuller, records a standard English view as preserved in the old saying *"I will use you as bad as a* Jew" (*History of the Worthies*, 2d 198). David Katz is helpful in clarifying the status of Jews in England in the 1650s.   [9]One might compare Brome's *Antipodes* (*"our Trauailes in th'* Antipodes" [L4v]); Greville's "Treatie of Warres" ("Nor by the *Warres* doth God reuenge alone, / He sometimes tries, and traueleth the good" [76]); and Willan's preface to *Orgula* ("o'reburdened with the travell of private or publique Negotiations" [a2r]).

tempted to see here a reference to comfortable, private performance (projected, actual, or both) under one of Compton's roofs. In any case, though *Love in Travell* is highly derivative, the dramatist's own frustration with the times, coupled with his energy and interest in the task at hand, seems to have been sufficient to infuse the play with a good deal more dramatic life than he was able to conjure up in his made-to-order *Banish'd Shepheardesse.*[10]

A cavalier dramatist of quite another sort—at once less conventional and less skilled—was Mildmay Fane, Earl of Westmorland. Unlike Killigrew, Fane was no libertine and no wanderer. Unlike Manuche, he was of gentle birth and not a man of arms. And unlike both Killigrew and Manuche, his position as a royalist—indeed, a royalist of Puritan background—appears equivocal.[11] In the summer of 1642 Fane was ordered to provide funds for the royal army and to serve as one of the commissioners of array in Northamptonshire (Fane, *Raguaillo* [ed. Leech] 13-14). Soon, however, according to his autobiography, "after various fortunes of war, he and about thirty others were taken prisoner [at Edgehill?], before their second battle. And pursuant to the orders of that Parliament which remained, he [was] handed over to the guard and custody of the Tower" (quoted in Morton, *Biography* 36). Rather amazingly, Fane then proceeded to use some of his incarceration time to write a dramatic show, dated December 1642. He hoped to "preuent / The Languishments of an Imprisonment" and "beguile tyme" (*Change* 50v). This work, called *The Change*, comes to a less than resoundingly royalist conclusion, however, with the insight "A king's a Man" (68r). Not until April 1643 was Fane paroled to his house in St. Bartholomew's, and not until mid-February 1644 was he released. Apparently it signified little that his wife, Mary, was a sister of the wife of Thomas, Lord Fairfax, leader of Parliament's Yorkshire forces ever since war broke out. In fact, Fairfax is the subject of some of Fane's satire.

However one decides to read such matters, Fane's public stance vis-à-vis King and Parliament was to prove of particular historical interest. The origin of so-called compounding was Parliament's promise as of 30 January 1644 to pardon nobles, knights, and gentlemen who were not "prime authors" of the war, provided they subscribed to the Covenant and "compounded"—that is, paid Parliament—for their delinquency.[12] Mildmay

---

[10]Manuche also wrote and dedicated to Compton a comedy called *The Feast*. Though omitted from discussion here (it is clearly a product of the Restoration), *The Feast* provides still further evidence of the breadth of Manuche's taste and talent.   [11]In his autobiography, recalling his trip from Italy to Switzerland, Fane describes himself as "rejoicing in the vicinity of Calvinistic truth" (BL MS Add. 34220, 5, cited in Morton, *Biography* 18).   [12]As of 9 June 1643, "the whole Kingdom," in order to preserve "the true Protestant Reformed Religion, and the Liberty of the Subject," was supposed to swear loyalty to Parliament in its struggle "against the Forces raised by the King without their Consent" (Firth and Rait 1:175).

Fane is noteworthy for being the first peer so to compound (Hardacre 20-21). Pondering Fane's action, Gerald Morton has concluded reasonably that his "dealings with those in power, necessary to secure his release, were motivated not nearly so much by conscience, as his final petition indicates, as by the belief that if he did not secure his release he and his family would be finally stripped of both wealth and position" (*Biography* 38).

Though never cured of his contempt for the opposition, Fane was allowed to return to his estate of Apethorpe in Northamptonshire. Here he had previously either constructed a theater or (more likely) modified his home, Apethorpe Hall, so that he could indulge in the pleasure of home-grown theatricals that required machinery, including something so newfangled as flat revolving wings. Prior to *The Change* he had produced the masquelike *Raguaillo D'Oceano* (1640) and two rather a-generic works called *Candia Restaurata* (1641) and *Tymes Trick upon the Cards* (1642). *Candia Restaurata*, written shortly before war erupted, depicted an island realm that had been ailing for thirteen years—that is, since 1629 and Charles's dismissal of Parliament. Somewhat surprisingly, considering that he wrote as late as 1641, Fane apparently thought that Candia might be restored by the wise ministrations of one Dr. Synodarke (Parliament).[13] In all likelihood—and despite his subscribing to the Covenant in 1644—Fane was fundamentally a royalist who believed in a government consisting of both a parliament and a king. In a poem dated July 1643 he writes, "but who are you for? ye King / Or Parlement? as if a body & head / Could severd be yet not ye party dead."[14] In his prologue to *Tymes Trick*, at any rate, Fane already looks back to Candia and suggests that its Synodarkian "restoring" was no great success. As a piece of writing, *Tymes Trick* proves to be characteristically packed with social and political allusion and allegory. It also proves to be the most unfocused and frustrating of all Fane's dramatic efforts.

In 1644, pleased with his return to country seclusion ("I hugg my quiet" [*Otia* 174]), Fane next produced *Vertues Triumph* (1644), followed by *Don Phoebo's Triumph* (1645) and then *De Pugna Animi* (1650). For the most part, his heteroclyte dramatic writings—seven in all—are confused and confusing self-indulgences.[15] Wearying to read, especially in manuscript, they nevertheless provide a variety of insights into amateur drama of the day

---

[13]Sometimes the doctor's name appears in the manuscript as "Psunodarke." Granting it apparent that the name alludes to Parliament, Leech explains that "Psunodarke" derives from the Greek for leader of a caravan (Fane, *Raguaillo* 34). One might also note that "Synodarke" is suggestive of "Synedrion," a term related to "Sanhedrin" that refers to a judicial or representative assembly. Jasper Mayne in his *Amorous Warre* writes of "the factious Members / Of our *Synedrium*" (63–64). [14]This poem, "The Times Steerage," is given in its entirety by Morton (*Biography* 123). [15]An eighth Fane work, now lost, is recorded by Hazlitt (*Manual* 127) from a sale at Sotheby's on 17 July 1888. Called *Ladrones*,

(for example, concerning double casting) and into the mind of their more or less cavalier creator.

Vertues Triumph and *De Pugna Animi* are probably Fane's best works. In the former he shows how Ambition ("A Tyrannicall Vsurper" [70v]) consorts with Impudence, who in turn relies on Lyes and Deceipts (disguised as Vertue and Trueth). A beleaguered character called Nobilitye is depicted as "A Statesman, But poore" (70v). Married to Learninge, and together with her the parent of Trueth, Nobilitye is sufficiently fortunate, even in adversity, to retain as his "honest bond Servant" the titular and true Vertue (70v). Secluded at Apethorpe in "Blest Privacie" (*Otia* 8), the author felt sufficiently free to write of the "Rapings and thefts maintaind and Cherisht / Under the name of Reformation" (*Vertues Triumph* 96v).

In *De Pugna Animi* Fane continued to indulge his allegorical bent. Though he called this work a comedy, even pointing out that it ends "wth Matrimony according to Custome" (124v), it might also be considered a latter-day morality play, a seventeenth-century *Psychomachia* that is more economical, more lively linguistically, and somewhat better built than his other works. Here, because he exercises a certain artistic self-discipline, Fane achieves greater clarity. This time his central character is Lord Mens (that is, Mind, Understanding, Reason, somewhat oddly represented as "A German Rhinegraue" [125r]), whose chief attendants are Sir Ratio Prudens, a valiant captain, and Sir Eurocledon Tempest, admiral and general at sea. His councillors—all colonels and commanders—are ffeall, Chaste Lyon, Patience, Curtoys, Temperance, ffrayanck (that is, Bounty), and D'accordes. Unfortunately, Mens has lost contact with Sir Ratio Prudens, thereby opening himself up to the dangers of the revolted Five Senses, each attended by an appropriate sense organ and each a prince who has made his own advances on the "little world of man" (124v).[16]

Within this rather complicated scheme of moral allegorizing, Fane analyzes the consequences of a faltering monarch's inability to understand and work with his supporters. Clearly, therefore, we should not overlook the relevance here of a cavalier's painful perception of how things had gone wrong with Charles. "Discord rakes through my Hull like a great Shott," says Lord Mens (128r). Even more than this, Morton would have us see *De Pugna Animi* as a dramatized version of the political philosophy espoused in a treatise by Fulvius Pacianus that was translated by Fane as *Of the Art of Well Governing a People* (now BL Add. MS 34251).

Though Fane was every inch an amateur (we may safely dismiss

it presumably was "An opera in a Romansike Way" and probably composed about the same time as Fane's other dramatic writings (1640-50).   [16]Harbage observes similarities with Nabbes's 1637 *Microcosmus* (*Cavalier Drama* 201). Much useful information on Fane is to be found in Leech's edition of Fane's *Raguaillo D'Oceano* and *Candy Restored*.

Herrick's claim that he "writes sweet Numbers well as any can" ["To the Right Honourable Mildmay, Earle of Westmorland," l. 2][17]), his best dramatic writings are analytic, moralistic, allegorical comedies (or quasi-comedies) that broach some of the major national problems of his day. Occasionally they reveal a specific awareness of other English writers such as Marlowe, Jonson, and Davenant ("I wisht for Gundobarts Contriuer by mee," says Naso in *De Pugna Animi* [140v]), but Fane himself was incapable of literary ascent. In the words of his Nobilitye in *Vertues Triumph*, he was "Christend Caualeir / Yet sett on foote" (89v). Politically speaking, nonetheless, Fane's royalist credentials would be revalidated in 1660, when he became commander of the eastern division of horse volunteers in Northamptonshire and joint Lord Lieutenant of that county.

The fourth figure chosen here to suggest the spectrum of cavalier writing was not a soldier like Killigrew or Manuche or a country gentleman like Fane, but probably he was the most articulate royalist of them all. Indeed, Abraham Cowley acquired during his lifetime—then barely outlived—a reputation for being the greatest poet of his day.[18] As a young man at Cambridge (B.A., 1639; M.A., 1643), where he was a friend of Richard Crashaw, Cowley was for political reasons ejected from the University—along with a good many others—in the spring of 1643.[19] He therefore went to join the King at Oxford, and whatever other activity engaged him there, he spent a good deal of time on a massive poem called *The Civil War.* His obvious aim was to paint a rosy royalist picture of the conflict ("To *Oxford* next Great *Charles* triumphant came" [l. 345]), but he abandoned the project in September, following the King's defeat at the First Battle of Newbury. Probably it was in Oxford that Cowley met Henry Jermyn, later Lord Jermyn. In any case, he soon became secretary to Jermyn, who in turn was Chamberlain to the Queen. Cowley is said to have served as cipherer for most of the coded letters traveling between the King and Queen, and when Henrietta Maria left England for France the following spring, Cowley joined the band of royalist expatriates in Paris. Not surprisingly, then, when he returned to England in 1654, apparently as a spy, he was arrested and imprisoned. In fact, Cromwell himself interrogated him. Released in 1655,

[17]Herrick, in fact, urges Fane to make his verses known ("Expose your jewels," l. 11). It was also to Fane that Herrick addressed his memorable poem "The Hock-Cart." All in all, as Morton points out, ample evidence exists to suggest that Fane was Herrick's patron (*Biography* 70) [18]Edward Phillips in his *Theatrum Poetarum* (1675) wrote of Cowley as "The most applauded Poet of our Nation both of the present and past Ages" (*Moderns* 1). [19]Hibbert writes that "eventually twelve heads of colleges and 181 Fellows and other senior members of the University were deprived of their positions, sent away to earn their livings as best they could, and replaced by acknowledged Puritans" (68).

Cowley wrote the next year in his *Poems* about the reasonableness of accommodation.

Cowley's efforts to resolve an intolerable political and personal situation are interesting both for their own sake and for the insight they provide into more or less comparable cases. Beginning rather disingenuously (contrary to what he implies, his *Civil War* poem certainly survived), Cowley proceeds here with what appears to be cool-headed pragmatism:

> I have cast away all such pieces as I wrote during the time of the late troubles, with any relation to the differences that caused them; as among others, *three Books of the Civil War it self,* reaching as far as the first *Battel* of *Newbury.* . . . Now though in all *Civil Dissentions,* when they break into open hostilities, the *War* of the *Pen* is allowed to accompany that of the *Sword,* and every one is in a maner obliged with his *Tongue,* as well as *Hand,* to serve and assist the side which he engages in; yet when the event of battel, and the unaccountable *Will* of *God* has determined the controversie, and that we have submitted to the conditions of the *Conqueror,* we must lay down our *Pens* as well as *Arms,* we must *march* out of our *Cause* it self, and *dismantle* that, as well as our *Towns* and *Castles,* of all the *Works* and *Fortifications* of *Wit* and *Reason* by which we defended it. *We* ought not sure, to begin our selves to revive the remembrance of those times and actions for which we have received a *General Amnestie,* as a *favor* from the *Victor.* The truth is, neither *We,* nor *They,* ought by the *Representation* of *Places* and *Images* to make a kind of *Artificial Memory* of those things wherein we are all bound to desire like *Themistocles,* the *Art* of *Oblivion.* [a4r]

True to his policy of practical flexibility, Cowley composed an impressive poem called "Ode, upon the Blessed Restoration" when Charles II came to the throne. Not surprisingly, however, there was a cost to be paid for his previous trimming: Charles is said to have refused to let Cowley kiss his hand.

The two plays by Cowley that concern us are *The Guardian* (performed 1642; published 1650) and *Cutter of Coleman Street* (performed 1661; published 1663), the second of which is a complete reworking of the first. *The Guardian,* presented before the Prince of Wales at Trinity College, Cambridge, on 12 March in the year the war broke out, was among the last half dozen plays known to have been performed before plays were banned.[20] The King at the time was on the road with his troops. In fact, he entered

---

[20]Something of the contemporary atmosphere is preserved in Cowley's own reconstruction of the performance. *The Guardian,* he recalls, was "made and acted before the *Prince,* in his passage through *Cambridge* towards *York,* at the beginning of the late unhappy War; or rather neither *made* nor *acted,* but *rough-drawn* onely, and *repeated;* for the haste was so great, that it could neither be *revised* or *perfected* by the *Author,* nor *learnt without-Book* by the *Actors,* nor set forth in any measure tolerably by the *Officers* of the *College*" ([a]1r). Kawachi's *Calendar of English Renaissance Drama* is helpful for dealing with dating problems of the pre-closure period.

York on the afternoon of 17 March. Already Cowley could write in his prologue that "we contemn the fury of these dayes" (Wiley 6).

Since the Prince of Wales was not yet twelve at the time, the kind of play deemed appropriate for his entertainment is of some interest. The guardian referred to in the title is one Captain Blade, a roisterer whose estates have fallen into the hands of an old Puritan widow—who therefore must be wooed. The ward for whom Blade is guardian is his niece Lucia, whose estate will come to him if she marries without his consent. He is also father to Aurelia, a cool-headed young woman whose ingenuity sparks various amorous complications. As if this were not enough, more complications are provided by the fact that the old widow has a daughter, Tabytha, who is sought by Blade's counterfeit-cavalier friend, Colonel Cutter.

A witty intellectual himself, Cowley packed his dialogue with satiric darts, colloquialisms, and enlivening allusions. He has the widow complain, for instance, that she is not used to having "such hee-hee-heeing fellows" as Blade and Cutter for boarders, but "O the father! the Colonel's as full of waggery as an egg's full of meat" (A3v). Particularly interesting are some references to London's theatrical milieu. When the sentimental heroine, Lucia, seems doomed to poverty, Cutter callously anticipates her fate: "How is't? twelve pence a time, I warrant, in these clothes," perhaps "at the Play house i' the six-peny-room sometimes" (D2v)—which adumbrates one of the practices decried by the theaters' foes. When Captain Blade thinks the widow will be his, he plans to cast off his rascally companions, leaving Dogrel the poet to "make and sell smal Pamphlets i'the playhouse, or else Tobacco, or else snuffe Candles" (D3r). There were pamphlets aplenty to be peddled in the theaters, we recall, just before the outbreak of war, but equally *déclassé* must have been the job of snuffing candles after a play. As for the widow, Blade plans to reform her Puritan ways: "I'll carry her to Plays, in stead of Lectures: she shall see them, as well as the dancing o' the ropes, and the Puppet-play of Nineve" (E1v). Naturally Cowley's own play ends comically, with multiple couplings, but there surely was irony as well as satire for readers in 1650 who found Aurelia predicting that her father's bride's "first pious deed will be, to banish *Shakespear* and *Ben. Johnson* out of the parlour" (E1v). Instead of going to see plays, puppets, or rope-dancing, the widow-bride will censor even the reading of plays in her new household. Aurelia's prognostications are designed to be comically ominous, of course, and yet they stand at no great distance from what Cowley dared to say in his prologue:

> *We perish if the Roundheads be about:*
> *For now no ornament the head must wear,*
> *No Bays, no Mitre, not so much as Hair.*

> *How can a Play pass safely, when we know,*
> *Cheapside-Cross falls for making but a show.*
>
> [A2r]

Since the Cheapside "show" was not closed until 1643, one might question how much revision Cowley's play underwent between its performance in 1642 and its printing in 1650.

When Cowley decided to rewrite *The Guardian* as *Cutter of Coleman-Street*, he *"fell upon the changing of it almost wholly"* (A2r). Most obviously, and despite the fact that what one is likely to remember best about both plays is a colorful collage of characters, "Cutter the pretended Cavaleer" has now been promoted to the title position. Cowley is careful to have him confess in an epilogue that *"To you who always of that Party were, / I never was of any; up and down / I rowld, a very Rakehell of this Town"* (71). Broadening the comic possibilities, Cowley now provides the pretended colonel with a companion, a pretended captain named Worm. On the other hand, Captain Blade has metamorphosed into Colonel Jolly, who like his predecessor is presented as both the wooer of a Puritan widow (formerly the spouse of Colonel Fear-the-Lord Barebottle) and the crooked guardian of a sentimentally correct niece.

With the Restoration accomplished, Cowley was appalled to find that some in the first audiences understood his *Cutter of Coleman-Street* as *"a piece intended for abuse and Satyre against the Kings party"* (A2v). In his 1663 preface he exclaims, *"Good God! Against the Kings party? After having served it twenty years during all the time of their misfortunes and afflictions, I must be a very rash and imprudent person if I chose out that of their Restitution to begin a Quarrel with them. I must be too much a Madman to be trusted with such an Edg'd Tool as Comedy"* (A2v). He goes so far as to protest *"that the vices and extravagancies imputed vulgarly to the Cavaliers, were really committed by Aliens who only usurped that name, and endeavoured to cover the reproach of their Indigency or Infamy of their Actions with so honourable a Title"* (A3r). As for Jolly, says Cowley, he is intended to be not a paragon but *"an ordinary jovial Gentleman"* (A3r) whose "Estate was sold for [his] being with the King at *Oxford*" (B3r). Probably Cowley should have thought twice about depicting Jolly planning to sell his young ward to Cutter or Worm for a thousand pounds. On the other hand, in the form in which it comes to us, this representation of teeming London life in 1658—Cromwell's final year—leaves little doubt about its basic political bearings. Worm calls down "a Pox on the Poll, of old Politique *Noll*," and Jolly proposes a toast to "the Royal Travailer" (E1v).

Having considered even briefly some works by Killigrew, Manuche, Fane, and Cowley, we have amassed considerable evidence that the subject of cavalier playwrights and playwriting is capable of widely variant permutations. (Chapter 15 will provide a closer look at the quite astonishing involvement with drama of one particular cavalier family.) If we also stay alert to cavalier elements in other and further plays, however, we will achieve a broader and hence better sense of midcentury comedy. In the remainder of this chapter we will examine, first, a well-known professional dramatist or two, then an array of lesser-known writers in whom topicality tends to break out particularly boldly, and, finally, a small but varied group of anonymous works that provide some of the most appealing features of all.

We have seen already that when the playhouse lights were ordered snuffed in 1642, the two dominating comic dramatists were Richard Brome and James Shirley. Brome's *Joviall Crew*, though first published in 1652, dates back to 1641; after this date we have no fresh drama from Brome. Brome himself (mentioned by Jonson as early as 1614 in *Bartholomew Fair*) apparently did not live to see the Protectorate. Shirley, however, whose final prewar play was licensed on 26 April 1642 (after the Queen had left for Holland and the King had been denied entry into Hull by Sir John Hotham), lived to see both Protectorate and Restoration, and in fact survived until 1666, when he and his wife perished in the Great Fire.[21] Along the way Shirley served under William Cavendish in the royalist army, assisted Cavendish with some dramatic projects, furnished the "Address to the Reader" for the Beaumont and Fletcher folio, and wrote grammar texts for his students, as well as some masquelike Interregnum entertainments.

Shirley's last antebellum play, *The Sisters*, came equipped with a prologue reminding its original auditors that the King had left town: "I hear say / *London* is gone to *York*" (A3r). Moreover, a reminder of the potential of real club-law hovered in the warning presented to Paulina, the presumed heiress in the play: "Madame, we are all undone, the Clubs are up, / Your Tenants are turn'd Rebels, and by this time / Entred the Hall" (27). Shirley's term *Clubs* here and the compound *club-law*, which had been current for many decades, referred generally to such physical citizen force as might be raised from time to time. Predictably it was often useful at midcentury. Hyde reports that "club-men," who were often "farmerly men," arose "in great numbers in several parts of the country" (4:54) and became capable of major mischief.[22]

---

[21]After Shirley's *The Sisters*, the only play to be licensed and entered in Henry Herbert's pre-war office-book was timely but now lost work called *The Irishe Rebellion* (*Dramatic Records* 39).   [22]It appears that Clubmen tended to spring up in favor of whichever side was strongest in their territory—their main objective being to end the fighting nearest them. That they were a serious cause of concern is clear. As Malcolm writes, "The 'peaceable army,' or club movement, grew until some fifteen counties and thousands of civilians were involved" (22). One might recall here the droll called *The Club-Men* that was extracted from Beaumont and Fletcher's *Philaster* (see chapter 8).

Despite a light scattering of such touches, *The Sisters* for the most part is best characterized as an efficient, somewhat mechanical, but verbally intelligent ordering of conventional dramatic material. Its quasi-allegorical signs point us more toward moral than political realms: the two sisters of the title are Paulina the proud and Angellina the angelically humble. Not surprisingly, the queenlike Paulina is finally proved a person of low birth, and Angellina, the rightful heir, is paired off with the Prince of Parma.

Another late Shirley work, *Honoria and Mammon* (1658), manifests its lateness in a number of ways. In an address to his reader, Shirley writes, "What is now presented, I hope will appear a genuine and unforc'd Moral, which though drest in Drammatique Ornament, may not displease, in the reading, persons of ingenuity" (A3v). All the more interesting, therefore, is the fact that *Honoria and Mammon* is derived from Shirley's 1632 *Contention for Honour and Riches*. As he puts it, "A Small part of this Subject, many years since . . . drop'd from my pen" (*Honoria* A3r). Interesting, too, is the extent to which this work may be related to Shirley's other comedies, including *The Sisters*. Here again there are two central, contrasting, figural females, and here again we learn of their nature and the world's by observing them and the kinds of men they magnetize. Honoria is sought by a soldier, a scholar, and a courtier, and Mammon by a townman and a countryman.

Set in an English "*Metropolis*, OR *NEW-TROY*" (title page) and equipped with a full, five-act development, this comedy strikes many notes that are at once safely and suggestively current. The scholar Alworth (that useful name again) is early assured by Honoria, "Depend upon my care, I know your parts" (12). Alworth is so stressed by subsequent events, however, that Honoria must call a physician to care for him. Indeed, she spends part of the play thinking him dead. As things go bad, the lawyer kidnaps Honoria, planning to marry her and retain Lady Mammon as his concubine. Like their counterparts in *The Sisters*, however, the citizens here also rise up, specifically to protest that Fulbank, the cityman, has presumed to claim Lady Mammon. The soldier, Colonel Conquest, observes, "Pity these Gentlemen should want Civil War" (60). Toward the close, even Alworth finds it necessary (as had Shirley himself) to appear for a while as a soldier. For another while, Conquest himself has both riches and honor in his power: "Ambition write *non ultra*, fix, fix here, / The two great darlings of mankinde are mine, / Both Excellent, and yet but one Divine" (80; i.e., 78). The scholarly Alworth is correct to be suspicious of the soldier's fine words, and yet at the end an enlightened Conquest assures him,

> . . . I am no enemy
> To Arts, but can take pleasure to reward
> Learning, with all due honour, be your self
> The example.   [87]

This sounds like wishful thinking on the playwright's part. Meanwhile Mammon, who has found no suitable man, places herself equally improbably at Honoria's feet.

In short, this Interregnum play is not merely a moralized comedy (or a comedic morality) but also a dramatic tract for the times, an obvious but safely general depiction of forces at work in the period. Composed from a scholar's-eye-view, it also constitutes the schoolteacher-dramatist's farewell as a playwright. Seventeen years after Brome's final play, Shirley now tells readers that "nothing of this nature shall after this, engage either my pen or invention" (A3v).

At least so far as abstract typological characterization is concerned, it is no giant step from *Honoria and Mammon* to the topical comedies of Samuel Sheppard and John Tatham—or, indeed, to Brathwaite's *Mercurius Britanicus*. Shirley's work invariably shows the surer hand, the greater smoothness, and the more restraint, but these other plays often have a brighter flash and deeper bite.

Sheppard was a part of the Mercurius Pragmaticus team and author of the two-part *Committee-Man Curried* (1647), *The Socratick Session* (1651), and *The Joviall Crew* (1651). In *The Committee-Man Curried* we find a bitter commentary on the sequestration of royalist or "malignant" estates. The prolonged process of sequestering was managed partly by committees scattered across the counties, but then it was pursued by the so-called Goldsmiths' Hall Committee in London and finally referred to Parliament. Adding to the victims' anguish over such procedures and to the severe fines that ensued were the abuses in which some committeemen indulged— hence the name of Sheppard's committeeman: Suck-Dry. The name of Suck-Dry's henchman, Common-Curse, an exciseman, is also understandable as soon as we begin to encounter documents of the day relating to excises.[23] So bad were the offenses of certain excisemen that officialdom itself found it necessary to pass a special "Ordinance to prevent fraudulent Entries of excisable Commodities" (Firth and Rait 1:626). Whatever thoughts the authorities may have had about royalist victims of fraud, clearly they were concerned that some excisemen left "no Means unpractised to defraud the State" itself (Firth and Rait 1:691). Adding to the vigor of Sheppard's dramatic skewering of such fellows, and possibly helping to determine the shape of his work, was the renewed legislation forbidding stage-plays in the very month—July 1647—that his *Committee-Man Curried* first appeared. The prologue of part 1 points out that "*since tis enacted / That*

[23]Morrill and Walter observe that the excise—introduced to defray the costs of war—caused "riots in both the larger cities (London, Norwich) and smaller communities" (143). Such disturbances reached their height in the years 1645–49 (145).

nought but fiery Faction shall be acted" and since *"Fooles onely speake* Cum privilegio," the author will do no more than provide words appropriate to a committeeman (A1v).

What follows is a satiric fifteen-page playlet, proclaimed a comedy, in five-act form. Its matter is described on its title page, which comes boldly complete with the author's name. We read that here is to be found *"A piece discovering the corruption of Committee-men, and Excise-men; the unjust sufferings of the Royall party, the divellish hypocrisie of some Round-heads, [and] the revolt for gaine of some Ministers."* The cavalier Loyalty, who has fought with Prince Rupert and presumably is about to leave for France, is significantly non-committal about the King himself:

> *Charles,* like a huge Pyramid, hath overthrown
> Himselfe with his own weight—and in his fall
> Hath crusht his props to nothing—he may take
> Root againe, and beare his Kingdome up—firme
> As the mighty Atlas doth his heaven. Fortunes wheele
> Ever turns. . . .
>
> [A2v]

There is nothing equivocal, however, about Sheppard's handling of the committeeman. The "currying" (beating or thrashing) of Suck-Dry that is promised by the title comes at the close. During one of his visits to Light-Heele, the wife of citizen Horne, Suck-Dry is driven naked from her bed and beaten with a stick by the ruffian Dammee, the woman's accustomed lover.

In the following month—August 1647—Sheppard put forth *The Second Part of the Committee-Man Curried.* This opens with the news that Common-Curse's clerk Shallow-Braines has married a widow ("a kinde of chewed meat" [A3r])—which triggers some of the most misogynistic words of the period from Suck-Dry's clerk, Sneake: "I nere yet affected a woman but as an house of office, to exonerate nature for that time" (A3v). This scene and a jumble of succeeding ones thoroughly blur the animus against the committeeman himself. Loyalty, for instance, makes another appearance, carrying a sword (contrary to the order that "no Cavalier shall mannage steele" [A4r]) and still determined to depart for France.[24] When Time-Server the priest makes love to Harlato, Shallow-Braines's new wife, her gleeful

---

[24]Sheppard alludes here to either or both of two recent ordinances: (1) as of 10 July 1647 the Committee of the Militia of London could seize the arms of anyone they had cause to suspect, including "all Popish Recusants or other Persons who have or shall discover their ill Affection to the Parliament"; and (2) as of 3 August 1647 the same committee and also the Committee of Safety were empowered "to disarm persons disaffected to the safety and defence of the Parliament and City" (Firth and Rait 1:987 and 3:1v).

husband manages to tumble the pair down through a trapdoor and into a vault of "mire not water" (B2r). And under the threat of another currying, this time from his own sometime sidekick Common-Curse the exciseman, Suck-Dry confesses (more to the reader, of course, than to Common-Curse) that he has merely pretended zeal to God while extolling traitors, hoarding others' money, and working against peace (B3r).

A third effort by Sheppard, a short verse drama called *The Socratick Session*, bound with his *Epigrams* (1651), seems not to have been noticed previously. A step aside from specific Interregnum topicality, if not from midcentury evaluations, it offers such characters as Juvenal, Aristophanes, Seneca, and Euripides, as well as Mercury and Apollo, and sets about depicting (as the subtitle puts it) *The Arraignment and Conviction, of Julius Scaliger*. The comic intent of the piece is to defend Homer from his great Renaissance critic and generally to reorganize the prevailing hierarchy of ancient writers.

That same year the same author took aim at the Ranters in what one might describe as a "playable pamphlet." With obvious reference to Brome's comedy from the previous decade, Sheppard's *The Joviall Crew; or, The Devill Turn'd Ranter* features Lucifer himself: "I've blinded them with pleasures of this world," says he, "by putting on a mask of Religion to make't no sin" (2).[25] There is nothing new about the satiric linkage of licentiousness and a decried religion, but Sheppard mocks here the recently emergent Ranters' own belief that they could proclaim their salvation by blasphemy and sexual license (cf. figure 36). Sheppard's unusually large proportion of female characters suggests a special targeting of women's failings. In the main action two citizens' wives, Mrs. Idlesby and Mrs. Doe-Little, decide to go to the Lime-Hound Tavern to become "convertites" to the Ranters. When their husbands arrive to berate them, Byas Doe-Little asks his wife: "Impudent whore, is this your zeal to goodnesse, to journey every morn e're six a clock unto S. Antholins to hear a Lecture, with a great Bible of Geneva print; your Table-book too, to take Sermon notes?" (14).[26]

The Ranters certainly caused a good many observers besides Sheppard to worry: the Blasphemy Act of 9 August 1650 was passed because of the political threat perceived to be posed by Ranters. On the other hand, *The Joviall Crew; or, The Devill Turn'd Ranter* appears to draw additionally upon a plentiful supply of personal spleen. Though its intemperateness has a

---

[25]In May 1651 John Taylor reported the Ranter claim that one John Robins was "God the Father, and Father of our Lord *Jesus Christ,* and that the childe which is yet unborn, and now in the womb of *Joan Robins* (the wife of the aforesaid *John*) shall be the Saviour of all those that shal be saved" (*Ranters of Both Sexes* 2). [26]One of the most interesting references to St. Antholin in Watling Street—which was indeed known for its morning lectures—occurs in W.S.'s *The Puritan* (1607): the rascal of the play is named Nicholas St. Antlings.

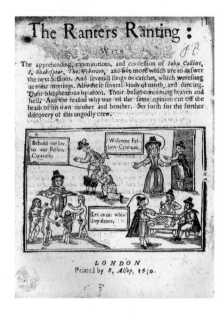

Figure 36. The title page of a pamphlet on Ranters from 1650. Among other activities, Ranters sang "blasphemous songs in the tune of *Davids* Psalms" (*Ranters Ranting* A2v). (By permission of the Folger Shakespeare Library.)

certain fascination, giving the work considerable energy, Sheppard's *Joviall Crew* is itself an instance of topical ranting in comedic form.

Much of Sheppard's output—which we have seen partially expressed in *The Famers Fam'd* (1646), *The Committee-Man Curried* (July 1647), *The Second Part of the Committee-Man Curried* (August 1647), *The Socratick Session* (1651), and *The Joviall Crew* (1651)—was very much attuned to the current events of the day. It is all the more interesting, therefore, to observe that Sheppard first esteemed and then became disillusioned with Cromwell, grew more sympathetic to the suffering Charles, endured imprisonment for his own expressions of loyalty, reconciled himself to accepting the power of Parliament, and finally, without forgetting Charles, came once more to esteem the Lord Protector Cromwell for his better qualities.[27] Interesting, too, is the fact that in a postscript to his most ambitious work, the lengthy *Faerie King,* Sheppard tried to distance himself from such of his publications as we have been considering: "only let mee beg," he writes, "of those who have had the Ill-hap to peruse my former (printed) Absurdities to consider that those spungie Sarcasms (whose being I would obliterate with my best blood) found birth meerly from a mercenary dizzinesse" (336).[28] Thus does

[27]This sentence is based on Rollins's helpful overview of Sheppard's career in his 1927 essay "Samuel Sheppard and His Praise of Poets."   [28]Presumably composed in the prisons of Lambeth Palace, Petre House, and Newgate beginning in 1648, Sheppard's *Faerie King* was prepared by him for the press, but it remained in manuscript until Klemp's recent edition.

Sheppard provide us with a clear-cut example of a writer who, having donned it repeatedly, was nonetheless concerned about setting aside the rude satirist's mask. In retrospect he would have us think that through the years he had been motivated more by Plutus than by politics.

For our present purposes, Sheppard may be coupled with John Tatham. Considered here earlier as a frequent writer of civic shows and as the concerned author of *The Distracted State* (1650-51), Tatham also produced two satiric and explicitly topical comedies: *The Scots Figgaries* (1652) and *The Rump* (1660). Tatham's versatility was for some reason mocked by Sheppard, who claimed that his admirers were broom-criers and watermen (*Epigrams* 142), but actually Tatham is a rather better writer than Sheppard himself. Tatham, too, is empowered by ire, but he is also more careful and controlled.

As in Tatham's *Distracted State*, *The Scots Figgaries* offers plentiful mocking of the Scots. (A "fegary" or "figary" is a prank or freak, a whim or eccentricity, and "to fig" is to pick pockets.) Jocky brags in an opening monologue that he has "creept thus firr intolth' Kingdom, like an Erivigg [earwig] intoll a mons lug [ear], and sall as herdly be gat oout" (1), all of which is reminiscent of sentiments that had been felt by some Englishmen ever since the ascent of James in 1603. Jocky continues: "I a Scot Theff may pass for a trow Mon here; Aw the empty Weomb [belly] and thin hide I full oft bore in *Scotlond*, an the geod fare I get here!" Wherever an Englishman stood in matters political or religious in the early 1650s, he was likely to disdain the Scots—who had not only alienated the royalists by betraying the King but had also estranged many others to the extent of triggering Cromwell's grimly successful march to the north. In *The Scots Figgaries*, besides the beggars Jocky and Billy, Tatham creates a Scottish soldier with the telltale name of Scarefoole. In some ways most intriguing of all, however, he depicts a Scottish "Court Foole" named Folly. Tatham's labeling calls to mind Archibald Armstrong, the court fool to both James and Charles, who lived through to the Restoration and on the way managed to make himself obnoxious to many. Still, the figure of Folly appears to stand here for generic Scottish "figgary" at the English court. Whenever the play was composed, and though it certainly resonates with latter-day disapproval of the Scots, one should note that it still specifically depicts a world with a court. According to Folly, "Thes Kingdom's mickle sick, tha Curt o tha Cety, tha Cety o tha Curt, an tha Contre o beoth, an aw o 'um o tha Kirke, an tha Law" (13). With the common metaphor of illness comfortably in hand, Tatham has Folly recommend that the two beggars pretend to be doctors (Billy in the country, Jocky in the city and court), ready to prescribe whether their victims be ill or well.

During the course of a fifty-two-page play there is time for some non-Scottish targets as well. Most notable among these is a brotherhood of English "Blades of the Times" (reminding one of a slew of other cavalier dammees, especially Cowley's Captain Blade), men who live by gulling "bubbles" such as Witwud and Wantwit and thereby provide an English counterpoint to the Scottish tricksters.

At the end we return to the Scots, who are hauled off when a good magistrate recognizes them to be "Meere Mountebanks" who have "instead of Cure / Bred strange Diseases, and distempers" (51). During a period when Englishmen were still pitted against Englishmen, quietly or otherwise, a satiric comedy such as Tatham offered here may have had a slightly ameliorative effect. Despite all other strifes and probably aside from the playwright's intent, mutually felt animosity against the Scots had the potential of serving as a unifying force among English readers.

Be this as it may, English unification was assuredly not the goal of Tatham's *The Rump*. Appearing some months after the final expelling of the Purged Parliament (that is, the Rump Parliament) in October 1659, this play, like all those we have just been considering, grew out of (and has many affinities with) the pamphlet satires, particularly those in dialogue form, that burgeoned during the preceding two decades. Whereas *Canterburie His Change of Diot* (1641) was a satiric pamphlet tricked out like a play, however, Tatham's *Rump* is a full-length satiric comedy. Performed in June 1660, the first month after the new King's return, it is, as Harold Love says, a "raucous howl of joy at the end of Puritan rule." Because of its nature and its placement in time, moreover, Love is also moved to state, "It is this play which marks the real starting-point of Augustan political drama" (1).

Opening with a conversation among soldiers ("The Town's Our own, Boys" [*Rump* 1]), Tatham soon reveals his intention to pillory in particular John Bertlam—that is, Major General John Lambert—who is presented as a principal contestant for the Protectorship after the demise of Oliver's son Richard (which occurred in May 1659). Lambert had indeed at one point had Cromwell's promise of the succession. Probably the most capable and certainly the most powerful of the men close to the Protector, "Honest John Lambert" had in effect been sent home to Wimbledon in 1657 when he declined to swear an oath of loyalty to Cromwell (his tulip-raising there is depicted here in figure 37). In Richard's time, however, he emerged from retirement and sided with the republican opposition to the Protectorate, and when Richard fell he resumed his army commands. What is more, in October 1659 Major General Lambert followed in the steps of their Highnesses Charles and Oliver by shutting down Parliament. In order to describe Bertlam/Lambert within the play, Tatham brings on the notorious astrologer William Lilly, who terms him "subtle, politick, and crafty" and "proud, inconstant, and deceitful" (52). Lady Bertlam, equally proud, plans

Figure 37. Major General John Lambert as he appears in a pack of Restoration playing cards. Both the background and the flower reflect Lambert's interest in gardening, but the tulip may also have political implications. (By permission of the Special Collections Library, Duke University.)

to be called "her Highness" (15). When Cromwell's widow ("Gammer *Cromwell*" [17]) enters, it is to rail against Bertlam, claiming that he "fool'd my Son in Law to betray the Innocent Babe my poor Child *Richard,* that Our Fames are now brought to the Slaughter houses" (17). The son-in-law whom Gammer calls Woodfleet was actually Lieutenant General Charles Fleetwood, second husband of the Cromwells' daughter Bridget. (According to Hyde, Fleetwood was "very popular with all the praying part of the army" [6:144].) Now it would appear that he and Bertlam/Lambert are the two main competitors for a Protectorship that is available for the taking.[29]

As viewed by Tatham's play, little or nothing good might be expected from the Committee of Safety that had been established by the army under

[29]The whole complex situation is treated also in the mock romance called *Don Juan Lamberto* (1661). Chapter 11 is headed "How the Knight of the *Golden Tulep* [Lambert] and the Knight of the *mysterious Allegories* [Henry Vane] came to the Castle of Sir *Fleetwood* the contemptible Knight, where they mett with the grim Gyant *Desborough*, and how they went all three and pulled the *Meek Knight* who was then chiefe Soldan out of his Palace by night" (B4r). Although the tulip reference alludes to the fact that Lambert was an avid gardener, known to spend large sums on tulips, it has been said also that during his rustication, when he and other army officers were conspiring to wrest power away from Parliament, they adopted a yellow tulip as their badge (Goldsmid 16).

Lambert's command, presumably to plan for a new government. According to the play, the committee was presided over by one Stoneware—obviously a personating of the Scottish statesman Archibald John*ston*, Lord *War*riston, who had been a member of both Oliver's and Richard Cromwell's House of Lords and, before that, Advocate General to the King. Stoneware afforded Tatham another opportunity to try his hand at Scottish dialect and at the same time to dramatize accusations of how some men in high places had begun to "Divide the Kingdomes Treasure" (*Rump* 37). Another such character is Lockwhite (Bulstrode Whitelocke), presented here as Bertlam's current confidante. Bertlam considers him

> . . . a Man
> Has run all hazzards, with as good success,
> Except Old *Noll*, as any Man I know;
> He was his Creature, and he now is mine. . . .   [7]

With a generally hated and partly military junto at its head, England had in fact been lurching toward disaster. In the play, Tatham suggests this in part by bringing onstage a band of right-thinking apprentices who carry clubs and vow to "spend life and limbe for *Magna Charta* and a *Free Parliament*" (39). Club-law is soon bested, however, and the boys dispersed by John Hewson. "Whoop Cobler," cry the apprentices, running off to drink the King's health. In actuality, Hyde reports, the former shoemaker Hewson managed to put down the apprentices by killing some of them. It was only a Tiananmen victory, however, for "the loss of that blood inflamed the city" (6:158).

In the midst of an array of characters with names that specifically indicate actual persons, the name of General Philagathus (suggesting love of good) is notable for its relative indirection. But no one is likely to be confused. In a later scene with the apprentices we learn that "the Noble General *Philagathus* lay at *Barnet* last night" (*Rump* 55)—a reminder of General George Monck's arrival north of London in late January 1660, preceding his entry into the city on 3 February. Though one cannot date Tatham's play exactly, Virgil Scott has pointed out that it cannot be earlier than Lambert's imprisonment, which occurred on 3 March (118). As the play puts it, "pityful, dityful *Lambert*"—and the name is now printed thus, not as Bertlam is in the Tower, and "the Phanaticks are trotting out of town" (55).[30]

When at last the apprentices reenter, jubilantly carrying "*Rumps of*

---

[30]One might compare *Lamberts Last Game Plaid, Set Out in a Mock-Comedy* (1660), a pamphlet mini-drama set in the Tower and featuring "divers Sisters of the Phanatique Crew." Regarding the latter, Lambert's man Roger says, "I'le be hanged if one had not better have dealt with a company of *Turnball-street* Ladies" (A4r).

Mutton upon Spits" and whooping "Roast the *Rump*, Roast the *Rump*" (61), the dramatist is engaging in some strikingly effective literalization, transforming a major metaphor of the day into a palpable, satirocomic stage property. No great inventiveness was required in the matter, though. Rumps at the time really were roasted in many bonfires in the city (Cobbett 1578; see figure 38).

Finally, bringing all to a close, Tatham has Stoneware selling ballads, Lady Bertlam cheese and cream, and Mrs. Cromwell "Kitchin-stuffe."[31] One-eyed Hewson, now returned to his trade, is looking for old boots to mend (67). The epilogue summarizes: "*You have here in a* MIRROUR *seen the Crimes / Of the late Pageantry Changeling Times*" (68).

This play that would be incomprehensible played before audiences of a subsequent age was in its own time a forceful expression of widespread joy and relief, a comic editorial akin to many of the partisan pamphlets that preceded it. Rather than attempting to shape popular thinking by countering or readjusting it (though Tatham may have felt some such motivation), it has more the air of riding the crest of public opinion, not unlike some of our own political cartoons. Not only was *The Rump* played repeatedly in 1660 "At the Private House in *Dorset*-Court," but it then moved on to the Red Bull. A second, revised edition was called for the following year, and as long as two decades later Aphra Behn borrowed from it heavily for *The Roundheads; or, The Good Old Cause* (1681; published 1682). In short, "currying" the Protectorate took a long and satisfying while.[32]

For a final cluster of comedies, we turn now to four anonymous works

---

[31]A short while later *The Court & Kitchin of Elizabeth . . . Cromwel* would seek to demean the former Protector's wife by linking her to lowly domestic activities even at the time of her husband's greatest power. An odd combination of satire and cookery book, the volume disdains what it terms her "*sordid frugality* and *thirfty basenesse*" (B3r) and relates that "she . . . kept two or three Cowes in St. *James's* Park, and created a new Office of a Dairy in *Whitehall*, with Dairy Maids" (D3v). Perhaps most noteworthy of all, *The Court & Kitchin* alludes to Tatham's play: "nor is all that Droll, which is mentioned of her in a Play, called *The Rump*" (13v). [32]Other lesser but more or less comparable works of the same season include pamphlet dramas called *A Phanatick Play* and *The Tragical Actors*. The intended targets of the former are suggested in the title page words "as presented before and by the Lord *Fleetwood*, Sir *Arthur Hasilrig*, Sir *Henry Vane*, the Lord *Lambert*, and others, last Night, with Master *Jester* and Master *Pudding*." Hasilrig—who had in fact become the recognized leader of Parliament—plays the devil, Pudding initiates a game of cards, and Lambert says he will play for a crown. But then a north wind interrupts the game. Hasilrig would like to keep the king permanently out of the game ("Upon my life . . . , he shall be a King and no King" [A4r]), but as the work ends, Lambert and Hasilrig have been put into "a great Bird-Cage" (A4v)—thus echoing, some twenty years later, the caging of Laud. *The Tragical Actors* looks back more specifically to earlier years. In fact, it proves to be a summary in dialogue form of the machinations presumably undertaken by George Joyce (who in 1647 turned Charles over to the army at Newmarket), Cromwell, Hesilrige, Hewson, and Bradshaw in order to ensure the death of the King.

Figure 38. The "Rump" being roasted. Frontispiece of Alexander Brome's *Rump* (1662). (By permission of the Folger Shakespeare Library.)

from the 1650s: *The Prince of Priggs* (1651), *The Hectors* (1656), *Lady Alimony* (1659), and *The London Chaunticleres* (1659). All are anonymous, and each, thrusting in its own idiosyncratic direction, helps to demonstrate the breadth of midcentury comedic possibilities.

Reasonably termed either a closet comedy or a pamphlet comedy (the author insists on the label "comedy"), the fourteen-page *Prince of Priggs* belongs also to England's rich cache of rogue literature. A prig is a thief (Shakespeare applies the term to Autolycus [*Winter's Tale* IV.iii.101]), and the "prince" of the moment is the famous highwayman James Hind. In fact, the tone-setting title page advertises Hind's "Pranks" and "Tarltonian Mirth"—thus connecting the hero to Richard Tarleton—as a prince's "REVELS."[33] Though the author offers no brief for stage-players ("the Apes and Parrots of the Stage, / Are silenc'd by the Clamours of the Age" [prol. 1]), he means for us to enjoy Hind's skillful acting, and specifically the shape-shifting that makes possible his "*wilie Couzenage*" (2) of a Bristol merchant (act I), a beautiful widow (act II), some aldermen of York (act III),

---

[33]The historical Tarleton (d. 1588) was a clownish comic actor known for his jigs, songs, and extemporaneous versifying.

and some citizens of London (act IV). There is little to prepare us for the closing action, however, save a notable aside in act II: "Me thinks I feel a civil war within me, / Egging me on for to proceed from this, / And get the substance of celestial blisse" (10).

The fact is that the comic mythologizing of the highwayman Hind is finally combined with the romantic mythologizing of Prince Charles. The victory of Cromwell over Charles at Worcester took place on 3 September 1651, and it may be that an underlying motive of the author, writing several weeks later (George Thomason's copy of the play is dated 11 November 1651), is to link Hind's shape-shifting, acting, and mobility with what was to become Charles's famous disguising and wandering between the time of his defeat in battle and his flight to France on 15 October. Beyond such parallels between the two "princes," in any case, the lives of both men really were briefly linked, insofar as Hind had served in Charles's army at Worcester. The fifth act of the mini-comedy takes this fact as a basis for embroidery, claiming that "*The Scots King being overthrown at the battel of* Worc[e]ster, *accepts of* Hinds *conduct (knowing how well he was acquainted with the Country) who carries him safe away*" (13). "Let me be hang'd," Hind assures the King, "if I prove false to you" (14). The author goes on to say in an epilogue that he would have continued beyond this point, but Hind has been apprehended. Back in London, in fact, Hind was captured in the Strand, taken before the Council of State, and sentenced to execution, not for his career as a thief but "for complying with Charles Stuart, and engaging against the Commonwealth of England" (*True and Perfect Relation* 6). When dramatic fancy collided with history this time, comic myth gave way to tragic fact.

In contrast, *The Hectors*, said on its title page to have been written in 1655, is a full-length, full-blooded comedy—in fact, according to Harbage, the only comedy "of any significance" produced during the Commonwealth (*Cavalier Drama* 81). An introductory poem promises that it will provide "Comick mirth . . . mix't with serious lines," and, explicitly sidestepping any reasons for closing the playhouses, it proceeds to offer a text for reading.[34] The titular term *hectors*, borrowed from the fabled Trojan soldier, had become ironic slang of the time.[35] A ballad from 1653 called "A Total Rout" goes thus:

---

[34]The quotation is from the recto of a leaf following the title page. [35]An exhaustive definition of the word is given in *A Notable and Pleasant History of the Famous Renowned Knights of the Blade, Commonly Called Hectors* (1652). The first sentence reads in part: "There was no sooner an end put to the Wars of *England,* but a great company of Officers and Souldiers being discarded, they repaired to the famous City of *London,* in hope that new troubles would arise, to maintain them in the same disordered courses they formerly practiced in the Armies, but missing fewell to feed the fire of their desires, they began to study living by their wits" (A2r).

You princely hectors of the town,
Who like the Devil strut up and down,
Come leave your God-dammees, and herken to me,
O! 'tis pitty that fuel for hell you should be. . . .

[Thomas Wright 131]

The fact that such rogues acquired so many pejorative labels (hectors, dam-mees, rooks, blades, and cutters were all molded from the same clay) is a good reason, of course, for recognizing their visibility as a postwar social phenomenon.

Still, we do not meet the hectors here until act II. The cunning gamesters Caster and Slur (their die are loaded with quicksilver) and their new associate Had-Land are preceded in the play by some old-time Jonsonian humour characters. These include young Know-Well and Wel-Bred and a gentleman of slender judgment named La-Gull. A braggart duelist, La-Gull is ripe for shocking out of his humour. Especially distaste-ful is the specificity of his bragging when, presumably describing a recent duel with a gentleman at the Devil Tavern, he claims to have "run at him just thus, as my Lord *Shandos* killed *Compton*" (10).[36]

Particularly interesting in *The Hectors* is the range of women created to interact with all these men: Mrs. Crisis, a discreet gentlewoman; her witty cousin Mrs. Love-Wit; young Mrs. Bud, who attends school in London; Mrs. Pate, a "cunning" gentlewoman (who formerly could serve a troop in about five nights and, more recently, moved to town, is charging "much about the same price" as a hackney coach [64][37]); Pate's maid Susan; and even streetwomen who sell oranges and apricots. Along with an alert concern for social relationships and settings (there are references to Chan-cery Lane, Hyde Park, Maribone Park, and Charterhouse Garden) and with some of the liveliest dialogue of the period, one finds here a surprisingly sympathetic concern for women. Mrs. Crisis muses over the difficulties experienced by a woman of intelligence: "it frights off all that have no wit, and they that have will never come on, except it be for an Afternoon or so, to exercise their tongues" (3). When her crusty father is angered by her appearance (it has taken her nearly an hour to dress, and now he rails at her powdering and patching), Know-Well defends her so reasonably (the "civillest Ladies of her yeares and quality" do, indeed, dress so [35]) that the old man backs down a bit. Most striking of all, however, are Mrs. Crisis's words to Know-Well on women: "You see, Sir, I am a woman, one of the

---

[36]The allusion is to George Brydges, Baron Chandos, and his mortal wounding of Colonel Henry Compton in a duel on Putney Heath on 13 May 1652. After a year of imprisonment, Chandos was found guilty of manslaughter.   [37]That is, she charges two shillings the first hour and one shilling each subsequent hour.

most undervalued Creatures living; we never yet by any polity were allowed to meddle with any thing but a needle: We are not esteemed to know ought of rational [*sic*] but our wills; nay, some will not allow us for to know our wills. And should I but consider my self by what some Satyrick Wits say of us, I could not but believe my self one of the most despicable things in Nature" (43). Rather than perceiving such a passage as ahead of its time, we should be willing to acknowledge that it—like the references to patching, Prince Rupert, and the "*Peazza, in Lincolnes* Inne fields" (61)—is itself a sign of the time.

The hectors, then, prove to be but one element in an unusually alert, well-plotted, well-languaged play. Far less involved with political matters than are many plays, and more immediately concerned with aspects of social life than most, *The Hectors* is studded with details of its time and place. A worthy way station between Shirley's *Hyde Park* (1632), say, and any of a number of Restoration comedies, it includes, toward the end, an extended passage in which La-Gull is bombarded by advice on how to comport himself after moving into the country ("a hop-ground may find you good imployment" [50]). Here we find Know-Well recommending for a rainy day not only Foxe's old *Book of Martyrs* (1563) but also the current *Scout* and *Weekly Intelligence* as sources of news, Bacon's *Natural History* (1626 *et seq.*), Browne's *Vulgar Errors* (1646; revised 1650), and Henry Parker's *Holy War* (1651). Whereupon Mrs. Love-Wit is allowed to add, "Sometimes to your wife you may read a piece of *Shak-speare, Suckling,* and *Ben. Johnson* too, if you can understand him" (50). Thus in this play that the dramatist presumably expects to be read, not played, the playwright has one character recommend to another the companionable reading aloud of plays, including Jonson's—but only provided the reader be less dense than the writing. Hectoring is clearly only part of the story here.

It is also part of the story in *Lady Alimony* (1659), an anonymous comedy wherein we meet not merely hectors but also hacksters, bravoes, trepanners, and runagadoes. The major social spark behind this work, however, is caught in the word *alimony*. Published some fourteen years after Milton's divorce pamphlets, the opening speech informs us that "Divorces are now as common, as scolding at *Billingsgate*. O Alimony, Alimony a Darling incomparably dearer, then a seere-icy Bed possest of the spirit of a dull unactive Husband!" (A2v).

Problems relating to alimony were frustratingly numerous at the time. In the years up through 1641, writes Roland Usher, most of the cases heard by the Court of High Commission "were of a disciplinary or matrimonial nature." In fact, "[s]uits for alimony, divorce, desertion, abuse, and the like seem to have been the first in point of number" (256). Still more specifically, in the year 1640 there appear to have been about three times more cases dealing with alimony than with the next most common problem, adultery (279). Furthermore, the subsequent demolition of the ecclesiastical courts, the failure of the Interregnum government to replace them with any comparable instrument, and the resultant chaos when it came to solving matrimonial difficulties made private—and therefore varied—separation agreements a necessity.[38] Such agreements were often less than agreeable, and not surprisingly someone decided to write a play on the subject.

Whatever Englishman actually wielded the quill here, and despite the fact that the setting is said to be Seville, the putative playwright of *Lady Alimony* is Timon. Traditionally Timon had found human inadequacy limited to neither sex, but in his present incarnation he is another misogynist, in fact the "Smock-satyr" and match of any "*Swetnam*" in England (A2v).[39] The term *lady* in the title refers to no particular individual in the play but instead creates a satiric abstraction distilled from the excesses of six "*Alimonial Ladies*" (B4v): Mesdames Fricase, Caveare, Julippe, Joculette, Medler, and Tinder. These "mad-mettal'd Girles," these "brave Braches," "Bona-Roba's," "She-Myrmidons," "gallant *Messalinas*," and "gamesome macquerellas" (B3r-v) have managed to shed their husbands on grounds of, respectively, incapacitating youth (Sir Amadin Puny), stupidity (Sir Jasper Simpleton), cowardice (Sir Arthur Heartless), deformity (Sir Gregory Shapeless), sexual shortcoming (a Shandean forerunner, Sir Tristram Shorttool), and promiscuity (Sir Reuben Scattergood).

With neat, comic symmetry the playwright also provides each of the divorcées with a male friend. Moreover, by the simple device of making all of the latter "Platonick Confidents" (A2r), he makes a mockery of whatever was left of the fashionable cultivation of platonic love. James Howell had explained back in the 1630s that platonic love is "abstracted from all corporeall gross impressions, and sensuall Appetit, but consists in contemplation and Idaeas of the mind, not in any carnall fruition" (*Epistolae Ho-Elianae* 202-3). James Shirley, therefore, a playwright *à la mode*, might have a character in *The Dukes Mistris* (1636; published 1638) claim, "Mine's a *Platonicke* love, give me to soule, I care not what course flesh, and blood inshrine it" (F1r). And a gentleman suitor in one of Margaret Cavendish's plays might protest, "I desire our friendship may be Platonick" (*Several Wits* 107). But there long had been a less ethereal countercurrent recognizing, as does Cavendish's heroine, that platonic love is "dangerous, for it of times

---

[38]Stone explains that "there are several reasons for believing that formal private separation deeds only began in the 1650s" (150).   [39]Joseph Swetnam, author of *The Araignment of Lewd, Idle, Froward, and Unconstant Women* (1615), was known as the Woman-Hater. His name was strikingly spotlighted in an anonymous comedy called *Swetnam the Woman-Hater Arraigned by Women* (1617–19).

proves a Traytor to Chastity." A more positive spin is put on the subject by the playwright Cowley in his poem called "Platonick Love":

> Indeed I must confess
> When *Souls* mix 'tis an *Happiness;*
> But not compleat till *Bodies* too combine,
> And closely as our minds together join. . . .
>
> [ll.2-3, in *Poems*]

The present playwright also—along with still others like Thomas Killigrew (*Parsons Wedding*) and Richard Brome (*Court Beggar*)—saw that highly idealized rhetorical professions of platonic love could easily become preludes to more customary expressions of physical desire. The problem, according to a poem by George Daniel, is that "in Platonicke Love thou canst doe more / With yeilding Females, then in Lust before" (56). However well received it had been in writings at the court of her Queen, Margaret Cavendish opined in her own *Worlds Olio* (1655) that "Platonick Love is a Bawd to Adultery" (109). Paradoxically, platonic love became a kissing cousin of libertinism.

The comic display of the ladies and their "Platonick Confidents," as well as their displaced mates, is the *raison d'être* of *Lady Alimony*. Apparently in order to postpone setting everything right at the end, however, the dramatist suddenly turns in act III to a largely extraneous hodgepodge of a subplot that serves as a "vindication of the Merchants honour" (F3v), introduces a duke who leads an expedition against the Salamancans, produces within itself a parallel action in which various kinds of riffraff go off to war, and includes a long soliloquy by a ghost named Gallerius, whose closing words trigger the entrance of Mephistophilus! When all else is said and done, the subplot does at least provide some underclass parallels to the main plot and, as well, the means of correcting the six erring wives. Finally the alimony ladies are given a choice of returning to their husbands or entering a cloister (a choice and no choice), and their platonic suitors are banished to some convenient quarries.[40]

Throughout much of its course, *Lady Alimony* displays such authorial intelligence, care, and energy that one hesitates to damn its interior fragmentation more than to suggest that in its present form the play is a pastiche. As for dating, it certainly bears some marks of the 1650s.

---

[40]After considering the patchy nature of this play, Kenneth Richards concludes: "The anonymous *Lady Alimony* may be neither an original composition of 1658/59, nor a revision of a Caroline play, but a made-up piece, utilizing material drawn from more than one old play." Richards then adds, less convincingly, that "the motive for the compilation would have been to evade official disapproval of a play proper" ("Anonymous *Lady Alimony*" 196).

Obviously the reference to "Crop=ear'd Histriomastixes, who cannot endure a civil, witty Comedy" (A4r) was not written before Prynne's sentencing in 1634, about eight years before the theaters closed. A notable touch suggesting a later time, however, is the character Benhadad, a Quaker. The term *Quaker* was first applied to George Fox and his followers in 1650. Here Benhadad enters with a company of ragtag soldiers (his scriptural namesake was a militarist [1 Kings 20]) and may be intended as a comic recognition of the early Quakers' ambiguous stand on violence.[41] Then again, it was in 1659—the year the play was published—that pacificism first emerged clearly as a key Quaker tenet, and subsequently Benhadad could be recognized as an all-too-familiar example of religious hypocrisy.

Bringing us most surely up to *Lady Alimony*'s publication date of 1659, however, is the play's reference to the sort of inferior dramatic work that offers "a *Monkey* dancing his Trick-a-tee [i.e., tricotee, a lively dance] on a Rope, for want of *strong lines* from the Poets pen," dramatic invention so bad that it stoops to "deluding an ignorant Rabble with the sad presentment of a roasted Savage" (A3v). Given such specificity, one is almost certainly meant to recall Davenant's *Cruelty of the Spaniards in Peru* (1658). In the first entry of *The Cruelty* "a Rope descends out of the Clowds, and is stretcht to a stiffness by an Engine," at which point two apes appear; one "leaps up to the Rope" and dances to "a Rustick Ayre" (6). In the fifth entry of the same show, Davenant calls for two Spaniards, one "turning a Spit, whilst the other is basting an *Indian* Prince" (19; see figure 22). Whatever one makes of these parallels from the preceding year, one may safely suppose that Davenant was not the author of *Lady Alimony*.

The final comedy to be noted here is *The London Chaunticleres*, also anonymous, also published in 1659, and also more social than political in its thrust. Writers of our own time have shown that virtually any writing has a political dimension, and this play's concentration on characters drawn from the underclass surely might be approached with the power tools of political analysis. However, one might just as reasonably be inclined to accept the prologue's assurance that "*all our Plot is but to make you smile*" (A2v). The play reminded Langbaine "of the Basse Comedy, writ by the *French;* the Scene lying entirely amongst Persons of the lowest Rank" (*Account* 538). Whatever its progenitors, the appeal of the piece derives largely from its suggestion of the lively language of seventeenth-century English tradespeople. Bristle, for in-

---

[41]As Morrill and Walter observe, the ideas of the Quakers "were more subversive than their actions, but there was nothing quietist about the early Quaker leaders. Their calculated disrespect for rank and degree, their disturbance of the worship of 'steeple houses' and of the preaching of 'hireling priests,' their encouragement of tithe-strikes aroused fear and bewilderment" (162).

stance, comes on crying, "Buy a save-all, buy a save-all; never more need, come, buy a save-all; buy a comb-brush, or a pot-brush, buy a flint or a steel or a tinder-box" (*London Chaunticleres* 2)—which economically tells most of us nowadays more about brush men than we ever previously knew.[42] Whatever details of urban life the original audience may or may not have known, the play purports to provide an echo, for those who cannot be there (then or now, one might interpolate), of the raucous, "*clamorous voice*" (A2v) of bustling, midcentury London. Even in England's darkest days, no matter what high tragedies transpired, common life provided a chorus of continuity, and here a comic writer has attempted to catch the sound and feel of it in sympathetic words. Whatever year the play was composed, we have here in this 1659 volume a sequence of scenes conveyed in a selection of the language really used by people in the city. A little rudimentary plotting is useful, of course, for keeping the dialogue flowing: after various tricks from a brush man, a broom man, and a tooth drawer (Bristle, Heath, and Gumb), a tinker matches with a fresh-cheese-and-cream woman, and a ballad man with an apple wench. The final scenes take place at a tavern and in typical comic fashion involve companionable song and drink. The slightness and indeed artifice of all this are part and parcel of the play's overall pleasant effect. Nor is it mere antiquarianism to respond sympathetically to such details as Bristle's reference to the silver cock atop Paul's steeple (2) or to Heath's jibe that Gumb is "dress'd up just like the woodden boy's on Haberdasher's stalls" (25). In fourteen short scenes (the lack of act division inclined Langbaine to call the piece an interlude) *The London Chaunticleres* touches life more surely than many a play that provides merely another king and queen.

Numerous as are the comedies noted in this chapter, yet a few others might be cited for discussion or conjecture. We have surely seen enough, however, to observe the heterogeneous nature of the kind. We have seen enough, perhaps, to suggest that these plays are not likely to be covered satisfactorily by any single umbrella term such as *cavalier*, however broadly that term may be interpreted. As with other dramatic genres of the day, indeed, the free-ranging, protean variety of our comedies almost inevitably resulted from the fact that dramatists after 1642 were largely released from the needs, demands, and expectations of a theater audience.

Generalizations that ring true about such a range of works are hard to forge, but certainly a major one would be that characterization in these plays is resolutely typological. Whether or not one believes in the interiority of a Falstaff, certainly no such characterizing manifests itself in these comedies. Rather than returning to Shakespearean or even Fletcherian realms, these

---

[42]A save-all is a device for holding a candle end in a candleholder so as to enable the entire candle to burn (*OED*).

writers are for the most part pursuing Jonsonian possibilities. We have here a drama that is very much possessed of the satiric edge implicit in the old term *komoidein,* and at its best it is a drama of energy, vitality, and wit.

Like all comedy, these plays rely on laughter (figurative, literal, or both) as a distractor. "Yes, Laughter is my object," Thomas Randolph had the character called Comedy say in *The Muses Looking-Glasse* (1638): "tis a propertie / In man essentiall to his reason" (10). Probably more important than ever in these later years, laughter was used to alchemize pain into pleasure. No one could expect to be altogether successful in "Converting all your sounds of woe / Into hey nonny nonny" (*Much Ado* II.iii.68-69), but some anxieties might be ameliorated by comic projections of such figures as Jews and Quakers, Scots and Ranters. (As the playwright Francis Osborne would have it, Scots *were* Jews—but "more nasty, & mangie" [*True Tragi-Comedie* 21r].) In other words, besides a predictable, general targeting of such things as overblown avarice, double-dealing, and self-love, in whose deflation laughter participates as a conservator of virtue, we find that midcentury playwrights often take aim at rather specific sources of social tension. The dramatic presentation of these latter targets presumably furnished a certain amusing relief for writers of the time. For us they are more likely to help by bringing the age into better focus. For instance, when we come across Suck-Dry the committeeman and Common-Curse the exciseman, as well as the alimony wives, the platonic lovers, and a whole battery of dammees, hectors, and blades, we can see not only that they reflect various timeless and universal human failings but also that they are immediate outgrowths of their own time and place. To the extent that they touch on more or less specific sources of pain or distress within seventeenth-century society, furthermore, they also are likely to be the playwrights' bid to enlist laughter on the side of conservatism, to protect whatever it is that such figures threaten. Harder to see is the playwrights' use of laughter to encourage forward motion of some sort. What we usually find instead is a nudging toward a future that appears to be merely a better-ordered version of the past. It is a nudging all the same, however, an incitement to laughter that suggests the need to do what one can to negate the uncurbed excesses of, say, ranters, rumpers, and assorted runagadoes.

Whatever approach we choose to take to these writings—and their complexity opens up very different avenues—clearly a significant number of writers continued to occupy themselves with comedy during these troubled years in England after, as Shirley put it, "the Scene of Drammatick Poetry . . . changed into a wilderness" (*The Sisters* A2r). Whether or not a given individual gave the matter much thought, common sense probably dictated to many that, indeed, "Laughter is . . . / In man essentiall to his reason."

[15]

THE CAVENDISH PHENOMENON

Ca'ndish whom every *grace* and every *Muse,*
Kist at his birth, and for their owne did choose.
Soe good a *Wit* they meant not should excell
In *Armes;* but now they see't, and like it well.
— Abraham Cowley, *The Civil War* (1643)

The Court, the City, Schools and Camp agree,
Welbeck to make an University,
Of *Wit* and *Honour,* which has been the Stage,
Since 'twas your *Lords* the Heroe of this Age. . . .
— *Letters and Poems in Honour of . . . Margaret,*
Dutchess of Newcastle (1676)

But Noble Readers, do not think my Playes,
Are such as have been writ in former daies;
As Johnson, Shakespear, Beaumont, Fletcher *writ;*
Mine want their Learning, Reading, Language, Wit. . . .
— Margaret Cavendish, *Playes* (1662)

Thence home; and there, in favour to my eyes, stayed at home read-
ing the ridiculous history of my Lord Newcastle wrote by his wife,
which shows her to be a mad, conceited, ridiculous woman, and he
an asse to suffer her to write what she writes to him and of him.
— Samuel Pepys, *Diary* (1668)

TO MOVE FROM A discussion of comedy to a discussion of Cavendish
family writings requires no giant step, for the latter are in the main comedic.
Why might the Cavendishes warrant a chapter of their own? Simply put,
we rarely find so many members of a single family concerned with writing
drama, and nowhere else do we find a playwright who was himself both a
friend and a patron of dramatists from Ben Jonson to John Dryden. Fur-
thermore, the appearance of no fewer than three women dramatists in the
family is a phenomenon worth special attention.[1]

---

[1]Probably the two other most intriguing configurations of related dramatists in the last half
of the century would be Edward, Henry, and Robert Howard and their cousin James Howard;
and Henry, William, and Thomas Killigrew and their cousin William Berkeley (sometime
Governor of Virginia).   Recent investigation suggests that the work of Sir William Killigrew

In April 1645, newly arrived in Paris, William Cavendish, Marquess of Newcastle, went to pay his respects to Henrietta Maria at the Louvre. Both she and King Charles regarded this cultivated, immensely wealthy, French-speaking Englishman so highly that for several years he had served not only as a member of the Privy Council but also as governor to the Prince of Wales. When the Scottish rebellion erupted in 1639, his contributions to the royal cause further strengthened his position at court, but it was during the Civil Wars, as General of the King's forces in the North, that he really became the observed of all observers. His own White Coats, a regiment of foot, brought him as much honor as military valor is likely to bring any commander, until at last, on 2 July 1644, at Marston Moor, he and Rupert were badly defeated by Fairfax and Cromwell.[2] Thus ended Cavendish's devoted but somewhat uneven military career, and thus began his life abroad in Hamburg, Paris, Rotterdam, and Antwerp.

In Paris he for the first time met Margaret Lucas, one of the Queen's maids of honor. A shy woman of about twenty-one, some thirty years younger than he, she soon became the Marquess's second wife and thence proceeded to become the most prolific woman dramatist of the century. William Cavendish himself, meanwhile, having poured nearly a million pounds into the royal cause, was rewarded by his opponents—as King Charles himself had been—with a sentence of death (14 March 1649).

It is noteworthy that when the satiric author of *The Character of an Oxford-Incendiary* (1645) went after Cavendish, it was to mock him as a soldier who "would be *fornicating* with the *Nine Muses*" (7). Cavendish was, in fact, a writer. One of the major authorities of the day on horses, he eventually produced *La Méthode nouvelle et invention extraordinaire de dresser les chevaux* (1658) and, in 1667, *A New Method and Extraordinary Invention to Dress Horses* (see figure 39). The satirist, however, had in mind Cavendish's penchant for more frivolous fare: as both patron and writer, he was fascinated by drama. One of the most thoroughly Jonsonized of the Sons of Ben, Cavendish many years previously had commissioned Jonson's *Entertainment at the Blackfriars* (1620) for the christening of his son Charles: "As soone as wee heard the Prince would be heere, / wee knewe by his comming wee should haue good cheere" (778). Later on, he may even have consulted Jonson on the education of his sons. (The chief evidence appears to be Jonson's *De liberis educandis* in *Timber: "It pleas'd* your Lordship of late, to ask my opinion, touching the education of your sonnes" [613].) Jonson certainly had high praise for Cavendish in *The Underwood* (poems 53 and

---

(1606–95), always considered by scholars to have been a product of the Restoration, may have had its beginnings as early as the 1640s—and thus may merit attention in future studies of midcentury drama (Vander Motten 148, 154).   [2]Regarding the royalists, Cromwell wrote on 5 July 1644 that "God made them a stubble to our swords" (*Writings* 1:287–88).

LA BATAILLE GAIGNEL.

Figure 39. William Cavendish, Marquess (later Duke) of Newcastle (1592-1676), as depicted in his *Méthode nouvelle . . . de dresser les chevaux* (1658). (By permission of the Folger Shakespeare Library.)

59)—specifically for his skill in horsemanship and fencing.[3] He also was evidently Jonson's model for the admirable Lord Lovel in *The New Inne* (Riggs 302). More conspicuously, however, Cavendish was the generous host who commissioned from Jonson *The Kings Entertainment at Welbeck*, performed on 21 May 1633, when Charles was on his way to Scotland to be crowned—Welbeck Abbey being Cavendish's seat in Nottinghamshire. "Our *King* is going now . . . / To see his Native *Countrey*," wrote Jonson. "O Sister *Scotland!*" (802). Then in the following year, on 30 July, Cavendish provided another entertainment for Charles by Jonson, *Loves Wel-come . . . at Bolsover*, this time at the second of his major estates, five miles away from Welbeck, in Derbyshire.

Jonson's death in 1637 by no means terminated Cavendish's affinity for plays and playwrights. On the contrary, he appears to have turned to James Shirley for help in the shaping and refining of his own works. Certainly such a liaison would help to explain the strange view of playmaking expressed by Cavendish's wife: "*I Have heard that such Poets that write Playes, seldome or never join or sow the several Scenes together; they are two several Professions.*"[4] During the Civil Wars Cavendish chose the dramatist William Davenant to be his Lieutenant General of Ordnance. Later still, exiled and living at least relatively "meanely" in a suburb of the French capital, he was reputed to have "writ severall things for the English Company that did lately act in *Parris* which sheweth in him either an admirable temper and settledness of mind, . . . or else an infinite and vaine affection unto Poetry, that in the ruines of his Country and himselfe to can be at the leisure to make Prologues and Epilogues for players" (*Kingdomes Weekly Intelligencer* 23 Feb.-2 March 1647, 438). In fact, some thirty years after Jonson's death, Cavendish appears to have been a patron of both Dryden and Shadwell, and perhaps to have collaborated with each on the writing of plays. Drama was one of the enduring passions of his life.

As a writer of comedy, Cavendish is best remembered for *The Country Captaine* and *The Varietie*.[5] Published respectively at The Hague (by Samuel Broun) and in London (by Humphrey Moseley) in the year of the King's

---

[3]Robert Evans's analysis of these two poems yields some interesting insights regarding the Cavendish-Jonson association. He writes, for example, "The confidence the poems embody must have been born of Jonson's prior, deeper confidence in himself, the Earl, and the integrity of their relations" (75).   [4]Quoted from *Playes*, the opening words of the eighth (of nine) passages headed "To the Readers."   [5]Never published until recently, *Witts Triumvirate; or, The Philosopher* is Cavendish's earlier and thoroughly Jonsonian effort to capture "Some . . . fresh humours, heretofore / Not touch'd, or els new-dress'd" (2r). Apparently this work was performed during the mid-1630s—at least once before a paying audience and once before the King and Queen. First described in 1964 by Samuel Schoenbaum and edited in 1975 by Cathryn Nelson, it was for the first time attributed to Cavendish by Hilton Kelliher in 1993 ("Donne, Jonson" 152).

beheading, both had earlier been presented by His Majesty's servants at the Blackfriars, perhaps in 1640 and 1641.[6] The characters in both spring from the Jonsonian well of humours, but Cavendish's main aim in them seems to be relaxed, good-natured amusement. Without a firm foundation of Jonsonian morality or a deep commitment to learning, the plays offer a loose sort of brisk, colloquial *divertissement*. We are told, for instance, that a beribboned Englishman wearing color-encoded French clothes, Device in *Country Captaine*, is supposed to be seen as "a walkinge mirth" (16). Ridiculous enough simply for being "governd by the mode" (11), Device becomes more so when, to impress a lady, he decides to acquire a reputation as "a fighting Cavalier" (50).

The strongest feature of both plays is the dialogue, which, like Jonson's, achieves some of its vitality by means of colloquial wit and evocative detail. In the opening scene of *The Country Captaine*, when Underwit, a newly made captain of a trained band, is about to go down to the country with Sir Richard Huntlove, we have an exchange between Underwit and his servant Thomas about what to pack:

> *Tho.* First and formost, Item a buffe coate, and a payre of breeches of the same cloath,—*Writes.*
> *Vnd.* A payre of bootes and spurs and a paire of shoos without spurs.
> *Tho.* Spurs—*Writes.*
> *Vnd.* A paire of gray stockens, thick dapple gray stockens. With a belt to be worne either about my shoulder or about my waste.
> *Tho.* Wast.—*Writes.*
> *Vnd.* A London dutch felt, with out a band with a Feather in it.
> *Tho.* With out a Feather in it.—*Writes.*
> *Vnd.* An old fox blade, made at houndslow heath, and then, all the bookes can bee bought, of martiall discipline which the learned call Tacticks.
> *Tho.* Ticktacks. . . . [5]

One is slightly better off if one recognizes that *fox* was cant for an English-made sword and that ticktacks was a backgammonlike game. In any case, a chief pleasure of the play lies in such quasi-realistic exchanges. The overall structure of both works remains scattered—as a title such as *The Varietie* warns.

The Country Captaine takes place shortly after "the leager at Barwick" (5), which ended the First Bishops' War in the summer of 1639. (Cavendish had contributed an impressive ten thousand pounds to the King's cause at

---

[6]Though these two plays were bound and issued together in 1649, Greg observes that they obviously are "bibliographically independent." He adds that while *The Country Captaine* must have been intended for publication at The Hague, "There is no evidence that the book . . . was ever issued in its original form" (*Bibliography* 2:801).

that time and had equipped and led some 120 knights and gentlemen whom he called the Prince of Wales's Troop.) We find eventually that Underwit, the titular captain who finally wins a lady's maid, is going to share our attention with the mistress herself, Lady Huntlove. The latter plans to cuckold her husband with the aid of Sir Francis Courtwell (who says, Faust-like, "I grow immortall with my hopes" [57]), and Master Courtwell (a nephew of Sir Francis) is brought in to woo and win the lady's sister. Cavendish's full acceptance here of human sexuality as a valid source of comedy shows—as does his liberated but not libertine life—that he felt comfortable in bypassing the affected courtly fashion, so dear to his Queen, of platonic love.[7] When Courtwell tells Lady Huntlove that he has married her sister, he makes no bones about declaring that with "a possett and foure naked thighs in a bed to night, wee'le bid faire earnest for a boy" (89). Repression of the libido was simply not much fun either in life or letters. Besides, platonic love's substitution of sentiment and rhetoric was too often a hypocritical blind. Everything considered, *The Country Captaine* had (and has) some appeal. For a revival in about 1690 Shadwell even ventured to claim that the "Noble Authour drew / Such Images, so pleasing and so true, / That after forty years they still are new" (50).

In his other best-known comedy, *The Varietie*, Cavendish creates a Lady Beaufield, who as "the only Magnetick widdow i'th Town" (2) is bound to call to mind Jonson's *Magnetic Lady*. Students have also found echoes here of James Shirley and Richard Brome, but when we come across an "Academy" of ladies (Mistress Voluble, chair), we are most likely to think of the Ladies Collegiate in *Epicoene* or of comparable "academies" in *Cynthia's Revels* and *The Devil Is an Asse*. There are also some jeerers and even a reminiscence—indeed, a parody—of a Jonson song: "*Have you smelt of the bud of the Rose? / In his pudding hose*" (*Varietie* 57).

More thought-provoking is the character of Master Jack Manly, who affects the ways of old and better days. In particular, Manly is wont to put on the "habit of *Leister*" (3)—that is, Robert Dudley, Earl of Leicester, Queen Elizabeth's favorite. Cavendish's use of humours is especially effective in this instance because it animates both a singular character and a theme of the play: "these things were worne when men of honor flourish'd, that tam'd the wealth of Spaine, set up the States, help'd the French King, and brought Rebellion to reason" (39). A nostalgic reminder of good times

---

[7]Cavendish's wife later recorded—somewhat enigmatically—that "he has been a great lover and admirer of the Female Sex; which whether it be so great a crime as to condemn him for it; I'le leave to the judgment of young Gallants and beautiful Ladies" (*Life* 149–50). A little more than a decade earlier she had observed more generally that "Dishonour and Inconvenience comes not by Adultery of the Husband, as the Wife; for the Children receive no dishonour by the Fathers Liberty, nor the Wife very much" (*Worlds Olio* 76).

past, the character of Manly is pleasantly conducive to smiles and at the same time useful as an inverted means of commenting on the failings of the present. Even within the comic construct of the play, one character observes that nowadays "the times are dangerous." These are "warlike times" (7).

The dancing master Galliard in *The Varietie* is a character somewhat like Device with regard to frivolity, and somewhat like Manly with regard to thematic usefulness. He is also a character of special interest for indicating the willingness of Cavendish to mock foolishness in one of Henrietta Maria's native countrymen and for touching the English funnybone sufficiently to be extracted for an Interregnum droll called *The Humours of Monsieur Galliard* (noted here in chapter 9). The passages chosen to make up the droll include some further reminiscences of Jonson—specifically his frustration as a masque writer—as well as a use of the word *variety* that may help us interpret the title of Cavendish's play. When Galliard speaks of producing a masque and Sir William inquires whether he will write it himself, Galliard responds that what counts is the "spirit, de fancie, de brave scene, de varietie of de Antimasque, de nimble a foot, no matre de sence" (*Varietie* 18-19). This from the pen of a patron of Jonson who had hearkened to Ben's latter-day grumbling. Further on we find Galliard saying, "Me tell you, ven dey are so bissey to learne a de dance, dey vil never tinke of de Rebellion, and den de reverence is obedience to Monarchy, and begar obedience is ale de ting in de varle" (36). Masquing as a means of distraction is a risible suggestion here, but soberingly close to some advice that we shall eventually find Cavendish offering seriously to his royal advisee. A respectful "obedience to Monarchy," we may be sure, meant much to Cavendish himself, but what might distract determined Englishmen from thoughts of rebellion was more than he or anyone else knew.

Probably the play's most striking juggling of perspective relates to Master Newman, a suitor to Lucy, Lady Beaufield's daughter. We learn that "The Taverne he frequents he has made his Theater at his own charge to act intemperance; o're the great Roome he uses to be drunk in, they say, he has built a heaven, a Players heaven, and thence a Throne's let down, in which, well heated, successively they are drawn up to the clouds to drink their Mistris health" (34-35). Here the intermingling of life and art, conceivably evocative to some degree of a real-life blending of the two (plays are said to have been put on in taverns), brings the world of the theater into that of the dramatically conceived tavern. Furthermore, when performed at the Blackfriars, Cavendish's play would have brought the enacted world of the tavern into the actual theater in such a way as to utilize the machinery of the latter: the ascending throne on which Lady Beaufield's tipsy gentleman usher was sent to heaven with a wench was presumably part of the actual equipment at the Blackfriars. During its comic course, *The Varietie* offers many songs, varied characters, and interesting incidents, but finally it comes to an ending so congested that one wonders if, indeed, the play doctor Shirley was ever called in on the case. Whether he was or not, we may have here an example of noble negligence, an aristocratic impatience with polishing that is sometimes, fairly enough, associated with the word *cavalier.*

Yet another Cavendish work, *A Pleasante & Merye Humor off a Roge* (ca.1658[8]), deals less with humours and throws over any pretense of plot in favor of a set of scenes connected mainly by the recurrence of a shape-shifting rogue. Whatever its background may be (one recalls that Jonson had a lifelong penchant for rogues), the string-of-onions structure here is strongly remindful of Spanish picaresque narrative—for example, the anonymous *Lazarillo de Tormes* (to which Cavendish seems to refer); Alemán's *Guzmán de Alfarache,* translated by Jonson's friend James Mabbe as *The Rogue* (1622); and Carlos García's *Desordenada codicia,* translated as *The Sonne of the Rogue* (1638). Among the varied professional shapes assumed by Cavendish's English rogue are those of a peddler (indebted to Shakespeare's *Winter's Tale*) and a "Notable Gipsye" (indebted to Jonson's *Gypsies Metamorphos'd*), and also a braggart soldier who claims, "I doe not loue to thriue by Rebellion, I haue more honor / In mee" (18).

Derivative but lively, the *Humor off a Roge* was later remodeled—perhaps with the aid of Thomas Shadwell—and, when Cavendish was in his eighties, put forth as *The Triumphant Widow* (1674). Whatever Shadwell may have contributed to the Restoration updating, Carolyn Kephart has pointed out that every scene in the earlier play reappears, somewhat modified, in the later one (269). Thus Kephart concludes *The Triumphant Widow* to be "at once old-fashioned and *avant-garde,*" a newly song-filled play that "looks backward to the Caroline comedies of Massinger and Shirley and forward to no less innovative work than *The Beggar's Opera*" (266).[9]

From about the same time as the *Roge,* toward the end of the Protectorate, we have a strong hint regarding Cavendish's long-sustained royalist hopes. Lynn Hulse has learned that in February 1658 "Charles II and his siblings were the recipients of a lavish spectacle staged in the Duke's lodgings at Antwerp."[10] Unfortunately the text of this show has been lost,

---

[8]First published in an edition by Francis Needham in 1933.   [9]Mention should be made here also of *The Humourous Lovers* (1667), on which Cavendish may have had the assistance of Dryden, Davenant, or Shadwell. In that same year, furthermore, Dryden apparently created *Sir Martin Mar-All* from Cavendish's versions of Molière's *L'Etourdi* and Quinault's *L'Amant indiscret.*   [10]All of the information regarding this show and the next has been kindly furnished by Dr. Hulse, either in private correspondence or via prepublication copy.

but it now appears that from two years later we have one further extant effort on Cavendish's part to catch the conscience of the King. *The King's Entertainment* dates from some time shortly after both men had returned from exile and before the Cavendishes had made their way back to Welbeck—that is, sometime between May and October or November 1660.[11] Apparently designed for performance in Cavendish's London lodgings, probably at Dorset House, *The King's Entertainment* is a full-fledged example of a royal entertainment, the overall fiction of which proves to be a strikingly transparent version of the actual situation. Hulse summarizes: "On discovering that Newcastle is to host a second visit from the monarch, the poet invokes the muses ... , but he is unable to devise a speech worthy of Charles and falls into an unconscious state. His friend, a gentleman, consults a doctor in the hope of finding a cure. The physician recommends several poetical remedies, but only music has the power to inspire the poet. The sick poet scenes frame a lengthy monologue and a ballad in honour of Wales, followed by a song mocking the Frenchified court."

Among Cavendish's more specific topical gestures here is the creation of a jocular Welshman who praises both the erstwhile Prince of Wales and the ongoing fidelity of the Welsh, then proceeds to compare Charles to the scriptual "Kinge Tavid" who killed "Golias" (*King's Entertainment* 6r). Boldest of all, perhaps, and yet presumably acceptable to the restricted audience for which it was designed, is the Welshman's assertion that "I doe ferily beleive / my Cozen Kinge Tavid did love a pritty Wench" (6r). If any Bathsheba-like woman was present, she is perhaps most likely to have been the married and beauteous Barbara Villiers, Charles's current major mistress. Then again, the Welshman's bold reference might pass muster as an allusion merely to Charles's well-known general interest in the fair sex. Be this as it may, this late example of a nobleman's royal entertainment is of interest not only for itself but also because it provided a substantial amount of material that was later—and rather extraordinarily—integrated into Cavendish's *Triumphant Widow*.

Very different contributions to the Cavendish phenomenon were made by two of Cavendish's daughters by his first wife, Elizabeth Bassett Cavendish. Back in 1642 Elizabeth's namesake, at age sixteen, was married to John Egerton, the nineteen-year-old Lord Brackley, son of the Earl of Bridgewater. (A few years earlier still, in 1634, young Brackley had appeared in both Carew's *Coelum Britannicum* and Milton's *Comus*.) For some time after the marriage the bride was considered "too young to be bedded,"

---

[11]The handwriting on the manuscript (Portland Collection, Nottingham University Library MS PwV23) is that of Cavendish's secretary, John Rolleston of Sokeholme, Nottinghamshire. Hulse considers it to represent "the summation of his calligraphic style."

as her stepmother later phrased it (*Life* 95), and she apparently continued to live with her own family. Possibly she remained with what was left of it in August 1644 when the royalist garrison at the great Cavendish estate of Welbeck fell to the parliamentarians under Edward Montagu, second Earl of Manchester. Earlier, when the thunderclouds of war had begun to gather, Cavendish had fortified his homes at both Welbeck and Bolsover. In 1643, however, while he and his sons Charles and Henry were away serving the King in the field, his wife died. In July of the following year came defeat at Marston Moor, followed a month later by the fall of Welbeck. Fortunately the victorious Manchester was willing to promise that the still-resident daughters would not be harmed.

This was the context in which Jane Cavendish and Elizabeth Egerton (Jane being the elder by about two years) decided to write something that would both amuse themselves and please their father. The result was a collaborative volume called *Poems, Songs, a Pastorall, and a Play.*[12] Because of these writings one may point to the Cavendish sisters as the first known female playwrights of our period. Indeed, as female English dramatists they have only a tiny handful of forerunners from any period at all.[13]

The works that have come down to us from the Cavendish daughters raise in a special way a question that is raised implicitly by all of our manuscript plays that were not intended for publication. If we perceive these particular writings to be even more private in nature than the unpublished work of, say, Mildmay Fane and Cosmo Manuche, should we make allowances—or perhaps different allowances—when considering them? How many of us would wish judgment of our writing to be based on what we have returned to the drawer? Whatever answers we are most comfortable with, it seems fair to say that these two Cavendish sisters, necessarily lacking their father's experience with plays, playwrights, and playhouses but daring to venture into a field they knew he loved, produced

---

[12]Kelliher, who has identified the copyist of *Witts Triumvirate* as John Rolleston ("Donne, Jonson" 153), cites the observation of Herford and the Simpsons that this volume by Cavendish's daughters is also in Rolleston's hand (*Jonson* 7:767). Apparently Cavendish kept Rolleston with him during his military campaigns, left him in England during his own exile, and eventually appointed him steward at Welbeck. A copy of the poems and pastoral is held also at the Beinecke Library, Yale (Osborn MS b 233).   [13]Setting aside a medieval liturgical drama, a pastoral dialogue, and a small handful of translations, the oldest surviving English play by a woman appears to be Elizabeth Cary's *Mariam* (ca. 1602–5; published 1613). According to Nancy Cotton's study, Queen Henrietta Maria's courtly entertainments came next (a masque in 1626 and, just possibly, *Florimène* in 1635), followed by the Cavendish works now under discussion. To help place such facts in their historical context, one might turn to David Cressy's observation that "Close to 90% of the women in seventeenth-century England could not even write their names" (41).

rather weak but nonetheless intriguing dramatic works that they called *The Concealed Fansyes* and *A Pastorall*.

The Concealed Fansyes presents two young sisters, Luceny and Tattiney, who endeavor to conceal their own "fancies" (the word here means, roughly, "preferences" especially "amorous preferences") and thus to frustrate and reprogram their respective suitors, Courtly and Praesumption.[14] Motherless daughters of an idolized, absentee father, Lord Calsindow (in other words, the basic situation of the fictive sisters is transparently that of their creators), they are targeted by one Lady Tranquility, who hopes to enlist them in her campaign to win Calsindow's hand. The likely aim of the playwrights is to relate Lady Tranquility (who keeps to her bed so as "to plumpe vpp" her face [94]) to Margaret Lucas, whom, as we have seen, Cavendish had met in Paris in April 1645.[15] That meeting, it would seem, furnishes a *terminus a quo* for the play as we have it. One should hasten to observe, moreover, that Calsindow is finally protected from the wiles of Lady Tranquility when the young playwrights marry her off to another character for his money. Actually Cavendish married Margaret Lucas late in the same year they met. Unless one sees some point in fretting about locking barn doors after the horse has run away, therefore, one probably will accept this historical marriage as providing a *terminus ad quem* for the play. But it did not necessarily end the concern on the part of all the family members involved. In a passage called "Of a Second Wife," Margaret Lucas Cavendish later wrote "that when a second Wife comes into a Family, all the former Children, or old Servants, are apt to be Factious, and do foment Suspicions against her, making ill Constructions of all her Actions; were they never so well, and innocently meant" (*Worlds Olio* 81).

Of particular interest in *The Concealed Fansyes*—and a new element in the present study—is a sense that we are involved with feminine discourse: "Ladyes I beseech you blush not to see / That I speake a Prologe being a Shee," we read in the first prologue. And in the second, " 'tis woman all ye way / For you'll not see a Plott in any Act" (87). And again, "wee haue beene brought vpp in the creation of good Language which will make vs euer our selues" (112). As Margaret Ezell suggests, the theme of self-possession, based in part on "the mastery of one's words, is manifested in all the female characters, even the unattractive and presumptuous Lady Tranquility and the outspoken serving maids" (289). One of the briefest, freshest scenes in the work concerns an outspoken young woman charged with ironing the

---

[14]One suitor tells another of Luceny, the lady he himself fancies, that she is "soe Courtly coy, I knowe not what to make of hir, for when shee smiles I knowe not whether 'tis a scorne or a grace" (91).   [15]Lady Tranquility's late rising may be traceable to the fact that Henrietta Maria and her ladies kept to their beds in cold weather "for want of fuel and food and . . . money" (Kathleen Jones 39).

marriage "lynnings": "I am sure," says she, "I haue burnt my fingers wth smoothinge" (145; see figure 40). Even while Luciney and Tattiney are attempting to re-form their suitors (who also have concealed fancies) and delighting in their own freedom and female wit, they are basically—and perhaps not surprisingly—conveying some very conservative attitudes. "Ho! my ffather indeede," exclaims Luceny, "that Gentleman shall bee my Alpha & Omega of Gouernem^{t}" (108). King Lear himself would have approved.

In the midst of such matters we suddenly encounter a fresh set of characters. "Come, what a Seige!" says Mr. Proper, a gentleman usher. Mr. Friendly replies, "By God I thinke soe, but where's the releife / I'm sure our partie is now as flatt as a flunder" (113). A sort of double exposure is utilized here to present very different aspects of the young ladies' lives. While Messrs. Proper and Friendly have been talking, Mr. Devinity has been measuring—"and the workes are not made high enough for [with-standing] ye Enemyes if shott will enter into euery Chamber of ye Howse" (114). As if all this were not a sufficient shifting of focus (clearly we are not concerned with realistic or linear drama), we soon come across the stage direction "Enter an Angell" (115).

The upshot is that, as matters grow dire, the grief-stricken Luceny and Tattiney don the garb of nuns. Nathan Starr believes that this turn of events suggests that Jane and Elizabeth were at the time writing at Ashridge, the home of Lord and Lady Brackley, which was formerly a religious house (837). We also are introduced rather belatedly to Luceny and Tattiney's two brothers, for some reason called "Stellowes" (a form of *star* plus *fellows*, perhaps).[16] In any case, Lord Calsindow is at the end safely united with his children, each young lady is married to the suitor of her choice, and the fifth act concludes. There then follows an extraordinary postnuptial, post-fifth-act dialogue between Luceny and Tattiney in which we find that the suitors, Courtly and Praesumption, are still being trained. As Tattiney puts it, the goal "is an equall marryage" (154). Then finally, ending everything, each new wife delivers an epilogue and joins with her sister in yet another.

Though the Cavendish sisters refer to *The Concealed Fansyes* as a comedy—and it is no other nameable thing—one may have the impression, for better or worse, that self-expression has triumphed here over genre. By dramatizing something like their own circumstances, the two collaborators could in a sense control them. The working out of it all does not make for

---

[16]Jordan refers to "stellified" heroes in *Fancy's Festivals* (D3v), and Carew, in *Coelum Britannicum*, to "the stellifying of our British Heroes" (*Poems* 183). Jonson is the most perspicuous: "*Good men* are the Stars, the Planets of the Ages wherein they live, and illustrate the times" (*Timber*, ll. 1100–1101). Simplest of all is Shakespeare, who writes of "star-like nobleness" (*Timon* V.i.63).

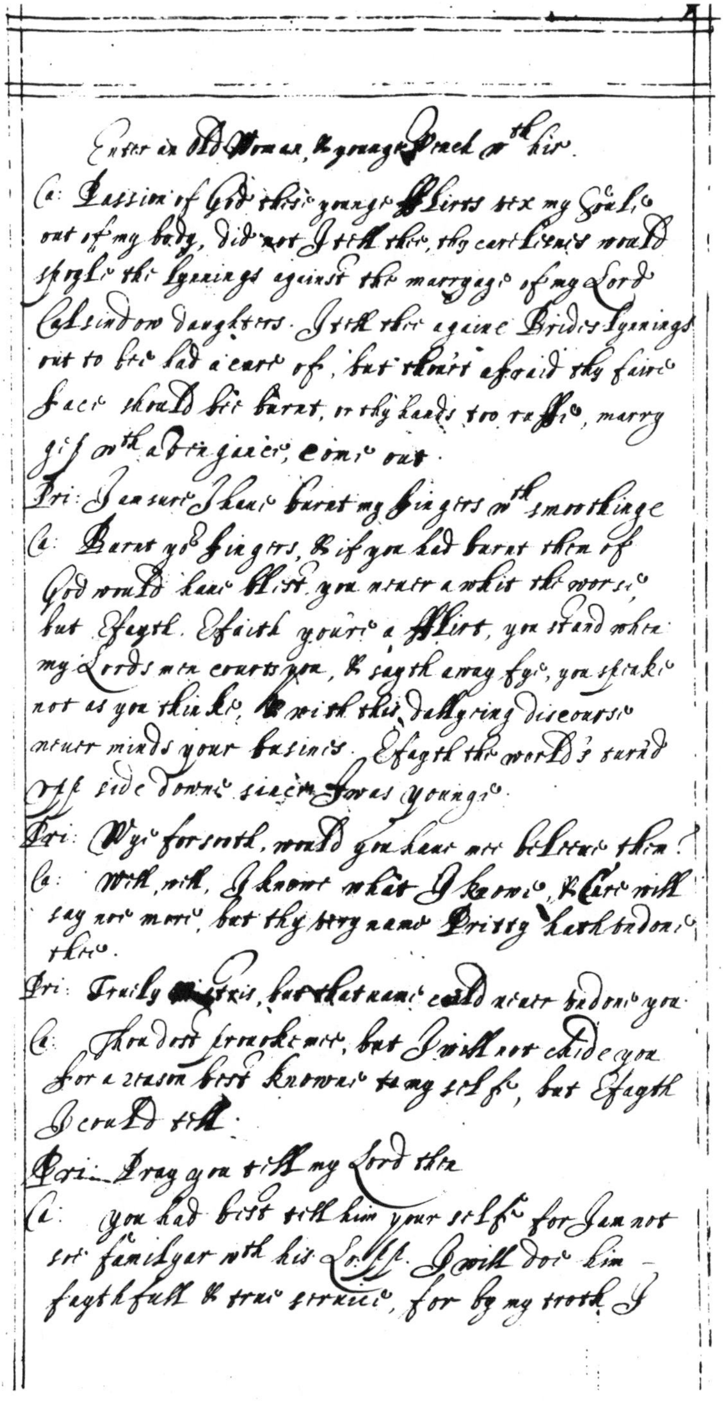

Enter an Old Woman, & younge Prick wth hir.
Ca: Passion of God this younge Flirts vex my soule out of my body, did not I tell thee, thy cart Livers would spoyle the lynnings against the marryage of my Lord Calsindow daughters. I tell thee againe Brides lynnings out to bee had a care of, but thou'rt afraid thy faire face should bee burnt, or thy hands too roffe, marry gif wth a vengance; come out.
Pri: I am sure I have burnt my fingers wth smoothinge
Ca: Burnt yor fingers, & if you had burnt them of God would have blist you neuer a whit the worse but Efaygth. Efaith you're a Flirt, you stand when my Lords men courts you, & sayth away fye, you speake not as you thinke, & with this dallyring discourse neuer minds your businis. Efaygth the world's turnd upside downe since I was younge.
Pri: Why forsooth, would you have mee beleeue them?
Ca: Well, well, I knowe what I knowe, & there will say noe more, but thy very name Prissy hath undone thee.
Pri: Truly Mistris, but that name could neuer undone you.
Ca: Thou dost mocke mee, but I will not chide you for a reason best knowne to my selfe, but Efaygth I could tell.
Pri: Pray you tell my Lord then
Ca: You had best tell him your selfe for I am not soe familyar wth his Lordshipp. I will doe him faythfull & true seruice, for by my troth I

Figure 40. A page from *The Concealed Fansyes* by Jane Cavendish and Elizabeth Egerton (Bodl. Rawl. MS Poet 16, p. 145). (By permission of the Bodleian Library.)

altogether satisfying art, but perhaps it was not a bad game for a couple of beleaguered young women to play. Neither they nor anyone else knew, of course, that their father would be exiled for some sixteen years.

Elizabeth and Jane's *Pastorall*, not surprisingly, proves to be both *sui generis* and also relatable to the dramatic pastorals that we discussed here in chapter 10. One also might recall that Queen Henrietta Maria herself, coming to England in 1625 as a girl of sixteen, had that same year written, directed, and performed at court a pastoral play. Beyond doubt, pastorals had been and for a while would remain in vogue. In their own particular homegrown specimen the Cavendish sisters produced a work that, like Jonson's *Masque of Queens*, opens with an antimasque of witches. "Hath not our mischeife made warr," asks one of them, "and that a miserable one, to make Brother hate brother" (*Pastorall* 52). "Lords," brags another, "we send beyond Seas at our pleasure" (52). The special delight of one witch is "makeinge Ladyes Captiues" (53). Another gloats about "how hansomely wee tye Ladyes Tongues" (53)—thus explicitly calling attention to the widely felt need of the day to substitute pens for tongues. In the second antimasque some country folks (including Goodman Rye and Goodman Hay) sing of their losses ("I haue Lost my melch Cow," one laments [61]), but basically there is once again a kind of aristocratic gynocentrism operative here. When the shepherds and shepherdesses come on, the autobiographical light burns bright in such lines as "Your Fathers absence makes you alwaies owne / Your selfe though hansom, still to bee alone" (66). In the margin of the manuscript a scattering of the initials J.C. and E.B. suggests how the collaborators' tasks were apportioned, and in a song toward the close that we know to be Jane's she concludes: "Our Summer is, if that could bee / Father, Brothers, for to see" (78). Finally, to the entire work she appends a poem that makes explicit a view that we have had no trouble deducing: "Soe what becomes mee better then / But to bee your Daughter in your Penn" (84). Through imitation, that is, both Jane and Elizabeth strove to honor their only begetter. By the time he arrived home, however, Jane would be married to a former royalist soldier from Northamptonshire, Captain Charles Cheyne, Elizabeth would be Countess of Bridgewater, and Cavendish himself would have his second wife, Margaret, to whom he had been married for about fifteen years.

The most phenomenal part of the Cavendish phenomenon proved to be Margaret herself, Marchioness (later Duchess) of Newcastle. Margaret Lucas Cavendish was the first English woman to publish her husband's biography, the first to publish her own autobiography, the first to publish her scientific writings ("Of Double-Tides," "Of Metamorphosed Elements," "Of Colours," etc.), the first to publish her science fiction, and the first to publish her remarks on Shakespeare and Jonson. All of these firsts are in a sense inseparable from the fact that she was also the first English woman to write and publish her collected plays, and, what is more, to do so in two folios (the first in 1662 and the second in 1668) of the sort that until that time had been used for enshrining the works of Jonson, Shakespeare, and Beaumont and Fletcher. All in all a very attemptive spirit, Margaret Cavendish was determined to put herself on record, to make known her uniqueness as a person and especially the fertility of her fancy. Her first collection of plays, published eight years before Aphra Behn's earliest play, appears to have been written after about 1653, during the exile that she shared with her husband. The volume would have been printed somewhat earlier had a previous manuscript for it not sunk with the ship that was taking it to England (Kathleen Jones 130). At the time of publishing her first book, *Poems, and Fancies* (1653), Cavendish explained that "*my* Lords Estate *being taken away, [I] had nothing for* Huswifery, *or thrifty* Industry *to imploy my selfe in*" (A7r). While this is true, true also is her claim that she was strongly and explicitly motivated by a desire for fame ("my ambition of extraordinary Fame, is restless, and not ordinary" [*Natures Pictures* bii,v]) as well as by what in modern terms may be termed an ambivalent but ardent feminism.

Situated between her own stepdaughters in age, Margaret Lucas Cavendish was born the daughter of Thomas Lucas, a wealthy gentleman of St. John's Abbey near Colchester in Essex. After his early death she was reared by her mother, Elizabeth. Though painfully shy (bashfulness is a recurring motif in her writing), she chose to become a maid of honor to Henrietta Maria. Hence she was part of the small entourage that accompanied the Queen in her flight to France in 1644.[17] Meeting and marrying William Cavendish there the following year ("All my Misfortunes they are gone," he wrote to her, "Now wee are one" [*Phanseys* 22]), she proceeded to share her husband's long exile—except for one trip that she made to England in 1651-53.

While they were living in Rotterdam the Marquess and his wife learned that her girlhood home at Colchester had become the site of a deadly siege in June 1648. Many weeks later, at the end of August, her youngest brother, Charles, who at one time had served as Lieutenant General of Horse under General Cavendish himself, and who had played a chief role in the defense of Colchester, was shot by a parliamentarian firing squad. This event, as we have seen earlier (chapter 6), provided part of the rage and dismay that

---

[17]She later wrote, "In truth, my bashfulness and fears made me repent my going from home to see the world abroad." Fortunately, "my Lord the Marquis of Newcastle did approve of those bashful fears which many condemned, and would choose such a wife as he might bring to his own humours" (*True Relation* 162).

empowered *The Famous Tragedie of King Charles I.* The bodies of Margaret's mother and sister were taken from their graves, and their hair was cut off and some of their bones removed to adorn the victors' hats.

Furthermore, as the great Cavendish estates in England were sequestered and plundered, and their parks devastated, and as the expenses for living abroad mounted, the couple slid into a morass of debt. Thus it is all the more remarkable that the imposing Englishman somehow managed to obtain sufficient credit to lease a fine house in Antwerp that the painter Rubens had previously created for himself, a beautiful place known now as the Rubenshuis Museum.

The Marchioness, always encouraged in her writing by her husband, poured forth a torrent of letters, discourses, orations, poems, and plays. As if such an output were not enough to distinguish her, and despite her enduring bashfulness, she had by this time chosen to fashion herself as a fantastic original—a sort of humours character, one might say—known especially for *outré* costumes. "I took great delight in attiring," she writes. "Also I did dislike any should follow my fashions, for I always took delight in a singularity, even in accoutrement of habits" (*True Relation* 175). It is therefore of interest to find a character in one of her dramas saying, "I am obliged more to my fancie, than my wealth, for this finerie" (*Several Wits* 90).[18] When at last the Restoration enabled the couple to return to England and the new King had intimated that he had little desire for advice from an antiquated mentor, William Cavendish gravitated back to Welbeck and his horses. *Beatus ille, qui procul negotiis.* . . . He requested a dukedom, however, and in June 1665 the King granted him one. Meanwhile and constantly, his wife continued to write.

Even in her plays, Margaret Cavendish was more set on expressing herself than on writing drama. In *Orations of Divers Sorts* (1662) she acknowledges that her plays have been criticized "as having no Plots, Designs, Catastrophes and such like I know not what," and readily she admits, "I had not Skil nor Art to Form them, as they should be" (a2r). All this is true. What was casual in her husband's writing is careless, even reckless, in her own. She is the most un-Jonsonian playwright imaginable. Further, her insistence on noting what she does not know calls attention not only to gaps in her knowledge but also to her writerly willfulness regarding them. In the introductory matter of the 1662 collection of plays she affirms that "*as for the nicities of Rules, Forms, and Terms, I renounce, and profess, that if I did understand and know them strictly, as I do not, I would not follow them*" (*Playes*

---

[18]Having visited the Duke and Duchess at their Clerkenwell house, John Evelyn wrote in his diary for 18 April 1667 that he was "much pleasd, with the extraordinary fancifull habit, garb, & discourse of the *Dutchesse*" (478).

THE CAVENDISH PHENOMENON 329

A5v). She even points out that "*some of my Scenes have no acquaintance or relation to the rest of the Scenes, although in one and the same Play*" (A4r).[19] More damaging observations than this a critic hardly can offer, though Henry Perry comes close when he proclaims that Cavendish produced "closet drama so lifeless and so dull that one shrinks from it even on the printed page" (214). In fairness to Cavendish one might cite also what may be the most generous statement made about her in a later age: "Perhaps like Gertrude Stein or Virginia Woolf," writes Jacqueline Pearson, "she had decided that the conventional polished classic sentence was 'unsuited for a woman's use' because it was 'devised by men out of their own needs for their own uses' and was searching for other means of expression" (125).[20] Then again, perhaps one should recall that Cavendish herself said her dramas were "*like dull lead statues, which is the reason I send them forth to be printed, rather than keep them concealed in hopes to have them first Acted*" (*Playes* A3r).

Accepting at once that these works were designed for the closet, we need not be blinkered to their insistent exploration of various ideas and themes of the day (platonic love, for instance, and women's education), nor need we refrain from exonerating them somewhat by acknowledging that many kinds of dialogue were then in vogue. In fact, in her 1668 *Plays, Never before Printed* Cavendish tells her reader that "*having pleased my Fancy in writing many Dialogues upon several Subjects, and having afterwards order'd them into Acts and Scenes, I will venture, in spight of the Critics, to call them Plays; and if you like them so, well and good; if not, there is no harm done.*"[21] Someone so bashful as Margaret Cavendish, whose speaking was limited to English, would have cut a poor figure in a Parisian salon of the period (the Marquise de Rambouillet was then in full career), but in the give-and-take of a written colloquy with herself, her plain English could be a sort of response to fashionable *préciosité*.

Though Cavendish's immersion in the culture of the foreign countries where she lived was apparently only nominal, one still might choose to argue that she had at least observed and more or less consciously accepted the mid- to late seventeenth-century French penchant for *négligence* and

---

[19]While such statements are faithful to the plays she wrote, Cavendish also was capable of writing the following problem-filled paragraph labeled "Of Comedies" for her *Worlds Olio:* "A Comedy should present vertue, and point at vice, for a Comedy should be to delight, and not to displease, a good Comedian wit, will onely reprove not reproach; but a satirrical wit will present the vices of two or three, in the person of one but a gentle spirit whch is a true Commical wit, will rather take the vice of one, and represent them in two or three persons, Satyr is more proper for a Comedy Tragedy [in 1671 revised to '*Tragi-Comedy*' (19)] then for pure Comedy; not that a true Comedy will flatter vice, but palliat it" (10).   [20]See also Harbage, *Cavalier Drama* 230.   [21]Quoted from the verso of a leaf following the title page.

badinage, for *le naturel* and *caprice*. In *The Worlds Olio* (1655) she wrote, "*I being of a lazy disposition, did choose to let it go into the World with its Defects, rather than take the pains to refine it*," and even "*I am . . . well armed with carelesness*" (A3v).

Such rationalization about Cavendish's writing will take us only so far, however. It will not finally bypass the fact that as a writer she is almost totally without discipline. As she has a character called Perfection say in *The Several Wits*, "my thoughts doth fly about my brain, like birds in Sun-shine weather" (102). She could claim at one point that "*I did my best indeavour, and took great pains in the ordering and joining*" of play parts, "*sowing*" several scenes together "*without any help or direction*."[22] Everything considered, however, trying to catch bright birds in sunshine weather was what she prized most: spontaneity, improvisation, and personal expression, with an ever-fresh hope that there might be a bird in the net.

For her best work, her *Life of the Thrice Noble, High and Puissant Prince William Cavendishe* (1667), she clearly had the aid of her husband. Here, uncharacteristically, she aims for "Brevity, Perspicuity and Truth" (B1r) and earns a significant measure of the fame for which she yearned. The very next year, however, she could be seen at her weakest when she indulged herself in her second folio of plays by publishing the names of characters in a "Farse" she never so much as began.[23]

Seeking aid with her plays from her devoted, indulgent husband, Margaret Cavendish complicated both of their canons. In part 2 of *Loves Adventures*, for instance, the musicians at a wedding say, "We desire your Excellence will give us leave to present you with a Song written by my Lord *Marquiss* of *New-Castle*" (76). More typical, however, is the Marquess's contribution of some of the dialogue. In *The Publique Wooing*, where the Lady Prudence takes control by insisting that she be wooed in public, her first wooer, a soldier, is appropriately given a speech that is labeled as the work of the former royalist General. To him also is assigned the suit of the country gentleman: "I am not young, nor yet condemn'd to age" (379). In *The Lady Contemplation*, part 1, he contributed scene xvii (between Lord Title and Mall Mean-Bred) and scenes xx and xxiv; and in part 2, scenes xxv and xxxv. Along the way, other, unlabeled signs of his input appear, as when Lady Contemplation observes, "This gallant and wise man, my Husband and your General, his Discourses have been my Tutors, and his Example hath and shall be my Guide" (pt. 2, 221).

Most intriguing of all, however, is the lack of accrediting in *The Sociable Companions*, where we find a coarser tone. This play opens with the news

---

[22]Quoted from the verso of a leaf inserted between A5 and A6 of *Playes* (1662).   [23]The names are given on the last of five page 2's in the volume.

"that the Army shall be disbanded, and all the Soldiers Cashiered" (1st 1), and the complaint "When a War is ended, Soldiers are out of Credit" (2). A lieutenant observes ruefully that "all the Cavalier Party lost their Wits when they lost their Estates" (8).

Tied though it is to its time and to her husband, Margaret Cavendish's drama is above all an exercise in self-projection. In play after play we find more or less cryptomorphic versions and inversions of herself. In *Loves Adventures*, for instance, we find that "*Lady* Bashfull *stands trembling and shaking, and her eyes being cast to the ground, and her face as pale as death*" (pt. 1, 9). Bashfull laments, "O in what a torment I have been in; hell is not like it" (10). In contrast, the Lady Sansparelle (*Youths Glory, and Deaths Banquet*) and Mademoiselle Grand Esprit (*Natures Three Daughters*) are presented as public lecturers who attract admiring throngs. In some of her plays Cavendish seems to be refracted into more than one character. In *Loves Adventures* we meet not only the aforementioned Lady Bashfull but also the brave, self-sacrificing Affectionata, who, disguised in male attire, appears to be "the sweetest, and most beautifullest young Cavalier, as ever I saw" (pt. 2, 67). Eventually, one might add, Affectionata wins the great general, Lord Singularity.

Most striking of all are the many passages in Cavendish's work that deal with a woman's place in the world. In her *Worlds Olio* of 1655 she observes, "It cannot be expected I should write so wisely or wittily as Men, being of the Effeminate Sex, whose Brains Nature hath mix'd with the coldest and softest Elements." Still, and typically, she maintains in this same passage that "*in Nature we have as clear an understanding as Man*" (A4r). At least since the time of Aristotle, men had discerned women to be the weaker sex, and now she, a self-published and self-proclaimed "poetresse," writes mockingly, "Women make Poems? burn them, burn them" (*Wits Cabal* 270). Though she never learned French during her stay in France, Cavendish must have been aware of the current vogue there for the *femmes savantes* and *femmes fortes*. The latter were especially lauded in Pierre Le Moyne's *Gallerie des femmes fortes* (1647) and exemplified outstandingly in Henrietta Maria's niece, Anne Marie de Montpensier, known as the Grande Mademoiselle, who fought with her troops in the French civil wars (the Fronde) of 1648-53 (Kathleen Jones 56-57). Whatever models Cavendish encountered, however, and whatever constraints she felt as a committed, dutiful, admiring, subservient wife (from the first, she vowed always to subject her will to her husband's), she produced plays that enabled her to ascend into a realm of the imagination where women could amaze with their intelligence, strive successfully for women's equity, and simultaneously win dazzled respect.

Some of the most explicit handling of such material occurs in the two-part (ten-act) *Bell in Campo*. Here the Lord General, "one of the gallantest and noblest persons in this Kingdome" (579), is married (as an allegorically inclined general might wish to be) to the Lady Victoria. Instead of being allowed to accompany him into battle, however, Victoria and the other women are sent away. Since things go badly for the men, it is lucky that Victoria has decided to improve her hours by rallying some five or six thousand supportive women troops whom she addresses as "Noble Heroickesse" (588). Proclaiming herself their Tutoress, Generalless, and Commanderess, she cries out that "we are fit to be Copartners in their Governments, and to help rule the World, where now we are kept as Slaves forced to obey; wherefore let us make our selves free, either by force, merit, or love" (588-89). To become worthy, these women will train themselves not in turkey-work (that is, handiwork imitating Turkish tapestry) but in "Wrastling, Running, Vaulting, Riding, and the like exercise" (592), and when they move as an army, they will "sing in their march the heroical actions done in former times by heroical women" (592). Within the world of this play Cavendish was moved to write as well as she ever did:

> now or never is the time to prove the courage of our Sex, to get liberty and freedome from the Female Slavery, and to make our selves equal with men: for shall Men only sit in Honours chair, and Women stand as waiters by? shall only Men in Triumphant Chariots ride, and Women run as Captives by? shall only men be Conquerors, and women Slaves? shall only men live by Fame, and women dy in Oblivion? no, no, gallant Heroicks raise your Spirits to a noble pitch, to a deaticall height, to get an everlasting Renown, and infinite praises. [609]

If people of her own time were more inclined to mock than admire what she wrote or did here or elsewhere, she was nonetheless at liberty to envision Lady Victoria's triumphal entrance in a gilt chariot drawn by eight horses covered with cloth of gold and wearing great plumes, with Victoria's hair curled attractively, flowing loosely, and crowned with laurel. In the world of *Bell in Campo*, if not in Cavendish's own, it is proclaimed that "all women shall hereafter in this Kingdome be Mistriss in their own Houses and Families" (631). In reading the speeches of any drama, one needs to be alert to the interpretative pitfalls that underlie even such apparent objectivity as Keats termed negative capability. Margaret Cavendish, however, is probably the most subjective of all English dramatists, and what reads here very much like wish-fulfillment inflated by romancing in the grand manner may in fact also be a sort of gilded *cri de coeur*, possibly even a communiqué to the Marquess himself. In any case, Lady Victoria's figure is ordered cast in brass so that it may be erected in the center of the city (cf. figure 41).

Margaret Cavendish is capable sometimes of sounding so startlingly

Figure 41. Margaret Cavendish, Duchess of Newcastle (1624-74), from the frontispiece of her *Plays* (1668). (By permission of the Bodleian Library.)

outspoken that she should, indeed, be included in any study of the beginnings of radical English feminism. Nevertheless, her various submissions and concessions, and especially her acknowledgment of her husband's variety of powers, make it difficult to deny the fundamental ambivalence of her stand. Though she strove always to be a striking original, she was very much a conservative, royalist, aristocratic woman of her time. Concerning the problem of how she could write so much on so many subjects (whether informed about them or not) and how she could write so inconsistently, Moira Ferguson has suggested, "The only consistency is her virtuosity and rich imagination, her talent and courage." Margaret Cavendish, says Ferguson, is not an enigma but a complex woman (317). This last part is surely true, and one might observe, long after the fact, that the two greatest disparities in her work—claims of shyness and fantasies about fame—are likely to share a single source in her self-absorption. This does not explain what she achieved, of course, achieved sometimes almost in spite of herself. It may, however, help us see that underneath everything there is really but one Margaret.

All in all, Margaret, Duchess of Newcastle, was neither the madwoman that Samuel Pepys beheld nor the "brightest beauty and the sharpest wit" that Etherege claimed to perceive (14). The not-so-simple fact is that with a minimum of education and against every sort of societal expectation and caveat, she not only wrote but also published over twenty original plays. Though her sense of humor had less range than her husband's and, conversely, though some of her work is so expansively protean as to escape the normal boundaries of genre, her basic dramatic instinct is to comedize. This said, the truth remains that her still stronger instinct is toward free-flowing self-expression. This woman who found speech in public difficult made up for the deficiency by turning to her pen, and in the process she produced a series of dramas that, for all their self-contradiction and oddity, have come to be recognized as constituting something not unlike Victoria's statue in brass. Though the crushing truth is that she never wrote a good play, Margaret Lucas Cavendish deserved what might be called an award for lifetime achievement.

Viewed together, the members of the Cavendish family provide us with a unique array of insights into the drama of the time (see figure 42).[24] The great Duke himself, in relationships variously compounded of patronage, friendship, and collaboration, touched the lives and careers of an extraordinary range of writers, from Ben Jonson to John Dryden, and including

---

[24]The picture of the Cavendish family reproduced here as figure 42 represents an unachieved ideal. The family was never all together in one place.

Thus in this Semy-Circle, wher they Sitt,
Telling of Tales of pleasure & of witt.
Heer you may read without a Sinn or Crime,
And how more innocently pass your tyme.

Figure 42. The Duke and Duchess of Newcastle and their family as depicted at storytelling time in Margaret Cavendish's *Natures Pictures* (1656). Both husband and wife are crowned with laurel. (By permission of the Folger Shakespeare Library.)

Brome, Shirley, Davenant, Shadwell, and Flecknoe.[25] It was to cavendish that Flecknoe dedicated his essay called *A Short Discourse of the English Stage* (1664; see Appendix B). As Langbaine put the case, "we may truly call him our *English Mecaenas*" (*Account* 386). By encouraging his wife to write and by collaborating with her (she held him to be "the best *Lyrick* and *Dramatick* Poet of this Age" [*Life* 146]), he extended still further such literary relationships as he had enjoyed with the professionals. These relationships were also echoed discreetly in the private collaborations of his daughters. Back in England, Jane and Elizabeth attempted awkwardly but high-spiritedly to sketch in dramatic form something like their own situation. Coming as early as they did in the line of women English dramatists, they immediately preceded their stepmother—who, like them, proved to be inspired and heartened by the dramatic interests of their father. Moreover, the feminist notes in the daughters' works are sounded again and greatly amplified in the work of their stepmother.

Whereas Margaret Cavendish created a unique female voice that is ubiquitous in her plays, even plays that are peopled with abstractions, her husband was inclined to create a more normative, less personal drama that was constituted mainly of a colorful but rather casually patterned mosaic of humour characters. Having come under the influence of Jonson in the reign of King James, and having survived the staggering blows of civil war and exile, his lordship finally returned to Restoration England an old man, but still a cavalier, still a Son of Ben.

---

[25]Some of the complexity of these relationships may be glimpsed in Harold Love's argument for the old Duke's implicit involvement in the satire of Dryden's "Mac Flecknoe." Love points out that Cavendish "was the common factor linking the ostensible victims Shadwell, Flecknoe and Shirley" ("Shadwell, Flecknoe and the Duke of Newcastle" 24).

TRAGICOMEDIES

Tragie-Comedy sho'd neither end Comically or Tragically, but betwixt both.
. . .

—Henry Burnell, *Landgartha* (1641)

We have *Joy* and *Dolor*, both commixt.
          —Mercurius Melancholicus, *Craftie Cromwell* (1648)

With Tragick sights this Play it doth begin,
But afterwards with mirth it sought to win. . . .
          —Thomas Meriton, *The Wandring Lover* (1658)

. . . we have invented, increas'd and perfected a more pleasant way
of writing for the Stage then was ever known to the Ancients or
Moderns of any Nation, which is Tragicomedie.
          —John Dryden, *Of Dramatick Poesie* (1668)

WHILE THE SUBJECT of tragicomedy brings new plays to the fore here,
it also calls for a salutary reprise. In the three most recent chapters we
have seen the contrasting genres of tragedy and comedy, but almost from
the outset we also have had glimpses of their convergence in tragicomedy.
Setting aside John Rowe's moralizing *Tragi-Comoedia*, which narrates the
real-life tragic ending that God presumably devised for a 1653 perform-
ance of the old comedy *Mucedorus*, we have noted the politico-journalistic
Scottish Politike Presbyter (1647) and the Man in the Moon's *New-Market-
Fayre*, parts 1 and 2 (1649), as well as Brathwaite's *Mercurius Britanicus*
(1641), Mercurius Melancholicus's *Craftie Cromwell* (1648) and Mercurius
Pragmaticus's *Crafty Crumwell* (1648), and *Cromwell's Conspiracy* (1660)—all
self-styled tragicomedies. In a chapter concerned with the military we
have seen Burnell's *Landgartha* (1639-40; published 1641), *The Female
Rebellion* (1657-59), perhaps by Birkhead, Chamberlaine's *Love's Victory*
(1658), and Howard's *Blind Lady* (1660), tragicomedies all. Having dis-
cussed Davenant's *Siege of Rhodes* (1656) as a new kind of show, perhaps as
a proto-opera, we should not lose sight of the fact that, with its military
threats dissolving into happiness, it may be viewed also as a late-blooming
sport of tragicomedy. In fact, the masquing tradition that undergirds *The
Siege of Rhodes* had itself for years drawn part of its effect from the sudden
displacement of evil by good. And the flowers of pastoralism that crop up
in various fields of drama throughout the period proved to be especially

suited to tragicomedy. We have noted the pastoral tragicomedies that William Lower brought forth as *The Enchanted Lovers* (1658) and *The Noble Ingratitude* (1659). We have seen Leonard Willan's romance-based *Astraea* (1651), where the noble heroine is constrained to seek "the humble Sanctuary of a *Pastorical* condition" in order "to avoid the Military Fury of debording Multitudes" (A4r). And we have glanced at Forde's *Love's Labyrinth* (1660), appearing at the end of our period but reaching back to Greene's Elizabethan *Menaphon* for its plot.

Especially noteworthy is the foreign-born *Faithful Shepherd* of Guarini, a turn-of-the-century tragicomedy that became newly available in English in 1647. Though the term *tragicomoedia* may be traced to Plautus, the focal point in modern discussions of Renaissance tragicomedy is generally Guarini's *Il pastor fido* (1590), together with his *Compendio della poesia tragicomica* (1601). In these works Guarini attempted to define, justify, and exemplify the genre. A half century later, in a translation of *Il pastor fido* called *The Faithful Shepherd*, Sir Richard Fanshawe reasserted the worth of Guarini's efforts to till a middle ground between tragedy and comedy, and at the same time he evinced his own fidelity to the royalist cause. Royalist motivation is apparent also in the 1647 publication of the Beaumont and Fletcher folio—which of course included, among other tragicomedies, Fletcher's Guarini-inspired *Faithfull Shepheardesse*. Writing back in the first decade of the century, Fletcher, for whom tragicomedy would prove the most characteristic form, provided not only an English model but also a preliminary guide to the genre. "A tragie-comedie is not so called in respect of mirth and killing," he explained, "but in respect it wants deaths, which is inough to make it no tragedie" (¶2v).

Throughout the first half of the century, on into the 1650s, and even for a while after the Restoration theaters opened, tragicomedy continued to be a dominant kind. During this period, of course, different writers tended to view tragicomedy differently. Thomas Meriton proclaimed of his *Wandring Lover,* "With *Tragick sights . . . it doth begin, / But afterwards with mirth it sought to win*" (31)—a modern version of which might be that tragicomedy is a tragedy with a happy ending. (An example more familiar than *The Wandring Lover* would be Nahum Tate's *Lear* [1681], which allows Cordelia to live.) On the other hand, one might argue that the word *tragicomedy* is made up of a noun and its modifier—that a tragicomedy is, in other words, a comedy whose happy ending is preceded, threatened, and qualified by tragic elements. (Witness, for instance, Shakespeare's *Cymbeline.*) The reverse presumably might be said of Margaret Cavendish's "come-tragedy" called *The Matrimonial Trouble,* which begins with fairly normal social subterfuge but ends when Sir Francis Inconstant murders his wife and dies with his mistress.[1] In most of the works that concern us, nonetheless, we shall find that a mix ("*Joy* and *Dolor*, . . . commixt") or a compound of comic and tragic elements has resulted in an intermediate form that is itself neither comic nor tragic. Drawing its chief sustenance from the worlds of the court and the prose romance (not only pastoral romance, but also sentimental and heroic romance); returning time and again to the subjects of love and honor, as well as to their common correlatives, war and politics; and often displaying a dash of satire, the midcentury tragicomedy is perhaps easier to recognize than it is to define.[2]

Though discussion is more the goal here than definition, a bit of both may be achieved by noting the title page that Fletcher's friend Jonson published with his *Workes* back in 1616 (figure 43; cf. figure 44). Represented here in two niches of an architectural construct are the contrasting female figures of Tragedy and Comedy. On a separate and centered perch, placed above and equidistant from the two, stands Tragicomedy. The fact that she is a smaller and therefore literally lesser figure than Tragedy and Comedy may represent an evaluation of the genre or suggest simply that Tragicomedy is the youngest of the three. In either case, her costume incorporates elements from the attire of the two larger figures. On her head she wears a crown, as does Tragedy, and on her feet she wears the socks of Comedy, indicating her connection with both. Two other figures stand more immediately beneath her: a satyr on the left, a shepherd on the right. That the natures of both contribute to her own nature is suggested by the satyr's staff and the shepherd's crook, both of which point toward her and reach well into her space. The satyr, of course, is a natural resident of pastoral realms, but in this instance, granted that the shepherd represents pastoralism, the satyr reminds us that the realm of Tragicomedy is not without satire.

When we turn to specific examples of tragicomedy on the earlier borders of our period—a quarter century after Jonson's folio—we find works by the poets Habington (*The Queene of Arragon*, 1640), Quarles (*The Virgin Widow*, 1641), and Suckling (whose *Aglaura* [1638] was equipped with alternative happy and sad endings). Some further examples that remained unpublished until well within our chronological frame include William Cartwright's *Lady-Errant* and *The Siedge* (both 1628-38; published 1651), the busy miscellanist Tatham's *Love Crowns the End* (1640; published 1657), and the comic writer Richard Brome's highly uncharacteristic *Love-Sick Court* (1632-40; published 1659).

---

[1]There being little new under the sun, it is not surprising that Anaxandrides, a much respected writer of Greek middle comedy, wrote a work called *Comoedotragoedia,* or that Alcaeus and Dinolochus, both comic poets, later produced plays with the same name (Ristine 8–9).   [2]Waith, nevertheless, offers a useful eight-part analysis of the genre (36–41).

Figure 43. Title page of Ben Jonson's *Workes* (1616). (By permission of the Folger Shakespeare Library.)

Figure 44. Frontispiece of James Shirley's *Six New Playes* (1653). (By permission of the Special Collections Library, Duke University.)

Also in the 1650s, as we have seen, Humphrey Moseley published a tidy little volume by James Shirley called *Six New Playes* (1653). The fact that three of the plays in this collection are tragicomedies parallels the fact that roughly half of Shirley's total output was devoted to the genre. This particular group of three (*The Imposture, The Doubtful Heir,* and *The Court Secret*) is therefore only a relatively small part of the evidence for the claim made by Shirley's friend Thomas Stanley: "So when immortall Fletcher left the Age, / Thou didst step in, and prop the sinking stage" (*Poems* 357). Whatever Jonsonian clouds he trailed, Shirley owed his greatest debt to Fletcher.

Among the tragicomedies in *Six New Playes, The Court Secret* probably has the strongest claim on our attention here, since it was "prepared for the Scene at BLACK-FRIERS" so late in 1642 that it could not be produced. Dedicated to William, Earl of Strafford, the son of King Charles's ill-fated friend, and apparently circulated in manuscript ("*it hath been read and honour'd with the Allowance of some men*" [A3r]), the play is neither especially Fletcherian nor exemplary of Shirley's best. In fact, the plot is resolutely confusing. Set in Madrid and peopled by the royal families of Spain and Portugal, it is centrally concerned with the facts that Carlo is known as Manuel and Julio as Carlo. Moreover, both of these youths, together with a third young man, Antonio, have at different times had as father or surrogate father a king, a duke, and a nobleman and *quondam* pirate. Complicating matters still more, the three young men are amorously involved with Maria, Isabella, and Clara. Intricacy and mystery are common traits in tragicomedies as well as in their cousins the prose romances, but Shirley's extensive and rather mechanical management of them in *The Court Secret* helps one to comprehend if not actually endorse a response recorded in Pepys's diary for 18 August 1664: "My wife says the play . . . is the worst that ever she saw in her life" (5:246).

Given the general nature of *The Court Secret,* manifested fairly enough by its tangled character deployment, a reader is likely to find it striking that a few unmistakable signs of midcentury English provenance occur in the fifth act. The most notable of these, perhaps, is an allusion made by the princess of Portugal to the people's tendency to "wa[i]ve their duty, / As they are prescrib'd by Faction, or lewd Pamphlets" (F4r-v).

Among the writers who turned to tragicomedy in the years after the theaters closed, naturally we reencounter a significant handful whose work in other genres we have noted previously. Besides Margaret Cavendish with her *Matrimonial Trouble*, these include Killigrew, Compton, Manuche, and Flecknoe—all of whose tragicomedies appear to be further products from the latter part of our period.

Killigrew turned out no fewer than four tragicomedies: *Cicilia and Clorinda,* parts 1 and 2 (1649-50), and *Bellamira Her Dream*, parts 1 and 2 (1652), all finally published in his imposing collection of 1664. Killigrew—whose travel to Spain we glimpsed in chapter 14—reported that he composed the first part of *Cicilia and Clorinda* in Turin, where he arrived in November 1649 on a mission from the young Charles to the Duke and Duchess of Savoy. If his recollection is accurate, the fledgling diplomat worked rapidly, for he next went on to visit Genoa, Leghorn, and Florence—he reports having written part 2 in Florence—before proceeding in mid-February 1650 to his destination of Venice, where he was to serve as English Resident for the next two years and where, he says, he wrote both parts of *Bellamira*.

Though aristocratic Savoyards, Romans, and Lombards play major roles in *Cicilia and Clorinda* (one wonders if the Duke and Duchess of Savoy were amused), of course the plays have their Englishry. One need not make much of the matter, but the fact that the most prominent of the works' two heroines bears the name Cicilia is apparently a belated compliment to one of Henrietta Maria's maids of honor, Cicilia Crofts, whom Killigrew had married in June 1636. The final act of part 2 concludes with a song against jealousy and Killigrew's note that it was written by "M. *Thomas Carew*, Cup-bearer to *Charles* the First; and sung in a Masque at *White-hall, Anno* 1633. And I presume to make use of it here, because in the first design, 'twas writ at my request upon a dispute held betwixt Mistress *Cicilia Crofts* and my self, where he was present" (309).[3] Killigrew dedicated part 1 of *Cicilia and Clorinda* to Lady Anne Villiers and part 2 to Lady Dorothy Sidney.

Whatever their ties to fact, all four of these Killigrew works are bound closely to the literary traditions of tragicomedy and prose romance. For *Cicilia and Clorinda* he was indebted in particular to Scudéry's *Artamène; ou, Le Grand Cyrus*. A reader's own acquaintance with the customary extreme length of such narratives may make Killigrew's presentation of comparable material in dramatic form seem almost economical. Too verbose for comfortable production on a stage—though of course, as we have seen, Killigrew's plays could be pruned—these tragicomedies were nevertheless a means of providing the matter of romance in an alternative form.[4]

Part 1 of *Cicilia and Clorinda* opens with Prince Orante of Lombardy,

---

[3]The song is included in Carew's *Poems* (1640) under the title "Foure Songs by Way of Chorus to a Play, at an Entertainment of the King and Queene, by My Lord Chamberlaine." Cicilia died on 1 January 1638 (Carew 59–60, 244–45). [4]Opinions on the subject of performability vary. For example, Visser writes: "It would seem that all the plays in the Killigrew folio were originally designed for the stage of a private playhouse, very possibly Blackfriars" (122). Whatever the case may be, Margaret Cavendish is indisputably correct in the following statement on her own work: *"for the Readers, the length of the Playes can be no trouble, nor inconveniency, because they may read as short or as long a time as they please, without any disrespect to the Writer"* (*Plays*, from the second of nine introductory passages labeled "To the Readers").

who appears to be a sort of Richardian villain. Dressed in black, *"with black Feathers, black Perriwig, his person . . . crooked and ugly, with a Dagger by his side"* (217), Orante exudes an ominous potential for evildoing that is effectively unleashed near the end of part 2. Lest we misperceive the matter, Killigrew has the nonpareil Cicilia specify that Orante's "person is not his crime, he made it not"; rather, "his soul is as crooked as his body" (220). Orante himself holds that "Nature, unkind Nature was my original enemy, who has not only set the world, but my self against my self" (243). For most of part 2, in any case, he eschews his villain's garb. From part 1, scene iv, through to his death in the final scene of the second play (or, one might say, the tenth act), he is, rather oddly, disguised as another sort of (presumably ugly) creature, namely *"an old Beggar-woman"* (271). The main business of the work, however, is love and honor (the subtitle of *Cicilia and Clorinda* is *Love in Arms*), and the wonder is that so much rhetorical analysis of both does so little to convey a sense of individual character. The most obvious explanation may be the right one: the ideal in art is generally underfeatured.

Bellamira Her Dream, parts 1 and 2, is a looser and more interesting pair of works. Here, in addition to complicated relations within the royal families and courts of Naples and Sicily, Killigrew assays a Calibanesque satyr, a couple of Spanish villains, and not one but three black Moors. The opening speech in part 1 confirms at once the work's affinity with prose narrative and the likelihood that, as written, it will be performed only in a reader's mind. It goes thus: " 'Tis for certain, the people at last have found a head, to whom *Clytus* is joyned; and I fear will follow the Revenge with as little mercy as the King shew'd his brother, our dead Master, the Royal *Ortho;* whose invasion though we neither counsell'd, nor assisted, yet such is the fate of Courts, when the People Arm against their Princes; which we have sadly proved, who now suffer that punishment which was meant to the Authors of the unnatural War" (467).

We soon learn that young Genorio, the displaced Prince of Sicily and Naples, is much beloved by the people, and that it is "indeed his Interest, ioyned with his noble Sisters, which these late years has kept the people quiet" (467). Though the drama provides no replay of contemporary English events, Killigrew surely was conscious of the effects he would create when he had the same speaker continue: "But the prince and *Palantus* [General of the Horse and perhaps reminiscent of Charles's greatest horseman, William Cavendish] being absent in these late disorders, our Friends have taken hold of the occasion, and prevailed so far, that the people are now Armed in the Name of our long lost prince [suggestive of the royalist uprisings projected in England from time to time]; which hope, joyned with their hatred of the present Government, has begot a danger" (468). Says Nigro, "Now or Never must we regain our Countrey, Prince and Liberty" (468).

Naturally everything is much more complicated than first meets the eye. For one thing, no Prince Genorio appears in the *dramatis personae*. For another, the current King's daughter, Bellamira, is our heroine, whom we soon find dressed as a boy and attempting to escape "this Beast the Multitude" (470). Fortunately, the dream that provides the title for both plays provides a sort of prophetic plot summary. Fortunately, too, it is interpreted by a hermit who says:

> *Your Highness walk by the Sea-side in a quiet Evening.*
> Signifies, the peace and security drawing to an end will be
> Interrupted by the unconstancy of the People; For the Evening
> Signifies the conclusion of a happiness.
> *And the cloud that landed a Knight in Forreign habit* [this stranger
>   proves to be Genorio], *who*
> *Kick'd up the sand in your Faces, in a dangerous proportion;*
> Signifies a forreign Invasion, which discontents will
> Countenance; for *Raising the dust* is raising the people, whose
> Hieroglyphique Sand and dust are, *Flying in your Faces,* is
> Rebellion, which knows no bound, nor respect . . .
> *The flying from the Dust, and loss of the King, in it;*
> My fears apprehend his loss in this Rebellion;
> *Your succour in a wood, where shepherds beat down the dust, with*
>   *boughes,*
> Signifies a happy relief in the faith and loyalty of the Countrey
>   People. . . .
>   [484]

In another scene but still within the opening act of part 1 we meet two of these young "Countrey People," presumably foresters, the brother and sister Pollidor and Phillora—who may remind readers of Shakespeare's country-bred princes disguised as Polydore and Cadwal. Killigrew specifies that "*The Scene must be a fine Land-skip, and a* Cave *must be in the Scene*" (475). Upon catching sight of the invading soldiers, Phillora, Miranda-like, exclaims, "An Army!—I never saw so glorious a sight before.—There is a beauteous horrour in't" (478). And when she sees Prince Leopold, she asks: "Is it a God or a Man?" (487). On the other hand, we have already been presented with her much more modish claim to have learned the "rules of Love and Honour" (481). A major recognition scene in act III of part 2 brings together a number of these main characters and is carefully introduced: "*The Scene opens and discovers a Prison, where* Pollidor *and* Phillora *appear next the Stage chained to a Ring . . . , and in a darker part of the Scene lies* Palantus *chained behinde them . . . ,* Bellamira *chained, and afar off in prospective other Prisoners and dead Carcases*" (542). The "*other Prisoners*" eventually prove to include two of the Moors, notably Arcus, who is really Prince Pyrrhus. At the end, Pollidor kills the crafty Spaniard Almanzor and is himself revealed to be a suitable match for the beauteous Bellamira, since he is really none other than the long-hidden and rightful Prince, Genorio.

Though the sheer number of words provided to convey the action of these plays is sobering, one can still understand why Killigrew became interested in penning them and why Lady Mary Villiers and Lady Anne Villiers—both of a family that had been close to the Stuarts since James's time—might have appreciated being named their dedicatees. Part 1 was for Mary, Duchess of Richmond and Lennox, daughter of the first great Duke of Buckingham (King Charles gave away the bride in 1637); and part 2 was for her cousin Anne, daughter of Buckingham's brother Christopher, who was wedded to the Earl of Sussex. Though Sussex himself was not exactly dependable politically, Killigrew clearly set his social sights high.

A far more private course was chosen by James Compton, the playwriting third Earl of Northampton, whom we have noted earlier as both a playwright and a translator of plays. Unfortunately, while the unnamed and unpublished tragicomedy that is apparently his handiwork comes down to us in two manuscripts, neither is complete. One breaks off after only a few pages (BL Add. MS 60278), and the other lacks both beginning and end(BL Add. MS 60279). Nevertheless, the play deserves notice as one of Compton's best. Recently and provisionally titled *Leontius, King of Cyprus*, it begins with news of the quelling of a rebellion and Leontius's particular delight because presumably he and his fellow Cypriots can now turn "from Mars to Hymen" (2r).[5] More specifically, he is ready to rejoice because of the anticipated union of his daughter Olinda and the noble young soldier Lucius, Prince of Corsica. The play is still just getting under way when, with gratitude and enthusiasm, the King turns to Garamantus, a powerful older soldier who has been instrumental in putting down the rebels. Invited by the King to say what reward he will have, Garamantus replies simply, "Nothing." Leontius then asks, "How's that?" The old soldier gives the dire response, "you haue disposed of all; / twas for Olinda that I tooke up armes" (2r). Worse yet, we soon overhear Garamantus's private resolve to "enjoy Olinda, and be revenged too" (2v). To achieve these goals he goes over to Leontius's foes, and war erupts again.

Compton's interest in military matters permeates the play. His embittered veteran Garamantus muses thus:

> how many winter nights haue I indured
> to ly in the feild when downy snow

---

[5]Wolf utilizes the title *Leontius, King of Cyprus* in his essay and also discusses authorship of the play. All quotations in this section come from BL Add. MS 60279.

hath covered the face of the frozen earth?
how many midday marches, when the Sun
hath cranyed the earth wth his
scorching beames?

[3v]

Though Garamantus sounds here like Shakespeare's Antony as described
by Octavius, he also can sound like an uncomic Falstaff. When a henchman
asks whether Garamantus's great reputation will suffer from his defection,
he replies, "What's honour but an aeriall sound"? (4r).[6] The second act
opens with a scene of bored soldiers on guard duty. One asks permission
to fetch his fiddle, and a kindly captain brings them all something to drink,
along with the admonition, "Drinke as long as you please, but see you
keepe yor selues sober" (5r). The third act opens with a contrasting group
of commanders on the night before an attack. Asks one, "shall we to make
vs valiant taste a cup of the best"? (11r).

Compton creates many characters and episodes here, but eventually he
unites the separated and long-suffering Lucius and Olinda and has the unhappy
Garamantus kill himself. He also finally presents explicitly a royalist message
that has been implicit throughout: "there can be no cause / to make a Subiect
lift his hand against his King" (30v). Though the final details in the
resolution of the play are now lost, the upbeat tone of the ending is perfectly
clear: King Leontius says, "This is proued a happy day" (31v). All in all,
and despite its damaged form, Compton's play deserves honorable notice
among the tragicomedies of its time.

Dedicated to Compton and his wife, Isabella, are two further tragi-
comedies called *The Just General* and *The Loyal Lovers*, both the work of
Compton's protégé Cosmo Manuche. Viewed side by side, this pair of plays
demonstrates not only some interesting continuities but also sufficient
contrasts to suggest, overall, a wider range than one might expect from even
a talented amateur. In *The Just General* (1652), a play he describes as "*the
first I wrote*" (A3r), the former Major Manuche was moved to present a
military protagonist named Bellicosus. Presumably we are whisked away
to far-off Sicily, but the fact is that Manuche never really allows us to forget
the England of his day. The "Valiant General," for instance, is said to have
"to[o] much honesty, mixt with knowledg, to / Condescend, to any thing
can prejudice / Our King and Country" (1). This statement contains noth-
ing specifically English and yet under the circumstances invites a dual
perception. We soon learn that young King Amasius is melancholy because
a letter from General Bellicosus has discouraged his love for Aurelia "as a
match too far beneath him" (1). This conceivably may recall the new young

---

[6]At this point BL Add. MS 60278 breaks off.

English King's well-known penchant for amorous action. Recorded in the Stationers' Register on 29 November 1651, only a couple of months after Charles's defeat at Worcester, the play has its king wonder in soliloquy, "What are we Princes, bove other men, more then in, / Our care?" (3). Such elements are conventional, of course, and the play goes its own way, complete with lively tavern scenes and a comic subplot involving some would-be soldiers (for instance, Captain Thunder) and a usurer's foolish son (young Goldcalf, a character type left over from Jacobean city comedy). The latter is in pursuit of the proud and wicked heiress Artesia, who in turn, jealous of the King's beloved, Aurelia, would like that lady to be murdered. When Aurelia prudently disappears, the King resolves to disguise himself as a pilgrim to go find her.

Manuche's use of a disguised prince is obviously another device with many precedents in earlier English drama. It had proved to be an element both interesting in itself and useful for exploring the relationship between the king as man and the king as symbol. On the other hand, such figuring was by no means totally fictive. For one thing, back in 1623 Charles I, when Prince of Wales, had assumed a false name and beard at the outset of his madcap Spanish wooing expedition. More immediately, Prince Rupert was reported to have disguised himself occasionally as an apple woman. Prince James actually escaped to Holland clad in women's clothes in 1648, and Prince Charles is said to have found that various disguises, including that of a woman, made possible his survival after Worcester in 1651. For good measure one might add that Sir George Booth, after his failed rebellion in 1659, was captured at Newport Pagnell in female garb. The fact that living parallels are pertinent here, moreover, we may deduce from the words of the noble Antonio, who comes seeking the young King. His procedure is to examine every young man, even as he realizes that perhaps he should be examining women too, "It being now in fashion for Princes to make escapes in / Womens habit" (46). So also thought one Captain Macey, who during the period of the royal post-Worcester flight mistook one of the daughters of Sir Hugh Wyndham for Charles (Eva Scott 262).

Manuche's Aurelia, meanwhile, has turned shepherdess, and as such she encounters a couple of singing shepherds named Strephon and Amintor. When the presumed pilgrim encounters the presumed shepherdess, he thinks her a goddess. Antonio, on the other hand, wonders if she may be Amasius himself:

> . . . Well my young King, if I
> Do chance to find you in the smock habit, I
> May hap to make you look red i'th cheeks,
> Without the help of Spanish paper.
> You gods, I'l pray my beads o'r twice a day

The more, should this stray shepheardess
But prove my King.

[47]

Those beads, one might note, are a rather Roman touch.

As the play draws to a close, Artesia and her accomplice (Delirus, son of the General) repent and marry, but the Just General himself, now serving as King, sentences them both to death. In the final Big Scene, for which the setting is specified to be "*a black Stage*" (63), we find the executioner, the condemned, and assorted others to whom the now-returned King Amasius reveals himself and to whom he presents the lost Aurelia "*in rich attire*" (65). The Just General weeps for joy, the threatened deaths are averted, and all ends happily.

The Loyal Lovers (1652) is a very different sort of work. Here again, nevertheless, we find miscellaneous military men (Manuche introduces himself as a "Major" on the title page), some lively tavern dialogue, a dupe who gets his comeuppance, a heroine who takes flight and disappears, some threatened executions, and villains who reform. Despite such parallels with *The Just General*, however, this play—probably Manuche's best—creates an altogether different effect. For one thing, it is set not in romance-land but in Amsterdam. Equally important, its "loyal" characters are contrasted to characters who are scornfully called Gripe-Man and Sodome. The former is a "Committee-man" ("his griping way of gain" [27] calls to mind Sheppard's *Committee-Man Curried*), and the latter, "One of the Synod," is a "zealous brother troubled with rebellious flesh" (*Loyal Lovers* 5). Langbaine comments on both this pair and another one: "In this Play our Author lashes the old Committee-men, and their Informers, in the Persons of *Gripeman* and *Sodom*, and I believe he meant to expose *Hugh Peters*'s Adventure with the Butcher's Wife of St. *Sepulcher*'s, with his Revenge thereupon, under the Characters of Phanaticus and *Fly-blow*. If my Conjecture prove true I hope no sober man will be angry, that *Peters* should be personated on the Stage, who himself had ridicul'd others, when he acted the Clown's part in *Shakespear*'s Company of Comedians, as I have read in Dr. *Young*'s Relation of his Life" (*Account* 339).[7]

Hugh Peters's prominence as virtual jailer to Charles I before his death, and later as chaplain to the Council of State, with lodgings at Whitehall, had certainly led to his becoming a frequent satiric and comic butt. Eventually it would occasion an entire jestbook devoted to him: *The Tales and Jests of Hugh Peters* (1660). In 1652, therefore, he may well have proved a tempting target for a royalist playwright. In any case, "*Phanaticus a Priest*"

---

[7]Langbaine refers to William Yonge's scurrilous *England's Shame; or, The Unmasking of a Politic Atheist*, published in 1663, three years after Peters's execution.

and "*Fly-blow a Butcher*" are "personated"—that term again—in a tavern skit that is rehearsed within Manuche's play. Whatever theatrical history we may be tempted to extract from the situation and the site, the temper of the skit may be indicated by noting that the main stage property it requires is "*a Bulls pizil*" (*Loyal Lovers* 17).

Gripe-Man the committeeman, a more central character, is the father of the heroine, Letesia. In the opening scene we learn that his creature Sent-Well has attempted to entrap old Firmstand, though "not a syllable, tending to th' States abuse, / I e're could hear him utter." No matter, replies Gripe-Man, "*Perjurus* and you shall swear." And off goes Gripe-Man to see "about sharing the Widdows goods / Wee caus'd to be plundered" (3).

The central story concerns not just the lovers Letesia and Adrastus but also Adrastus's "Loyal Comrades" Albinus and Symphronio. That the titular adjective *loyal* is likely to have layered meanings is obvious even before Albinus (his name suggestive of "Albion") vows to Adrastus, "if I faile to serve Thee, to my last drop of blood, / My miserie enforce mee take up arms against / My naturall Prince" (8). An old nurse is described somewhat awkwardly as one "whose milk / Innocent, as the Livory it wore, still sympathized / With Loyal bloud" (47). Even the villain's repentance is couched in political terms. Gripe-Man exclaims,

> My horrid treason against my just, and sacred Prince for vengeance cal's aloud.
> The ruine of my Country, which (to my best of power) I have been actor in. [44]

At the close of the play some threatened executions are averted, the loyal lovers are paired off, the main villains repent, and Gripe-Man, unlikely though it may seem, invites everyone home for a feast. Langbaine concluded that the play might "pass Muster amongst those of the third Rate" and that Manuche's "Muse was *travesté en Cavileer*" (*Account* 339).

The muse of the prolific Richard Flecknoe was comparably attired. Flecknoe's tragicomedies, however, are more simple, careful, controlled, and rarified—and also more pretentious. Flecknoe claimed that his *Temple of Friendship*, a tragicomedy in progress, was designed to be a ravishing depiction of friendship that presented "Ladies, after the like example of the Queen and her Ladies here formerly, & of the greatest Ladies & Princesses in *Spain, France[,] Flandres*, and else where, [because] I thought none reasonably could take exceptions, nor think me too ambitious in't, especially I having been long Time train'd up & conversant in the Courts of the greatest Queens and Princesses in *Europe*" (*Relation* 147). The fact is that Flecknoe had managed to encounter a good many foreign ladies because, as a good Catholic and perhaps a priest, he had found it advisable to leave England for a number of years.

Love's Dominion, his tragicomedy that now comes before us, was originally created for Beatrix de Cusance, Duchess of Lorraine.[8] All the more startling, therefore, is Flecknoe's dedication of the 1654 printed version to Oliver Cromwell's favorite daughter, Lady Elizabeth ("Bettie") Claypole. Apparently that lady had addressed him positively concerning this work— or possibly an earlier form of it (now lost) entitled *Love in Its Infancy* (1650). When printed in 1654, in any case, it was described on its title page not as a tragicomedy but more hedgingly as "A Dramatique Piece, Full of Excellent Moralitie; Written as a Pattern for the *REFORMED STAGE*." Oliver's first Parliament opened in September of that year, and Bettie's husband, John, as protectoral Master of the Horse, rode immediately behind his father-in-law's coach. Flecknoe must have asked himself who could be better than a princess of the Protectorate to win sympathy for performances on a "reformed" stage. Nevertheless, he cautiously takes pains to reassure her that "*I dare not Interest you in its more publique Representation, not knowing how the palat of the Time may relish such Things yet, which, till it was disgusted with them, was formerly numbred amongst its chiefest Dainties, and is so much longed for still, by all the nobler and better sort, as could it but be effected by your mediation, you, should infinitely oblige them all*" (A3r-v). *Noblesse oblige*, indeed!

In his preface Flecknoe goes on to argue that the theater is capable of being "an Academy of choicest language, a Map of the best manners and behaviour; and finally a Mirrour representing the Actions of men (and therefore by a better title than that of *Plays*, called *Actions* by some, and *Operaes*, or works, by others) proposing the good for our example and imitation, and the bad to deter us from it, and for the avoiding it" (A4r). Such fadoodling with terminology (more famously exemplified in Davenant's publications) is followed here by a passage that, with a boldness uncharacteristic of Flecknoe, transmits a sense that the times might be changing in the earlier 1650s. He writes of the period as one

> when we are rid of our sullen Masters, of so *Cynick* a devotion, as they would enforce men to serve *God* spight of *Humanity,* and shake us into Religion with fear and trembling, not remembering that we are oftner invited to it (in the *Holy Scripture*) with rejoycing and jubilation, chearfulness having been always accounted the exterior mark of true piety and devotion. And it is that for my part I labour to introduce, as a thing no doubt more acceptable to Almighty God . . . than to see us go about his service with a sad countenance, and sullen chear. [A5r-v]

---

[8]Flecknoe enjoyed the patronage of the Duchess for several years (Mayer, in Flecknoe, *Prose Characters* xl, lxi).

Flecknoe then offers some comments on *Love's Dominion* that are as interesting as the play itself. In fact, they constitute something of a preview of issues that would be explored later in Dryden's essay *Of Dramatick Poesie:* "For the *Plot,* I have taken a middle way betwixt the *French* and *English,* the one making it too plain, and the other too confused and intrigued. I imagining one of these pieces not like a simple *Alley,* where one walks alwayes in the same track; nor as a *Wilderness,* where one is lost through so many diversions: but as a pleasant *Garden* composed of divers walks, with variety and uniformity so mixt, as one part handsomly introduces you into another, & every one has correspondence amongst themselves, and to the whole" (A7r). As he draws the preface to a close, Flecknoe continues to provide evidence that he is a very conscious creator. He writes, "I have observed all the Rules of Art in handling it, the Scene at *Amathonte* in *Cypres,* never going out of view, nor out of the Precincts of *Love's Temple;* Continued to the End of the Act, to make an intire piece of every Act, and some distinction (by cleering of the Stage) betwixt the end of an Act, and the ending of a Scene; The Time only from Morning till Night" (A7v).

The play itself offers unity of place, unity of time ("from Morning till Night"), and unity of action (after six months of residence all strangers on the island must swear they love someone there or leave—and the lovely Bellinda's time is up). Given Flecknoe's Catholic background, one may understand why his high priest of Love, the Governor of Cypres, is supposed to appear "in Pontificial Ornaments, a Tyara on his head, &c." (A8r), and even why the play opens with Love's priests "*lustrating the place*" with "*Asperges and Thuribles.*" These striking details are soon contained a bit when the high priest launches into a long speech on platonic love: "It's *outre tendance* most commonly falls fowl / O'th' Body in its passage towards the Soul" (B6v). Still, it is noteworthy that Flecknoe thought all this a plausible way to impress Cromwell's daughter.

It is interesting also that to a far greater degree than most playwrights, Flecknoe is overtly concerned with the look of his play. Euphanes is clad "like your antient Heroes in Military array, a Javelin in his hand" (A8r), and Philena appears "in long Taffata robes to the mid-legg, with a Tynsel mantle of different colour, fastned on the one shoulder, and hanging down under the other arm, silver'd Buskins with falls of white Tynsel on either side; . . . with a Coronet of Roses or Mirtle, white gloves, a collar of Pearl about her neck, &c." (A8r-v). All this helps one visualize the world in which Flecknoe's action is supposed to take place. The opening setting is "*a Boscage, with the adjacent Prospect of a delightfull Valley, here and there Inhabited, with a magnificent Temple afar off discovered*" (B1r). For any observer of a performance of *Love's Dominion,* furthermore, the visual communication presumably would be enhanced by the inset "Pastoral shew, or Rural masque" performed by "neighbour Swains" and intended, "in Dance, to personate / The Emblem of a Lovers state" (F4r). Indeed, the aural effects throughout were important to Flecknoe. Skillful lutenist and singer that he was, he calls for frequent songs.

All in all, *Love's Dominion* has an admirable cleanness of story line, clarity of writing, and carefulness of presentation, as well as a singleness of subject—the nature of love. Though few plays could live up to such outsized authorial pride as Flecknoe's public persona projects, *Love's Dominion* is one of the better English pastoral dramas of the day.

Following the text of the play in the 1654 volume, Flecknoe appends the statement that "*if ever it be acted, I intitle my right in it, (not departing in the mean time with my right of altering my mind) [to] Mr.* Will. Beeston, *who by Reason of his long Practice and Experience in this way, as also for having brought up most of the Actors extant, I think the fittest Man for this Charge and Imployment*" (80).[9] As it turns out, Flecknoe did see the play produced by Davenant at the Duke's Theatre in 1664. Scholars of our own time who delight in evidence of textual uncertainties might take note, therefore, that a play that began abroad, very probably in French, and later became known as *Love in Its Infancy* and then developed into *Love's Dominion*, eventually came to the boards of the Duke's Company as *Love's Kingdom*. Finally—supposedly finally—still further revision of the work was manifested in volumes published in 1664 and 1674.

These later volumes brought the presumably noble reader much more than the text (or *a* text) of a play. Besides a dedication to that inveterate lover of drama William Cavendish, Marquess of Newcastle, Flecknoe provided a self-righteous explanation and justification of his dramatic goals and also *A Short Discourse of the English Stage*. Because the latter makes available to us more thoroughly and directly than any other single document the theatrical perspective of one of our dramatists regarding the whole sweep of prior drama in early modern England, it is included here as Appendix B. Considering its appraisals of Shakespeare, Jonson, and Beaumont and Fletcher, its statement on the *modus operandi* of Burbage, and its views on theatrical scenes and machines, it is a discourse worth knowing. It may even be, as Langbaine observed, the most valuable thing Flecknoe ever wrote (*Account* 203).

Without belaboring the question of quality, one should acknowledge also the existence of Flecknoe's *Erminia* (1661), a tragicomedy written we

---

[9]The King and Queen's Young Company (alias "Beeston's Boys") was a prewar troupe comprised mainly of boy actors who performed at the Cockpit (or Phoenix). This passage appears in BL 643.B.27, a copy that has a "Preface to the Reader" rather than the Claypole dedication in BL 162.C.48.

know not when and printed "to pass to private hands, not to the publick" (A3r). For this play the author explicitly claims a mooring in historical fact. In his dedication to Lady Southcote, Flecknoe avows, "*From you I took the pattern of the Plot; from you the spirit of writing it; nor am I ever more Poet, then when I am with you at* Mestham." Recalling the hospitality he has received there, Flecknoe goes on to assure his dedicatee that "*Your green Walks are my* Parnassus" (A2r-v). An old Catholic family, the Southcotes had acquired the seat of Albery in the parish of Merstham, down in Surrey, back in Elizabeth's time. In the time of Charles I they equipped their only male scion, John, with horses and arms for himself and two or three others and sent him off to fight for the King.[10] Somewhat undercutting Flecknoe's devotion to Lady Southcote in 1661, however, is his later assertion that a subsequent version of the play, slightly camouflaged as *Emilia* (1672), was inspired by none other than Margaret Cavendish, Duchess of Newcastle. Moreover, after the death of the latter in December 1673, Flecknoe made bold to address the same avowal to the Duchess of Monmouth.[11]

Lest anyone puzzle over the meaning of the play's original name, *Erminia*, Flecknoe has his heroine herself comment on the great caution required of women who wish to preserve "their Ermine purity" (8).[12] Shortly after she enters, in fact, Erminia gives a speech on wives who live honorably when their husbands are away (her husband is General Cleander), and toward the middle of the play Cleander enters disguised as an Ethiope, the better to eye his wife's doings. He decides that Erminia, though sorely tempted by aristocratic wooers, "is as white . . . / as is her name or innocence it self" (50). She has yet to surmount the news of his own supposed death, however. This being a tragicomedy, moreover, we have yet to find him drawing his sword to kill both her and her presumed lover (a lovely "boy" who is actually the Princess Cyrena of Argos). Then again, this being a reasonably neat tragicomedy, Princess Cyrena is soon matched with an appropriate prince, and in the final speech the now-enlightened Cleander praises his newly vindicated, ermine-pure wife.[13]

All things considered, it is clear that Flecknoe never really arrived at Parnassus. Langbaine had it right: Flecknoe knew the nobility better than the muses (*Account* 199). As a matter of fact, Flecknoe himself had it right, too. In a striking passage of self-appraisal he acknowledges, "For his Minde 'tis neither very good, nor very bad" (*Heroick Portraits* I2r). As an inveterate

---

[10]Morris provides a great deal of relevant information on the Southcotes—including the fact that John Southcote somehow came into particular favor with Cromwell's daughter Elizabeth (393). [11]These later attributions are explored by Harold Love ("Richard Flecknoe"). [12]One might compare the playwright Fountain's "This Ermyne will not be / Perswaded from the whiteness she so loves" (6–7). [13]Of *Emilia*, Canfield writes, "the most interesting additions are perhaps veiled allusions to Charles II" (4).

dilettante, he strove for pleasure, not profundity, and as a writer bent on survival, he tossed endless bouquets to people of position.[14] Whatever one may think of his variously manifested social opportunism, Flecknoe was not only a decent writer of conventional, quasi-courtly tragicomedy but also the first person ever to attempt an historical survey of English drama. From both of these perspectives he is interestingly different from that Flecknoe who is known to readers only through the satire of Marvell and Dryden.

Besides the several foregoing tragicomedies, whose fairly busy authors we have encountered previously as writers of other genres (Shirley, Killigrew, Compton, Manuche, and Flecknoe), some miscellaneous additional plays also invite attention. Each has its individual attractions and weaknesses, most offer more by way of literary interest than literary merit, and together all serve to demonstrate that the breadth of the tragicomic genre in its latter days was greater than most of us have realized. To facilitate discussion of the group, we shall designate two that may be taken for the extremes of "romance" and "history" within the genre (unstable though such terms may be), and then range some further exemplars between them.

The White Ethiopian (ca. 1650), an anonymous work that comes down to us in manuscript, probably a holograph, takes its plot directly from the famed *Aethiopica* of Heliodorus. In chapter 2 we noted briefly Gough's *Strange Discovery* (1640), another specific and more or less contemporary return to the old story of Theagenes and Chariclea. The fact is that Heliodoran (like Sidneian) elements are to be found scattered throughout the plays of the period. The present specimen may be the worst of them all. Obviously the work of an amateur, it is so unconcerned with the nature of actable drama that it assigns the thwarted lovers' ostensible father, old Calasiris, a speech that goes on for forty-eight pages (36v-60r). Worse, the couplet form chosen by the author sometimes lures him over the brink of folly—as in "Chariclea had a Cabbin, in yᵉ ship / where only wᵗʰ her nurce shee mou'd the lipp" (65r). Though interesting for such elements as its early and extended use of couplets in drama, its detailed stage directions, and a prologue and epilogue that assume performance (the speaker of the prologue is instructed to point to the ladies), *The White Ethiopian* is sufficiently lame to inspire readerly gratitude that the manuscript as we have it ends with "Scena decima octava" of the fourth act. In this version of their story, Theagenes and Chariclea are forever left imprisoned and in chains, forever to be blessed.

In contrast, *The True Tragi-Comedie Formarly Acted at Court & Now Reui[u]ed by ane Eie Witnes* (ca. 1654) is a cold-eyed work far removed from

---

[14]Love lists twenty-seven poems that Flecknoe dedicated to members of the Cavendish family alone, apparently beginning with "Consolation to the Lord of Newcastle, in These Calamitous Times," published in 1653 ("Richard Flecknoe" 47-49).

any realm of romance. Indeed, one might argue that despite the play's title, this tragicomedy is "really" something else. Typological perils are pandemic, however, and taking the author's labeling seriously is probably the surest way to appreciate the ironies of the whole. An anonymous work in manuscript—though Lois Potter in her edition has attributed it to Francis Osborne—*The True Tragi-Comedie* is unique for turning back to the time of King James and offering a direct representation of actual persons at the Jacobean court. In particular, it treats events leading up to the Overbury scandal.[15] Both in the play itself and in some character sketches ("characters or pictures" [1v]) preceding it, the author appears to take bitter satisfaction in the firsthandedness of his knowledge. He assures us, for instance, that Lady Frances Howard's second bridegroom-to-be, Robert Carr, Earl of Somerset, was among the first to frizzle and powder his hair, and that he became King James's "Minnion" not because "of any humor resident in him" but because he was a sheep possessed of "flece" that was coveted by the royal shepherd (3v-4r). Scholars who debate whether James was a practicing homosexual should be aware of the evidence of this play. On the other hand, James is credited here with even more terrible malfeasance: "if I am not foulely mistakne," the playwright observes, "the Late war grew from the so-far-dilated extent & marciles tirany of this Court" (9v). Not that Osborne (assuming it was he) holds any brief for the Puritan opposition: "now thay haue had thair full swing in reformetion, I wold faine know whoe is the better for it" (10v). Potter suggests that by placing the blame elsewhere, the dramatist is in effect lightening the burden on Charles's shoulders (" 'True Tragicomedies' " 208).[16] For our purposes, furthermore, his outlook also manifests itself interestingly in the remark that at midcentury the drama was hurting badly: "the Stage . . . lies now undar a heuier censure, then any wise nation euer loaded her with" (18r).[17]

The True Tragi-Comedie opens with some salvos that include depiction of the Scots as "insatient," "nasty," "mangie" beggars (19r, 21r) and King James himself as crude ("still grabling in his Codpiece" [20r]). The action gets under way with a discussion between Lady Frances and her sister

---

[15]Sir Thomas Overbury was a friend and mentor of Robert Carr, a handsome young Scot who became one of the favorites of King James. Overbury opposed Carr's proposed marriage to Frances, Countess of Essex, who in the play is not yet divorced from young Robert Devereux, third Earl of Essex. Sent to the Tower on the flimsy grounds that he had declined diplomatic appointment, Overbury was there poisoned slowly by agents of the Countess. Eventually four accomplices were hanged, but Frances and her husband Carr, both convicted, were pardoned.   [16]Probably significant is the fact that in his *Historical Memoires* Osborne refers to Charles as James's "more wise and innocent successour" (4).   [17]Other observations by the author on drama include his admission that "I amonst others hissed Seianus of the stage, yet after sate it out, not only patiantly, but with content, & admiration" (*True Tragi-Comedie* 1v).

about the shortcomings of Frances's first bridegroom, young Robert Devereux, third Earl of Essex, who is reputedly no more a man than "the bake of your hand" (22r). Soon after the wedding, Frances's mother (Kate, Countess of Suffolk) enters, anxious to learn "how many courses" Essex has "made at the Ring Prince harry tooke so oftne at Richmond" (23v). Thence the gossip-laden old story runs its scabrous course, carrying along also an account of the sexual adventures of the Duke of Lennox and the Countess of Hartford; incorporating though not emphasizing Sir Thomas Overbury's advice to Somerset not to marry Frances; providing a conversation between King James and his next favorite, George Villiers, about sexual preference (says George, "I confess your Matie hath conuinc'd my reson / Though my Sense stands stiffest for feminin Embraces" [42v]); and closing with the nuptials of Frances and Carr—and the acknowledgment that further pursuit of the story might "proue a Tragedy" (46r). Not surprisingly, given its subject and the nature of its genre, *The True Tragi-Comedie* proves to be our tragicomedy that is closest to historical fact, however distorted. It is also the sourest and darkest. As the author has rationalized in his prologue, "within a Court whoe spreds his Scenes, must be Tangled with filth, or baser flatterie, & he that harbors all the truth he meets cannot auoid the fouling of his Sheets" (18v). Turning back some forty years for his material, the hard-bitten old "Eie Witnes" has produced a play that is, in Potter's words, and for all its voyeuristic appeal, "impossible to act and difficult to read" ("'True Tragicomedies'" 209).

The only other tragicomedy in this group that comes close to *The True Tragi-Comedie* in toughness of tone is *The Governor.* Likewise surviving only in manuscript, it poses problems of both dating and authorship.[18] While the manuscript is specifically inscribed 1656, a play by the same name was performed in 1636 by the King's Men, and the same or another of the same title was registered with the Stationers on 9 September 1653 (Briscoe 1:428). Was there only one play with this name, or were there two or three? That the 1656 text (or the text it was based on) was originally composed a number of years earlier has seemed plausible to some students because of the play's concern with soldiering in the Low Countries. One should not forget, however, that a fair number of Englishmen who left their homeland during the century's middle decades found themselves marching to different drums on the Continent. Then again, what is one to make of the mild handling here of the Puritans? Little animus may be found in the remark

---

[18]As for who wrote *The Governor,* one Sir Cornelius Formido has been suggested because that name appears in the Stationers' Register entry (Briscoe 1:428). Unfortunately the information avails us little because we know nothing else of the man. Neither does the inscription of the name "Samuel" on the title page of the manuscript do much to help, even though the hand does resemble one of those used subsequently in the text.

of one Vigetto, a citizen, that "I have lost as little of this story as a Puritan does / of a sermon when he writes short hand" (37v). Nor does the even-handed presentation of the all-Spanish (and therefore all-Catholic) *dramatis personae* help much with dating. To be sure, we are given a cynical account of how the unscrupulous Governor of Barcelona, Nicholaio, together with an abbot of the church, uses religion as an "excellent Cloake," specifically recognizing what advantages inhere in having a bishop available "wth power to iudge in secular affaires" (43r). The author is more concerned with Nicholaio's personal wickedness, however, than with failings of church or state. In fact, one of the Governor's tools, a quack doctor ("I am sure . . . wee kill more then wee cure" [14r]), comes in for about as much implicit criticism as the bishop. Whatever one decides to make of such straws in the wind, they suggest that the play does not spring very obviously from any recognizable midcentury milieu.

The action of *The Governor* is somewhat garbled in the manuscript, but plain as rain is the fact that it concerns the titular hero's—Nicholaio's—attempt to bed Sabina, the dalliance-prone wife of a gentleman named Facundo. Sabina assures her wooer, "I am a Proteus to serve yor ends" (19v). She also has the presence of mind to bind the Governor to a set of precoital vows. Before actually giving herself to him, moreover, Sabina decides not to carry through with their agreement, whereupon Nicholaio has her cast down into a dismal vault in his house. Afterward she appears with a broken arm in a "scarfe" (47r). One of the play's most interesting elements, also conveyed to a reader with the aid of stage directions, is a pair of vaults, the entrances to which are situated on opposite sides of the stage. During the course of the play these vaults are presumably connected by means of a tunnel dug by some of the good characters, making possible at last the rescue and "draweing vpp" of the now-reformed "treasure" Sabina (42v). Long and wordy though the play is, its basic plot is simple, and its tone urban and hard for a tragicomedy. On the other hand, it has both the tragic potential and the comic ending that the author most likely had in mind when affixing to his work the label of "Tragi Comedy."

One might be forgiven for not thinking of the tragicomic label at all when first reading of a play called *Titus; or, The Palme of Christian Courage*, and especially after learning that it was designed "To be exhibited by the Schollars of the Society of IESVS, at Kilkenny, *Anno Domini* 1644." Here, one might suppose, is another martyr play—such as *Herminigildus*, perhaps. But appearances can be deceiving. All we have for evidence, unfortunately, is a printed scenario, not a text, but the five-act, scene-by-scene scenario is sufficient to show beyond doubt that the completed play was a tragicomedy. Moreover, it clearly was both relatable to historical fact (no surprise there) and also (a surprise, indeed) equipped with a Japanese hero. The concise

opening line of the play's epitome conveys clearly that the full version of
the prologue told how "Divine love extolleth the *Iaponian's* courage."[19] In
an "argument" given on the title page, furthermore, we find that the play
was set in Bungo, which at one time was a province in Kyushu, Japan. The
entire argument reads thus: "*Titus* a noble Gentleman more illustrious for his
Christian courage, then parentage: was sollicited by the King of *Bungo*, to
desert his Religion by severall, most artificious infernall plots, all which he
sleighted and dashed with his invincible courage, and generous Christian
resolution, whereat the King amazed, restored him to his liberty, wife and
children, and granted him the freedome of his Religion, with all his lands
and possessions of which before he was bereaved as traitor to the Crowne."

Whether or not *Titus* "personates" an actual historical figure, it helps
to know that early Japanese converts to Catholicism "were regularly given
a 'Christian' name at baptism" (Drummond 41). But why Titus? Of a
handful of ancient Tituses we might be expected to call to mind, the most
likely is the one said to have received a letter from Paul. Whatever Pauline
author really wrote them, the major concern of all three of the so-called
pastoral epistles (i.e., 1, 2 Timothy and Titus) is the threat that heretical
teaching poses for Christianity. More specifically, the mission of the New
Testament Titus, living on the island of Crete, surrounded by immoral
Cretans, is to be a blameless Christian model who holds fast to the Holy
Word, both exhorting the native naysayers and persuading them of the
rightness of his stand (Titus 1.9). Not surprisingly, in other words, the name
of the play's hero is an important key to the parable he enacts.

Conjectures about dating the action in *Titus* are not much aided by the
author's inclusion of a cameo appearance by the ghost of St. Francis Xavier,
despite the fact that Xavier (1506-52), an apostle to Japan (he arrived there
in August 1549), was not canonized until 1622. Far more helpful is a
somewhat confused note on the title page of the scenario. Here we find
that the play was based on a work by François Solier (1558-1628), a French
Jesuit who produced a two-volume *Histoire ecclésiastique des isles et royaumes
du Iapon* (1627-29). Difficult of access though this source is today, tracking
it proves fruitful, for in it Solier not only addresses Xavier as the dedicatee
of his first volume, but also includes in his second volume a chapter called
"Des Roiaumes de Bungo, Chiungocù & Xicocù, & autres nouuelement
découuerts." More precisely, he finds occasion there to memorialize one
"Tite Gentil-homme, & ses vertus" (2.639). Under the date 1620 we are
first introduced to an unnamed Japanese Christian who quickly abandons
his faith as soon as he is subjected to political threats. Set against such a
foil, obviously, Titus's virtue is supposed to shine all the brighter. When

---

[19]Quoted from the verso of the scenario's title page.

Solier's Titus is urged to forsake his Christianity, he responds, "I'attends & desire de plus grandes peines qu'on ne me propose." And when the Prince threatens to put him in the chains of a slave, he replies that for him "Ce sera ma vraie & plus douce liberté." Such constancy does Solier's Titus display, in fact, that "diuine majesté" is moved to provide miraculous signs of approval. On the night when Titus is taken before his judges, the bedchamber of his wife is somehow illumined with blazing torches that are held by no human hands, and as the next day dawns, the servants of his household see torches moving here and there on his rooftop.

It is against such a background, then, that the Emperor in the play "commands the edict against Christians to bee proclaimed."[20] Historically speaking, this edict is but one of a series stretching back into the preceding century. In 1588 a particularly cruel one, effective throughout all of Japan, was issued by one Cambacundono (Solier 1.602ff.). A well-known one of 1614 articulated the need to expel both foreign missionaries and all they had converted. Not until 1622, however, did the so-called Great Martyrdom (thirty persons beheaded, twenty-five burned) take place at Nagasaki (Cary 1:203). Though Solier's *Histoire* extends only to 1624, the period between 1623 and 1637 saw the number of martyred Christians climb to about thirteen hundred. Thus the man named Titus in this play—a work subtitled *The Palme of Christian Courage*—is but a single sterling example of a courageous commitment made over a period of time by "a large segment of the Japanese population," a commitment that "to the astonishment and consternation of the authorities . . . created heroes of steadfastness" (Drummond 103). Drummond goes so far as to say that "The proportion of martyrs in comparison with the total Christian population is probably greater than that of any other period or place in the history of the church" (104).

The joyous, miraculous, and indeed tragicomic twist at the close of the play *Titus* is that when the would-be martyr will not recant, his persecutor relents. That a group of schoolboys on the island of Ireland might be found enacting such an upbeat ending in 1644, demonstrating the happy results of diehard commitment despite terrible pressure, is hardly surprising. It must have been a bracing sight to see the brave and long-suffering Titus regain not only his liberty but also his lands and freedom of religion. Unfortunately, neither in Japan nor in Ireland was suffering rewarded so well as it could be on the stage.

Lying much closer to *The White Ethiopian* in the spectrum that stretches between that play and *The True Tragi-Comedie, The Governor,* or even *Titus* is Thomas Meriton's *Wandring Lover* (1658). With all due caution one may say that Meriton's play is bad. Dedicated to his friend Francis Wright, *The*

---

[20]Quoted from the first page of the scenario.

Wandring Lover—labeled a "TRAGY-COMEDIE" on its title page—is the third play that young Meriton attempted. His first two efforts, kept "private," were a comedy called *The Severall Affairs* and a "Romance" called *The Chast Virgin*.[21] The wanderer of the play is one Euphrates, lover of a woman unfortunately called Greceana. The name does not sound well: "*Cupid and my Greceana plaid* / *At Cards for Kisses*" (17; borrowed, of course, from Lyly). On the very first page a reader may begin to suspect trouble when Euphrates proclaims that "I am no Orator, much less no Hudorigrapher," and that "Many words umbrage dissimulation." Thence he rises to rhyme concerning Greceana:

> If she be dead and here me left,
> Of life mortal she hath bereft
> Me; and I wish I had run the race,
> That I might her sweet Corps embrace.
>
> [1]

There is a schoolboy naïveté about all this. *Swelling* is one word that Langbaine applies to the play, and *unintelligible* another (*Account* 369). Nevertheless, the play is said to have been "Acted severall times privately at sundry places by the Author and his friends with great applause" (title page), and reading it is one way to inform oneself about some midcentury tastes, perceptions, presumptions, attitudes, and aspirations.

The False Favourite Disgrac'd (1657) is a much better play. Though it brings onstage a prince of Sicily, it is situated geographically in Florence and generically in the dependable old realm of Fletcherian courtly romance. It may call to mind Massinger's *Great Duke of Florence* (1627), because of Massinger's comparable but more mildly expressed antipathy to King James's final favorite, Buckingham. Written by George Gerbier D'Ouvilley and described on its title page as "A Tragi-Comedy. / Never Acted," *The False Favourite Disgrac'd* was launched with notable care. Friendly poems were provided by James Howell, E. Aldrich (who lamented that the cothurne—or buskin—was now laid aside, "The Actors dead, Spectators terrify'd" [a5r]), and J. Cole (who rationalized that "*Wee'l read, and like, and think we see thy Play*" [a7r]).

A former soldier himself, D'Ouvilley dedicated his *False Favourite* to Aubrey de Vere, twentieth Earl of Oxford; to William Craven, Baron of Hampsted (and later Earl of Craven); and to John Belasyse, Baron of Worlaby. He claimed not only that he had written for the "particular *divertisments*" of these three but also and more specifically that in three of his characters—Sicanio, Martiano, and Honorio—he had tried to convey their qualities, "especially *that of Honour*" (a3r). Craven was a military man

---

[21]Both are lost. In chapter 5, however, we briefly considered Meriton's tragedy *Love and War.*

of considerable repute. He was also "My Noble Lord and Collonel" (a1r)—that is, one to whose drum D'Ouvilley himself had marched in earlier years on the Continent. In Craven's service D'Ouvilley had risen to the rank of captain. Furthermore, Craven was a generous supporter and friend of Elizabeth of Bohemia (she lived for a while in his London mansion) and was widely known as a generous man. Here in D'Ouvilley's list of dedicatees he appears second, just as Martiano—whose name certainly has a martial cast—is second in his naming of characters. "A sword, and horse have ever bin my minnions," says Martiano (F7v). Similar paralleling would lead one to associate the third character noted in the dedication, Honorio (whose name keeps honor to the fore), with Belasyse, the third-named dedicatee. Having served at Edgehill, Newbury, Newark, and Naseby, Belasyse in his day was also greatly esteemed as a soldier. The man to whom D'Ouvilley gives precedence, however, his first-named model and dedicatee, likewise a soldier, courtier, and royalist, was Aubrey de Vere. One might be tempted to suggest that there is a special relationship between him and Prince Sicanio (Latin *Sicania* means Sicily), the first-named and highest-ranking of the three characters in the drama singled out for praise. Clearly some degree of "personating" (as D'Ouvilley terms it [a3r]) is operative here. However, one cannot gauge the differing degrees to which D'Ouvilley hoped that the general reader or a friend might relate reality and romance. One cannot say, for instance, how accurately or specifically the dramatist's friend A. Prissoe is thinking when he ventures to say

> Well, we dare Read, and Judge, and think we know
> This man's *Honorio*, that's *Hypolito;*
> And hope that *Lucabella* once shall smile,
> And wrong'd *Pausanio* be call'd from Exile. . . .
>
> [a6r]

In any case, considering the number of characters presented negatively in the play, D'Ouvilley probably was wise to claim that he had "some years since Extracted" his story "out of the *Italian Annals*" (a2v). Such a statement may call to mind Hamlet's information that *The Mouse-Trap* "is the image of a murther done in Vienna," and "the story . . . written in very choice Italian" (III.ii.238-39, 262-63). A little later D'Ouvilley adds—perhaps protests—that his characters are "*Tuscans; who have no relation at all to our English Actions*" (*False Favourite* a3v).

The play's titular favorite ("our Masters Minnion" [B5v]) is the conniving and powerful Hippolito, who hopes to supplant his patron, the Duke of Florence, and is finally supplanted himself by the honorable Honorio. Clearly the subject of favorites was not outdated during the time of either the exile or the reign of Charles II. Sir Balthazar Gerbier, a relative of the playwright, had not long since published, at The Hague, *Les Effects pernicieux de meschants favoris et grands ministres d'estat* (1653). In other words, the play could be taken by its contemporaries as both a reminder and an admonition.

Chief among the wronged outsiders in the play is the banished General Pausanio. Hence much of our attention is directed to his admirable children, Martiano and Lucebella, who remain behind and must decide on their courses of action. Like Hamlet, Martiano is intent on gathering evidence before pursuing revenge. Lucebella, meanwhile, has to deal with the inconvenient fact that she likes the Duke, the man she holds responsible for her father's exile. Much of the action in the play, it turns out, concerns who is wooing whom how, how long, and with what justification. Even the old-fashioned subplot involving cowardly Daw and LaFoole-like duelists ("mimique gallants" [D2v]) relates to wooing. In a number of ways, then, *The False Favourite Disgrac'd* is determinedly derivative, sometimes the more interesting for being so. The mistress-heroine's traditional "cruelty," for example, is better motivated here than usual. Also interesting is D'Ouvilley's penchant for utilizing an occasional out-of-the-way word. A handful such as "tardity" (A5r), "impetrate" (B3v), "memorative" (C3v), and "ubiquitary" (E5r) were sufficiently eccentric to trigger a charge against the play of "uncouth diction" in the *Dictionary of National Biography* (5:1281).

The technique of personating and the potentially dangerous subject of favorites remain important when we turn to a final tragicomedy, George Cartwright's *Heroick-Lover* (published in 1661). Cartwright, a gentleman of Fulham, west of Chelsea, dedicates his work to King Charles himself and in the process goes so far as to claim that "It is a Poem, consisting more of fatal Truth, then flying Fancy" (A3r). To be sure, George Cartwright (not to be confused with William Cartwright) gives us here a tragicomedy bearing the typical marks of its genre. Still, he has constructed both the play itself and its introductory matter so as to provoke frequent thoughts of historical facts. For example, he observes in the dedication that the play was "penn'd many years ago . . . [when one found] the Muses among our sad misfortunes here, suffering an Ecclipse: which I hope Your most Illustrious Rayes will over-power" (A3r). He reminds Charles, now King, of "the many, and extraordinary favours Your Majestie received at the Spanish Court, in Your sad, necessitated retirement thither who next to Heaven, were both the Preservers and Restorers of Your Royal Person here" (A2v). Such an authorial observation, especially coupled with Cartwright's main title and subtitle—*The Heroick-Lover; or, The Infanta of Spain*—calls to mind thoughts of Anglo-Spanish marriage discussions relating to more than one royal prince. Indeed, Cartwright does have an eye on Charles I. The twist is that the Prince in this play finally marries the Princess of Spain—though he has previously expressed his love for a handsome lady named, suggestively, Francina. In other words, the playwright gives us parallels and no parallels.

As a title, *The Heroick-Lover* might appeal especially to Charles II. Certainly the play takes place in a Poland that has many resemblances to the England of Charles I's day. It opens with a discussion by two servants of the royal household. One says,

> The City's weary, and the Countrey too,
> And something shortly, murmure for to do.
> They will no longer, have the King abus'd,
> Nor let themselves, so rigidly be us'd.
> But how to do't, they are not yet agreed,
> Out of the Court, such netles for to weed.
>
> [2]

If King, city, and country are all hurting because of them, it would seem reasonable to remove the nettles from the garden of the court. Most of them have been sown by the royal favorite, however, in this play a Cardinal. Calling to mind James Shirley's shadowing of Laud in *The Cardinal* back in 1641, one is better prepared to see the Cardinal here presented as a royalist writer's scapegoat for much of what is turning things rank in Poland. For instance, notice is taken of unreasonable taxation for which the Cardinal is to blame.

As the opening scene has foreshadowed, the King is eventually visited by two characters named Zorates and Selucious—who, Allardyce Nicoll suggested, shadow forth John Pym and John Hampden (228). Pym certainly moved the impeachment of Laud in 1640, Hampden's opposition to the Ship Money tax was probably his chief claim to fame, and both men became members of the so-called war party. In the play, Zorates and Selucious present the King with a petition urging him to "quit the *Cardinal*. / And leave him to the mercy of the Law, / Which he contemns, and will not stand in awe" (B6r). The King, however, dismisses the pair with a warning, and eventually we hear him go to the extreme of proclaiming the Cardinal one "Whom 'bove our life, and Kingdom, we do love!" (C6r).

The more amorous sort of love that is intimated in the combined title and subtitle of the play soon shares the stage with (and becomes part of) the political action. After the King and his advisers decide that the Prince must marry the Spanish *infanta*, the Cardinal recommends that the Lord Controuler go as ambassador to demand her of Spain. (We learn little of this ambassador, but it may be worth observing that Edward Hyde, later Earl of Clarendon, became Chancellor of the Exchequer in 1643, and that he and Francis Cottington served as ambassadors to Madrid for the exiled court from May 1649 to March 1651.) Secretly, however, the Prince loves Francina—who in turn loves another man, indeed none other than the confidante used by the Prince as his ambassador of love. Such complications are usual in tragicomedy. Quite unusual is the fact that both Francina and her young friend Symphrona eventually choose to enter a nunnery.

Meanwhile, Zorates and Selucious (who bear the titles of Lord High Chamberlain and Lord President) prepare for war. Not surprisingly, such would-be "weeders" prove more disruptive than those they would weed. For one thing, they try to subvert the virtuous Lord High Admiral by saying that they have not only gold but also "a pretence, that's somewhat fair" (C2r).[22] In the discourse of these three we have a thought-provoking mosaic of such arguments as tormented Englishmen for years. Zorates holds that while a king cannot live without subjects, subjects can live without a king; but regarding the present monarch the Admiral protests, "Were he a Tyrant, or a Prince unjust, / It were no argument, to break my trust" (C2v)—and even, "I'le faithful be; be what he will" (C3r). When the Admiral proves unyielding in the face of temptation by the King's enemies, he is arrested and carried off to the "castle." One might argue that his predicament is reminiscent of Strafford's. Nor is it any less so when we hear Zorates announce that next they will formally try the Admiral, "Whom if we find, by Law to merit Death, / We must not spare, to take away his breath" (D6v). Certainly the historical Pym took a major role in the impeachment and trial of Strafford. In Cartwright's play the King is incredulous upon hearing of the capture of his Admiral, but he is hesitant to strike against his subjects. Nevertheless, he would "be King, or else not King at all," and calls for the heads of the "Monsters" Zorates and Selucious (C7v).

As for dismissing the Cardinal, the King remains firm: "wee'le rather die, / Then either him, or else his Counsel flie" (C6r). This does not keep the opposition party from apprehending the Cardinal in his own palace and carting him off to the "castle" (E5r). (Laud, we recall, was held prisoner in the Tower for more than two years before being tried.)

Despite all the preceding action, and claiming the freedom of an artist—and a royalist—to paint and varnish history to suit his own gilded frame, Cartwright depicts the King as victorious at last. The "City flies / To him for mercy" (F3r), the traitors Zorates and Selucious are condemned to death, the Cardinal and Admiral are freed rather than executed, and the Prince enters upon the final scene with his Spanish bride—who speaks but

---

[22]Nicoll suggests that the Admiral shadows Edward Hyde (228). England's Lord Admiral was Algernon Percy, Earl of Northumberland, as of 19 October 1642, and Francis, Lord Cottington, assumed the post in December 1643.

one speech in the play. Then, lest anyone miss the ameliorating revisionism that has gone on here, the printed play is followed by a short, bleak poem "Upon Hells High-Commission Court, Set to Judge the King" (F5r). And next comes a poem called "Upon the Horrid, and Unheard of Murther, of Charles the First" (F5v). One may fairly conclude that in this drama that has been composed with passion and thought, and ordered in careful though sometimes awkward couplets, Cartwright sends down to us an example of drama used as a wishful corrective to history. With his fictive monarch's military put-down of dissension and with the questionable reintegration of the Cardinal into the scheme of things, Cartwright was obviously romancing. Tragicomedy was for him a near-perfect dramatic vehicle.

For most other playwrights as well, tragicomedy was the genre of choice. In fact, it is to be hoped that the present volume has conveyed a sense of the pervasiveness of tragicomedy in the century's two middle decades—mainly the 1650s—not merely through the plays noted in this chapter but also through those mentioned previously.

To anyone disinclined toward the form, the phenomenon apparently is (and probably always was) difficult to understand. As with other social and literary phenomena, however, one may conjecture how it came to be. For instance, we are dealing with a high percentage of amateur work here, and tragicomedy was probably easier than either tragedy or comedy for an amateur to write. Questions of quality aside, an amateur might more safely launch into a work in which, at different points, any tone or device could be justified, a genre in which variety was a positive goal. Then, too, tragicomedy had gained a good deal of momentum among the professionals in the years before the theaters closed. Since it was a well-established form with wide appeal, it was the more tempting to imitate. Another part of the picture was the current popularity of prose romances. Tragicomedy was by all odds the dramatic form most compatible with the assumptions and elements of such books. Though one might have expected that Sidney's *Arcadia* and, especially, Heliodorus's *Aethiopica* would have run their course by this time, not only the story elements themselves but also certain other qualities of these works proved transferable to drama—sometimes modified, of course, in Fletcherian ways, and sometimes modernized in keeping with the popular French romances of the day.

One might also suspect and argue, if never finally prove, that writing and reading these plays had a special appeal at midcentury because they seemed to have a fundamental relevance. Other writings of the time are brimful of instances of real bravery, nobility, and suffering, as well as a sense of getting on with the everyday details of living; and probably few of our dramatists wrote without some hope, for themselves and for their country, that eventually a better day would dawn. In other words, and insofar as genre in itself can speak, it may be significant that the period as a whole—and especially the decade of the 1650s—turned more often to tragicomedy than to tragedy or comedy. Of course we have glimpsed compelling tragic bleakness in such plays as Wase's *Electra* and the anonymous *Marcus Tullius Cicero*, but the tragicomedies implicitly and continuously insinuate that, whatever threats or losses come our way, a happy ending is possible.[23]

Potter conjectures that "the product of the tragicomedy model may have done the royalist cause more harm than good" because its stress on the importance of the ruler and Providence may have induced royalists "to abdicate responsibility and leave matters in the hands of fate" (" 'True Tragicomedies' " 214). About such matters we can only hypothesize. There will never be clues sufficient to lead to a sure answer. On the one hand, Dr. William Chamberlaine, author of *Love's Victory*, looking back in his poem *England's Jubile* (1660), wrote how those "Who durst live here spectators of those times, / Do now in tears repent our passive crimes" (298). Then, too, and despite some necessary accommodation to the powers that be, many Englishmen continued to work as best they could—and Cromwell knew it—to restore the Stuarts to the throne. Though Chamberlaine himself was aware that "Some loyal subjects had prepared the road" for Charles's return (301), people of the time of course had no way of knowing whether or not they were living during an interregnum. In fact, one of the paradoxes of the day is that even some Cromwellians came to hope that they were.

Meanwhile, tragicomedy provided an appealing way to tell a story, old or new, in a tried-and-true dramatic form. Tragicomedy was fun, and after some travail it always proved positive. Moreover, those writers who chose it could have their say on all manner of matters of the day, from kings to commons and soldiers to shepherds, expressing themselves sometimes obliquely and sometimes directly, hoping frequently to persuade and always to entertain. At the same time they could hold out for themselves and others the hope of better days to come. Lovelace wrote of this last matter with characteristic neatness: "That mighty breath which blew foul winter hither / Can eas'ly puff it to a fairer weather" ("Advice to My Best Brother," ll. 51-52). The playwright-poet Cowley looked specifically toward the royal Charles: "*You are our Morning-star, and shall b'our Sun*" (*Guardian* A2r).

---

[23]Though her focus is on Restoration drama, Maguire makes a compatible point when she writes, "The very nature of tragicomedy (that is, . . . drama which turns tragedy to comedy) made the genre suitable for marketing a restored king with a decapitated father" (*Regicide* 13).

THE RISING SUN

As in a tedious Winter, ev'ry Plant,
Seems dead, and out of life, and all for want
Of the Suns presence; so Great *Charles* did we,
Like dead men seem, and all for want of thee.
　　　　　—George Cartwright, "To Charles the Second,"
　　　　　　　　in *The Heroick-Lover* (1661)

Heaven, to restore our lost light, sent us him,
Without whose raise our sphere had still been dim.
Dim as in that dark interval, when we
Saw nothing but the clouds of anarchy,
Raised by the witchcraft of Rebellion. . . .
　　　　　—William Chamberlaine, *England's Jubile* (1660)

Kings and *queens* may appear
Once again in our *Sphere,*
Now the *Knaves* are turn'd out of door,
And drive the cold Winter away.
　　　　　—"The Second Part of St. George for England," to the
　　　　　tune of "To Drive the Cold Winter Away," in *Rump* (1662)

Welcome, welcome royal May,
Welcome long desired Spring.
　　　　　—Alexander Brome, "On the King's Return,"
　　　　　　　　in *Songs and Other Poems* (1661)

AFTER OLIVER CROMWELL'S death during a great storm in September 1658, he was succeeded briefly by his son Richard. A much stronger man than "Tumble-Down Dick" would have been required to reconcile the Rump Parliament and the army leaders, however, to say nothing of the miscellaneous myriarchy of presbyterians, independents, sectaries, royalists, and protectarians.

Despite some justifiable uncertainties about the views of General George Monck, royalists and parliamentarians alike joined to invite him to come down from Scotland to stave off chaos. In November 1659 the members of the Council of State named Monck commander in chief of all forces in the two kingdoms, and on the first day of 1660 he crossed the Tweed into England. On 3 February he entered London, and on 21 February, speaking at Whitehall, he came out for a legal dissolution of the

Long Parliament. Then on 16 March an act was passed terminating the remnants of that old Parliament and calling for a new one as of 25 April. Thus Samuel Pordage (whom we have seen as the translator of Seneca's *Troades*) exulted that *"George* most bravely has the *Dragon* slain" (*Poems* B3r). Thus, too, we have such pamphlet drama as *The Rump Despairing* and *The Famous Tragedie of the Life and Death of Mrs. Rump.* Obviously the main point of these was to crow. John Tatham's *The Rump*, a relatively complex, full-length play (discussed in chapter 14), is also given over to such cock-a-doodle-doings. Assuming a more refined stance, the player-playwright-civic poet Thomas Jordan produced *A Speech Made to His Excellency the Lord General Monck and the Council of State at Goldsmiths Hall* on 10 April, and two days later he furnished not only another speech for His Excellency but also (as we have seen in chapter 8) *Bacchus Festival . . . Being a Musical Representation . . . at Vintners-Hall.* Perhaps even more interesting, Jordan produced for the next day yet another speech for Monck and the Council, this one at "Fishmongers-Hall," in which, after a "SONG of difference" between a lawyer, a soldier, a citizen, and a countryman, he called for a rhyming speech by the ghost of that famous "MASSIANELLO Fisher-man of Naples."

About a month later the rambling-headed divine Anthony Sadler had in print "A Sacred MASQUE" called *The Subjects Joy for the Kings Restoration* (Thomason's copy is dated 17 May). Dedicating his work to Monck, Sadler claimed somewhat nervously that *"This Peece (I confess) is Theatrical, New, and Strange; Strange, but yet Pertinent; New, but yet Serious; and Theatrical, but yet Sacred"* (A2r-v). Perhaps as a safeguard and certainly as a claim to legitimacy, he turned to two old precedents: "Apollinarius *and* Nazianzen . . . *are known to be exemplary in this very way"* (A2v). Calling for six *"Shewes,"* ten speeches, and three songs, his text derived its general character from Davenant and its narrative underpinning from the rebellion of Jeroboam (he of the golden calf) against Judah's legitimate dynasty—"In which Rebellion, when he had continued eighteen years: then began *Abijah . . .* to reign over *Juda"* (B4r). Though flattery should not be discounted as a contributory motive, Sadler's ostensible main reason for writing is to decry rebellion and to show by means of scriptural parallels that *"Religion and Allegience, are the wings of the soul"* (A2v). He invites each reader "by Application, to resolve; / That this Sad-Sacred-pleasing-Scene, is laid; / To make the Good, rejoyce; the Bad, afraid" (C1v). In short, Sadler invokes the powers of parallelism and application on behalf of both himself and his masque.

A proclamation for the restitution of monarchy in the person of Charles Stuart had been issued on 8 May, and Sir Thomas Fairfax was named to head Parliament's commission to meet Charles at The Hague.[1] Soon thereafter, on 25 May, the rising royal son touched shore at Dover. He delayed his entry into London, however, probably in order that his birthday on 29 May might coincide with his rebirth-day and thus expand the celebratory symbolism of the occasion. In any case, Elias Ashmole had time to write a six-page poem called *Sol in Ascendente; or, The Glorious Appearance of Charles the Second, upon the Horizon of London* (1660), and James Shirley composed *An Ode upon the Happy Return of King Charles II. to His Languishing Nations, May 29, 1660*. The sixty-four-year-old playwright thanked both God and Monck, rejoiced in the hundreds of men who marched joyously in "plush and pride" and in "Buff and gold lace / As thick as grass," and even noted that the water conduits for the nonce "Pist Claret wine" (22-23). To set these words to music so they might be sung, Shirley turned to Charles Coleman, who four years earlier had composed some of the music for Davenant's *Siege of Rhodes*. Meanwhile, Charles Stuart's boyhood governor, the redoubtable soldier, equestrian, dramatist, and patron of playwrights William Cavendish, set himself the tasks of writing out both a welcoming royal entertainment (as we saw in chapter 15) and a more sober work offering such counsel as he deemed fit for a king. Though Charles's attention was no longer focused very frequently on the outdated old courtier, Cavendish, still striving to be politic and hoping to be of use, now observed of plays—and also of rope-dancing, juggling, and tumbling—that "These divertissements will amuse the people's thoughts, and keep them in harmless action which will free your Majesty from faction and rebellion" (*English "Prince"* 168). Coming from one who had lived so long and seen so much, the admonition was disappointingly off the mark.

Of all the entertainments celebrating Charles's return, the most glorious involved a set of triumphal arches, pageants, and musical offerings made for his grand procession from the Tower to Whitehall on 22 April 1661, the day before his coronation. The chief begetter of this extravaganza was John Ogilby, former dancer at the court of Charles I, former tutor to Strafford's children, former translator of Virgil, later cartographer and inventor of the odometer, and clearly—despite Dryden's jibes—an all-around bright fellow. Ogilby's complex show was first described in *The Relation of His Majesties Entertainment* (1661), then delineated in more detail the following year in an illustrated folio called *The Entertainment of His Most Excellent Majestie Charles II*. In the latter we find engravings of the four great coronation arches, which are believed to have been designed with the aid of that quondam master of ceremonies under Charles I, Sir Balthazar

---

[1]As early as May 1655, Lord Jermyn had reported to Charles from Paris that the common word there was that Fairfax had dispatched an emissary "to offer you his service" (Lambeth Palace Library MS 646, no. 28).

Gerbier.[2] The first arch depicted Britain's Monarchy supported by Loyalty and threatened by Rebellion. The second was devoted to naval themes, the third presented the Temple of Concord, and the last, the Garden of Plenty. All were packed with symbols, common and uncommon, antique and modern. One way and another, Ogilby and his fellow craftsmen managed to imply that Charles was an Aeneas (an heroic wayfarer), a St. George (his father's last gift to him was his George), a Neptune, an Augustus (presently about to launch a new Augustan Age), and, of course, a sun (see figure 45). Though all of these are potentially negative or at least ambivalent signs, it would be pointless to misread them as anything other than the glorious positives for which Ogilby strived. Now, presumably, all England might rejoice to think *"The Clouds blown o're, which long our joys o'recast, / And the sad Winter of Your absence past"* (165).

We also find in Ogilby's work a stunning example of quasi-dramatic art holding up a specific individual to scorn. In the central painting of the first arch, and apparently fleeing from Charles, the grotesque figure of Usurpation was depicted *"with many ill-favoured Heads, some bigger, some lesser, and one particularly shooting out of his Shoulder, like* CROMWEL'S*"* (28). This same arch had another painting of *"A Trophy with decollated Heads"* together with the motto "ULTOR A TERGO DEUS"—"God's Vengeance Rebels at the Heels pursues" (21; see figure 46). Exhilarated as the designers, participants, and most of their public may have been, such touches should suffice to remind us that some English people could only wear frowns or false smiles when they saw such a "Trophy" or read about it.[3] The first of thirteen retributive executions, that of Major General Thomas Harrison, had taken place on 13 October 1660, and the body of Cromwell himself was exhumed from Westminster Abbey, then hanged and beheaded at Tyburn on 30 January 1661—the twelfth anniversary of Charles's death.[4] Now John Ogilby, looking forward hopefully to a new Augustan Age, masterminded here what was to be one of England's last great royal entries.[5]

---

[2]Knowles argues thus in his 1988 introduction to Ogilby's *Entertainment*. [3]Conversely, perhaps one should also acknowledge that those who had always remained faithful royalists had cause to be frustrated when twelve of the thirty seats on the Privy Council in 1661 went to men who had borne arms against Charles's father. MacKay's collection (209) includes "The Cavalier's Complaint": "My coyne is spent, my time is lost, / And I this only fruit can boast, / That once I saw my King. / But this doth most afflict my mind: / I went to Court in hope to find / Some of my friends in place; / And walking there, I had a sight / Of all the crew, but, by this light! / I hardly knew one face." [4]For 13 October 1660 Pepys wrote that "it was my chance to see the King beheaded at White-hall and to see the first blood shed in revenge for the blood of the King at Charing-cross" (1:265). [5]Richards calls Tatham's *Aqua Triumphalis* (1662)—London's welcome to Catherine of Braganza when she came by water from Hampton Court to Whitehall—"the last grand Stuart public spectacle" ("Restoration Pageants" 69).

Figure 45. The crown and the rising sun as medallic images of Charles II. (From Pinkerton, *The Medallic History of England to the Revolution* [1790].)

Long before the coronation, professional performances of plays had resumed. Even before 21 August 1660, when Davenant and Killigrew received their warrants entitling them to a monopoly on professional theatrical performances in London, at least a few scattered performances had occurred. Details of the matter are now scarce and controversial, but William Van Lennep is able to list a number of performances during the 1659-60 season (*London Stage* 9-13). He also reminds us that on 23 April Monck and the Council of State put out an order forbidding stage-plays (10). Whatever impact the latter may have had was not long-lived, for the royal warrants of Davenant and Killigrew came that summer.

As was perfectly natural, men of the theater wishing to start over again turned first not only to old theaters but also to old plays.[6] On 6 June 1660 Pepys reported that the Dukes of York and Gloucester had "the other day" seen Jonson's *Epicoene* at the Red Bull (1:171). Sir Robert Stapleton was soon warning audiences, however, not to expect from their own time the wonders of a Jonson or a Shakespeare, or a Beaumont and Fletcher, "*For, Men are shrunk in Brain as well as Stature*" (A3v). Nevertheless, Stapleton upheld the value of theatergoing, arguing that "*our Plays recreate the Mind, | Instruct the Judgment, which Mens Nature learns, | And how to manage Low and High Concerns*" (A3r). In contrast, Henry Adis in November 1660, bemoned already "the revived and daily continued Acts of abomination in *Stage-playes, May-games,* and *Pastimes,* with the many *bitter* and *most horrid Oaths*

---

[6]Hume observes, in fact, that there was something of a "scramble for play rights in 1660" ("Securing" 158).

Figure 46. Cromwell's head on a pole, pictured on one of the arches in Ogilby's *Entertainment of His Most Excellent Majestie* (1662). (By permission of the Special Collections Library, Duke University.)

and *Execrations,* uttered almost in *every corner*" (*Fannaticks Mite* 3r-v).[7] For all that things had changed, they were in some ways much the same. Unlike Stapleton and Adis, we latecomers have the advantage of knowing not only the polar-opposite writings they produced but also what subsequent years of the Restoration would bring, good and bad. We know also that Dryden, at the end of his career and looking back over the period, had a painfully acute and counterbalancing rejoinder for those who would claim that the Restoration stage stood guilty of infecting the age: "*sure, a banisht Court, with Lewdness fraught, | The Seeds of open Vice returning brought.*"[8]

Five months after Jonson's *Epicoene* was performed at the Red Bull, the same play was chosen as the first to be presented at court. The performance was sponsored by General Monck himself (who doubtless had his reasons for an about-face regarding drama) and presented by Killigrew's company on 19 November 1660 in the Cockpit at Whitehall. Whoever wrote the new prologue for the old play (Davenant seems a good possibility), he seized on what was, theatrically speaking, an historical turning point and thus reflected on both past and present:

> *Greatest of Monarchs, welcome to this place*
> *Which* Majesty *so oft was wont to grace*
> *Before our Exile, to divert the Court,*
> *And ballance weighty Cares with harmless sport,*
> *This truth we can to our advantage say,*
> *They that would have no* KING, *would have no* Play:
> *The* Laurel *and the* Crown *together went,*
> *Had the same* Foes, *and the same* Banishment. . . .
> . . . .
> *Affrighted with the shadow of their Rage,*
> *They broke the Mirror of the times, the Stage;*
> *The Stage against them still maintain'd the War,*
> *When they debauch'd the* Pulpit *and the* Bar.
> *Though to be* Hypocrites, *be our Praise alone,*
> *'Tis our peculiar boast that we were none.*
> *What er'e they taught, we practis'd what was true,*
> *And something we had learn'd of honor too,*
> *When by Your Danger, and our Duty prest,*
> *We acted in the Field, and not in Jest;*
> *Then for the* Cause *our Tyring-house they sack't,*

---

[7]The epithet *fanatic* that Adis incorporates in his title was given him, he reports, "by the tongue of Infamy" (title page).   [8]Dryden hurled this accusation in the epilogue he wrote for Sir John Vanbrugh's adaptation in 1700 of Fletcher's *The Pilgrim* (*Poems* 4:1760). For *The Secular Masque* in the same play, Dryden produced the famous closing lines " '*Tis well an Old Age is out, | And time to begin a New*" (4:1765).

And silenc't us that they alone might act;
And (to our shame) most dext'rously they do it,
Out-act the Players, and out-ly the Poet;
But all the other Arts appear'd so scarce,
Ours were the Moral Lectures, *theirs the* Farse. . . .

With allusions here to the "cause" and to drama's criticism by "shadowing" and to the "hypocrites" who closed the theaters, this prologue is an interesting document to juxtapose with other writings in earlier years by men such as Davenant and Flecknoe. Particularly notable is the claim that *"The Stage against them still maintain'd the War."* Whoever the author may have been, there is no reason to doubt his delight that now once again a King was in the Cockpit.

A reader of this book will hardly be surprised that the Restoration period, especially at its outset, witnessed the survival and revival of earlier plays.[9] Robert Hume observes that it was not until the season of 1663-64 that a substantial offering of new plays occurred (*Development* 20).[10] Furthermore, and also not surprisingly, when changes in drama did come, they generally tended to be outgrowths from something earlier. The forms in which language was packaged—blank verse, couplets, and prose—were all explored before as well as after 1660. Genres, of course, were trans-shifting, as genres always do, but we should not lose track of the fact that the tragicomedies considered here in chapter 16 play an important role in the genealogy of the new heroic drama. Then, too—thinking of these later, larger-than-life shows—one might suggest that their splendid costuming had plenty of progenitors in the Caroline masques. On the other hand, Charles's gold and scarlet coronation robes came to the boards in 1661 adorning a play (*Love and Honour*) that Davenant had written back in 1634 (Downes 52). To be sure, the use of scenery and music took on a new life during the new reign—yet both of these also had prewar and Interregnum precedents. Probably few would deny that the Restoration tendency toward realism on the stage was enhanced by the appearance of women playing women—apparently beginning in December 1660 when a now-unknown woman ventured to play Shakespeare's Desdemona. "Shall we

---

[9]Hume writes: "By my count, the King's Company mounted at least thirty-nine old plays during the 1660–1 season" ("Securing" 161). In comparison with this score, however, "We have certain record of only fourteen plays performed by the Duke's Company this season" (161). Apparently what forced the Duke's Company "to turn fairly quickly to new plays was, very simply, lack of old ones" (165)—that is, lack of available rights. Sorelius's *"Giant Race before the Flood"* explores the subject at length. Gewirtz's study, though concerned mainly with Restoration adaptations of earlier comedies, is also generally helpful. [10]This is an updated and reinforced version of an observation made by Palmer back in 1913: "For four complete years of the reign of Charles II . . . the English theatre was the theatre of Charles I. restored" (3).

count that a crime *France* calls an honour?" Thomas Jordan asked (*Royal Arbor* 22). Women on the public stage might now provide visible objects of desire for men in the audience, and, for women, a greater potential for identification (Rothstein and Kavenik 60). But the way for such appearances had been prepared not only in Henrietta Maria's (and even Anne's) day but also and more recently by Davenant and the attractive Catherine Coleman.[11] As for other players, the study of certain lawsuits has led to the discovery recently of "exciting . . . evidence . . . about the continuity of the King's Company with Commonwealth and pre-Commonwealth troupes." Members of the King's Company "clearly conceived themselves as part of an ongoing and unbroken 'Socyety of Actors' " (Milhous and Hume 509). Of course, the awarding of theatrical warrants to Killigrew and Davenant on 21 August 1660 was bound to bring about major differences—and yet Hume sensibly points out that the warrants were assigned to men who had been writing and seeing their plays performed back in the days of the first Charles. Moreover, Sir Henry Herbert now reclaimed and regained— though in somewhat diminished form—his prewar position as Master of the Revels. No one can deny that time brought change to the Restoration stage. That, however, is someone else's story to tell. Here it must suffice to suggest that much was carried forward from the drama of earlier days.

Most pertinent for the present study, the penchant for allusiveness continues to be discernible in plays of the Restoration.[12] Examples range from Robert Howard's *The Committee* (1662), which curries yet again the old Sequestration Committee that had caused so many royalists so much pain, to Edward Howard's *The Usurper* (1664), which disguises Cromwell as Damocles and Hugh Peters as Hugo da Petra, and on to the two parts of Aphra Behn's *The Rover* (1677, 1681), with their recollection of Thomaso Killigrew's wanderings on the Continent.

Memories of the Good Old Cause or the bad old days would survive for lifetimes and more, but dramatists turned also to more immediate subjects, positive and negative. Samuel Tuke assured Henry Howard of Norfolk not only that *The Adventures of Five Hours* (1663) was based on Howard's garden at Aldbury, but also that "I design'd the Character of *Antonio* as a Copy of Your Stedy Virtue" (A2v). In striking contrast, a production of Robert Howard's *The Country Gentleman* (1669) never opened because the text had been modified to include such savage satire of William Coventry that that gentleman threatened to undertake some nose-

---

[11]One should note also that in his traveling troupe on the Continent, George Jolly, the English actor-manager, appears to have engaged women even before Davenant did.　[12]Backscheider suggests that "the royal theaters and their courtier-playwrights produced plays so rich in political content that they could be reaccentuated for propagandistic statement for over a hundred years" (xvii).

slitting.[13] The most spectacular instance of dramatic attack, however, may be Thomas Otway's excoriation of Anthony Ashley Cooper as the driveling, baby-talking, sex-hungry Antonio of *Venice Preserved* (1682). In other words, English dramatists continued to enliven their work by indulging in parallels, examples, and personatings. Otway's epilogue to *Venice Preserved* begins with the line *"The Text is done, and now for Application"* (A3v). We should not be amazed. It had always been the task of viewers and readers to engage in appropriate application.

One might consider it a convenient happenstance that in our own *fin de siècle* years we have learned—or learned again—that no book can mean the same to any two people, whether they be situated in the same or different centuries, the same or different countries, or, indeed, the same or different sectors of a particular bed. When one is trying to determine meanings of dramatic writings from a period of censorship, furthermore, calculated indeterminacy and ambiguity in the text are particularly problematic, intriguing, and significant. The case, of course, is not that a battery of new techniques had to be invented in the middle of the seventeenth century in order to achieve such ends. Rather, the tried-and-true methods of previous years continued to be practiced. Consequently—and even during times of notable repression—examples of both subtle indirection and bold directness could be found side by side.

True, a number of our writers were actually imprisoned—including Cowley, Fanshawe, Fane, Killigrew, Manuche, Davenant, and Compton—but it was not because of their politics as expressed in their plays. Naturally each of these writers had his own story, but among them we find no series of reprisals via incarceration that might echo the experience, say, of Jonson and Nashe for their writing of *The Isle of Dogs* back in Queen Elizabeth's day. Christopher Wase did, to be sure, get in trouble for his *Electra*, but such an instance seems rather to test the generalization than negate it. By way of explaining the situation, one might suggest that some of our playwrights worked very privately, that each repetition of a governmental constraint tended to signal the limited effectiveness of prior ones, and even that, throughout the period, the authorities seem to have been more concerned with play performances than with play-texts. Meanings conveyed by the plays, moreover, were (as they still are) dependent on what a reader might discern and create.[14] And even a reader suspicious of something subversive might well decide not to take any action. It is also a truism, furthermore,

---

[13]This "lost" play, now edited by Scouten and Hume, has been placed by Winton in the larger picture of Restoration dramatic censorship. [14]The question of meaning becomes vastly more complex if one takes actual stage presentation into consideration, with variables contributed by a particular production, an individual performance of that production, a specific audience, and even specific members of that audience.

that whatever good interpretative ideas come into our own heads regarding these plays, latter-day readers can never know exactly what any given seventeenth-century reader or even an impossibly hypothetical "typical" reader might have discerned and created from even so much as a single speech in a single play.

Nevertheless, we do have the printed books and the handwritten manuscripts, and we may rest assured that allusions aplenty are often there to be discerned and pondered. Whatever form they take, we can hardly be surprised that few of their creators came out with signpost statements so bold as that in *The Female Rebellion*, whose author's expressed aim is "to silence, if not reconcile," his opponents (176r). Few plays afford such pellucid claims of intention as *The Unfortunate Usurper: "True Monarchy's supported by our play."* [15] Occasionally, of course, we find an authorial claim to "shadowing," but much more frequently we are invited only implicitly to participate in the inexact game of application.

However we choose to approach them, the fact remains that our plays are all tied in complex ways to their time. Not only do all make use of generic assumptions of their day (hence the usefulness of an approach that takes genre into account), but virtually all touch issues of their day. Though different scholars working with these same materials might make more of such subjects as the Scottish connection or the radical presence (both of which are touched on here), the fact remains that the most pervasive of topically oriented subjects in these midcentury works are clearly kingship and war. Neither sprang full-grown from anyone's forehead in 1642, and yet we have here a body of drama that is tireless in its treatment of these subjects, exploring them sometimes casually and sometimes searchingly, but exploring them endlessly.

On the other hand, given that most of these plays are the fruits of a basically inhospitable season of repression, perhaps we should not be surprised that few appear to embody more or less complete figurative statements or systems. (Exceptions that might prove the rule are *Marcus Tullius Cicero*, Wase's *Electra*, and Manuche's *Banish'd Shepheardesse*.) This being true, readers are likely to fare best and see most not by seeking overall configurations but by staying alert to apparently random allusions, occasional characters, speeches, and situations, and clustered or scattered details that may suggest patterns of reference.

Relationships of plays to their times have been a particular concern

---

[15]In such a place, says the author, it is suitable to acknowledge what has been acted on "*Englands Stage*" in "*this Age*": "*Let* Nevill, Lambert, Vane, *and all that crew / To their Usurping Power bid Adieu, / Those Meteors must vanish*, Charles *our Sun, / Having in* Englands *Zodiack begun / His course*" (*Unfortunate Usurper* 71).

here, but still more broadly important are the variety, vitality, and inherent interest of this body of writing. Largely neglected because it is correctly perceived to be less great than the Renaissance drama that preceded and the Restoration drama that followed, these plays sometimes deal with manners, sentiment, and rhetoric seemingly for their own sake. To return to Jonson's figure, they are sometimes only cream-bowl deep. Then, too, in many ways they are endlessly imitative of the works of their great predecessors—usually Jonson, Shakespeare, and Beaumont and Fletcher. Yet another trait that enervates some is pointed out by Flecknoe, who complains of "our huddling too much matter together, and making them too long and intricate; we imagining we never have intrigue enough, till we lose our selves and Auditors, who shu'd be led in a Maze, but not a Mist" (*Short Discourse* G4v).

Flipping to the positive side of the coin, however, we have seen enough evidence along the way to suggest the varied charms, curiosities, and virtues of these plays. If asked to single out their most characteristic virtue, one might, at the end of a long trail, point to the realization that a fairly large number of our playwrights demonstrate a sense of liberated enjoyment. One cannot say when or whether this sort of happy valiancy is traceable to the fact that many were amateurs unfettered by professional experience or that a confining sense of actual theater facilities did not threaten them or that normal commercial considerations did not obtain or even that the anguish of the age somehow energized them. One can suggest, however, that when the hurly-burly of war was done (at different times for different men), some Englishmen, and especially royalists, must have had more time on their hands than before, time for growing tulips (as did Lambert, though no royalist he), training horses (Cavendish), and planting fruit trees (Fanshawe), as well as time for building libraries, translating classics, and working on plays. Generalizations tend to be leaky devices, but one can point to Fane, for instance, who in prison or out gives every indication of writing as he pleased. Or to Killigrew, who does so too. And, surely, to that old "Eie Witnes" who wrote the *True Tragi-Comedie*. As he puts the matter in a passage preserved with his play, "if the nice rules of a Dramatike Poem be uiolated, I desire the redar to considar, how feue haue obsarued them" (18r).

To conclude the inconcludable—for all of us are finally responsible for our own applications—one might venture the claim that these dramatic writings, the fruits of what many at the time perceived as a long, cold winter, continued to be composed, translated, revived, transmuted, read, and sometimes even acted throughout the official hiatus in playing. The dramatic tradition that had fascinated the English in earlier years continued to provide writers, readers, and sometimes audiences with many different forms of expression, whether for persuasion or pleasure or both. As for ourselves, at the same time that these plays offer endless recollections of earlier drama and intimations of drama to come, they take on new life and meaning of their own when we know something of the context that produced them. Indeed, they offer a challenge to readers of any time, a challenge not only to understand but also, with a little sympathy and perseverance, to appreciate and enjoy.

APPENDIX A

The Preface to Leonard Willan's *Orgula* (1658)[1]

To the most accomplisht Lady,
the Lady FRANCES WILDEGOSS.[2]

MADAM,

Having long since renounced all sorts of civill homage, which either Custome hath blindly tenderd, or Arrogance insolently assumed, as the affected rights of Greatness, being but an ostentive Coloss, nor accessible nor communicable.[3]

I now can figure to my thoughts no nobler Object of Respect than a clear, high and regular Intellect, whose Endowments may challenge a more Plausible and Legitimate Acquisition in such publique addresses of Honour, as may sometime reach to a more remote Posterity; in pursuit of which consequence, *Madam,* judging the Dignity of your Minde the most perfect Model of so equal a Designe, I have presumed (from the obscurity of many years) to tender this piece to your view. The nature whereof, though vilified with vulgar Obloquie (the unrestrained Fury of whose Ignorance, hath not[,] of late, left the most high and Sacred Mysteries unimpeachable[4]) can gain no further access on your Inclinations, than what a clear and sollid Argument impartially may produce, which to unfold, it will be requisite to distinguish the *Nature,* and the *Use* of this our subject now in Agitation.

In Order to which, the *Nature* thereof is (without all opposition) *Poesie.* What that is, cannot in my Apprehension be more Elegantly and perspicuously delineated than the agreable Philos[o]pher hath formed it in his convertible definition. *Poesie is a speaking Picture: A Picture is a dumb Poesie.*[5] From which Sence we may

---

[1]From A2r-a2v of *Orgula,* which was printed by Thomas Mabb for Stephen and Thomas Lewis and sold "at the signe of the *Book-binders* in *Shoo-lane.*" The transcription here incorporates five corrections provided in Willan's own list of errata and four corrections of obvious typographical errors. For the sake of clarity, a few brackets are added, and the paragraphing is slightly modified. Willan refers to the document as a preface, an introduction, and an essay, and its running heads term it an "*Epistle Dedicatory.*" [2]Lady Frances was of the Wildigos family of Iridge Court, Saleshurst, Sussex. [3] In this opening participial unit, paragraphed separately, Willan's political disaffection and retreat provide the background for all that follows. [4]Willan compares what he perceives as the vilification of drama with attacks on religion itself. [5]Conceivably Willan recalls here Simonides of Amorgos and a saying of his quoted in the *De gloria Atheniensium* (3.346F); or perhaps he has in mind the more famous related statement by Horace, "Ut pictura poesis" (*Ars poetica,* l. 361). In any case, the comparison was considered commonplace by Plutarch (*De audiendis poetis* 3.F2-3), and it became so again during the Renaissance.

extract, that Poesie only is an Art of lively representation of bodies Natural, Simply, without referrence to other, or Compositively with circumstance to their mutual communities, either Natural or Civil. Real in respect of their precedent, present, or future condition: or Imaginary in relation to their possibility. In the extent of which Exposition some particulars may probably at first Appearance seem Dubious, some Erronious.

Dubious, As how it may fall within compass of humane capacity: to figure to anothers sence what falls not under the dimension of our own; our purpose is not here to search into the causes of so high an illumination, it is sufficient proof to our Position, to affirm such an inspection evident in its Nature, as may be instanc'd from the sacred Raptures of the Judahack-Prophets & the Gentique-Sybills,[6] whom though we seem improperly to include with the tractators[7] of our *Subject*, inspired by a nobler Object; yet in referrence to the Analogy of form in their Discourses, preceding Ages have indifferently implied the intimation of their Nature under one and the same Denomination[,] *Vates*, To which usage we have extended this our Exposition.[8]

Erronious, In that the Fancie herein doth assume too vast a Libertie, to figure forms [that] are visibly to natural and to civil Rules inconsonant.[9]

As in referrence to the *First*, Satyrs, Centaures, transmutation of Forms and the like. In answer whereto although it be not difficult to prove, that ev'n herein the *Art* doth only Nature imitate, who oftentimes from the Inaptitude of matter doth err from her intention in the Form; and in her Ministry doth frequently produce a Prodegie. Yet these inventions may by mean capacities be distinguished, to be but Metaphors to a Moral sence.

In relation to the *Second*, inserting things *Prophane, Obscene, Fabulous* and *Proposterous*.

Prophane, As the figuration of their Gods invested with our humane Imperfections. In reply whereto we may alleadge, that in reference to the Civil frame, intended are hereby, the Potentates of the earth, [and] an allusion may be produc'd from Sacred proofs to form it warrantable. In relation to the natural texture, are secretly herein involved Moral, Phisical, or metaphisical Mysteries, perhaps yet undiscovered, which from the vulgar Eye should be conceal'd, as the Adulterers of Philosophy.

Obscene, To clear which charge we might inferr, that if the indecen[t]'st form hereof were figured, it rather would imply an imperfection in our civil Commerce than any Imputation to the Art, whose End is only to expose each Circumstance and accident inherent to the subject, in their most proper and essential Colours, Beauties, or Deformities. Yet will we not so farre insist on the strict Rules of the Art, as not to impute such indiscretion to the Artists Errour. Who may if skilful, nay who ought (according to the true rules of his pattern, Nature) so gracefully to overshadow the less decent parts, as might not raise a stain on the most modest Cheek to view them publiquely.

---

[6]Old Testament prophets and, presumably, gentile or pagan prophets. [7]Writers of tractates—or, more simply, of literary works. [8]Latin *vates* (prophet, soothsayer, seer) had from ancient times been used to mean also singer, bard, poet. [9]I.e., "forms that are visibly inconsonant with natural and civil rules."

Fabulous, This subject bears so little weight in an objection, that it might rather infer the ignorance of the Impeacher, than the Impostury of the Artist. All sorts of Arts having some secret Gloss and reservation of their mysteries, to support their Honour and Advantage: This only and alone, pretending unto none[,] declareth things for such as it delivers them, Fained or Essential, Imaginary or Historical; though in some textures of the latter kinde may possibly be interwoven certain enlargements and digressions (as graces but peculiar to the Art) not properly consistant with the dignity, weight, use of such a Subject, [which] requireth simple Truth in every circumstance.[10] Yet ev'n herein a clear Intelligence will suddenly distinguish shadows by the position of the Natural light; like perfect ears in Musick still retain the Grounds,[11] Orders, Times of every note, though the Musitians hand, to grace his Harmony, cast various flourishes on the suspended Measures[.] [T]o lend more weight unto the usage of invention in this rejected Art, we shall not need to instance the excellence of the nature thereof to Instruction, to which the choicest of essential similitudes cannot exactly reach, wanti[n]g such forms of circumstances as might enlighten the intention of the Deliverer, restrained and obscured in a real Narrative. It may suffice to silence opposition, to alledge we find our most authentique precepts couched in such forms of texture, as Allegories or Parables; a winning method to attract the grossest tempers, and infix in All most durable impressions.

From the freedome of this latter objected subject, issues the objection of the last (*Preposturous*) in that it is suppos'd the unprescribed Fancy, having assumed a liberty to rove, will suddenly contract extravagant mixtures in her compositions, to form a Prodigie in the civill frame, as formerly in the natural.

To this conjecture we may make reply: That no Absurdity can be imagined so irregular, which may not meet a parralel in the occurrences of civil Actions. Be it, that we should suppose the most evident Truth condemned for the grossest Errour: That Wisedom should be confuted by Ignorance: Integrity ejected by Hypocrisie, Valour overcome by Lachety,[12] Industry supplanted by Sloth, the Innocent suffer by the Criminal, Justice smothered by Iniquity, Love rewarded with Hate; which without further proof to verify, I only, *Madam,* will appeal to your own observation. If any shall aledge such accidents to be but the effects of our corruption which guids us still to satisfie our sence, rather than an infeasable impropriety in a civill usage, which the licentiousness of the Art doth often figure; not to decline the smallest shadow of an objected scruple; we shall in some example devest the action of his pretended object, leaving the occurrence immaterial or void in any consequence what ever.[13] Can humane sence reflect upon a more Preposterous transaction, than *That the Monarch of the world should in the height of all his Glory, and in the*

---

[10]Willan works here with the problem of adding artistic "graces" to "simple [historical] Truth."   [11]A ground-bass is a bass passage of four or eight bars, constantly repeated but with variations of melody and harmony (*OED*).   [12]A variant related to *lachedness* and *laches:* laxness or slackness, remissness, negligence (*OED*).   [13]This passage is probably Willan's densest. A paraphrase might go thus: If anyone alleges that our perception (that wisdom, integrity, valor, industry, innocence, justice, and love are confuted by ignorance, hypocrisy, laxness, sloth, etc.) emanates from our corruption, which art often depicts, I shall with an example negate this objection, showing it to be inconsequential.

Eye of all the world magnificently solemnize Nuptials with another Man; the most abject of his Domesticks. Yet such a real precedent we may authenickly collect from the Records of N*ero*'s Infamy.[14]

Having thus briefly (as the capacity of our Preface will give leave) discussed of the Nature of our *Subject*[,] Order requires that we should next insist upon the use *Thereof;* Whereon depends the real worth of every Piece, in Nature or in Art, which to pursue methodically, we should in course unfold the several kinds thereof, in their particulars; as *Odes, Elegies, Epigrams,* and the like: But since the nature of our present subject may include them all, as several species under their proper gender,[15] we only will adhere to agitate thereon, raising our introduction from the first view of the whole *Frame,* without distinction of the Parts thereof.

If intercourse in civill commerce may conduce to form the Judgement, compose the mind, or rectify the manners (as none who hath receiv'd impression thereof, can deny) no form of institution humane reason can reflect upon, more suddenly and more perfectly can attain thereto, than can the well composed illustrations of a *Theater.* Where in few hours we may take full view of such variety in circumstance, as many Ages cannot represent; and from the consequence of events collect such rules, may guide our undertakings with successe to their peculiar Objects. Whilst being uninteressed Spectators only, are to us distinguished the secret source of each Transactors purposes, whose actions leave so sensible an impression of their Character in our thoughts, that seldom in our own particular community we encounter such an inclination, but that the prepossession of their figure streight illuminates our sences to disclose their Tract;[16] whereby our Fortunes, Lives, Liberties and Fames, are timely oftentimes secur'd from secret Trains.[17]

To yeeld a true allay[18] to the distempers of the Soul, no Art can form a fairer methode, than thus to represent the wilde distractions of her irregular motives, transported with licentious fury, to execute the giddy will, with violation to each strict prescription. Outrage to it self, with the disasters frequently ensue so stubborn a revolt from that interior light, should lend her dignity: if the deformity of the figure may reduce the minde to a more happy and decent Regulation of her Faculties. To which pattern was among the *Spartans* introduced a custom to inebriate their Slaves, they might expose their loose Demeanors to their childrens view, that such a loathsome spectacle might imprint a lasting Detestation of so bruitish a distemper.[19]

Nor yet to regulate our manners can the most powerfull precepts form the Minde, so willingly susceptible of her intended Object: If intimation of the glory and successe of virtue may inflame the Soul to noble enterprises; or the Infamy and punishment of Vice, deterre from shamefull practises, which are the principall Objects, a well compiled Piece still viseth at:[20] or, seldome in the most imperfect

---

[14]Suetonius, *Lives of the Caesars* 6.28-29.   [15]*Gender* is used here in its obsolete sense of genus (*OED*).   [16]The course or continuity of a narrative or other writing (*OED*).   [17]*Trains* is used here figuratively in the sense of a line of combustible material leading to an explosive charge. Willan is unusually expansive in his claims regarding the dangers to be averted by some knowledge of drama [18]An allay is something that quells or diminishes.   [19]Plutarch records the custom in his *Lycurgus* (28.4).   [20]*Viseth*: looks at or regards closely (*OED*).

are omitted. First, in regard the minde is here no way subordinate unto a more supream sufficience than her own. Secondly, in that such forms of Institution do pretend unto no servile impositions, the most materiall impediments, why the authentick'st guides so seldome meet successe in the Intention of their elaborate prescriptions. Subjects of this nature propounding no other object, but delight, unto the Auditory, the sensuall minde is easily inticed to view such spectacles, where left unto the freedome of her proper Inclination, she insensibly assumes a voluntary propension[21] to those forms [that] are represented in the fairest Characters, with an aversion to the impeachable.

These are the essentiall uses of our subject; nor yet are the Collaterall lesse materiall: as, The Community of a Prince unto his people (at whose peculiar charge were formerly erected such magnificent receipts for publique Spectacles[)], either to ingratiate himself with his subjects in a mutuall participation of delight, as an endearing entertainment from himself, or else to represent the object, by circumstance and issue of some eminent expedition, enterprise or treaty within his proper jurisdiction, or with foreign States transacted by himself or substitutes, unto the illiterate and orebusied multitude: who usually want vacancy or capacity to peruse, conceive, or retain the sence thereof under the tedious, abstruse forms of publique manifests: which figured in such Interludes were even obvious, to their very children.[22] A happy piece of policy to inform with delight the meanest member of the civill frame in what he is concerned. The means to our security becoming once to us a mysterie, may justly by us be suspected for disguised Furbery.[23]

To this advantage herein doth succeed the benefit which ariseth from the Peoples intercourse with one another, not onely in the introduction and pursuit of Commerce or Affairs: but in the initiation and support of mutuall Amities, sprung frequently from civill and unsought abodes, and cherished with gracefull entertainments in Society, which here not limited to particulars, may possibly be dispensed through the civill structure to the Composure of a generall Union, the strength and glory of a Commonwealth. From whence also ensues the requisite relaxation of Minde and Body, (o'reburdened with the travell of private or publique Negotiations) in a plausible divertisment, whereby become refresht, both may with fuller vigour and Alacrity, reassume the pursuit of their civill Functions.

Nor is the Action of a Theatre lesse usefull in the Education of our Youth (a frequent exercise in Forreign Seminaries, Societies and Schools[)],[24] to inanimate their spirits, render them plyant and susceptible to every form, [that] might either frame them more agreeable in their society, or more successefull in their private Commerce; as also, to lend a more assured gracefull unconstrain'd Demeanour to their persons and in such Habits, to indue them with undaunted Confidence, Facility, and readinesse to communicate in discourse the Image of their Thoughts

---

[21]*Propension:* propensity, inclination.   [22]It is noteworthy that Willan assumes civic entertainments to be a significant part of his subject.   [23]Variant of *fourbery:* deception, fraud, imposture (*OED*).   [24]At least three of the plays discussed in the present volume began thus: Buchanan's *Tyrannicall-Government*, Compton's *Herminigildus*, and the Kilkenny *Titus*. McCabe writes that thousands of boys on the Continent participated in such productions (67).

to an attentive multitude, an acquisition of no little moment, in publique Consult-ations, Conferences and pleas: In managing whereof, who hath not gained this Dexterity, shall finde the weightiest Reasons in his Argument silenc'd, smotherd, o'resway'd by the lesse pertinent clamor of an insisting Impudence.

These are the generall *Objects*, which we but cursorarily have onely pointed at, omitting them to amplifie or illustrate[25] with the Honour or Example of Antiquity, in due conformity to the quality of our Introduction, and the more clear inspection into the nature of our present Subject, which possibly might appear to rigid Tempers of far lesse validity, o're-shaddowed with such formalities, as if they were but artificiall Ornaments, no proper or essentiall lusters.

The particular Objects have a vaster influence, which (not to err from our prescription) we will contract to one united couplet to crown the closure of our Texture, affirming that *Poesie* investeth vertues, Glory with Eternity on Earth: and inspiring life in Harmony, lends Zeal wings to scale the vault of Heaven. If this Essay may in your Honour, Madam, but pretend to the first branch hereof; my next Endeavour shall in your Piety attempt to reach the latter.

Madam,
Your humbly Devoted Servant

L.W.

---

[25]I.e., "omitting to amplify or illustrate them."

APPENDIX B

Richard Flecknoe's *A Short Discourse of the English Stage to His Excellency, the Lord Marquess of Newcastle* (1664)[1].

My Noble Lord,

I Send your Excellency here a short Discourse of the *English Stage,* (which if you pleas'd you could far better treat of then my self) but before I begin it, I will speak a word or two of thôse of other Countreys.

About the midst of the last Century, Playes, after a long discontinuance, and civil death in a manner, began to be reviv'd again, first in *Italy* by *Guarino, Tasso, de Porta,* and others; and afterwards in *Spain* by *Lopes de Vega,* the French beginning later by reason of their Civil Wars, Cardinal *Richlieu* being the first that brought them into that Vouge[2] and Esteem as now they are; well knowing how much the Acting noble and heroick Playes, conferr'd to the instilling a noble and heroick Spirit into the Nation. For ûs, we began before them, and if since they seem to have out-stript us, 'tis because our Stage ha's stood at a stand this many years; nor may we doubt, but now we shall soon out-strip them again, if we hold on but as we begin. Of the Dutch I speak nothing, because they are but slow, and follow other Nations onely afar off: But to return unto our present subject.

Playes (which so flourisht amongst the Greeks, and afterwards amongst the Romans) were almost wholly abolished when their Empire was first converted to Christianity, and their Theaters, together with their Temples, for the most part, demolished as Reliques of Paganisme, some few onely reserved and dedicate to the service of the True God, as they had been to their false gods before; from which time to the last Age, they Acted nothing here, but Playes of the holy Scripture, or Saints Lives; and that without any certain Theaters or set Companies, till about the beginning of Queen *Elizabeths* Reign, they began here to assemble into Companies, and set up Theaters, first in the City, (as in the Inn-yards of the *Cross-Keyes,* and *Bull* in *Grace* and *Bishops-Gate Street* at this day is to be seen) till

---

[1]This brief historical survey first appeared at the back of Flecknoe's *Love's Kingdom* (G3r-G8r), which was printed in 1664 by R. Wood for the author. It is of particular interest for providing an overview by one of our dramatists of the drama up to and during the period under discussion. Its addressee was, of course, both a dramatist himself and a patron of dramatists. In this transcription, one typographical error has been corrected. [2]An obsolete variant of *vogue* (*OED*).

that Fanatick Spirit which then began with the Stage, and after ended with the Throne, banisht them thence into the Suburbs, as after they did the Kingdom, in the beginning of our Civil Wars.[3] In which time,[4] Playes were so little incompatible with Religion, and the Theater with the Church, as on Week-dayes after Vespers, both the Children of the Chappel and St. *Pauls,* Acted Playes, the one in *White-Friers,* the other behinde the Convocation-house in *Pauls,* till people growing more precise,[5] and Playes more licentious, the Theatre of *Pauls* was quite supprest, and that of the Children of the Chappel, converted to the use of the Children of the Revels.

In this time were Poets and Actors in their greatest flourish, *Johnson, Shakespear,* with *Beaumont* and *Fletcher* their Poets, and *Field,* and *Burbidge* their Actors.[6]

For Playes, *Shakespear* was one of the first, who inverted the Dramatick Stile, from dull History to quick Comedy, upon whom *Johnson* refin'd, as *Beaumont* and *Fletcher* first writ in the Heroick way, upon whom *Suckling* and others endeavoured to refine agen; one saying wittily of his *Aglaura,* that 'twas full of fine flowers, but they seem'd rather stuck, then growing there; as another of *Shakespear's* writings, that 'twas a fine Garden, but it wanted weeding.

There are few of our English Playes (excepting onely some few of *Johnson*s) without some faults or other; and if the French have fewer then our English, 'tis because théy confine themselves to narrower limits, and consequently have less liberty to erre.

The chief faults of ours, are our huddling too much matter together, and making them too long and intricate; we imagining we never have intrigue enough, till we lose our selves and Auditors, who shu'd be led in a Maze, but not a Mist; and through turning and winding wayes, but sô still, as they may finde their way at last.

A good Play shu'd be like a good stuff,[7] closely and evenly wrought, without any breakes, thrums, or loose ends in 'um, or like a good Picture well painted and designed; the Plot or Contrivement, the Design, the Writing, the Coloris, and Counterplot, the Shaddowings, with other Embellishments: or finally, it shu'd be like a well contriv'd Garden, cast into its Walks and Counterwalks, betwixt an Alley and a Wilderness, neither too plain, nor too confus'd. Of all Arts, that of the Dramatick Poet is the most difficult and most subject to censure; for in all others, they write onely of some particular subject, as the Mathematician of Mathematicks, or Philosopher of Philosophy; but in thât, the Poet must write of every thing, and every one undertakes to judge of it.

A Dramatick Poet is to the Stage as a Pilot to the Ship; and to the Actors, as an Architect to the Builders, or Master to his Schollars: he is to be a good moral

---

[3]Plays were performed at the Cross Keys Inn on Gracechurch Street from some time before 1579 and at the Bull Inn on Bishopsgate Street from some time before 1575. Moving hastily and writing broadly in this passage, Flecknoe traces the "Fanatick Spirit" to Elizabeth's day and, in the process, considerably oversimplifies the historical facts pertaining to drama. [4]Flecknoe at this point resumes his observations on the early days. [5]I.e., puritanical. [6]Nathan Field (1587-1620?) and Richard Burbage (ca. 1567-1619), both of the King's Men. Flecknoe passes over the fact that Field was also a playwright. [7]A textile fabric.

Philosopher, but yet more learned in Men then Books. He is to be a wise, as well as a witty Man, and a good man, as well as a good Poet; and I'de allow him to be so far a good fellow too, to take a chearful cup to whet his wits, so he take not so much to dull 'um, and whet 'um quite away.

To compare our English Dramatick Poets together (without taxing them) *Shakespear* excelled in a natural Vein, *Fletcher* in Wit, and *Johnson* in Gravity and ponderousness of Style; whose onely fault was, he was too elaborate; and had he mixt less erudition with his Playes, they had been more pleasant and delightful then they are. Comparing him with *Shakespear,* you shall see the difference betwixt Nature and Art; and with *Fletcher,* the difference betwixt Wit and Judgement: Wit being an exuberant thing, like *Nilus,* never more commendable then when it overflowes; but Judgement a stayèd and reposed thing, always containing it self within its bounds and limits.

Beaumont and *Fletcher* were excellent in their kinde, but they often err'd against *Decorum,* seldom representing a valiant man without somewhat of the *Braggadoccio,* nor an honourable woman without somewhat of *Dol Common* in her:[8] to say nothing of their irreverent representing Kings persons on the Stage, who shu'd never be represented, but with Revêrence: Besides, *Fletcher* was the first who introduc't that witty obscenity in his Playes, which like poison infused in pleasant liquor, is alwayes the more dangerous the more delightful. And here to speak a word or two of Wit, it is the spirit and quintessence of speech, extracted out of the substance of the thing we speak of, having nothing of the superfice, or dross of words (as clenches, quibbles, gingles, and such like trifles have[9]) it is thât, in pleasant and facetious discourse, as Eloquence is in grave and serious; not learnt by Art and Precept, but Nature and Company. 'Tis in vain to say any more of it; for if I could tell you what it were, it would not be what it is; being somewhat above expression, and such a volatil thing, as 'tis altogether as volatil to describe.

It was the happiness of the Actors of those Times to have such Poets as these to instruct them, and write for them; and no less of those Poets to have such docile and excellent Actors to Act their Playes, as a *Field* and *Burbidge;* of whom we may say, that he was a delightful *Proteus,* so wholly transforming himself into his Part, and putting off himself with his Cloathes, as he never (not so much as in the Tyring-house) assum'd himself again until the Play was done: there being as much difference betwixt him and one of our common Actors, as between a Ballad-singer who onely mouths it, and an excellent singer, who knows all his Graces, and can artfully vary and modulate his Voice, even to know how much breath he is to give to every syllable. He had all the parts of an excellent Orator, (animating his words with speaking, and Speech with Action) his Auditors being never more delighted then when he spake, nor more sorry then when he held his peace; yet even thên, he was an excellent Actor still, never falling in his Part when he had done speaking; but with his looks and gesture, maintaining it still unto the heighth, he imagining

---

[8]The name "Dol Common" conveys its own meaning, but Flecknoe cannot have written it without thinking especially of Jonson's roguish trollop in *The Alchemist* (1610).   [9]A clench is a play on words, a pun, or a quibble, and *gingle* is an obsolete form of *jingle* (*OED*).

Age quod agis, onely spoke to him:[10] so as those who call him a Player do him wrong, no man being less idle then he, whose whole life is nothing else but action; with only this difference from other mens, that as what is but a Play to them, is his Business; so their business is but a play to him.

Now, for the difference betwixt our Theaters and those of former times, they were but plain and simple, with no other Scenes, nor Decorations of the Stage, but onely old Tapestry, and the Stage strew'd with Rushes, (with their Habits accordingly) whereas ours now for cost and ornament are arriv'd to the heighth of Magnificence; but that which makes our Stage the better, makes our Playes the worse perhaps, they striving now to make them more for sight, then hearing; whence that solid joy of the interior is lost, and that benefit which men formerly receiv'd from Playes, from which they seldom or never went away, but far better and wiser then they came.

The Stage being a harmless and innocent Recreation; where the minde is recreated and delighted, and that *Ludus Literarum,* or School of good Language and Behaviour, that makes Youth soonest Man, and man soonest good and vertuous, by joyning example to precept, and the pleasure of seeing to that of hearing. Its chiefest end is, to render Folly ridiculous, Vice odious, and Vertue and Noblenesse so amiable and lovely, as, every one shu'd be delighted and enamoured with it; from which when it deflects; as, *corruptio optimi pessima;*[11] of the best it becomes the worst of Recreations. And that his Majesty well understood, when after his happy Restauration, he took such care to purge it from all vice and obscenity; and would to God he had found all bodies and humours as apt and easie to be purg'd and reform'd as thât.

For Scenes and Machines they are no new invention, our Masks and some of our Playes in former times (though not so ordinary) having had as good or rather better then any we have now.

They are excellent helps of imagination, most grateful deceptions of the sight, and graceful and becoming Ornaments of the Stage, transporting you easily without lassitude from one place to another; or rather by a kinde of delightful Magick, whilst you sit still, does bring the place to you. Of this curious Art the Italians (this latter age) are the greatest masters, the *French* good proficients, and we in *England* onely Schollars and Learners yet, having proceeded no further then to bare painting, and not arriv'd to the stupendious wonders of your great Ingeniers, especially not knowing yet how to place our Lights, for the more advantage and illuminating of the Scenes.

And thus much suffices it briefly to have said of all that concerns our Modern Stage, onely to give others occasion to say more.

FINIS

---

[10]That is, Burbage applied to himself an adage that means, literally, "Do what you are doing." Best known in this form and perhaps deriving from Plautus, *Miles Gloriosus* ("Age si quid agis" [l. 215]), it probably can be understood in the present context to mean "Maintain your role whether you are speaking or not." [11]"The corruption of the best is the worst." Hugh Percy Jones gives as a variant "The fallen Saint is the worst kind of sinner" (24). Cf. Shakespeare's "Lilies that fester smell far worse than weeds" (Sonnet 94).

WORKS CITED

Asterisks are placed before entries of all dramatic writings, including various forms of masques, drolls, jigs, civic entertainments, and some of the more playlike pamphlet dialogues. Translations are generally listed under the names of translators. Unless otherwise indicated, the place of publication of sixteenth- and seventeenth-century titles is London. A reader desiring separate listings of plays and playwrights will find most of those named here in the Harbage-Schoenbaum-Wagonheim *Annals of English Drama.*

The Actors Remonstrance, or Complaint: For the Silencing of Their Profession. 1643.

Adis, Henry. *A Fannaticks Mite.* 1660.

Adler, Jeremy. "Rehearsing a Merry Revolution." *London Times Literary Supplement* 22-28 Dec. 1989: 1412-13.

Aggeler, Geoffrey D. "The Rebellion in Cavalier Drama." *Western Humanities Review* 32 (1978): 53-75.

*Alphonsus Emperor of Germany. 1654.

Altieri, Joanne. *The Theatre of Praise: The Panegyric Tradition in Seventeenth-Century English Drama.* Newark: U of Delaware P, 1986.

Andrews, Michael C. "The Sources of *Andromana.*" *Review of English Studies* ns 19 (1968): 295-300.

Anselment, Raymond A. *Loyalist Resolve: Patient Fortitude in the English Civil War.* Newark: U of Delaware P, 1988.

Arber, Edward. *A Transcript of the Registers of the Worshipful Company of Stationers, 1554-1640.* 5 vols. London: privately printed, 1875-94. Gloucester, Mass.: Peter Smith, 1967. [See also Briscoe, G.E.]

Arundell, Dennis. *The Critic at the Opera.* London: Ernest Benn, 1957.

Ashmole, Elias. *Sol in Ascendente; or, The Glorious Appearance of Charles the Second, upon the Horizon of London.* 1660.

Aston, Margaret. *England's Iconoclasts.* Oxford: Clarendon, 1988.

Atkyns, Richard. *The Vindication of Richard Atkyns. . . .* Ed. Peter Young and John Gwyn. Hamden, Conn.: Archon, 1968.

Ausonius. *Ausonius.* Trans. Hugh G. Evelyn White. Vol. 2 of 2. 1921. Cambridge, Mass.: Harvard UP, 1967.

**B., H.H. [Henry Burnell?], trans. *The World's Idol, or Plutus.* From Aristophanes. 1659.

*B., T. *The Rebellion of Naples; or, The Tragedy of Massenello.* 1649.

Backscheider, Paula R. *Spectacular Politics: Theatrical Power and Mass Culture in Early Modern England.* Baltimore: Johns Hopkins UP, 1993.

Bacon, Francis. *The Essayes or Counsels, Civill and Morall.* Ed. Michael Kiernan. Cambridge, Mass.: Harvard UP, 1985.

Baker, Richard. *Theatrum Redivivum; or, The Theatre Vindicated.* 1662.

*Balshaw, John. [Untitled jig]. BL Add. MS 68891. 1660.

Barish, Jonas. *The Antitheatrical Prejudice.* Berkeley: U of California P, 1981.

Baron, Robert. *The Cyprian Academy.* 1647.

*———. *Mirza: A Tragedie, Really Acted in Persia, in the Last Age.* 1655.

———. *Pocula Castalia.* 1650.

*Baskervill, Charles Read. *The Elizabethan Jig and Related Song Drama.* 1929. New York: Dover, 1965.

The Bastard. 1652.

Bates, George. *Elenchus Motuum Nuperorum in Anglia.* Trans. A. Lovell. 2 pts. 1685.

Battaile on Hopton-Heath in Staffordshire betweene His Majesties Forces under the Right Honourable the Earle of Northampton, and Those of the Rebels. 1643.

*Beaumont, Francis, and John Fletcher. *Comedies and Tragedies.* 1647.

———. *A King and No King.* 1655.

Beheaded Dr. John Hewytt's Ghost Pleading. 1659.

Beilin, Elaine. "Elizabeth Cary and *The Tragedie of Mariam.*" *Papers on Language and Literature* 16 (1980): 45-64.

Bentley, Gerald E. *The Jacobean and Caroline Stage.* 7 vols. Oxford: Clarendon, 1941-68.

———. "John Cotgrave's *English Treasury of Wit and Language* and the Elizabethan Drama." *Studies in Philology* 40 (1943): 186-203.

———. *The Profession of Dramatist in Shakespeare's Time.* Princeton, N.J.: Princeton UP, 1971.

———. *Shakespeare and Jonson: Their Reputations in the Seventeenth Century Compared.* 2 vols. Chicago: U of Chicago P, 1945.

———. "The Theatres and the Actors." *The Revels History of Drama in English.* vol. 4. Ed. Philip Edwards et al. Methuen: London, 1981. 69-124.

Bergeron, David M. *English Civic Pageantry, 1558-1642.* Columbia: U of South Carolina P, 1971.

Bevington, David M. *Tudor Drama and Politics: A Critical Approach to Topical Meaning.* Cambridge, Mass.: Harvard UP, 1968.

*Birkhead, Henry(?). *The Female Rebellion.* Bodleian MS Tanner 466, 174r-199v. ca. 1657-59.

The Bloody Court; or, The Fatal Tribunall. 1649.

Bold, John. *John Webb: Architectural Theory and Practice in the Seventeenth Century.* Oxford: Clarendon, 1989.

Bond, John. *The Poets Recantation, Having Suffered in the Pillory.* 1642.

Bone, Quentin. *Henrietta Maria: Queen of the Cavaliers.* Urbana: U of Illinois P, 1972.

The Bouncing Knight; or, The Robers Rob'd. Elson. 47-59.

Bowers, Rick. "Players, Puritans, and 'Theatrical' Propaganda, 1642-1660." *Dalhousie Review* 67 (1987): 463-79.

Boyce, Benjamin. *The Polemic Character, 1640-1661*. New York: Octagon, 1969.

Bradley, Jesse Franklin. "Robert Baron's Tragedy of *Mirza*." *Modern Language Notes* 34 (1919): 402-8.

The Braggadocia Souldier; and, The Civil Citizen. 1647.

*Brathwaite, Richard. *Mercurius Britanicus*. 1641.

A Briefe Discourse upon Tyrants and Tyranny. 1642.

Briggs, Julia. *This Stage-Play World: English Literature and Its Background, 1580-1625*. Oxford: Oxford UP, 1983.

Briscoe, G.E., ed. *A Transcript of the Registers of the Worshipful Company of Stationers . . . from 1640-1708*. 3 vols. London: privately printed, 1913-14. Gloucester, Mass.: Peter Smith, 1967. [See also Arber, Edward.]

Bristol, Michael D. *Carnival and Theater: Plebeian Culture and the Structure of Authority in Renaissance England*. New York: Methuen, 1985.

*Brome, Alexander. *The Cunning Lovers*. 1654.

———. *Rump; or, An Exact Collection of the Choycest Poems and Songs Relating to the Late Times*. 1662.

———. *Songs and Other Poems*. 1661.

*Brome, Richard. *The Antipodes*. 1640.

*———. *Five New Playes*. Ed. Alexander Brome. 1653.

*———. *Five New Playes*. 1659.

*———. *A Joviall Crew; or, The Merry Beggars*. 1652.

Buc, George. *The History of the Life and Reigne of Richard the Third*. 1647.

*Buchanan, George. *A Critical Edition of George Buchanan's "Baptistes" and of Its Anonymous Seventeenth-Century Translation "Tyrannicall-Government Anatomized."* Ed. Steven Berkowitz. New York: Garland, 1992.

*———. *Tyrannicall-Government Anatomized; or, A Discourse Concerning Evil-Councellors*. Anon. trans. of *Baptistes, siue Calumnia, tragoedia*. 1643.

*Bulteel, John. *Londons Triumph; or, The Solemn and Magnificent Reception of That Honourable Gentleman, Robert Tichburn*. 1656.

*Burkhead, Henry. *Cola's Furie; or, Lirenda's Miserie*. Kilkenny, 1646.

Burne, Alfred H., and Peter Young. *The Great Civil War*. London: Eyre and Spottiswoode, 1959.

*Burnell, Henry. *Landgartha*. Dublin, 1641.

Burton, Robert. *The Anatomy of Melancholy*. 1638.

Bush, Douglas. *English Literature in the Earlier Seventeenth Century, 1600-1660*. 1945. Rev., Oxford: Clarendon, 1962.

Bushnell, Rebecca W. *Tragedies of Tyrants: Political Thought and Theater in the English Renaissance*. Ithaca, N.Y.: Cornell UP, 1990.

Butler, Martin. "A Case Study in Caroline Political Theatre: Brathwaite's *Mercurius Britannicus* (1641)." *Historical Journal* 27 (1984): 947-53.

———. *Theatre and Crisis, 1632-1642*. Cambridge: Cambridge UP, 1984.

Butler, Samuel. *Mercurius Menippeus: The Loyal Satyrist*. 1682.

C., R. "To Mr. Alexander Goughe." *The Queene*. 1653.

Calendar of the Proceedings of the Committee for Advance of Money, 1642-1656. 3 vols. Ed. Mary Anne Everett Green. London: HMSO, 1888.

Calendar of State Papers, Domestic Series . . . 1640. Ed. William Douglas Hamilton. London: Longman, 1880.

Calendar of State Papers, Domestic Series, 1649-1650. Ed. Mary Anne Everett Green. London: Longman, 1875.

*Campion, Thomas. *The Discription of a Maske . . . in Honour of the Lord Hayes.* 1607.

Canfield, J. Douglas. "The Authorship of *Emilia:* Richard Flecknoe's Revision of *Erminia.*" *Restoration* 3 (1979): 3-7.

**Canterburie His Change of Diot, A New Play Called.* See Overton, Richard.

*Carew, Thomas. *Poems.* Ed. Rhodes Dunlap. Oxford: Clarendon, 1949.

Carey, Patrick. *Trivial Poems.* London: John Murray, 1820.

*Carlell, Lodowick. *The Deserving Favorite.* 1659.

Carlton, Charles. *Archbishop William Laud.* London: Routledge & Kegan Paul, 1987.

Carpenter, Richard. *Experience, Historie, and Divinitie.* 1641.

*———. *The Jesuit and the Monk.* 1656.

*———. *The Pragmatical Jesuit New-Leven'd.* ca. 1660-65.

Carter, Tim. "Lowbrow and Lifelike." *London Times Literary Supplement* 13 March 1992: 19.

*Cartwright, George. *The Heroick-Lover; or, The Infanta of Spain.* 1661.

*Cartwright, William. *The Lady-Errant. Comedies, Tragi-Comedies, with Other Poems.* 1651.

*———. *The Plays and Poems of William Cartwright.* Ed. G. Blakemore Evans. Madison: U of Wisconsin P, 1951.

*———. *The Royall Slave. Comedies, Tragi-Comedies, with Other Poems.* 1651.

*———. *The Siedge; or, Love's Convert. Comedies, Tragi-Comedies, with Other Poems.* 1651.

Cary, Otis. *A History of Christianity in Japan: Roman Catholic and Greek Orthodox Missions.* 2 vols. New York: Fleming H. Revell, 1909.

Cassidy, Frederic C., ed. *Dictionary of American Regional English.* Vol. 1. Cambridge, Mass.: Belknap P of Harvard UP, 1985.

A Catalogue of the Names of So Many of Those Commissioners as Sate and Sentenced the Late King Charles to Death. 1660.

Catalogue of the Pamphlets, Books, Newspapers, and Manuscripts Relating to the Civil War, the Commonwealth, and Restoration, Collected by George Thomason, 1640-1661. 2 vols. London: British Museum, 1908.

*Caussin, Nicholas. *Herminigildus.* See Compton, James.

*Cavendish, Jane, and Elizabeth Egerton. *The Concealed Fansyes. Poems, Songs, a Pastorall, and a Play.* Bodleian MS Rawlinson Poet. 16. ca. 1644-46.

*———. *A Pastorall. Poems, Songs, a Pastorall, and a Play.* Bodleian MS Rawlinson Poet. 16. ca. 1644-46.

*Cavendish, Margaret. *Bell in Campo. Playes.* 1662.

*———. *The Comicall Hash. Playes.* 1662.

———. *Description of the New World.* 1666.

*———. *The Lady Contemplation. Playes.* 1662.

————. *The Life of the Thrice Noble, High and Puissant Prince William Cavendishe.* 1667.

*————. *Loves Adventures. Playes.* 1662.

*————. *The Matrimonial Trouble. Playes.* 1662.

————. *Natures Pictures Drawn by Fancies Pencil.* 1656.

*————. *Natures Three Daughters. Playes.* 1662.

————. *Orations of Divers Sorts.* 1662.

*————. *Playes.* 1662.

*————. *Plays, Never before Printed.* 1668.

————. *Poems, and Fancies.* 1653.

*————. *The Presence. Plays, Never before Printed.* 1668.

*————. *The Publique Wooing. Playes.* 1662.

*————. *The Several Wits. Playes.* 1662.

*————. *The Sociable Companions. Plays, Never before Printed.* 1668.

————. *A True Relation of My Birth, Breeding, and Life. The Life of William Cavendish.* Ed. C.H. Firth. London: Routledge and Sons, 1906. 155-78.

*————. *The Unnatural Tragedy. Playes.* 1662.

*————. *Wits Cabal. Playes.* 1662.

————. *The Worlds Olio.* 1655.

*————. *Youths Glory, and Deaths Banquet. Playes.* 1662.

*Cavendish, William. *The Country Captaine.* 1649.

————. *An English "Prince": Newcastle's Machiavellian Political Guide to Charles II.* Ed. Gloria Italiano Anzilotti. Pisa: Giardini, 1988.

*————. *The King's Entertainment.* Nottingham University Library, Portland Collection, MS RwV23. 1660.

————. *La Méthode nouvelle et invention extraordinaire de dresser les chevaux.* Antwerp, 1658.

————. *A New Method and Extraordinary Invention to Dress Horses.* 1667.

————. *The Phanseys of William Cavendish Marquis of Newcastle Addressed to Margaret Lucas and Her Letters in Reply.* Ed. Douglas Grant. London: Nonesuch P, 1956.

*————. *A Pleasante & Merye Humor off a Roge.* Ed. Francis Needham. *Welbeck Miscellany I.* Bungay, Suffolk: Clay & Son, 1933.

*————. *The Variety.* 1649.

*————. *Witts Triumvirate; or, The Philosopher.* BL Add. MS 45865.

*————. *Witts Triumvirate; or, The Philosopher.* Ed. Cathryn Anne Nelson. 2 vols. Salzburg: Institut für Englische Sprache und Literatur, 1975.

*Chamberlain, Robert. *The Swaggering Damsel.* 1640.

Chamberlaine, William. *England's Jubile.* Saintsbury 1:296-303.

*————. *Love's Victory.* 1658.

————. *Pharonnida.* Saintsbury 1:1-295.

The Character of an Oxford-Incendiary. 1645.

Charles I. *His Speech Made upon the Scaffold.* 1649.

————. *The Letters, Speeches, and Proclamations of King Charles I.* Ed. Charles Petrie. New York: Funk and Wagnalls, 1968.

Chester, Allan G. *Thomas May: Man of Letters, 1595-1650.* Philadelphia: U of Pennsylvania, 1932.

Cicero. *Brutus.* Trans. G.L. Hendrickson. London: Heinemann, 1962. 2-293.

——. *De Oratore.* Trans. H. Rackham. 3 vols. 1942. London: Heinemann, 1960.

——. *Philippics.* Ed. and trans. D.R. Shackleton Bailey. Chapel Hill: U of North Carolina P, 1986.

Clare, Janet. *"Art made tongue-tied by authority": Elizabethan and Jacobean Dramatic Censorship.* Manchester: Manchester UP, 1990.

Clark, Ira. *Professional Playwrights: Massinger, Ford, Shirley, and Brome.* Lexington: UP of Kentucky, 1992.

Cleveland, John. *The Poems of John Cleveland.* Ed. Brian Morris and Eleanor Withington. Oxford: Clarendon, 1967.

*The Club-Men. Elson. 146-50.

Cobbett, William. *Cobbett's Parliamentary History of England.* Vol. 3, Oct. 1642– April 1660. London: T. Curson Hansard, 1808.

A Coffin for King Charles: A Crowne for Cromwell: A Pit for the People. 1649.

**Cokayne, Aston. *A Masque Presented at Bretbie. A Chain of Golden Poems.* 1658.

*——. *The Obstinate Lady.* 1657.

*——. *Trappolin Suppos'd a Prince.* 1658.

Coltrane, Robert. "Cowley's Revisions in *Cutter of Coleman Street.*" *Restoration* 13 (1989): 68-75.

**Compton, James, trans. *Agamemnon.* From Seneca. BL Add. MS 60276.

*——. *Bassianus.* BL Add. MS 60281.

——. "The former constitution of y^{is} realm. . . . " BL Add. MS 60282.

*——, trans. *Hercules Furens.* From Seneca. BL Add. MSS 60276 and 60277.

*——, trans. *Herminigildus.* From Nicolas Caussin. BL Add. MS 60276.

*——. *Leontius, King of Cyprus.* BL Add. MSS 60278 and 60279. ca. 1649.

*——, trans. *The Mandrake.* From Niccolò Machiavelli, *La Mandragola.* BL Add. MS 60278.

*——. *Mariamne.* BL Add. MS 60280.

——. *The Martird Monarch.* BL Add. MS 60282. 1649-50.

*——. Untitled fragment of a tragedy concerning Sophius and Caliphilus. BL Add. MS 60281.

Compton, William Bingham. *History of the Comptons of Compton Wynyates.* London: John Lane, 1930.

A Conference Held between the Old Lord Protector and the New Lord General. 1660.

Coonan, Thomas L. *The Irish Confederacy and the Puritan Revolution.* Dublin: Clonmore and Reynolds, 1954.

**"The Copt Hall Interlude." Essex Record Office MS D/DWZ. (Beginning "There's more tradesmen broke this yeare ith city.")

**Corneille, Pierre. *Polyeucte.* Paris, 1643.

Cotton, Nancy. *Women Playwrights in England, c. 1363-1750.* Lewisburg: Bucknell UP, 1980.

Coughlan, Patricia. " 'Enter Revenge': Henry Burkhead and *Cola's Furie.*" *Theatre Research International* 15 (1990): 1-17.

The Court & Kitchin of Elizabeth, Commonly Called Joan Cromwel, the Wife of the Late Usurper. 1664.

Cowley, Abraham. *The Civil War.* Ed. Allan Pritchard. Toronto: U of Toronto P, 1973.

*————. *Cutter of Coleman-Street*. 1663.

————. *A Discourse by Way of Vision. Essays, Plays, and Sundry Verses*. Ed. A.R. Waller. Cambridge: Cambridge UP, 1906. 342-76.

*————. *The Guardian*. 1650.

————. *Poems*. 1655.

*Cox, Robert. *Acteon and Diana; with A Pastoral Storie of the Nimph Oenone: Followed by the Several Conceited Humours of Bumpkin the Huntsman. Hobbinol the Shepherd. Singing Simpkin, and John Swabber the Seaman*. 1656. See also Kirkman, *The Wits*.

Craftie Cromwell. See Mercurius Melancholicus.

Cressy, David. *Literacy and the Social Order: Reading and Writing in Tudor and Stuart England*. Cambridge: Cambridge UP, 1980.

Cromwell, Oliver. *By the Lord Protector*. Proclamation of 23 May 1654.

————. *Orders of His Highness the Lord Protector . . . for Putting in . . . Execution the Laws, Statutes, and Ordinances, Made and Provided . . . for the Further Regulating of Printing*. 1655.

————. *The Writings and Speeches of Oliver Cromwell*. Ed. Wilbur Cortez Abbott. 4 vols. Cambridge, Mass.: Harvard UP, 1947.

Cromwell's Conspiracy: A Tragy-Comedy. 1660.

Crouch, John. See The Man in the Moon.

The Cryes of Westminster. 1648.

Cunningham, Dolora. "The Jonsonian Masque as a Literary Form." *English Literary History* 22 (1955): 108-24.

Cutts, John. "The Anonymous Masque-like Entertainment in Egerton MS 1994, and Richard Brome." *Comparative Drama* 1 (1967): 277-87.

————. "The Dramatic Writing of Martin Llewellyn." *Philological Quarterly* 47 (1968): 16-29.

The Cyprian Conqueror; or, the Faithless Relict. BL Sloane MS 3709, 1v-51v. ca. 1640-42.

*Daborne, Robert. *The Poor-Mans Comfort: A Tragi-Comedy*. 1655.

The Dagonizing of Bartholomew Fayre. 1647.

*Dancer, John, trans. *Aminta*. From Torquato Tasso. 1660.

Daniel, George. *The Selected Poems of George Daniel of Beswick, 1616-1657*. Ed. Thomas B. Stroup. Lexington: UP of Kentucky, 1959.

*Daniel, Samuel. *Tethys Festival. The Complete Works in Verse and Prose*. Ed. Alexander B. Grosart. Vol. 3 of 5. 1885. New York: Russell and Russell, 1963. 301-23.

*Davenant, William. *Britannia Triumphans*. 1638.

*————. *The Cruelty of the Spaniards in Peru*. 1658.

*————. *The First Day's Entertainment at Rutland-House*. 1657.

*————. *The History of Sr Francis Drake: The First Part*. 1659.

*————. *Salmacida Spolia*. 1640.

*————. *The Siege of Rhodes*. [Pt. 1]. 1656.

*————. *The Siege of Rhodes: The First and Second Part*. 1663.

*————. *The Triumphs of the Prince d'Amour*. 1635.

*Davenport, Robert. *King John and Matilda*. 1655.

Davis, J.C. *Fear, Myth, and History: The Ranters and the Historians*. Cambridge: Cambridge UP, 1986.

Dawson, William Harbutt. *Cromwell's Understudy: The Life and Times of General John Lambert.* London: William Hodge, 1938.

Deedes, Cecil, ed. *Royal and Loyal Sufferers.* London: F. E. Robinson, 1903.

A Deep Sigh Breath'd Through the Lodgings at White-Hall. 1642.

*Denham, John. *The Sophy.* 1642.

*Denny, William. *The Sheepheard's Holiday.* BL Add. MS 34065. 1651.

*Dent, Edward J. *Cupid and Death: Matthew Locke and Christopher Gibbons. Musica Britannica.* Vol. 2. London: Stainer and Bell, 1951.

A Description of the Passage of Thomas Late Earle of Strafford, over the River of Styx. 1641.

The Devill and the Parliament. 1648.

The Dictionary of National Biography. Ed. Leslie Stephen and Sidney Lee. 22 vols. Oxford: Oxford UP, 1921-22.

The Disease of the House; or, The State Mountebanck. 1649.

The Disloyall Favorite; or, The Tragedy of Mettellus. Bodleian MS Rawlinson D.1361, 285r-305v. 1650s.

Disraeli, Isaac. "The History of the Theatre During Its Suppression." *Curiosities of Literature* 2 (1837): 281-92.

Don Juan Lamberto. 1661.

Donald, Peter. *An Uncounselled King: Charles I and the Scottish Troubles, 1637-1641.* Cambridge: Cambridge UP, 1990.

Donne, John. *Biathanatos.* 1648.

*D'Ouvilley, George Gerbier. *The False Favourite Disgrac'd.* 1657.

Downes, John. *Roscius Anglicanus.* Ed. Judith Milhous and Robert D. Hume. London: Society for Theatre Research, 1987.

Drayton, Michael. *Pastorals. The Works of Michael Drayton.* Vol. 2 of 2. Ed. J. William Hebel. Oxford: Shakespeare Head P, 1961. 515-73.

Drummond, Richard Henry. *A History of Christianity in Japan.* Grand Rapids, Mich.: Eerdmans, 1971.

*Drury, William. *Aluredus sive Alfredus.* See Knightley, Robert.

Dryden, John. *Of Dramatick Poesie, An Essay. The Works of John Dryden.* Vol. 17 of 20. Ed. Samuel H. Monk et al. Berkeley: U of California P, 1971. 3-81.

———. *The Poems of John Dryden.* Ed. James Kinsley. 4 vols. Oxford: Clarendon, 1958.

———. Preface to *Ovid's Epistles, Translated by Several Hands.* 1680.

*———. *The Spanish Fryar.* 1681.

Duppa, Bryan, ed. *Jonsonus Virbius.* 1638.

Dutton, Richard. *Mastering the Revels: The Regulation and Censorship of English Renaissance Drama.* Iowa City: U of Iowa P, 1991.

The Earle of Straffords Ghost Complaining 1644.

Edmond, Mary. *Rare Sir William Davenant: Poet Laureate, Playwright, Civil War General, Restoration Theatre Manager.* New York: St. Martin's, 1987.

Edmundson, Henry. *Comes Facundus in Via.* 1658.

*Edwards, Richard. *Damon and Pithias.* 1571.

Egerton, Elizabeth. *See* Cavendish, Jane, and Elizabeth Egerton.

An Elegie upon the Death of Our Dread Soveraigne. 1649.

An Elegy on the Murder Committed at Colchester upon Sir C. Lucas and Sir G. Lisle. 1648.

Elizabeth, Queen of Bohemia. ALS to Prince Charles. Lambeth Palace Library MS 645, no. 83. 27 Dec. 1655.

Elsky, Martin. *Authorizing Words: Speech, Writing, and Print in the English Renaissance.* Ithaca, N.Y.: Cornell UP, 1989.

*Elson, John James, ed. *The Wits; or, Sport upon Sport.* Ithaca, N.Y.: Cornell UP, 1932.

England's Black Tribunall: Set Forth in the Triall of K. Charles I. 1660.

Etherege, George. *The Poems of Sir George Etherege.* Ed. James Thorpe. Princeton, N.J.: Princeton UP, 1963.

Evans, John, comp. *Hesperides; or, The Muses Garden.* Folger MS V.b.93. ca. 1655.

Evans, Robert C. " 'Making Just Approaches': Ben Jonson's Poems to the Earl of Newcastle." *Renaissance Papers, 1988.* Ed. Dale B.J. Randall and Joseph A. Porter. Durham, N.C.: Southeastern Renaissance Conference, 1988. 63-75.

Evelyn, John. *The Diary of John Evelyn.* Ed. E.S. de Beer. Vol. 3 of 6. Oxford: Clarendon, 1955.

———. *Numismata: A Discourse of Medals.* 1697.

Ewbank, Inga-Stina. " 'These pretty devices': A Study of Masques in Plays." *A Book of Masques in Honour of Allardyce Nicoll.* Ed. T.J.B. Spencer et al. Cambridge: Cambridge UP, 1967. 405-48.

An Exact Description of a Roundhead, and a Long-Head Shag-Poll. 1642.

Ezell, Margaret J.M. " 'To Be Your Daughter in Your Pen': The Social Functions of Literature in the Writings of Lady Elizabeth Brackley and Lady Jane Cavendish." *Huntington Library Quarterly* 51 (1988): 281-96.

Fairfax, Thomas. "The Poems of Thomas Third Lord Fairfax." Ed. Edward Bliss Reed. *Transactions of the Connecticut Academy of Arts and Sciences* 14 (1909): 237-90.

The Famous Tragedie of King Charles I. 1649.

Fane, Francis. *Letters and Poems in Honour of . . . Margaret, Dutchess of Newcastle.* 1673.

*Fane, Mildmay. *Candia Restaurata.* BL Add. MS 34221, 1v-18v. 1641.

*———. *The Change.* BL Add. MS 34221, 50r-68v. 1642.

*———. *De Pugna Animi.* BL Add. MS 34221, 124v-147r. 1650.

———. *Otia Sacra (1648).* Introduction by Donald M. Friedman. Delmar, N.Y.: Scholars' Facsimiles and Reprints, 1975.

*———. *Raguaillo D'Oceano.* BL Add. MS 34221, 107v-123r. 1640.

*———. *Raguaillo D'Oceano, 1640, and Candy Restored, 1641.* Ed. Clifford Leech. *Materials for the Study of the Old English Drama.* Ed. Henry de Vocht. Ns, vol. 15. Louvain: Ch. Uystpruyst, 1938.

*———. *Tymes Trick upon the Cards.* BL Add. MS 34221, 19v-49r. 1642.

*———. *Vertues Triumph.* BL Add. MS 34221, 69v-106v. 1644.

*Fanshawe, Richard, trans. *The Faithful Shepherd.* From Giambattista Guarini, *Il pastor fido.* 1647.

*———, trans. *Festivals Presented at Aranwhez.* From Antonio Hurtado de Mendoza. 1670.

*————, trans. *Querer por solo querer: To Love Only for Love Sake*. From Antonio Hurtado de Mendoza. 1670.

————. *Shorter Poems and Translations*. Ed. N.W. Bawcutt. Liverpool: Liverpool UP, 1964.

Farley-Hills, David. *The Benevolence of Laughter: Comic Poetry of the Commonwealth and Restoration*. London: Macmillan, 1974.

Feinberg, Anat. " 'Like Demie Gods the Apes Began to Move': The Ape in the English Theatrical Tradition, 1580-1660." *Cahiers Elizabethains* 35 (1989): 1-13.

Ferguson, Moira. "A 'Wise, Wittie and Learned Lady': Margaret Lucas Cavendish." *Women Writers of the Seventeenth Century*. Ed. Katharina M. Wilson and Frank J. Warnke. Athens: U of Georgia P, 1989. 305-40.

Fidoe, J., T. Jeanes, and W. Shaw. *The Parliament Justified in Their Late Proceedings against Charls Stuart*. 1649.

Filmer, Robert. *The Necessity of the Absolute Power of All Kings: And in Particular, of the King of England*. 1648.

Firth, C.H., and R.S. Rait, ed. *Acts and Ordinances of the Interregnum, 1642-1660*. 3 vols. London: HMSO, 1911.

Five Most Noble Speeches Spoken to His Majestie Returning Out of Scotland into England. 1641.

*Flecknoe, Richard. *Ariadne Deserted by Theseus, and Found and Courted by Bacchus*. 1654.

————. *Enigmaticall Characters, All Taken to the Life*. 1658.

*————. *Erminia*. 1661.

————. *Heroick Portraits*. 1660.

————. *The Idea of His Highness Oliver*. 1659.

————. *The Life of Tomaso the Wanderer*. Ed. G. Thorn-Drury. London: P.J. and A.E. Dobell, 1925.

*————. *Love's Dominion*. 1654.

*————. *Love's Kingdom*. 1664.

*————. *The Mariage of Oceanus and Brittania*. 1659.

————. *Miscellania; or, Poems of All Sorts*. 1653.

————. *The Prose Characters of Richard Flecknoe: A Critical Edition*. Ed. Fred Mayer. New York: Garland, 1987.

————. *A Relation of Ten Years Travells*. [1654?].

————. *A Short Discourse of the English Stage. Love's Kingdom*. 1664.

*Fletcher, John. *The Faithfull Shepheardesse*. 1609.

*————. *The Wild-Goose Chase*. 1652.

———— and Beaumont. *See* Beaumont, Francis, and John Fletcher.

*Forde, Thomas. *Love's Labyrinth*. 1660.

————. *The Times Anatomiz'd in Severall Characters*. 1647.

Forker, Charles R. "Bishop Laud and Shirley's *The Cardinal*." *Transactions of the Wisconsin Academy of Sciences, Arts, and Letters* 47 (1958): 241-51.

Foucault, Michel. *Discipline and Punishment*. Trans. Alan Sheridan. New York: Random House, 1979.

*Fountain, John. *The Rewards of Vertue*. 1661.

Frank, Joseph. *The Beginnings of the English Newspaper, 1620-1660*. Cambridge, Mass.: Harvard UP, 1961.

———. *Cromwell's Press Agent: A Critical Biography of Marchamont Nedham, 1620-1678*. Lanham, Md.: UP of America, 1980.

———. *Hobbled Pegasus: A Descriptive Bibliography of Minor English Poetry, 1641-1660*. Albuquerque: U of New Mexico P, 1968.

Fraser, Antonia. *Royal Charles: Charles II and the Restoration*. New York: Knopf, 1979.

Freehafer, John. "Brome, Suckling, and Davenant's Theater Project of 1639." *Texas Studies in Literature and Language* 10 (1968): 367-83.

Freeman, Arthur. "William Drury, Dramatist." *Recusant History* 8 (1966): 293-97.

*Fuller, Thomas. *Andronicus: A Tragedy, Impieties Long Successe, or Heavens Late Revenge*. 1661.

———. *Andronicus; or, The Unfortunate Politician*. 1646.

———. *The Church-History of Britain*. 1655.

———. *The Historie of the Holy Warre*. 1639.

———. *The History of the Worthies of England*. 1662.

———. *The Holy State and the Profane State*. 1642.

Gair, W.R. "The Politics of Scholarship: A Dramatic Comment on the Autocracy of Charles I." *The Elizabethan Theatre III*. Ed. David Galloway. Hamden, Conn.: Shoestring, 1973. 100-118.

———. "The Salusbury Circle at Llewenni." *Research Opportunities in Renaissance Drama* 11 (1968): 73-79.

Gardiner, Samuel Rawson, ed. *The Constitutional Documents of the Puritan Revolution, 1625-1660*. 3d ed. Oxford: Clarendon, 1906.

———. *History of the Commonwealth and Protectorate*. 3 vols. 3d ed. London: Longmans, Green, 1901.

*Gates, William Bryan. *The Dramatic Works and Translations of Sir William Lower with a Reprint of "The Enchanted Lovers."* Philadelphia: U of Pennsylvania, 1932.

Gauden, John. *Cromwell's Bloody Slaughter-House*. 1660.

*Gayton, Edmund. *Charity Triumphant; or, The Virgin-Shew*. 1655.

———. *Pleasant Notes upon Don Quixot*. 1654.

Gerbier, George D'Ouvilley. See D'Ouvilley, George Gerbier.

Gewirtz, Arthur. *Restoration Adaptations of Early 17th Century Comedies*. Lanham, Md.: UP of America, 1982.

The Ghost; or, The Woman Wears the Breeches. 1653.

Gilbert, John T., ed. *History of the Irish Confederation and the War in Ireland*. 7 vols. Dublin: Gill and Sons, 1882-91.

Gildersleeve, Virginia C. *Government Regulation of the Elizabethan Drama*. New York: Columbia UP, 1908.

Gimmelfarb-Brack, Marie. *Liberté, égalité, fraternité, justice!: La Vie et l'oeuvre de Richard Overton, Niveleur*. Berne: Lang, 1979.

Girouard, Mark. *Life in the English Country House*. Harmondsworth, Middlesex: Penguin, 1980.

*[Glapthorne, Henry?]. *Revenge for Honour*. 1654.

Glover, Henry. *Cain and Abel Parallel'd with King Charles and His Murderers*. 1664.

*Goffe, Thomas. *The Careles Shepherdess*. 1656.

Goldberg, Jonathan. *James I and the Politics of Literature*. Baltimore: Johns Hopkins UP, 1983.

Goldsmid, Edmund. *Explanatory Notes of a Pack of Cavalier Playing Cards*. Edinburgh: E. and G. Goldsmid, 1886.

*Goldsmith, Francis, trans. *Hugo Grotius, His Sophompaneas*. From Hugo Grotius, *Tragoedia Sophompaneas*. 1652.

Goodwin, John. *Anti-Cavalierisme; or, Truth Pleading as Well the Necessity, as the Lawfulnesse of This Present Warre*. 1643.

The Gossips Braule; or, The Women Weare the Breeches. 1655.

*Gough, John. *The Strange Discovery*. 1640.

The Governor. BL Add. MS 10419. 1656.

Granville-Barker, Harley. "On Translating Plays." *Transactions of the Royal Society of Literature* 3d ser., 5 (1925): 19-42.

The Grave-Makers. Elson. 111-18.

Graves, Thornton S., "Notes on Puritanism and the Stage." *Studies in Philology* 18 (1921): 141-69.

———. "Some Allusions to Religious and Political Plays." *Modern Philology* 9 (1911-12): 545-54.

Greenblatt, Stephen. *Renaissance Self-Fashioning from More to Shakespeare*. Chicago: U of Chicago P, 1984.

Greene, Robert. *Menaphon*. 1589.

Greg, Walter W. *A Bibliography of the English Printed Drama to the Restoration*. 4 vols. London: For the Bibliographical Society at the University P, Oxford. 1939-59.

———. *Pastoral Poetry and Pastoral Drama*. 1905. New York: Russell and Russell, 1959.

Greville, Fulke. "A Treatie of Warres." *Certaine Learned and Elegant Workes*. 1633. 70-82.

Griswold, Wendy. *Renaissance Revivals: City Comedy and Revenge Tragedy in the London Theater, 1576-1980*. Chicago: U of Chicago P, 1987.

Grobiana's Nuptialls. Bodleian MS Bodley 30, 13r-25r. [1640?]

Habington, William. *The Poems of William Habington*. Ed. Kenneth Allott. London: Hodder and Stoughton, 1948.

*———. *The Queene of Arragon*. 1640.

*Hackluyt, John. See Mercurius Melancholicus, *Mistris Parliament*.

Hall, John. *The True Cavalier Examined by His Principles*. 1656.

Hamilton, William Douglas, ed. *Calendar of State Papers, Domestic Series . . . 1639*. Vol. 14. London: Longman, 1873.

Hammond, Charles. *Truth's Discovery*. 1664.

Harbage, Alfred. *Annals of English Drama, 975-1700*. 1940. 2d ed., rev. Samuel Schoenbaum, 1964. 3d ed., rev. Sylvia Stoler Wagonheim. London: Routledge, 1989.

———. *Cavalier Drama*. New York: MLA, 1936.

———. "Elizabethan-Restoration Palimpsest." *Modern Language Review* 35 (1940): 287-319.

———. *Thomas Killigrew: Cavalier Dramatist, 1612-83*. Philadelphia: U of Pennsylvania P, 1930.

Hardacre, Paul H. *The Royalists During the Puritan Revolution.* The Hague: Martinus Nijhoff, 1956.

*Harding, Samuel. *Sicily and Naples.* Oxford, 1640.

Haythornthwaite, Philip. *The English Civil War, 1642-1651.* Poole, Dorset: Blandford, 1985.

Hazlitt, William Carew. *A Manual for the Collector and Amateur of Old English Plays.* London: Pickering and Chatto, 1892.

———. *The English Drama and Stage under the Tudor and Stuart Princes, 1543-1664.* London: Roxburghe Library, 1869.

The Hectors. 1656.

*Hedbäck, Ann-Mari, ed. *Sir William Davenant, The Siege of Rhodes: A Critical Edition.* Uppsala: Acta Universitatis Upsaliensis, 1973.

Hegg, Robert. *The Legend of Saint Cuthbert.* 1626. Rpt. 1717.

Heinemann, Margot. *Puritanism and Theatre: Thomas Middleton and Opposition Drama under the Early Stuarts.* Cambridge: Cambridge UP, 1980.

*Heminges, William. *The Fatal Contract: A French Tragedy.* 1653.

Henfrey, Henry W. *Numismata Cromwelliana.* London: John Russell Smith, 1875.

Herbert, Henry. *The Dramatic Records of Sir Henry Herbert.* Ed. Joseph Quincy Adams. New Haven, Conn.: Yale UP, 1917.

Herbert, Thomas. *A Relation of Some Yeares Travaile, Begunne Anno 1626.* 1634.

Herrick, Robert. *The Poetical Works of Robert Herrick.* Ed. L.C. Martin. Oxford: Clarendon, 1963.

Heyleyn, Peter. *A Briefe and Moderate Answer, to the Seditious and Scandalous Challenges of Henry Burton.* 1637.

Heywood, Thomas. *The Exemplary Lives and Memorable Acts of Nine the Most Worthy Women of the World.* 1640.

Hibbert, Christopher. *Cavaliers and Roundheads: The English at War, 1642-1649.* London: HarperCollins, 1993.

Hill, Christopher. "Literature and the English Revolution." *Seventeenth Century* 1 (1986): 15-30.

Hilton, John. *Catch That Catch Can; or, The Musical Companion.* 1667.

Hines, Samuel Philip, Jr. "English Translations of Aristophanes' Comedies, 1655-1742." Ph.D. diss., U of North Carolina at Chapel Hill, 1967.

Hirst, Derek. "The Politics of Literature in the English Republic." *Seventeenth Century* 5 (1990): 133-55.

Holland, Samuel. *Don Zara del Fogo.* 1656.

Horace. *Carminum Liber. The Odes and Epodes.* Trans. C.E. Bennett. 1927. Cambridge, Mass.: Harvard UP, 1968. 2-347.

———. *Epistolarum. Satires, Epistles, and Ars Poetica.* Trans. H. Rushton Fairclough. London: Heinemann, 1929. 247-441.

Hotson, Leslie. *The Commonwealth and Restoration Stage.* Cambridge, Mass.: Harvard UP, 1928.

*Howard, Robert. *The Blind Lady.* 1660.

*———. *The Country Gentleman: A "Lost" Play.* Ed. Arthur H. Scouten and Robert D. Hume. Philadelphia: U of Pennsylvania P, 1976.

Howell, James. *Epistolae Ho-Elianae.* 1650.

————, trans. *An Exact Historie of the Late Revolutions in Naples.* From Alessandro Giraffi. 1650.

*————, trans. *The Nuptialls of Peleus and Thetis, Consisting of a Mask and a Comedy.* Perhaps from Francesco Buti, *Le nozze di Peleo e di Theti.* 1654.

————. *A Winter Dreame.* 1649.

Hulse, Lynn. " 'The King's Entertainment' by the Duke of Newcastle." Forthcoming in *Viator.*

The Humble Petition of Us the Parliaments Poore Souldiers. 1648.

Hume, Robert D. *The Development of English Drama in the Late Seventeenth Century.* Oxford: Clarendon, 1976.

————. "Securing a Repertory: Plays on the London Stage, 1660-5." *Poetry and Drama, 1570-1700.* Ed. Antony Coleman and Antony Hammond. London: Methuen, 1981. 156-72.

The Humour of Simple; or, Simpleton the Smith. Elson. 165-74.

The Humours of Simpkin. Elson. 180-86.

Hunter, G.K. "Seneca and English Tragedy." *Seneca.* Ed. C.D.N. Costa. London: Routledge, 1974. 166-204.

Hunton, Samuel. *His Highness the Lord Protector-Protected.* 1654.

*Hurtado de Mendoza, Antonio de. *Fiesta que se hizo en Aranivez.* Madrid, 1623.

————. *Querer por solo querer.* In *Fiesta que se hizo en Aranivez.*

Hyde, Edward (Earl of Clarendon). *The History of the Rebellion and Civil Wars in England.* Ed. W.D. Macray. 6 vols. Oxford: Clarendon, 1888.

James I. *Basilikon Doron.* Edinburgh, 1603.

————. *The Political Works of James I.* Ed. Charles Howard McIlwain. Cambridge, Mass.: Harvard UP, 1918.

*Jaques, Francis. *The Queen of Corsica.* Facsimile prepared by Henry D. Manzen et al. Oxford: University Printing House, 1989.

*————. *The Queene of Corsica.* BL MS Lansdowne 807. 1642.

Jardine, Lisa. *Still Harping on Daughters: Women and Drama in the Age of Shakespeare.* Brighton, Sussex: Harvester, 1983.

Jermyn, Henry. ALS to Charles. Lambeth Palace Library MS 646, no. 28. 14 May 1655.

John Swabber. Elson. 191-203.

Johnson, Vivienne Stevens. "Images of Power: Oliver Cromwell in Seventeenth-Century Writings." Ph.D. diss., Duke U, 1990.

Jones, Hugh Percy, ed. *Dictionary of Foreign Phrases and Classical Quotations.* Edinburgh: John Grant, 1963.

Jones, Kathleen. *A Glorious Fame: The Life of Margaret Cavendish, Duchess of Newcastle, 1623-1673.* London: Bloomsbury, 1988.

*Jonson, Ben. *The Alchemist.* Ed. C.H. Herford and Percy Simpson. In *Ben Jonson.* Vol. 5 of 11. Oxford: Clarendon, 1954. 273-408.

*————. *Bartholomew Fair.* Ed. C.H. Herford, Percy Simpson, and Evelyn Simpson. In *Ben Jonson.* Vol. 6. Oxford: Clarendon, 1954. 1-141.

*————. *Catiline.* Ed. C.H. Herford and Percy Simpson. *Ben Jonson.* Vol. 5. Oxford: Clarendon, 1954. 409-550.

*————. *Cynthia's Revels.* Ed. C.H. Herford and Percy Simpson. *Ben Jonson.* Vol. 4. Oxford: Clarendon, 1954. 1-184.

*————. *An Entertainment at the Blackfriars.* Ed. C.H. Herford, Percy Simpson, and Evelyn Simpson. *Ben Jonson.* Vol. 7. Oxford: Clarendon, 1963. 765-78.

————. *Epigrammes. The Workes of Beniamin Jonson.* 1616.

*————. *Every Man Out of His Humour.* 1600.

*————. *Hymenaei.* Ed. C. H. Herford, Percy Simpson, and Evelyn Simpson. *Ben Jonson.* Vol. 7. Oxford: Clarendon, 1963. 203-41.

*————. *The Kings Entertainment at Welbeck.* Ed. C.H. Herford, Percy Simpson, and Evelyn Simpson. *Ben Jonson.* Vol. 7. Oxford: Clarendon, 1963. 787-803.

*————. *The New Inne; or, The Light Heart.* 1631.

*————. *Sejanus.* Ed. C.H. Herford and Percy Simpson. *Ben Jonson.* Vol. 4. Oxford: Clarendon, 1954. 327-471.

*————. *A Tale of a Tub.* Ed. C.H. Herford and Percy Simpson. *Ben Jonson.* Vol. 3. Oxford: Clarendon, 1954. 1-92.

*————. *Timber; or, Discoveries.* Ed. C.H. Herford, Percy Simpson, and Evelyn Simpson. *Ben Jonson.* Vol. 8. Oxford: Clarendon, 1954. 555-649.

————. *The Underwood.* Ed. C.H. Herford, Percy Simpson, and Evelyn Simpson. *Ben Jonson.* Vol. 8. Oxford: Clarendon, 1954. 123-295.

*————. *The Vision of Delight.* Ed. C.H. Herford, Percy Simpson, and Evelyn Simpson. *Ben Jonson.* Vol. 7. Oxford: Clarendon, 1963. 461-71.

*————. *Volpone.* Ed. C.H. Herford and Percy Simpson. *Ben Jonson.* Vol. 5. Oxford: Clarendon, 1954. 1-137.

*————. *The Workes of Beniamin Jonson.* 1616.

Jonsonus Virbius. See Duppa, Bryan.

*Jordan, Thomas. *Bacchus Festival . . . Being a Musical Representation . . . at Vintners-Hall.* 1660.

*————. *The Cheaters Cheated.* 1659.

*————. *Cupid His Coronation.* Ed. W.H. Lindgren III. *Neuphilologische Mitteilungen* 76 (1975): 108-29.

*————. *Cupid His Coronation in a Mask.* Bodleian MS Rawlinson B.165, 107r-113v. 1654.

*————. *Fancy's Festivals: A Masque.* 1657.

————. *A Royal Arbor of Loyal Poesie.* 1664.

————. *A Speech Made to His Excellency George Monck General, &c.* 1660.

————. *A Speech Made to His Excellency the Lord General Monck and the Council of State at Goldsmiths Hall.* 1660.

————. *A Speech Made to His Excellency the Lord General Monck and the Council of State at Fishmongers-Hall.* 1660.

*————. *The Walks of Islington and Hogsdon.* 1657.

Journals of the House of Commons. Vols. 3, 7. London: House of Commons, 1742.

Journals of the House of Lords. Vol. 5. London: House of Lords, n.d.

Katz, David S. *Philo-Semitism and the Readmission of the Jews to England, 1603-1655.* Oxford: Clarendon, 1982.

Kawachi, Yoshiko. *Calendar of English Renaissance Drama, 1558-1642.* New York: Garland, 1986.

Kegel-Brinkgreve, E. *The Echoing Woods: Bucolic and Pastoral from Theocritus to Wordsworth.* Amsterdam: J.C. Gieben, 1990.

Kelliher, Hilton. "Donne, Jonson, Richard Andrews, and the Newcastle Manuscript." *English Manuscript Studies* 4 (1993): 134-73.

———. "A Hitherto Unrecognized Cavalier Dramatist: James Compton, Third Earl of Northampton." *British Library Journal* 6 (1980): 158-87.

The Kentish Fayre; or, The Parliament Sold to Their Worth. 1648.

Kenyon, J.P. *The Stuart Constitution, 1603-1688: Documents and Commentary.* Cambridge: Cambridge UP, 1966.

Kephart, Carolyn. "An Unnoticed Forerunner of 'The Beggar's Opera.' " *Music and Letters* 61 (1980): 266-71.

Ker, A. *XII. Resolves Concerning the Disposall of the Person of the King.* 1646.

A Key to the Cabinet of the Parliament. 1648.

Kiefer, Frederick. "Senecan Influence: A Bibliographic Supplement." *Research Opportunities in Renaissance Drama* 28 (1985): 129-42.

———. "Seneca's Influence on Elizabethan Tragedy: An Annotated Bibliography." *Research Opportunities in Renaissance Drama* 21 (1978): 17-34.

*Killigrew, Henry. *Pallantus and Eudora.* 1653.

*Killigrew, Thomas. *Bellamira Her Dream.* Pts. 1 and 2. *Comedies, and Tragedies.* 1664.

*———. *Cicilia and Clorinda.* Pts. 1 and 2. *Comedies, and Tragedies.* 1664.

*———. *Comedies, and Tragedies.* 1664.

*———. *The Parsons Wedding. Comedies, and Tragedies.* 1664.

*———. *The Pilgrim. Comedies, and Tragedies.* 1664.

*———. *The Princesse. Comedies, and Tragedies.* 1664.

*———. *Thomaso; or, the Wanderer.* Pts. 1 and 2. *Comedies, and Tragedies.* 1664.

King, Henry. *Poems.* Saintsbury 3:161-273.

King, John N. *English Reformation Literature: The Tudor Origins of the Protestant Tradition.* Princeton, N.J.: Princeton UP, 1982.

The King and the Cause. Beinecke Library, Osborn MS b.94. [1642?]

King Charles His Defence against Some Trayterous Observations, upon King James. 1642.

King Charls His Speech Made upon the Scaffold. 1649.

Kingdomes Weekly Intelligencer no. 188, 16-23 Feb. 1647, and no. 189, 23 Feb.–2 March 1647.

Kirkman, Francis. "The Stationer, to the Judicious Reader." *A Cure for a Cuckold.* 1661.

———. "The Stationer to the Reader." *The Thracian Wonder.* 1661.

———. *A True, Perfect, and Exact Catalogue of All the Comedies, Tragedies, Tragi-Comedies, Pastorals, Masques and Interludes, That Were Ever Yet Printed and Published, Till This Present Year 1661.*

*———. *The Wits; or, Sport upon Sport.* Pt. 2. 1673. Also Elson. 267-367.

*Klause, John L., ed. *Andronicus Comnenus (Acted 1617-18).* By Samuel Bernard. *Renaissance Latin Drama in England,* 1st ser., vol. 6. Hildesheim: Georg Olms, 1986.

*Knightley, Robert, trans. *Alfrede; or, Right Reinthron'd.* From William Drury, *Aluredus sive Alfredus.* Bodleian MS Rawlinson Poet. 80. 1659.

*———, trans. *Alfrede; or, Right Reinthron'd*. Ed. Albert H. Tricomi. Binghamton, N.Y.: Medieval and Renaissance Texts and Studies, 1993.

Knights, L.C. *Public Voices: Literature and Politics with Special Reference to the Seventeenth Century*. Totowa, N.J.: Rowman and Littlefield, 1972.

Knolles, Richard. *The Generall Historie of the Turkes*. 5th ed. 1638.

Kogan, Stephen. *The Hieroglyphic King: Wisdom and Idolatry in the Seventeenth-Century Masque*. Rutherford, N.J.: Fairleigh Dickinson UP, 1986.

*Lady Alimony. 1659.

*Lamberts Last Game Plaid, Set Out in a Mock-Comedy. 1660.

*The Lame Common-Wealth. Elson. 78-84.

Lamont, William. "Pamphleteering, the Protestant Consensus and the English Revolution." *Freedom and the English Revolution*. Ed. R.C. Richardson and G.M. Ridden. Manchester: Manchester UP, 1986. 72-92.

Langbaine, Gerard. *An Account of the English Dramatick Poets*. 1691.

———. *Momus Triumphans*. 1688.

La Primaudaye, Pierre de. *The Second Part of the Frenche Academie*. Trans. of *Academie françoise*, trans. T. Bowes. 1594.

Larkin, James F., ed. *Stuart Royal Proclamations*. Vol. 2. Oxford: Clarendon, 1983.

Laud, William. *The History of the Troubles and Tryal of the Most Reverend . . . William Laud*. 1700.

Lawler, John. *Book Auctions in England in the Seventeenth Century*. London: Stock, 1898.

Leech, Clifford. "Francis Jaques: Author of *The Queene of Corsica*." *Durham University Journal* 39 (1947): 111-19.

Lehmann, Gary Paul. "A Critical Analysis of the Works of John Day." Ph.D. diss., Duke U, 1980.

Leighton, Alexander. *A Shorte Treatise Against Stage Playes*. Amsterdam, 1625.

Leslie, Henry. *The Martyrdome of King Charles*. The Hague, 1649.

Letters and Poems in Honour of the Incomparable Princess, Margaret, Dutchess of Newcastle. 1676.

*The Levellers Levell'd. See Mercurius Pragmaticus.

Levin, Harry. *Playboys and Killjoys: An Essay on the Theory and Practice of Comedy*. Oxford: Oxford UP, 1987.

The Liberty of the Imprisoned Royalist. 1647.

The Life and Death of King Charles. 1649.

**Lindgren, W.H., III. See Jordan, *Cupid His Coronation*.

Lindley, David, ed. *The Court Masque*. Manchester: Manchester UP, 1984.

Lodge, Edmund. *Life of Sir Julius Caesar, Knt*. London: Hatchard, 1827.

Loewenstein, Joseph. "Guarini and the Presence of Genre." *Renaissance Tragicomedy: Explorations in Genre and Politics*. Ed. Nancy Klein Maguire. New York: AMS, 1987. 33-55.

*The London Chaunticleres. 1659.

Love, Harold. "Richard Flecknoe as Author-Publisher." *Bibliographical Society of Australia and New Zealand Bulletin* 14 (1990): 41-50.

———. "Shadwell, Flecknoe and the Duke of Newcastle: An Impetus for *Mac Flecknoe*." *Papers on Language and Literature* 21 (1985): 19-27.

————. "State Affairs on the Restoration Stage, 1660-1675." *Restoration and Eighteenth-Century Theatre Research* 14 (1978): 1-9.

Lovelace, Richard. In *Cavalier Poets: Selected Poems.* Ed. Thomas Clayton. Oxford: Oxford UP, 1978. 255-325.

Lowe, Dr. [Deposition concerning Archbishop Laud's dealings with Richard Carpenter.] Lambeth Palace Library MS 943, no. 729.

*Lower, William, trans. *The Amourous Fantasme.* From Philippe Quinault, *Le Fantôme amoureux.* The Hague, 1660.

*————, trans. *Don Japhet of Armenia.* From Paul Scarron, *Don Japhet d'Arménie.* BL Add. MS 28723. 1657.

*————. *The Dramatic Works and Translations of Sir William Lower.* See Gates, William Bryan.

*————. *The Enchanted Lovers.* The Hague, 1658.

*————, trans. *Horatius: A Roman Tragedy.* From Pierre Corneille, *Horace.* 1656.

*————, trans. *The Noble Ingratitude.* From Philippe Quinault, *La Généreuse Ingratitude.* The Hague, 1659.

*————, trans. *Polyeuctes; or, The Martyr.* From Pierre Corneille, *Polyeucte.* 1655.

The Loyal Citizens. Elson. 119-22.

The Loyal Sacrifice. 1648.

Ludlow, Edmund. *The Memoirs of Edmund Ludlow Lieutenant-General of the Horse in the Army of the Commonwealth of England.* Ed. C.H. Firth. 2 vols. Oxford: Clarendon, 1894.

McAlindon, Thomas. *English Renaissance Tragedy.* Vancouver: U of British Columbia P, 1986.

McCabe, William H. *An Introduction to the Jesuit Theater: A Posthumous Work.* Ed. Louis J. Oldani. St. Louis: Institute of Jesuit Resources, 1983.

MacKay, Charles, ed. *The Cavalier Songs and Ballads of England from 1642 to 1684.* London: Griffin Bohm, 1863.

Maguire, Nancy Klein. *Regicide and Restoration: English Tragicomedy, 1660-1671.* Cambridge: Cambridge UP, 1992.

————, ed. *Renaissance Tragicomedy: Explorations in Genre and Politics.* New York: AMS, 1987.

————. "The Theatrical Mask/Masque of Politics: The Case of Charles I." *Journal of British Studies* 28 (1989): 1-22.

Malcolm, Joyce Lee. *To Keep and Bear Arms: The Origins of an Anglo-American Right.* Cambridge, Mass.: Harvard UP, 1994.

*The Man in the Moon. *The Second Part of the Tragi-Comedy Called New-Market-Fayre: Or Mrs Parliaments New Figaryes.* 1649.

*————. *A Tragi-Comedy, Called New-Market-Fayre.* 1649.

*Manuche, Cosmo. *The Banish'd Shepheardesse.* Huntington Library MS EL 8395; BL Add. MS 60273. 1660.

*————. *The Feast.* BL Add. MS 60274. ca. 1663-64.

*————. *The Just General.* 1652.

*————. *Love in Travell.* BL Add. MS 60275. 1655.

*————. *The Loyal Lovers.* 1652.

Marcus Tullius Cicero, The Tragedy of That Famous Roman Oratour. 1651.

Marinelli, Peter V. *Pastoral.* London: Methuen, 1971.

*Marlowe, Christopher. *Doctor Faustus.* Ed. John D. Jump. Cambridge, Mass.: Harvard UP, 1962.

*Marmion, Shackerley. *The Antiquary.* 1641.

*Marsh, Henry, ed. *The Wits; or, Sport upon Sport. Select Pieces of Drollery.* 1662.

*Marston, John. *The Parasitaster; or, The Fawne.* 1606.

Martial. *Martial: Epigrams.* Trans. Walter C.A. Ker. Vol. 1 of 2. Cambridge, Mass.: Harvard UP, 1968.

Marvell, Andrew. *The Poems and Letters of Andrew Marvell.* Ed. H.M. Margoliouth; rev. Pierre Legouis with E.E. Duncan-Jones. 2 vols. Oxford: Clarendon, 1971.

Maule, J.F. "Robert Baron's *Cyprian Academy* (1647)." *Notes and Queries* 33 (1986): 393-94.

May, Thomas. *The History of the Parliament of England: Which Began November the Third M.DC.XL.* 1647.

———. Ed. *The Kings Cabinet Opened* 1645.

*———. *The Tragedie of Julia Agrippina.* 1654.

Maycock, A.L. *Nicholas Ferrar of Little Gidding.* London: SPCK, 1938. Grand Rapids, Mich.: Eerdmans, 1980.

*Mayne, Jasper. *The Amorous Warre.* Oxford, 1648.

———. *Certaine Sermons and Letters of Defence and Resolution.* 1653.

*———. *Two Plaies: The City Match . . . and The Amorous Warre.* 1658.

Meiklejohn, Norman. "Cimarrón." *Encyclopedia of Latin America.* Ed. Helen Delpar. New York: McGraw-Hill, 1974.

Mercurius Democritus; or, A True and Perfect Nocturnall. 2-9 March 1654.

*Mercurius Melancholicus. *Craftie Cromwell; or, Oliver Ordering Our New State.* 1648.

*———. *Ding Dong; or, Sᵣ Pitifull Parliament, on His Death-Bed.* 1648.

*———. *Mistris Parliament Brought to Bed of a Monstrous Childe of Reformation.* 1648.

Mercurius Pragmaticus. Communicating Intelligence from All Parts, Touching All Affaires, Designes, Humors, and Conditions. 5-9 May 1648.

*Mercurius Pragmaticus. *The Levellers Levell'd; or, The Independents Conspiracie to Rout out Monarchie.* 1647.

———. *The Reverend Alderman Atkins (The Shit-Breech) His Speech.* 1648.

*———. *The Second Part of Crafty Crumwell; or, Oliver in His Glory.* 1648.

Mercurius Urbanicus. Newes from London and Westminster. 9 May 1648.

*Meriton, Thomas. *Love and War.* 1658.

*———. *The Wandring Lover.* 1658.

Middleton, Thomas, William Rowley, and Philip Massinger. *The Old Law.* 1656.

Mildmay, Humphrey. "The Records of Sir Humphrey Mildmay." Bentley, *Jacobean and Caroline Stage* 2:673-81.

Milhous, Judith, and Robert D. Hume. "New Light on English Acting Companies in 1646, 1648, and 1660." *Review of English Studies* 42 (1991): 487-509.

*Miller, Arthur. *Arthur Miller's Collected Plays.* New York: Viking, 1957.

Milton, John. *Areopagitica.* Ed. Ernest Sirluck. Vol. 2 of 8 vols. *Complete Prose Works of John Milton.* New Haven: Yale UP, 1959. 480-570.

———. *A Defence of the People of England.* Ed. William J. Grace. Trans. Donald C.

Mackenzie. *Complete Prose Works of John Milton.* Vol. 4, pt. 1. New Haven, Conn.: Yale UP, 1966. 285-537.

————. *Eikonoklastes.* Ed. Merritt Y. Hughes. *Complete Prose Works.* Vol. 3. New Haven, Conn.: Yale UP, 1962. 335-601.

————. *Of Education.* Ed. Donald C. Dorian. *Complete Prose Works.* Vol. 2. New Haven, Conn.: Yale UP, 1959. 357-415.

————. *Poems of Mr. John Milton.* 1645.

————. *The Reason of Church-Government.* Ed. Ralph A. Haug. *Complete Prose Works.* Vol. 1. New Haven, Conn.: Yale UP, 1953. 736-861.

*————. *Samson Agonistes.* Ed. Frank Allen Patterson. *The Works of John Milton.* Vol. 1, pt. 2, of 18 vols. New York: Columbia UP, 1931. 331-99.

————. *A Second Defence of the English People.* Ed. Donald A. Roberts. Trans. Helen North. *Complete Prose Works.* Vol. 4, pt. 1. New Haven, Conn.: Yale UP, 1966. 538-686.

————. *The Tenure of Kings and Magistrates.* 1649.

Miner, Earl. *The Cavalier Mode from Jonson to Cotton.* Princeton, N.J.: Princeton UP, 1971.

**Mistris Parliament Brought to Bed of a Monstrous Childe of Reformation.* See Mercurius Melancholicus.

*Montagu, Walter. *The Shepheard's Paradise.* 1659.

Montrose, Louis Adrian. "Of Gentlemen and Shepherds: The Politics of Elizabethan Pastoral Form." *ELH* 50 (1983): 415-59.

Morrill, J.S. *The Revolt in the Provinces.* London: Allen and Unwin, 1976.

———— and J.D. Walter. "Order and Disorder in the English Revolution." *Order and Disorder in Early Modern England.* Ed. Anthony Fletcher and John Stevenson. Cambridge: Cambridge UP, 1985. 137-65.

Morris, John, ed. *The Southcote Family. The Troubles of Our Catholic Forefathers Related by Themselves.* London: Burns and Oates, 1872. 363-410.

Morton, Gerald W. *A Biography of Mildmay Fane, Second Earl of Westmorland, 1601-1666.* Lampeter, Dyfed, Wales: Edwin Mellen, 1990.

*————. "A Critical Edition of Mildmay Fane's *De Pugna Animi.*" Ph.D. diss., U of Tennessee at Knoxville, 1984.

Nathanson, Alan J. *Thomas Simon: His Life and Work, 1618-1665.* London: Seaby, 1975.

Neale, J.E. *Elizabeth I and Her Parliaments, 1584-1601.* 2 vols. London: Cape, 1957.

Nedham, Marchamont. *The Case of the Commonwealth of England, Stated.* Ed. Philip A. Knachel. Charlottesville: UP of Virginia, 1969.

Neill, Michael. " 'Exeunt with a Dead March': Funeral Pageantry on the Shakespearean Stage." *Pageantry in the Shakespearean Theater.* Ed. David M. Bergeron. Athens: U of Georgia P, 1985. 153-93.

Nelson, Carolyn, and Matthew Seccombe. *Periodical Publications, 1641-1700: A Survey with Illustrations.* London: Bibliographical Society, 1986.

**Newes Out of the West; or, The Character of a Mountebank.* 1647.

Newman, P.R. *The Old Service: Royalist Regimental Colonels and the Civil War, 1642-46.* Manchester: Manchester UP, 1993.

A New Play Called Canterburie His Change of Diot. See Overton, Richard.

Nicoll, Allardyce. "Political Plays of the Restoration." *Modern Language Review* 16 (1921): 224-42.

No-Body His Complaint. 1652.

North, Dudley. *A Narrative of Some Passages in or Relating to the Long Parliament.* 1670.

A Notable and Pleasant History of the Famous Renowned Knights of the Blade, Commonly Called Hectors. 1652.

Nuñez, Benjamin. *Dictionary of Afro-Latin American Civilization.* Westport, Conn.: Greenwood, 1980.

Occhiogrosso, Frank Victor. "Sovereign and Subject in Caroline Tragedy." Ph.D. diss., Johns Hopkins U, 1969.

*Oenone. Elson. 305-15.

**Ogilby, John. *The Entertainment of His Most Excellent Majestie Charles II.* 1662.

*———. *The Entertainment of His Most Excellent Majestie Charles II.* Introduction by Ronald Knowles. Binghamton, N.Y.: Medieval and Renaissance Texts and Studies, 1988.

———. *The Fables of Aesop Paraphras'd in Verse. . . .* 2d ed. 1668.

———. *The Relation of His Majesties Entertainment Passing through the City of London to His Coronation.* 1661.

Oliver Cromwell, the Late Great Tirant. 1660.

Olson, Marilynn Strasser. "*Nil Medium:* Noble Soldiers in the Drama in English, 1625-1660." Ph.D. diss., Duke U, 1975.

Orgel, Stephen. *The Illusion of Power: Political Theater in the English Renaissance.* Berkeley: U of California P, 1975.

———. *The Jonsonian Masque.* Cambridge, Mass.: Harvard UP, 1967.

Osborne, Francis. *Historical Memoires on the Reigne of Queen Elizabeth and King James.* 1658.

———. *A Miscellany of Sundry Essayes, Paradoxes, and Problematicall Discourses, Letters and Characters.* 1659.

*———. *The True Tragi-Comedie Formarly Acted at Court & Now Reui[u]ed by ane Eie Witnes.* BL Add. MS 25348. ca. 1654.

*———. *The True Tragicomedy Formerly Acted at Court.* Ed. Lois Potter. New York: Garland, 1983.

*Otway, Thomas. *Venice Preserved.* 1682.

Ovatio Carolina: The Triumph of King Charles. 1641.

Overton, Richard. *The Baiting of the Great Bull of Bashan.* 1649.

*———. *A New Play Called Canterburie His Change of Diot.* 1641.

———. *Vox Borealis.* 1640-41.

Ovid. *Metamorphoses.* Trans. Frank Justus Miller. 2 vols. 1921. Cambridge, Mass.: Harvard UP, 1966.

———. *Remedia Amoris. Ovid in Six Volumes.* Trans. J.H. Mozley. Vol. 2. Cambridge, Mass.: Harvard UP, 1979.

The Oxford English Dictionary. 2d ed. Prepared by J.A. Simpson and E.S.C. Weiner. Oxford: Clarendon, 1989.

P., J. *Tyrants and Protectors Set Forth in Their Colours.* 1654.

P., R. *A Discreet and Judicious Discourse betweene Wisdome and Pietie.* 1642.

Palmer, John. *The Comedy of Manners.* London: G. Bell, 1913.

Partridge, Eric, ed. *A Dictionary of Slang and Unconventional English.* New York: Macmillan, 1984.

Paster, Gail Kern. "The Idea of London in Masque and Pageant." *Pageantry in the Shakespearean Theater.* Ed. David M. Bergeron. Athens: U of Georgia P, 1985. 48-64.

Patterson, Annabel. *Censorship and Interpretation: The Conditions of Writing and Reading in Early Modern England.* Madison: U of Wisconsin P, 1984.

———. *Pastoral and Ideology: Virgil to Valéry.* Berkeley: U of California P, 1987.

*Peaps, William. *Love in It's Extasie.* 1649.

Pearson, Jacqueline. *The Prostituted Muse: Images of Women and Women Dramatists, 1642-1737.* New York: St. Martin's, 1988.

Pepys, Samuel. *The Diary of Samuel Pepys.* Ed. Robert Latham and William Matthews. 11 vols. Berkeley: U of California P, 1970-83.

Perella, Nicolas J. *The Critical Fortune of Battista Guarini's "Il Pastor Fido."* Florence: Olschki, 1973.

Perfect Occurrences 102 (Dec. 1648).

Perrinchief, Richard. *A Messenger from the Dead.* 1658.

———. *The Royal Martyr; or, The Life and Death of King Charles I.* 1676.

———. *The Syracusan Tyrant; or, The Life of Agathocles.* 1661.

Perry, Henry Ten Eyck. *The First Duchess of Newcastle and Her Husband as Figures in Literary History.* Harvard Studies in English 4. Boston: Ginn, 1918. New York: Johnson Reprint, 1968.

Phelps, Wayne H. "Cosmo Manuche, Royalist Playwright of the Commonwealth." *English Language Notes* 16 (1979): 207-11.

Philetis and Constantia. Elson. 283-90.

Phillips, Edward. *Theatrum Poetarum.* 1675.

Phillips, John, trans. *The Tears of the Indians.* From Bartolomé de las Casas, *Breuissima relación de la destruycíon de las Indias.* 1656.

Pinkerton, John. *The Medallic History of England to the Revolution.* 1790.

Plato. *The Symposium. Plato in Twelve Volumes.* Trans. W.R.M. Lamb. Vol. 3. 1925. Cambridge, Mass.: Harvard UP, 1967. 73-245.

*Plautus. *Miles Gloriosus.* Trans. Paul Nixon. 1924. London: Heinemann, 1963. 119-285.

Plutarch. *De Audiendis Poetis.* Ed. Ernesto Valgiglio. Turin: Loescher Editore, 1973.

———. *Lives: Lycurgus.* Trans. Bernadotte Perrin. Vol. 1 of 11. 1914. Cambridge, Mass.: Harvard UP, 1967. 203-303.

Pollux, Julius. *Onomasticon.* Frankfurt, 1608.

Ponet, John. *A Short Treatise of Politique Power.* [Paris?], 1639.

Pordage, Samuel. *Heroick Stanzas on His Maiesties Coronation.* 1661.

———. *Poems upon Several Occasions.* 1660.

*———, trans. *Troades.* From Seneca. 1660.

Potter, Lois, ed. "The *Mistress Parliament* Dialogues." *Analytical and Enumerative Bibliography* ns 1 (1987): 101-70.

———. "The Plays and the Playwrights, 1642-60." *The Revels History of Drama in English.* Vol. 4. Ed. Philip Edwards et al. London: Methuen, 1981. 261-304.

———. *Secret Rites and Secret Writing: Royalist Literature, 1641-1660*. Cambridge: Cambridge UP, 1989.

———. " 'True Tragicomedies' of the Civil War and the Commonwealth." *Renaissance Tragicomedy: Explorations in Genre and Politics*. Ed. Nancy Klein Maguire. New York: AMS, 1987. 195-217.

Powell, Anthony. *John Aubrey and His Friends*. New York: Charles Scribner's Sons, 1948.

Powell, Robert. *The Life of Alfred; or, Alured: The First Institutor of Subordinate Government in This Kingdom*. 1634.

*The Presbyterian Lash; or, Noctroff's Maid Whipt. 1661.

Prestage, Edgar. *The Diplomatic Relations of Portugal with France, England, and Holland from 1640 to 1668*. Watford, Hertfordshire: Voss and Michael, 1925.

*Prestwich, Edmund, trans. *Hippolitus*. From Seneca, *Phaedra*. 1651.

Price, Curtis. "Baroque Opera: England." *History of Opera*. Ed. Stanley Sadie. New York: Norton, 1990. 38-48.

*The Prince of Priggs. 1651.

The Princely Pelican. 1649.

*The Prologue to His Majesty at the First Play . . . Novemb. 19. 1660.

A Prospect of Bleeding Irelands Miseries. 1647.

Prynne, William. *A Breviate of the Life of William Laud*. 1644.

———. *Histrio-mastix*. 1633.

———. *A New Discovery of Free-State Tyranny*. 1655.

*Pullen, John, trans. *Filli di Sciro*. From Guidobaldo della Rovere Bonarelli. Folger MS V.b.243.

Puttenham, George. *The Arte of English Poesie*. 1591.

*Quarles, Francis. *The Virgin Widow*. 1649.

Quarles, John. "Upon the Incomparable Tragedy Called *Mirza*." Baron, *Mirza*.

*The Queene. 1653.

Quinn, David B. *Explorers and Colonies: America, 1500-1625*. London: Hambledon, 1990.

Quintilian, M. Fabius. *Institutio oratoria*. Trans. H.E. Butler. Vol. 1 of 4. 1920. Cambridge, Mass.: Harvard UP, 1969.

*R., T., trans. *The Extravagant Sheepherd*. From Thomas Corneille, *Le Berger extravagant*. 1654.

Randall, Dale B.J. *Gentle Flame: The Life and Verse of Dudley, Fourth Lord North (1602-1677)*. Durham, N.C.: Duke UP, 1983.

———. "The Head and the Hands on the Rostra: *Marcus Tullius Cicero* as a Sign of Its Time." *Connotations* 1 (1991): 34-54.

———. "Some New Perspectives on the Spanish Setting of *The Changeling* and Its Source." *Medieval and Renaissance Drama in England*. Ed. Leeds Barroll and Paul Werstine. Vol. 3. New York: AMS, 1986. 189-216.

*Randolph, Thomas. *Amyntas*. 1640.

*———. *Hey for Honesty, Down with Knavery*. Augmented by F.J. 1651.

*———. *The Muses Looking-Glasse*. 1638.

The Ranters Ranting. 1650.

*Rawlins, Thomas. *The Rebellion*. 1640.

Read and Wonder: A Warre between Two Entire Friends, the Pope and the Divell. 1641.

*Reymes, William, trans. *Selfe Intrest; or, The Belly Wager.* From Nicolò Secchi, *L'Interesse.* Folger MS V.b.128.

*———, trans. *Selfe Intrest; or, The Belly Wager.* Ed. Helen Andrews Kaufman. Seattle: U of Washington P, 1953.

Reynolds, John. *The Triumphs of Gods Revenge against the Crying and Execrable Sinne of (Wilfull and Premeditated) Murther.* 1640.

Richards, Kenneth R. "The Anonymous *Lady Alimony* (1659)." *Archiv für das Studium der Neueren Sprachen und Literaturen* 205 (1968): 192-96.

———. "The Restoration Pageants of John Tatham." *Western Popular Theatre.* Ed. David Mayer and Kenneth Richards. London: Methuen, 1977. 49-73.

Ridpath, George. *The Stage Condemn'd.* 1698.

Riggs, David. *Ben Jonson: A Life.* Cambridge, Mass.: Harvard UP, 1989.

The Right Picture of King Oliure. 1650.

Ristine, Frank Humphrey. *English Tragicomedy: Its Origin and History.* New York: Columbia UP, 1910.

*Roberts, Joan W. "*Sicily and Naples; or, the Fatall Union:* A Critical Edition." Ph.D. diss., U of Cincinnati, 1975.

Robinson, John W. "On the Sources of the English Biblical Puppet Plays (1600-1700)." *Theatre Survey* 12 (1971): 151-54.

Rogers, Hugh C.B. *Battles and Generals of the Civil Wars, 1642-1651.* London: Seeley Service, 1968.

Rollins, Hyder E. *Cavalier and Puritan Ballads and Broadsides Illustrating the Period of the Great Rebellion, 1640-1660.* New York: New York UP, 1923.

———. "The Commonwealth Drama: Miscellaneous Notes." *Studies in Philology* 20 (1923): 52-69.

———. "A Contribution to the History of the English Commonwealth Drama." *Studies in Philology* 18 (1921): 267-333.

———. "Samuel Sheppard and His Praise of Poets." *Studies in Philology* 24 (1927): 509-55.

Rombus the Moderator; or, The King Restored. 1648.

Rothstein, Eric, and Frances M. Kavenik. *The Designs of Carolean Comedy.* Carbondale: Southern Illionis UP, 1988.

Rowe, John. *Tragi-Comoedia.* Oxford, 1653.

Rump; or, An Exact Collection of the Choycest Poems and Songs. See Brome, Alexander.

Rupert, Prince. *A Speech Spoken by His Excellence Prince Rupert.* 1642.

Russell, Conrad. *The Fall of the British Monarchies, 1637-1642.* Oxford: Clarendon, 1991.

———, ed. *The Origins of the English Civil War.* New York: Barnes and Noble, 1973.

Rymer, Thomas. *A Short View of Tragedy.* 1693.

*S., J. *Andromana; or, The Merchant's Wife.* 1660.

*———. *The Prince of Priggs.* 1651.

*Sadler, Anthony. *The Subjects Joy for the Kings Restoration, Cheerfully Made Known in a Sacred Masque.* 1660.

*Sadler, John. *Masquarade du Ciel.* 1640.

Saintsbury, George, ed. *Minor Poets of the Caroline Period.* 3 vols. Oxford: Claren-
don, 1905-21.

*Salusbury, Thomas. *Love or Money.* National Library of Wales MS 53900, 70-109.
ca. 1638-42.

*———. *A Masque . . . at Knowsley.* National Library of Wales MS 53900, 34-45.
1641.

*———. *A Masque . . . at Knowsley.* R.J. Broadbent, "A Masque at Knowsley."
Transactions of the Historic Society of Lancashire and Chesire 41 (1926): 1-16.

*———. *A Show or Antimasque of Gipseys.* National Library of Wales MS 53900,
50-55. 1641.

*Sandys, George, trans. *Christs Passion.* From Hugo Grotius, *Christus patiens.* 1640.

Scott, Eva. *The King in Exile: The Wanderings of Charles II. from June 1646 to July
1654.* London: Constable, 1905.

Scott, Virgil Joseph. "A Reinterpretation of John Tatham's *The Rump; or, The
Mirrour of the Late Times.*" *Philological Quarterly* 24 (1945): 114-18.

The Scottish Politike Presbyter, Slaine by an English Independent. 1647.

Seccombe, Thomas. "Thomas Urquhart." *Dictionary of National Biography.* Vol.
20. Oxford: Oxford UP, rept. 1920-21. 46-50.

Selden, John. *Table-Talk: Being the Discourses of John Selden Esq.* 1689.

Seneca the Elder. *Controversiae. The Elder Seneca.* Trans. M. Winterbottom. Vol. 2
of 2. Cambridge, Mass.: Harvard UP, 1974. 2-483.

Sexby, Edward. *Killing Noe Murder.* 1657.

*Shadwell, Thomas. *The Miser.* 1672.

*———. *The Volunteers.* 1693.

*Shakespeare, William. *The Riverside Shakespeare.* Ed. G. Blakemore Evans et al.
Boston: Houghton Mifflin, 1974.

Sharpe, Kevin. *Criticism and Compliment: The Politics of Literature in the England of
Charles I.* Cambridge: Cambridge UP, 1987.

———. *The Personal Rule of Charles I.* New Haven, Conn.: Yale UP, 1992.

Shaw, Catherine M. "*Landgartha* and the Irish Dilemma." *Eire-Ireland* 13 (1968):
26-39.

*Sheppard, Samuel. *The Committee-Man Curried.* 1647.

———. *Epigrams.* 1651.

———. *The Faerie King (c. 1650).* Ed. P.J. Klemp. *Elizabethan and Renaissance
Studies.* Salzburg Studies in English Literature 107.2. Salzburg: Institut für
Anglistik und Amerikanistik, 1984.

———. *The Famers Fam'd.* 1646.

*———. *The Joviall Crew; or, The Devill Turn'd Ranter.* 1651.

*———. *The Second Part of the Committee-Man Curried.* 1647.

*———. *The Socratick Session.* 1651.

*Sherburne, Edward, trans. *Medea.* From Seneca. 1648.

———. *The Poems and Translations of Sir Edward Sherburne, 1616-1702.* Ed. F.J.
Van Beeck. Assen: Van Gorcum, 1961.

*Shirley, Henry. *The Martyr'd Souldier.* 1638.

*Shirley, James. *The Bird in a Cage.* 1633.

*———. *The Brothers. Six New Playes.* 1653.

*————. *The Cardinal. Six New Playes*. 1653.

*————. *The Contention of Ajax and Ulysses, for the Armor of Achilles. Honoria and Mammon*. 1658.

*————. *The Court Secret. Six New Playes*. 1653.

*————. *Cupid and Death, a Masque*. 1653.

*————. *The Dukes Mistris*. 1638.

*————. *Honoria and Mammon*. 1658.

*————. *The Imposture. Six New Playes*. 1653.

*————. *The Maid's Revenge*. 1639.

————. *An Ode upon the Happy Return of King Charles II. to His Languishing Nations*. 1660.

————. *Poems &c.* 1646.

————. *Rudiments of Grammar: The Rules Composed in English Verse for the Greater Benefit and Delight of Young Beginners*. 1656.

*————. *The Sisters. Six New Playes*. 1653.

*————. *The Triumph of Beautie*. 1646.

A Shorte Treatise against Stage-Playes. See Leighton, Alexander.

Sidney, Philip. *An Apologie for Poetrie*. 1595.

————. *The Countesse of Pembrokes Arcadia*. 1598.

Siebert, Fredrick S. *Freedom of the Press in England, 1476-1726*. Urbana: U of Illinois P, 1952.

The Siege of Colchester. Map. 1648.

Simpson, Claude M. *The British Broadside Ballad and Its Music*. New Brunswick, N.J.: Rutgers UP, 1966.

Simpson, Richard. "The Political Use of the Stage in Shakspere's Time." *Transactions of the New Shakespeare Society* 2 (1874): 371-95.

Sir Francis Drake Revived. 1653.

Smith, Courtney Craig. "The Seventeenth-Century Drolleries." *Harvard Library Bulletin* 6 (1952): 40-51.

Smith, H. ALS to Hugh Smith of Long Ashton. Folger MS x.c.48. 3 May 1659.

Smuts, Malcolm. "The Political Failure of Stuart Cultural Patronage." *Patronage in the Renaissance*. Ed. Guy Fitch Lytle and Stephen Orgel. Princeton, N.J.: Princeton UP, 1981. 165-87.

Solier, François. *Histoire ecclésiastique des isles et royaumes du Iapon*. 2 vols. Paris, 1627-29.

Sorelius, Gunnar. *"The Giant Race before the Flood": Pre-Restoration Drama on the Stage and in the Criticism of the Restoration*. Uppsala: Almqvist & Wiksells, 1966.

Speaight, George. *The History of the English Puppet Theatre*. 1955. Carbondale: Southern Illinois UP, 1990.

The Speech of a Cavaleere to His Comrades. 1642.

The Stage-Players Complaint. 1641.

Stallybrass, Peter, and Allon White. *The Politics and Poetics of Transgression*. Ithaca, N.Y.: Cornell UP, 1986.

*Stanley, Thomas, trans. *The Clouds*. From Aristophanes. *The History of Philosophy*. Vol. 1 of 2. 1655.

————. *The Poems and Translations of Thomas Stanley*. Ed. Galbraith Miller Crump. Oxford: Clarendon, 1962.

*Stapleton, Robert. *The Slighted Maid*. 1663.

Starr, Nathan Comfort. "*The Concealed Fansyes:* A Play by Lady Jane Cavendish and Lady Elizabeth Brackley." *PMLA* 46 (1931): 802-38.

The Statutes at Large, from the First Year of James the First to the Tenth Year of the Reign of King William the Third. Vol. 3. 1763.

Stephens, Frederic George. *Catalogue of Prints and Drawings in the British Museum.* Vol. 1 of 5. London: Trustees of the British Museum, 1870.

Stone, Lawrence. *Road to Divorce: England, 1530-1987.* Oxford: Oxford UP, 1990.

*Stoppard, Tom. *Dogg's Hamlet, Cahoot's Macbeth.* New York: Samuel French, 1980.

*Strode, William. *The Floating Island.* 1655.

Strong, Roy. *Art and Power: Renaissance Festivals, 1450-1650.* Berkeley: U of California P, 1984.

*Suckling, John. *The Plays.* Ed. L.A. Beaurline. Vol. 2 of *The Works of Sir John Suckling.* Oxford: Clarendon, 1971.

Suetonius. *The Lives of the Caesars.* Vol. 2 of 2. Trans. J.C. Rolfe. London: Heinemann, 1970.

Swetnam, Joseph. *The Araignment of Lewd, Idle, Froward, and Unconstant Women.* 1615.

*Swinhoe, Gilbert. *The Unhappy Fair Irene.* 1658.

Talbot, Gilbert. ALS to Charles. Bodleian MS Clarendon 51. March 1656.

*————, trans. *Fillis of Scirus.* From Guidobaldo della Rovere Bonarelli. BL Add. MS 12128. 1657.

*Tatham, John. *Daphnes, a Pastorall.* 1651.

*————. *The Distracted State.* 1650 or 1651.

————. *The Fancies Theater.* 1640.

*————. *Londons Glory Represented by Time, Truth, and Fame.* 1660.

*————. *Londons Triumphs, Celebrated . . . in Honour to the Truly Deserving Richard Chiverton.* 1657.

*————. *Londons Tryumph, Presented by Industry and Honour.* 1658.

*————. *London's Tryumph, Celebrated . . . in Honour of the Much Honoured, Thomas Allen.* 1659.

*————. *London's Tryumphs Presented in Several Delightfull Scoenes.* 1661.

*————. *Love Crowns the End.* 1657.

*————. *Neptunes Address to His Most Sacred Majesty Charls the Second.* 1661.

*————. *The Royal Oake with Other Various and Delightfull Scenes.* 1660.

*————. *The Rump.* 1660.

*————. *The Scots Figgaries; or, A Knot of Knaves.* 1652.

Taylor, John. *Crop-Eare Curried.* 1644.

————. *The Generall Complaint of the Most Oppressed, Distressed Commons of England. Works.* 4th collection. Manchester: Spenser Society, 1877.

————. *The Great Eater of Kent.* 1630.

————. *Ranters of Both Sexes. Works.* 4th collection. Manchester: Spenser Society, 1877.

————. *Tailors Travels, from London, to the Isle of Wight. Works.* 4th collection. Manchester: Spenser Society, 1877.

———. *The Whole Life and Progresse of Henry Walker the Ironmonger. Works.* 1st collection. Manchester: Spenser Society, 1870. Reptd. New York: Burt Franklin, 1967.

Temple, John. *The Irish Rebellion.* 1646.

The Terrible, Horrible, Monster of the West. 1649.

Thomas, Keith. "The Puritans and Adultery: The Act of 1650 Reconsidered." *Puritans and Revolutionaries.* Ed. Donald Pennington and Keith Thomas. Oxford: Clarendon, 1978. 257-82.

Thomas, P.W. "Two Cultures? Court and Country under Charles I." *The Origins of the English Civil War.* Ed. Conrad Russell. New York: Barnes and Noble, 1973. 168-93.

*Time's Distractions. BL MS Egerton 1994, 212r-223r. 1643.

*Time's Distractions. Ed. Diane W. Strommer. College Station: Texas A&M UP, 1976.

*Titus; or, The Palme of Christian Courage. Waterford, 1644.

*Tomkis, Thomas. *Lingua; or, The Combat of the Tongue, and the Five Senses.* 1657.

Torshell, Samuel. *The Womans Glorie.* 1645.

To the Supream Authoritie, the Parliament of the Common-Wealth. 1650.

*Townshend, Aurelian. *The Poems and Masques of Aurelian Townshend.* Ed. Cedric C. Brown. Reading, Berkshire: Whiteknights, 1983.

The Tragedy of the Cruell Warre. 1643.

Travitsky, Betty S. "Reconstructing the Still, Small Voice: The Occasional Journal of Elizabeth Egerton." *Women's Studies* 19 (1991): 193-200.

Trevelyan, G.M. *The Tudors and the Stuart Era.* Vol. 2 of *History of England.* 1926. Garden City, N.Y.: Doubleday, 1952.

Tricomi, Albert H. *Anti-Court Drama in England, 1603-1642.* Charlottesville: UP of Virginia, 1989.

A True and Perfect Relation of the Taking of Captain James Hind. 1651.

*The True Tragi-Comedie Formarly Acted at Court. See Osborne, Francis.

*Tuke, Samuel. *The Adventures of Five Hours.* 1663.

Turner, James. *Memoirs of His Own Life and Times.* Edinburgh, 1829.

Turner, James. *The Politics of Landscape: Rural Scenery and Society in English Poetry, 1630-1660.* Oxford: Clarendon, 1985.

Turner, Robert Y. "Responses to Tyranny in John Fletcher's Plays." *Medieval and Renaissance Drama in England.* Ed. Leeds Barroll and Paul Werstine. Vol. 4. New York: AMS, 1989. 123-41.

The Tyranny of Tyrannies. 1648.

Underdown, David. *Revel, Riot, and Rebellion: Popular Politics and Culture in England, 1603-1660.* Oxford: Clarendon, 1985.

———. *Royalist Conspiracy in England, 1649-1660.* New Haven, Conn.: Yale UP, 1960.

———. "The Taming of the Scold." *Order and Disorder in Early Modern England.* Ed. Anthony Fletcher and John Stevenson. Cambridge: Cambridge UP, 1985. 116-36.

*The Unfortunate Usurper. 1663.

Usher, Roland G. *The Rise and Fall of the High Commission.* 1st pub. 1913. Oxford: Clarendon, 1968.

Valency, Maurice J. *The Tragedies of Herod and Mariamne.* New York: Columbia UP, 1940.

Vander Motten, J.P. *Sir William Killigrew (1606-1695): His Life and Dramatic Works.* Ghent: Rijksuniversiteit te Gent, 1980.

Van Lennep, William. *The London Stage, 1660-1800.* Pt. 1, *1660-1700.* Ed. Emmett L. Avery and Arthur H. Scouten. Carbondale: Southern Illinois UP, 1965.

———. "Thomas Killigrew Prepares His Plays for Production." *Joseph Quincy Adams Memorial Studies.* Ed. James G. McManaway, Giles E. Dawson, and Edwin E. Willoughby. Washington, D.C.: Folger Shakespeare Library, 1948. 803-8.

Vaughan, Henry. *The Complete Poetry of Henry Vaughan.* Ed. French Fogle. New York: New York UP, 1965.

Veevers, Erica. *Images of Love and Religion: Queen Henrietta Maria and Court Entertainments.* Cambridge: Cambridge UP, 1989.

Vicars, John. *A Sight of ye Trans-Actions of These Latter Yeares.* 1646.

Vindiciae contra Tyrannos: A Defence of Liberty against Tyrants. 1648.

Virgil. *Virgil.* Trans. H. Rushton Fairclough. Vol. 1 of 2. Cambridge, Mass.: Harvard UP, 1978.

Visser, Colin. "The Killigrew Folio: Private Playhouses and the Restoration Stage." *Theatre Survey* 19 (1978): 119-38.

Vox Borealis. 1641. See Overton, Richard.

Waith, Eugene M. *The Pattern of Tragicomedy in Beaumont and Fletcher.* New Haven, Conn.: Yale UP, 1952. Hamden, Conn.: Archon, 1969.

Walker, George. *Anglo-Tyrannus; or, The Idea of a Norman Monarch Represented in the Paralell Reignes of Henrie the Third and Charles Kings of England.* 1650.

Walker, John. *An Attempt towards Recovering an Account of the Numbers and Sufferings of the Clergy of the Church of England.* 1714.

Wallace, John M. "The Case for Internal Evidence ... : The Date of John Tatham's *The Distracted State.*" *Bulletin of the New York Public Library* 64 (1960): 29-40.

———. " 'Examples Are Best Precepts': Readers and Meanings in Seventeenth-Century Poetry." *Critical Inquiry* 1 (1974): 273-90.

Waller, Edmund. *Poems, &c.* 2 vols. in 1. 1694.

A Warning for Fair Women. 1599.

Warwick, Philip. *Memoires of the Reigne of King Charles I.* 1701.

Wase, Christopher, trans. *Cicero against Catiline.* 1671.

*———, trans. *Electra.* From Sophocles. The Hague, 1649.

*Webster, John. *Appius and Virginia.* 1654.

Wedgwood, C.V. *Poetry and Politics under the Stuarts.* Cambridge: Cambridge UP, 1960.

The Weekly Accompt 27 Sept.–4 Oct. 1643.

*Werstine, Paul, ed. "1. *New-Market-Fayre.*" *Analytical and Enumerative Bibliography* 6 (1982): 71-103.

The White Ethiopian. BL MS Harley 7313. ca. 1650.

Whitelocke, Bulstrode. *Memorials of the English Affairs.* 1682.

Whitlock, Richard. *Zootomia.* 1654.

*Wild, Robert. *The Benefice*. 1689.

Wilding, Michael. *Dragons Teeth: Literature in the English Revolution*. Oxford: Clarendon, 1987.

Wiley, Autrey Nell. Ed. *Rare Prologues and Epilogues, 1642-1700*. Reissued Port Washington, N.Y.: Kennikat P, 1970.

*Willan, Leonard. *Astraea*. 1651.

———. *The Exact Politician; or, Compleat Statesman*. 1670.

*———. *Orgula; or, The Fatall Error*. 1658.

———. *The Phrygian Fabulist*. 1650.

Williams, C.M. "The Anatomy of a Radical Gentleman: Henry Marten." *Puritans and Revolutionaries*. Ed. Donald Pennington and Keith Thomas. Oxford: Clarendon, 1978. 118-38.

*Williams, William P., ed. "*Canterbury His Change of Diet*." *Analytical and Enumerative Bibliography* 1 (1977): 37-65.

———. "The Castle Ashby Manuscripts: A Description of the Volumes in Bishop Percy's List." *Library* 6th ser., 2 (1980): 391-412.

———. "Evidence of Performance." *English Language Notes* 30 (1992): 11-16.

Wiltshire Tom. See Kirkman, *The Wits*.

Winstock, Lewis. *Songs and Marches of the Roundheads and Cavaliers*. London: Leo Cooper, 1971.

Winton, Calhoun. "Dramatic Censorship." *The London Theatre World, 1660-1800*. Ed. Robert D. Hume. Carbondale: Southern Illinois UP, 1980. 286-308.

Wiseman, Susan J. "History Digested: Opera and Colonialism in the 1650s." *Literature and the English Civil War*. Ed. Thomas Healy and Jonathan Sawday. Cambridge: Cambridge UP, 1990. 189-204.

Wither, George. *The Dark Lantern*. 1653.

———. *Mercurius Rusticus*. 1643.

Wolf, William D. "The Authorship of *The Mandrake* and *Leontius, King of Cyprus*." *Library* 6th ser., 2 (1980): 456-60.

Wood, Anthony à. *Athenae Oxonienses*. 2 vols. 1691-92.

Wood, James O. "Thomas Fuller's Oxford Interlude." *Huntington Library Quarterly* 17 (1954): 185-208.

Wright, James. *Historia Histrionica: An Historical Account of the English-Stage*. 1699.

Wright, Louis B. "The Reading of Plays during the Puritan Revolution." *Huntington Library Quarterly* 5 (1934): 73-108.

Wright, Thomas, ed. *Political Ballads Published in England during the Commonwealth*. London: Percy Society, 1841.

Yates, Patricia Haim. "English Dialogue Pamphlets of the Mid-Seventeenth Century, 1640-1660." Ph.D. diss., Duke U, 1978.

Yonge, William. *England's Shame; or, The Unmasking of a Politic Atheist*. 1663.

Zwicker, Steven N. "Politics and Panegyric: The Figural Mode from Marvell to Pope." *Literary Uses of Typology*. Princeton, N.J.: Princeton UP, 1977. 115-46.

INDEX